AF770399

Judicial Process in America

Thirteenth Edition

To the memory of Brian Rainer and his surviving wife Gloria, greatly valued and much-cherished friends for over fifty years.

—R. A. C.

To Marcia, Katie, and Kenny.

—K. L. M.

To Meghan, Lee, Jessica, Lizzy, and Sydney.

—L. M. H.

To my husband, Gavin Bowie, and my family.

—J.B.

Judicial Process in America

Thirteenth Edition

Robert A. Carp

University of Houston

Kenneth L. Manning

University of Massachusetts Dartmouth

Lisa M. Holmes

University of Vermont

Jennifer Bowie

University of Richmond

Sage | CQ PRESS

FOR INFORMATION:

2455 Teller Road
Thousand Oaks, California 91320
E-mail: order@sagepub.com

1 Oliver's Yard
55 City Road
London, EC1Y 1SP
United Kingdom

Unit No. 323-333, Third Floor, F-Block
International Trade Tower
Nehru Place, New Delhi – 110 019
India

18 Cross Street #10-10/11/12
China Square Central
Singapore 048423

100% Paper from well-managed forests

Acquisitions Editor: Anna Villarruel

Content Development Editor: Bailey Witterholt

Production Editor: Astha Jaiswal

Copy Editor: Talia Greenberg

Typesetter: diacriTech

Designer: Scott Van Atta

Marketing Manager: Jennifer Haldeman

Copyright © 2026 by CQ Press, an imprint of Sage.

All rights reserved. Except as permitted by U.S. copyright law, no part of this work may be reproduced or distributed in any form or by any means, or stored in a database or retrieval system, without permission in writing from the publisher.

All third party trademarks referenced or depicted herein are included solely for the purpose of illustration and are the property of their respective owners. Reference to these trademarks in no way indicates any relationship with, or endorsement by, the trademark owner.

Printed in the United States of America

Library of Congress Cataloging-in-Publication Data

Names: Carp, Robert A., 1943-, author. | Manning, Kenneth L. (Kenneth Luis) author. | Holmes, Lisa M., 1969- author. | Bowie, Jennifer Barnes, author.

Title: Judicial process in america / Robert A. Carp, University of Houston; Kenneth L. Manning, University of Massachusetts Dartmouth; Lisa M. Holmes, University of Vermont; Jennifer Bowie, University of Richmond.

Description: Thirteenth. | Thousand Oaks : CQ Press, 2025. | Previous edition 2023. | Includes bibliographical references and index.

Identifiers: LCCN 2024059344 (print) | LCCN 2024059345 (ebook) | ISBN 9781071934425 (paperback) | ISBN 9781071934432 (epub)

Subjects: LCSH: Justice, Administration of—United States. | Courts—United States. | Judicial process—United States.

Classification: LCC KF8700 .C37 2025 (print) | LCC KF8700 (ebook) | DDC 347.73—dc23/eng/20241212

LC record available at https://lccn.loc.gov/2024059344

LC ebook record available at https://lccn.loc.gov/2024059345

This book is printed on acid-free paper.

25 26 27 28 29 10 9 8 7 6 5 4 3 2 1

BRIEF CONTENTS

DETAILED CONTENTS

PREFACE

Since the publication of the twelfth edition of *Judicial Process in America* in 2023, the United States has seen a great deal of uncertainty and discord, and the courts have certainly not been cut off from this turmoil. Some of the most prevalent issues surrounding the federal courts in recent years have concerned increased partisan polarization of the judiciary, the implications of President Donald Trump's success in appointing conservative judges across the federal courts, declining support for the Supreme Court by the public, and President Joe Biden's successful efforts at diversifying the federal judiciary.

Partisan polarization has been increasing in the United States, including among the public and among our elected officials. Recent scholarship points to a Supreme Court that has also seen a dramatic increase in partisan polarization in recent years, "perhaps more so than ever in its history."[1] This increased polarization has affected Supreme Court decision-making across many policy areas, including voting rights and campaign finance, religious liberty, and cases involving business. In other words, there is more disagreement today than there used to be in resolving campaign finance or religious liberty cases between justices appointed by Democratic versus Republican presidents.[2]

We are now a few years into the 6-3 conservative supermajority brought about by the hardball tactics utilized in appointing two of President Trump's three appointees to the Court (as we address in Chapter 6). Justice Ketanji Brown Jackson's selection in 2022 as President Biden's sole appointee to the nation's highest court, while unprecedented from the perspective of representation, did little to alter the ideological composition of the Court, given that she replaced liberal Justice Stephen Breyer. Decades of work by conservative interests and Republican political leaders are in the process of coming to fruition in expanding gun rights, empowering individual religious liberty claims over antidiscrimination policies, ending race-based affirmative action in college admissions, and limiting the power of administrative agencies, among other areas. Indeed, at the close of the 2023-2024 term, one longtime Court observer noted that the justices had "taken on a stunning array of major disputes and [assumed] a commanding role in shaping American society and democracy."[3]

Two such major disputes from the Court's 2023 term directly involved President Donald Trump. In a 6-3 decision mirroring the Court's partisan composition, the majority ruled that a president is entitled to full immunity for actions within his core constitutional authority and at least presumptive immunity from criminal prosecution for all of his official acts.[4] This ruling calls into question some of the ongoing criminal trials involving Trump, as we address in Chapter 10. In the other case, the Court ruled in a unanimous per curiam opinion that Section 3 of the Fourteenth Amendment did not empower the state of Colorado to exclude Trump from the primary ballot, even with a trial court determination that he had "engaged in insurrection" by intentionally inciting the breach of the US Capitol on January 6, 2021.[5] The ballot access case demonstrates that even in this era of increased polarization on the Court, the resolution of some high-profile cases does not always reflect our expectation of the justices' ideological leanings.

Most high profile among recent Court rulings, however, has been the overturning of decades of abortion law in *Dobbs v. Jackson Women's Health Organization*,[6] in a 6-3 decision along ideological lines. The ramifications of the *Dobbs* decision have been seismic, in multiple ways. Newly empowered to chart their own course on abortion law, many states across the country passed restrictive abortion laws. According to the Guttmacher Institute, forty-three clinics in eleven states had stopped providing abortion care within thirty days of the *Dobbs* decision in June 2022.[7] The number of states with lesser or no access to abortion care have increased since then. The success achieved by pro-life advocates in the *Dobbs* decision has also encouraged further efforts at bringing additional cases to the courts regarding abortion care, although not all of these cases have achieved the goals sought by the conservative plaintiffs. In Chapter 4, for example, we discuss the as yet unsuccessful efforts at overturning the Food and Drug Administration's approval and regulation of mifepristone, a drug used in medication abortions in the United States.

Beyond the ramifications of *Dobbs* on abortion law and policy around the country, the decision influenced electoral politics in the United States. In the 2022 midterm elections, Democrats were expected to suffer the wrath of voters upset about inflation and economic concerns. Instead, voters' views on abortion were more critical than were views on the economy to shifting votes from one party to the other in the 2022 midterms.[8] Since a larger number of voting Americans supported rather than opposed legal abortions, the Democratic Party exceeded expectations by barely losing control of the House and gaining a seat to their slim majority in the Senate in the midterms that year.

The legacy of the *Dobbs* decision continued into the 2024 presidential election. In her time as vice president, Democratic presidential candidate Kamala Harris served as "the White House's voice of unflinching support for reproductive health rights," and this experience in discussing abortion followed her on the presidential campaign trail.[9] For his part, Donald Trump was challenged in reconciling his role in appointing justices who voted to overturn *Roe* with the electoral blowback for Republicans that has come in the wake of *Dobbs*. Ultimately, early exit poll analyses of the 2024 election indicated that those who voted to support reproductive rights in the states that had abortion-related measures on the ballot did not break for Harris to the extent that her campaign needed to defeat Trump, especially in battleground states like Arizona and Nevada.[10]

The implications of party polarization and appointment politics on the judiciary extend beyond the US Supreme Court. In Chapter 4, we consider how the ideological composition of lower federal courts has contributed to litigants filing cases strategically in the hopes of drawing judges particularly sympathetic to the litigants' arguments. This intense form of "forum shopping" on the part of litigants has drawn pushback from other actors in the political system, including the Judicial Conference of the United States.

At the state level, discord between the political branches and the judiciary remains prevalent in some states. As we discuss in more detail in Chapter 5, for instance, Republican legislators in Wisconsin threatened to impeach a newly elected state supreme court justice if she did not recuse herself from an important redistricting case.

Given these events, it is perhaps not surprising that we are currently seeing historically low levels of approval of the US Supreme Court expressed by the public, with the Court's approval dropping a full 23 percentage points between 2020 and 2024.[11] As would likely be expected, given our polarized society, the decrease in support for the Supreme Court has a partisan hue, with support among Democrats dropping especially sharply.[12] In addition, the steady stream of ethics scandals following some of the justices has also been a likely contributor to the decrease in support. These widely reported scandals, and the Court's tepid response to them, have spurred a call for increased judicial ethics reform, as we discuss in Chapter 6. In that chapter, we also give attention to President Biden's judicial reform plan, including his proposal for term limits and judicial ethics provisions specifically targeting the justices of the nation's highest court.

Alongside noticeable trends toward increased partisan polarization and decreased public support for the Supreme Court, another obvious trend has been the dramatic increase in diversity in judicial appointments during the Biden presidency. From the perspective of racial, ethnic, and gender diversity, President Biden has had a tremendous impact on the courts. Justice Ketanji Brown Jackson is the first Black woman, the second woman of color, and only the sixth woman appointed in the Court's history. Justice Jackson's previous experience as a public defender also reflects Biden's approach to diversifying the professional backgrounds of his judicial appointees. With more opportunity to shape the composition of the lower federal judiciary, Biden's record on diversifying the district and circuit courts is unprecedented. In Chapter 6, we provide updated data on the demographic, educational, and professional backgrounds of Biden's appointees to the circuit and district courts.

In this current edition, we also include updated original data on the voting patterns of US trial court judges. We provide additional analysis of the decisions made by the judges appointed by President Trump, and also give a full assessment of the voting behavior of Biden's trial court cohort in Chapter 7. Given the particularly diverse identities and professional backgrounds of the Biden judges, the decision-making behavior of his judicial appointees will be important to track in the coming years.

The results of the 2024 elections will, of course, have a significant influence over the direction of US law and policy moving forward. Although the confirmation process has settled into a post-nuclear option reality, where a filibuster is no longer able to deny confirmation, partisan control of the presidency and the Senate are critical to who is appointed to all levels of the judiciary. President Trump will benefit from unified government in the 119th Congress, with a Senate controlled 53 to 47 by Republicans, clearing the path toward confirmation for a new cohort of Trump judges without the need for bipartisan support.

The implications of the 2024 presidential election will also be seen in the leadership and priorities of the US Department of Justice (DOJ). With a newly elected president, we expect new appointees to serve in key positions within the DOJ. As we discuss in Chapter 8, these new appointees will influence the direction of law and policy in the United States for the near future, at least. At the state level, the increasing amount of money spent on certain judicial elections has shown little sign of abating in recent election cycles, as we address in Chapter 5. In that chapter, we also discuss how the elected branches have attempted to influence the judiciary in some states through hardball political tactics, often in response to electoral victories or defeats.

State court systems have also recently demonstrated why states are often seen as "laboratories of democracy." The COVID-19 pandemic caused monumental obstacles for access to court systems across the country, and state judiciaries responded as they often do, through innovations designed to allow courts to continue hearing cases as the pandemic raged. As the nation has moved forward from the most disruptive days of the crisis, many states have retained innovations deemed useful in providing greater access to these courts, although these reforms have come with their own drawbacks and problems, as we address in Chapter 3.

In considering all of these topics, and many others throughout the book, we have taken care to prepare a text that is highly readable for both academic and general audiences. The primary emphasis is on full coverage of the federal courts, state judicial systems, the role of the lawyer in American society, the nature of criminal and civil law, and public policy concerns that color the entire judicial fabric. The book is designed as a primary text for courses in judicial process and behavior; it is also useful as a supplement in political science classes in constitutional law, American government, and law and society. Likewise, it may serve as interesting reading in law-related courses in sociology, history, psychology, and criminology.

We also provide a variety of comparative references and examples throughout the book, continuing to highlight relevant aspects of the US judicial system that are uniquely American and that may be compared with the judicial practices of other nations. In providing some comparative insight, we have endeavored to include a wide variety of countries as the sources of our comparisons—not just Canada and the United Kingdom, whose judiciaries are mostly like the US system.

Throughout the text, we have endeavored to use minimal jargon and theoretical vocabulary of political science and the law without condescending to the reader. We believe it is possible to provide a keen and fundamental understanding of the court systems and their impact on Americans' daily lives without assuming that all readers are budding political scientists or lawyers. At times, it is necessary and useful to employ technical terms and evoke theoretical concepts. Still, we address the basic questions on a level that is meaningful to an educated layperson.

We have also avoided stressing any theoretical framework for the study of courts and legal questions, such as a systems model approach or a judicial realist perspective. Instructors partial to the tenets of modern behaviorism will find much here to appreciate, but we have also included some of the insights that more traditional scholarship has provided over the years. The book reflects the contributions not only of political scientists and legal scholars but also of historians, psychologists, court administrators, think tanks and research groups, and journalists.

For students who may desire more specialized explanations or who wish to explore further some of the issues we discuss, the glossary, notes, and suggested resources contain ample leads. We have added new websites to the suggested resources at the end of each chapter, for those who wish to pursue the subject matter in greater depth. As an additional learning aid, we encourage readers to visit the Cornell University Law School Supreme Court website (https://www.law.cornell.edu/supremecourt/text/home), from which they can obtain, without cost, summaries of Supreme Court decisions immediately after they are handed down by the justices. For those interested in current developments in Supreme Court jurisprudence, we also suggest the free, award-winning website *SCOTUSblog.com*, sponsored by Bloomberg Law. *SCOTUSblog.com* has become a go-to source for many Court watchers.

Throughout the text we are constantly mindful of the interrelation of the courts and public policy. We have worked from the premise that significant portions of citizens' lives—both as individuals and as part of a nation—are affected by what federal and state judges choose to do and what they refrain from doing. We reject the common assumption that only liberals make public policy and only conservatives practice restraint. We believe that to some degree all judges engage in the inevitable activity of making policy. The question, as we see it, is not whether American judges make policy but which directions their policy decisions take. In the chapters that follow, we explain why this has come to be, how it happens, and what the consequences are for the United States today.

We intend for the thirteenth edition of this book to provide the same balance between rigor and readability seen in previous editions. But evolution is inevitable, and we would like to highlight one major change with this current edition. We are delighted to announce that Dr. Jennifer Bowie, associate professor of political science at the University of Richmond, has brought her wealth of expertise with her as this project's newest coauthor. We cannot highlight all of Dr. Bowie's impressive teaching and scholarly accomplishments here, but her contributions to this latest edition have been vast, and she is a valued and important new member of the *Judicial Process in America* team.

In terms of chapter organization for this text, we set the theoretical stage in Chapter 1, noting Americans' ample respect for the law and also their traditional willingness to violate the law when it is morally, economically, or politically expedient to do so. We also examine sources of jurisprudence in the United States and several of the major philosophies concerning the role and function of law.

In Chapter 2, we examine the organizational structure and workloads of the federal judicial system, and we have updated all the tables to reflect new caseload statistics for all three levels of the federal judiciary. In this thirteenth edition, we provide a deeper discussion of the work at each level of the federal judiciary and devote more attention to the importance of the federal courts of appeals and district courts.

Chapter 3 focuses on the judicial systems in the various states. There is also expanded coverage of courts of limited jurisdiction including juvenile courts, of the increasing use of administrative hearings (in place of litigation), and of the expanding role of state supreme courts in critical areas of policymaking such as same-sex marriage and legislative apportionment. We also discuss the significant impact that post-pandemic innovations have had on state judicial administration. Finally, the statistical tables in this chapter reflect the most recent available data.

In Chapter 4, we outline the jurisdiction of the several levels of US courts and discuss the political and nonjusticiable realms of American life into which judges in principle are not supposed to enter. In this edition, we highlight a number of recent developments of relevance to this chapter. We include a new discussion of "forum shopping," the practice (when available) of filing a case in the court that is expected to be the most sympathetic to the plaintiff's argument. We also address contemporary debates concerning proposals to alter the Supreme Court's appellate jurisdiction and we update some examples by incorporating *FDA v. Alliance for Hippocratic Medicine*[13] and *303 Creative v. Elenis*[14] into the chapter.

Chapter 5 focuses on the role and work of state judges with an emphasis on the selection, retention, and removal of state judges. We emphasize the balance between judicial accountability and judicial independence in this chapter, focusing on tensions between the elective branches and the judiciary. We include new material in this chapter on judicial oversight and in particular judicial misconduct commissions in the states. The statistical information includes the most recent data available.

Focusing on the federal courts in Chapter 6, we use newly collected original data to take a close look at the men and women serving the federal judiciary. What are their backgrounds and qualifications for office? How are they chosen? How are they socialized into their judicial roles, under what circumstances can they be removed from office, and when do they choose to leave their lifetime tenured seats? As noted, President Joe Biden had a profound influence on the composition of all levels of the federal judiciary, particularly with respect to the unprecedented racial, ethnic, and gender diversity among his appointees. We also expand the discussion of judicial ethics, focusing on recent controversies centering on Justice Clarence Thomas, and give attention to President Biden's actions with respect to judicial reform initiatives. Lastly, we discuss the relevance of the 2024 elections to the judiciary moving forward.

Chapter 7 examines the work and decision-making patterns of federal judges, those appointed by Presidents Franklin Roosevelt through Joe Biden. We find a discernible link among the values of most of the voters in a presidential election, those of the appointing president, and the subsequent policy content of decisions made by the judges nominated by the chief executive. And through original research, using significant amounts of our own new and updated data, we offer an in-depth assessment of recent presidents' impact on the ideological orientation of the federal judiciary. Finally, we provide an updated analysis that compares and contrasts the judicial nomination and appointment strategies of Presidents Trump and Biden.

Chapter 8 discusses the role of lawyers in American society—their training, values, and attitudes, and the public policy goals of their professional associations. We provide an expanded and updated discussion of the issues facing law students and law schools themselves in recent decades. The legal profession has rebounded well but not completely, since the darkest days of the Great Recession. The student debt crisis remains a problem, especially for law students from traditionally marginalized backgrounds. In this chapter, we also provide a discussion of the role of litigants and interest groups in the judicial process, including the rise and success of conservative legal groups in recent years. We have updated statistics and examples throughout the chapter.

In Chapter 9, we focus on the nature of crime and on the various procedures prior to a criminal trial: the arrest, the appearance before a magistrate, the grand jury process, the arraignment, and the possibility of a plea bargain. We provide new crime examples throughout the chapter and we further discuss the adversarial process as it exists in American courtrooms. We also place more attention on plea bargaining, highlighting that plea bargaining is the norm and not the exception in the US system. We provide new statistical information in this chapter.

Chapter 10 explores the criminal trial and its aftermath. We examine the procedural rights of the criminal defendant, the process of selecting a jury, the roles of judge and juries during the trial, the sentencing process, and the possibility of an appeal. To illustrate the various stages of a criminal trial, we rely on Donald Trump's 2024 conviction on charges related to paying off Stormy Daniels in the leadup to the 2016 presidential election. We also provide current statistics throughout the chapter.

Chapter 11 examines the civil court process, beginning with an analysis of the distinct types of civil cases and the options available to the complainant and the respondent. We then proceed through the various methods of alternative dispute resolution, followed by a discussion of pretrial hearings and jury selection. Finally, we discuss the trial and judgment. In addition to updates to statistics and examples, this chapter gives

1 FOUNDATIONS OF LAW IN THE UNITED STATES

CHAPTER GOALS AND OBJECTIVES

In this chapter, readers will learn that . . .

- It is important that we understand what we mean by the word *law*.
- There are a variety of types of law in the United States, and each one has a separate function for society.
- Americans have historically had rather ambivalent attitudes about whether the law should always be obeyed and about whether there are legitimate reasons for ignoring the commands of legal statutes.
- The United States is a very litigious society, and there are reasons why this might be a good thing.

They called themselves the Memphis Seven. Coworkers at a Starbucks location in Memphis, Tennessee, they were all fired in February 2022 after being accused by the coffee giant of violating company safety and security policies. But the baristas believed the *real* reason they lost their jobs was in retaliation for their efforts to unionize their local branch of the national chain. Starbucks management claimed that the employees had violated company rules when they unlocked a door to the store after hours and allowed unauthorized TV media representatives into the building to conduct employee interviews as part of the workers' attempts to publicize their unionization efforts. It was also alleged by the company that the Memphis Seven had not followed the company's COVID-era protocols regarding mask-wearing, imperiling the health and safety of those in the store.[1]

Starbucks Workers United, a union spearheading efforts to unionize the company's workers across the United States, filed a legal challenge on behalf of the fired employees, arguing that the workers were victims of unfair labor practices. The union claimed that "Starbucks chose to selectively enforce policies that have not previously been consistently enforced as a pretext to fire union leaders."[2] The baristas pointed out that some of the supposed violations were common practices at the coffee shop and that employees had not been previously disciplined over them. They noted, for example, that off-duty workers frequently had been admitted into the closed store to check their schedules, which are posted there.[3] The union also argued that companies are prohibited by federal law—in particular, by the National Labor Relations Act—from retaliating against workers for leading unionization efforts. Companies may not like unions—in fact, news reports noted that the Seattle-based coffee company had a history of being anti-union.[4] But legally, employers cannot harm or otherwise disadvantage workers who push to organize and fight for collective bargaining. The union claimed that that is exactly what Starbucks had done.

"The Memphis Seven" — seven former employees of a Starbucks coffee shop in Memphis, Tennessee, who claimed they were fired in 2022 for their efforts to unionize their store's employees.

Patrick Lantrip/Daily Memphian via AP

So, who was correct in this "David versus Goliath" dispute? Was Starbucks legally allowed to fire the employees for clearly violating company rules? Were the workers right that the rules violation was just an excuse that the company used to illegally dismiss staff who were leading unionization efforts?

The dispute was initially heard by the National Labor Relations Board (NLRB), the government agency that enforces a federal law known as the National Labor Relations Act (NLRA) by investigating allegations of wrongdoing brought by workers, unions, employers, conducting organizing elections, and deciding and resolving cases.[5] After a formal hearing process in which both sides were given the opportunity to present their cases, the NLRB ruled in favor of the baristas. The board concluded that Starbucks unlawfully fired the Memphis employees for supporting the union drive and that the company had done so, at least in part, to send a threatening message to other workers about supporting the union.

But this decision by itself did not end the matter. The NLRB finding in their favor did not automatically give the workers their jobs back. For that to happen, there would have to be an order issued by a federal judge to force the company to rehire the employees. And that's exactly what the NLRB got when it requested such an order from US District Judge Sheryl Lipman, who ruled in favor of the employees and granted an injunction compelling Starbucks to rehire the workers. Consistent with its right under federal law, the coffee chain appealed Judge Lipman's injunction to the US Court of Appeals for the Sixth Circuit, which upheld the judge's ruling.[6]

Starbucks then appealed to the US Supreme Court. But the company made a claim on appeal to the High Court that raised a new and interesting legal question, increasing the likelihood that the justices would agree to hear the case. In particular, Starbucks questioned the standard that judges should use to determine whether to issue such a preliminary injunction. In other words, Starbucks didn't dispute the specific *facts* in the case; rather, the company challenged Judge Lipman's *legal authority* to issue the injunction mandating that the company rehire the baristas. In particular, the company's appeal questioned how hard it should for the NLRB to win an injunction.[7] As it turns out, the NLRA law doesn't say much about this, simply providing that a court can grant "such temporary relief . . . as it deems just and proper." But this imprecise language conflicted with existing precedent, which had a stricter standard for granting an injunction. Starbucks argued that the judge didn't have the legal power to order the company to rehire the workers because the NLRA's vague standard unfairly gave too much leeway to judges.[8] And if the company's argument that Judge Lipman didn't have the legal authority to grant the order was correct, then her injunction was null and void. The workers would not get their jobs back.

On June 13, 2024, the US Supreme Court settled the dispute when it handed down a ruling in favor of Starbucks. In a decision that was said to hinder future efforts to organize workers, the Court ruled that the legal test the district court judge used to make their decision was too broad and inconsistent with precedent.[9] The NLRB ruling in favor of the Memphis Seven was not reversed, but the judge's order forcing the company to rehire the workers was ruled improper and thus overturned.

This was an outcome in which both sides could claim at least some vindication. The workers won a key public relations and moral victory when the NLRB ruled that they had been fired improperly by Starbucks. "It's exciting to know, us baristas in Memphis, Tennessee, in the South, an area where they aren't very pro-union, that we were able to create an atmosphere and really drive forward the labor union," said twenty-five-year-old Memphis Seven member Nabretta Hardin.[10] And some observers have suggested that high-profile litigation over labor organizing efforts has led Starbucks to soften its stance toward unions.[11] But the company prevailed in the dispute about being forced to rehire the dismissed employees — the baristas did not win back their jobs. Starbucks issued a statement that said, in part, "Consistent federal standards are important in ensuring that employees know their rights and consistent labor practices are upheld no matter where in the country they work and live."[12]

This dispute reveals much about the United States and the rule of law, and it suggests themes that we will articulate not only in this chapter but throughout the book. What happens when there are conflicts between two lawful and well-motivated propositions: the desire to engage in union organization and a company's right to enforce its policies consistent with established legal principles? Both desires are legitimate, but sometimes, they may come into conflict with one another. And if distinctions are to be made in our society between conflicting interests, which institutions should be empowered to make these determinations: legislatures, courts, local executives, or election officials?

We begin our discussion of the foundations of law in the United States with a look at the law itself. This is appropriate because without law, there would be no courts and no judges, no political or judicial system through which disputes could be settled and decisions rendered. In this chapter, we examine the sources of law in the United States—that is, the institutions and traditions that establish the rules of the legal game. We discuss the types of law that are used and define some of the basic legal terms. Likewise, we explore the functions of law for society—what it enables citizens to avoid and accomplish as individuals and as a people that would be impossible without the existence of some commonly accepted rules. Finally, we examine America's ambivalent tradition vis-à-vis the law—that is, how a nation founded on an illegal revolution and nurtured with a healthy tradition of civil disobedience can pride itself on being a land where respect for the law is ideally taught at every mother's knee. We also take note of the degree to which American society has become highly litigious and why this is significant for the study of the American judicial system.

DEFINITION OF LAW

A useful definition of American **law** postulates that "law is a social norm the infraction of which is sanctioned in threat or in fact by the application of physical force by a party possessing the socially recognized privilege of so acting."[13] This definition suggests that law comprises three basic elements—force, official authority, and regularity—the combination of which differentiates law from mere custom or morals in society.

In an ideal society, force would never have to be exercised; in an imperfect world, the threat of its use is a foundation of any law-abiding society. Although substitutes for physical force may be used, such as confiscation of property or imposition of fines, the possibility of physical punishment must nevertheless remain to deter a potential lawbreaker. The right to apply this force constitutes the official element of the definition of law. The party that exercises this right of physical coercion represents a valid legal authority. Finally, the term *regularity*, as used in the legal sense, can be likened to its use by scientists. Although the term does not reflect absolute certainty, it does suggest uniformity and consistency. The law calls for a degree of predictability, of regularity, in the way individuals are expected to behave or to be treated by the state. In American society, this emphasis on regularity is manifested by adherence to prior court decisions and precedents (the **common law** doctrine of **stare decisis**) and by the mandate of the Fourteenth Amendment to the US Constitution, which forbids the states to "deny to any person within its **jurisdiction** the *equal protection* of the laws" (emphasis added).[14]

SOURCES OF LAW IN THE UNITED STATES

Where does law come from in the United States? At first, the question seems a bit simpleminded. A typical response might be, "Law comes from legislatures; that's what Congress and the state legislatures do." This answer is not wrong, but it is far from adequate. Law comes from a large variety of sources.

Constitutions

The US Constitution is the primary source of law in the United States, as it claims to be in Article VI: "This Constitution . . . shall be the supreme Law of the Land; and the Judges in every State shall be bound thereby, any Thing in the Constitution or Laws of any State to the Contrary notwithstanding." Thus, none of the other types of law may stand if they conflict with the Constitution. Similarly, each state has its own separate constitution, and all local laws must yield to its supremacy.

Acts of Legislative Bodies

Laws passed by Congress and by state legislatures constitute a sizable bulk of law in the United States. Statutes requiring the payment of income tax to Uncle Sam and state laws forbidding the robbing of banks are both examples. But many other types of legislative bodies also enact statutes and ordinances that regulate the lives of US residents. County commissioners (also known as county judges or boards of selectmen), for example, act as legislative bodies for the various counties within the states.

Likewise, city councils serve in a legislative capacity when they pass ordinances, set property-tax rates, establish building codes, and so on at the municipal level. Then there are almost fifty thousand "special districts" throughout the country, each of which is headed by an elected or appointed body that acts in a legislative capacity. Examples of these would be school districts, fire prevention districts, water districts, and municipal utility districts.

Decisions of Quasi-Legislative and Quasi-Judicial Bodies

Sprinkled vertically and horizontally throughout the US governmental structure are thousands of boards, agencies, commissions, departments, and so on, whose primary function is not to legislate or to adjudicate but that still may be called on to make rules or to render decisions that are semilegislative or semijudicial in character. The job of the US Postal Service is to deliver the mail, but sometimes it may have to act in a quasi-judicial capacity. For example, a local postmaster may refuse to deliver a piece of mail because he or she believes it contains hazardous materials. (Congress has mandated that "hazardous materials" may not be sent through the mail.) The postmaster is acting in a semi- or quasi-judicial capacity in determining that a particular item is "hazardous" and hence not subject to being delivered.

The US Securities and Exchange Commission (SEC) is not a lawmaking body, either, but when it determines that a particular company has run afoul of the security laws or when it rules on a firm's qualification to be listed on the New York Stock Exchange, it becomes a source of law in the United States. In effect, the SEC makes rules and decisions that affect a person or a company's behavior and for which penalties are imposed for noncompliance. Although decisions of such agencies may be appealed to or reviewed by the courts, they are binding unless they are overturned by a judicial entity.

A university's board of regents may also be a source of law for the students, faculty, and staff members covered by its jurisdiction. These boards may set rules on matters such as which persons may lawfully enter the campus grounds, procedures to be followed before a staff member may be fired, or definitions of plagiarism. Violations of these rules or procedures carry penalties backed by the full force of the law.

Orders and Rulings of Political Executives

Civics classes teach that legislatures make the law and executives enforce the law. That is essentially true, but political executives also have some lawmaking capacity. This lawmaking occurs when presidents, governors, mayors, or others fill in the details of legislation passed by legislative bodies, and sometimes when they promulgate orders purely in their executive capacity.

When Congress passes reciprocal trade agreement legislation, the goal is to encourage other countries to lower trade and tariff barriers to US-produced goods, in exchange for which the United States will do the same. But there are so many thousands of goods, almost two hundred countries, and countless degrees of setting up or lowering trade barriers. What to do? The customary practice is for Congress not only to set basic guidelines for the reciprocal lowering of trade barriers but also to allow the president to decide how much to regulate a given tariff on any given commodity for a particular country. These executive orders of the president are published regularly in the *Federal Register* and carry the full force of law. In fact, at the national level, more than 80,000 pages of new rules are churned out each year.[15] At the present time, the *Code of Federal Regulations*, dealing mainly with economic activity and published in the *Federal Registrar*, now runs over 200,000 pages.[16]

In his first several months in office, President Joe Biden made extensive use of his power to issue executive orders. For instance, on January 20, 2021, he revoked President Donald Trump's plan to exclude noncitizens from the census; on January 25, he declared that transgender persons could serve in the military; and on January 27, he ordered that climate change be elevated as a **national security** concern.[17]

Likewise, at the state level, when a legislature delegates to the governor the right to "fill in the details of legislation," the state executive uses his or her **ordinance-making power**, which also is a type of lawmaking capacity. Political executives may promulgate orders that, within certain narrow but important realms, constitute the law of the land. For example, during the height of the COVID-19 pandemic in 2020, many governors and mayors issued orders limiting or prohibiting certain kinds of public gatherings of individuals in order to prevent the spread of the virus. The governor of the state of Kentucky issued an order limiting religious gatherings to ten people.[18] In California, that state's governor issued a similar order requiring that people in houses of worship maintain a six-foot distance from one another. Violators were subject to a fine of up to $1,000 or up to ninety days imprisonment.[19] Although limited and usually temporary, such orders are law, and violations invoke penalties.

Judicial Decisions

Civics classes also teach that judges interpret the law. So, they do, but judges make law as they interpret it. And judicial decisions themselves constitute a body of law in the United States. All the thousands of court decisions that have been handed down by federal and state judges for the past two-and-a-half centuries are part of the **corpus juris**—the body of law—of the United States.

Judicial decisions may be grounded in or surround a variety of entities: any of the abovementioned sources of law, past decisions of other judges, or legal principles that have evolved over the centuries. (For example, one cannot bring a lawsuit on behalf of another person unless that person is one's minor child or ward.) Judicial decisions may also be grounded in the common law—that is, those written (and sometimes unwritten) legal traditions and principles that have served as the basis of court decisions and accepted human behavior for many centuries. For instance, if a couple lives together as husband and wife for a specified period of years, the common law may be invoked to have their union recognized as a legal marriage.

TYPES OF LAW

After examining the wellsprings of American law, it is appropriate to take a brief look at the vessels wherein such laws are contained—that is, to define or explain the formal types of categories of law. (Note that types of law are not necessarily mutually exclusive.)

Codified (or Code) Law

Unlike the United States, most countries (including most of Europe and Latin America) refer to themselves as code law countries. A code is merely a body of laws, but it is one that consists of statutes enacted by a national parliament. These laws address virtually all aspects of the body politic; are often detailed; and are arranged in an orderly, systematic, and comprehensive manner. The US legal system is often seen from abroad as a hodgepodge of legislative acts, judicial decisions, unwritten legal traditions, and so on.

Statutory Law and Common Law

Statutory law is the type of law enacted by a legislative body such as Congress, a state legislature, or a city council, although it could also include the written orders of various quasi-legislative bodies. The key is that the enactments be in written form and be addressed to the needs of society. Examples of statutory law would be a congressional act increasing Social Security payments or a statute passed by a state legislature authorizing the death penalty for first-degree murder. Statutory law is often contrasted with the common law, which is a less orderly compilation of traditions, principles, and legal practices that have been handed down from one generation of lawyers and judges to the next. Because much of the common law is not systematically codified and delineated, as is statutory law, it is sometimes referred to as the unwritten law. However, this is not entirely accurate. Much of the common law exists in the form of court decisions and legal precedents that are in written form. The common law is known for its flexibility and capacity to change as it evolves in response to the changing needs and values of society.

Civil Law and Criminal Law

Civil law deals with disagreements between individuals—for example, a dispute over ownership of private property. It also pertains to corporations, admiralty matters, and contracts. **Criminal law** concerns offenses against the state itself—actions that may be directed against a person but that are deemed to be offensive to society. **Crimes** such as drunken driving, armed robbery, and so on are punishable by fines or imprisonment.

Equity

Equity is best understood when contrasted with law; the primary difference between the two terms is in the remedy involved. In law, the only remedy is financial compensation; in equity, a judge is free to issue a remedy that will either prevent or cure the wrong that is about to happen. Because in many circumstances monetary settlements are inappropriate or inadequate, equity allows judges a degree of flexibility that they would not otherwise have. For example, say you were the owner of an old cabin located in the center of town and that this structure was the first built in the community. You wish to preserve it because of its historic value, but the city decides to expand the adjacent street and thereby destroy the cabin. Your remedy at law is to ask the city for monetary compensation, but to you, this is inadequate. The cabin has little intrinsic value, although as a historic object, it is priceless. Thus, you may wish to ask a judge to issue a writ in equity that might order the city to move the cabin to another site or to reconsider its plan to widen the street.

Private Law

Private law deals with the rights and obligations that private individuals and institutions have when they relate to one another. Much civil law is in this category because it covers subjects such as contracts between private persons and corporations and statutes pertaining to marriage and divorce.

Public Law

Public law addresses the relationship that individuals and institutions have with the state as a sovereign entity. The government makes laws in its capacity as the primary political unit to which all owe allegiance; in turn, the government is obliged to preserve and protect the citizens who live within its jurisdiction. Public law also deals with obligations that citizens have to the government, such as paying taxes or serving in the armed forces, or it may pertain to services or obligations that the state owes to its citizenry, such as laws providing for unemployment compensation or statutes protecting property rights. Criminal law also falls into this broad category, as do laws that deal with such diverse subjects as defense, welfare, and taxation. Two subheadings in this category are administrative law and constitutional law.

Administrative Law

The decisions and regulations set forth by the various administrative agencies of the government are the substance of administrative law. Agencies, such as the SEC or a city health department, are empowered to oversee implementation or carry out specific mandates established by a legislative body. When one of these agencies promulgates rules or guidelines about how it intends to carry out its regulatory functions, the rules become part of administrative law.

Constitutional Law

Basically, constitutional law is the compilation of all court rulings on the meaning of the various words, phrases, and clauses in the US Constitution. Although all courts have the authority to perform this function, the US Supreme Court has the final say about questions of constitutional law. For example, in 1952, during the Korean War, the United States was faced with a strike by the unions against the nation's steel producers. President Harry S. Truman believed that a steel strike would impair the production of armaments needed for the war. He decided to seize and run the steel mills in the name of the United States. He claimed that he had "inherent powers" under Article II of the Constitution to do this—for example, his power as "Commander in Chief of the Army and Navy" and the fact that "the executive power shall be vested in [the] president." The Supreme Court disagreed with Truman and ruled that the chief executive did not have inherent authority to seize and operate the steel mills—even in times of emergency—without specific congressional authorization.[20]

State Law and Federal Law

Laws passed by one of the fifty state legislatures, ordinances promulgated by a state governor, and decisions handed down by a state court all constitute the corpus juris of a single state. They are compelling only for the citizens of that state and for outsiders who reside or do business there. State laws must not conflict with either federal law or anything in the US Constitution. Examples of state law are Illinois' income tax for those who reside within its boundaries and Utah's law that approves the use of firing squads for executions "when no lethal-injection drugs are available."[21] Federal law is made up of acts of Congress, presidential orders, US court decisions, and so on. This body of law applies throughout the United States and usually pertains to topics that are relevant to persons in more than just one state. Examples include a congressional act forbidding the transportation of a stolen car across state lines and a US Supreme Court decision outlawing prayer in the public schools. As with state law, federal law must be in harmony with the strictures of the US Constitution.

FUNCTIONS OF LAW

What is the function of law in the United States (or in any country, given that the function of law is universal)? What would the negative consequences be if there were no law? Or conversely, what positive things could be done through law that would be impossible without it? Few would deny that, in today's world, law is essential for ensuring that people live together amicably. As populations expand and modern transportation and communication link people together even more, every action that everyone takes affects others, either directly or indirectly, possibly causing harm. When conflict results, it must be resolved peaceably, using a rule of law. Otherwise, disorder, death, and chaos reign. Some common set of rules must exist that all agree to live by—in other words, a rule of law and order.

But what kind of law and order? Anarchists (those who are opposed to laws in general) argue that laws restrict personal freedom, and certainly in many cases that is so. If there are too many rules, laws, and restrictions, totalitarianism results. This result may be just about as bad as a state of anarchy. The trick is to strike a balance so that the positive things that law can do are not strangulated by the tyranny of the law and order offered by the totalitarian state.

Assuming, then, that both anarchy and totalitarianism are rejected, what are the positive functions of law when it exists to a reasonable degree? Legal theorists denote several benefits.

Providing Order and Predictability in Society

The world is often chaotic and uncertain. People win lotteries while the price of oil fluctuates dramatically; more and more people are living to the age of one hundred, while millions around the world died of COVID; the availability of agricultural commodities ebbs and flows based upon fickle weather patterns, geopolitical concerns, industrial accidents, and supply chain disruptions. Laws can neither avert most natural disasters nor prevent random episodes of misfortune, but they can create an environment in which people can work, invest, and pursue happiness with a reasonable expectation that their activity is worth the effort. Without an orderly environment based on and backed by law, the normal activities of life would be lacerated with chaos.

For example, rules must be established that determine which side of the road to drive on, how fast cars can safely go, and when to slow down and stop. Without rules of the road, horrible traffic jams and terrible accidents would result because no driver would know what to expect from the others. Without a climate of law and order, no parent would have the incentive to save for a child's college education. The knowledge that the bank will not close and that one's savings account will not be arbitrarily confiscated by the government or by some powerful party gives the parent an environment in which to save. Law and the predictability it provides cannot guarantee a totally safe and predictable world, but they can create a climate in which people believe it is worthwhile to produce, to venture forth, and to live for the morrow.

Resolving Disputes

No matter how benign and loving people can be at times, altercations and disagreements are inevitable. How disputes are resolved between quarreling individuals, corporations, or governmental entities reveals much about the level and quality of the rule of law in a society. Without an orderly, peaceful process for dispute resolution, there is either chaos or a climate in which the largest gang of thugs or those with the strongest fists prevail.

Suppose a new fraternity house is built next to the home of Mr. Joe Six-Pack, a man who likes his peace and quiet. After Joe's sleep has been disrupted for the umpteenth time by loud music coming from the fraternity house, Joe decides to get even. About sunrise one Sunday, after another sleepless night, Joe angrily runs over to his neighbors' driveway and systematically begins to let air out of the tires of the students' cars—"just to teach those damn kids a lesson." He is caught in the act by several well-soused fraternity boys marking the end of a raucous night. Angry words are exchanged; "manhood" and "right-and-wrong" are at stake. A brawl ensues, resulting in bloodshed and injury all around. How much better the outcome would have been if Joe had turned this grievance over to the police, the courts, or campus authorities—all empowered by the law to peacefully resolve such matters.

Protecting Individuals and Property

Even libertarians, who take a narrow view of the role of government, will readily acknowledge that the state must protect citizens from the outlaw who would inflict bodily harm or steal or destroy their worldly goods. Because of the importance of the safety of persons and their property, many laws on the books deal with protection and security. Not only are laws in the criminal code intended to punish those who steal and do bodily harm, but civil statutes also permit many crime victims to sue for monetary **damages**. The law has created police and sheriffs' departments, district attorneys' offices, courts, jails, and death chambers to deter and punish the criminal and to help people feel secure. This is not to say that there is no crime; everyone knows otherwise. But without a system of laws, crime would be much more prevalent and the fear of it would be much more paralyzing. Unless everyone could afford to hire his or her own bodyguards and security teams, people would be in constant anxiety about the potential loss of life, limb, and property. However imperfect the system of law, prevention, and enforcement may be, it is certainly better than none.

Providing for the General Welfare

Laws and the institutions and programs they establish enable a society to do corporately what would be impossible, or at least prohibitive, for individuals to do. Providing for the common defense, educating young people, putting out forest fires, controlling pollution, and caring for the sick and aged are all examples of activities that could be done only feebly, if at all, by an individual acting alone but that can be done efficiently and effectively as a society. Citizens may disagree about which endeavors should be undertaken through the government by law. Some may believe, for example, that the aged should be cared for by family members or by private charity; others see such care as a corporate responsibility. Although citizens can disagree about the precise activities that the law should require of government, few would deny that many significant and beneficial results are achieved through corporate endeavors. After all, the foundation of the American legal system, the Constitution, was ordained to "establish Justice, ensure domestic tranquility, provide for the common defense, promote the general Welfare, and secure the Blessings of Liberty to us and our Posterity."

Protecting Individual Liberties

Law should protect the individual's personal and civil rights against those forces that would curtail or restrict them. These basic freedoms might include those provided for in the Bill of Rights, such as freedom of speech, of religion, and of the press; the right to a fair trial; and freedom from cruel and unusual punishment. They might also include some that are not stated in the Bill of Rights but are implied, such as the right to personal privacy, or they might be rights that Congress has provided through legislation, such as the right to be free from job discrimination based on gender or ethnic origin. Potential violators of these freedoms might be the government itself (for example, a law denying American citizens accused of terrorist acts the right to a civilian trial) or one's fellow citizens (for example, a conspiracy among private individuals to discourage certain persons from voting). Although disagreement may arise about which freedoms are basic or about how extensively they should be provided for, it is fair to say that unless the law protects certain basic immutable rights, the nation's citizens are no more than cogs in a machine. It is the meaningful provision for these basic liberties that ensures the dignity and richness of the life of the individual.

THE UNITED STATES AND THE RULE OF LAW

Americans pride themselves on being a law-abiding people, and to the casual observer, they are. Few would question Abraham Lincoln's admonition that respect for the law should be taught to every child at his or her mother's knee, and most are glad to proclaim that the United States has a government of law, not of individuals. The United States has one of the highest incarceration rates in the world—the US prison population was 1,230,100 in 2022.[22] Indeed, the United States locks up around 20 percent of the Earth's prisoners, even though it is home to less than 5 percent of the world's inhabitants. But this is seen by many not as evidence that society is lawless but as proof that in the United States respect for the law is paramount and disobedience of the law is punished.[23] A careful analysis of US history and traditions reveals, however, that this view of the law has in reality been ambivalent. A few examples will illustrate Americans' love–hate relationship with the rule of law.

The Revolutionary War

An appropriate place to begin is the Revolutionary War. Few Americans can look back on that seven-year struggle and feel anything but pride when certain images come to mind: the bold act of defiance of the Boston Tea Party; the shot fired at Concord, Massachusetts, that was "heard 'round the world"; and George Washington's daring attack on the Hessian troops at Trenton, New Jersey. Despite the goose bumps raised in this patriotic reverie, one bothersome fact is lost: the Revolution was illegal. The wanton destruction of private property wrought by the Boston Tea Party and the killing of British troops sent to America for the colonists' protection were illegal in every sense of the word. The founders were so keenly aware of this fact that they prepared a Declaration of Independence to justify to the rest of the world why a bloody and illegal revolt against the lawful government is sometimes permissible:

> When in the course of human events, it becomes necessary for one people to dissolve the political bands which have connected them with another-. . ., a decent respect to the opinions of mankind requires that they should declare the causes which impel them to the separation . . . [W]hen a long train of abuses and usurpations . . . evinces a design to reduce them under absolute Despotism, it is their right, it is their duty, to throw off such Government, and to provide new Guards for their future security.

The irony of America's birth is often overlooked. This citadel of law and order was born under the star of illegality and revolution.

John Brown at Harpers Ferry

Another example is John Brown's famous raid on the US arsenal at Harpers Ferry, West Virginia, in the fall of 1859. With thirteen White men and five Black men, this militant opponent of slavery launched his plan to lead a mass insurrection among the slaves and to create an abolitionist republic on the ruins of the South and its plantation economy. After a small but bloody battle that lasted several days, Brown was captured, given a public trial, and duly hanged for murder and other assorted crimes. But were Brown's flagrantly violent and illegal actions justifiable, given the nobility of his vision? Many in the North believed so. Its moral and cultural elite took the line that Brown might have been insane, but his acts and intentions should be excused on the grounds that the compelling motive was divine. Horace Greeley wrote that the Harpers Ferry raid was "the work of a madman," but he had not "one reproachful word." Ralph Waldo Emerson described Brown as a "saint." Henry David Thoreau, Theodore Parker, Henry Wadsworth Longfellow, William Cullen Bryant, and James Lowell—the whole Northern pantheon—took the position that Brown was an "angel of light," and that it was not Brown but the society that hanged him that was mad. It was also reported that "on the day Brown died, church bells tolled from New England to Chicago; Albany fired off one hundred guns in salute, and a governor of a large Northern state wrote in his diary that men were ready to march to Virginia."[24] Again, the ambivalence is evident. One ought always to obey the law—unless one hears a divine call that transcends the law.

The Civil Rights Movement

The civil rights movement beginning in the 1950s conflicted many Americans between their natural desire to obey the law of the land and their call to change the system. As the Reverend Martin Luther King Jr. sat in a Birmingham, Alabama, jail, he wrote a now famous letter to supporters who were disturbed by his having disobeyed the law during his civil rights protests:

> You express a great deal of anxiety over our willingness to break laws. This is certainly a legitimate concern. Since we would diligently urge people to obey the Supreme Court's decision in 1954 outlawing segregation in the public schools, at first glance it may seem rather paradoxical for us consciously to break laws. One may well ask: "How can you advocate breaking some laws and obeying others?" The answer lies in the fact that there are two types of laws: just and unjust. I would be first to advocate obeying just laws. One has not only a legal but a moral responsibility to obey just laws. Conversely, one has a moral responsibility to disobey unjust laws. Thus, it is that I can urge men to obey the 1954 decision of the Supreme Court [*Brown v. Board of Education*, 347 U.S. 483 (1954)], for it is morally right; and I can urge them to disobey segregation ordinances, for they are morally wrong.[25]

Even a member of the Supreme Court of the United States sanctioned civil disobedience during the heady days of the civil rights movement. Justice Abe Fortas said,

> If I had been a Negro living in Birmingham or Little Rock or Plaquemines Parish, Louisiana, I hope I would have disobeyed the state laws that said that I might not enter the public waiting room in the bus station reserved for "Whites." I hope I would have insisted upon going into parks and swimming pools and schools which state or city law reserved for "Whites." I hope I would have had the courage to disobey, although the segregation ordinances were presumably law until they were declared unconstitutional.[26]

More recently, we note the action of a forty-nine-year-old Kentucky county clerk, Kim Davis, who refused to issue marriage licenses to same-sex couples based on her beliefs as an Apostolic Christian. In September 2015, a federal judge temporarily jailed her for contempt of court because of her refusal to obey his orders to issue the contested marriage licenses. Davis was eventually sued for her inaction and in 2024 was ordered by the courts to pay over $360,000 in compensation and damages for refusing to follow the law.[27]

We should also note that in today's world, civil disobedience to morally offensive statutes is not limited to the United States. For example, in 2007, former Pope Benedict XVI told a group of Catholic pharmacists that they have a moral right to use "conscientious objection" to avoid dispensing emergency contraception or euthanasia drugs, and that they should also inform patients of the ethical implications of using such drugs. "Pharmacists must seek to raise people's awareness so that all human beings are protected from conception to natural death, and so that medicines truly play a therapeutic role," Benedict said. He added that conscientious objector status would "enable them not to collaborate directly or indirectly in supplying products that have clearly immoral purposes such as, for example, abortion or euthanasia."[28] Civil disobedience does not need a divine call. Ample illustrations exist of the wholesale avoidance of laws that were thought to be economically harmful and unfair or that were seen as beyond the rightful authority of the state to enact.

Examples of Civil Disobedience in the United States

American farmers are probably as law-abiding a segment of the population as any, but they too can thwart the law when their economic livelihood is at stake. During George Washington's administration, state militias were activated and sent out to quash what came to be known as the Whiskey Rebellion, a series of lawless acts by tillers of the soil who objected to the federal tax on their homemade elixirs. And during the terrible Great Depression of the 1930s, when, for example, one-third of the state of Iowa was being sold into bankruptcy, farmers often revolted. Thousands with shotguns held at bay local sheriffs who tried to serve papers on fellow farmers about to be dispossessed.

During the Prohibition era, from 1919 to 1933, many Americans refused to obey a law they regarded as unfair and more than the legitimate bounds of state authority. Not only did the laws prohibiting the production and sale of alcohol prove to be ineffective and unenforceable, but Americans also seemed to relish flouting the law. The statistics on Prohibition enforcement reveal how the laws were honored in the breach. In 1921, the government seized a total of 95,933 illicit distilleries, stills, still worms, and fermenters; this number rose to 172,537 by 1925, and it jumped to 282,122 by 1930.[29] By 1932, President Herbert Hoover, who had originally supported Prohibition, began to talk about "the futility of the whole business."[30] More recently, the "Occupy movement" was a focus of civil disobedience in the United States (and elsewhere in the world). Beginning in September 2011, literally tens of thousands of Americans "camped out" in public places such as parks or in private and public buildings to protest what they believed are severe inequalities in our economic and social systems. There were almost eight thousand arrests in 122 different cities resulting from these acts of civil disobedience.[31] In many states, it is against the law to engage in certain sexual activities, such as fornication and adultery. "Fornication" is voluntary sexual intercourse between two unmarried persons, while "adultery" is voluntary sexual intercourse between a married person and someone other than his or her lawful spouse. Indeed, at the present time, it is illegal in the state of Mississippi for couples to live together without being married.[32] An identical law was repealed in Michigan only in 2023,[33] while a court in North Carolina overturned that state's law banning cohabitation in 2006, though it has never been officially repealed by the legislature.[34] The fact that laws like these are seldom obeyed or enforced is a secret to no one. Although most Americans still approve of forbidding sexual practices and acts that they find personally distasteful, few have much enthusiasm for putting police officers in bedrooms or for strictly enforcing laws that touch on very personal issues.

Concluding Thoughts on the United States and the Rule of Law

So, are Americans a law-abiding people or not? Is respect for the law only superficial and the belief that everyone ought to obey the law mere cant? The truth, it would appear, is that Americans do honestly have great respect for the law and that their abhorrence of lawbreakers is genuine. But it is also fair to say that mixed with this tradition and orientation is a long-standing belief that sometimes people are called to respond to values higher than the ordinary law and thereby to engage in illegal behavior. However, one person's command to disobey the law and follow the dictates of conscience will appear to another as mere foolishness. Furthermore, Americans have a hefty, pragmatic tradition vis-à-vis the law. Laws that drive citizens to the wall economically (such as farm foreclosures during the 1930s) and laws that are seen to needlessly impinge on personal matters (such as Prohibition and laws prohibiting couples from living together without being married) are just not taken as seriously as those that forbid bank robbery and first-degree murder.

A LITIGIOUS SOCIETY

Like the law, judges are viewed ambivalently by Americans. In general, judges are held in inordinately high esteem, and most Americans would be proud if a son or daughter achieved this position. Yet, Americans can be quick to condemn judges whose rulings go against deeply held values or whose decisions are not in the best interests of their pocketbooks.[35] Whether this is hypocrisy or merely the complex and ambivalent nature of humankind is perhaps in the eye of the beholder.

The raw statistics reveal that Americans readily look to the courts to redress their grievances. The over 380,000 cases that are filed in the federal courts each year[36] are dwarfed by the 13.7 million civil suits filed in the courts of the fifty states and the District of Columbia.[37] That works out to approximately one new lawsuit for every twenty-three people in America.[38] Although some of these suits deal with relatively minor matters, at least three-fourths deal with substantive legal issues. The financial cost of these lawsuits is staggering: though firm statistics are not regularly compiled on such matters, one pro-business interest group estimated in 2022 that the annual bill for such litigation is around $443 billion (at least half of which likely represents legal fees and expenses).[39] Furthermore, the number of lawyers in the United States is comparatively quite large: 1,331,290 as of January 1, 2023, according to the American Bar Association—more per capita than most other countries.[40] And the figure is growing. Over the past decade or so, the number of attorneys nationwide has risen by more than 63,000—an increase of 5 percent from 2013 to 2023.[41] As one expert once noted:

> Ours is a law-drenched age. Because we are constantly inventing new and better ways of bumping into one another, we seek an orderly means of dulling the blows and repairing the damage. Of all the known methods of redressing grievances and settling disputes—pitched battle, rioting, dueling, mediating, flipping a coin, suing—only the latter has steadily won the day in these United States.
>
> Though litigation has not routed all other forms of fight, it is gaining public favor as the legitimate and most effective means of seeking and winning one's just deserts.
>
> The impulse to sue is so widespread that "litigation has become the nation's secular religion," and a growing array of procedural rules and substantive provisions is daily gaining its adherents.[42]

It is useful to see Americans' love affair with lawsuits in some type of comparative perspective. Cross-national comparisons reveal that while the United States is a litigious society, citizens in many other industrialized nations are even more litigious. For example, in the United States in 2011, for every 1,000 people, some 74.5 lawsuits were filed. However, in Germany the number was 123.2; in Sweden it was 111.2; in Israel it was 96.8; and in Austria it was 95.9. So, contrary to much popular belief, America is not the most litigious nation in the world.[43]

This virtual explosion of primarily civil litigation in the United States has led the courts to consider cases that in years past were settled privately between citizens or were issues that often went unresolved. Some cases deal with momentous subjects, such as the right of the states to curtail abortion and efforts by the Environmental Protection Agency to enjoin polluters of the environment. But some suits are surprisingly audacious or trivial:

> [Americans] sue doctors over misfortunes that no doctor could prevent. They sue their school officials for disciplining their children for cheating. They sue their local governments when they slip and fall on the sidewalk, get hit by drunken drivers, get struck by lightning on city golf courses—and even when they get attacked by a goose in a park (that one brought the injured plaintiff $10,000). They sue their ministers for failing to prevent suicides. They sue their Little League coaches for not putting their children on the all-star team. They sue their wardens when they get hurt playing basketball in prison. They sue when their injuries are severe but self-inflicted, and when their hurts are trivial and when they have not suffered at all.[44]

While such suits may be frivolous, they still require the time and efforts of the jurists who must at least consider their merits in the seventeen thousand courthouses throughout the United States.

Despite this plethora of less than monumental lawsuits, the judicial system appears to be fighting those who attempt to use the courts to advance frivolous causes. Rule 11 of the Federal Rules of Civil Procedure forbids the filing of worthless petitions, and this was made stronger in 1983, when US trial judges were given the authority to impose sanctions for the filing of frivolous suits. (Critics of the rule have charged that it has had a chilling effect on civil rights suits, but law school studies have largely refuted that claim.)[45] In 1991, the US Supreme Court handed down two key decisions that reaffirmed the imposition of large fines on those filing specious lawsuits—sending a strong message to the legal community that violations of Rule 11 will be taken seriously.[46] More recently, in May 2018, the Supreme Court handed down a very important ruling that held that companies can require their employees to settle employment disputes through *individual arbitration* rather than filing class actions in federal court.[47] This decision affects as many as twenty-five million workers.[48]

Furthermore, the individual states are also electing to combat those who inundate their legal tribunals with worthless petitions.[49] The American Tort Reform Association now has a nationwide network of state-based liability reform coalitions backed by 135,000 grassroots supporters, and it claims "an unparalleled track record of legislative success."[50] But as with many things in the judiciary, the matter of human judgment is all-important: what is frivolous to one person might be deadly serious to another.

Although a burst of litigation has been evident in the United States during the past several decades, Americans have always been litigious people. As early as 1835, the highly perceptive French observer Alexis de Tocqueville noted that "there is hardly a **political question** in the United States which does not sooner or later turn into a judicial one."[51] As one contemporary scholar has said, "To express amazement at American litigiousness is akin to professing astonishment at learning that the roots of most Americans lie in other lands. We have been a litigious nation as we have been an immigrant one. Indeed, the two are related."[52] This scholar goes on to argue that US history was made by diverse groups who wanted to live according to their own customs but found themselves drawn haphazardly into a larger political community. As these groups bumped into one another and the edges became frayed, disputes resulted. But given a strong common law legal tradition, such disputes were channeled, for the most part, into the courtroom rather than onto the battlefield. Many reasons can be cited as to why Americans have been and continue to be highly litigious, and it is beyond the scope of this chapter to examine them all systematically. Suffice it to say that in the United States, the courthouse has been and is the anvil on which a significant portion of personal, societal, and political problems are hammered out.

Although America is a litigious society, this trend may be part of a worldwide phenomenon. For example, class action lawsuits in Europe increased over 120 percent between 2017 and 2022.[53] In India, that country's already woefully overloaded judicial system has seen the backlog of cases double over the past two decades.[54] Even countries that historically made little use of public law courts are seeing increasing use of these tribunals as their citizens gradually deem it appropriate and useful to bring grievances before the courts, which in earlier times would have been borne in silence or at least viewed as unsuitable for a judicial tribunal. A case in point is China, which in 2008 saw a lawsuit on an issue that at one time would have been considered unthinkable: parents sued the government for the death of their children, which resulted from shoddy workmanship on a collapsed schoolhouse. This stemmed from the horrendous earthquake that occurred in western China in May 2008. The quake left eighty-eight thousand people dead or missing, including up to ten thousand schoolchildren, as thousands of classrooms and dormitories collapsed across the quake zone. The government conceded that in the rush to build schools during the Chinese economic boom, poor workmanship or faulty planning might have contributed to the school's collapse during the quake.[55] In the past, to bring a lawsuit against the Chinese government in such an instance would have been unheard of at best and an act of treason at worst. The lawsuit was eventually dismissed by a court,[56] but the case itself was evidence of a potentially new phenomenon in a changing China.

These facts suggest that modern life and the increasing use of law courts may go hand in glove. Because America's judicial caseload is so enormous and far-ranging, the courts must be examined to understand fully how the nation is governed and how its resources are allocated. Given the significance of courts in formulating and implementing public policy in the United States, it is important to know who the judges are, what their values are, and what powers and prerogatives they possess. And it is essential to study how decisions are made and how they are implemented if the judicial game is to be understood.

SUMMARY

In this chapter, we looked briefly at law in the United States—the wells from which it springs, its basic types, and its functions in society. We also examined the ambivalent attitude Americans have about the rule of law; this is a nation born in an illegal revolution, yet it is proud of its respect for law and order. Finally, we noted that Americans' contentiousness as a people has been channeled largely through the legal and court systems. Consequently, the high priests of the judicial temples, the judges, play a significant role in Americans' personal lives and in their evolution as a society and political entity.

FURTHER THOUGHT AND DISCUSSION QUESTIONS

1. In the introduction to this chapter, we discussed the case of the Memphis Seven, employees of a Starbucks coffee shop who believed they were fired improperly for trying to join a labor union. On the other hand, the company contended that the workers were dismissed for directly violating clear company policies and, in doing so, had threated health and safety. Which side was right? Is there an inherent conflict between what citizens often want to do and what is allowed under the law? How should such conflicts be resolved in a democracy: by popular vote, by the courts, by legislative action, by decisions of elected executive officials?
2. In the United States today, over 1.2 million people are incarcerated in jail or prison. Is this a sign of the inherent lawlessness of the American people, or is it evidence that the United States is a nation that believes in strict law enforcement?
3. Americans are known internationally for their high numbers filing lawsuits, but many other nations, particularly developing countries, are beginning to close the gap. Is this a sign of progress or regression on their part?
4. How many US citizens would be willing to break the law and risk imprisonment if their economic survival depended on it? If they believed the law were illegal and unjustified? If they felt the law violated a higher moral or religious belief? If they felt the law unfairly violated their individual liberties?

SUGGESTED RESOURCES

Calvi, James V., and Susan Coleman. *American Law and Legal Systems*, 8th ed. Boca Raton, FL: Taylor & Francis, 2017. A systematic discussion of all the major types of law in the United States.

Hall, Kermit L., and Karsten Peter. *The Magic Mirror: Law in American History*. New York, NY: Oxford University Press, 2008. A discussion of the historical interactions of law with events in the social and political realms.

Howard, Philip K. *Life Without Lawyers: Restoring Responsibility in America.* New York, NY: W. W. Norton, 2009. This legal reformer argues that we are being choked to death by lawyers and with too much law. His critique is directed mainly toward the realms of health care, education, and the plaintiffs' bar.

Irons, Peter. *The Courage of Their Convictions: Sixteen Americans Who Fought Their Way to the Supreme Court.* New York, NY: Penguin, 1990. Examines sixteen case studies of strong-minded individuals who fought their legal battles all the way to the Supreme Court.

May, Larry, and Jeff Brown. *Philosophy of Law: Classic and Contemporary Readings.* West Sussex, UK: Wiley-Blackwell, 2010. A wide selection of readings about various philosophies of law, punishment, liberty, legal reasoning, and so on.

Sarat, Austin, and Patricia Ewick, eds. *Studies in Law, Politics, and Society,* Vol. # 23. Bingley, UK: Emerald Books, 2012. A collection of readings on diverse topics such as the purpose of law, the dilemmas inherent in social organization, and the discretionary aspects of the judicial system.

Vago, Steven. *Law and Society,* 11th ed. New York, NY: Routledge, 2018. A good summary of law and society issues in the United States, with an excellent comparative perspective on these issues.

KEY TERMS

Civil law
common law
corpus juris
Crimes
Criminal law
damages
Equity
jurisdiction
law
national security
ordinance-making power
political question
Private law
Public law
Statutory law

2 THE FEDERAL JUDICIAL SYSTEM

CHAPTER GOALS AND OBJECTIVES

In this chapter, readers will learn that . . .

- Before we can understand the federal judicial system as it is today, we must first learn about its historical development.
- There are three primary levels of the federal judiciary: the Supreme Court, the courts of appeals, and the federal district courts.
- The federal court system has many different actors and institutions that support it: law clerks and magistrate judges. Also, the Administrative Office of the US Courts and the Federal Judicial Center.
- The federal courts make important policy decisions at all levels of the federal judiciary.
- It is important to understand the size and nature of the federal judicial workload.

One of the most important, most interesting, and most confusing features of the judiciary in the United States is the dual court system—that is, each level of government (state and national) has its own set of courts. Thus, there is a separate court system for each state, one for the District of Columbia, and one for the federal government. Some legal problems are resolved entirely in the state courts, whereas others are handled entirely in the federal courts. Still others may receive attention from both sets of tribunals.

To simplify matters, we discuss the federal courts in this chapter and the state courts in Chapter 3. Because knowledge of the historical events that helped shape the national court system can shed light on the present judicial structure, our discussion of the federal judiciary begins with a description of the court system as it has evolved over more than two centuries. We first examine the three levels of the federal court system in the order in which they were established: the Supreme Court, the courts of appeals, and the district courts. The emphasis in our discussion of each level will be on policy-making roles and decision-making procedures.

Built in 1935, this edifice is the home of the United States Supreme Court.

Courtesy of the Library of Congress, Prints and Photographs Division

In a brief look at other federal courts, we focus on the distinction between constitutional and legislative courts. Next, we discuss the individuals and organizations that provide staff support and administrative assistance in the daily operations of the courts. Our overview discussion concludes with a brief look at the workload of the federal courts.

THE HISTORICAL CONTEXT

Prior to ratification of the Constitution, the country was governed by the Articles of Confederation. Under the Articles, almost all functions of the national government were vested in a single-chamber legislature called Congress. There was no separation of executive and legislative powers.

The absence of a national judiciary was considered a major weakness of the Articles of Confederation. Both James Madison and Alexander Hamilton, for example, saw the need for a separate judicial branch. Consequently, the delegates gathered at the Constitutional Convention in Philadelphia in 1787 and expressed widespread agreement that a national judiciary should be established. A good deal of disagreement arose, however, on the specific form that the judicial branch should take.

The Constitutional Convention and Article III

The first proposal presented to the Constitutional Convention was the Virginia Plan, which would have set up both a Supreme Court and inferior federal courts. Opponents of the Virginia Plan responded with the New Jersey Plan, which called for the creation of a single federal supreme tribunal. Supporters of the New Jersey Plan were especially disturbed by the idea of lower federal courts. They argued that the state courts could hear all cases in the first instance and that a right of appeal to the Supreme Court would be sufficient to protect national rights and provide uniform **judgments** throughout the country.

The conflict between the states' rights advocates and the nationalists was resolved by one of the many compromises that characterized the Constitutional Convention. The compromise is found in Article III of the Constitution, which begins, "The judicial Power of the United States, shall be vested in one supreme Court, and in such inferior Courts as the Congress may from time to time ordain and establish." Thus, the conflict would be postponed until the new government was in operation.

The Judiciary Act of 1789

Once the Constitution was ratified, Congress acted quickly to create the federal judiciary. When the new Congress convened in 1789, its first major concern was judicial organization. Discussions of Senate Bill 1 involved many of the same participants and arguments that were involved in the Constitutional Convention's debates on the judiciary. Once again, the question was whether lower federal courts should be created at all or whether federal claims should first be heard in state courts. Attempts to resolve this controversy split Congress into two distinct groups.

One group, which believed that federal law should be adjudicated in the state courts first and by the US Supreme Court only on appeal, expressed the fear that the new government would destroy the rights of the states. The other group of legislators, suspicious of the parochial prejudice of state courts, feared that litigants from other states and other countries would be dealt with unjustly. This latter group naturally favored a judicial system that included lower federal courts. The law that emerged from the debate, the Judiciary Act of 1789, set up a judicial system comprising a Supreme Court, consisting of a chief justice and five associate justices; three circuits with eleven circuit courts (one in each of the judicial districts in states that had ratified the Constitution), each with two justices of the Supreme Court and a district judge; and thirteen district courts, each presided over by one district judge.[1] The power to create inferior federal courts, then, was immediately exercised. Congress created not one but two sets of lower courts.

THE US SUPREME COURT

A famous jurist once said, "The Supreme Court of the United States is distinctly American in conception and function and owes little to prior judicial institutions."[2] To understand what the framers of the Constitution envisioned for the Court, another American concept must be considered: the federal form of government. The founders provided for both a national government and state governments; the courts of the states were to be bound by federal laws. However, final interpretation of federal laws could not be left to state courts and certainly not to several state tribunals, whose judgments might disagree. Thus, it was decided the Supreme Court must interpret federal legislation. Another of the founders' intentions was for the federal government to act directly on individual citizens as well as on the states. The Supreme Court's function in the federal system may be summarized as follows:

> In the most natural way, as the result of the creation of Federal law under a written constitution conferring limited powers, the Supreme Court of the United States came into being with its unique function. That court maintains the balance between State and Nation through the maintenance of the rights and duties of individuals.[3]

Given the high court's importance to the US system of government, it was perhaps inevitable that the Court would evoke great controversy. A leading student of the Supreme Court said,

> Nothing in the Court's history is more striking than the fact that, while its significant and necessary place in the Federal form of Government has always been recognized by thoughtful and patriotic men, nevertheless, no branch of the Government and no institution under the Constitution has sustained more continuous attack or reached its present position after more vigorous opposition.[4]

The Impact of Chief Justice Marshall

John Marshall served as chief justice from 1801 to 1835, and although he was not the nation's first chief justice, he dominated the Court to a degree unmatched by anyone who came after him. Marshall's dominance of the Court enabled him to initiate some major changes in the way opinions were presented. Before his tenure, the justices ordinarily wrote separate opinions (called seriatim opinions) in major cases. Under Marshall's stewardship, the Court adopted the practice of handing down a single opinion, and the evidence shows that from 1801 to 1835, Marshall himself wrote almost half the opinions.[5] In addition to bringing about changes in opinion-writing practices, Marshall used his powers to involve the Court in the policymaking process. Early in his tenure as chief justice, in *Marbury v. Madison* (1803), the Court asserted its power to declare an act of Congress unconstitutional.[6]

In this decision, Marshall declared Section 13 of the Judiciary Act of 1789 unconstitutional because it granted **original jurisdiction** to the Supreme Court in excess of that specified in Article III of the Constitution. Thus, the Court's power to review and determine the constitutionality of acts of Congress was established. This decision is rightly seen as one of the single most important decisions the Supreme Court has ever handed down. A few years later, the Court also claimed the right of **judicial review** of actions of state legislatures. During Marshall's tenure it overturned more than a dozen state laws on constitutional grounds.[7] Inferior federal and state courts also exercise the power to review the constitutionality of legislation. Judicial review is one of the features that set American courts apart from those in other countries. Judicial scholar Herbert Jacob said that "the United States is the outlier in the extraordinary power that its ordinary courts exercise in reviewing the constitutionality of legislation; France and Germany occupy intermediate positions, and the Japanese courts are the least active."[8] Constitutional challenges to legislation do occur in France and Germany, but ordinary judges sitting in ordinary courts do not exercise these powers. In Japan, the Supreme Court, although possessing the power of constitutional review, rarely exercises it. Judicial review in the United Kingdom is basically of administrative actions.[9]

The Supreme Court as a Policymaker

The Supreme Court's role as a policymaker derives from the fact that it interprets the law. Public policy issues come before the Court in the form of legal disputes that the Court determines must be resolved:

> Courts in any political system participate to some degree in the policymaking process because it is their job. Any judge faced with two or more interpretations and applications of a legislative act, executive order, or constitutional provision must choose among them because the controversy must be decided. And when the judge chooses, their interpretation becomes policy for the specific litigants. If the interpretation is accepted by the other judges, the judge has made policy for all jurisdictions in which that view prevails.[10]

In an article about the European Court of Justice, which serves the twenty-five member states of the European Union, judicial scholar Sally J. Kenney said that this court, similar to the US Supreme Court, "is grappling with the most important policy matters of our time—separation of powers, the environment, communications, labor policy, affirmative action, sex discrimination, and human rights issues."[11] Fundamental human rights issues in the European Court of Justice are typically raised in the context of trade, however.[12]

An excellent example of US Supreme Court policymaking may be found in the area of racial equality. Public school racial segregation was contested in the famous *Brown v. Board of Education* case of 1954.[13] Parents of Black schoolchildren made the case that state laws requiring or permitting segregation deprived them of equal protection of the laws under the Fourteenth Amendment. The Supreme Court ruled that separate educational facilities are inherently unequal, and therefore, segregation constitutes a denial of equal protection. In the *Brown* decision, the Court overturned the separate-but-equal doctrine and established a policy of desegregated public schools.

In an average year, the Court decides, with signed opinions, approximately sixty-five to seventy-five cases.[14] Thousands of other cases are disposed of without full treatment. Thus, the Court deals at length with a very select set of policy issues that have varied throughout its history.

In a democracy, broad matters of public policy are, at least in theory, presumed to be left to the elected representatives of the people—not to judicial appointees with life terms. In principle, US judges are not supposed to make policy, but in practice, they cannot help but do so to some extent, as the examples discussed earlier demonstrate.

The Supreme Court, however, differs from legislative and executive policymakers. Especially important is the fact that the Court has no self-starting device. In other words, the justices must wait for cases to be appealed to them; there can be no judicial policymaking if there is no litigation. The president and members of Congress have no such constraints. Moreover, even the most assertive Supreme Court is limited to some extent by the actions of other policymakers, such as lower court judges, Congress, and the president. The Court also depends on others to implement its decisions (more on that in Chapter 14).

The Supreme Court at Work

As we discuss in greater detail in Chapter 4, the Supreme Court has both original and **appellate jurisdiction**. Original jurisdiction means that a court has the power to hear a case for the first time; Article III of the Constitution outlines the Court's original jurisdiction. On the other hand, appellate jurisdiction means that a higher court has the authority to review cases originally decided by a lower court.

The Supreme Court is overwhelmingly an appellate court because most of its time is devoted to reviewing decisions made by lower courts such as the US courts of appeals and state courts of last resort. The Supreme Court is the highest appellate tribunal in the country, and as such, it has the final word in the interpretation of the Constitution, acts of legislative bodies, and treaties—unless the Court's decision is altered by a constitutional amendment or, in some instances, by an act of Congress.

By law, the formal session of the Supreme Court, known as terms, starts on the first Monday in October and ends until the business of the term is completed, customarily in late June or in rare instances early July. The Court's term is divided into sittings, each lasting approximately two weeks, during which the justices meet in open session and hold internal conferences and recesses. During this time, the justices work behind closed doors to consider cases and write opinions. The sixty-five to seventy-five cases per term that receive the Court's full treatment follow a routine pattern, which is described below.

Case Selection

The Supreme Court generally picks which cases it wants to review and decide. Since 1925, a device known as certiorari has allowed the high court to exercise discretion in deciding which cases it should review. Under this method, a litigant who lost in the courts below may request Supreme Court review of a lower court decision; this is known as a petition for certiorari or a **cert petition**. The litigant seeking review by the Supreme Court will explain in their petition why the Court should review their case. The justices determine whether the request should be granted. In order for a cert petition to be granted at least four justices must decide the case is worthy of review. This is known as the rule of four. If review is granted, the Court issues a **writ of certiorari**, which is an order to the lower court to send up a complete record of the case. When certiorari is denied, the decision of the lower court stands. It should be noted that granting review is extremely rare. For instance, in a typical year the Court receives on average seven thousand cert petitions and the Court grants less than eighty of those petitions for full review. For example, during the twelve-month period ending on September 30, 2023, the Supreme Court granted review to only sixty-eight cases.[15]

Law clerks play an indispensable role in helping justices decide which cases should be heard. At the suggestion of Justice Lewis Powell in 1972, as a way to ease the Court's workload, a majority of the Court's members began to participate in the "certpool": the participating justices pool their clerks, divide up all the cert petition filings, and circulate a single clerk's certiorari memo to all those participating in the pool.[16] The memo summarizes the facts of the case, the questions of law presented, and the recommended course of action—whether the case should be granted a full hearing, denied, or dismissed. To put it another way, law clerks at the Supreme Court play a crucial part in helping the justices decide which cases they will review. Participating in the cert pool is not mandatory, and some justices opt not to be part of the pool. For example, Justices Samuel Alito's and Neil Gorsuch's clerks do not participate in the cert pool.[17] Justice Ketanji Brown Jackson, the Court's newest justice, decided to join the cert pool when she joined the Court.[18]

Written Briefs

If the Supreme Court grants review, the litigants in the case will submit written arguments known as briefs. Per the Supreme Court's rules, the litigant making the appeal, known as the Appellant or Petitioner, must submit their written arguments within forty-five days from when the Court granted the writ of certiorari.[19] Similarly, the Respondent or Appellee has thirty days to file their arguments from receipt of the Appellant brief. The Supreme Court has specific rules governing the written briefs, from page length, formatting, and word limits to the number of copies that must be filed with the Court. Once the briefs have been submitted to the Court, the Clerk of the Court ensures that each justice receives copies of the briefs along with the lower court record. The justices and their law clerks will spend considerable time reviewing the lower court opinion and the litigant briefs as they prepare for oral arguments. As should be no surprise to any student of the Supreme Court, the written briefs, along with the lower court opinion, provide an essential roadmap for the justices in determining how the case should be decided.

Law clerks are essential in helping their justices prepare for oral arguments. After the written briefs are submitted, the law clerks carefully read through them and prepare a bench memorandum that outlines the arguments for the Appellant and Respondent, along with providing an overview of the most relevant precedent. Bench memos may also make recommendations on how the case should be decided. And some justices meet with their law clerks to discuss the merits of the case prior to oral argument.

Oral Argument

Oral arguments are the most visible part of the Supreme Court's work because it is the only part of the process that is open to the public. Oral arguments are generally scheduled on Monday through Wednesday during the sittings. The sessions typically run from 10:00 a.m. to noon, and very rarely will be held in the afternoon beginning at 1:00 p.m. Formal arguments are held in a large courtroom that seats just over four hundred people; however, only fifty of those seats are reserved for the general public viewing.[20] At the front of the courtroom is the bench where the justices are seated. When the Court is in session, the chief justice, followed by the eight associate justices (the number since 1869) in order of seniority (length of continuous service on the Court), enters through the purple draperies behind the bench and takes a seat. Seats are arranged according to seniority, with the chief justice in the center, the senior associate justice on the chief justice's right, the second-ranking associate justice on the left, and continuing this pattern in descending order of seniority. Because the procedure is not a trial or the original hearing of a case, no jury is assembled, and no witnesses are called. Instead, the two opposing attorneys present their arguments to the justices. The general practice is to allow thirty minutes for each side, although the Court may decide that additional time is necessary. For example, when the Court heard oral arguments in the same-sex marriage case (*Obergefell v. Hodges*) on April 28, 2015, it allotted two-and-a-half hours. The Court normally hears two cases per day of arguments.

During oral argument the Appellant (or Petitioner) goes first, followed by the Respondent (or Appellee). The Appellant and Respondent attorneys presenting oral arguments are frequently interrupted with probing questions from the justices; however, according to the Supreme Court's *Guide for Counsel*, during the first two minutes of oral argument justices are generally not permitted to ask questions.[21] After the first two minutes the justices, in a free-for-all manner, will question the attorney. Per the *Guide for Counsel*, once the attorney's time has expired, "each Justice will have the opportunity to question that attorney individually. Questioning will proceed in order of seniority."[22]

The exchange below between Justice Sonia Sotomayor and Lisa Blatt, the attorney defending the school district, in a recent First Amendment student speech case illustrates the back-and-forth dance that happens during oral argument. The *Mahoney Area School District v. B. L.* centers on a high school cheerleader who went on a profanity-laden rant on Snapchat when she did not make the varsity cheer team. She had posted a picture of herself giving the middle finger with a caption that read, "Fuck school fuck softball fuck cheer fuck everything," and all of this occurred off school grounds.[23] When coaches saw screenshots of her Snapchat, she was suspended from the JV cheer team because the school claimed her post violated school and team rules. The student challenged her suspension as a violation of her First Amendment rights. The Third Circuit US Court of Appeals ruled in her favor, which led the school district to appeal the decision to the Supreme Court. In prior school free speech cases, the Court has held that while schoolchildren "do not shed their constitutional rights at the schoolhouse gates," schools may regulate speech that is substantially disruptive to the functioning of the school.[24] During this exchange, Justice Sotomayor wanted to know if the school could regulate cursing at home. The following back-and-forth occurred:

Sotomayor: Let me start with just this case. Can you punish the student for cursing at home—

Blatt: Absolutely—

Sotomayor: —or at her parents' home?

Blatt: —absolutely not, nor could you do that—

Sotomayor: Can you—can you curse—can you punish her for cursing in her conversations as she walks to school?

Blatt: Absolutely not, although, under Respondent's test, I guess you can. But absolutely not.

Sotomayor: All right. Now, if you can't punish them for doing that, you're punishing her here because she went on the Internet and cursed and used a curse word related to what? To her unhappiness with the school and cheering, right?

Blatt: Yes, she berated her coaches, the sport, and other teammates—

Sotomayor: Well—

Blatt: —and that—

Sotomayor: —we could quibble with that, but my point is, I'm told by my law clerks, that among certain populations—a certain large percentage of the population, how much you curse is a badge of honor. That would surprise many parents. However, if it is true, where do we draw the line with respect to it targeting a school? Kids basically talk to their classmates. Most of their conversation is about school. Most of their exchanges have to do with their perceptions of the authoritarian nature of their teachers and others. And why isn't this any different than just that the coach of this team took personal offense?[25]

As the example above illustrates, oral argument is about the back-and-forth between the justices and attorney and is considered particularly important by both attorneys and justices because it is the only stage in the process that allows such personal exchanges in real time.

The Conference

When the Court is in session there are two conferences scheduled per week, one on Wednesday afternoon and the other on Friday. At the Wednesday conference meeting, the justices discuss the cases argued on Monday. At the longer conference on Friday, they discuss the cases that were argued on Tuesday and Wednesday, plus any other matters that need to be considered. The most important of these other matters are the certiorari petitions along with any emergency petitions that have been filed.

The chief justice administers the conference meetings. This means that the chief justice speaks first, and the rest of the justices speak in order of seniority with the most junior justice speaking last. The Court follows a norm that every justice has a chance to talk before they can speak again. Justices have commented on the unique role the most junior justice position has. At times, the junior justice can be the deciding vote, meaning by the time the tentative vote reaches them, the breakdown is 4–4. Other times, there is a clear majority by the time the most junior justice speaks. Justice Ruth Bader Ginsburg made the following observation about the conference: "Justices who speak later do have one advantage. They have an opportunity to adjust their statements to take account of views expressed earlier by others. To do that effectively one must be both well prepared and a good listener."[26]

A quorum for a decision on a case is six members; obtaining a quorum is seldom difficult. Cases are sometimes decided by fewer than nine justices because of vacancies, illnesses, or nonparticipation resulting from possible conflicts of interest. Supreme Court decisions are made by a majority vote. In the event of a tie, the lower court decision is upheld.

Opinion Writing

After a tentative decision has been reached in conference, the next step is to assign an individual justice to write the Court's opinion. The chief justice, if voting with the majority, either writes the opinion or assigns it to another justice who voted with the majority. When the chief justice votes with the minority, the most senior justice in the majority makes the assignment. They can also assign the opinion to themselves or another member of the majority.

After the conference, the justice who will write the Court's opinion begins work on an initial draft. Other justices may work on the case by writing alternative opinions. The completed opinion is circulated to justices in both the majority and the minority groups. The writer seeks to persuade justices originally in the minority to change their votes and to keep their majority group intact. A bargaining process ensues, and the wording of the opinion may be changed to satisfy other justices or obtain their support.

Justice Ginsburg notes this bargaining process is called "Dear [insert the justice's first name]" letters. Justice Ginsburg explains, "In all intra-Court correspondence, we use only first names. 'Dear Ruth' letters not uncommonly read: 'Please consider adding, deleting, dropping, revising to say [thus and so] . . . or 'I will join your opinion if you will take out, put in, alter, or adjust as follows.'"[27]

Sometimes a deep division in the Court makes it difficult to achieve a clear, coherent opinion and may even result in a shift in votes or in another justice's opinion becoming the Court's official ruling. For example, in 1991, the Court heard a school prayer case called *Lee v. Weisman*.[28] In this case a Rhode Island public middle school invited a rabbi to speak and offer a prayer at the graduation ceremonies. During the initial conference vote, a 5–4 majority prevailed upholding prayer at graduation ceremonies. Chief Justice William Rehnquist assigned the majority opinion to Justice Anthony Kennedy. However, by the spring of 1992, and after several attempts to write the opinion, Justice Kennedy came to the position that prayer at public school graduation ceremonies violated the Establishment Clause of the First Amendment. Justice Kennedy "left his chambers and walked down the hall to see Rehnquist. Apologetic and embarrassed, Kennedy delivered the news. In writing the opinion for the majority to allow the prayer, Kennedy had changed his mind about the result. He'd written a decision ruling instead that the prayer was unconstitutional."[29] Kennedy's vote switch meant that Justice Harry Blackmun, the most senior justice in the majority, could reassign the opinion. To maintain this newfound majority, Blackmun strategically kept Kennedy as the majority opinion author. In Blackmun's "Dear Anthony" letter, he wrote, "I have read your draft opinion with interest. As you indicated in your note to me, we have disagreed on the proper approach to the Establishment Clause in the past, but you have done good work in finding common ground in the case. With some changes, it will be an opinion I could join."[30]

In most cases, a single opinion does obtain majority support, and several rulings are often unanimous. However, those who disagree with the **opinion of the Court** are said to dissent. A dissent does not have to be accompanied by a **dissenting opinion**, but usually a justice in the dissent will write one. Whenever more than one justice dissents, each may write an opinion, or all may join in a single opinion. Dissents play an important role in the decision-making process. Political scientists and leading experts on dissenting opinions Pamela Corley, Amy Steigerwalt, and Artemus Ward explain:

> Dissents by their very nature proclaim publicly that important disagreements exist on the Court over the legal question at hand. Dissents highlight the source of these disagreements, allowing justices to spell out precisely how and why they believe their colleagues have erred. They showcase the reality that many legal and policy issues are difficult and complex, lacking clear answers or easy compromises. And dissents ensure that the nature and scope of this disagreement is enshrined in the public record, available to be read by the other justices, lower court judges, members of Congress, and the executive branch, state actors and members of agencies, and the broader public alike.[31]

On occasion, a justice will agree with the Court's decision but differ in their reason for reaching that conclusion. Such a justice may write what is called a **concurring opinion**. A classic example is Justice Sandra Day O'Connor's concurring opinion in *Lawrence v. Texas* (2003).[32] In that case, the majority relied on the Due Process Clause of the Fourteenth Amendment to declare a Texas statute banning same-sex sodomy unconstitutional. Justice O'Connor agreed with the majority that the statute should be struck down, but she based her conclusion on the Fourteenth Amendment's Equal Protection Clause. As sodomy between opposite-sex partners is not a crime in Texas, the state treats the same conduct differently based solely on the sex of the participants. According to Justice O'Connor, that violates the Equal Protection Clause.

An opinion labeled "concurring and dissenting" agrees with part of a Court ruling but disagrees with other parts. Finally, the Court occasionally issues a **per curiam** opinion—an unsigned opinion that is usually brief. Such opinions are often used when the Court accepts the case for review but gives it less than full treatment. For example, it may decide the case without benefit of oral argument and issue a per curiam opinion to explain the disposition of the case. However, it is important to note that the Court can issue per curiam opinions in bigger cases like *Trump v. Anderson* (the case that decided Donald J. Trump could not be removed from the Colorado ballot).[33]

The "Shadow Docket"

In recent years, scholars have begun to take notice of what has been termed "the shadow docket" of the Supreme Court.[34] This refers to the ever-increasing attempts by presidential administrations to seek emergency relief from the Supreme Court on a variety of measures. Such a tactic allows the administration and often states to try to bypass federal appeals courts by asking the Supreme Court to block or undo a federal district court decision of which the administration disapproves. It also allows the Supreme Court to issue rulings, sometimes controversial ones, without opinions.[35] For instance, during the Trump presidency, his administration requested "emergency relief" forty-one times and the Court granted that relief twenty-eight times. To place this increased use of the shadow docket in perspective, the Bush and Obama administrations made these "emergency relief" requests eight times between the two administrations and the Court granted only four of them.[36] In a 2024 study, political scientist EmiLee Smart found evidence that the increased use of the shadow docket leads to less public support for decisions stemming from this procedure.[37]

THE US COURTS OF APPEALS

The **courts of appeals** have been described as "perhaps the least noticed of the regular constitutional courts."[38] They receive less media coverage than the Supreme Court, in part because their activities are simply not as dramatic. However, one should not assume that the courts of appeals are unimportant to the judicial system. For example, in its 2022 term, the Supreme Court handed down decisions with full opinions in only sixty-eight cases; this means, as one set of scholars explain, "the courts of appeals have increasingly become in practice the courts of last resort for the vast majority of litigants."[39]

The courts of appeals were officially created in 1891 under the Evarts Act. The law created nine courts of appeals, one for each judicial district. Over time Congress has expanded the number of circuits and courts of appeals.[40] Although these intermediate appellate courts have been headed at one time or another by circuit judges, courts of appeals judges, district judges, and Supreme Court justices, they now are staffed by 179 authorized courts of appeals judges.

The courts of appeals in each of the twelve regional circuits are responsible for reviewing cases appealed from federal district courts (and in some cases from administrative agencies) within the boundaries of the circuit. Figure 2.1 depicts the appellate and district court boundaries and indicates the states contained in each.

FIGURE 2.1 ■ District and Appellate Court Boundaries

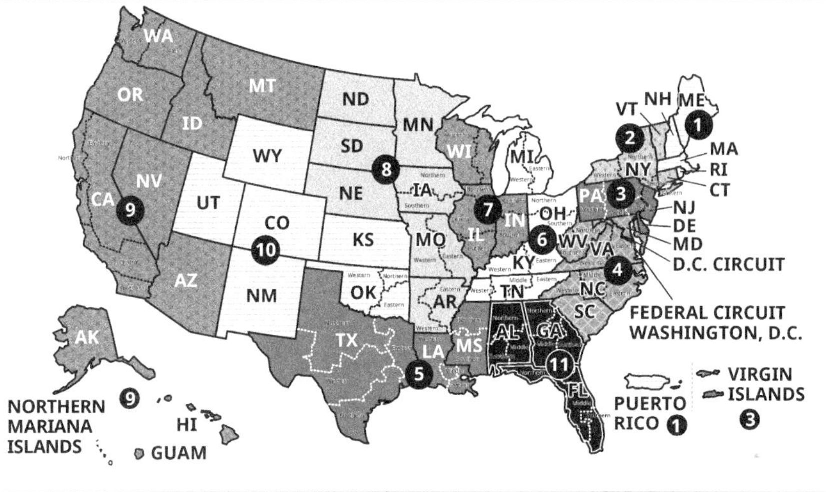

Note: The large numerals indicate the courts of appeals; the dashed lines indicate district boundaries. Number and composition of circuits set forth by 28 U.S.C. § 41.

Source: Administrative Office of the United States Courts, www.uscourts.gov/uscourts/images/CircuitMap.pdf.

A specialized appellate court came into existence in 1982, when Congress established the Federal Circuit, a jurisdictional instead of a geographic circuit. The US Court of Appeals for the Federal Circuit was created by consolidating the Court of Claims and the Court of Customs and Patent Appeals.

The Review Function of the Courts of Appeals

Although the Supreme Court has had discretionary control of its docket since 1925, the courts of appeals still have no such luxury. Instead, their docket depends on how many and what types of cases are appealed to them.

Most of the cases reviewed by the courts of appeals originate in the federal district courts. Litigants disappointed with the lower court decision may appeal the case to the court of appeals of the circuit in which the federal district court is located. The appellate courts have also been given authority to review the decisions of certain administrative agencies. Well over a thousand administrative law judges now perform judicial functions within the executive branch of the federal government. In adjudicating cases, they conduct formal trial-type hearings, make findings of fact and law, apply agency regulations, and issue decisions.[41] This type of case normally enters the federal judicial system at the court of appeals level instead of at the federal district court level.

Because the courts of appeals have no control over which cases are brought to them, they deal with both routine and incredibly important matters. At one end of the spectrum are frivolous appeals or claims that have no substance and little or no chance for success. At the other end of the spectrum are the cases that raise major questions of public policy and evoke strong disagreement. Decisions by the courts of appeals in such cases are likely to establish policy for society, not just for the specific litigants. Civil liberties, reapportionment, religion, and education cases provide good examples of the kinds of disputes that may affect all citizens.

The main purpose of the court of appeals is error correction from the judgement below. Judges in the various circuits are called on to monitor the performance of federal district courts and federal agencies and to supervise their application and interpretation of national and state laws. In doing so, the courts of appeals do not seek out new factual evidence but instead examine the record of the lower court for errors. In the process of correcting errors, the courts of appeals also settle disputes and enforce national law.

The Courts of Appeals as Policymakers

The Supreme Court's role as a policymaker derives from the fact that it interprets the law and Constitution; the same holds true for the courts of appeals. The scope of the courts of appeals' policymaking role takes on added importance because they are the courts of last resort in most cases. A study of three circuits, for example, found that the US Supreme Court reviewed only nineteen of the nearly four thousand decisions of those tribunals.[42] As an example of the impact of circuit court judges, consider a decision in a case involving the Fifth Circuit. After the Supreme Court overturned the *Roe v. Wade* precedent in the *Dobbs v. Jackson Women's Health Organization* (2022) case, many abortion rights opponents have since sought to restrict further abortion access, including access to mifepristone (a medication that can end a pregnancy before the tenth week). A group of doctors opposed to abortion filed a lawsuit in a federal district court in Texas challenging the Food and Drug Administration's (FDA) approval of the drug in 2000, along with two more recent FDA decisions that expanded access to this medication. The district court ruled in favor of the doctors and issued a nationwide suspension of FDA approval of the drug. The case was immediately appealed to the Fifth Circuit. The Fifth Circuit three-judge panel affirmed, in *Food and Drug Administration v. Alliance for Hippocratic Medicine*, the district court's ruling to suspend the FDA expanded access approvals. The Supreme Court agreed to review the case and placed the Fifth Circuit's decision on hold pending its decision. On June 13, 2024, the Supreme Court, in a unanimous ruling, dismissed the case because the doctors bringing the suit lacked the right to sue; this is known as standing (more on standing in Chapter 4).[43] While the Supreme Court skirted ruling on the merits of the case, for now, this ruling means that mifepristone will be available in the United States.

A major difference in policymaking by the Supreme Court and by the courts of appeals should be noted. Whereas there is one high court for the entire country, each court of appeals covers only a specific region. Thus, the courts of appeals decisions only apply to the states and districts within the circuit. Still, as evidenced by the recent mifepristone case, they are part of the federal judicial system and "participate in both national and local policy networks, their decisions becoming regional law unless intolerable to the Justices."[44]

The Courts of Appeals at Work

The courts of appeals do not have the same degree of discretion as the Supreme Court to decide whether to accept a case for review. Nevertheless, circuit judges have developed methods for using their time as efficiently as possible. Additionally, the work of the court of appeals shares many similarities with the Supreme Court.

Screening

After the written briefs from the Appellant and Respondent are filed with the circuit court of appeals the judges and their staff screen the cases. During the screening stage, the judges decide whether to give an appeal a full review or to dispose of it in some other way. The docket may be reduced to some extent by consolidating similar claims into single cases, a process that also results in a uniform decision. In deciding which cases can be disposed of without oral argument, the courts of appeals increasingly rely on law clerks or staff attorneys who read petitions and briefs and then submit recommendations to the judges on whether the case should receive oral arguments. As a result, many cases are decided without receiving oral argument. For example, in 2023, 80 percent of the cases were terminated without oral argument.[45]

Three-Judge Panels

Cases given the full treatment (oral argument) are normally considered by panels of three judges rather than by all the judges in the circuit. The three-judge panels are generally randomly selected and judges will sit in panel on a rotating basis for each sitting period. This means that several cases can be heard at the same time by different **three-judge panels**, often sitting in different cities throughout the circuit.

Panel assignments are typically made by the clerk of the circuit or the circuit executive, and then the clerk randomly assigns cases to the panel (taking into account any conflicts of interest). Because all the circuits now contain more than three judges, the panels change frequently so that the same three judges do not sit together permanently. Regardless of the method used to determine panel assignments, one fact remains clear: a decision reached by a three-judge panel may not necessarily reflect the views of most of the judges in the circuit.

Oral Argument

Cases that have survived the screening process and have not been settled by the litigants are scheduled for **oral argument**. Attorneys for each side are given a short amount of time (in some cases this can range from ten to fifteen minutes and in some instances up to twenty minutes) to discuss the points made in their written briefs and to answer questions from the three-judge panel. Judicial scholars Jennifer Bowie, Donald R. Songer, and John Szmer interviewed over sixty court of appeals judges. One judge they interviewed explained oral arguments in this way:

> Oral argument is always interesting—it is your chance to see what the attorneys will be arguing and what the perspective of the other judges are, because usually this is your first chance to get an idea of what your colleagues are thinking about the case.[46]

The Conference and Decision

Just like the Supreme Court, court of appeals judges meet for conference following oral arguments. The most senior active judge on the panel is called the presiding judge and runs the conference. The judges discuss the case and take a tentative vote. Generally, the conference follows this typical process as explained by one court of appeals judge:

> We first go around the table junior to senior—everyone indicates how they see the first case, then there may be a good bit of back-and-forth to see if there is a way to reach consensus—it is all collegial. I can't think of a single conference in why any hostility was expressed even when we disagreed.[47]

If the presiding judge is in the majority, they may assign the opinion to themselves or another member of the majority. In one study, scholars found evidence that presiding judges assign majority opinions to themselves, especially in important cases.[48] But the presiding judge may also consider other factors when assigning opinions such as judge expertise.

After the opinion assignment is made, the opinion writer will begin the process of writing the opinion of the court. Once the opinion has been drafted, the opinion writer will circulate it to the other panel members for comment. Similar to the Supreme Court, there will be some back-and-forth in the language of the opinion. In a study that interviewed court of appeals judges, one judge commented,

> I have definitely written what you would probably call a "bargaining memo" in response to a draft opinion from a colleague—something like, "If you are willing to change X then I will not dissent."[49]

Once the opinion has been finalized, the court of appeals will make it public. If a judge on the panel disagrees with the majority they can write a dissenting opinion. If any of the panel judges agree with the majority but have different reasons they wish to articulate, they may write a concurring opinion. However, it is necessary to note that separate opinion writing is rare in the court of appeals. Unlike the Supreme Court, most courts of appeals decisions are decided unanimously. Relatedly, because of growing caseloads most opinions in the courts of appeals are issued as unpublished. In 2023, for example, approximately 13 percent of the opinions written were published.[50] This is partly due to the routine clear-cut cases that are appealed to them. Each circuit has rules related to when an opinion should be published. For example, the Fourth Circuit US Court of Appeals *Appellate Procedure Guide* suggests that an opinion should be published if it meets one of the following criteria:

> It establishes, alters, modifies, clarifies, or explains a rule of law within this circuit: or it involves a legal issue of continuing public interest; or it criticizes existing law; or it contains an historical review of a legal rule that is not duplicative; or it resolves a conflict between panels of this court or creates conflict with a decision in another circuit.[51]

It becomes clear from the listed criteria that not every decision will meet the guidelines for opinion publication. When an opinion is published it becomes binding precedent on that circuit (where unpublished opinions are not considered binding precedent).

En Banc Proceedings

Occasionally, different three-judge panels within the same circuit may reach conflicting decisions in similar cases. To resolve such conflicts and to promote circuit unanimity, federal statutes provide for an **en banc** procedure, in which all the circuit's judges sit together on a panel and decide a case. For instance, in the Fourth Circuit Court of Appeals this would mean all fifteen judges would rehear the case if the en banc hearing is granted. The exception to this general rule occurs in the large Ninth Circuit, where assembling all twenty-nine judges becomes too cumbersome. There, en banc panels normally consist of ten judges randomly selected plus the chief judge of the circuit for a total of eleven judges. Interestingly, because of the random selection it is possible for the original three-judge panel members to not be selected to sit on the en banc panel. En banc rehearings rarely happen; when they do, however, the case usually concerns an issue of extraordinary importance. The procedure may be requested by the litigants or by the judges of the circuit. A majority of the judges in the circuit must agree to rehear the case en banc (this is different from the Supreme Court, where only four justices—a minority—are required). The circuits themselves have discretion to decide if and how the procedure will be used. Clearly, its use is the exception, not the rule. If the circuit decided to rehear a case en banc, the litigants will submit new written briefs, the court will hold a new oral argument, and issue a new decision.

US DISTRICT COURTS

The US district courts represent the basic point of input for the federal judicial system. Although some cases are later taken to a court of appeals or perhaps even to the Supreme Court, most federal cases never move beyond the US trial courts. In terms of sheer numbers of cases handled, the district courts are the workhorses of the federal judiciary. However, their importance extends beyond simply disposing of many cases.

Current Organization of the District Courts

The practice of respecting state boundaries in establishing district court jurisdictions began in 1789, and it has been periodically reaffirmed by statutes ever since. As the country grew, new district courts were created. Congress eventually began to divide some states into more than one district. California, New York, and Texas have the most, with four each. Other than consistently honoring state lines, the organization of district constituencies appears to follow no rational plan. Size and population vary widely from district to district. Over the years, a court was added for the District of Columbia, and several territories have been served by district courts. US district courts now serve the fifty states, the District of Columbia, Guam, Puerto Rico, the Virgin Islands, and the Northern Mariana Islands. Today, there are ninety-four districts in the federal court system.

Congress often provides further organizational detail by creating divisions within a district. In doing this, the national legislature precisely lists the counties included in a particular division as well as the cities in which court will be held. For instance, the Southern District of California is made up of two divisions composed of San Diego County and Imperial County.[52]

As indicated, the original district courts were each assigned one judge. With the growth in population and litigation, Congress has periodically added judgeships to the districts, bringing the current total to 677. The Southern District of New York, which includes Manhattan and the Bronx, currently has twenty-eight judges and is the largest. On the other end of the spectrum, Vermont and North Dakota represent the smallest number of judges, each with two.

The District Courts as Trial Courts

Congress established the district courts as the trial courts of the federal judicial system and gave them original jurisdiction over virtually all cases. They are the only federal courts in which attorneys examine and cross-examine witnesses. The factual record is thus established at this level. Subsequent appeals of the trial court decision will focus on correcting errors, not on reconstructing the facts. The task of determining the facts in a case often falls to a jury, a group of citizens from the community who serve as impartial arbiters of the facts and apply the law to the facts.

The Constitution guarantees the right to a jury trial in criminal cases in the Sixth Amendment and the same right in civil cases in the Seventh Amendment. The right can be waived, however, in which case the judge becomes the arbiter of questions of fact as well as matters of law. Such trials are referred to as **bench trials**. Two types of juries are associated with federal district courts. The **grand jury** is a group of people convened to determine whether probable cause exists to believe that a person has committed the federal crime of which they have been accused. Grand jurors meet periodically to hear charges brought by the US attorney. **Petit jurors** are chosen at random from the community to hear evidence and determine whether a **defendant** in a civil trial has liability or whether a defendant in a criminal trial is guilty or not guilty. Federal rules call for twelve jurors in criminal cases but permit fewer in civil cases. The federal district courts generally use six-person juries in civil cases. We discuss juries in greater detail in Chapter 10.

Norm Enforcement by the District Courts

Some students of the judiciary make a distinction between norm enforcement and policymaking by the courts.[53] Trial courts are viewed as engaging primarily in norm enforcement, whereas appellate courts are seen as having greater opportunity to make policy.

Norm enforcement is closely tied to the administration of justice because all nations develop standards considered essential to a just and orderly society. Societal norms are embodied in statutes, administrative regulations, prior court decisions, and community traditions. Criminal statutes, for example, incorporate concepts of acceptable and unacceptable behavior into law. A judge deciding a case concerning an alleged violation of that law is basically practicing norm enforcement. Because cases of this type rarely allow the judge to escape the strict restraints of legal and procedural requirements, they have little chance to make new law or develop new policy. In civil cases, too, judges are often confined to norm enforcement; opportunities for policymaking are infrequent. Rather, such litigation generally arises from a private dispute whose outcome is of interest only to the parties in the suit.

Policymaking by the District Courts

The district courts also play a policymaking role. One leading judicial scholar explains how this function differs from norm enforcement:

> When they make policy, the courts do not exercise more discretion than when they enforce community norms. The difference lies in the intended impact of

the decision. Policy decisions are intended to be guideposts for future actions; norm-enforcement decisions are aimed at the case at hand.[54]

The discretion that a federal trial judge exercises should not be overlooked, however. As Americans have become more litigation-conscious, disputes that were once resolved informally are now more likely to be decided in a court of law. The courts find themselves increasingly involved in domains once considered private. What does this mean for the federal district courts? According to one study, "These new areas of judicial involvement tend to be relatively free of clear, precise appellate court and legislative guidelines; and as a consequence the opportunity for trial court jurists to write on a clean slate, that is, to make policy, is formidable."[55] In other words, when the guidelines are not well established, district judges have a great deal of discretion to set policy.

A recent decision by US District Court Judge Robert Hinkle, a President Clinton appointee in the Northern District of Florida, is a case in point. In 2023, the Florida legislature passed a law signed by Governor Ron DeSantis that bans doctors and nurses from providing gender-affirming care, including prescribing any medications such as puberty blockers, sex reassignment, and hormone therapy, among other restrictions to minors. Four families sued the state in federal court over the new law, arguing the law violates the Equal Protection Clause of the US Constitution. On June 11, 2024, Judge Hinkle ruled the Florida ban is unconstitutional. He wrote in the decision, "Whether based on morals, religion, unmoored hatred, or anything else, prohibiting or impeding a person from conforming to the person's gender identity rather than the person's natal sex is not a legitimate state interest."[56] He further argued that while a state has an interest in safeguarding health care for minors, prohibiting gender-affirming care "across the board" for all minors instead of regulating the care does not serve a legitimate state purpose.[57] While the decision is likely to be appealed, it is nonetheless of monumental policy significance.

Three-Judge District Courts

From time to time, Congress has passed legislation permitting certain types of cases to be heard before a **three-judge district court** rather than a single trial judge. Such courts are created on an ad hoc basis and must include at least one judge from the federal district court and at least one judge from the court of appeals. Appeals of decisions of three-judge district courts go directly to the Supreme Court.

At one time, Congress provided that private citizens challenging the constitutionality of state or federal statutes and seeking injunctions to prohibit their further enforcement could bring the case before a three-judge district court. That is what happened in the famous abortion case of *Roe v. Wade* (1973).[58] Jane Roe (a pseudonym), a single, pregnant woman, challenged the constitutionality of the Texas antiabortion statute and sought an injunction to prohibit further enforcement of the law. The case was initially heard by a three-judge court consisting of District Judges Sarah T. Hughes and W. N. Taylor and Fifth Circuit Court of Appeals Judge Irving L. Goldberg. The three-judge district court held the Texas abortion statute invalid but declined to issue an injunction against its enforcement on the ground that a federal intrusion into the state's affairs was not warranted. Roe then appealed the denial of the injunction directly to the Supreme Court. For the most part today, three-judge district court panels are used for apportionment cases.

CONSTITUTIONAL COURTS, LEGISLATIVE COURTS, AND COURTS OF SPECIALIZED JURISDICTION

The Judiciary Act of 1789 established the three levels of the federal court system in existence today. Periodically, however, Congress has exercised its power, based on Article III and Article I of the Constitution, to create other federal courts. Courts established under Article III are known as constitutional courts, and those courts created under Article I are called legislative courts. The former handles the bulk of litigation in the system, and for this reason, they will remain the focus of this discussion. The Supreme Court, courts of appeals, and federal district courts are constitutional courts or Article III courts. The Administrative Procedure Act (APA) was passed in 1946, with the goal of ensuring fairness and due process in executive agency actions or proceedings involving rulemaking and adjudications. To meet these goals, the APA created the position of administrative law judge (ALJ) within the federal government. Originally called hearing examiners, the ALJs are employees of federal agencies who function like trial judges in the executive branch. These judges and courts are often referred to as Article I courts or judges.

The two types of courts may be further distinguished by their functions. Legislative courts, unlike their constitutional counterparts, often have administrative and quasi-legislative as well as judicial duties. Another difference is that legislative courts are often created to help administer a specific congressional statute. For example, more than two hundred immigration judges in more than fifty immigration courts throughout the United States adjudicate cases pursuant to the Immigration Reform and Control Act of 1986 and the Immigration Act of 1990. Their decisions are appealable to the Board of Immigration Appeals, a fifteen-member administrative body housed in the US Department of Justice. All board decisions are subject to review in the federal courts.[59]

Finally, the constitutional and legislative courts vary in their degree of independence from the other two branches of government. Article III (constitutional court) judges serve during a period of good behavior or what amounts to life tenure. Because Article I (legislative court) judges have no constitutional guarantee of good-behavior tenure, Congress may set specific terms of office for them. Judges of Article III courts are also constitutionally protected from salary reductions while in office. Those who serve as judges of legislative courts have no such protection. Bankruptcy courts provide a good example. The bankruptcy judges are appointed for fourteen-year terms by the court of appeals for the circuit in which the district is located and have their salaries set by Congress.

ADMINISTRATIVE AND STAFF SUPPORT IN THE FEDERAL JUDICIARY

The daily operation of federal courts requires a myriad of personnel. Although judges are the most visible actors in the judicial system, a large supporting cast is also needed to perform the tasks for which judges are unskilled or unsuited, or for which they simply do not have adequate time. Some members of the support team, such as law clerks, may work specifically for one judge. Others—for example, US **magistrate** judges—work for a particular court. Still others may be employees of an agency serving the entire judicial system, such as the Administrative Office of the United States Courts.

United States Magistrate Judges

To help federal district judges deal with increased workloads, Congress passed the Federal Magistrates Act in 1968. This legislation created the office of US magistrate to replace the US commissioners, who had performed limited duties for the federal trial courts for several years. In 1990, with passage of the Judicial Improvements Act, their title was changed to US magistrate judge. Magistrate judges are formally appointed by the judges of the district court for eight-year terms, although they can be removed for "compelling cause" before the term expires.

The magistrate judge system constitutes a structure that responds to each district court's specific needs and circumstances. Within guidelines set by the Federal Magistrates Acts of 1968, 1976, and 1979, the judges in each district court establish the duties and responsibilities of their magistrate judges. Of most significance, the 1979 legislation permits a magistrate judge, with the consent of the involved parties, to conduct all proceedings in a nonjury civil matter; to enter a judgment in the case; and to conduct a trial of persons accused of **misdemeanors** (less serious offenses than felonies) committed within the district, provided the defendants consent.

In other words, Congress has given federal district judges the authority to expand the scope of magistrate judges' participation in the judicial process. Because each district has its own needs, a magistrate judge's specific duties may vary from one district to the next and from one judge to another. The decision to delegate responsibilities to a magistrate judge is still made by the district judge, so that a magistrate judge's participation in the processing of cases may be narrower than that permitted by statute.

Law Clerks

Several thousand law clerks now work for federal judges, bankruptcy judges, and US magistrate judges.[60] In addition to the law clerks hired by individual judges, all appellate courts and some district courts hire staff law clerks who serve the entire court.

A law clerk's duties vary according to the preferences of the judge for whom they work. They also vary according to the type of court. Law clerks for federal district judges often serve primarily as research assistants, spending a good deal of time examining the various motions filed in civil and criminal cases. They review each motion, noting the issues and the positions of the parties involved, then research important points raised in the motions and prepare written memoranda for the judges. Because their work is devoted to the earliest stages of the litigation process, law clerks may have a substantial amount of contact with attorneys and witnesses. Law clerks at this level may also be involved in the initial drafting of opinions. As one federal district judge said, "I even allow my law clerks to write memorandum opinions. I first tell him what I want and then he writes it up. Sometimes I sign it without changing a word."[61] At the appellate level, the law clerk becomes involved in a case first by researching the issues of law and fact presented by an appeal. Saving the judge's time is important. Consider the courts of appeals. As we have discussed earlier in this chapter these courts do not have the same discretion that the US Supreme Court has to accept or reject a case. Nevertheless, the courts of appeals now use certain screening devices to differentiate between cases that can be handled quickly and those that require more time and effort. Law clerks are an integral part of this screening process.

Beginning around 1960, some courts of appeals began to use staff law clerks who work for the entire court as opposed to a particular judge. They began to be used primarily because of the rapid increase in the number of pro se matters (generally speaking, those involving indigents) coming before the courts of appeals. Today, some district courts also have pro se law clerks for handling prisoner petitions. In some circuits, the staff law clerks deal only with pro se matters; in others, they review nearly all the cases on the court's docket. As a result of their review, a truncated process may be followed—that is, no oral argument or full briefing is made.

As cases are scheduled for oral argument, law clerks assist the judges in preparing for them. Intensive analysis of the record by judges before oral argument is not always possible. Judges seldom have time to do more than scan pertinent portions of the record called to their attention by law clerks. As one judicial scholar aptly noted, "To prepare for oral argument, all but a handful of circuit judges rely upon bench memoranda prepared by their law clerks, plus their own notes from reading briefs."[62] Once a decision has been reached by an appellate court, the law clerk frequently participates in writing the order that accompanies the decision. The clerk's participation generally consists of drafting a preliminary opinion or order pursuant to the judge's directions. A law clerk may also be asked to edit or check citations in an opinion written by the judge.

Because the work of the law clerk for a Supreme Court justice roughly parallels that of a clerk in the other appellate courts, all aspects of their responsibility do not need to be restated here. However, a few important points about Supreme Court law clerks deserve mention. Once the justices have voted to hear a case, the law clerks, like their counterparts in the courts of appeals, prepare bench memoranda that the justices may use during oral argument. Finally, law clerks for Supreme Court justices, like those who serve courts of appeals judges, help to draft opinions.

Administrative Office of the US Courts

The administration of the federal judicial system is managed by the Administrative Office of the US Courts, which essentially functions as "the judiciary's housekeeping agency."[63] Since its creation in 1939, it has handled everything from distributing supplies and negotiating with other government agencies for court accommodations in federal buildings to maintaining judicial personnel records and collecting data on cases in the federal courts.

The Administrative Office also serves a staff function for the Judicial Conference of the United States, the central administrative policymaking organization of the federal judicial system. In addition to providing statistical information to the conference's many committees, the Administrative Office acts as a reception center and clearinghouse for information and proposals directed to the Judicial Conference.

Closely related to this staff function is the Administrative Office's role as liaison for both the federal judicial system and the Judicial Conference. The Administrative Office serves as advocate for the judiciary in its dealings with Congress, the executive branch, professional groups, and the public. Especially important is its representative role before Congress, where, along with concerned judges, it presents the judiciary's budget proposals, requests for additional judgeships, suggestions for changes in court rules, and other key measures.

The Federal Judicial Center

The Federal Judicial Center, created in 1967, is the federal courts' agency for continuing education and research. Its duties fall generally into three categories: (1) conducting substantial research support for the federal courts, (2) making recommendations to improve the administration and management of the federal courts, and (3) developing educational and training programs for personnel of the judicial branch.

Since the inception of the Federal Judicial Center, judges have benefited from its orientation sessions and educational programs. In recent years, magistrate judges, bankruptcy judges, and administrative personnel have also been the recipients of educational programs. The Federal Judicial Center's extensive use of videos and satellite technology enables it to reach large numbers of people.

FEDERAL COURT WORKLOAD

Table 2.1 shows the number of civil and criminal cases entering the federal district courts during the twelve-month periods ending September 30, 2020, through September 30, 2023. The number of civil cases varied over the time period of this table, but the total number of such cases is over 130,000 higher in 2020 than in 2023. Criminal cases, also, have generally decreased over time, from over 74,000 cases in 2020 to 66,000 cases in 2023.[64]

TABLE 2.1 ■ Cases Filed in US District Courts during Recent, Twelve-Month Periods Ending September 30, 2020, through September 30, 2023: By Case Type

	2020	2021	2022	2023
Civil	470,581	344,567	274,771	339,731
Criminal	73,879	74,465	68,482	66,157

Source: Compiled from data available online at https://www.uscourts.gov/us-district-courts-judicial-business-2023 (accessed June 6, 2024).

Table 2.2 provides figures on the total number of appeals commenced in the courts of appeals from 2020 to 2023. The number of appellate court cases has generally declined in recent years, from over 48,000 cases in 2020 to just under 40,000 cases in 2023. Not surprisingly, the bulk of the appeals come from the district courts and federal administrative agencies.[65] In Table 2.3, we look at caseload data for the US Supreme Court. The total number of cases on the Court's docket has steadily declined from a high of 7,622 in 2018 to a low of 4,878 in 2022. The decline may be attributed to the general decline in the number of pauper's petitions, that is, those brought by indigent people for whom the filing fee and requirement of multiple copies are waived by the Court. For example, there were 2,353 less pauper petitions filed in the 2022 term than the 2018 term.

TABLE 2.2 ■ Appeals Filed in US Courts of Appeals during Recent, Selected Twelve-Month Periods Ending September 30, 2020, through September 30, 2023

2020	2021	2022	2023
48,190	44,546	41,839	39,987

Source: Compiled from data available online at https://www.uscourts.gov/us-courts-appeals-judicial-business-2023 (accessed June 6, 2024).

TABLE 2.3 ■ Cases on the Docket, Argued, and Disposed of by Full Opinions in the US Supreme Court, October Terms 2018 through 2022

Cases	2018	2019	2020	2021	2022
Paid	1,915	1,818	2,137	1,996	1,529
Pauper	5,702	4,706	3,982	3,796	3,349
Original	9	10	10	5	4
Argued	73	73	72	79	68
Disposed of by Full Opinions	69	69	69	63	66

Source: Compiled from data available online at https://www.uscourts.gov/sites/default/files/data_tables/supcourt_a1_0930.2023.pdf (accessed June 6, 2024).

The key point to remember about the workload of the Supreme Court is that the justices themselves have discretion to decide which cases merit their full attention. As a result, the number of cases argued before the Court may fluctuate from session to session. In the 2022 term, sixty-eight cases were argued, but only sixty-six were disposed of by full opinions.

A final word about the workload of the federal courts deserves mention before concluding our discussion. That deals with the fact that only Congress can create new judge positions for specific circuits and districts to help alleviate heavy workloads. Efforts to do that, however, have run into political resistance in recent years. The result is a major backlog of civil cases piling up in some of the nation's federal trial courts but, as the data illustrate in Table 2.1, the district court civil and criminal case load has been trending downward in recent years.

However, while numbers are trending downward in the Article III courts the same can't be said for some Article I courts. In particular, there has been a massive backlog of immigration cases. A 2017 study concluded that, "The massive backlog of immigration cases is a real problem. Since 2011, the number of pending cases has doubled to more than 600,000, bogging down lawyers and miring immigrants in an average of nearly two years of uncertainty before their fate is decided."[66] According to the pending immigration case backlog data, by December 2020, the number doubled again to a massive 1,290,766 cases and by May 2024 that number skyrocketed to over 3.5 million.[67] In the United States, wait times average 762 days. For example, in the nation's two largest states, California and Texas, respective wait times are 840 and 794 days.[68] In an effort to address the backlog, the Biden administration hired just over 300 new immigration judges and in their latest budget request asked for funding for 150 more judges.

SUMMARY

In this chapter, we offered a brief historical review of the development of the federal judiciary. A perennial concern has existed since preconstitutional times for independent court systems.

We focused on the three basic levels created by the Judiciary Act of 1789, noting, however, that Congress has periodically created both constitutional and legislative courts. The bulk of federal litigation is handled by US district courts, courts of appeals, and the Supreme Court.

We also briefly examined the role of magistrate judges and law clerks associated with the federal judiciary, noting the crucial roles they play in the work of the federal judiciary.

Finally, we looked at administrative assistance for the federal courts as this relates to the Administrative Office of the US Courts and the Federal Judicial Center. We concluded our discussion with a brief look at the workload of each of the three levels of the federal judiciary.

FURTHER THOUGHT AND DISCUSSION QUESTIONS

1. Should federal courts have policymaking powers?
2. How can a democracy justify the fact that federal judges appointed for life possess the power to nullify federal and state laws that were enacted by elected representatives?
3. Since Article III judges are appointed for life and are independent of one another, what guarantees exist that justice is consistently and equitably dispensed?

SUGGESTED RESOURCES

Administrative Office of the US Courts website. Available online at www.us-courts.gov/adminoff.html. A useful site for caseload data compiled for each level of the federal judiciary.

Barrow, Deborah J., and Thomas G. Walker. *A Court Divided: The Fifth Circuit Court of Appeals and the Politics of Judicial Reform*. New Haven, CT: Yale University Press, 1988. An excellent study of the politics involved in the splitting of the Fifth Circuit Court of Appeals.

Baum, Lawrence. *The Supreme Court*, 15th ed. Washington, DC: CQ Press, 2023. A brief look at all aspects of the US Supreme Court.

Bowie, Jennifer, Donald R. Songer, and John Szmer. *The View from the Bench and Chambers: Examining Judicial Process and Decision Making on the U.S. Courts of Appeals*. Charlottesville, VA: University of Virginia Press, 2014. A thorough study of the US courts of appeals that includes the perspectives of the judges.

Burrows, Vanessa K. "Administrative Law Judges: An Overview." *Congressional Research Service* (April 13, 2010). Available online at www.crs.gov. A good introduction to administrative law judges in the federal government.

Federal Administrative Law Judges Conference Website. Available online at www.faljc.org. Provides useful information about administrative law judges in the federal government.

Federal Judicial Center Website. Available online at www.fjc.gov. The website of the federal courts' continuing education and research agency.

Federal Judiciary Website. Available online at www.uscourts.gov. The single most important source of information about all aspects of the federal judiciary. Provides links to individual district courts, courts of appeals, and bankruptcy courts, as well as to other useful Internet sites.

Legal Information Institute Website. Available online at www.law.cornell.edu. An excellent source of information about all aspects of the US Supreme Court, including recent and historical decisions.

Oyez Website. Available online at www.oyez.org. Another useful site for recent and historical Supreme Court decisions; it also is the most complete source for all of the Court's oral argument and opinion announcement audio since the installation of a recording system in October 1955.

Rowland, C. K., and Robert A. Carp. *Politics and Judgment in Federal District Courts*. Lawrence, KS: University Press of Kansas, 1996. A thorough study of the various factors that influence the decisions of federal district judges.

US Supreme Court Website. Available online at www.supremecourtus.gov. Provides information about all aspects of the nation's highest court.

Vladeck, Stephen. *The Shadow Docket: How the Supreme Court Uses Stealth Rulings to Amass Power and Undermine the Republic*. New York, NY: Basic Books, 2023. A thorough and excellent overview of the shadow docket and its consequences.

KEY TERMS

appellate jurisdiction
bench trials
cert petition
concurring opinion
defendant
dissenting opinion
grand jury
judgments
judicial review
magistrate
misdemeanors
opinion of the Court
oral argument
original jurisdiction
three-judge district court
writ of certiorari

3 STATE JUDICIAL SYSTEMS

CHAPTER GOALS AND OBJECTIVES

In this chapter, readers will learn that . . .

- To fully understand the state court systems of today, we must first learn about their historical development.
- There are four basic levels of the state judiciaries: trial courts of limited jurisdiction, trial courts of general jurisdiction, intermediate appellate courts, and courts of last resort.
- There are several basic functions of state tribunals: norm enforcement, administrative hearings, and policymaking.
- Many innovations that began in response to the COVID-19 global pandemic have continue to help courts administer justice more efficiently.
- The Courts' workload is immense, but the burden is shared by court administrators and other important staff members.

HISTORICAL DEVELOPMENT OF STATE COURTS

No two states are exactly alike when it comes to the organization of courts. Each state is entirely free to adopt any organizational scheme it chooses, create as many courts as it wishes, name those courts whatever it pleases, and establish their jurisdiction as it sees fit. Thus, the organization of state courts does not necessarily resemble the clear-cut, three-tier system found at the federal level. For instance, in the federal system, the trial courts are called district courts, and the appellate tribunals are known as circuit courts. However, in well over a dozen states, the circuit courts are known as *trial courts*. Several other states use the term *superior court* for their major trial courts. Perhaps the most bewildering situation is found in New York, where the major trial courts are known as *supreme courts*.

Although a great deal of confusion surrounds the organization of state courts, there is no question regarding its importance. Because statutory law is more extensive in the states than at the federal level, covering everything from the most basic personal

Judge Ural Glanville, who presided over the Jeffrey Wiliams (aka rapper "Young Thug") criminal racketeering trial. Judge Glanville was removed from the case once it came to light that he had a secret meeting with prosecutors and witnesses without defense counsel present.

Bob Andres/Atlanta Journal-Constitution via AP

relationships to the state's most important public policies, the state courts handle a wide variety of cases. One study of state supreme courts says that the main categories of cases include:

> appeals in major felonies; state regulation of business and professions; a wide range of private economic disputes, including business contracts and real estate; wills, trusts, and estates; divorce, child custody, and child support; and personal injury suits involving automobile accidents, medical malpractice, job-related injuries, and the like.[1]

State courts also interpret their own state constitutions,[2] which sometimes have broader protections for their citizens than are found in the US Constitution. In fact, "since the 1970s, state courts (particularly the highest courts of the states) have issued hundreds of opinions interpreting their constitutions to protect rights beyond the federal minima."[3] Former US Supreme Court Justice William Brennan, in an influential 1977 *Harvard Law Review* article, is generally credited with encouraging state courts to interpret their own constitutions to provide greater protection of citizens' rights.[4] One study of this development, known as "new judicial federalism," indicates that there was a dramatic increase in state courts' reliance on state declarations of rights in civil liberties cases over the latter part of the twentieth century.[5] A recent example of this is a 2019 decision of a three-judge superior court in Wake County, North Carolina. The decision overturned the process of political gerrymandering of state legislative districts. It ruled that the plaintiffs proved that the consequence of the "partisan" maps drawn by the state legislature was that "in all but the most unusual election scenarios, the Republican party will control a majority of both chambers of the

General Assembly." The North Carolina court ruled that "the Free Elections Clause of the North Carolina Constitution guarantees that all elections must be conducted freely and honestly to ascertain, fairly and truthfully, the will of the People and that this is a fundamental right of North Carolina citizens, a compelling governmental interest, and a cornerstone of our democratic form of government."[6] (Federal courts for the most part have stayed clear of ordinary gerrymandering issues in recent years.)

Early State Courts

Following the American Revolution, the powers of the government were not only taken over by legislative bodies but also greatly reduced in scope. The former colonists were not eager to see the development of a large independent judiciary, given that many of them harbored a distrust of lawyers and the common law. As one scholar describes,

> Given the low esteem in which colonial courts were held and the high esteem in which legislatures were held, the idea of a strong and independent state judiciary overseeing legislative activity was laughable when the first state constitutions were drafted. . . . The Revolution left the states with governments dominated by their legislatures—legislatures had been the heroes of the Revolution and were believed to be the authentic expression of the public voice. By contrast, judges had been agents of the British Crown.[7]

As a result, state legislatures carefully watched the courts, and in some instances, they removed judges or abolished specific courts because of unpopular decisions. However, the basic structure of the state judiciaries was not greatly altered.

Increasingly, a distrust of the judiciary developed as courts declared legislative actions unconstitutional. Conflicts between legislatures and judges, often stemming from opposing interests, became more prevalent. For example, legislators seemed more responsive to policies that favored debtors, whereas courts generally reflected the views of creditors. As the country expanded, new demands were placed on state judiciaries, which were largely considered inefficient and fragmented. Additionally, frustrations over legislative power began to develop and there was a growing "belief that a check on legislative behavior was required."[8] A consensus emerged that the most obvious candidate to check the legislative branch were the courts.[9] These differences were important because "out of this conflict over legislative and judicial power . . . the courts gradually emerged as an independent political institution."[10]

Modern State Courts

From the Civil War to the early twenty-first century, the state courts confronted still other problems. Increasing industrialization and the rapid growth of urban areas created new types of legal disputes and resulted in longer and more complex court cases. The state court systems, largely fashioned to handle the problems of a rural agrarian society, were now faced with a crisis of backlogs as they struggled to adjust.

One typical response was to create new courts to handle the increased volume of cases. Courts were often simply piled on top of one another with overlapping jurisdictions. Another strategy was the addition of new courts, coupled with a careful specification of their jurisdiction in terms of geographic area. Still another response was to create specialized courts to handle one case. Small claims courts, juvenile courts, and domestic relations courts, for example, became increasingly prominent.

The result of all this activity was a confusing array of courts, especially in the major urban areas, where growth tended to be more pronounced. One observer noted that:

> each court was a separate entity; each had a judge and a staff. Such an organizational structure meant there was no way to shift cases from an overloaded court to one with little to do. In addition, each court produced political patronage jobs for the city political machines.[11]

The largely unplanned expansion of state and local courts to meet specific needs led to a situation many have referred to as fragmentation. A multiplicity of trial courts was only one aspect of fragmentation. Many of these courts had very narrow jurisdictions. Furthermore, the jurisdictions of the various courts often overlapped. This meant that a case could be tried in a few courts depending on the advantages each one offered. Court costs, court procedures, court delays, and the reputation of the judge all entered the decision of which court to choose. For example, an attorney filing a civil suit on behalf of a client might seek a court known for its complex procedures to draw the other side into a confusing web of legal technicalities. Political considerations were also involved in the choice of a court. The justice of the peace courts were especially political because many of them operated on a fee basis. Justices of the peace (J.P.s) were often willing to trade favorable decisions for court business. Critics of this model at the time remarked the initials J.P. were often said to stand for "Justice for the Plaintiff" because many J.P.s were compensated from fees that plaintiffs paid.[12]

In the early twentieth century, some legal scholars began to advocate a series of reforms known as court unification. The best-known advocate was Roscoe Pound, dean of the Harvard Law School.[13] He called for the consolidation of trial courts into a single set of courts or two sets of courts, one to hear major cases and one to hear minor cases. The court unification movement has not been as successful as many would like, although proponents of court reform have secured victories in some states.

STATE COURT ORGANIZATION

It is generally understood that no two state court systems are structured exactly the same way, however many states have moved closer to a unified court system, whereas others still operate with a complex network of courts with overlapping jurisdiction. The California court system, shown in Figure 3.1, is an example of a simplified state court system that looks similar to the federal courts. Like the federal court system described in Chapter 2, it consists of one level of trial courts, regional courts of appeals, and one high court.

FIGURE 3.1 ■ Court System of California

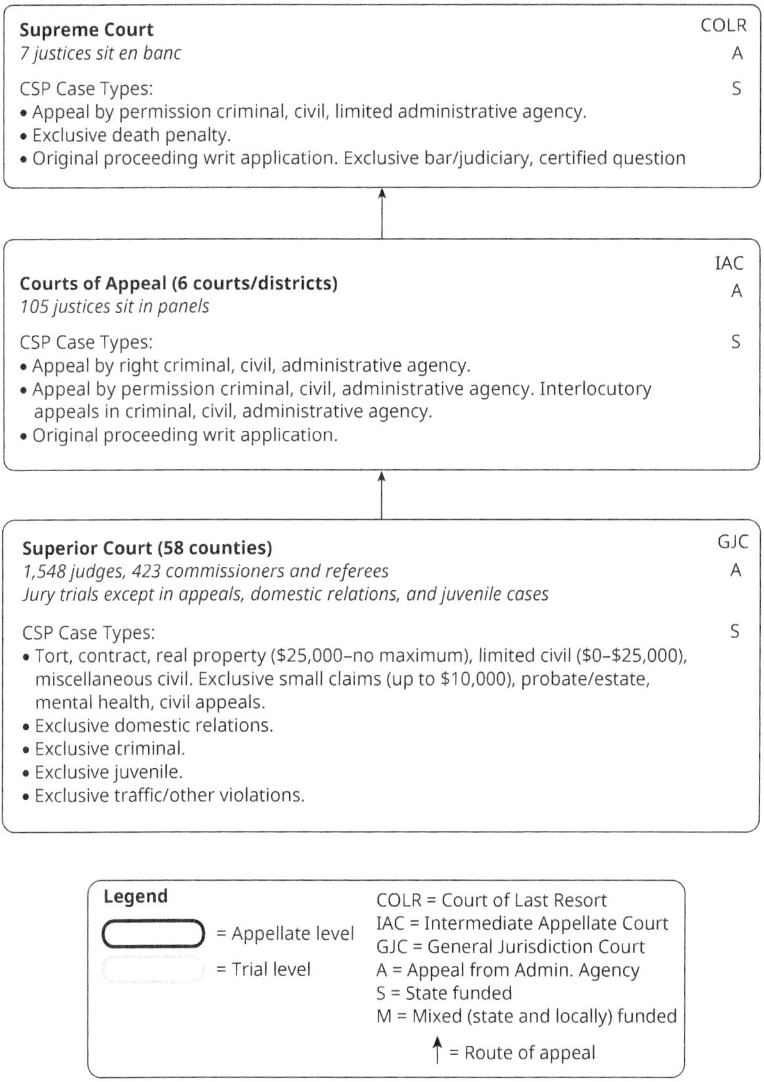

Note: CSP indicates that these case types are included in the Court Statistics Project of the National Center for State Courts.

Source: Used with permission from the National Center for State Courts, Court Statistics Project, www.courtstatistics.org, 2015.

On the other hand, the equally busy New York court system provides an example of a state with a more complex network of courts. A look at Figure 3.2, indicates that there are ten trial courts, two appellate courts, and one high court in the state. These courts are staffed by more than 3,500 judicial officials known in different courts as judges, justices, or surrogates.

FIGURE 3.2 ■ Court System of New York

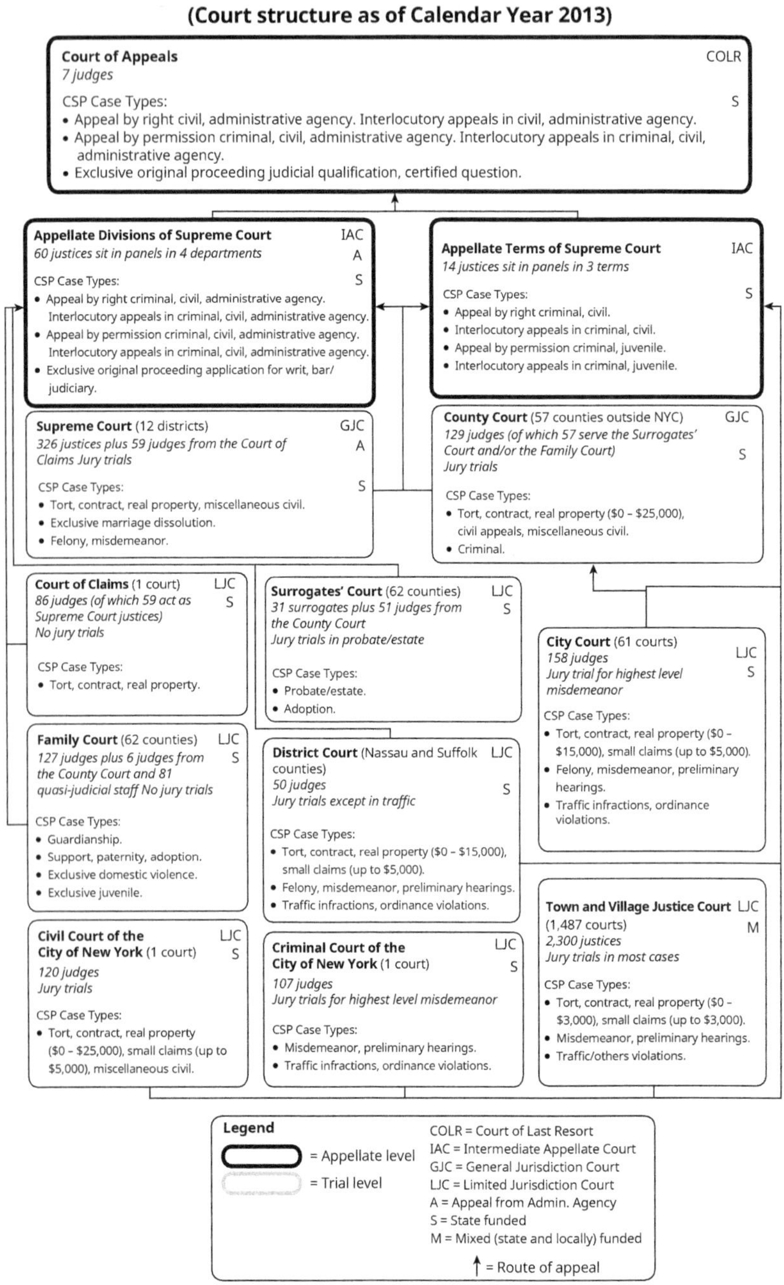

Note: CSP indicates that these case types are included in the Court Statistics Project of the National Center for State Courts.

Source: Used with permission from the National Center for State Courts, Court Statistics Project, www.courtstatistics.org, 2015.

Most states, falling somewhere between the two extremes, illustrated in Figures 3.1 and 3.2, are divided into four extensive categories or levels: trial courts of limited jurisdiction, trial courts of general jurisdiction, intermediate appellate courts, and courts of last resort. While the state court organization may be slightly different than their federal court counterpart, keep in mind that state courts do function similarly when it comes to the work and duties at each level of the judicial hierarchy.

Trial Courts of Limited Jurisdiction

Trial courts of limited jurisdiction handle the bulk of litigation in this country each year and constitute about 85 percent of all courts in the United States.[14] They have a variety of names: small claims courts, justice of the peace courts, magistrate courts, municipal courts, city courts, county courts, juvenile courts, domestic relations courts, and metropolitan courts, to name the more common ones.

The jurisdiction of these courts is limited to minor cases. In criminal matters, for example, state courts deal with three levels of violations: infractions (the least serious), misdemeanors (more serious), and felonies (the most serious). Trial courts of limited jurisdiction typically handle infractions and misdemeanors. They may impose only limited fines (usually no more than $1,000) and jail sentences (generally no more than one year). In civil cases, these courts are usually limited to disputes under a certain amount, such as $10,000. In addition, these types of courts are often limited to certain kinds of matters: traffic violations, domestic relations, or cases involving juveniles, for example. Another difference is that in many instances these limited courts are not courts of record. Because their proceedings are not recorded, appeals of their decisions usually go to a trial court of general jurisdiction for what is known as a **trial de novo** (new trial).

New York is one of about thirty states that rely on many local trial courts of limited jurisdiction to dispense justice at the lowest level. One such group, the nearly 1,500 Town and Village Justice Courts, has more than two thousand judges spread throughout all areas of the state except New York City. Although judges presiding over the Town and Village Justice Courts are generally nonlawyers (less than half have law degrees) with only six days of training classes at the start of their tenure and a twelve-hour required refresher course each year thereafter, they perform some essential duties.[15] For instance, Justice Courts in New York handle a variety of matters such as setting **bail**, traffic violations and misdemeanor tickets, misdemeanor and **felony** arraignments, eviction proceedings, small claims cases, jury trials for misdemeanor offenses, and in some instances performing civil marriage ceremonies.[16] In short, courts of limited jurisdiction are vitally important to the functioning of state judiciaries in the United States. For example, in 2022, the courts of limited jurisdiction across the United States handled approximately forty million cases.[17]

Trial Courts of General Jurisdiction

Most states have one set of major trial courts that handle the more serious criminal and civil cases. In addition, in many states, special categories—such as juvenile criminal offenses, domestic relations cases, and probate cases—are under the jurisdiction of the general trial courts.

In most states, these courts also have an appellate function. They hear appeals in certain types of cases that originate in trial courts of limited jurisdiction. These appeals are often heard in a trial de novo or tried again in the court of general jurisdiction.

General trial courts are usually divided into judicial districts or circuits. Although the practice varies from state to state, the general rule is to use existing political boundaries such as a county or a group of counties in establishing the district or circuit. For example, Virginia's courts of general jurisdiction are divided up into thirty-one circuits (in Virginia, there is a circuit court in each county and city in Virginia).[18] In rural areas, the judge may travel from one town to another within the district or circuit to hold court in various parts of the territory according to a fixed schedule. In urban areas, judges hold court in a prescribed place throughout the year. In larger counties, the group of judges may be divided into specializations. Some may hear only civil cases; others try criminal cases exclusively.

The courts at this level have a variety of names. The most common are district, circuit, and superior court. However, Ohio and Pennsylvania still use the title "court of common pleas" and New York is undoubtedly the most confusing of all; its trial court of general jurisdiction is called the supreme court (see Figure 3.2). The judges at this level are required by law in all states to have law degrees. These courts also maintain clerical help because they are courts of record. In other words, a degree of professionalism is evident at this level that is often lacking in the trial courts of limited jurisdiction.

Intermediate Appellate Courts

The intermediate appellate courts are relative newcomers to the state judicial scene. Only thirteen such courts existed in 1911, whereas forty-two states now have them. Their basic purpose is to relieve the workload of the state's highest court called the court of last resort.

In most instances, they are called courts of appeals, although other names are occasionally used. Most states, such as Hawaii, Massachusetts, and Virginia, have one court of appeals with statewide jurisdiction. Other states, such as California, Ohio, and Texas, have created regional appellate courts to hear appeals from trial courts in a specific area. Alabama and Tennessee have separate intermediate appellate courts for civil and criminal cases. And a handful of states, such as Vermont, do not have an intermediate appellate court (litigants who lose in the trial court would appeal to the court of last resort).

The names of these intermediate appellate courts vary. The size of intermediate courts also varies from state to state. The court of appeals in Alaska, for example, has only three judges. At the other extreme, California, with the largest court system in the nation, has 106 court of appeals judges.[19] In some states, the intermediate appeals courts sit en banc, whereas in other states they sit in permanent or rotating panels.

The jurisdiction of intermediate appellate courts is mandatory because Americans hold to the view that parties in a case are entitled to at least one appeal. In numerous instances, these are the courts of last resort for litigants in the state court system.

Courts of Last Resort

Every state has a court of last resort with the exception of Oklahoma and Texas, which have two high courts. Interestingly, both states have a supreme court with jurisdiction limited to appeals in civil cases and a court of criminal appeals for criminal cases. Most states call their highest courts supreme courts; other designations are the court of appeals (Maryland and New York), the supreme judicial court (Maine and Massachusetts), and the supreme court of appeals (West Virginia).

The courts of last resort range in size from five to nine judges (called justices in most states). They typically sit en banc and usually, although not necessarily, in the state capital. A majority vote is required for a decision, although in two states (Nebraska and North Dakota) a supermajority is required to overturn a state statute.

The highest courts have jurisdiction in matters pertaining to state law and are the final arbiters in such matters. In states that have intermediate appellate courts, the court of last resort's cases come primarily from these midlevel courts. In this situation, the high court typically is allowed to exercise discretion in deciding which cases to review. For instance, in 2022, 846 petitions for review were filed in the Supreme Court of Virginia and the court accepted forty-eight them.[20] Thus, it is likely to devote more time to cases that deal with the important policy issues of the state. When there is no intermediate court of appeals, cases generally go to the state's highest court on a mandatory review basis. This is likely to create a role of error correction for the court of last resort in routine cases and to reduce its opportunities for policymaking.[21] In most instances, the state courts of last resort resemble the US Supreme Court in that they have a good deal of discretion in determining which cases will occupy their attention. Most state supreme courts also follow procedures like those of the US Supreme Court. That is, when a case is accepted for review, the opposing parties file written briefs and later present oral arguments. Amicus curiae briefs are also filed quite frequently in such states as California, Illinois, Michigan, Oklahoma, Pennsylvania, and Wisconsin.[22] After reaching a decision, the judges issue written opinions explaining that decision.

Juvenile Courts

Even the most casual reading of a daily newspaper or the viewing of a nightly news broadcast acquaints one with the fact that Americans are increasingly concerned about the handling of cases involving juveniles. Not surprisingly, states have responded to the problem in a variety of ways.[23] Some have established a statewide network of courts specifically to handle matters involving juveniles. They are commonly called juvenile courts or family courts. Georgia, for example, has juvenile courts throughout the state. Rhode Island and South Carolina provide good examples of another approach. These two states have family courts, which handle domestic relations matters as well as those involving juveniles. Still other states have juvenile courts, family courts, or both in limited areas. In Colorado, there is a juvenile court for Denver. Louisiana has created four juvenile courts for the state and one family court in East Baton Rouge Parish.

The most common approach is to give one or more of the state's limited or general trial courts jurisdiction to handle situations involving juveniles. In Alabama, for example, the circuit courts (trial courts of general jurisdiction) deal with juvenile matters. In Virginia, however, juvenile courts are considered trial courts of limited jurisdiction—the district courts.

Finally, some states apportion juvenile jurisdiction among more than one court. Recall the juvenile court in Denver. No one would believe that problems among juveniles in Colorado are limited to the city of Denver. Instead, the state has given jurisdiction over juveniles to district courts (general trial courts) in areas other than Denver, but in Denver there is a specific juvenile court.

As might be expected, the states vary in determining when jurisdiction belongs to an adult court. States set a standard age at which defendants are tried in an adult court. In addition, many states require that younger offenders be tried in an adult court if unusual circumstances are present. In Illinois, for instance, the standard age at which juvenile jurisdiction transfers to adult courts is seventeen. The age limit drops to fifteen, however, for first-degree murder, aggravated criminal sexual assault, armed robbery, robbery with a firearm, and unlawful use of weapons on school grounds. For instance, California law demands individuals under the age of eighteen be tried in juvenile court unless they have committed a serious felony offense (such as murder, robbery, forcible sexual assault, and kidnapping) and are sixteen or seventeen at the time of the crime, and for judges to decide whether to transfer the case from juvenile to adult court. In 2021, the California Supreme Court upheld a 2018 law prohibiting fourteen- and fifteen-year-olds from being tried as adults, even for serious felony offenses.[24]

Recently, states have also taken measures to institute best practices and innovations when it comes to handling juvenile cases. For instance, all new judges in Maryland are required to take a week-long orientation that addresses how best to handle juvenile cases. By statute, Oklahoma requires any judge overseeing juvenile cases to take an annual twelve-hour training course on juvenile court policies and best practices. And New Jersey created a judicial mentorship program offering all new judges a judge mentor with experience in family and juvenile court. Additionally, judges in New Jersey received specific training on family and juvenile matters and must complete two hours of coursework on diversity, inclusion, and bias.[25]

NORM ENFORCEMENT IN THE STATE COURTS

As described in Chapter 2, norm enforcement is closely tied to the administration of justice and the maintenance of societal norms embodied in statutes, administrative regulations, and community traditions. Since statutory law is so extensive in the states, it is only natural that much of the work of state courts, especially in trial courts of limited jurisdiction, involves norm enforcement rather than policymaking. According to one recent study describing the work of state judges:

> Some of their workload is administrative (for example, the probating of wills). Another part involves conflict resolution (for example, deciding which party is correct in contested divorce settlements and property disputes). And still another area of responsibility includes the criminal prosecution and appeals process.[26]

The handling of criminal cases in the state courts is especially important because "anyone who looks at the local news, reads the newspapers, listens to talk shows, or gossips with the neighbors knows that crime, criminal justice, and criminal courts attract nearly everyone's enduring interest and morbid fascination."[27] Even though similar rules and processes are used to prosecute criminal cases throughout the United States, careful observers tell us that there are also notable differences from one courthouse to another. How do we explain these differences, which exist not only among courts in different cities but also among different judges' courtrooms in the same city?

One plausible explanation, prominent in the social science literature, notes that the culture of a community—that is, its shared beliefs and attitudes—influences how its members behave. These shared beliefs and attitudes may help explain the actions of entire nations or smaller communities within a nation. Many legal scholars argue that a local legal culture—norms shared by members of the local court community—determines how criminal cases will be prosecuted in a particular courtroom.[28] The values and norms shared by judges, attorneys, clerks, bailiffs, probation officers, and others who work in the court system influence court operations in three important ways.[29] First, they help participants distinguish between "our" court and other courts. Attorneys and judges will often boast that they process cases more efficiently than do other courts within the city or state. Second, norms tell members of a court community how they should treat one another. Third, norms describe how cases should be processed in a particular court. In short, the local legal culture helps us understand why different courts handle things differently, even though the formal rules of criminal procedure are basically the same.

THE COURTROOM WORK GROUP

Implicit in the notion of courts as communities is the belief that courts are permanent organizations rather than occasional gatherings of strangers who resolve a particular conflict and then go their separate ways.[30] To put it another way, "court communities rely on predictable case processing strategies between familiar attorneys in stable work-groups."[31] The most visible members of this permanent organization are judges, prosecutors, and defense attorneys. Commonly referred to as the **courtroom work group**, each is generally associated with a specific function. Prosecutors push for convictions of those accused of criminal offenses against the government, defense attorneys seek acquittals for their clients, and judges serve as neutral arbiters to guarantee a fair trial. Members of the courtroom work group share certain values and goals and are not the fierce adversaries that many Americans imagine. Cooperation among judges, prosecutors, and defense attorneys is the norm.

The most important goal of the courtroom work group is to handle cases expeditiously. Because of high caseloads, judges, prosecutors, and defense attorneys share the goal of resolving cases efficiently, expeditiously, and quickly. In many jurisdictions, public defender offices often lack adequate resources and staff, and therefore appreciate the quick disposition of their caseload. A second important goal of the courtroom work group is to maintain group cohesion. Conflict among the members makes work more difficult and interferes with the expeditious handling of cases. Therefore, the work group stresses cooperation and censures those who violate this norm. Finally, the courtroom work group is interested in reducing or controlling uncertainty. In practice, this means that all members of the group strive to avoid trials. Trials, especially jury trials, produce a great deal of uncertainty, given that they require substantial investments of time and effort without any reasonable guarantee of a desirable outcome.

To attain the goals of handling cases expeditiously, maintaining group cohesion, and reducing uncertainty, work group members use several techniques. Although unilateral decisions and adversarial proceedings occur, negotiation is the most used technique in both criminal and civil cases. The members negotiate on a variety of issues—continuances, hearing dates, and exchanges of information, among other matters. Without a doubt, however, in criminal cases plea bargaining is the most heavily publicized subject of negotiation among members of the courtroom work group (more on plea bargaining in Chapter 9).

ADMINISTRATIVE HEARINGS IN THE STATES

For more than half a century, there has been a movement in the United States, at both the national and state levels, to separate agency hearings from their regulation and enforcement functions. The idea is that there should be "an independent and impartial forum for citizens and businesses to dispute state agency action against them."[32]

In 1945, the California legislature became the first state lawmaking body to establish a quasi-judicial court to hear administrative disputes. Known as the Office of Administrative Hearings, it is one of the largest such agencies in the United States.[33] Today, the staff of some seventy-five administrative law judges handle upwards of fourteen thousand cases annually.[34] Since that beginning, more than half the states have established a central agency to resolve citizen disputes with various state agencies and administrative boards.[35]

The state of Oregon provides an interesting and informative case study of this process in action.[36] Before 2000, Oregon, along with several other states, permitted hearing officers within the regulating agency to hear complaints by citizens and businesses who disputed the agency's action. That changed when the Oregon legislature created the Office of Administrative Hearings (OAH) in 1999, and it began operating in 2000. Today, the OAH has 130 permanent employees, including 65 administrative law judges, and is headed by a chief administrative law judge. According to the Oregon OAH website, the administrative law judges hold more than thirty thousand hearings per year for about seventy state agencies. That number represents 90 percent or more of all the contested orders issued by agencies in Oregon.

States vary widely in the number and scope of cases handled by administrative law judges. In Washington, for example, during fiscal year 2023, 99 percent of its cases came from two state departments: the Department of Social and Health Services and the Employment Security Department.[37] According to Alaska's *OAH Annual Report*, submitted in January 2023, the bulk of its cases dealt with the Medicaid program and Department of Labor (unemployment) cases.[38] A deeper look at Alaska's *OAH Annual Report* indicates that of the 1,494 contested cases in 2022, approximately 529 involved unemployment benefit disputes, about 373 cases pertained to Medicaid benefits, and 262 cases involved child abuse and neglect cases.[39] Finally, it should be noted that administrative law judges may do more than simply hold hearings in cases involving citizen disputes with state agencies, boards, departments, and commissions. In some states, for instance, they are also trained mediators who work to bring about a mutual decision between the adversaries in a dispute.[40] For example, the Minnesota Office of Administrative Hearings website boasts that "All Administrative Law Judges have received training as mediators and several have extensive mediation experience."[41]

POLICYMAKING IN THE STATE COURTS

State courts do more than simply enforce norms. There are also opportunities to engage in shaping policies in the state. One good example of policymaking by state high courts involves the issue of school districts within a state spending vastly unequal amounts on the education of their students. When the US Supreme Court held in *San Antonio Independent School District v. Rodriguez* (1973) that different spending patterns in poor and wealthy school districts within a state do not violate equal protection rights under the US Constitution,[42] several legal challenges were mounted in state courts, arguing that unequal educational opportunities violate various clauses in state constitutions. This strategy has proven successful. One observer notes that:

> State supreme courts in more than half the states have held that reliance on local property-tax revenues to fund public schools violates the right to a free public education contained in their respective state constitutions.[43]

State courts have also been innovative in the realm of voting and civil liberties rights. A recent example of this is the decision of Pennsylvania's high court in 2018. Here, the state's supreme court—interpreting the state and not the US Constitution—ruled that the congressional districts in Pennsylvania were unconstitutional because the "boundaries put partisan interests above neutral line-drawing criteria, such as keeping districts compact and eliminating municipal and county divisions."[44] The decision was the first time that a state court had ever thrown out congressional boundaries in a partisan gerrymandering case.

Same-sex relationships have also been protected as domestic partnerships and civil unions, but the availability and rights of these alternatives have varied greatly from state to state.[45] Indeed, there are many ancillary issues related to same-sex unions that are still unresolved. For example, can same-sex couples adopt children? Are states and local governmental bodies required to grant employee benefits to the spouses and adopted children of same-sex couples? And not all state judicial activism in the realm has favored same-sex equality. A case in point is the decision of the Texas Supreme Court on June 30, 2017, in the case of *Pidgeon v. Parker*.[46] Here, the Texas high court ruled in effect that states did not have to provide government employee benefits to all married persons, regardless of whether their marriages are same sex or opposite sex.[47] Thus, the Texas Supreme Court chose to take a very restrictive view of the prior year's US Supreme Court ruling that held that the right to marry is guaranteed by both the Due Process Clause and the Equal Protection Clause of the US Constitution.[48] In effect, the Texas tribunal said that the technical right to marry does not carry with it all of the rights and benefits often associated with marriage. Between 2015 and the present day there have been a variety of laws passed by state legislatures (and challenged by their respective state courts) on the subjects of LGBTQ rights.[49]

As this brief look at the same-sex marriage issue illustrates, state court judges possess important tools that permit them to be quite active in expanding the rights of state citizens. Whether they are willing and politically able to do so is a different matter. A combination of ideology, judicial role, interpretation, and political pressures may dictate that state high court judges do not venture far from the status quo.

INNOVATION IN STATE COURTS

Given the wide variety of problems facing state courts and the increasing numbers of fights over scarce budget resources, it is not surprising that a substantial amount of innovation has occurred in the state judiciaries. As noted earlier, some states have created specialized courts to handle types of cases, ranging from water courts (which resolve legal disputes over water rights in states with scarce water supplies), to probate courts, to others dealing with domestic relations, small claims, and juveniles.

Over the past few decades, court-connected **alternative dispute resolution (ADR)** has spread throughout the country as an alternative to lengthy court involvement in certain types of cases. According to the National Center for State Courts, every state now has some type of court-connected ADR at some level.[50] Innovations have also been made in the way cases are placed on a court's docket, so that less complicated cases may be resolved more quickly and not be delayed during more complicated cases. Changes in the courts' calendar systems have made it easier to track cases and keep all involved parties up to date on the status of the case. Increasing use of technology has also been a priority in many state court systems, as computer records and electronic filing systems (often called "efile") have largely replaced paper trails in everything from the filing of cases to the publication of final decisions. Perhaps more important, state judicial systems have begun to examine the very reasons for the existence of courts. It is to that issue that we next turn our attention.

By the latter part of the twentieth century, a developing trend saw some state courts changing from adversarial arenas to problem-solving courts focusing on the underlying behavior of criminal defendants. Drawing on a concept known as therapeutic jurisprudence, these new problem-solving courts were expected to include services along with judicial case processing.[51] Perhaps the best-known examples are the drug treatment courts that now exist in many states. These courts emphasize therapeutic measures to reduce recidivism and generally include such essential elements as immediate intervention, nonadversarial adjudication, hands-on judicial involvement, treatment programs with clear rules and structured goals, and a team approach that brings together judges, prosecutors, defense attorneys, treatment providers, and corrections personnel.[52] In Harris County (in the Houston, Texas, metro area), for example, there are "eighteen specialty courts serving adults, juveniles and families. Veterans, those who struggle with mental health issues, and juveniles involved in human trafficking and gang activities benefit from these programs."[53] Other types of problem-solving courts have also become popular, among them mental health courts, teen courts, domestic violence courts, DWI courts, community courts, gambling courts, truancy courts, gun courts, child support courts, tobacco courts, fathering courts, homeless courts, veteran courts, and reentry courts. Some are permanent courts, while others are pilot or model programs. Still others exist as specialized dockets of established courts.[54]

Post-Pandemic Innovations

More recently, the immediate impact of COVID-19 was considerable and required state courts to be creative in processing cases. However, many of the pandemic-related innovations have remained in effect and have been seen as positive reforms that make the courts more accessible for the participants involved. For example, the Arizona Mohave Superior Court allows for remote participation in many court proceedings, which has helped reduce scheduling conflicts for litigants, attorneys, and judges.[55] Another example can be seen in Florida. The 17th Judicial Circuit took steps to continue with remote hearing options. Additionally, judges in this district have the discretion to decide whether hearings should be in person, virtual, or hybrid, which allows judges to consider the needs and limitations of the participants involved. These changes have produced positive results, such as increased attendance rates at various hearings where remote or hybrid options have been available.[56] The Washington Olympia Municipal Court has taken a different approach to increase accessibility issues. The Washington court has implemented a drive-thru window to streamline services where individuals can make payments, request court documents, submit case filings, and submit juror summons paperwork.[57] Finally, because of West Virginia's geographically diverse and rural regions, the West Virginia Intermediate Court of Appeals developed five regional satellite locations where court participants can go instead of traveling to the capitol of West Virginia. The regional locations are equipped with secure, state-of-the-art teleconferencing equipment and have provided more accessibility to the intermediate appellate courts while also decreasing the cost of litigation.[58] According to the current chief judge of the West Virginia Intermediate Appellate Court, the changes have generally been positive. He states,

> The majority of the time, our remote oral arguments have gone smoothly, and it is difficult to identify any disadvantage to those who have chosen to present their oral argument remotely rather than in person in the ICA's main courtroom in Charleston, West Virginia. There have certainly been a few isolated glitches, or technological problems, and it is still a work in progress, but, overall, it has gone smoothly, and the ultimate goal remains to make the remote and hybrid satellite hearings as seamless and effective as those in the main courtroom.[59]

While there has been general support for the post-COVID-19 innovations, there are some that are less enthusiastic of the benefits. As an illustration, a report by the National Center for State Courts (NCSC) on remote proceedings in Texas state courts discovered that virtual processes tend to be more time-consuming compared to in-person ones.[60] Criminal justice scholars Elizabeth Webster, Beth Huebner, Alessandra Milagros Early, and Luis Torres explain that "Texas judges attributed the length to technical difficulties, connectivity problems, and challenges in sharing screens or uploading documents."[61] What is clear: whatever the specific approach, state courts are willing and imaginative innovators.

ADMINISTRATIVE AND STAFF SUPPORT IN THE STATE JUDICIARY

The daily operation of the federal courts requires the efforts of many individuals and organizations. This is no less true for the state court systems.

Magistrates

State magistrates, who may also be known in some states as commissioners or referees, are often used to perform some of the work in the initial stages of civil and criminal case processing. In this way, they are like US magistrate judges. In some jurisdictions, they hold bond hearings, issue warrants, and conduct preliminary investigations in criminal cases. They are also authorized in some states to make decisions in minor cases. In North Carolina, for example, the magistrates who lend support to the state's district courts may accept guilty pleas on certain traffic violations as well as preside over small claims cases.

Law Clerks

State courts, like federal courts, utilize law clerks. The majority of law clerk positions are typically found in the courts of general jurisdiction and appellate courts. Courts of limited jurisdiction normally do not employ law clerks. The utilization of law clerks varies depending on the court's level and individual judge practices. For instance, in some state courts, law clerks are assigned to a particular judge, whereas in other states, law clerks are shared among multiple judges.

Administrative Office of the Courts

Every state now has an administrative office of the courts or a similarly titled agency that performs a variety of administrative tasks for its court system. The size of the administrative office and its operating budget vary from state to state, so that some of these agencies perform more tasks than others. Among the duties more commonly associated with administrative offices are budget preparation, data processing, facility management, judicial education, public information, research, and personnel management. Several administrative offices have total or partial responsibility for one or more of these tasks.

Court Clerks and Court Administrators

The clerk of the court has traditionally handled the day-to-day routines of the court. This includes making courtroom arrangements, keeping records of case proceedings, preparing orders and judgments resulting from court actions, collecting court fines and fees, and disbursing judicial monies. In many states, these officials are elected and may be referred to by other titles.

In many areas, the traditional court clerks have been replaced by court administrators. In contrast to the court clerk, who managed the operations of a specific courtroom, the modern court administrator may assist a presiding judge in running the entire courthouse. Even more broadly, in some states, the administrator may work for a statewide organization that oversees all the state court systems at the city or county level.

STATE COURT WORKLOAD

The lion's share of the nation's judicial business exists at the state, not the national, level. That federal judges adjudicate several hundred thousand cases in a year is impressive; the fact that total caseloads in the state trial courts (limited and general jurisdiction) hover around 65 million is overwhelming (and at their peak in 2008 state trial courts dealt with an influx of over 106 million cases).[62] Interestingly, data trends show that almost half of the total cases come from traffic courts (approximately 30 million cases a year).[63]

Completely reliable data on the number of cases filed in the state courts are somewhat difficult to come by as not all states make their data available. Record-keeping is much better in some states than in others, and some of the lower-level courts, which are sometimes not courts of record, often greatly vary. Nonetheless, the National Center for State Courts and the Courts Statistics Project do an excellent job of tracking the figures for the states' trial courts. We begin at the trial court level, where we examine both civil and criminal case filings.

Tables 3.1 and 3.2 show the number of civil and criminal cases filed in state trial courts of general jurisdiction, limited jurisdiction, and single trial courts in 2022. Although the numbers are similar for the three types of state trial courts, it is important to note that the greatest number of cases are found in limited jurisdiction courts.

The number of cases filed in state intermediate appellate courts and courts of last resort in 2022 are detailed in Table 3.3. They are broken down by those cases the two courts are obligated to hear, those granted by right, those granted by permission of the court, and those that are handled in the first instance or for some other reason. As the numbers indicate, a far greater number of cases are handled in the intermediate courts of appeals than in the state courts of last resort.

TABLE 3.1 ■ Total Number of Civil Cases Filed in State Trial Courts in 2022, by Type of Court

Court of General Jurisdiction	Court of Limited Jurisdiction	Single Trial Court
3,761,017	6,919,516	1,975,902

Source: Data compiled from https://www.courtstatistics.org/court-statistics/interactive-caseload-data-displays/csp-stat-nav-cards-first-row/csp-stat-overview (accessed June 6, 2024).

TABLE 3.2 ■ Total Number of Criminal Cases Filed in State Trial Courts in 2022, by Type of Court

Court of General Jurisdiction	Court of Limited Jurisdiction	Single Trial Court
2,367,552	9,753,919	1,596,556

Source: Data compiled from https://www.courtstatistics.org/court-statistics/interactive-caseload-data-displays/csp-stat-nav-cards-first-row/csp-stat-overview (accessed June 6, 2024).

TABLE 3.3 ■ Total Incoming Caseload Composition in State Appellate Courts, 2022

Case Type	Total Incoming Cases	Courts of Last Resort	Intermediate Appellate Courts
Appeal by right	100,463	14,488	85,975
Appeal by permission	45,470	21,704	23,766
Original/other	16,980	6,572	10,408
All cases	169,503	49,354	169,503

Source: Data compiled from https://www.courtstatistics.org/court-statistics/interactive-caseload-data-displays/csp-stat-nav-cards-first-row/csp-stat-overview (accessed June 6, 2024).

SUMMARY

In this chapter, we offered a brief historical review of the development of state judicial systems. The picture that emerges is that no two state court systems are alike. However, there are four basic levels within the states: trial courts of limited jurisdiction, trial courts of general jurisdiction, intermediate appellate courts, and courts of last resort. We examined the work done at each of these four levels. Our discussion also included a brief look at the handling of juvenile cases within the states. In addition, we briefly discussed norm enforcement, administrative hearings, policymaking by state courts, and innovation—primarily in the context of problem-solving courts and innovations that have continued in light of the COVID-19 global pandemic.

In discussing administrative assistance for the state courts, our review centered on administrative offices of the courts, law clerks, court clerks and court administrators, and magistrates. We concluded with a brief look at the workload of the state trial and appellate courts.

FURTHER THOUGHT AND DISCUSSION QUESTIONS

1. Does a unified court system provide the best way for state courts to handle their legal issues?
2. Why are state courts not as commonly recognized for their policymaking activities as the federal courts?
3. Why is the courtroom work group essential to the functioning of state courts?
4. What conclusions may be drawn from a comparison of state and federal court caseload statistics?

SUGGESTED RESOURCES

Bureau of Justice Statistics. Available online at http://www.ojp.usdoj.gov/bjs/courts.htm. Important information and statistics on state courts.

Court Statistics Project. Available online at https://www.courtstatistics.org/. Provides comprehensive state court data and information regarding state court organization.

Eisenstein, James, Roy B. Flemming, and Peter F. Nardulli. *The Contours of Justice: Communities and Their Courts*. Lanham, MD: University Press of America, 1999. Excellent study of the processing of felony criminal cases in nine medium-size courts in three states. The study examines how different courts in different communities incorporate local norms into court procedures.

FindLaw. Available online at http://www.findlaw.com. Useful information about individual state courts and state laws.

Gray, Virginia, Russell L. Hanson, and Thad Kousser (Eds.). *Politics in American States: A Comparative Analysis*, 11th ed. Thousand Oaks, CA: Sage, 2017. An excellent reader of the day-to-day politics and operations of state courts in America.

National Center for State Courts. Available online at http://www.ncsc.org. Excellent source of information and statistics related to the work of state courts. Also contains links to individual state court systems.

National Drug Court Institute. Available online at http://www.ndci.org. Institute distributes information about drug court programs and training for officials.

National Institute of Justice. Available online at https://nij.ojp.gov/. The NIJ is a research agency that focuses on criminal justice and juvenile issues.

Solimine, Michael E., and James L. Walker. *Respecting State Courts: The Inevitability of Judicial Federalism*. Westport, CT: Greenwood Press, 1999. A good book about the relationship between the federal and state court systems.

Tarr, G. Alan. *Understanding State Constitutions*. Princeton, NJ: Princeton University Press, 2000. Informative book about the development and interpretation of state constitutions.

Tarr, G. Alan. *Without Fear or Favor: Judicial Independence and Judicial Accountability in the States*. Stanford, CA: Stanford University Press, 2012. The focus of the text is on the tension between judicial independence and the accountability of state jurists. He examines both the challenges and possible solutions inherent in these two concepts.

Zackin, Emily. *Looking for Rights in All the Wrong Places*. Princeton, NJ: Princeton University Press, 2013. An excellent book that takes an in-depth historical approach to understanding how state constitutions have enshrined many of our rights.

KEY TERMS

alternative dispute resolution (ADR)
bail
courtroom work group
felony
trial de novo

4 JURISDICTION AND POLICYMAKING BOUNDARIES

CHAPTER GOALS AND OBJECTIVES

In this chapter, students will learn that . . .

- The concept of jurisdiction structures the workload of the US judiciary at the federal and state levels, with different courts having or sharing jurisdiction over different kinds of disputes.
- Legislative politics and jurisdiction are often intertwined, although the extent of the legislature's power to alter jurisdiction is at times legally and politically questionable.
- Sometimes litigants have a choice of where to file a case among the various courts that may properly have jurisdiction. This can allow litigants some opportunity to strategize as to which courts might be the most receptive to that litigant's side in the dispute.
- There are ten important maxims of judicial self-restraint that help to keep our judiciary in check. However, judges themselves play a key role in determining the boundaries of these restraints.

Jurisdiction is the power of a court to adjudicate cases and as such may be thought of as the cornerstone of the legal system. In setting the jurisdictions of courts, Congress and the US Constitution—and their state counterparts—mandate the types of cases each court can hear. The judiciary in the United States is a complex structure where jurisdiction is split or shared among a variety of courts at the state and federal levels. In this chapter, we examine how jurisdiction operates across the various levels in federal and state court.

Beyond jurisdiction, we also provide a detailed discussion of judicial self-restraint, examining ten principles that govern a judge's decision about whether or how to resolve a case. Derived from legal tradition and constitutional and statutory law, judges are constrained by the types of matters that a court may adjudicate, or whether a case is in a proper form to be adjudicated. Although all ten principles discussed in this chapter constrain the behavior of judges in the exercise of their power to resolve issues and influence policy, judges—especially at the appellate level—have a good deal of ability to define the boundaries of these constraints.

JURISDICTION OF FEDERAL COURTS

As we have discussed in previous chapters, the federal court system is divided into three separate levels: the trial courts, the appellate tribunals, and the US Supreme Court. Next, we examine each in turn with an eye toward the jurisdiction at play at each level.

US District Courts

In the United States Code, Congress has set forth the jurisdiction of the federal district courts. These tribunals have original jurisdiction in federal criminal and civil cases—that is, by law, the cases must be heard first in these courts, no matter who the parties are or how significant the issues. US Code also specifies how many federal districts exist within each state, as well as which locations (or divisions) within each district will hold court.[1]

Although the formal processes of criminal and civil trials are discussed in greater detail in Chapters 10 and 11, respectively, here we focus specifically on federal criminal and civil cases from a jurisdictional perspective.

US District Court Judge Matthew Kacsmaryk is the only judge currently hearing cases in the Amarillo Division of the District Court for the Northern District of Texas. Judge Kacsmaryk's rulings since his appointment in 2019 have made Amarillo a particularly attractive location for conservative groups to file in order to draw a like-minded judge to preside over the case.

Senate Judiciary Committee via AP

Criminal Cases

Federal criminal cases typically represent offenses that transcend state boundaries or that violate federal laws. After obtaining an **indictment** from a federal grand jury, the US attorney files charges against the accused in the district court in which they serve.

Criminal activity as defined by Congress covers a wide range of behavior, including interstate theft of an automobile, involvement in terrorist activities, illegal importation of narcotics, conspiracy to deprive persons of their civil rights, and even the killing of a migratory bird out of season.

Specific categories of cases tend to dominate the federal district court docket. In the fiscal year ending in 2023, violation of immigration laws and drug laws were the offenses prosecuted most frequently in the US trial courts, accounting for 29 percent and 28 percent of all filings, respectively.[2] Firearms/explosives, fraud, and a variety of other criminal cases constituted the remainder of the criminal docket in federal district courts in the United States.

Some federal crimes, such as robbery, are comparatively uniform in occurrence in each of the ninety-four US judicial districts, whereas others are endemic to certain geographic areas. For example, those districts next to the Mexican border get an inordinate number of illegal drug and immigration cases. In the US Court for the Southern District of Texas, for example, it is not unusual for drug and illegal entry cases to constitute at least three-fourths of all criminal filings for any given year.

Congress is the key actor in determining the content of the criminal code in the United States and as such has a major influence over the caseload and subject matter of criminal (and civil) cases in the various district courts. In setting federal law, however, Congress is constrained by its own constitutional authority. In a 5–4 decision in 1995, for example, the Supreme Court ruled that the Gun Free School Zones Act of 1990, which forbade anyone "knowingly to possess a firearm at a place [known to be] . . . a school zone," unconstitutionally exceeded Congress's power.[3] Legislators justified the law as an extension of their Article I power to regulate interstate commerce. The justices in the majority disagreed, ruling that having a gun in a school was not an economic activity. As such, while the student possessing the gun in this case may justly have been tried in state court for the offense (he had initially been charged in state court in Texas, where the misdeed occurred), it was unconstitutional for Congress to turn the action into a crime against the United States.

Civil Cases

Most of the district court caseload is civil in nature—that is, suits between private parties or between the US government, acting in its nonprosecutorial capacity, and a private party. Civil cases that originate in the US district courts may be placed in several categories. The first is litigation concerning the interpretation or application of the Constitution, acts of Congress, or US treaties. Examples of cases in this category include the following: a petitioner claims that one of their federally protected civil rights has been violated; a litigant alleges that they are being harmed by a congressional statute that is unconstitutional; and a plaintiff argues that they are suffering injury from a treaty that is improperly affecting them. The key point is that a **federal question** must be raised for the US trial courts to have jurisdiction. It is not enough to say that the federal courts should hear a case because it involves a critical issue or the public cares a lot about it. Unless one can invoke the Constitution or a federal law or treaty, the case must be litigated elsewhere—probably in the state courts.

Some minimal dollar amount traditionally had to be in controversy in some types of cases before the trial courts would hear them, but such amounts have been waived if the case falls into one of several broad categories. For example, an alleged violation of a civil rights law, such as the Voting Rights Act of 1965, must be heard by the federal instead of the state judiciary. Other types of cases in this category are patent and copyright claims, passport and naturalization proceedings, admiralty and maritime disputes, and violations of the US postal laws.

Another broad category of cases over which the US trial courts exercise general original jurisdiction includes citizenship disputes involving parties from different states or between an American citizen and a foreign country or citizen. Thus, if a citizen of New York were to be injured in an automobile accident in Chicago, by a driver from Illinois, the New Yorker could sue in federal court because the parties to the suit were of "diverse citizenship." The requirement that the matter in controversy must exceed the sum or value of $75,000 in a **diversity of citizenship suit** keeps relatively less consequential disputes out of federal court, while providing access to the district courts for more substantial civil claims.

Federal district courts also have jurisdiction over petitions from convicted prisoners who contend that their incarceration (or perhaps their denial of parole) is in violation of their federally protected rights. In many of these cases, prisoners ask for a writ of **habeas corpus**, an order issued by a judge to determine whether a person had been lawfully imprisoned or detained. The judge would demand that the prison authorities either justify the detention or release the petitioner. Prisoners convicted in a state court must take care to argue that a federally protected right was violated—for example, the right to be represented by counsel at trial. Otherwise, the federal courts would have no jurisdiction. Federal prisoners have a somewhat wider range for their appeals, given that all their rights and options are within the penumbra of the US Constitution.

Finally, the district courts have the authority to hear any other cases that Congress may validly prescribe by law. For example, although the Constitution grants to the US Supreme Court original jurisdiction to hear "cases affecting Ambassadors, [and] other public Ministers and Consuls,"[4] Congress has also authorized the district courts to have concurrent original jurisdiction over cases involving such parties.

US Courts of Appeals

The US appellate courts have no original jurisdiction whatsoever; every case or controversy that comes to one of these intermediate-level panels has been first argued in some other forum. These tribunals, like the district courts, are the creations of Congress, and their structure and functions have varied considerably over time. Basically, Congress has granted the circuit courts appellate jurisdiction over two extensive categories of cases. The first of these are ordinary civil and criminal appeals from the federal trial courts, including the US territorial courts, the US Tax Court, and some District of Columbia courts. In criminal cases, the appellant is the defendant because the government is not free to appeal a verdict of not guilty. (However, if the question in a criminal case is one of defining the legal right of the defendant, the government may appeal an adverse trial court ruling.) In civil cases, the party that lost in the trial court is usually the appellant, although the winning party can appeal if it is not satisfied with the lower court judgment.

The second broad category of appellate jurisdiction includes appeals from certain federal administrative agencies and departments and from important independent regulatory commissions, such as the Securities and Exchange Commission and the National Labor Relations Board. Traditionally, less than 10 percent of the civil docket has consisted of administrative appeals. However, this jumped to more than 20 percent in 2005, because of a surge of causes related to Board of Immigration Appeals decisions. By 2023, however, the percentage had backed off to less than 11 percent of the total appellate case filings.[5]

US Supreme Court

The US Supreme Court is the only federal court mentioned by name in the Constitution, which spells out the general contours of the high court's jurisdiction.[6] Although the Supreme Court is usually thought of as an appellate tribunal, it does have some general original jurisdiction. Probably the most important subject of such jurisdiction is a suit between two or more states.

Cases over which the Supreme Court has original jurisdiction are often important, but they could create logistical and time-management problems were they to take a large portion of the Court's caseload each year. Cases taken on its original jurisdiction put the Court in the position of acting simultaneously as the trial court and the court of last resort. In most of these cases, the time-consuming activities related to conducting a trial motivate the Court to appoint a Special Master to assist in managing the case and make initial findings of fact and legal conclusions.[7]

To avoid getting dragged into petty disputes between states, the justices generally reserve the exercise of original jurisdiction to a narrow class of disputes. In recent years, these cases have typically involved disagreement between two states over state boundaries or water resources and have accounted for less than 1 percent of the high court's docket. The Court only issued one opinion in a case on original jurisdiction during the 2021–2022 term, and only two cases in the previous year.[8]

In addition, the high court shares original jurisdiction with the US district courts in certain cases brought by or against foreign ambassadors or consuls, in cases between the United States and a state, and in cases commenced by a state against citizens of another state or against citizens of another country. In situations such as these, where jurisdiction is shared, the courts are said to have **concurrent jurisdiction**.

The vast majority of cases handled by the US Supreme Court come to that tribunal on its appellate jurisdiction. The US Constitution declares that the Supreme

Court "shall have appellate Jurisdiction . . . under such Regulations as the Congress shall make."[9] Over the years, Congress has passed much legislation setting forth the "regulations" determining which cases may appear before the nation's apex judicial body. In essence, appeals may reach the Supreme Court through two main avenues. First, appeals may be heard from all lower federal constitutional and territorial courts and from most, but not all, federal legislative courts. Second, the Supreme Court may hear appeals from the highest court in a state—provided there is a substantial federal question.

As discussed in fuller detail in Chapter 2, most of the high court's docket consists of cases in which it has agreed to issue a writ of certiorari—a discretionary action. Such a writ (which must be supported by at least four justices, according to the **rule of four**) is an order from the Supreme Court to a lower court demanding that it send up a complete record of a case so that the high court can review it. Historically, the Supreme Court has agreed to grant the petition for a writ of certiorari in only a tiny proportion of cases—usually less than 10 percent of the time, and in recent years, the number has been closer to 1 percent.

Another method by which the Supreme Court exercises its appellate jurisdiction is **certification**. This procedure is followed when one of the appeals courts asks the Supreme Court for instructions regarding a question of law. The justices may choose to give the appellate judges binding instructions, or they may ask that the entire record be forwarded to the Supreme Court for review and final judgment.

JURISDICTION OF STATE COURTS

The jurisdictions of the fifty separate state court systems in the United States are established in virtually the same manner as those within the national court system. Each state has a constitution that sets forth the authority and decision-making powers of its various trial and appellate judges. Likewise, each state legislature passes laws that further detail the specific powers and prerogatives of judges and the rights and obligations of those who bring suit in the state courts. Because no two state constitutions or legislative bodies are alike, it is not surprising that the jurisdictions of state courts vary from one state to another. For example, one state constitution may give its supreme court original jurisdiction over all cases in which a state is suing one of its counties, while another state constitution may confer such jurisdiction only on the low-level circuit courts. Similarly, one state legislature might define felony theft as the stealing of $3,000 or more, sending the case automatically to a county criminal court, whereas a case involving less than $3,000 would go to a municipal court authorized to handle only minor crimes. In another state, the legislature might draw the line between felony and petty theft at a different dollar amount. In their civil courts, states also define the jurisdiction of their small claims tribunals to cases with varying maximum dollar values at stake.

Thus, while court jurisdictions vary from one state to another and from the national model, they are all derived in part from a constitution and in part from enactments of legislative bodies. The heavy workload of state judiciaries nationwide requires careful attention to matters of jurisdiction within the state's judicial system. In addition, the power of a state's political branches over the jurisdiction of state tribunals allows the elected branches an avenue to alter jurisdiction in ways intended to ensure compliance with the wishes of those in power in the state.[10]

JURISDICTION AND LEGISLATIVE POLITICS

One political reality regarding the jurisdiction of the federal and state courts that must be remembered is that, for all intents and purposes, Congress and the fifty state legislatures determine the types of issues and cases the courts in their separate realms will hear. And equally important, what the legislative branches give, they may also take away. Some judges and judicial scholars argue that the US Constitution (in Articles I and III) and the respective state documents confer a certain inherent jurisdiction on the judiciaries in some key areas, independent of the legislative will. Nevertheless, the jurisdictional boundaries of American courts clearly are a product of legislative judgments—determinations often flavored with the bittersweet spice of politics. The sensitivity of the US Supreme Court to the moods of Congress was explored empirically by a recent study. The author found that between 1877 and 2006, when the Court perceived the congressional mood toward it to be "hostile," the justices were more likely to exercise self-restraint and less likely to use judicial review to invalidate acts of Congress.[11]

Congress may advance a particular cause by giving courts the authority to hear cases in a public policy realm that previously had been forbidden territory for the judiciary. For example, when Congress passed the Civil Rights Act of 1968, it gave judges the authority to penalize individuals who interfere with "any person because of his race, color, religion or national origin and because he is or has been . . . traveling in . . . interstate commerce."[12] Prior to 1968, the courts had no jurisdiction over incidents that stemmed from interference by one person with another's right to travel. Likewise, Congress may discourage a particular social movement by passing legislation to make it virtually impossible for its advocates to have any success in the courts.[13]

Perhaps the most vivid illustration of congressional power over federal court jurisdiction occurred just after the Civil War, and the awesome nature of this legislative prerogative haunts the judiciary to this day. On February 5, 1867, Congress empowered the federal courts to grant habeas corpus to individuals imprisoned in violation of their constitutional rights. The Supreme Court was authorized to hear appeals of such cases. William McCardle was incarcerated by the military government of Mississippi for being in alleged violation of the Reconstruction laws. McCardle was alleged to have published "incendiary and libelous" articles that attacked his "unlawful restraint by military force." He sought relief in the circuit court, but it was denied. He then appealed to the Supreme Court, which agreed to take the case.

After the arguments had been made before the high court (but prior to a decision), Congress got into the act. Its anti-Southern majority feared that the Court would use the *Ex Parte McCardle* case as a vehicle to strike down all or part of the Reconstruction acts—something Congress had no intention of permitting. And so, over President Andrew Johnson's veto, the following statute was enacted: "That so much of the act approved February 5, 1867 [as] authorized an appeal from the judgment of the Circuit Court to the Supreme Court of the United States, or the exercise of any such jurisdiction by said Supreme Court, on appeals which have been, or may hereafter be taken, [is] hereby repealed." Thus, while the Court was in the process of deciding the case, Congress removed the subject matter from the federal docket. Was all of this strictly legal and constitutional? Yes, indeed. Stunned by Congress's action but obedient to the Constitution, the Court limply ruled that McCardle's appeal must now "be dismissed for want of jurisdiction."[14]

More recently, a regular pattern has been seen where controversial decisions by the Supreme Court have resulted in bills introduced in Congress to strip the Court of its appellate jurisdiction in those particularly salient policy areas (such as abortion, school prayer, LGBTQ rights, and religious liberty).[15] Although such bills are introduced regularly, they are rarely passed into law today.

That recent history does not mean that Congress could not start passing laws removing jurisdiction more regularly in coming years. Proponents of "jurisdiction stripping" have no "inherent partisan valence and [jurisdiction stripping] could be utilized to serve the ideological goals of nearly any constituency with the political capacity to enact it."[16] With the hardball nature of the politics involved in appointing Justices Neil Gorsuch and Amy Coney Barrett to the Supreme Court (discussed more fully in Chapter 6) and the resulting decisions of the 6–3 conservative supermajority on the Court, some Democrats have recently expressed interest in removing the Court's jurisdiction to hear cases in areas including abortion, LGBTQ rights, and the constitutionality of a hypothetical wealth tax. That said, arguments in favor of altering the Court's appellate jurisdiction are often motivated by ideological preferences in how these policy areas should be resolved. Jurisdiction stripping is also supported by those who argue that it could be designed to make the Court more accountable or improve our democracy by diverting policymaking power away from unelected judges to the more representative political branches.

Proposals to alter the Court's jurisdiction bring with them uncertainty as to their legality, in part because the historic weight of *McCardle* as precedent for a similar situation has been questioned over time.[17] Congress is clearly granted power to limit the Supreme Court's appellate jurisdiction, but such power is not unlimited and the boundaries of Congress's authority are unclear. In addition, the feasibility of such proposals resulting in a better-functioning democracy is also uncertain. Stripping the Supreme Court alone of jurisdiction to hear a category of cases may have little influence on empowering the elected branches to resolve these policy debates unless jurisdiction is similarly removed from lower federal or even state courts as well. On the other hand, more expansive jurisdictional proposals that strip the power of lower federal and state courts to hear cases raise even more serious questions about the constitutionality of those proposals, compared to those focused only on the Supreme Court's jurisdiction.

Additionally, although jurisdiction stripping has been somewhat successful in other countries in making courts more politically accountable, it also opens avenues for political manipulation or the elimination of the ability of judicial tribunals to check and balance the other branches of government. Israel's legislature (the *Knesset*), for example, sparked turmoil in the country in 2023 when it passed a bill stripping Israel's Supreme Court of the power to declare government decisions unreasonable.[18] The Knesset passed the "Reasonableness Bill" by a vote of 64–0, after members of the opposition left the 120-seat chamber in protest.

These debates and concerns may help explain why jurisdiction stripping has taken something of a back seat in the contemporary debate over possible Supreme Court reform, in favor of proposals instituting term limits or binding judicial ethics reform on current or future justices. In the summer of 2024, for example, President Joe Biden did not include any attention to jurisdiction stripping as part of his broader Court reform proposal. (The Biden proposal will be discussed in more detail in Chapter 6.)

Readers may agree or disagree with those who encourage the political branches to utilize the power to alter a court's jurisdiction more vigorously to isolate public policy from judicial review. Even with the uncertainty as to the precise limits of this power, we should not lose sight of the fact that the jurisdiction of US courts is established by "the United States of America in Congress assembled."[19] Likewise, the jurisdictions of courts in the states are very much governed by—and are the political product of—the will of the state legislatures.

JURISDICTION AND FORUM SHOPPING

With respect to jurisdiction, one final consideration relates to litigant options that may be available when more than one court has proper jurisdiction over a case or when litigation of national significance may be instigated by potential plaintiffs across the country. In such situations, an advantage may be found with respect to where the case is filed. One high-profile example has been playing out recently in federal cases filed in Texas. For example, in 2023, US District Court Judge Matthew Kacsmaryk suspended the Food and Drug Administration's (FDA) approval of mifepristone, one of the two drugs used in medication abortions. As will be discussed later in this chapter, the US Supreme Court eventually ruled that the pro-life medical associations and doctors that filed the case lacked the standing to bring the litigation.

With respect to the current topic of jurisdiction, the relevance of this case is where it was filed in the first place. The Alliance for Hippocratic Medicine (AHM) served as the lead litigant challenging mifepristone's approval. Given that the drug is used in medication abortions nationwide, potential plaintiffs may have decided to file their case in any number of district courts across the country. AHM filed the case in the Amarillo Division of the US District Court for the Northern District of Texas. The Northern District of Texas contains seven divisions, and cases are assigned to an available judge in the specific geographic division in which the case is filed. It is not required that cases are assigned this way. In some other federal districts, cases are assigned randomly to any judge within the district, rather than to one in the smaller division in which it is filed.

The Northern District of Texas has twelve active district court judges when fully staffed,[20] but Kacsmaryk alone is currently located in the Amarillo Division of the Northern District. Litigants filing cases in that division can therefore predict with near certainty who will preside over their case, an advantage that would not be available were cases to be randomly assigned to any of the judges serving the full district.

Prior to his appointment to the district court by President Donald Trump in 2019, Kacsmaryk worked as deputy general counsel for First Liberty, a Texas-based legal organization focused on religious liberty-centered litigation.[21] Given the regularity with which Kacsmaryk rules in favor of conservative interests, it is not a coincidence that like-minded litigants have flocked to that specific division. Indeed, the Alliance for Hippocratic Medicine only opened an office in Amarillo three months before filing their case in what has effectively become Kacsmaryk's court.[22]

Additional examples of potential judge shopping in Amarillo or elsewhere in Texas are not difficult to identify. Of the first twenty lawsuits filed against the Biden administration by Republican Attorney General of Texas Ken Paxton, thirteen were filed in divisions with only a single judge. The single available judge was appointed by President Trump in every case.[23]

These events have hardly gone unnoticed. The Judicial Conference of the United States, part of the executive branch and responsible for considering and recommending federal policy related to the judiciary, recently reiterated its long-standing preference for random case assignment and recommended that districts adopt policies that would avoid the ability to judge shop, especially in cases where litigants seek to affect policy at a statewide or national level.[24]

Congressional leaders in both parties have questioned case assignment protocols that exacerbate the prevalence of strategic **forum shopping**.[25] Although most of the more recent disapproval has come from Democrats, Republican leaders in Congress have also criticized when liberal interests seek out favorable judges in divisions with only one or two like-minded judges. In the wake of the 2024 recommendation of the Judicial Conference regarding district-level case assignment, both party leaders in the Senate introduced legislation addressing the problem, although finding common ground between the parties' solutions is, of course, the bigger challenge.

We should expect, then, that conservative and liberal interests with the ability to choose where to file litigation will continue to act strategically in seeking out courts and even individual judges who are expected to be particularly amendable to those groups' arguments. One legal scholar has highlighted that even with rules intended to limit the practice, forum shopping in the United States is "broad in scope, widespread in practice, and quintessentially American in design."[26] The American legal culture of litigant autonomy and zealous legal advocacy contributes to the general acceptance that forum shopping (between federal and state court, within the federal level, between states, or even homing in on one specific judge) is legitimate advocacy, so long as it is not abused.

JUDICIAL SELF-RESTRAINT

Beyond questions related to jurisdiction, courts in the United States are restrained by a variety of other considerations that affect the kinds or forms of cases that can be resolved by judges. These restraints serve to limit the extent of judicial power to weigh in on particular disputes. That said, these considerations are often referred to as examples of "judicial self-restraint," because the judges themselves (and especially the justices of the US Supreme Court) are often responsible for defining the specific contours of these limitations. Still, the exercise of judicial power is limited—at least in theory, if not always in practice—by these principles.

The activities that judges are forbidden from engaging in, or at least are discouraged from engaging in, deal not so much with technical matters of jurisdiction as with **justiciability**—the question of whether judges in the system ought to hear or refrain from hearing certain types of disputes. In the following sections, ten separate aspects of judicial self-restraint, ten principles that serve to check and contain the power of American judges, will be examined.[27] These maxims originate from a variety of sources—the US Constitution and state constitutions, acts of Congress and of state legislatures, the common law tradition—and when possible, their roots and the nature of their evolution will be noted. Although the primary examples provided will be illustrative of the federal judiciary, most apply to state judicial systems as well.

A Definite Controversy Must Exist

The US Constitution states that "the judicial Power shall extend to all Cases, in Law and Equity, arising under this Constitution, the Laws of the United States, and Treaties made . . . under their Authority" (Article III, Section 2). The key word here is *cases.* Since 1789, the federal courts have chosen to interpret the term in its most literal sense; there must be a controversy between legitimate adversaries who have met all the technical legal standards to institute a suit. The dispute must concern the protection of a meaningful, nontrivial right or the prevention or redress of a wrong that directly affects the parties to the suit. Three corollaries to this general principle breathe a little life into its rather abstract-sounding admonitions.

The first is that the federal courts do not render **advisory opinions**, which is a court's nonbinding interpretation of law. Such requests would typically come from the legislative or executive branches as they consider legislative or policy change, and ask judges to address questions that are still hypothetical. Absent an authentic clash between actual adversaries, there is no real dispute at the center of a request for an advisory opinion.

Although federal judges do not rule on abstract or hypothetical issues, as of 2002, "high courts in eleven states (and a number of countries) provide advisory opinions on pending legislation when requested by the executive or legislative branch of government."[28] Some federal legislative courts, such as the Court of Federal Claims, may give advisory opinions as well. Also, American judges are empowered to render **declaratory judgments**, which define the rights of various parties under a statute, will, or contract. The judgments do not entail any type of coercive relief. As Justice William Rehnquist once put it, "A declaratory judgment is simply a statement of rights, not a binding order."[29] Although a difference exists between an abstract dispute that the federal courts must avoid and a situation where a declaratory judgment is in order, the line between the two is often a difficult one for jurists to draw in practice.

A second corollary of the general principle is that the parties to the suit must have proper **standing**. This deals with the matter of who may bring litigation to court. Although the term *standing* has many aspects, the most prominent component is that the person suing must have suffered (or be immediately about to suffer) a direct and significant injury. As a rule, a litigant cannot bring a claim on behalf of others (except for parents of minor children or in special types of suits called **class actions**). In addition, the alleged injury must be personalized and immediate—not part of some generalized **complaint**.

In 2024, doctrine related to standing provided the resolution to the challenge to FDA's approval of the abortion drug mifepristone, discussed previously in this chapter. Recall that the Alliance for Hippocratic Medicine filed their case in the Amarillo Division of the Northern District of Texas. The gambit paid off when Judge Matthew Kacsmaryk "in effect enjoined FDA's approval of mifepristone, thereby ordering mifepristone off the market."[30] In the process of doing so, Kacsmaryk ruled that the plaintiffs, four pro-life medical associations and several individual doctors in Texas, had standing to bring the suit. On appeal, the conservative Fifth Circuit agreed on the standing issue, although the appeals court partially granted a stay of the district court order pending appeal, temporarily reinstating FDA's approval of mifepristone.

In a unanimous decision, the Supreme Court disagreed with the lower courts on the standing issue. In his majority opinion for the Court, Justice Brett Kavanaugh summarized that "to sue in federal court, a plaintiff must show that he or she has suffered or likely will suffer an injury in fact."[31] In addition, the plaintiffs must demonstrate causation between the government's actions (FDA's approval of mifepristone) and the asserted injury to themselves. The plaintiffs in this case, pro-life doctors and medical associations that do not perform abortions or prescribe mifepristone, were unable to do so to the satisfaction of any member of the Supreme Court.

As Justice Kavanaugh summarized in his opinion for the Court:

> The plaintiffs have sincere legal, moral, ideological, and policy objections to elective abortion and to FDA's relaxed regulation of mifepristone. But under Article III of the Constitution, those kinds of objections alone do not establish a justiciable case or controversy in federal court. Here, the plaintiffs have failed to demonstrate that FDA's relaxed regulatory requirements likely would cause them to suffer an injury in fact. For that reason, the federal courts are the wrong forum for addressing the plaintiffs' concerns about FDA's actions. The plaintiffs may present their concerns and objections to the President and FDA in the regulatory process, or to Congress and the President in the legislative process. And they may also express their views about abortion and mifepristone to fellow citizens, including in the political and electoral processes.[32]

Having strong and sincere beliefs about a matter of public policy is not the same thing as having the legal standing to challenge that policy. Although future litigants might be able to satisfy standing requirements to challenge the approval of mifepristone, for the time being, FDA regulations regarding mifepristone remain in effect nationwide.

The third corollary of this general principle that there must be a definite controversy involving legitimate adversaries is that courts ordinarily will not hear a case that has become **moot**—when the basic facts or the status of the parties has significantly changed in the interim between when the suit was filed and when it comes before the judge(s). The death of a litigant or the fact that the litigants have ceased to be warring parties would render a case moot in most tribunals.

In 2020, a majority of justices on the US Supreme Court ruled in a per curiam opinion that a challenge to a New York City policy banning the transport of licensed handguns outside the city was mooted.[33] After the Supreme Court granted certiorari to the case and seemed poised perhaps to rule that the policy violated the Second Amendment, New York City amended the rule to now allow the transport of firearms to a shooting range or second home outside the city. Regardless of the city's motivations for changing their policy, the Court decided that since the petitioners could now do exactly what they indicated they were seeking the right to do, their specific challenge to the old policy no longer contained a live controversy. In dissent, Justice Samuel Alito (along with Justices Clarence Thomas and Neil Gorsuch) argued that the Court had allowed "our docket to be manipulated [by the City of New York] in a way that should not be countenanced."[34]

The New York City example demonstrates that sometimes judicial self-restraint delays rather than denies forever the courts the ability to rule on a specific set of issues. In the NYC gun case, for example, Justice Brett Kavanaugh agreed that the challenge to the amended NYC law was moot but wrote a concurring opinion noting that he shared the dissenters' concerns about the constitutionality of many gun restrictions on the books, and signaled that the Court should address these issues soon, "perhaps in one of the several Second Amendment cases with petitions for certiorari now pending before the Court."[35] Just because one case had been rendered moot did not affect the other legal challenges to gun regulations that remained in effect at the time.

In addition, sometimes judges for their own reasons may decide that a case is still ripe for adjudication, even though the status of the facts and parties would seem to have radically altered. Examples include cases where someone has challenged a state's refusal to permit an abortion (such as in *Roe v. Wade*[36]). In such cases, by the time the suit reaches an appellate court, the woman may already have given birth, as was the case with Jane Roe in *Roe v. Wade*. In this case, the justices believed that the issues were so important that they needed to be addressed by the court. To declare the case moot would, practically speaking, prevent it from ever being heard in time by an appellate body.

A great deal of flexibility and common sense is built into the US legal system. Judges may not decide an issue unless there is an actual case or controversy. From this, it follows that they do not consider abstract, hypothetical questions; they do not take a case unless the would-be litigants can demonstrate direct and substantial personal injury; and they (usually) do not take cases that have become moot. They may rule only on concrete issues brought by truly injured parties directly affected by the facts of a case.

That said, the word *self* in the phrase "judicial self-restraint" is important to keep in mind, and there can at times be room for innovation and disagreement in determining whether a legal dispute contains an actual case brought by a properly invested litigant (such as among the justices in the New York City gun regulation example). Another very recent example came in the 2023 decision in *303 Creative v. Elenis*,[37] where Lorie Smith successfully challenged a Colorado law that prohibited nearly all public-facing businesses in the state from denying anyone the full and equal enjoyment of services based on race, creed, disability, or sexual orientation.[38] In pursing the litigation, Smith alleged that she recently "decided to expand her [graphic design company's] offerings to include services for couples seeking websites for their weddings," and she was concerned that the Colorado law would require her to provide services for same-sex weddings and thus would "force her to express views with which she disagrees."[39]

Earlier in the litigation, Smith's attorneys filed documents indicating that her company had been contacted by a man named "Stewart" with an inquiry about hiring 303 Creative (Smith's company) to provide web-related services for his wedding to another man. Mere days before the Supreme Court ruled in favor of Smith in this case, a reporter with *The New Republic* used court documents to identify and call Stewart, who claimed that he had never contacted 303 Creative about a wedding website, and at the time the inquiry was submitted to Smith's company, Stewart was already married to a woman.[40]

Smith and her lawyers contended that the inquiry was submitted and that either Stewart gave the reporter inaccurate information or someone else submitted the request on behalf of Stewart, for whatever reason. Regardless, in a contentious and high-profile case where the key litigant had not yet engaged in business practices that would bring her within the scope of the law she was challenging, this new information added fuel to the fire of criticism from those opposed to the *303 Creative* ruling. Some news outlets centered on the "sham" or "fake" nature of the factual record in the case, and legal experts debated the standing issue in the aftermath of the Supreme Court's decision that the state of Colorado had violated Smith's free speech rights.[41]

Even though US courts may not rule on abstract questions or on matters for which no significant injury can be found, this is by no means the pattern throughout the rest of the world. In Norway, for example, the Parliament may ask its Constitutional Court for advice about the constitutionality of a law before it is ever passed. In Ireland, the president is permitted to ask the courts for an opinion about a bill's constitutionality before they sign it into law. In Canada, members of the executive cabinet may ask the country's Supreme Court for advisory opinions on almost any topic, including bills pending in or enacted by the provincial legislative bodies. And in Germany, the *Land* (state) governments may petition the Constitutional Court for abstract opinions about legal matters. Yet, even in these countries, obtaining advisory opinions from the courts is mainly a prerogative of government officials and agencies—not private citizens.

A Plea Must Be Specific

Another constraint on the judiciary is that judges will hear no case on the merits unless the petitioner is first able to cite a specific part of the Constitution as the basis for the plea. In other words, judges will give short shrift to anyone who comes to court arguing that circumstances have treated her unfairly or that he is unhappy with his lot in life. We witnessed this late in 2020 when President Donald Trump's reelection campaign appealed to the Third Circuit Court of Appeals (which has jurisdiction over Pennsylvania) to reverse the certification of the voting results in Pennsylvania, a state that had voted for Joe Biden.[42] The Trump team had claimed that the election was "a total scam," that he "won by a lot," and that the news media "refuse to report the real facts."

A three-judge panel, consisting of all Republicans, unanimously turned aside the Trump arguments. Judge Stephanos Bibas, a Trump appointee, began his opinion by writing that:

> Free, fair elections are the lifeblood of our democracy. Charges of unfairness are serious. But calling an election unfair does not make it so. Charges require specific allegations and then proof. We have neither here.[43]

Let us look at another example of this principle where the parties clearly did cite a specific part of the Constitution as the basis of their plea and who also presented some credible evidence. The First Amendment forbids government to make a law "respecting an establishment of religion," which means, among other things, that the government may not provide direct financial aid to religious entities. To improve some of its poorly rated public school systems, the state of Ohio enacted its Pilot Project Scholarship Program, which provides financial assistance to families in any Ohio school district that is or has been "under federal court order requiring supervision and operational management of the district by the state superintendent."[44] (Cleveland became the only Ohio school district to fall within that category.) In the 1999–2000 school year, fifty-six private schools participated in the program, and of these, forty-six (or 82 percent) had a religious affiliation. Furthermore, of the 3,700 students who participated in the scholarship program, 96 percent enrolled in religiously affiliated schools. In 2002, this program was challenged in the Supreme Court by those who argued that this flow of government aid to schools with a religious affiliation violated the First Amendment's ban on governmental "establishment of religion." Ultimately, the Supreme Court, in a divided vote, disagreed with the petitioner, arguing that the aid to religion was indirect rather than direct because the government money went primarily to the parents. But no one could deny that the original petitioners had relied on a specific portion of the Constitution (the Establishment Clause) as part of their plea.

However, if one went into court and contended that a particular law or official action "violated the spirit of the Bill of Rights" or "offended the values of the founders," a judge would dismiss the proceeding on the spot. If judges were free to give concrete, substantive meaning to vague generalities such as these, there would be little check on what they could do. Who is to say what is the "spirit of the Bill of Rights" or the collective motivation of those who hammered out the Constitution?

Despite what has just been said, in the real world, this principle is not as simple and clear-cut as it sounds because the Constitution contains many clauses that are open to a wide variety of interpretations. For example, the Constitution forbids Congress to pass any law abridging "freedom of speech," but such a term has been virtually impossible for jurists to define with any degree of precision. The Eighth Amendment prohibits "excessive bail" for criminal defendants, but what is excessive? The Fourteenth Amendment, Section 1, forbids states to abridge "the privileges and immunities of citizens of the United States," but who is to say what these privileges and immunities are? The Constitution gives hardly a clue. Although petitioners must cite a particular constitutional clause as the basis for their plea—as opposed to some ambiguous concept—there are enough vague clauses in the Constitution to give federal judges plenty of room to maneuver and make policy.

The United States is not the only country with a federal Constitution that contains ambiguous wording and potentially conflicting clauses to which judges have felt free to give new and imaginative meanings. For instance, Article 40 of the Irish Constitution "guarantees liberty for the exercise" of the rights of citizens "to express freely their convictions and opinions" and "to assemble peaceably without arms." But this same article also stipulates that all these rights are "subject to public order and morality." And it specifically hedges these guarantees by excluding from the protected realm speech that is "blasphemous, seditious, or indecent" and assemblies that serve "to cause a breach of the peace or to be a danger or nuisance to the general public." Reconciling these various provisions leaves room for disagreement over determining the boundary between regulations that do or do not violate the Irish Constitution.

Beneficiaries May Not Sue

A third aspect of judicial self-restraint is that a case will be rejected out of hand if the petitioner has apparently been the beneficiary of a law or an official action that they have subsequently chosen to challenge. Suppose that Farmer Brown has long been a member of the Soil Bank Program (designed to cut back on grain surpluses). Under the program, he agreed to take part of his land out of production and periodically was paid a subsidy by the federal government. After years as a participant, he learns that his lazy, ne'er-do-well neighbors, the Joneses, are also drawing regular payments for letting their farmland lie fallow. The idea that his neighbors are getting something for nothing starts to offend Farmer Brown, and he begins to harbor grave doubts about the constitutionality of the whole program. Armed with a host of reasons why Congress had acted illegally, Brown challenges the legality of the Soil Bank Act in the local federal district court. As soon as it is brought to the judge's attention that Farmer Brown had himself been a member of the program and had gained financially from it, the suit is dismissed. One may not benefit from a particular governmental endeavor or official action and subsequently attack it in court.

Appellate Courts Rule on Legal—Not Factual—Questions

A working proposition of state and federal appellate court practice is that these courts will generally not hear cases if the grounds for appeal are that the trial judge or jury wrongly amassed and identified the basic factual elements of the case. It is not that trial judges and juries always do a perfect job of making factual determinations. Rather, they are believed to be closer, sensorially and temporally, to the parties and physical evidence of the case. The odds are, so the theory goes, that trial judges and juries will do a much better job of making factual assessments than would an appellate body reading only a stale transcript of the case some months or years after the trial.

However, legal matters—which laws to apply to the facts of a case or how to assess the facts in light of the prevailing law—are appropriate for appellate review. On such issues, collegial, or multijudge, appellate bodies presumably have a legitimate and better capacity "to say what the law is," as Chief Justice John Marshall put it.[45]

In the real world, appellate court justices often find it difficult to tell whether a particular legal dispute is a question of who did what to whom (the facts of the case) or of how to weigh and assess a series of events (the legal interpretation of the facts). Some additional qualification must also be offered. In most jurisdictions, appellate courts will hear appeals under *the clearly erroneous rule*—that is, when the petitioner contends that the trial court's determination of the facts was obviously and utterly wrong. The issue would not be a minor quibble about what the facts were but a belief that the trial court had made a finding that totally flew in the face of common sense.

Likewise, appellate courts may be willing to review an administrative agency's factual determinations that were allegedly made *without substantial evidence.* Despite these qualifications, it is still fair to say that trial courts are the primary determiners of the facts or evidence in cases, even though such determinations are not always conclusive.

For example, if a person was convicted of a crime, and the sole grounds for her appeal were that the judge and jury had mistakenly found her guilty (that is, incorrectly sifted and identified the facts), the appeals court would probably dismiss the case out of hand. However, assume that same person provided evidence that she had asked for and been denied access to a lawyer during her FBI interrogation and that the trial judge ruled against the defendant's motion that the Fifth Amendment's right against self-incrimination was violated during her interrogation. Such a ruling could be appealed because the issue is one of legal, not factual, interpretation.

The Supreme Court Is Not Bound (Technically) by Precedents

If the high court is free to overturn or circumvent past supposedly controlling precedents when it decides a case, this might appear to be an argument for judicial **activism**—not restraint. However, even at the Supreme Court, the overturning of precedent is a serious action that requires extensive explanation and justification. Justices of the nation's highest court must be able to overturn precedent from time to time, or the nation and its people would forever be saddled with the legacy of some of the worst rulings in US history, such as the "separate but equal" doctrine established in *Plessy v. Ferguson.*[46]

That said, how often and in what cases the Court overturns precedent are important considerations. We often see nominees to the Supreme Court questioned repeatedly about how they would approach the important task of considering when to overturn precedent if seated on the nation's highest tribunal. The phrase *super precedent* has been used in recent judicial confirmation hearings, with senators asking whether some precedents have been around for so long and have been confirmed so many times that they are all but unable to be overturned. In her 2020 confirmation hearings, for example, Justice Amy Coney Barrett was asked by Senator Amy Klobuchar (D-MN) to explain her views on "super precedents." Barrett, a former law professor who had written on the topic, defined "super precedents" as "cases that are so well settled that no political actors and no people seriously push for their overruling."[47] Although Barrett categorized cases like *Brown v. Board of Education* (banning racial segregation in public schools) and *Marbury v. Madison* (establishing the power of judicial review) as "super precedents," she argued that *Roe v. Wade*'s holding on abortion rights was not.

The overturning of *Roe* by the Court in 2022 demonstrates that no amount of questioning of judicial nominees by senators can overcome the fact that the justices of the Supreme Court may overturn precedent at will. At times they may do so at least somewhat trepidatiously, due to concerns over consistency in the law and to stave off criticism from the public or the other branches of government. The fate of *Roe v. Wade* demonstrates that at the end of the day, today's justices may overturn yesterday's precedent, even those precedents that some view as particularly significant and well-established.

Other Remedies Must Be Exhausted

Another principle of self-restraint that often frustrates the anxious litigant but is essential to the orderly administration of justice is that courts in the United States will not accept a case until all other remedies, legal and administrative, have been exhausted. Although this caveat is often associated with the US Supreme Court, it is a working principle for virtually all American judicial tribunals. In its simplest form, this doctrine means that any possible administrative relief must be sought before turning to the courts, and as well that the principle of a three-tiered judicial hierarchy is adhered to.

Administrative relief might be in the form of an appeal to an administrative officer, a hearing before a board or committee, or formal consideration of a matter by a legislative body. Available nonjudicial remedies cannot be overlooked in favor of rushing to court prematurely.

In terms of the hierarchical judicial system, federal cases must first be heard by the US trial courts, then reviewed by one of the appellate tribunals, and finally heard by the US Supreme Court. This orderly procedure generally will occur despite the importance of the case or of the petitioners who filed it. For instance, in 1952, President Harry S. Truman seized the American steel mills to prevent a pending strike that he believed would imperil the war effort in the Korean conflict. Both labor and management were suddenly told they were now working for the US government. The mill owners were furious and immediately sued, charging that the president had abused the powers of his office. A national legal–political crisis erupted.

One might think that the Supreme Court would immediately take a case of this magnitude. Not so. In the traditional and orderly fashion of American federal justice, the controversy first went to the local district court in Washington, DC, just as if it were the most ordinary dispute. Not until after the district court had ruled did the nation's highest tribunal sink its teeth into this case. (The Supreme Court did, however, concede the need for expeditious action by granting certiorari before the court of appeals could rule on the merits of the case, thereby shortening the normal appellate process.)

Thus, judicial restraint means that judges are not to jump immediately into every controversy that appears to be important or that strikes their fancy. The restrained and orderly administration of justice supposes that before any court may hear a case, all administrative and inferior legal remedies must first be exhausted.

Courts Do Not Decide "Political Questions"

US judges are often called on to determine the winner of a contested election, to rule on the legality of a newly drawn electoral district, or to get involved in voting rights cases. How, then, can the argument be made that those political questions are out of bounds for the American judiciary? The answer lies in the narrow, singular use of the word *political*. To US judges, the executive and legislative branches of government are political in that they are elected by the people for the purpose of making public policy. The judiciary, in contrast, was not designed by the founders to be an instrument manifesting the popular will and is therefore not generally responsible for resolving particular "political" questions.

According to this line of reasoning, a political question is one that ought properly to be resolved by one of the other two branches of government. When judges determine that something is a political question (and therefore not appropriate for judicial review) they are saying that the issue falls within the purview of the other branches and the involvement of the courts will only confuse the issue and potentially run at cross-purposes with the decisions of those constitutionally empowered to resolve the question.

For example, in 2003, Americans witnessed a circus-like political scenario in the state of Texas that some wanted the courts to resolve, but the judges would have none of it. In this instance, the Republican-dominated legislature attempted to redraw congressional boundaries in the state to give the GOP four to seven additional seats in the Texas delegation to the US House of Representatives. The Democratic minority in the Texas Senate, unable to defeat the redistricting bill in a straight party-line vote, opted to physically leave the state, thereby depriving the Senate of a quorum and preventing the bill from being passed. During the regular session of the legislature, the Democratic senators fled to Oklahoma, and when the governor called a special session of the legislature for redistricting purposes, the Democrats hightailed it to the protective confines of New Mexico, where the Texas Rangers were without jurisdiction. The Republican governor and GOP Senate members repeatedly attempted to have the Texas courts order the wayward Democratic senators back to their posts, but even the all-Republican state supreme court unanimously refused to enter the fray. Putting aside the judges' legalese, the courts said that this was basically a political matter, a dispute to be settled within the framework of the political process and/or ultimately by the voters of Texas. The courts do not enter what Justice Felix Frankfurter once called "the political thicket."[48]

When President Jimmy Carter acted on his own initiative to end the Mutual Defense Treaty between the United States and Taiwan, this action was challenged in the courts by a few senators and representatives. The high court, consistent with tradition in the area of foreign policy, refused to involve itself in this political question.[49] Attempts were also made to challenge the legality of the wars in Afghanistan and Iraq. None of these cases reached the Supreme Court, and lower courts showed no interest in blocking what they regard as essentially a political, nonjusticiable matter.

The Burden of Proof Is on the Petitioner

Another weighty principle of self-restraint is the general agreement among the nation's jurists that an individual who would challenge the constitutionality of a statute bears the burden of proof. This is just a separate way of saying that laws and official deeds are all presumed to be legal unless and until proven otherwise by a preponderance of evidence. The question of who has the burden of proof is of keen interest to lawyers because it means, in effect: Which side has the bigger job to perform in the courtroom? And which party must assume the lion's share of the burden of convincing the court—or lose the case entirely? Thus, if one were attacking a particular statute, one would have to do more than demonstrate that it was "questionable" or "of doubtful constitutionality." One must persuade the court that the evidence against the law was clear-cut and overwhelming—not often an easy task. In giving the benefit of the doubt to a statute or an executive act, judges have yet another area in which to exercise restraint.

The only exception to this burden of proof principle is in the realm of civil rights and liberties. Some jurists who are strong civil libertarians have long contended that when government attempts to restrict basic human freedoms, the burden of proof should shift to the government. And in several specific areas of civil rights jurisprudence, that philosophy now prevails. For example, the US Supreme Court has ruled in a variety of cases that laws that treat persons differently on the basis of their race or gender are automatically subject to "special scrutiny." This means that the burden of proof shifts to the government to demonstrate a compelling or overriding need for this differential treatment.

Laws Are Overturned on the Narrowest Grounds Only

Sometimes during a trial, a judge clearly sees that the strictures of the Constitution have been offended by a legislative or executive act. Even here, however, judges typically can exercise restraint in how they proceed, resolving the case on narrower grounds and rejecting the opportunity to rule in a broader way.

What do we mean by ruling on the narrowest grounds possible? One manifestation of this is that when the opportunity exists, a judge should invalidate an official action on statutory rather than constitutional grounds, or rule that the enactment of a statute in a particular circumstance is inappropriate rather than striking down the statute itself. For example, the Supreme Court recently decided a case in which a Colorado baker, Jack Phillips, refused to prepare a designer wedding cake for two newly married men.[50] The baker did so because of religious objections to same-sex marriage. The couple then filed a complaint with the Colorado Civil Rights Commission. The complaint was based on a Colorado civil rights law dealing with public accommodations, which basically said that once merchants open their businesses to the public, they could not discriminate among the customers they served. The Civil Rights Commission investigated that complaint and ruled that the rights of the couple basically trumped any religious objections that the baker might have to preparing a special wedding cake. After the baker appealed, the case eventually reached the Supreme Court, which ruled 7–2 in 2018 in favor of Jack Phillips. However, the high court's decision was a relatively narrow one. In essence, the Court said that Colorado had every legal right to enact a law forbidding discrimination in public accommodations. However, the justices said that *in this instance*, the Colorado Civil Rights Commission had not given due regard to the sincere religious convictions of Phillips. Thus, the statute was preserved and a direct confrontation between the courts and the state of Colorado was averted, at least for a while, but the Court gave Philips everything he wanted without ruling on the constitutionality of the law itself. (The same Colorado antidiscrimination law was later found to have unconstitutionally abridged Lorie Smith's free speech rights in *303 Creative*.)

Another opportunity to decide a case more narrowly is when a judge invalidates only that portion of a law found to be constitutionally defective instead of overturning the entire statute. For instance, in 1963, Congress passed the Higher Education Facilities Act, which provided construction grants for college buildings. Part of the law declared that for a twenty-year period, no part of the newly built structures could be used for "sectarian instruction, religious worship, or the programs of a divinity school." Because church-related universities as well as public institutions benefited from the act, the entire law was challenged in court as being in violation of the Establishment of Religion Clause of the First Amendment. The Supreme Court determined that the basic thrust of the law did not violate the Constitution, but it did find the "twenty-year clause" to be objectionable. After all, the Court reasoned, most buildings last a good deal longer than two decades, and a building constructed at public expense could thus house religious activities during most of its lifetime. Instead of striking down the entire act, however, the Court majority merely substituted the word "never" for the words "twenty years."[51] Thus, the baby was not thrown out with the bath water, and judicial restraint was maintained.

Rulings Are Not Made on the "Wisdom" of Legislation

This final aspect of judicial self-restraint is probably the least understood by the public and perhaps the most often violated by judges. What this admonition means, if followed strictly, is that the only basis for declaring a law or an official action unconstitutional is that it violates the Constitution. Statutes do not offend the Constitution merely because they are unfair, fiscally wasteful, or bad public policy. Official actions can be struck down only if they step across the boundaries clearly set forth in the Constitution. If taken truly to heart, this means that judges and justices are not free to invoke their own personal notions of right and wrong or of good and bad public policy when they examine the constitutionality of legislation.

A classic articulation of this phenomenon of judicial self-restraint is found in Justice Potter Stewart's dissenting opinion in the case of *Griswold v. Connecticut* in 1965. The Court majority had struck down the state's law that forbade the use of contraceptive devices or the dissemination of birth control information. Stewart said, in effect, that the law was bad, but that its weaknesses did not make it unconstitutional:

> Since 1897 Connecticut has had on its books a law which forbids the use of contraceptives by anyone. I think this is an uncommonly silly law. As a practical matter, the law is obviously unenforceable, except in the oblique context of the present case. But we are not asked in this case to say whether we think this law is unwise, or even asinine. We are asked to hold that it violates the United States Constitution. And that I cannot do.[52]

Another spin-off of this principle is that a law may be passed that all agree is good and wise but that is nevertheless unconstitutional; conversely, a statute may legalize the commission of an official deed that all know to be ill-considered and ineffective but that still does not offend the Constitution. Thus, when laws or official acts are at issue, the adjectives *goodness* and *constitutionality* are no more synonymous than are *badness* and *unconstitutionality*.

Although few legal scholars would disagree with what has just been said, virtually all would point out that the principle of not ruling on the "wisdom" of a law is difficult to follow in the real world and is often violated in practice, especially by appellate judges. Indeed, the regularity with which Supreme Court justices form ideologically like-minded cohorts on many of the most socially charged constitutional cases of the day indicate that the line between ruling on constitutionality and wisdom of legislation is likely quite blurry. Even so, the requirement that rulings be supported by written opinions at least requires the justices to justify their rulings with something more than a claim that the law at issue is bad or ineffective.

Throughout this discussion of what it means that courts should only resolve real cases with real litigants bringing disputes that are appropriate for the courts to resolve, we have emphasized that these considerations can and do serve as restraints on the exercise of judicial power. Litigants bringing cases that *clearly* violate any of these standards should not expect the courts to resolve the merits of the dispute at hand. Recall that even with lower courts determining that the Alliance for Hippocratic Medicine had standing to challenge FDA approval of mifepristone, a *unanimous* Supreme Court disagreed.

The boundaries of these considerations regarding judicial restraint are often determined by the justices themselves. Vagaries, whether in the relevant constitutional or statutory language, in the interpretation of applicable precedent, or even in the determination of the factual record of the case itself, open the possibility for personal preferences to have an influence on whether a case is deemed proper to be resolved in a court of law.

SUMMARY

In this chapter, we have focused on what federal and state courts are supposed to do and on what they are expected to refrain from doing. They adjudicate cases that come within their lawful original or appellate jurisdiction. Federal district courts hear criminal cases and civil suits that deal with federal questions, **diversity of citizenship matters**, prisoners' petitions, and any other issues authorized by Congress. The federal appellate courts, having no original jurisdiction whatever, take appeals from the district courts and from numerous administrative and regulatory agencies. The US Supreme Court has original jurisdiction over suits between two or more states and in cases where ambassadors or public ministers are parties to a suit. Its appellate jurisdiction, regulated by Congress, permits the justices to hear appeals from the circuit courts and from state courts of last resort.

Although issues related to jurisdiction are often noncontroversial and obvious, circumstances can arise when otherwise technical considerations of jurisdiction allow for tactical behavior. The power that legislators at the state and federal level have over setting jurisdiction may be attractive sources of raw political power, designed to circumvent judicial review or push cases to courts more likely to rule in the legislature's favor. Litigants as well may engage in forum—or even judge—shopping in deciding where to file a case, when such a choice is available. Such policy-motivated behavior is not necessarily limited to those on one side of the ideological spectrum or the other in the United States.

Finally, under the US legal system, a host of expectations come with Article III's command that the judicial power extends to "cases" with actual "controversies." State judges are also expected to follow most, but not all, of these principles. Much of the time, cases that transgress one or more of these principles will be thrown out without a ruling on the merits. Sometimes, however, judges will reach different conclusions about whether a real case with a real controversy exists.

FURTHER THOUGHT AND DISCUSSION QUESTIONS

1. Why do you figure members of Congress often introduce bills intended to strip the appellate jurisdiction of the Supreme Court when those bills almost always fail? How big of a concern are such bills given how rarely they are passed into law, at least at the federal level?
2. Do you support efforts at the state or federal level to alter the judiciary's ability to hear particular issues in response to judicial rulings that are contrary to the preferences of the political branches? Does this power hinder the independence of the judiciary, or does it provide a necessary check on judicial power?
3. Would it be a clever idea if the president, Congress, and other governmental agencies could get the courts to rule on the constitutionality of proposed governmental actions before they were put in place? Wouldn't considerable time and trouble be saved if courts were allowed to nip unconstitutional acts in the bud before they did any harm?
4. How much of a restraint is the constitutional demand that the judicial power extends to actual cases with real controversies?

SUGGESTED RESOURCES

Abraham, Henry J. *The Judicial Process*, 7th ed. New York, NY: Oxford University Press, 1998. A traditional but classic discussion of the judicial process, especially Chapter 9, which focuses on judicial self-restraint.

Administrative Office of the US Courts. Available online at www.uscourts.gov. This website provides much data and statistical information on the operation of the federal court system.

Epstein, Lee, Kevin T. McGuire, and Thomas G. Walker. *Constitutional Law for a Changing America: Institutional Powers and Constraints*, 11th ed. Thousand Oaks, CA: Sage, 2023. Chapter 2, on the judiciary, includes a discussion of jurisdiction and justiciability issues.

Hasian, Marouf, Jr. *In the Name of Necessity: Military Tribunals and the Loss of American Civil Liberties*. Tuscaloosa, AL: University of Alabama Press, 2005. A well-written history of the use of military tribunals during times of crisis, particularly relevant in the aftermath of September 11, 2001.

Jackson, Vicki C., and Mark V. Tushnet. *Comparative Constitutional Law*, 3rd ed. New York, NY: Foundation Press, 2014. The text discusses the activity and function of constitutional courts, such as the US Supreme Court, in other countries.

Judicature 81. 1998. The entire issue of this journal is dedicated to courts and justice abroad, with a special emphasis on matters of jurisdiction and policymaking boundaries.

Murphy, Walter F., C. Herman Pritchett, Lee Epstein, and Jack Knight, eds. *Courts, Judges, and Politics: An Introduction to Judicial Process*, 6th ed. New York, NY: McGraw-Hill, 2006. A rich and varied collection of some of the most important historical documents in the realm of judicial process and behaviour.

Presidential Commission on the Supreme Court of the United States: Final Report. December 2021. Chapter 4 includes a good discussion of the history of the Supreme Court's appellate jurisdiction.

Tarr, G. Alan. *Understanding State Constitutions*. Princeton, NJ: Princeton University Press, 2000. An important discussion of state courts as affected by changes in their own constitutions and by the effect of the new judicial federalism.

Tarr, G. Alan, and Robert F. Williams. *State Constitutions for the Twenty-First Century*, Vol. 1. Albany, NY: State University of New York Press, 2006. A review of issues at the center of the debate over revisions of modern-day constitutions.

Wetstein, Matthew E., and Cynthia Ostberg. *Value Change in the Supreme Court of Canada*. Toronto, ON: University of Toronto Press, 2017. An insightful discussion of the recent impact of the High Court of Canada, our closest counterpart in terms of a tribunal with the power of judicial review.

KEY TERMS

advisory opinions
certification
class actions
complaint
concurrent jurisdiction
declaratory judgments
diversity of citizenship matters
diversity of citizenship suit
federal question
forum shopping
habeas corpus
indictment
justiciability
moot
rule of four
standing

5 STATE JUDGES

CHAPTER GOALS AND OBJECTIVES

In this chapter, students will learn that . . .

- Collecting comprehensive information on the judges sitting on state tribunals throughout the country is a difficult endeavor. Recent research efforts have provided a picture of state judiciaries that typically lag in the gender, racial, and ethnic diversity of the state.
- A variety of methods are used to select judges among the fifty American states. Selection methods are often convoluted, differing within a state across the various levels of the state judiciary.
- The merit selection movement, which has cooled in recent decades, was intended to remove politics and patronage from the judicial selection process. However, research has not demonstrated that merit selection–appointed judges are of higher quality than those chosen through other methods.
- States attempt to hold judges accountable through terms of office, retention, conduct commissions, and removal mechanisms. Achieving an appropriate balance between judicial accountability and independence is very difficult.
- Policies and practices related to the selection, retention, and removal of judges at the state level are open to manipulation by the governor and/or the state legislature. Elites from both political parties attempt to alter these mechanisms for their own purposes, although recent efforts have come more often from states where conservatives control the political branches.

The focus in this chapter, as well as the following chapter, is on the judges who sit on courts at the state and federal levels. In this chapter, we look at judges at the state level. Given that each state has autonomy over how to select, retain, and remove judges, how are judges seated in the American states? Should we be concerned about the role of money and campaigning in states that elect their judges? How do states attempt to resolve problems associated with having very elderly, incompetent, or unprofessional judges serving on the bench? How do all these institutional decisions affect the diversity, quality, and independence of the state courts? Irrespective of judicial selection, retention, and removal mechanisms, how concerned should we be over efforts by the political branches to influence, even manipulate, a state's third branch?

In turning our attention to these questions, we consider some of the thorniest and most contentious issues facing state courts in the United States today. In the United States, there is a great deal of variation across and within the fifty states with respect to important questions concerning how judicial positions are filled. This variation not only exists from one state to the next, but within states, judges to different court levels are subjected to varied selection procedures. This institutional diversity extends to other relevant issues concerning the state courts, from terms of office to the filling of unexpected vacancies, to the presence or absence of mechanisms to remove elderly judges or judges who have acted improperly or in ways the public simply does not like. This variation makes it difficult, if not impossible, to summarize easily and simply how judges are selected at the state level. On the other hand, the variety of institutional rules governing the selection, retention, and removal of judges provides a wealth of opportunity to ask important social science questions concerning the pros and cons associated with the separate ways in which state judiciaries are staffed across the country. Before we examine the mechanisms by which state court judges are selected and retained in office, we begin by giving some attention to the backgrounds of the people who serve their states as judges.

On April 4, 2023, Janet C. Protasiewicz was elected to the Wisconsin Supreme Court and took office on August 1, 2023. After she took office, the Republican legislature threatened to impeach her if she did not recuse herself from an upcoming redistricting case, which she refused to do.

Sara Stathas for The Washington Post via Getty Images

BACKGROUND CHARACTERISTICS OF STATE JUDGES

It is difficult to get a comprehensive picture of the judges who serve on state judiciaries across the country. Unlike federal judges, whose background information (including educational and occupational experience) is readily available through the Federal Judicial Center, there is no such centralized repository for information on state judges. Recent efforts at collecting comprehensive information on the judges who serve on state judiciaries have provided us with some insight into the people in these important roles.

The most comprehensive data collection effort has been undertaken by scholars Tracey H. George and Albert H. Yoon. Before we dig into George and Yoon's key findings, some attention is warranted to the difficulties inherent in doing research on state judges. For this project, George and Yoon "collected biographical data for every judge sitting on a state appellate court or a state trial court of general jurisdiction as of December 2014."[1] That ambitious goal resulted in a dataset of more than ten thousand judges. Absent a centralized data source, George and Yoon collected their data from:

> Only sources that had the hallmarks of credibility and reliability. The sources included state government webpages, press releases, and directories; professional association, practitioner, and university publications; academic journals, newspapers; judges' official campaign websites; judicial and legal directories; and confidential telephone interviews with judges and lawyers.[2]

While the data collection effort by George and Yoon was impressive indeed, their findings, at least with respect to the level of diversity on state courts, were less encouraging.

Race, Ethnicity, and Gender Diversity on State Judiciaries

To examine racial, ethnic, and gender diversity on state courts, George and Yoon developed a measure they call the "Gavel Gap," developed on the idea that a "truly representative judiciary would have the same ratio of women and minorities on the bench as it does in the general population."[3] In other words, "[t]he Gavel Gap is how much the state falls short of that forecast."

What George and Yoon found was that state judiciaries across the country were lacking in racial, ethnic, and gender diversity. In no state in 2014 were women as well represented on the state judiciary as they were in the state's population. The Gavel Gap for gender was similar across the four geographic regions of the country (Northeast, Midwest, South, and West). Across all four regions, the percent of women in the population was just over 50 percent, but the percent of women on state courts ranged from 28.09 percent (in the South) to 32.93 percent (in the West).

With respect to racial and ethnic diversity, in only four states (Hawaii, Montana, South Dakota, and West Virginia) were racial and ethnic minorities represented on the state tribunals at a rate that was as high as or higher than in the state's population.[4]

Here, however, George and Yoon did find differences across regions of the country, with the Gavel Gap being greater in the Southern and Western regions of the country, compared to the Northeast and the Midwest, although racial and ethnic minorities were substantially underrepresented in all four regions.

Although George and Yoon's study is the most comprehensive, given that judges on all appellate and trial courts of general jurisdiction were included, it is not the most recent. In 2022, the Brennan Center for Justice published its latest report on diversity on state supreme courts (not including lower court judges). The Brennan Center reports that in twenty states, "no justices publicly identify as a person of color, including in 12 states where people of color make up at least 20 percent of the population."[5] Racial and ethnic minorities make up only 18 percent of justices on state high courts, compared to 40 percent of the US population. With respect to gender, women hold 39 percent of the seats on state supreme courts, and in nine states there is only one woman on the court. In South Carolina none of the justices are women, the only state supreme court in the nation without a woman. On a slightly more positive note, the data in 2022 show that the twenty-five newest justices are more reflective of our diverse population. For example, 60 percent of the new justices are women (fifteen in total) and 40 percent are people of color (ten in total).[6] Across the country and across different levels of the state judiciaries, state courts are not as diverse as the population those courts serve, even today.

One topic of interest to state court scholars has been the connection between state judicial selection method and diversity. We now turn to a discussion of the various selection methods utilized in states across the country. While understanding how these diverse selection mechanisms work is important in and of itself, we also consider the implications of selection methods, not only to court diversity, but to judge quality and judicial independence.

THE SELECTION PROCESS FOR STATE JUDGES

Basically, there are five routes to a judgeship in any one of the fifty states: partisan election, nonpartisan election, **merit selection**, gubernatorial appointment, and appointment by the legislature. Tables 5.1 and 5.2 indicate which states use each of the methods for selecting judges for full terms in the trial courts of general jurisdiction and the courts of last resort. But as is often the case in the political world, things are not always what they seem. For instance, in states that officially choose their judges for full terms by partisan elections, a substantial number of judges may receive their initial position through gubernatorial appointment. This occurs because a sitting judge may die or resign or a new judicial vacancy may occur, and the position is then filled by the governor in accordance with state law. The newly appointed judge may eventually have to run for another term in a general election, but most incumbent judges are easily reelected. Likewise, in states that are officially in the nonpartisan election category—for example, Minnesota—it is often no secret which judicial candidate is the Democrat, and which is the Republican, and the voters may respond accordingly. Sometimes states amend the way they choose their judges and justices. For example, beginning with the November 2022 election, state supreme court justices in Ohio are selected by partisan election. Prior to the November 2022 election, state supreme court justices in Ohio were selected via nonpartisan elections. The change from nonpartisan to partisan elections was motivated by two prior state supreme court elections where Republicans lost three of the four seats, altering the once 7–0 Republican majority to 4–3 majority Republican majority.[7]

TABLE 5.1 ■ Methods of Selecting Judges for Full Terms in State Trial Courts of General Jurisdiction

Method	State(s)
Partisan election	Alabama, Illinois, Indiana, Kansas,[a] Louisiana, Missouri,[b] New Mexico,[c] New York, North Carolina, Pennsylvania, Tennessee,[d] Texas
Nonpartisan election	Arkansas, California, Florida, Georgia, Idaho, Kentucky, Michigan, Minnesota, Mississippi, Montana, Nevada, North Dakota, Ohio, Oklahoma, Oregon, South Dakota, Tennessee,[d] Washington, West Virginia, Wisconsin
Merit selection	Alaska, Arizona,[e] Colorado, Connecticut, Delaware, Hawaii, Iowa, Kansas,[a] Maryland, Massachusetts, Missouri,[b] Nebraska, New Hampshire, Rhode Island, Utah, Vermont, Wyoming
Gubernatorial appointment	Maine, New Jersey
Legislative appointment	South Carolina, Virginia

Note: Some states use more than one method for various courts.

[a]Kansas allows for trial court judges to be chosen through merit selection or partisan election, at the option of each judicial district.

[b]Circuit judges in most counties in Missouri are selected in partisan elections. The Missouri Constitution requires merit selection for circuit judges in the city of St. Louis and in Jackson County, and it allows for the adoption of merit selection of circuit judges in other counties as well.

[c]New Mexico has a hybrid system of judicial selection that includes aspects of merit selection, partisan elections, and retention elections.

[d]Circuit judges in Tennessee are selected in partisan elections with exception to judges in Shelby County, where they are selected in nonpartisan elections.

[e]Arizona allows for merit selection in the most populated counties. Less populous counties may adopt merit selection with voter approval.

Source: Data on judicial selection compiled by the National Center for State Courts, https://www.ncsc.org/consulting-and-research/areas-of-expertise/court-leadership/judicial-selection (accessed July 12, 2024).

TABLE 5.2 ■ Methods of Selecting Judges for Full Terms in State Courts of Last Resort

Method	State(s)
Partisan election	Alabama, Illinois, Louisiana, New Mexico,[a] North Carolina, Ohio, Pennsylvania, Texas
Nonpartisan election	Arkansas, Georgia, Idaho, Kentucky, Michigan, Minnesota, Mississippi, Montana, Nevada, North Dakota, Oregon, Washington, West Virginia, Wisconsin
Merit selection	Alaska, Arizona, California, Colorado, Connecticut, Delaware, Florida, Hawaii, Indiana, Iowa, Kansas, Maryland, Massachusetts, Missouri, Nebraska, New Hampshire, New York, Oklahoma, Rhode Island, South Dakota, Tennessee, Utah, Vermont, Wyoming
Gubernatorial appointment	Maine, New Jersey
Legislative appointment	South Carolina, Virginia

[a]New Mexico has a hybrid system of judicial selection that includes aspects of merit selection, partisan elections, and retention elections.

Source: Data on judicial selection compiled by the National Center for State Courts, https://www.ncsc.org/consulting-and-research/areas-of-expertise/court-leadership/judicial-selection (accessed July 12, 2024).

With respect to the five routes to a judgeship, it is impossible to determine objectively which selection method is "best." Rather, each has different issues that may make that selection method appealing to those within a particular state. Three legitimate goals to be achieved in selecting judges may relate to diversity, quality, and independence for those on the bench. With respect to the goal of fostering a diverse judiciary, for example, research has found that states that elect judges take longer to select the first woman or non-White judge, compared to states with merit selection or appointment systems.[8] On the other hand, if the goal is developing a professional bench with judges who are the most capable of doing the job well, another recent study has concluded that while appointed judges write higher quality opinions (as measured by how often a judge's opinions are cited by judges from other states), elected judges are more productive (as measured by how many opinions a judge writes).[9]

In determining which selection method results in the most independent judges, we first must consider who it is that we want judges to be independent *from*. If what we seek are judges who are independent from their own expected partisan biases, then there is some evidence that partisan elections and appointment mechanisms result in judges who are more willing to cast votes in opposition to their partisan allies on the bench, compared to their counterparts chosen through nonpartisan elective or merit selection schemes.[10] If we are interested in developing a bench that is independent from the other branches, however, research indicates that judges dependent on the legislature or the governor to retain their seats are less likely to consider constitutional challenges to a state's laws in areas such as abortion policy or campaign and election law, compared to those who are not similarly beholden to the political branches for keeping their jobs.[11]

While it is clear, then, that there are strengths and weaknesses to each of the selection mechanisms, it is important to have a fuller understanding of how each selection method works. We now turn our attention more specifically to the distinct ways of choosing judges in the American states.

Partisan and Nonpartisan Election of Judges

The election of judges, on either a partisan ballot (candidate is listed on the ballot with a political party designation) or a nonpartisan ballot (candidate is listed on the ballot without a political party designation), is a quite common selection methodology among the states. Although almost unheard of in colonial days, this method became popular during the time of President Andrew Jackson—during an era when Americans sought to democratize the political process.

In practice, things have not always worked this way. Before the 1980s, judicial elections "were traditionally uncompetitive, and the major causes of turnover on the bench were retirements and resignations."[12] Furthermore, uncontested races typically involved modest spending and low levels of candidate visibility. Truly little information was imparted in judicial campaigns, and voters relied primarily on such cues as party affiliation and name familiarity.

This began to change in the late 1970s, and "the 1980s brought numerous examples of extremely competitive and remarkably expensive judicial elections."[13] The first signs of a modern style of judicial elections appeared in California, where deputy district attorneys in Los Angeles advertised in a local legal newspaper to recruit candidates to run against sitting trial court judges. This resulted in an unprecedented number of contested races and defeated incumbents. Subsequent judicial elections in California have been characterized by "preemptive fundraising and hiring political consultants early in the election season."[14] Naturally, they have also become quite a bit more expensive.

Money in Judicial Campaigns

Spending in judicial elections has increased dramatically over the last twenty years. Indeed, in total, state supreme court candidates in the United States spent more than $33 million in 2006, over $35 million in 2010, $39 million in 2015–2016, over $61 million in 2019–2020, and almost $55 million in 2021–2022.[15] The Brennan Center for Justice, a "nonpartisan law and policy institute," publishes regular reports on spending in judicial elections. Its most recent report, analyzing the 2021–2022 judicial election cycle, found $54.6 million in candidate spending across the seventeen states in which spending was documented.[16] While it may seem like candidate spending is retreating slightly from the previous cycle, the numbers for the 2019–2020 judicial election cycle included spending across the twenty-one states (2021–2022 included seventeen states) in which spending was documented. However, when outside interest money is calculated, almost $101 million was spent across the seventeen states in 2021–2022, which is an increase from 2019–2020.

Between candidate fundraising and outside interest donations, three states led the way in spending a total of $67.5 million, which accounted for approximately 67 percent of all spending in 2021–2022.[17] For one example, the Illinois Supreme Court races cost $28.6 million for three open seats (this figure includes candidate and special interest spending). In eight other state supreme court justice elections the spending exceeded $1 million (but less than $10 million).[18]

The 2021–2022 data show that outside spending in judicial elections has increased substantially in recent years.[19] In 2012, the first election cycle after the 2010 *Citizens United* decision prevented the government from limiting independent spending by corporations in elections, "interest groups and political parties increasingly spent money independently of campaigns."[20] This trend toward large amounts of money raised and spent in judicial elections is not limited to large or urban states, and all indications are that such increases will continue. In the 2021–2022 election cycle, outside spending by interest groups was estimated at $45.6 million and accounted for 45 percent of all election spending.[21] The Brennan Center reports that the top outside spender was the Republican State Leadership Committee (RSLC). The RSLC spent approximately $10 million in state judicial races.[22] Although there is a good deal of concern expressed over the role of money in judicial elections, much of the recent social science research in this area questions the conventional wisdom that more money on judicial elections is a terrible thing for the judiciary. For example, one 2008 study by Melinda Gann Hall and Chris Bonneau, two leading scholars in this field, concluded that expensive campaigns increase voter participation and give voters more ownership in the outcome of the election.[23] A 2013 study by these same authors found that, at least as far as voter willingness to participate in judicial elections is concerned, the use of attack ads in judicial campaigns does not alienate voters or discourage them from the electoral process. On the contrary, "attack ads are a *mobilizing* force in state supreme court elections,"[24] leading to increased voter participation in judicial elections.

Another important change in judicial elections involves the source of campaign funds—a subject that raises concerns about the susceptibility of judges to accusations of favoritism. Judicial candidates raise campaign funds from a variety of sources: individuals (including lawyers with business before the court), lobbyists, interest groups, labor unions, and political parties. Some judicial candidates spend their own money on their election. However, the data indicate that many monies raised and spent at the state supreme court level come from political interests and not the candidates themselves.

The US Supreme Court wrestled with this issue of campaign contributions and judicial conflict of interest in *Caperton v. A. T. Massey Coal Co.* in 2009, in a case that emerged out of West Virginia.[25] The Court ruled that excessive contributions to judges can create an unconstitutional threat to a fair trial because they pose a risk of "actual bias" in cases involving the judge's political benefactors.[26] The dispute centered on an executive, Don Blankenship, for the coal company Massey Energy. Blankenship spent $3 million in 2004 to help elect Brent Benjamin to the West Virginia Supreme Court, and once on the bench, Judge Benjamin voted to reverse a $50 million judgment against Massey Energy. Judge Benjamin declined calls to recuse himself from the case, even though the money that Blankenship spent was more than three times the total amount spent by Benjamin's campaign committee.[27] Given the set of facts in this case, the US Supreme Court ruled that due process of law had been violated by Benjamin's refusal to recuse himself from the Massey case.

The question of campaign contributions does not just involve wealthy business interests. Some suggest that lawyers make contributions to judicial candidates in the hopes of receiving favorable treatment in the courts. It is of some concern that lawyers may be *asked* to contribute to a judicial campaign, by a judicial candidate, a judge's staff, or the judge personally. Lawyers with business before the court may find it difficult to refuse a solicitation for a contribution, especially if it comes from a sitting judge. In 2015, former Alabama Chief Justice Sue Bell Cobb published an account of her discomfort with having to solicit millions of dollars to fund what was, in 2006, the costliest judicial election in the country.[28] In the title of her piece, Cobb noted that she was ashamed by what was needed to raise the necessary amount of money to win the election. She wrote:

> I felt trapped. I had made it to the top of my profession. I was the chief justice of Alabama, the first women to head the state Supreme court. It was, for a lawyer like myself, the pinnacle of achievement. And I'd earned it the hard way. To get to the justice's chambers, I had won the nation's most expensive judicial race that year. But at what cost?
>
> And while I was proud of the work I did for the next 4 ½ years, I never quite got over the feeling of being trapped inside a system whose very structure left me feeling disgusted. I assure you: I've never made a decision in a case in which I sided with a party because of a campaign donation. But those of us seeking judicial office sometimes find ourselves doing things that feel awfully unsavory.[29]

Most states that elect their judges prohibit judicial candidates from personally soliciting donations. In *Williams-Yulee v. The Florida Bar* in 2015, the Supreme Court ruled on whether it violated the First Amendment for judges in Florida to be prevented from personally soliciting campaign funds.[30] The Court ruled that Florida had a compelling interest in preserving the public's confidence in judicial integrity and that this interest was appropriately furthered by the restriction.

Coupled with the *Caperton* decision from 2009, *Williams-Yulee* seems to indicate that the Supreme Court is concerned about and attentive to some of the problems associated with bringing big-money campaigning to judicial elections. However, one analysis has concluded that these decisions are likely to have little influence on the operation of judicial campaigns.[31] In the wake of the *Caperton* decision, "attorneys and litigants who have cases before the particular court remain the largest contributors to these campaigns," irrespective of any worry that a judge may have to recuse herself.[32] As far as the *Williams-Yulee* ban on direct solicitation of campaign contributions is concerned, these authors note that there is no evidence that the public's faith in the judiciary is particularly harmed when donations are solicited directly from judges.[33] Furthermore, a ban on direct solicitations is unlikely to have any influence on the amount of money being spent on judicial campaigns.[34]

A recent example of corruption in judicial campaigning also highlights the limitations of direct solicitation bans on the integrity of judicial campaigns. The state of Arkansas, which joined a multistate amicus brief in support of Florida's direct solicitation ban in the *Williams-Yulee* case, has a provision like the Florida rule. Such a ban on direct campaign solicitations by judges, however, did not stop former Faulkner County Circuit Court Judge Michael Maggio from receiving a campaign donation in 2013, from the owner of a nursing home, and in turn reducing a $5.2 million verdict against the nursing home to $1 million.[35] Maggio pled guilty to a federal bribery charge in January 2015.[36]

In summary, state judicial elections no longer simply subject judges to a cursory review by voters. As the authors of one study put it:

> [N]ow that electoral uncertainty forces candidates to raise money and gain the support of interested groups, they are subject to electoral pressures that are remarkably like those experienced by legislators, mayors, and other elected officials.[37]

For states that use partisan or nonpartisan elections to select their judges, much concern has been expressed about the deleterious effects of money, campaigning, and negative advertising on the public's perception of the state's courts. One major study by political scientist James L. Gibson on the influence of campaigns on judicial legitimacy concluded that the legitimacy-conferring benefits of elections outweigh any of the negative consequences that may exist when judges are elected.[38] Although this research indicates that the negative aspects of campaigning are unlikely to harm the public's perception of the courts, some scholars still note other concerns regarding judicial elections, such as the link between elections and more punitive sentencing in criminal cases.[39] Clearly, a good deal of attention moving forward will continue to be given to concerns regarding judicial campaigns, the integrity of the judiciary, and if and how electoral concerns affect decision-making by those on the bench.

Merit Selection

Reformers have come up with a method other than nonpartisan elections to accomplish the goal of obtaining qualified state judges free from the taint of political bias. Merit selection, by whatever name, has been around since the early 1900s, as a preferred method of selecting judges. The first state to fully adopt such a method was Missouri, in 1940, and such schemes have since become known as generic variants of "the Missouri Plan."

The states with Missouri-type plans use a combination of elections and appointments. In effect, this type of plan provides much greater influence from lawyers than any other selection method. The governor appoints a judge from among several candidates recommended by a nominating panel or nominating commission of five or more people, usually including attorneys (often chosen by the local bar association), nonlawyers appointed by the governor, and sometimes senior judges. Either by law or by implicit agreement, the governor appoints someone from the recommended list. After serving for a fleeting period (usually a year or two), the newly appointed judge must stand for a retention election, at which time they, in effect, run on their record. (The voters are asked, "Shall Judge X be retained in office?") If the judge's tenure is supported by the voters, as is virtually always the case, the judge will serve for a regular and long term (usually eight or more years, depending on the state).

Does the Missouri Plan approach take politics out of the judicial selection process? After an exhaustive study of how this approach had operated in Missouri for over a quarter-century, two observers concluded that "it is naive to suggest . . . that the Plan takes the 'politics' out of judicial selection."[40] The merit selection scheme still has plenty of room for politics. One student of retention elections notes that special interest groups have discovered that judicial retention elections "are vehicles by which offending judges can be unseated and state judicial policy making can be influenced."[41] Furthermore, with respect to reformers' interests in selecting the highest-quality judges, one assessment of judicial ability and selection method found that while merit-selected judges served longer tenures than did those who were elected, merit-selected judges were no better than elected judges on their productivity or the quality of their written opinions, and they scored lower than elected judges on independence.[42]

Some highly publicized judicial retention contests in Iowa show what can happen when judges are asked to run on their records. Three justices on the state supreme court—including the chief justice—faced retention elections in 2010, which became a referendum on same-sex marriage.[43] The Iowa Supreme Court held unanimously in a 2009 case that the state could not prohibit gay couples from marrying. This opened the door to Iowa becoming the third state in the United States to allow same-sex marriage. The retention debate surrounding the three state supreme court justices the following year did not center upon the judges' ethics, qualifications, or character. Rather, the retention vote became an intense battle over the issue of same-sex marriage. Even though there were no credible allegations of judicial wrongdoing against any of the three jurists, nor did the retention vote have the potential to overturn the court's ruling in the gay rights case, all three justices lost their positions on the bench after social conservatives mounted a vigorous effort to remove them because of their votes in the marriage equality case. Same-sex marriage supporters were alarmed by the threat to judicial independence and worried about the possible chilling effect the vote might have on judges' willingness to defend the liberty interests of minority groups. On the other hand, marriage equality foes heralded the outcome. One person stated, "I think it will send a message across the country that the power resides with the people. It's we the people, not we the courts."[44] Recent research by Allison Harris, a political scientist, confirms this conjecture. In her study she analyzed how the 2009 Iowa same-sex marriage decision influenced the subsequent retention election. Harris found evidence that the high-profile decision increased voter participation in the retention election and led to the three justices losing their seats.[45]

The successful effort to unseat the Iowa justices in 2010 represented the first time since 1986 that multiple justices had lost retention election over a controversial state issue and the first time a sitting justice in Iowa would not be retained since merit selection was adopted in the state in 1962.[46] The financing for this campaign came largely from national groups targeting the Iowa retention election.[47] However, with respect to Missouri Plan states that rely on retention elections, the long-term picture is not one of spectacular defeats but of judges being retained in large numbers. A study covering the years 1964 through 2006 found that in only 56 of 6,306 judicial retention elections during that period were judges not retained.[48] As Charles Gardner Geyh noted in a 2018 article on state judicial selection methods:

> Retention elections are dreary by design. Who wants to go to the racetrack to watch a solitary horse run a time trial to see whether it qualifies to do it again next year? Nobody. And in the context of retention elections, that means nobody is energized enough to jeopardize incumbency.[49]

Iowa's retention election of state supreme court Justice David Wiggins in 2012 would revert somewhat to form. The 2012 effort to unseat Wiggins was less well funded, with $466,000 spent by anti-retention advocates in 2012, compared to nearly $1 million spent by those seeking to unseat the three justices in 2010.[50] Even with a cross-state "NO Wiggins" bus tour joined at times by former US Senator Rick Santorum and Louisiana Governor Bobby Jindal, Justice Wiggins, with the support of the Iowa State Bar Association and the state media, won retention with 54.5 percent of the vote.[51]

Although most of our discussion in this section has centered on states using a Missouri Plan–styled method of merit selection, it is important to note that some of the states identified in Tables 5.1 and 5.2 as relying on merit selection forgo retention election in favor of legislative confirmation. These states still rely on a merit selection approach in that the governor is constrained in having to nominate someone identified as appropriately qualified by a nominating panel. One former governor from a state with this sort of selection mechanism characterized the process as "subjective" and "inconsisten[t]" in that the members of the nominating panel on more than one occasion found a potential candidate to be qualified at one point in time but would later deem the same person to be unqualified for the position.[52]

Despite the unhappy anomalies that occasionally accompany this form of judicial selection and retention, it still has a number of supporters, the most famous being the late Supreme Court Justice Sandra Day O'Connor, who advocated for states to adopt Missouri Plan selection mechanisms for years after stepping down from the Court.[53] That said, the Missouri Plan has, according to noted state judicial selection scholar Herbert M. Kritzer, "fallen out of favor" in recent decades, with no state adopting it through constitutional amendment since 1985.[54] In particular, Kritzer finds that in some states, political efforts pushed primarily by Republicans in the governor's mansion or the state capitol have been attempting to terminate merit selection approaches in their state, in part due to concerns that the lawyers involved in such processes may help select more liberal judges to the state judiciary.[55]

Even apart from any partisan considerations involved in whether to adopt, retain, or remove a merit selection system from the state judicial selection protocol, most studies fail to document significant differences in the behavior of elected judges as compared with those selected under merit systems. Thus, support for merit selection may be more an act of faith than an argument based on well-documented findings.

Gubernatorial Appointment and Legislative Appointment

In the early days of the Republic, judges were chosen either by the governor or the state legislature, but today, such methods are used in only a handful of states. When judges are appointed by the governor, politics almost invariably come into play. In the dozens of appointment opportunities that arise, governors tend to select individuals who have been active in state politics and whose activity has benefited either the governor personally or the governor's political party or allies. Also, in making judicial appointments, the governor often bargains with local political bosses or with state legislators whose support is needed. A governor may also use a judgeship to reward a legislator or local politico who has given faithful political support in the past.

Only two states—South Carolina and Virginia—still allow their legislators to appoint state judges. Although legislative appointment of judges is rare in contemporary American state judicial politics, the Republican-controlled North Carolina legislature recently attempted to insert itself more forcefully in the judicial appointment process. The legislature forwarded a constitutional amendment that would nominally establish a merit selection scheme, whereby a merit selection commission would pass along its recommendations to the state legislature, which would then filter the list down before passing it along to the governor to appoint the judge. If the governor refused to appoint a judge from the final list forwarded by the General Assembly, the legislature would choose the judge directly.[56] North Carolina voters rejected the amendment by a 2 to 1 margin.

Selection of the Chief Justice: The Cautionary Tale of the Wisconsin Supreme Court

The process by which the position of the chief justice on a state supreme court is filled also warrants attention. In nearly half of the states in the country, the chief position is filled the same way as any other position on the state's supreme court. In these states, a person is elected or appointed to fill that slot for the term of office and then must be reelected or reappointed to the chief position just like any other justice wishing to retain their seat on the court.[57]

In about half of the states, the chief justice is selected among the justices already sitting on the supreme court. Most commonly in these states, the chief justice is chosen by their colleagues on the supreme court. The remaining states select the chief based on seniority among the cohort of justices on the court.

The process by which the chief justice is selected is not immune to political manipulation. In January 2015, for example, the Wisconsin State Assembly voted down party lines to move forward with a referendum that would amend the state constitution and alter how the chief justice would be selected.[58] Supported by Republicans, the constitutional amendment would end the practice in place for a century of choosing the chief based on seniority in favor of having the justices vote to select the position.[59] Largely seen as an effort to push liberal Chief Justice Shirley Abrahamson from the position and funded by $600,000 from the Wisconsin Manufacturers and Commerce Association, the referendum passed on April 7, 2015.[60] Abrahamson had been on the Wisconsin Supreme Court since 1976, and as its most senior member, had served as its chief since 1996.[61] In the wake of the certification of the constitutional amendment, the four conservative justices on the court outvoted their three liberal colleagues to place Justice Patience Roggensack as their new chief justice.[62] Roggensack herself cast the tie-breaking vote.[63] Abrahamson initially sued to hold her position as chief until her term expired in 2019, but Roggensack remained in the chief justice position after Abrahamson dropped her lawsuit in late 2015.

The chief justice situation is but one recent example of how ideology and partisan politics in Wisconsin have created a hostile climate, both within the Wisconsin Supreme Court and between the court and the state legislature. A particularly high-profile and disturbing manifestation of the tension on the Wisconsin Supreme Court occurred in June 2011, when a conversation among most of the court's justices about a recent case and Abrahamson's leadership of the court turned heated and then physical.[64] Justice Ann Walsh Bradley accused Justice David Prosser of putting her in a chokehold, while Prosser contended that he put his hands up to push her away after she charged him with her fists raised.[65]

Even more recently, the Wisconsin Supreme Court was central to another controversy that garnered national news attention. In April 2020, voters in Wisconsin turned out to cast their ballots in an early test of the challenges of holding an election during the COVID-19 pandemic. Much of the news coverage focused on long lines to cast ballots in person, particularly in urban centers in the state, after weeks of political and legal wrangling over whether to change the date of the election or the date by which absentee ballots needed to be received, due to health concerns related to the pandemic.[66] What generally received less attention at the time was the relevance of the ideological balance on Wisconsin's supreme court to this controversy. The main event in the April 7 election in Wisconsin that year, at least so far as the national media were concerned, was the presidential primary, particularly for the Democratic Party, which at the time was still engaged in a competitive contest between Joe Biden and Bernie Sanders. So far as the state's political elites were concerned, however, the reelection prospects of conservative incumbent supreme court justice Daniel Kelly, who was being challenged by liberal contender Jill Karofsky, were particularly salient. (In Wisconsin, judges are chosen through nonpartisan elections, but as is often the case, voters had a chance to know which candidate was supported by each political party in the state.)

As early as November 2018, local media in Wisconsin had reported that Republicans in the state legislature were considering moving the date of the presidential primary, out of concern for the implications of the juxtaposition of the presidential primary with the state high court election. Republicans anticipated, accurately, that the Democrats were more likely to have a robust and competitive presidential primary heading the ballot in April 2020. Republicans would not, given that President Trump was unlikely to have any serious competition for his party's nomination. Republicans fretted that the presidential primary vote, therefore, would draw out more Democrats than Republicans on April 7, hurting Justice Kelly's chances of retaining his seat.[67]

Unable to change the date of the presidential primary without violating party rules that would penalize the state, the primary election and the state supreme court election were both held on April 7. After last-minute, pandemic-related efforts by Democratic Governor Tony Evers to postpone the election or move to an all-mail election were rebuffed by the courts, voters unable to meet the rigid absentee ballot deadline were forced to the polls in person, which resulted in long lines of people waiting to vote—especially in Black neighborhoods, where the pandemic's impact was most severe. Once the electoral dust settled, though, Republican concerns over retaining Justice Kelly's seat were validated with Karofsky unseating Kelly by a decisive 55.3–44.7 percent margin.

The extent of the ideological and political tension on and surrounding the Wisconsin Supreme Court is unusual, in that few disagreements related to a state's judiciary lead to physical confrontations between state supreme court justices or nationwide attention to voting lines of the level seen in April 2020. However, what has been going on in recent years in Wisconsin does highlight concerns over the politicization of state judiciaries and how this can lead not only to political efforts to weaken courts or even particular justices but to discord among justices who must figure out how to continue working together in the wake of unpleasant and unfortunate disagreements and politically based maneuverings.

THE RETIREMENT, REMOVAL, AND JUDICIAL OVERSIGHT OF STATE JUDGES

Being burdened with judges too old and unfit to serve seems to be less a problem at the state level than at the federal level because states are free to set mandatory retirement rules. At least thirty-five states have mandatory retirement provisions. The US Supreme Court, in 1991, upheld such mandatory retirement plans by ruling that they do not violate federal law or the Equal Protection Clause of the Fourteenth Amendment.[68] Mandatory retirement ages vary across the states, typically ranging from seventy to seventy-five years old, with seventy being the most common (however, Vermont's mandatory retirement age is ninety). Fifteen states do not have a mandatory retirement age.

Removal

Retirement plans, no matter how effective in getting the older judge to resign, are still of little use against the younger jurist who is incompetent, corrupt, or unethical. Throughout American history, the states have used procedures such as impeachment, recall elections, and concurrent resolutions of the legislature to rid themselves of the judge gone bad. Interestingly, impeachment of state judges is rare and only two state judges have been impeached in the last thirty years. In 1994, a Pennsylvania Supreme Court justice was impeached and removed from his seat for secretly meeting with an attorney to decide case outcomes. In 2000, the New Hampshire House of Representatives impeached the state's supreme court chief justice, David Brock. The House alleged, among other things, that Brock lied under oath to impede an investigation of his court involving a fellow justice, Stephen Thayer. Thayer was accused of trying to influence the appointment of judges to hear an appeal in his own divorce case, and he resigned after the scandal became public in March 2000. Chief Justice Brock, however, was ultimately acquitted on all four counts brought against him.

What is less rare, however, are calls for state judge impeachment by state legislators. For example, as recently as 2023, Wisconsin Republican legislatures threatened to impeach Wisconsin Supreme Court Justice Janet Protasiewicz if she did not recuse herself from a redistricting case, which she refused to do. Republican state lawmakers eventually backed off the threat.[69] Over the last twenty years, legislators have issued various impeachment threats. In New Hampshire, the legislature proposed impeaching a judge for overstepping their authority; in Pennsylvania, the legislature threatened to impeach a judge for dismissing her own parking tickets; and in West Virginia, threats of impeachment transpired when a state supreme court justice used funds to lavishly renovate his office.[70] A 2010 report by the National Center for State Courts found some evidence of state legislatures threatening to use their impeachment power to remove judges for decisions they did not like. For example, in Iowa, Massachusetts, and New Jersey, bills were filed to remove judges who supported same-sex marriage rights, and in 2010 and 2011, a member of the Oklahoma legislature requested removal of a judge who accepted a plea deal in a child molestation case (all participants—prosecutor, defense, and victim's parents—approved the agreement).[71] The evidence suggests that methods for judicial discipline and removal are only minimally effective, either because they prove to be politically difficult to put into operation or because of their time-consuming, cumbersome nature.

Judicial Oversight Commissions

Every state has an oversight agency to address judicial misconduct, often made up of the judges themselves, to police their own members. One law professor describes the system as "judges judging judges."[72] Misconduct proceedings and sanctions are often kept confidential and at least thirty-eight states do not make public judicial misconduct sanctions.[73] For instance, one report showed that in Massachusetts nine of the ten judges sanctioned in 2020 were done so privately.[74] However, some states, like California, will publicly admonish a judge as part of their sanctions. In 2019, the California Commission on Judicial Performance publicly admonished Judge David Mason for an ongoing romantic relationship he had with an attorney who appeared before him in more than eighty cases.[75]

Judicial misconduct can be a matter of life and death. In 2009, for example, the presiding judge on the Texas Court of Criminal Appeals, Sharon Keller, faced a disciplinary hearing before the Texas Commission on Judicial Conduct in a high-profile death penalty case. Lawyers for a condemned man, Michael Richard, called the court on the afternoon of September 25, 2007, to ask that the offices be kept open late to receive a last-minute appeal after the US Supreme Court had issued an order earlier in the day in another death penalty case that provided grounds for delaying Richard's execution. (Requests for late filings due to late-breaking legal developments are routine in death penalty cases.) However, Keller refused: "We close at 5," she told Richard's lawyers. An appeal was never filed, and Richard was executed a few hours later, even though the US Supreme Court's ruling that day effectively stopped executions in the United States for months. The Commission on Judicial Conduct ultimately issued a public warning admonishing Keller for her actions in the Richard case. This rebuke, which was considered mild by most observers, was subsequently appealed by Keller. On appeal, all the charges were dismissed.[76] Keller thus never faced any official reprimand for her conduct in the matter. What's more, this was not the only ethical question surrounding Judge Keller. In 2010, she was fined $100,000 (later reduced to $25,000) for failing to follow state ethics law requirements that she disclose nearly $2 million in personal real estate holdings. Despite all this, Keller was reelected to her position as the presiding judge on the Texas Court of Criminal Appeals in 2012. In 2018, Keller narrowly defeated a Republican primary challenger who made Keller's ethics issues a major focus of his campaign, and Keller retained her seat after prevailing in the general election.[77]

Perhaps it is no surprise that reformers have given these types of judicial ethics and misconduct commissions only fair-to-poor marks. Critics suggest that the persons most familiar with the problem—the judges—are often loath to expose a colleague to public censure and discipline. A recent investigation of judicial misconduct of state judges identified that from 2008–2019, there were 1,509 cases where judges retired, resigned, or were disciplined following accusations, and another 3,613 cases in which states disciplined judges but kept the details of the misconduct a secret.[78] The report also found that several judges were allowed to return to the bench. Examples include a "California judge who had sex in his courthouse chambers, once with his former law intern and separately with an attorney; a New York judge who berated domestic violence victims; and a Maryland judge who, after his arrest for driving drunk, was allowed to return to the bench provide he took a Breathalyzer test before each appearance." In 2020, egregious acts of misconduct merely received reprimands. For instance, a Utah judge texted "a video of a man's scrotum to his court clerks"; three judges in Indiana got drunk at a conference, then started a brawl outside a White Castle restaurant "that ended with two of the judges shot"; and a Texas trial court judge entered a jury room while jurors were deliberating and "declared that God told him the defendant was innocent."[79] Clearly, policing the state judiciaries remains a challenge that beckons champions of good government.

Voter Recalls

Finally, a small number of states (roughly one in five) allows for voter recall of judges. In about half of these states, judges may only be recalled for some sort of malfeasance or impropriety. In the remaining handful of states, such as California, judges may be recalled for any reason. In 2018, Santa Clara County Superior Court Judge Aaron Persky was successfully recalled by voters after the 2016 conviction of Brock Turner for three felonies related to his sexual assault of another Stanford University student in 2015. Judge Persky sentenced Turner to six months in jail (with Turner serving three), three years of probation, and lifetime registration as a sex offender. Public backlash to this sentence, which Judge Persky justified in part on Turner's relatively youthful age, expressions of remorse, and Persky's conclusion that Turner did not pose a danger to others, was swift.[80] Stanford law professor Michele Dauber spearheaded a campaign to have Judge Persky removed from the bench following the sentencing. After collecting the requisite number of signatures to have the recall question placed on the ballot and defeating multiple efforts by Judge Persky to have the recall vote delayed via court order, in June 2018, Judge Persky became the first judge recalled in the state of California since 1932, after approximately 60 percent of voters cast a ballot favoring recall.

The Brock Turner trial, the sentence, and the recall effort all drew national attention. Throughout the recall process, varied concerns were expressed about recalling a judge for handing down a lenient sentence in a single criminal case. Some judges expressed concern over the impact of such a high-profile recall on judicial independence. Some public defenders expressed apprehension that the recall effort would discourage judges from extending leniency to people convicted in criminal court, which the public defenders argued would inadvertently cause lengthier prison sentences for many poor people and people of color. Lastly, another important consideration may be the fact that Judge Persky's sentence, while lenient, was within the law. If voters are unhappy with criminal sentences, should their anger be directed at the judges handing down the sentences or the legislators responsible for passing criminal statutes in the first place? Notably, on this last point, within months of Judge Persky's controversial sentencing of Turner, the California legislature enacted new mandatory minimum sentences in sexual assault cases and closed a loophole that allowed for more lenient sentences in cases where sexual assault victims were too intoxicated to physically resist their attackers.[81]

Judge Persky's recall demonstrates well the tension between accountability and independence with respect to judicial decision-making. The Recall Aaron Persky campaign noted that "California judges are accountable to voters, and that means considering judges' previous decisions." On the other hand, Jeffrey Rosen, the district attorney who prosecuted Turner and who expressed great disappointment with Turner's lenient sentence, argued that "[s]ubjecting judges to recall when they follow the law and do something unpopular undermines judicial independence . . . [and may cause judges to] lack the courage to stand up for the rights of minorities and others needing protection from powerful majorities."[82] Still others have argued that the Persky recall represents a perfect storm of sorts, coinciding with the #MeToo movement, and that it does not signal the need for any widespread concern over the independence of judges. Lastly, as Professor Dauber stated in response to a question about whether a single decision should be the basis for recalling a judge, "It is my belief that sometimes one case can be so bad that it does require strong action and strong repudiation."[83]

JUDICIAL INDEPENDENCE AND STATE COURTS

Underlying much of the discussion in this chapter is the consideration of judicial independence in state judiciaries. Given the varied selection methods, terms of office, judicial salaries, and removal mechanisms at play across the American states, there is opportunity for other state officials, especially legislators and governors, to manipulate these processes with an eye toward crafting a like-minded state judiciary. Political scientist Gbemende Johnson found significant evidence that when courts are vulnerable to executive retaliation they will engage in more deferential behavior toward the executive. She notes that excessive deference by the courts "raises concerns over judicial independence."[84] As highlighted in a previous section, Wisconsin has seen a good deal of tension between the legislature and the judiciary in recent years. Wisconsin is not alone, however. Legislators in Florida and Kansas have introduced bills to give the state legislature more control over selecting judges in those states.[85] In Pennsylvania, the state legislature has threatened impeachment in retaliation for a state supreme court decision that struck down a redistricting map.[86] In Arkansas, the legislature attempted to limit the supreme court's rulemaking power in response to a 2013 decision to strike down a tort reform law.[87]

In West Virginia in 2018, a bizarre set of circumstances resulted in a period when every justice on the state supreme court was under an impeachment investigation.[88] The controversy started when Justice Allen Loughry was indicted by a federal grand jury on multiple charges including fraud and witness tampering. Soon thereafter, Loughry's colleague Menis Ketchum retired with two years remaining on his term, after a report found that he had used state-owned vehicles for personal matters, leading to an agreement whereby Ketchum agreed to plead guilty to a federal charge of defrauding taxpayers through his personal use of the state car. Allegations of improper use of state resources surfaced against other justices on the West Virginia high court, and the state's Judicial Investigation Commission (JIC) considered bringing ethics complaints against the remaining three justices (Margaret Workman, Robin Davis, and Beth Walker—the last of whom had only joined the court in 2017). Although the JIC closed its investigation without bringing any charges against the remaining justices, in August of that year, the West Virginia House of Delegates voted to impeach all four remaining justices (Loughry, Workman, Davis, and Walker) on a variety of charges related to wasteful use of state resources. Davis resigned the day after the impeachment vote.

As for the vacancies left over by the sudden departures of Ketchum and Davis, both were filled by special election. However, in the interim, Republican Governor Jim Justice appointed two conservative Republicans (Evan H. Jenkins and Tim Armstead) to the seats, and these interim appointees retained the seats in the special election. Note that both Ketchum and Davis had been elected as Democrats. With respect to the remaining three justices, the West Virginia Senate rejected Walker's impeachment by a nearly unanimous vote. The impeachment proceedings against Justice Workman were blocked by a judicial order from moving forward, due to multiple problems with the impeachment articles. Workman would remain on the bench until her retirement at the end of 2020. Loughry, who had been suspended from the high court after his federal indictment, would eventually resign after Governor Justice called the legislature to a special session to consider impeachment charges related to Loughry's criminal behavior. Loughry's departure gave the Republican governor a third interim appointment to the five-member court. Governor Justice's selection, John Hutchinson, a friend of the governor, would go on to retain the seat in the special election in 2020.

These convoluted and political events in West Virginia and Wisconsin, while remarkable and consequential, are perhaps outdone by recent actions in the state of North Carolina, which has seen as much, if not more, discord between the state judiciary and the political branches in recent years. North Carolina is no stranger to recent legislative changes to how judges are selected. After an extended period (from 1868 to 1996) when the state saw no legislative reforms to judicial selection protocols, the state has seen a recent flurry of activity affecting the judiciary coming out of the state legislature.[89] In 2002, the state legislature passed the Judicial Campaign Reform Act, which changed the selection mechanism for state supreme court and court of appeals judges starting in 2004 from partisan elections to nonpartisan elections. Former North Carolina Supreme Court Justice Bob Orr argued that the state legislature, then controlled by the Democrats, wanted party affiliation to be taken off the ballot "because they thought too many Republicans were winning."[90]

More recently, the now Republican-controlled General Assembly in North Carolina has been pushing for many changes to how judges are selected to the state bench. In 2015, the legislature attempted to change to retention elections for supreme court justices, who would thereafter run alone in a simple up or down vote. Widely seen as an effort to protect the supreme court seat held by Republican Justice Bob Edmunds, the law was struck down as unconstitutional by the state judiciary.[91] Interestingly, the initial decision to strike down the law was made by a special three-judge panel of superior court judges and was then appealed to the state's highest court. With Justice Edmunds's decision to recuse himself, given that the law would have directly affected his upcoming election, the state's high court split 3–3 on the appeal, causing the lower court decision to stand and the law to be struck down.

With nonpartisan elections still in place during the 2016 election, Justice Edmunds lost his seat to Michael Morgan by nearly ten percentage points.[92] Unexpectedly, one factor that may have helped Morgan unseat Edmunds was another recent legislative change to the way in which judges are selected in North Carolina. Starting with the 2016 election, the order by which candidates are listed on the ballot for court of appeals selection would be done via a convoluted mechanism of "alphabetical order by party beginning with the party whose nominee for Governor received the most votes in the most recent gubernatorial election and in alphabetical order within the party," rather than by random ordering selection, which had previously been in place.[93] However, this ballot ordering change, which was expected to help Republicans on the ballot, only applied to court of appeals races, and not supreme court races. The court-of-appeals-specific ballot-ordering mechanism, coupled with the fact that court of appeals judges in North Carolina are elected in partisan races, meant that Republican candidates were listed first with party labels attached in the five statewide court of appeals elections. Supreme court candidates in North Carolina run without their party label on the ballot, and Michael Morgan (a Democrat) was listed first via the random ordering method.[94] This confusing situation may have tricked some voters into presuming that Morgan was also a Republican.

The failed effort at imposing retention elections and the convoluted method for placing court of appeals candidates on the ballot would prove to be only the beginning with respect to the importance of the 2016 election to the state judiciary's relationship with the political branches in North Carolina. Morgan's defeat of Edmunds tipped the state supreme court to a 4 (Democrat) to 3 (Republican) split. In addition, Democrat Roy Cooper defeated Republican incumbent Governor Pat McCrory in an extremely close and contested gubernatorial election. The Republican-controlled legislature (with the assistance of lame-duck Governor McCrory) moved quickly to limit the power of the incoming Democratic governor. Although rumors of a court-packing plan to add two seats to the state's highest court before McCrory left office never came to pass, the legislature extended a special session intended to address hurricane relief to pass a bill (signed into law by McCrory) that imposed partisan primaries on state supreme court elections and another (also signed into law by McCrory just before leaving office) that prevented state constitutional challenges from skipping the state court of appeals en route to the state supreme court. Recall that after the 2016 election, the state supreme court would consist of four Democrats and three Republicans. In 2016, on the other hand, the state's fifteen-member court of appeals consisted of eleven Republicans and only four Democrats, spurring opponents to allege that the change was made to bolster the influence of a court level controlled by Republicans at the expense of the higher court that was newly controlled by Democrats.

In the wake of the 2016 election, the state legislature also reduced the number of seats on the court of appeals, preventing the new Democratic governor from filling the vacancies expected to be created by three Republican judges approaching the state's mandatory retirement age.[95] Before this court-shrinking law, which the legislature passed over Democratic Governor Cooper's veto, went into effect, Republican Court of Appeals Judge Doug McCullough resigned in protest so Cooper could appoint his replacement. When announcing his surprise retirement, Judge McCullough stated, "I did not want my legacy to be the elimination of a seat and the impairment of a court that I have served on."[96] In 2017, the legislature overrode Cooper's veto to ensure that seats on all levels of the state judiciary would now be chosen in partisan elections.[97]

In addition to the above efforts, the Republican-controlled General Assembly attempted to amend the state constitution to insinuate itself into a "pseudo-merit selection system," of sorts, as discussed previously in this chapter.[98] This effort was rebuffed by voters in the state.

State Judicial Independence: Beyond Selection Method

Recent tensions between state legislatures and judiciaries in states such as North Carolina, West Virginia, and Wisconsin speak to problems that transcend the selection and retention of judges. They also fit with political science research on the use of court-curbing legislation in the states. One study by political scientist Meghan E. Leonard examined legislative efforts to pass court-curbing measures, which were defined as bills intended to reverse a judicial decision, prevent courts from ruling on certain issues, or alter the court for the purpose of producing a particular substantive outcome.[99] In this study, Leonard found that court-curbing efforts are largely unrelated to the selection method used in the state. Rather, court-curbing measures are more likely to be introduced in states where the legislature is more conservative, rather than more liberal. Also, the number of court-curbing bills increases as the legislature and the court become more ideologically distant. In other words, "court curbing in the states is more of a political event, rather than one driven by institutional conditions. State legislators use these introductions when they are ideologically most beneficial to them."[100] In a 2022 study, Leonard found that between 2008–2016 all states introduced some sort of court-curbing legislation.[101] Oklahoma and Tennessee led the way; during this time period, Tennessee had ninety-six bills introduced related to court curbing and Oklahoma had ninety-eight. Although state legislatures controlled by Democrats are not immune from partisan manipulation of the judiciary (as the 2004 change from partisan to nonpartisan elections in North Carolina demonstrates), many of the recent examples from North Carolina and other states are being instigated by legislatures controlled by Republicans.

In addition, the post-2016 election efforts at altering judicial selection in North Carolina demonstrate how a legislature may respond when it sees a state supreme court suddenly controlled by the opposing party. One conclusion that is quite clear from the state judicial selection research to date is that while no one selection method is objectively the "best" at choosing judges, the important process of seating and retaining judges is always vulnerable to political manipulation by those interested in seeing their preferred vision reflected in the composition of the state judiciary.

Indeed, in his recent book on state judicial selection, noted expert Herbert Kritzer concludes that state judicial observers should reconsider the conceptual framework away from one that balances judicial independence with accountability. Instead, Kritzer argues for recasting this tension as one between partisan politics and legal professionalism.[102] When asked what they most want to see in their state judges, especially at the state supreme court level, Kritzer found that respondents rated characteristics associated with legal professionalism higher than ideological or political considerations. However, many of the recent anecdotes discussed in this chapter highlight efforts to manipulate the state judiciary for partisan purposes, irrespective of voter preferences or considerations of judicial merit or professionalism. States that fall more on the "professionalism" side, on the other hand, would be expected to see less bare-knuckled brawling over the state's judiciary. While the processes by which state court judges are selected, retained, or removed are undoubtedly important to the composition and functioning of state courts around the country, interference from the political branches may always become a concern.

SUMMARY

Politics and the judiciary go hand in glove. If the governor appoints the judges, similarity in the values of the governor and the judicial nominees is the norm. If judges are elected—even on nonpartisan ballots—the political and judicial processes are still inexorably intertwined. Judicial decisions by state judges reflect both the process by which the judges are chosen and the values of those who choose them. True and total judicial independence is probably impossible to achieve, and it may not be fully desirable even if we could achieve it.

Merit selection systems—those incorporating retention elections and those that do not—are seen by many advocates as a way of selecting judges based on quality rather than ideology, partisan politics, or patronage. However, there is no unambiguous evidence that merit-selected judges are of higher quality than their elected and appointed peers. Furthermore, for Missouri Plan states, one student of the courts noted that "Judicial retention elections thus become another access point by which special interest groups can influence policy making,"[103] as was seen in the Iowa Supreme Court retention elections in 2010.

The disciplining and removal of corrupt or mentally unfit judges remain a problem. However, implementation of mandatory retirement plans and the establishment of peer policing commissions illustrate the states' commitment to addressing this problem, although these efforts are far from fool-proof. As the recall of Judge Aaron Persky highlights, removal of judges for making unpopular decisions is something that court actors warn us to do cautiously and thoughtfully, even when citizens may be supportive of such removal efforts.

Finally, we gave some attention to the recent controversies involving the judiciary in North Carolina, West Virginia, and Wisconsin. Recent incidents in these states highlight how politicization of the state courts can affect rules and resources related to the judiciary, such as how leadership positions are selected, how judges are chosen and retained, and even how candidate names are ordered on the electoral ballot. In some states, no election rule, however obscure it may seem, is beyond the reach of political manipulation if the elected branches are sufficiently motivated to do so.

FURTHER THOUGHT AND DISCUSSION QUESTIONS

1. How successful have states been in their efforts to remove politics from the judicial selection process? To what extent is it desirable, or even possible, to make judicial selection apolitical?
2. Are citizens well enough informed to evaluate judges' performances in retention elections, or should such decisions be left to attentive experts? Should we be satisfied that social science research indicates that increases in campaign spending and negative advertising in judicial campaigns appear to stimulate voter interest in these elections? Are there other reasons to be concerned about the role of money in judicial elections?
3. Should there be more public accountability when it comes to judicial misconduct sanctions? Should the general public be informed about judicial misconduct sanctions?
4. How protected from professional retribution should judges be for making unpopular decisions? Should voters remove judges, and if so, should that power only be allowed for professional misconduct? If we cannot entirely prevent judges from being accountable to someone, is it more appropriate for judges to be accountable to the public or to the members of the other branches of the state government?

SUGGESTED RESOURCES

Bonneau, Chris W., and Melinda Gann Hall. *In Defense of Judicial Elections.* New York, NY: Routledge, 2009. A definitive academic discussion of state judicial elections; the authors back up their arguments with solid data.

Bonneau, Chris W., and Melinda Gann Hall, eds. *Judicial Elections in the 21st Century.* New York, NY: Routledge, 2017. This edited volume is an excellent overview of trends and research on judicial elections.

Brennan Center for Justice. Available online at https://www.brennancenter.org/ (accessed July 12, 2024). Releases reports regularly on topics of interest to scholars of state courts. These include summary reports on judicial elections released after each election cycle.

DePaul Law Review 67, no. 2 (Winter 2018). This issue was dedicated to research on state judicial selection, including articles from several leading legal and political science scholars on the topic.

George, Tracey E., and Albert H. Yoon. "Gavel Gap: The Differences between the Race & Gender Composition of the Courts & the Communities They Serve." American Constitution Society. The "Gavel Gap" website includes links to the data collected by George and Yoon on all judges sitting on state courts in 2014. Available at https://www.acslaw.org/analysis/reports/gavel-gap/ (accessed July 12, 2024).

Gibson, James L. *Electing Judges: The Surprising Effects of Campaigning on Judicial Legitimacy.* Chicago, IL: University of Chicago Press, 2012. A comprehensive, empirical assessment of the impact of campaigns on the public's perception of the judiciary. The March/April 2013 issue of *Judicature* (Vol. 96, No. 5) was dedicated to research on judicial elections that came in the wake of the publication of Gibson's book.

Kritzer, Herbert M. *Judicial Selection in the States: Politics and the Struggle for Reform.* Cambridge: Cambridge University Press, 2020. An in-depth analysis of recent efforts across multiple states to alter how state judges are selected and retained.

National Center for State Courts. Available online at www.ncsconline.org. An excellent source of research and information on state courts.

Sample, James J., Charles Hall, and Linda Casey. "The New Politics of Judicial Elections." *Judicature* 94 (September–October 2010): 50–57. A discussion of the latest trends in judicial elections in the states.

KEY TERM

merit selection

6 FEDERAL JUDGES

CHAPTER GOALS AND OBJECTIVES

In this chapter, students will learn that . . .

- Judges at all levels of the federal judiciary have historically been selected from a relatively narrow pool of candidates from elite backgrounds. Serious efforts have been made to diversify the bench in recent years, although informal norms defining acceptable qualifications for a federal judgeship can work at cross-purposes with efforts to diversify.
- The process by which federal judges are selected is complicated and political and involves many people within the executive branch, the Senate, and outside interests. Key alterations to this process can influence the composition of the federal judiciary for decades to come.
- Federal judges in the United States undergo a process of largely informal socialization to assist them in getting up to speed with the demands of their work.
- The privilege of lifetime tenure that comes with a federal judgeship can create difficulties in terms of removing judges who are unfit to serve due to advanced age or improper behavior. Congress has instituted efforts over the years to help alleviate these problems, although as applied to the Supreme Court in particular, controversies remain over the consequences of justices having tenure for life.

The main actors in the federal system are the people who serve as judges and justices, and it is to them that we now turn our attention. In this chapter, we consider the background characteristics of federal judges, their selection and socialization to the bench, and the consequences of lifetime tenure that Article III judges enjoy. Although there are a lot of similarities among judges on different rungs of the judicial hierarchy, we give attention throughout this chapter to significant differences between the various levels of the federal judiciary. We also give attention to how the judges of the federal courts are affected by partisan politics and public opinion.

President Joe Biden had only one opportunity to appoint a Supreme Court justice. His 2022 selection of Judge Ketanji Brown Jackson to fill the seat vacated by Justice Stephen Breyer was reflective of Biden's general approach to filling vacancies across the judiciary. Biden's record of appointing women, people of color, and those with previous experience in public defense or legal aid work surpassed that of any president in US history. Justice Jackson is the first Black woman ever appointed to the Supreme Court, and the first justice with substantial experience in criminal defense to serve on the Court in decades.

Chip Somodevilla/Getty Images

BACKGROUND CHARACTERISTICS OF FEDERAL JUDGES

Before we turn our attention to the processes by which judges are nominated by the president and confirmed by the Senate, we begin with an assessment of the background of federal judges, with particular emphasis on the demographic background of the people who hold these positions, as well as their educational and occupational credentials. The US Constitution and federal statutes impose no formal qualifications on federal judges, in terms of age, residency or citizen restrictions, or educational or occupational background, beyond the requirement that judges serve "during good behavior." This distinguishes the United States from most other countries around the world. For example, many countries (including Austria, Egypt, France, Singapore, and Sweden) use some form of examination and training program to select their judges.[1]

Even absent formal requirements, the informal expectation is that federal judges in the United States be qualified for the position through their educational training, personal and professional character, and professional experience. Indeed, over time, certain informal norms have developed that help determine who is selected to join the federal bench, although these expectations at times differ based on whether a person is being appointed to the Supreme Court, one of the circuit courts, or to a district court.

Supreme Court Justices

As of 2024, 110 men and six women have sat on the bench of America's highest judicial tribunal. This includes Justice Ketanji Brown Jackson, who was appointed to replace Stephen Breyer in 2022. If we think of federal judges as being culled primarily from America's cultural elite, members of the US Supreme Court would likely be thought of as the crème de la crème of the legal profession.

As we discuss in Chapter 8, law schools and the legal profession historically excluded many from their ranks, including those from more modest backgrounds, women, and people of color. Unsurprisingly, these practices influenced the composition of the entire federal judiciary, and the Supreme Court in particular. Throughout much of US history, most justices "were not only from families in comfortable economic circumstances, but were chosen overwhelmingly from the socially prestigious and politically influential gentry class in the late eighteenth and early nineteenth century, or the professionalized upper class thereafter."[2]

Until the 1960s, the high court had been all White and all male, but in 1967, President Lyndon B. Johnson appointed Thurgood Marshall as the first Black member of the Court. When Marshall retired in 1991, President George H. W. Bush nominated Clarence Thomas, a man who shared Marshall's racial identification, though not his liberal views. In 1981, the gender barrier was broken when President Ronald Reagan named Sandra Day O'Connor to the Court; thirteen years later, she was joined by Ruth Bader Ginsburg, and this has been followed by the appointment of Sonia Sotomayor in 2009, who was also the first Hispanic justice. In 2010, Elena Kagan became the fourth woman to join the high court, followed by Amy Coney Barrett as the fifth in 2020. Ketanji Brown Jackson is the sixth woman and first Black woman to serve on the nation's highest court.

In terms of religious background, the membership of the Court has been overwhelmingly Protestant, and most of the justices over time have been affiliated with the denominations that are more likely to be members of the social elite (such as the Episcopal, Presbyterian, and Unitarian Churches). In recent decades, and in stark contrast to history, the Supreme Court has included more justices who identify (at least culturally) as Jewish and especially more justices of Roman Catholic backgrounds.[3]

While the contemporary Supreme Court is more diverse in these ways than it has been at any point in our history, it still falls short of resembling either America or the legal community. Whether considering demographic background, educational training, or professional résumé, the Supreme Court has always represented a particular model of legal qualifications that places a primary on pedigree. In recent years, the Court has been dominated by those who received their legal education at Harvard or Yale, with Barrett's degree from Notre Dame Law School being the current exception.

The Court has also recently been dominated by justices with a particular set of occupational qualifications, including court of appeals experience and previous Supreme Court clerkship over others, including electoral office and criminal defense work. Except for Elena Kagan, who had worked as US Solicitor General and dean of Harvard Law School prior to her appointment, every member of the Court in 2024 was serving as an appeals court judge prior to their elevation to the highest court. Many Court observers have bemoaned this state of affairs, because the work of the nation's highest court often brings the justices in contact with critical questions regarding separation of powers and the rights of the criminally accused.

President Biden's appointment of Justice Jackson perhaps represents a turning point with respect to the appointment of justices with substantial experience with criminal defense work. Jackson is the first justice in modern history to have worked in public defense. In addition, she is the first justice to serve on the Court with any experience in criminal defense, since Thurgood Marshall left the Court over thirty years ago. How important is it for the Court to contain those with varied professional backgrounds? Justice O'Connor commented on the importance of working alongside Justice Marshall, given that he was someone who "understood the vulnerabilities of the accused and established safeguards for their protection."[4]

As we move our attention to the judges on the courts of appeals and then the district courts, we will consider similarities and differences in the backgrounds of judges on these distinct levels of the judicial hierarchy. In doing so, readers should keep in mind that the lower courts represent something of a "farm team" for future appointments to the Supreme Court. Therefore, recent trends in the identities and backgrounds of the judges appointed to the circuit and district courts may tell us something about the future composition of the Supreme Court.

Court of Appeals Judges

Table 6.1 provides original data on the demographic, educational, and occupational backgrounds of all judges appointed to the US courts of appeals, starting with President Jimmy Carter and concluding with President Joe Biden.[5] Unsurprisingly, the two-term presidents (Reagan, Clinton, W. Bush, and Obama) tend to outperform the one-term presidents (Carter, H. W. Bush, Biden, and also Trump in his first term) with respect to the number of judges appointed, although Obama appointed fewer court of appeals judges (at 48) than did Trump (at 54) or Carter (at 56). Biden appointed a total of 43 judges[6] to the courts of appeals, placing him closer to President H. W. Bush (at 37) than to either Presidents Carter or Trump, in terms of the opportunity to influence the composition of the courts of appeals during a single term in office.

Digging into some of the statistics in Table 6.1 uncovers other significant differences in how recent presidents have approached appointing judges to the courts of appeals.

Race, Ethnicity, Gender, and Age

Historically, one clear norm was that federal judgeships were limited to White men, typically from more elite backgrounds. When Jimmy Carter was inaugurated as president in 1977, less than 2 percent of federal judgeships had ever been held by a member of a racial

TABLE 6.1 ■ Background Characteristics of Presidents' Court of Appeals Judges, Carter through Biden

	Carter	Reagan	H. W. Bush	Clinton	W. Bush	Obama	Trump	Biden
Race/ethnicity								
White, non-Latino	78.6%	97.4%	89.2%	73.8%	84.7%	66.7%	85.2%	32.6%
Minority	21.4	2.6	10.8	26.2	15.3	33.3	14.8	67.4
Gender								
Male	80.4	94.9	81.1	67.2	74.6	54.2	79.6	30.2
Female	19.6	5.1	18.9	32.8	25.4	45.8	20.4	69.8
Non-Latino White male	60.7	92.3	70.3	49.2	64.4	29.2	68.5	14.0
Mean age at appointment	52.3 yrs	50.4 yrs	49.5 yrs	52.3 yrs	51.0 yrs	53.1 yrs	47.6 yrs	49.0 yrs
Law school education								
Harvard/Yale	28.6%	21.8%	29.7%	27.9%	20.3%	29.2%	29.6%	30.2%
Ivy/elite[a]	60.7	37.2	37.8	41.0	39.0	41.7	59.3	51.2
Other law school	39.3	62.8	62.2	59.0	61.0	58.3	40.7	49.0
Job at appointment								
Private practice	32.1%	25.6%	27.0%	32.8%	25.4%	18.8%	37.0%	16.3%
US District Court	26.8	41.0	59.5	31.2	22.0	37.5	16.7	27.9
Nonprimary federal court	0.0	1.3	0.0	3.3	1.7	4.2	1.9	11.6
State/local judiciary	19.6	12.8	2.7	18.0	25.4	18.8	18.5	14.0
US DOJ	1.8	3.9	5.4	6.6	10.2	4.2	11.1	9.3
Academia	14.3	11.5	0.0	8.2	5.1	10.4	3.7	0.0
Other	5.4	3.9	5.4	0.0	10.2	6.3	11.1	20.9

(Continued)

TABLE 6.1 ■ Background Characteristics of Presidents' Court of Appeals Judges, Carter through Biden (*Continued*)

	Carter	Reagan	H. W. Bush	Clinton	W. Bush	Obama	Trump	Biden
All previous employment								
Private practice	92.9%	89.7%	86.5%	85.2%	91.5%	87.5%	96.3%	74.4%
Mean years in private practice[b]	13.8 yrs	13.5 yrs	14.9 yrs	14.3 yrs	11.8 yrs	10.3yrs	10.0 yrs	9.4 yrs
US District Court	26.8%	43.6%	59.9%	32.8%	22.0%	37.5%	16.7%	27.9%
Nonprimary federal court	0.0	1.3	0.0	3.3	1.7	6.3	1.9	20.9
State/local judiciary	33.9	28.2	16.2	31.1	42.4	27.1	22.2	23.3
US DOJ	21.4	23.1	24.3	32.8	35.6	56.3	51.9	37.2
State prosecutor	21.4	28.2	27.0	29.5	16.9	16.7	24.1	16.3
Public defender/ legal aid	3.6	1.3	0.0	4.9	6.8	12.5	0.0	27.9
SCOTUS clerkship	10.7	9.0	10.8	13.1	15.3	25.0	37.0	11.6
Other clerkship	19.6	23.1	27.0	39.3	47.5	68.8	88.9	74.4
Military	69.6	53.8	35.1	14.8	13.6	6.3	0.0	4.7
Total no. of appointees	56	78	37	61	59	48	54	43

[a]This category includes all judges who went to an Ivy League law school (Harvard, Yale, Columbia, Cornell, and Pennsylvania), plus judges who earned their degree from UC-Berkeley, Chicago, Michigan, or Stanford.

[b]Calculated only for those who previously worked in private practice, excluding those who did not.

Source: Data collected by Lisa M. Holmes, with assistance from Meredith Gensch (UVM '16), Isaac Salem (UVM '20), and Robin Olsen (UVM '24) from the Federal Judicial Center and the Library of Congress. We exclude judges on specialized or territorial courts in this analysis.

or ethnic minority group, and an even smaller percentage (about one-half of 1 percent) had been held by women. As president, Carter prioritized developing a federal judiciary that at least somewhat better resembled America, in terms of the racial, ethnic, and gender backgrounds of his nominees. Although Carter did not have an opportunity to appoint anyone to the Supreme Court, his presidency was gifted a huge opportunity to influence the composition of the lower courts, when Congress passed the largest expansion of the federal judiciary in US history in 1978. Executing his promise to appoint more diverse judges would prove to be difficult, however, in part because in the 1970s, relatively fewer racial minorities and women had access to the kinds of prestigious educational and occupational institutions that were expected of a highly qualified judicial nominee. This was particularly complicated given that Carter's second major commitment was to appointing judges based on merit rather than political expediency or patronage.

Even so, President Carter would eventually set into motion a new era in judicial appointment politics, where the federal courts would never again return to the days when they were staffed all but exclusively by White men.

Of the fifty-six judges Carter appointed to the courts of appeals, just over 21 percent were people of color, and nearly 20 percent were women. Although Carter only appointed one woman of color to the courts of appeals during his time in office, his record on diversity was truly seismic, with nearly 40 percent of his judges to these courts being either women or members of minority racial or ethnic groups.

Carter's Democratic successors were particularly interested in following his lead, with roughly half of Clinton's court of appeals judges being White men and just under 30 percent of Obama's judges from that group. The Biden presidency, however, has eclipsed all predecessors, in that two-thirds of his appointees to the courts of appeals identified as something other than White and non-Latino. And roughly 70 percent of seats on this level of the judiciary went to women. In appointing what is—far and away—the most racially, ethnically, and gender-diverse cohort of judges in US history, Biden made good on a key pledge made during the 2020 presidential campaign. Indeed, in publicly naming his nominees to the lower courts throughout his presidency, his administration often highlighted how particular nominees were breaking new ground in diversifying their respective courts on a variety of factors.

Although our focus here has been on race, ethnicity, and gender, Biden took a broader view toward diversification of the federal bench. For example, even before his inauguration, the Biden–Harris transition team announced that the president was interested in identifying "talented individuals who would bring to [the federal judiciary] a wide range of life and professional experiences, including those based on their race, ethnicity, national origin, gender, sexual orientation, gender identity, religion, veteran status, and disability."[7] With respect to professional background, the incoming president announced that he would be looking to nominate "individuals whose legal experiences have been historically underrepresented on the federal bench, including those who are public defenders, civil rights and legal aid attorneys, and those who represent Americans in every walk of life."[8]

For their part, recent Republican presidents have not kept pace with respect to racial, ethnic, and gender diversity, and the interparty difference is substantial. No Republican president has yet matched the diversity of even the Carter cohort, let alone that of Clinton, Obama, or Biden. However, from Reagan through George W. Bush, there was a notable drop in the percent of White men appointed to these seats, with each Republican president outpacing their same-party predecessor on diversity. That ended with President Trump. Instead of continuing the trend of outdoing the diversity of the previous same-party president's appointees, Trump awarded a higher proportion of court of appeals judgeships to White men, compared to W. Bush (68.5 percent to 64.4 percent). The gap between the racial, ethnic, and gender diversity of judges appointed by Democrats versus those appointed by Republicans has therefore become more dramatic in recent years.

With respect to the average age of a court of appeals judge upon joining that bench, one finding from Table 6.1 is that the cohort appointed by President Trump is the youngest (at an average of 47.6 years) of all the recent presidents, with Biden's judges being the next youngest, at roughly 49 years old, on average. Biden and Trump are also the only presidents in our analysis who appointed a younger cohort to the court of appeals than to the district courts (district court judges are discussed later in this chapter), although with Trump, the difference was more substantial.

Education

Although the courts of appeals are not as strongly dominated by judges educated at the most elite law schools, compared to recent justices appointed to the Supreme Court, many of the circuit judges are well acquainted with these most prestigious of educational institutions. All presidents since Carter have selected at least 20 percent (but no more than 30 percent) of their court of appeals judges from the Harvard or Yale ranks, although modern presidents of both parties display a willingness to appoint those who were trained at schools outside the Ivy League or most elite law schools to the courts of appeals.[9] The Carter administration in the 1970s represents the high water mark in terms of selecting circuit court judges who earned their law degrees from Ivy League or other particularly elite law schools. Recall that Carter was interested in appointing judges based on merit; elite law school pedigree represents one approach to pursuing that goal.

After Carter and through the Obama years, most circuit court judges gained their legal education somewhere other than the nation's most prestigious law schools. Interestingly, however, more than half of those appointed by Trump and Biden were trained at the more elite programs. Whether this demonstrates an informal expectation moving forward that court of appeals judges are educated at the nation's most prestigious law schools remains to be seen.

Previous Occupation

We provide data on two ways of conceptualizing previous occupation in Table 6.1. First, we consider what job the judge had immediately before joining the court of appeals. In other words, what kind of position was the person directly lured away from by a seat on the circuit court? In addition, we provide information on the entire employment history of each nominee to the courts of appeals since 1977, to assess more fully the professional experiences and backgrounds being reflected on the bench.

With respect to the position held at the time of appointment to circuit court, in recent decades judges have come predominantly from one of two occupations: elevation from a US district court position, or private practice. Over the last fifty years, more than half of all circuit court judges have come directly out of one of these two positions. In the decades leading up to Carter's election in 1976, however, appointing judges out of the public sector (including elevating sitting judges) had become trendier, with the consequence being that fewer people were coming to the bench out of private practice, by the 1970s.

Going back more than fifty years, why did the president start looking to elevate district court judges at numbers that rival or at times surpass the numbers of those being appointed out of the private sector, compared to earlier in our history? Nominating a sitting district court judge to the circuit court has some advantages. District court judges have already survived the vetting associated with the appointment process previously, and they have a legal track record that can be evaluated, perhaps to assure the president that the judge shares the president's preferred approach to judicial decision-making. In addition, Chief Justices William Rehnquist and John Roberts both fretted publicly that relatively modest judicial salaries, coupled with an uncertain and contentious appointment process, may be depressing interest in seeking a federal judgeship from those in private practice. According to Roberts, these long-term trends matter, because "[i]t changes the nature of the federal judiciary when judges are no longer drawn primarily from among the best lawyers in the practicing bar."[10]

As readers may note from Table 6.1, relatively fewer judges have come directly to the circuit court from positions other than elevation from the district court or from private practice. That includes appointing circuit court judges from a "nonprimary" federal seat (such as a position as a federal magistrate), a state judiciary, a position with the US Department of Justice, or legal academia.

With respect to our most recent president, a plurality of Biden's appointees were appointed directly from the district courts, but he appointed the lowest percentage of judges out of private practice of any president in at least the last fifty years. Instead, more than 20 percent of Biden's circuit judges came from "other" professional backgrounds.

What were these other occupations? One answer may be found by way of our data measuring the full employment history of each president's appointees over time, including data on those who worked at some point in their career as a public defender or in legal aid. Until recently, very few circuit court judges had any experience as public defenders, let alone be so immersed in that world that they would have been appointed to the bench immediately from a public defense or legal aid position. This began to change during the Obama administration. Recall that even before being inaugurated as president, Joe Biden signaled to Senate Democrats that his approach to diversifying the federal judiciary included expanding the professional backgrounds of his nominees, including by appointing more people with public defense and legal aid experience.

With respect to the overall professional experience brought to the circuit courts, roughly 28 percent of Biden's judges had experience in public defense or legal aid. This is a remarkable increase over even Obama's 12.5 percent with that experience, let alone compared to the other presidents under consideration. In some cases, the public defense experience of Biden's appointees was particularly extensive. Judge Eunice Lee, for example, worked with the Office of the Appellate Defender in New York City for more than two decades prior to her appointment to the Second Circuit Court of Appeals in 2021. Similarly, Judge Lara Montecalvo spent nearly her entire career with the Rhode Island Public Defender's Office, prior to her appointment to the First Circuit Court of Appeals in 2022.

This is as opposed to the appointment of judges with prosecutorial experience, either through the US Department of Justice (DOJ) or at the state level, backgrounds that have long been prevalent at all levels of the federal judiciary.

Although Biden's emphasis on appointing people with experience as public defenders is noticeable and intentional, in other ways, the professional background of his judges is more similar than different to what we've seen from other recent presidential appointees. For example, Biden's circuit judges have similar experience with the US Department of Justice or as state prosecutors to the circuit judges appointed by many recent presidents. In addition, nearly one-quarter of his judges have some background as a state court judge, in line with other presidents.

Lastly, Biden, like Obama and Trump before him, appointed more judges to the courts of appeals with clerkship experience. Some lower federal or state-level clerkship experience seems to have become the new normal for circuit court judges, at least since the Obama years. However, one interesting difference is that Biden has slowed the recent trend toward seeing more circuit judges with Supreme Court clerkships in their backgrounds. This prestige marker had been creeping up on the courts of appeals since Carter, with fully 37 percent of Trump's judges previously working as Supreme Court clerks. Only 12 percent of Biden's judges clerked with a Supreme Court justice—the lowest percent since the cohort appointed by President George H. W. Bush.

District Court Judges

The data on district court judges provided in Table 6.2 show that in some ways, judges appointed to this level of the judiciary have similar informal norms expected of them when compared to their counterparts on the courts of appeals. In other ways, though, the district courts draw from a different and broader pool of potential nominees than is the case for seats on the higher courts.

TABLE 6.2 ■ Background Characteristics of Presidents' District Court Judges, Carter through Biden

	Carter	Reagan	H. W. Bush	Clinton	W. Bush	Obama	Trump	Biden
Race/Ethnicity								
White, non-Latino	78.7%	92.4%	89.2%	74.4%	82.4%	63.8%	83.9%	41.7%
Minority	21.3	7.6	10.8	25.6	17.6	36.2	16.1	58.3
Gender								
Male	85.6	92.4	80.4	71.1	79.3	58.6	78.7	37.4
Female	14.4	7.6	19.6	28.9	20.7	41.4	21.3	62.6
Non-Latino White male	67.8	85.5	73.0	51.5	67.8	38.1	67.8	13.9
Mean age at appointment	50.1 yrs	49.2yrs	48.8 yrs	50.2 yrs	50.8 yrs	51.7 yrs	50.1 yrs	49.8 yrs
Law School Education								
Harvard/Yale	12.9%	9.7%	8.1%	15.1%	6.1%	17.2%	10.3%	17.1%
Ivy/elite[a]	22.3	20.3	23.6	25.9	14.9	30.2	19.5	29.4
Other	77.7	79.7	76.4	74.1	85.1	69.8	80.5	70.6
Job at Appointment								
Private practice	48.0%	48.3%	45.3%	39.0%	36.0%	36.6%	39.7%	20.3%
Nonprimary federal court	7.9	6.2	12.2	14.1	16.9	16.8	13.2	28.3
State/local judiciary	37.1	30.7	31.1	33.7	30.7	26.9	23.6	26.7
Academia	2.5	2.4	0.7	1.3	1.2	0.8	1.2	1.1
US DOJ	0.5	8.3	8.8	5.9	12.3	10.1	10.9	11.8
Other	4.0	4.1	2.0	5.9	3.1	9.0	11.5	11.8

(Continued)

TABLE 6.2 ■ Background Characteristics of Presidents' District Court Judges, Carter through Biden (*Continued*)

	Carter	Reagan	H. W. Bush	Clinton	W. Bush	Obama	Trump	Biden
All Previous Employment								
Private practice	94.1	94.1	90.5	89.5	86.6	88.8	91.4	85.0%
Mean years in private practice[b]	16.4 yrs	15.8 yrs	15.1 yrs	14.5 yrs	16.1 yrs	14.0 yrs	13.3 yrs	10.4 yrs
Nonprimary federal court	4.5%	5.5%	12.2%	12.5%	16.9%	17.5%	14.4%	27.3%
State/local judiciary	42.1	39.3	39.2	39.0	36.0	30.1	25.9	27.3
US DOJ	17.3	23.8	27.0	23.6	31.8	38.4	36.8	41.2
State prosecutor	35.1	31.4	27.7	32.8	30.3	25.4	28.2	15.0
Public defender/Legal aid	3.5	5.2	4.1	17.0	5.7	15.7	2.9	24.1
SCOTUS clerkship	3.0	0.3	1.4	1.6	2.7	4.1	5.7	2.7
Other clerkship	18.3	19.3	27.0	29.8	33.7	46.6	56.9	57.8
Military	64.9	53.1	39.9	16.1	16.9	6.3	10.9	3.7
Total no. of appointees	202	290	148	305	261	268	174	187

[a]This category includes all judges who went to an Ivy League law school (Harvard, Yale, Columbia, Cornell, and Pennsylvania), plus judges who earned their degree from UC-Berkeley, Chicago, Michigan, or Stanford.

[b]Calculated only for those who previously worked in private practice, excluding those who did not.

Source: Data collected by Lisa M. Holmes, with assistance from Meredith Gensch (UVM '16), Isaac Salem (UVM '20), and Robin Olsen (UVM '26), from the Federal Judicial Center and the Library of Congress. We exclude judges on specialized or territorial courts in this analysis.

For example, similar trends across political party and over time are seen with respect to the racial, ethnic, and gender diversity of district court judges as we saw previously for the appeals court cohort. Democrats appoint a more diverse set of judges to the district courts than do Republican presidents. Among the Republican presidents, diversity had been increasing over time, although once again, the racial and ethnic diversity of Trump's appointees was lower than that of the previous Republican president, George W. Bush. With respect to average age, district court judges tend to be a little younger when they are appointed than court of appeals judges, aside from the Trump and Biden cohorts, whose court of appeals judges were younger, on average.

Biden once again surpassed every president in US history, in terms of the racial, ethnic, and gender diversity of his district court appointees. Here again, Biden executed on his promise of appointing a more diverse judiciary. Roughly 86 percent of his nominees to the district courts were women, people of color, or both, and only about 14 percent of his district court judges have been White, non-Latino men.

With respect to educational background, substantial majorities of district court judges across each presidential administration were trained outside the Ivy League or most elite law schools. Although earning a law degree from an elite institution is increasingly expected of court of appeals nominees and (especially) Supreme Court justices, a broader educational pipeline remains available for seats on the district courts.

Similarly, experience as a Supreme Court clerk remains rare among district court judges, even today. As with legal education, the most exclusive professional markers, in the form of a Supreme Court clerkship, remain absent for most of those currently serving on the federal district courts. The percentage of those with non–Supreme Court clerkships in their background, on the other hand, has been growing. A majority of all Biden and Trump district court judges have experience as clerks at the lower federal or state level (or both).

On the question of professional experience, as with the circuit courts, over 24 percent of Biden's district judges have experience as public defenders or in legal aid—a higher number than for any previous president. Although some experience in public defense work has been more prevalent on the district courts than on the appellate courts since the 1990s, especially when Democratic presidents are doing the nominating.

Final Considerations on Judge Background

What should we make of the data concerning appointees to the federal bench in recent decades? One conclusion to be drawn here is that the informal norms dictating who is considered most readily "qualified" to be on the federal bench differ across the various levels of the federal judiciary, at least to some extent. The most obvious markers of "prestige," such as an Ivy League pedigree or a Supreme Court clerkship, remain less prevalent on the lower rungs of the judicial hierarchy. That said, across the most recent presidential administrations, these prestige markers are growing in their presence, particularly on the courts of appeals. Presidents of both parties appear to be increasingly interested in nominating judges with such obvious markers of prestige to those positions.

Another conclusion is that increased diversity is here to stay, although there is a widening partisan gap in how diversity is prioritized in the appointment process. At the end of his first term in office, President Trump left the federal judiciary less diverse (in terms of race, ethnicity, and gender) than he inherited it, demonstrating that some of these gains can be lost.[11] Even so, starting with President Carter in the 1970s, presidents of both parties have typically looked to appoint more women and people of color to the courts, at all levels, even though much more intensive commitment to diversity of these forms has come from Democrats.

President Biden has demonstrated a particularly strong commitment to diversity, not only in terms of race, ethnicity, and gender, but as well to factors including religion and sexual orientation, and as well to professional background. In particular, the appointment of such a large cohort of judges with extensive backgrounds in public defense and legal aid work will give scholars a lot to study in the coming years, in terms of how increased professional diversity on the bench may affect how those judges make decisions, compared to their colleagues with more traditional experience as prosecutors or from elite private practice.[12]

Finally, although we have so far given a lot of attention to presidents and have characterized judges by cohort based on the identity of the appointing president, it is important to keep in mind that other actors are involved in this process, and some of those actors may serve to constrain rather than empower a president's ambitions with respect to the judiciary. Given their role in confirming federal judges, the Senate serves as a particularly critical consideration in terms of who sits on the federal bench. We now continue our analysis by moving on to discuss in more detail the process by which federal judges are selected.

THE FEDERAL SELECTION PROCESS AND ITS PARTICIPANTS

The skeletal selection framework is the same for all federal judges, although the roles of the participants vary depending on the level of the US judiciary. All nominations are made by the president after due consultation with the White House staff, the attorney general's office, and certain senators. Furthermore, the FBI customarily performs a routine security check. Various interest groups that believe they have a stake in the appointment may lobby for or against a candidate. The candidate's qualifications will be evaluated by a committee of the American Bar Association (ABA). The candidate's name is sent to the Senate Judiciary Committee, which conducts a separate investigation of the nominee's fitness for the post. If the committee's vote is favorable, the nomination is sent to the floor of the Senate, where it is either approved or rejected by a vote of the full Senate. Within that skeletal framework, however, lies the opportunity for a good deal of variation in approach and politicization.

The President

Even with the attention we have already given to the president's role in nominating federal judges, a few added comments are warranted. Technically, the chief executive nominates all judicial candidates, but history has shown that the president manifests greater personal involvement in appointments to the Supreme Court than to the lower courts. There are two major reasons for this. First, Supreme Court appointments are regarded by the president—and by the public at large—as generally more important and politically significant than openings on the lower tribunals. Second, presidents are less likely to devote much attention to lower court appointments because tradition has enabled individual senators to influence and often dominate such activity. Historically, the practice known as **senatorial courtesy** has been a major restriction on the president's capacity to appoint district judges. This unwritten rule of the game has the following condition: senators of the president's political party who object to a candidate whom the president wishes to appoint to a district judgeship in their home state have a virtual veto over the nomination.

Based on the US Constitution's Recess Appointments Clause, the president also has authority "to fill up all Vacancies that may happen during the recess of the Senate, by granting Commissions which shall expire at the End of their next Session."[13] One reason why a chief executive may wish to make a **recess appointment** is to fill a judicial vacancy on a court that has a large backlog of business. The other reason is more political. A president may find it easier to secure confirmation for a sitting judge than for a candidate named while the Senate is in session. Of the 308 judicial recess appointments made since 1789, some 88 percent were successfully confirmed to the bench.[14]

Once a viable avenue for placing a judge on the federal judiciary, the recess power has been severely limited in recent years, due to political controversy surrounding its use and particularly in the wake of the Supreme Court decision in *NLRB v. Canning* in 2014. Keep in mind that this power only comes into play when the Senate is in recess, which begs the question of what does it mean for the Senate to be "in recess"? On its face, it may seem obvious when the Senate is or is not in session. However, over time, partisan gamesmanship in the Senate had gotten to the power where one party in the Senate would hold "pro forma" sessions over breaks in order to prevent a president from the other party from taking advantage of a recess to exercise the unilateral power to make appointments to the judiciary or other executive positions requiring Senate confirmation.

The US Supreme Court ruled in 2014 that short three-day intrasession breaks in the Senate's calendar were not sufficient to trigger the president's recess appointment power under the Constitution.[15] The Court also ruled that during longer breaks, the Senate's power to hold "pro forma" sessions, where they are technically in session but no business is being conducted and most senators are nowhere near Washington, DC, further limited the president's use of the recess power. Already, the use of recess appointments had become contentious and rare (it was last used to appoint a federal judge in 2004); 2014's *Canning* decision was a further limitation to a president's ability to place judges on the bench as recess appointments.

The Department of Justice

Assisting the president and the White House staff in the judicial selection process are key presidential appointees in the Department of Justice (DOJ), including the attorney general of the United States and the deputy attorney general. Their primary job is to seek out candidates who conform to general criteria set by the president. Once several names are obtained, the staff of the Justice Department will subject each candidate to further scrutiny. They may order an FBI investigation of the candidate's character and background; they will usually read copies of all articles or speeches the candidate has written or evaluate a sitting judge's written opinions; and they might check with local party leaders to determine that the candidate is a party faithful and is in tune with the president's major public policy positions.

In the case of district judge appointments, where names are often submitted by home state senators, the Justice Department's function is more as a screener than as an initiator. Regardless of who comes up with a basic list of names, the Justice Department's primary duty is to evaluate the candidate's personal, professional, and political qualifications. In performing this role, the department may work closely with the White House staff, with the senators involved in the nomination, and with party leaders who may wish to have some input in the choice of the potential nominee.

Research by noted scholar Sheldon Goldman, an expert on judicial appointment politics, highlights those tensions that have arisen over the years between the White House and the Justice Department. Goldman notes that Carter and Reagan ushered in a period where White House staff have taken on more influence over the nominee selection process, often at the expense of those in the DOJ.[16]

Interest Groups

Interest groups in the United States, representing the whole political spectrum from left to right, often lobby either for or against judicial nominations, particularly to the Supreme Court. Leaders of interested groups have little hesitation about urging the president to withdraw the nomination of someone whose political and social values are different from their own or about lobbying the Senate to support the nomination of someone who is favorably perceived. As noted in a study by Gregory A. Caldeira and John R. Wright,

> The participation of organized interests in judicial nominations in recent years extends well beyond the highly visible cases of [Robert H.] Bork, [David H.] Souter, and [Clarence] Thomas. Although these cases have obvious significance for cases reaching the Supreme Court, nominations for federal district judgeships, circuit judgeships, and other appointed positions in the executive branch that are subject to senatorial confirmation also have important implications for organized interests.[17]

Interest groups also play a role in the appointment process for lower federal court judges, and this influence has increased in recent years. According to an important book on the topic by political scientist Nancy Scherer, presidents respond to interest group attention to lower courts by forwarding nominees who pass a particular ideological litmus test or who appeal to groups interested in diversity and affirmative action.[18] With respect to the Senate's role in confirming judges, Scherer co-authored a follow-up study in 2008, concluding that while most lower court nominations are "rubber-stamped" by the Senate, occasionally interest groups may sound a fire alarm of sorts for a nominee, especially for those to the courts of appeals, whom they find particularly objectionable. The study noted that:

> once opposition to a nomination is voiced by interest groups, the political salience of this confirmation proceeding is now raised to a new level. Senators aligned with the opposing groups are now forced to consider this nomination or else face the wrath of interest groups come election time. Thus, opposed nominations will likely face a contentious and lengthy confirmation process. In many instances . . . it may mean the nomination is blocked completely and therefore will never make it to the floor for a vote.[19]

Interest groups are still more involved in the selection process for those at the appellate levels of the federal judiciary, and especially the Supreme Court, but when they do get involved and voice opposition to particular district court nominees, like-minded senators tend to make note and act accordingly.

Although many groups attempt to influence the appointment process, we now turn our attention to the two of the most significant: the American Bar Association (ABA) and the Federalist Society.

The American Bar Association

The ABA's unique role in the judicial appointment process began in 1946 with the creation of the ABA Standing Committee on Federal Judiciary, intended to evaluate the suitability of nominees to the federal courts.[20] The committee, whose fifteen members represent all the US circuits, evaluates candidates based on numerous criteria, including judicial temperament, age, trial experience, character, and intelligence. Each committee member rates the candidate as being "well qualified," "qualified," or "not qualified," meaning that some candidates may receive mixed ratings from the committee as a whole.

In 1956, President Dwight D. Eisenhower began the practice of having the ABA's evaluation of judicial candidates forwarded to the president for consideration prior to the president's selection of a nominee.[21] Thus began the decades-long period of the ABA having a unique and influential role in how judges are selected in the United States.

The traditional composition of the ABA committee has made it the subject of some controversy, in terms of its lack of professional and demographic diversity and in terms of whether committee members engage in ideological or partisan bias in their evaluative process. The committee's role in the appointment process is important because of the assumption, supported by scholarly studies, that a nominee with a low ABA rating is less likely to be confirmed by the Senate. Thus, bucking the recommendations of the committee is a risky business, and presidents infrequently nominate candidates tagged as being not qualified.[22]

In terms of the demographic and professional composition of the committee, one classic analysis by political scientist Elliot Slotnick of the ABA's role in the appointment process noted that "the committee has not enjoyed a good reputation among those concerned with increasing the ranks for the underrepresented on the federal bench."[23] Slotnick's subsequent analysis of nominees forwarded by President Carter in 1979 and 1980 found that White men were indeed rated more favorably than were women or minorities.[24] The ABA ratings favored nominees with more experience, meaning that the ABA favored "traditional candidates" with experience that was not as readily available to women and minorities fifty years ago.[25] This kind of exclusive view of what it means to be "qualified" for a judicial post hindered Carter's ability to diversify the bench while maintaining his other central commitment to appointing judges based on merit.

A few more recent studies have found continued evidence of troubling bias in the ABA rating system. Although the professional backgrounds of female and minority nominees have become more like those of White male nominees over time, ABA ratings for female and especially minority nominees lag behind those of their White, male counterparts.[26]

The other criticism of the ABA's role in the appointment process comes from those who argue that the ABA's committee members are **liberal** and therefore rate **conservative** nominees forwarded by Republican presidents less favorably. Ideological or partisan bias in the ABA rating process has been the focus of recent scholarly work, with somewhat mixed results. Although one study found no evidence that the ABA disfavored conservative or Republican nominees, another found evidence that higher ratings were given to nominees forwarded by Democratic presidents.[27] Still another study determined that partisan bias was only found when rating nominees to the courts of appeals and not for nominees to the district courts, most likely because of the greater policymaking role of judges on the courts of appeals.[28]

In March 2001, President George W. Bush's administration announced an end to the long-held practice of letting the ABA evaluate judicial candidates before they are nominated. In a letter to the ABA, White House counsel Alberto Gonzales said it was unfair to give the organization such a significant role in the judicial selection process, particularly because it takes stands on issues under litigation. Although President Obama reinstated the ABA's role in evaluating candidates prior to their nomination,

President Trump followed W. Bush's lead on expelling the ABA from the nominee vetting process. Upon taking office, President Biden announced that he would retain the Trump and W. Bush approach of not sending the names of potential candidates to the ABA until the nominee's name was forwarded to the Senate, to expedite the appointment process.[29] This perhaps signals a permanent end to the ABA's formalized role in the nominee selection process. The ABA still conducts an evaluation of every nominee, but only once the final choice for the seat has been selected by the president.

The Federalist Society

As noted, recent Republican presidents have been unwilling to submit the names of their potential nominees to the ABA. One group that has instead come into great prominence during Republican administrations is the Federalist Society for Law and Public Policy Studies. Founded in 1982 by conservative and libertarian law students at Yale and the University of Chicago, the Federalist Society was established to provide an alternative to the perceived liberal bend of the law school and legal culture at the time.[30] According to a 2015 study by Amanda Hollis-Brusky on the influence of the Federalist Society on legal culture in the United States, members now carry their shared beliefs and ideas in their professional capacities as academics, law clerks, and judges.[31]

When President George W. Bush removed the ABA from the prenominating stages of the judicial selection process, the Federalist Society was seen as filling that void, but with an "even more central judgemaking role than had ever been attributed to the ABA."[32] During the W. Bush administration, however, the Society's role was not particularly formalized; rather, Federalist Society members' informal networking skills were called to action in "essentially run[ning] large parts of the process in key positions in the White House and the White House Counsel's Office."[33] What is clear is that during the W. Bush administration, membership in the Federalist Society was one way in which a person seeking a federal judgeship could identify themselves as sharing the judicial philosophy that President Bush was looking for in a nominee.[34]

During the Trump administration, the Federalist Society's role went from somewhat informal to central and formalized. During the 2016 presidential campaign, Donald McGahn (a Federalist Society member), in his capacity as Trump's top campaign lawyer and future White House Counsel, proceeded with the idea to release a shortlist of possible replacements for deceased Justice Antonin Scalia[35] (Scalia died unexpectedly while on a hunting vacation on February 13, 2016). Leonard Leo, executive vice president of the Federalist Society, met with McGahn and Trump in March 2016 to discuss the possibility of filling Scalia's seat. Soon thereafter, in an interview with a *Breitbart*-hosted radio show, then-candidate Trump stated, "We're going to have great judges, conservative, all picked by the Federalist Society."[36]

Leo, who founded the Society's chapter at Cornell Law School in 1989, took a leave of absence from his position with the Federalist Society to advise President Trump on judicial appointments.[37] In actuality, "advise" is likely too soft a word to describe Leo's role in the judicial selection process under President Trump. As promised during the campaign, President Trump largely delegated the judicial selection process to Leo, not only in selecting the three justices Trump was able to appoint to the Supreme Court in his first term, but for appointments to the lower courts as well. This outsourcing of much of the work involved in identifying and vetting potential nominees likely contributed to the efficiency with which President Trump handled judicial appointments during his presidency.

In return, Trump appointed judges affiliated with the Federalist Society to all levels of the judiciary, particularly the appellate courts. All six Republican-appointed justices currently on the Court (including the three appointed by Trump) have ties to the Federalist Society. A recent study found that over 88 percent of Trump's nominees to the circuit courts were Federalist Society members, as were over 45 percent of his district court nominees.[38] Once on the bench, judges affiliated with the Federalist Society vote more conservatively than do those not affiliated with the Federalist Society, including nonmembers appointed by Republican presidents.[39]

The Federalist Society has clearly become a major player in determining the composition of the federal courts, particularly when a Republican controls the presidency. The presence of judges associated with the Federalist Society at all levels of the judiciary has influenced the decisions being made by those courts.

Once a nominee has been selected by the president, the name is referred to the Senate. It is at that point that the confirmation part of the appointment process formally begins.

The Senate Judiciary Committee

The rules of the Senate require its Judiciary Committee to pass on all nominations to the federal bench and to make recommendations to the Senate as a whole. Its role is thus to screen individuals who have already been nominated, not to suggest possible candidates. The committee by custom holds hearings on all nominations, at which time nominees are questioned by committee members and witnesses may be heard.

The chair of the Senate Judiciary Committee plays an incredibly significant role in how confirmations are handled. Key to this is the blue slip policy adopted by the chair. The **blue slip** is the form that senators, most notably from the nominee's home state, use to express their views about the candidate.[40] Senatorial courtesy does not apply to appellate court appointments, although presidents customarily defer to senators of their party from states that make up the appellate court circuit. An unwritten rule is that each state in the circuit should have at least one judge on that circuit's appellate bench, a practice typically followed when the vacancy is that of a state's only representative on the circuit bench.

In recent decades, committee chairs (especially on the Republican side) have altered how much power they allow individual senators to have in unilaterally stopping forward movement on a nominee's confirmation, to benefit the chair's political party. Thus, during periods of divided government, when the chair and the president belong to opposing parties, the Judicial Committee chair may strengthen the power of the blue slip to allow a single senator to more readily obstruct a nominee. During periods of unified government, on the other hand, the chair might weaken the blue slip to prevent such obstruction.[41] During the Trump administration, the two Republicans who chaired the Judiciary Committee (Chuck Grassley, followed by Lindsey Graham) maintained the power of the blue slip for district court judges, but refused to allow home state Democrats to halt the progress on nominations to the courts of appeals.

Soon after Biden's inauguration, chair Dick Durbin (D-IL) announced that he would follow the recent Republican lead, preventing recalcitrant Republican senators from unilaterally obstructing home state nominees to the circuit courts, while indicating that his intention was to allow blue slips to be used in the traditional way to prevent movement on district court nominees deemed unsatisfactory to the home state's senators.[42] Durbin retained this approach throughout the Biden presidency, even in the face of pressure from liberal groups that retaining this blue slip policy allowed Republican home state senators to obstruct appointments to the district courts. In 2023, for example, the nomination of William Pocan to serve on the District Court for the Eastern District of Wisconsin failed, after Republican home state senator Ron Johnson flipped from supportive to opposed to Pocan's appointment. Durbin expressed disappointment at Johnson's decision, but did not move forward to confirm Pocan, who would have become the first openly LGBTQ federal judge in Wisconsin.[43]

Race, Gender, and Confirmation Hearings

As noted, a key hurdle for every successful federal court nomination is the confirmation hearing before members of the Senate Judiciary Committee. In recent decades, how the hearing proceeds is often determined by two factors: the court level being filled and whether the nomination has been deemed controversial, often due to interest group opposition.

Confirmation hearings for district court nominations have been and remain largely perfunctory, low-stakes affairs.[44] For circuit court nominees targeted as controversial by interested groups, and for all Supreme Court nominees, the hearings become more personal and the vetting of the nominee is heightened.[45]

A major new study has added a third factor for consideration with respect to the tone and content of a confirmation hearing.[46] Christina L. Boyd, Paul M. Collins Jr., and Lori A. Ringhand analyzed the role of gender and race in Supreme Court confirmation hearings, finding that women and people of color are subjected to a nastier and more grueling experience in front of the Judiciary Committee, particularly when being questioned by senators of the other political party. Compared to their White and male counterparts, women and nominees of color face more extensive questioning, are asked more questions related to their competence, are more frequently interrupted, and receive more negative questions. (Interruptions are a relevant measure of potential hostility and disrespect toward a speaker because they are "closely linked with dominance, control, power, and status" that seize and build on the power of the interrupter by placing the interrupter in a dominant position relative to the one being interrupted.[47])

In addition, women and nominees of color may also be asked more questions that demonstrate subject matter stereotyping, in that women nominees are asked more questions than their male counterparts about issues (such as abortion or gender discrimination) stereotyped as being of more relevance to women. This study's authors also found evidence that Supreme Court nominees of color are asked more questions about racial discrimination and crime, compared to their White counterparts. Keep in mind that this research posits that the connection being expressed by the senators (typically of the opposing party) asking these questions points to an implicit bias in not only connecting an issue like crime to members of a particular racial group, but that a nominee who is a member of that racial group is being called to account on the issue of crime in a way that White nominees are not.

This study focused only on confirmation hearings for Supreme Court nominees, and no research has yet been published on whether findings related to the role race and gender play in contemporary Supreme Court confirmation hearings are generalizable to lower court hearings, which are typically less fraught, unless the nominee has been deemed controversial. As well, interesting and important questions remain as to whether and how nominees from other traditionally marginalized groups (based on such factors as religion, sexual orientation, or gender identity) or nominees with atypical professional experience (as a public defender, for example) may be treated differently in their confirmation hearings.

Even so, it is not difficult to identify examples of similar kinds of questioning for lower court nominees, particularly those from one or more underrepresented groups. For example, in 2023, President Biden nominated Adeel Abdullah Mangi to a position on the US Court of Appeals for the Third Circuit.[48] If confirmed, Mangi (a Harvard-educated Partner at the law firm Patterson Belknap) would have become the first Muslim American to serve on a federal appellate court, and only the third Muslim ever to serve on the federal judiciary at all. After Mangi's December 2023 hearing, the White House responded by calling out Republican Senators Ted Cruz, Josh Hawley, and Tom Cotton in particular for what the Biden administration referred to as their "cruel and Islamophobic" treatment of Mangi.[49]

At Mangi's hearing, held two months after the Hamas-led attack in Israel, Mangi was asked repeatedly about his views on the October 7 attack and its aftermath. Mangi was also questioned aggressively by Republicans about his involvement on an advisory panel to the Center for Security, Race, and Rights at Rutgers University, which had held an event featuring a controversial speaker on the twentieth anniversary of the September 11 terrorist attacks.

In response to Senator Cruz's questions about the Rutgers event, for example, Mangi asserted that he "never heard of this event prior to today—it was never brought to the advisory board, which met once a year to talk about academic issues," before being interrupted by Cruz. Soon thereafter, Committee Chair Durbin intervened, culminating in a back-and-forth between Durbin and Cruz during which Durbin advised Cruz that he "should not bully the witnesses, nor try to bully members of the committee."

Cruz responded by talking over Durbin's gavel and accusing the chair of intervening to "save" a Democratic nominee from questioning, before pushing Mangi again to condemn the Rutgers event "that was celebrating Islamic Jihad." Once given the opportunity to complete his response, Mangi closed out this line of questioning by Cruz by stating calmly that "I don't know anything about this event, or who these people are. I've never heard of any of them. If someone [at the Rutgers event] is a terrorist, I'd condemn them."

Although most nominees who go as far as the hearing part of the confirmation process are confirmed, in Mangi's case, the damage had been done. With no Republicans supporting Mangi's confirmation, and even a few Democratic senators expressing reservations, Mangi's nomination to the circuit court was ultimately unsuccessful.

Given the emphasis on expanding the experiences and identities represented on the federal courts in recent years, and by President Biden in particular, there is no shortage of new data to parse over, in the form of confirmation hearing transcripts. We expect to see new research on the questioning of lower court nominees in their confirmation hearings in the coming years.

The Senate

The ultimate step in the judicial appointment process for federal judges is a vote by the Senate. The Constitution states that the Senate must give its "advice and consent" to judicial nominations made by the president. Historically, for district and appeals court judges, once a nominee has been favorably voted on by the Senate Judiciary Committee, a confirmation vote in the full Senate happened quickly, often within a single day.[50] However, in recent years, Senate leadership has used its ability to schedule floor votes to further delay nominee confirmation, particularly in response to interest group opposition to a nominee.[51] Even so, for lower court appointments, most nominees that fail to be confirmed tend to do so at the hands of the Senate Judiciary Committee, whose chair simply refuses to hold a hearing or report the nomination to the full Senate.[52] Even today, most nominees that survive the committee hearing are confirmed by the full Senate, although voice votes are becoming increasingly unusual, and those with recorded votes are seeing more "Nay" votes cast against them.

The Filibuster and the "Nuclear Option"

One critical aspect of Senate procedure that we have not yet addressed is the relevance of the filibuster to Senate confirmation of federal judges. Historically, the confirmation process was subject to the same filibuster rules that applied to Senate procedure more generally. Beginning in 1917, then, a filibuster on a judicial nomination could be ended with a cloture vote that met the two-thirds majority requirement. Starting in 1975, when the Senate reduced the number of votes required for cloture to three-fifths (or 60 of the 100 senators), that rule applied as well for confirmation votes. As confirmation proceedings for circuit and even district court judges began to become increasingly contentious in the 1990s and 2000s, the filibuster and its place in the judicial appointment process began to be called into question. Unsurprisingly, the use of the filibuster became particularly vexing to presidents during periods of unified government, when their own party controlled the Senate, leaving the senators in the opposing party with the filibuster as their most powerful tool of obstruction.

During the final year of George W. Bush's first term as president, Senate Democrats were successful in blocking several of the president's appeals court nominations using the filibuster. President Bush retaliated by using recess appointments, which infuriated Democrats. (Recall that no president since W. Bush has used the recess power to appoint a judge.) Tensions eased when a deal of sorts was cut, whereby the president agreed to make no more recess appointments for the remainder of his first term, which ended on January 20, 2005. "In return, Democrats, who had been holding up action on all of Bush's judicial choices . . . protesting the recess appointments, agreed to allow votes on 25 mostly noncontroversial nominations to district and appeals posts over the next several weeks."[53]

This partisan détente largely held throughout the remainder of the Bush presidency. During the Obama presidency, however, the filibuster problem resurfaced vigorously, with the use of the filibuster by Senate Republicans increasing to unprecedented levels.[54] Democratic Senate leaders responded by invoking the so-called "nuclear option" on November 21, 2013. The nuclear option reformed filibuster protocol by allowing cloture (thus ending a filibuster) with a simple majority vote rather than the previous sixty-vote supermajority.[55] This reform applied to executive and judicial nominations, except for appointments to the Supreme Court. The response from Senate Republicans was strongly negative. Then–Minority Leader Mitch McConnell (R-KY) noted that Democrats would "regret" the nuclear option vote, possibly "a lot sooner than [they] think."[56]

The effect of the nuclear option on the treatment of Obama's lower court nominees was striking. Elliot Slotnick, Sheldon Goldman, and Sara Schiavoni, longtime scholars of judicial appointment politics, noted that because of the nuclear option, the confirmation rate for Obama's circuit court nominees was the highest in nearly twenty-five years.[57] However, Senator McConnell's predication that Democrats may regret the decision to enact the nuclear option would also prove relevant. Upon taking over as majority leader in 2015, after Republicans regained Senate control in the 2014 midterms, McConnell brought confirmations of Obama's nominees to a near halt, especially with respect to the courts of appeals and to Obama's nomination of Merrick Garland to replace Antonin Scalia on the Supreme Court.

Then, in 2017, at the dawn of the Trump presidency, the Republican-controlled Senate not only kept the nuclear option for lower court confirmations, but extended it to include Supreme Court confirmations, starting with President Trump's nomination of Neil Gorsuch and continuing with his nomination of Kavanaugh to replace Justice Anthony Kennedy and Barrett to replace Justice Ginsburg. Enjoying same-party control of the Senate in the post–nuclear option world was critical to President Trump's success in appointing so many judges to all levels of the federal judiciary.

Of course, President Biden, whose party was tenuously in control of the Senate throughout his four years in office, was also unconstrained by the filibuster, because Senate Democrats retained the simple majority threshold to end a filibuster on judicial appointments. We now appear to have a new normal with respect to judicial confirmation procedure: the filibuster no longer serves as a robust tool of obstruction by those in the minority party in the Senate. With a simple majority required to confirm any federal judge, nominees can be confirmed by a straight party-line vote when the president's party controls the chamber. This confirmation norm now applies to all levels of the judiciary, including the Supreme Court.

Upon receiving their commission (the official document empowering the individual to assume judicial office), a judge joins the bench. This period of professional transition is the focus for the next part of our analysis.

THE JUDICIAL SOCIALIZATION PROCESS

When scholars use the term **socialization**, they are referring to the process whereby individuals acquire the values, attitudes, and behavior patterns of the existing social system. Factors that aid the process include family, friends, education, coworkers, religious training, political party affiliation, and the media. Social scientists also apply the term *socialization* to the process by which a person is formally trained to perform the specific tasks of a particular profession.

Much significant socialization occurs before judges first mount the bench. From their parents, teachers, exposure to the news media, and so on, future judges learn the rules of the American political game. That is, by the time they are teenagers they have absorbed key values and attitudes that will circumscribe subsequent judicial behavior, such as the idea that judges ought to be fair and impartial or that the rights of political minorities should be protected. In college and law school, future judges acquire important analytical and communication skills, in addition to the basic substance of the law. After years of legal practice, the preparation for a judgeship is in its final stage. The future judge has learned a good deal about how the courts and the law work and has specialized in several areas of the law. Despite all this preparation, sometimes called "anticipatory socialization," most new judges in America still have much to learn even after donning the black robe.[58]

Regardless of previous background, new district court judges are expected to be experts on all legal subjects, are required to engage in judicial duties usually unrelated to tasks they may have performed previously (for example, sentencing), and are given a host of administrative assignments for which they may have no prior experience (for example, learning how to manage their docket efficiently).[59] The following statements by US trial judges reveal what it was like for each of them as the new kid on the judicial block. (Virtually all the judges who were interviewed for this book were promised anonymity; therefore, no references will appear.)

> Before I became a federal judge, I had been a trial lawyer dealing mainly with personal injury cases and later with some divorce cases. I knew almost nothing about criminal law. With labor law, I had had only one case in my life on this subject, and that was a case going back to the early days of World War II. In other words, when I became a federal judge, I really had an awful lot to learn about many key areas of the law.

> My legal background and experience really didn't prepare me very well for the kind of major judicial problems I face. For instance, most lawyers don't deal with constitutional issues related to the Bill of Rights and the Fourteenth Amendment; rather, they deal with much more routine questions, such as wills and contracts. Civil liberties questions were new to me as a judge, and I think this is true for most new judges.

At the appeals court level, there is also a period of first-year socialization—despite the circuit judge's possible prior judicial experience—and former trial judges appear to make the transition with fewer scars. As a couple of appeals judges said of their first days on the circuit bench: "I was no blushing violet in fields I knew something about. How effective I was is another question." Even an experienced former trial judge recalled his surprise that "it takes a while to learn the job—and I'm not addressing myself to personal relationships. That's a vastly different job." Another appeals judge, regarded by his peers as a leader from the beginning, said, "I don't know how I got through my first year."[60] During the transition time (the period of learning the ropes of the appellate court), circuit judges tend to speak for the court less frequently than do their more experienced colleagues. They often take longer to write opinions and defer more often to senior colleagues.

Given the need on the part of all new federal jurists for both first year and broader occupational socialization, where do they go for instruction? Although there are many agents of socialization for novice judges, the evidence is strong that the older, more experienced judges have the primary responsibility for this task. As one trial judge said, "My prime sources of help were the two judges here in [this city]. They sent me various things even before I was appointed, and I was glad to get them." Another recalled, "I had the help I needed right down here in the corner of this building on this floor," pointing in the direction of another judge's chambers. One district judge gave a more graphic description of his "schooling":

> They [the other trial judges] let me sit next to them in actual courtroom situations, and they explained to me what they were doing at every minute. We both wore our robes and we sat next to each other on the bench. I would frequently ask them questions and they would explain things to me as the trial went along. Other times I would have a few free minutes and I would drop into another judge's courtroom and just sit and watch. I learned a lot that way.

Likewise on the Supreme Court, more senior colleagues play a primary part in passing on to newer colleagues the essential rules and values on which their work is based. For example, Justice Ruth Bader Ginsburg recalled that when she was first appointed to the Court, Justice Byron R. White (whose seat Ginsburg was filling) had given her a manual outlining her work. "A new justice could not have had a clearer, more sensible introduction to the ways of the court," she said, adding that she had kept the manual up to date and intended to pass it on to her successor.[61]

An interesting recent study brought a new perspective to the analysis of how interactions between judges as colleagues encourage certain professional behaviors.[62] Leveraging novel data on where circuit judges' offices are located, the authors knew which judges from a particular circuit worked in the same city and even in the same building. This allowed them to analyze whether being in closer contact with colleagues (and thus being more likely to see and interact with them regularly) influenced judicial behavior. Being in closer contact with circuit colleagues reinforced norms of collegiality, particularly among colleagues who were ideologically distant from each other. To give one example of how this influence was manifest, a judge was less likely to write an opinion dissenting from a majority opinion written by an ideological foe if those two judges worked in the same building together, compared to those who did not.

In another recent study, political scientist Allison Harris studied the sentencing decisions of trial judges in three different courthouses in the same circuit court, in and around Chicago. She found that as the percentage of Black judges in a courthouse increased, White judges were less likely to sentence Black defendants to prison. Being in the presence of Black judges in the workplace altered the behavior of their White colleagues.[63]

This recent scholarship provides some fascinating insight into how judges are influenced by working in closer proximity to their colleagues, thus contributing to further socialization deeper into a judicial career. But let us return briefly to the question of socializing new federal judges, which is a particularly relevant inquiry, given that new federal judges come from a variety of backgrounds, with some having served extensively on lower federal or state courts, and others having not served on any court previously. How might judicial socialization be hindered for novice judges who are isolated from their more experienced colleagues, geographically or otherwise (such as due to the COVID-19 pandemic)? Would judges in these scenarios require much more time to learn the fine points of their profession?

One scenario of this sort has perhaps been playing out recently at the Fort Pierce location of the Southern District of Florida. Judge Aileen M. Cannon is the sole judge assigned to Fort Pierce, a "small fishing and citrus community on the edge of the Southern District."[64] Judge Cannon has drawn national attention as the presiding judge in the criminal case against Donald Trump over his handling of classified documents. Quite apart from her handling of the Trump case, some local attorneys who frequent Judge Cannon's courtroom have criticized the inefficiency with which she runs the typically low-profile trials that come to her court, pointing to her lack of previous trial experience (as a judge or a lawyer) and the isolation of her particular courthouse as possible causes.[65]

Judicial socialization may be most relevant and consequential soon after appointment to a new position, particularly for those with less of the sort of previous experience that might be brought to bear in navigating the technical aspects of the job. Much of the time, more experienced colleagues may be called upon to help fill in some of the gaps, as is surely the case in other professional environments as well. In other cases, however, circumstances are such that the less experienced judge may have less access to that kind of nearby collegial support.

Aside from this brief attention to how judges enter the judiciary, we leave to other chapters the critical questions related to how judges do the job of judging. Instead, we now jump ahead to issues related to the lifetime tenure enjoyed by federal judges. After discussing available remedies related to judicial misconduct, we discuss the options available for older judges thinking about departing from their positions.

THE CONSEQUENCES OF LIFETIME TENURE

All federal judges appointed under the provisions of Article III of the Constitution hold office "during good Behavior," which means, in effect, for life or until they choose to step down. In this section, we address some very recent debates concerning the implications of the lifetime tenure afforded to federal judges. On this issue, the United States is a clear outlier on the world stage. The United States is the only democracy in the world where high court judges enjoy life tenure. All other established democracies subject their justices to either term limits or mandatory retirement ages, or both.[66]

First, we will address constitutional and statutory mechanisms available to respond to misconduct. Then, we focus on the decision-making calculus involved when a judge with tenure for life is ready to leave the bench. In both discussions, we focus attention on current concerns and reforms under consideration.

Disciplinary Action against Federal Judges

The only way Article III judges can be removed from the bench is by **impeachment** (indictment by the House of Representatives) and conviction by the Senate. In accordance with constitutional requirements (for Supreme Court justices) and legislative standards (for appeals and trial court judges), impeachment may occur for "Treason, Bribery, or other high Crimes and Misdemeanors." An impeached jurist would face trial in the Senate, which could convict by a vote of two-thirds of the members present.[67]

The impeachment of a federal judge is a rare but not unheard-of event. In 2010, Judge G. Thomas Porteous of the Eastern District of Louisiana (New Orleans) was convicted by the US Senate of impeachment proceedings that were previously brought by the US House of Representatives, and he was removed from office. He was recommended for impeachment after a criminal investigation showed that he had accepted cash and other items of value from lawyers and that he had falsified federal court documents in his personal bankruptcy proceedings.

Since 1789, fifteen judges have been impeached by the House of Representatives; eight were convicted after a trial in the Senate, which thereby removed them from office.[68] Four others were acquitted, and three resigned after being impeached by the House.

These numbers, however, do not include judges who leave the bench to avoid possible (even likely) impeachment and forcible removal. In May 2015, US District Court Judge Mark Fuller resigned his position on the federal bench rather than face possible impeachment.[69] Fuller was charged with misdemeanor battery in Atlanta after his wife called the police during an argument in August 2014. Fuller eventually entered a plea deal that required he have an alcohol and drug evaluation and undergo counseling for twenty-four weeks through a domestic violence program.[70]

Disciplinary Options beyond Impeachment

The fact that so few judges in US history have been impeached, and even fewer have been convicted, speaks to how onerous the constitutional requirements are, particularly given the supermajority (two-thirds) vote needed to convict in the Senate. Much of the problematic behavior engaged in more commonly by judges will not rise to the level of what is considered impeachable and convictable by members of Congress.

In an effort to address such situations, on October 1, 1980, a new statute took effect, on which Congress had labored for several years. Titled the Judicial Councils Reform and Judicial Conduct and Disability Act, the law has two distinct parts.[71] The first part authorizes the Judicial Council in each circuit, composed of both appeals and trial court judges and presided over by the chief judge of the circuit, to "make all necessary and appropriate orders for the effective and expeditious administration of justice within its circuit."

The second part of the act establishes a statutory complaint procedure against judges. Basically, it permits anyone to file a written complaint with the clerk of the appellate court. The chief judge then reviews the charge and may dismiss it if it relates directly to the merits of a judge's decision or procedural rule, appears to be frivolous, or for a variety of other reasons. If the complaint requires a finding of fact to resolve, the chief judge must appoint an investigating committee consisting of him- or herself and an equal number of trial and circuit court judges. After an inquiry, the committee reports to the council, which has several options: (1) the judge may be exonerated; (2) if the offender is a bankruptcy judge or magistrate, that person may be removed; and (3) an Article III judge may be subject to private or public reprimand or censure, certification of disability, request for voluntary resignation, or prohibition against further case assignments. However, removal of an Article III judge is not permitted; impeachment is still the only recourse. If the council determines that the conduct "might constitute" grounds for impeachment, it will notify the Judicial Conference, which in turn may transmit the case to the US House of Representatives for consideration. Note that these disciplinary proceedings only apply to lower court judges; the act does not cover Supreme Court justices.

Since the act went into effect, there has been no shortage of complaints. For example, in the twelve-month period ending on September 30, 2023, some 1,363 complaints were filed against judges, with another 900 cases still pending from the previous year. At 57 percent, most were filed against district judges, with another 20 percent against circuit judges, 19 percent against magistrates, and the remainder filed against bankruptcy or Court of Federal Claims judges. By the end of that fiscal year, 1,338 complaints had been terminated as final.[72] The vast majority of these (1,286) were dismissed in whole or in part due to frivolousness, lack of sufficient evidence, or because the complaint was improperly related to a judge's judicial decision.

With respect to judicial conduct proceedings, corrective action does not mean that the judge is removed from office or even that any real disciplinary action is taken against the errant jurist. It often means only, for example, that a judge is asked to apologize for something they had done, or that the judge is asked to resign from a board on which they should not have been serving. "Remedial action" includes things such as the censure of a judge, case assignment suspension, request for voluntary retirement or resignation, and certification of disability.

In July 2024, District Judge Joshua M. Kindred (appointed to the District Court in Alaska by President Trump) resigned after the Judicial Council of the Ninth Circuit publicly reprimanded and admonished Judge Kindred for violating canons that require judges to "act at all times in a manner that promotes public confidence in the integrity and impartiality of the judiciary."[73] Through multiple actions, including having a sexual relationship with a clerk and then lying about it multiple times during the investigation, Kindred had engaged in conduct that "might constitute one or more grounds for impeachment," resulting in a request by the Judicial Council that Kindred voluntarily resign.

A more complicated situation arose in 2018, after complaints were filed based on DC Court of Appeals Judge Brett Kavanaugh's statements and behavior during his Supreme Court confirmation hearings related to the sexual assault allegations leveled against him by Christine Blasey Ford. On October 6, 2018, DC Court of Appeals Judge Karen LeCraft Henderson issued a statement indicating that

> after the start of Judge Brett Kavanaugh's confirmation hearings, members of the public began filing complaints in the D.C. Circuit about statements made during those hearings. The complaints do not pertain to any conduct in which Judge Kavanaugh engaged as a judge. The complaints seek investigations only of the public statements he has made as a nominee to the Supreme Court of the United States.[74]

Although Merrick Garland was the DC Circuit's chief judge at the time and would therefore normally be expected to decide which complaints to dismiss or consider, he recused himself from this matter, presumably due to the blocking of his previous Supreme Court nomination by Senate Republicans in 2016.[75] Judge Henderson dismissed some of the complaints but concluded that more than a dozen were substantive enough to warrant further investigation.[76] At the request of the Judicial Council of the DC Circuit, Chief Justice John Roberts eventually transferred the judicial conduct proceedings against Kavanaugh to the Judicial Council of the Tenth Circuit.[77] On December 18, 2018, the Judicial Council of the Tenth Circuit determined that all complaints against Kavanaugh must be dismissed. Due to Kavanaugh's elevation to the Supreme Court, the judges concluded that the complaints against him were no longer appropriate for consideration under the statute.

The Supreme Court and Judicial Ethics Reform

The ethics complaints filed against Judge-turned-Justice Kavanaugh proved to be only the tip of the iceberg, so far as recent ethics concerns against members of the Supreme Court are concerned. In 2023, *ProPublica* released an investigative report on the previously undisclosed relationship between Supreme Court Justice Clarence Thomas and billionaire Harlan Crow.[78] The details and regularity of the "luxury trips" Thomas took "virtually every year" over more than twenty years were deemed to have "no known precedent in the modern history of the U.S. Supreme Court," as *ProPublica* reported.

All federal judges, including Supreme Court justices, are required to adhere to the financial disclosure requirements established in the Ethics in Government Act of 1978, passed in the wake of the Watergate scandal.[79] In response to the wave of criticism inspired by the *ProPublica* story, Thomas issued a terse statement in which he characterized Harlan Crow (and Crow's wife) as among Thomas's "dearest friends" and justified the decision not to disclose the many trips by stating that early in his tenure, Thomas "sought guidance from [his] colleagues and others in the judiciary, and was advised that this sort of personal hospitality from close personal friends, who do not have business before the Court, was not reportable."

The dam had broken, however, and the *ProPublica* investigation launched a series of stories of financial, conflict of interest, and other ethical allegations against some of the justices. Further reporting uncovered a remarkable number of additional financial dealings between Thomas and Crow (or other wealthy benefactors).[80] Another example occurred when *ProPublica* released a report detailing a luxury fishing vacation Justice Samuel Alito took with a billionaire who later had cases in front of the Court.[81] One additional example was when the Associated Press reported that Justice Sonia Sotomayor's staff had pushed public institutions to purchase Sotomayor's books, when hosting the justice for a speech. (One judicial ethics expert noted that although the allegations against Sotomayor differed in that "dozens of undisclosed luxury junkets are far more serious than asking staff to boost book sales–judicial ethics principles must still be politically neutral," and applied equally to all justices.[82])

Chief Justice John Roberts has long contended that the justices are not exempt from the Code of Conduct, arguing in his *2011 Year-End Report* that all members of the Court "do in fact consult the Code of Conduct in assessing their ethical obligations."[83] Such arguments did little to stem the reporting, or the public's disapproval. The steady stream of ethics concerns targeting Thomas and Alito in particular coincided with opinion polls showing some of the lowest approval ratings ever recorded for the Court.

The Court so far has refused to adopt serious ethics reform, although some of the justices, including Elena Kagan, Amy Coney Barrett, and Brett Kavanaugh, publicly expressed support for an ethics code. A Code of Conduct for Justices of the Supreme Court of the United States, which contained no enforcement mechanism, was released by all nine justices in November 2023, but it did nothing to alleviate the criticism. In July 2024, President Biden announced a Supreme Court reform plan that included a proposal to enact a binding code of conduct for Supreme Court justices. In the *Washington Post* op-ed Biden released to announce his plan, he argued that the justices "should be required to disclose gifts, refrain from public political activity and recuse themselves from cases in which they or their spouses have financial or other conflicts of interest."[84]

President Biden's plan, released so close to the election, had little chance of success during Biden's term. Given that President Trump has demonstrated no interest in pursuing Supreme Court ethics reform, it is unlikely that we will see successful proposals in this area soon. However, the seriousness of the ethical lapses being reported, coupled with the cratering approval rating of the Court and the dissention emerging among the justices themselves on this issue, point to a scenario where the Court may now be in a more precarious position from which to fight off these challenges, should more such efforts come from the political branches in the future.

The Decision to Leave the Bench

Understanding that Article III judges enjoy lifetime tenure does not address the various avenues that exist for a federal judge to leave the bench. Some ways of departing a judgeship have remained consistent across US history. Judges have always been able to resign (that is, walk away from) their seats, perhaps to go back to private practice. And some judges have held their positions until death, whether death came unexpectedly early for the judge, or after a long, long life. Judges who are elevated to a higher federal court must relinquish their previous seat. Although rare, removal through impeachment and conviction has also always been an option.

Over time, Congress has created additional, better options for judges who are reaching an age when they may be thinking of bringing their judicial careers to a close. Congress has endeavored, with some success, to tempt the longer-serving judges into retirement by making it financially more palatable to do so, mostly through the creation of retirement benefits for judges. Starting in 1869, judges could continue to draw their existing salaries upon retirement, so long as the judge satisfied age and service-length requirements set by Congress.[85] Since 1984, federal judges have been permitted to retire with full pay and benefits under what is called the **rule of eighty**—that is, when the sum of a judge's age and number of years on the bench is eighty. According to political scientist David Yalof:

> For the Supreme Court, at least, the single most key factor for justices to leave the Court has been the presence of a formal retirement provision with generous benefits. Indeed, as retirement benefits for federal jurists have been enacted and expanded over the years, a much greater percentage of justices have chosen to leave on their own initiative, before illness (or in some cases death) forecloses the possibility of continued service.[86]

For aging Supreme Court justices, departing the bench is largely a "take it or leave it" decision. They stay on the Supreme Court in full, or they leave in full. This is because another option created by Congress to encourage aging judges to leave the bench applies differently to Supreme Court justices than to judges on the courts of appeals or the district courts. In 1919, Congress created an alternative to full retirement, called **senior status**. Senior status judges are permitted to retain their office and staff and—equally important for many—the prestige of being a federal judge. When a judge takes senior status and becomes a "senior" judge, her "active" seat is opened for the appointment of her successor.

Supreme Court justices may and often do take senior status, but they are currently not allowed to continue hearing Supreme Court cases in senior status. Rather, justices who take senior status may sit by designation of the chief justice on an appeals or district court.[87] Both Justice Sandra Day O'Connor and Justice David Souter, for example, served on appeals courts after departing the high court.

The senior status option provides an alternative for lower court judges in addition to the take it or leave it nature of full retirement, in that a senior status judge may continue hearing cases while opening up their active seat to be filled. Indeed, some prominent Republicans, including then–Senate Judiciary Committee Chair Lindsey Graham, tried to capitalize on this alternative in the waning months of Trump's first term in office. While being interviewed on Hugh Hewitt's radio show in May 2020, Graham urged conservative judges, especially those on the courts of appeals, to use the senior status option to vacate their active seats. Emphasizing the "historic" opportunity presented by unified Republican control of the presidency and the Senate at the time, Graham noted that if an aging judge was thinking of leaving the bench, "now would be a suitable time" to do so.[88]

Twenty or more years ago, the evidence was mixed as to whether lower court judges were being strategic about when they chose to leave the bench. Indeed, circuit and district court judges often took senior status soon after reaching eligibility age and then stayed on the bench continuing to hear cases for many years as senior status judges.[89] More recent research indicates that judges are showing more evidence that their departure decisions are motivated by strategic calculations related to partisan politics, including staying in active status longer to wait out a president.[90]

For example, Jake S. Truscott and Richard L. Vining Jr. point out that of the twelve circuit judges who stepped down during Biden's first year in office, ten were appointed by Democratic presidents.[91] This suggests that those judges, appointed by Presidents Clinton and Obama, were waiting for Trump's presidency to end, in the hopes of being able to leave their seats to be filled by a more like-minded president.

Although we have focused a good deal of attention on the ability of lower court judges to use senior status to enable a politically strategic departure, it is also important to emphasize the critical contributions made by many senior status judges. A 2012 study found that approximately 42 percent of the nation's more than 1,300 working judges were on "senior status" and have thus opted not to retire in full. These judges have been resolving a larger proportion of lower court cases in recent decades and continue to exert a potentially important ideological influence on their courts long after they move into senior status.[92] In his 2010 "Year-End Report on the Federal Judiciary," Chief Justice Roberts noted that although senior status judges "are under no obligation to do so, many of them continue to carry substantial caseloads."[93] Roberts emphasized that the lower courts "would be in dire straits without their services, and the country as a whole owes them a special debt of gratitude."[94]

Since the senior status option for Supreme Court justices does not allow them to continue hearing cases on the nation's highest court, aging justices can find themselves under tremendous pressure to depart the Court at a time that is convenient for their partisan allies. As the Obama presidency wound down, for example, Justice Ruth Bader Ginsburg was subjected to what one op-ed columnist referred to as "unprecedented public nagging" over her decision to remain on the Supreme Court.[95] In an interview with *Elle* magazine in 2014, Ginsburg was asked if she would leave the bench during the Obama administration. "If I resign any time this year, he could not successfully appoint anyone I would like to see in the court," was her reply.[96] She noted that the nuclear option that reformed the filibuster for lower court appointments did not apply (at that time, at least) to those nominated to the Supreme Court. Therefore, it was "misguided," in her view, for anyone to presume that Obama would be able to appoint someone like her. Although President Obama gently pushed back on Ginsburg's comments by touting his "pretty good track record" of appointing judges, he concluded by expressing his admiration for Ginsburg and his belief that life tenure means that "she gets to decide, not anyone else, when she chooses to go."[97] Of course, after Donald Trump's unexpected victory in the 2016 presidential election, Ginsburg was unable to hold her seat until the 2020 election, dying on September 18 of that year, a mere forty-six days before the election.

Lifetime tenure for Supreme Court justices in particular also means that all presidents do not have the same opportunity to shape the composition of the nation's highest court. President Trump appointed three justices in his first term to President Biden's one, during their respective four-year terms in office. For years, reforms have been suggested to impose some form of term limits on the justices. At the same time that he announced his intention to push for a binding ethics code for the justices, Biden announced support for eighteen-year term limits for Supreme Court justices, with one justice stepping down every two years, to "ensure that the court's membership changes with some regularity" and "reduce the chance that any single presidency radically alters the makeup of the court for generations to come."[98]

As with his Supreme Court ethics reform announcement, aspects of Biden's term limits proposal are highly unlikely to find support with President Trump. Even so, the simple fact that the former president proposed to limit or curb the Court's power and autonomy is a notable development. Research by Tom Clark demonstrates that the introduction of bills in Congress designed to restrict, remove, or otherwise limit judicial power can serve to constrain the Supreme Court, because these efforts signal that the Court's legitimacy with the public is waning.[99] Even when the bills are not enacted, they can serve to constrain the Supreme Court. Based on theories explaining the interaction between public opinion and judicial power, the justices should be taking serious note of the signals being sent that the Court's support among the public is waning. In such situations, previous research indicates that the justices would typically be expected to moderate their behavior so as to reverse such a troubling trend.

THE 2024 ELECTIONS AND THE FEDERAL JUDICIARY

With respect to many of the issues related to federal judges discussed in this chapter, the consequences of the 2024 elections are critical to what will likely happen moving forward. As we have discussed, partisan politics play a big role in the process by which federal judges are selected. The partisan affiliation of the president is critical, as is party control of the Senate. Since the nuclear option was extended to the confirmation of Supreme Court justices in 2017, the party that controls the presidency has also controlled the Senate. This has meant that there was little that senators from the opposition could do to prevent confirmation of the presidents' preferred nominees. (Although the blue slip policy enacted by the chair of the Judiciary Committee is of relevance to how confirmation politics proceed for district court seats.)

With the benefit of a Republican-controlled Senate and the filibuster no longer an effective tool for the minority party to derail judicial confirmations, President Trump should have a similarly clear path to single-party confirmation of his judicial nominees in his second term in office as he had in his first, at least in the 119th Congress. (The 2026 midterm elections will determine if the Republicans can retain the 53 seats they held in the Senate after the 2024 elections.) As will be discussed in more detail in the next chapter, presidents can only appoint judges or justices when seats are available to fill. As the second Trump presidency plays out, therefore, it will be important to pay attention to the decisions made by Supreme Court justices and lower court judges to depart from or remain on the bench.

SUMMARY

This chapter began with a collective portrait of the people who have served in the federal judiciary. Though formal qualifications for a seat on the bench are few, tradition has established several informal criteria. These informal norms at times differ across the various levels of the judiciary, although a recent trend has been for presidents to be more motivated by expanding the diversity of the courts. These efforts have been much more prevalent among recent Democratic presidents, compared to their Republican counterparts.

At the national level, the judicial selection process includes a variety of participants, despite the constitutional mandate that the president shall do the appointing with the advice and consent of the Senate. While political concerns have always affected the selection of judges at the higher levels of the judiciary, the selection process for lower court judges has become increasingly politicized in recent decades. This has led to the very consequential decision of Senate Democrats in 2013 to adopt the nuclear option and weaken the use of the filibuster against district and appeals court nominees; the nuclear option would be extended by Senate Republicans to include Supreme Court confirmations in 2017.

Although much judicial socialization occurs before the judges don their black robes, a good deal of learning takes place after they reach the bench. Interpersonal interactions can help a new judge acclimate to the job. Even beyond a judge's early years on the bench, interpersonal interactions and exposure to colleagues can affect how judges make decisions, well into a judicial career.

The disciplining and removal of corrupt or otherwise unfit judges is still a problem, although at the circuit and district court level it may be eased a bit because of the Judicial Conduct Act of 1980. The fact that some judges may time their departures to allow a president of similar party identification and values to appoint a replacement is additional evidence that the jurists themselves see a substantive link between the appointment process and the content of many of their decisions. The development of senior status has encouraged lower court judges to take this option to make room for a new active judge while the senior judge remains on the bench. At the Supreme Court level in particular, however, concerns over life tenure and judicial ethics are very prevalent. Although enacting such reforms would likely require bipartisan support in Congress, previous research informs us that the mere threat of measures intended to curb the Court's power can restrain the justices, who traditionally have been concerned about losing the public's faith in their institution.

FURTHER THOUGHT AND DISCUSSION QUESTIONS

1. Justice Sonia Sotomayor was harshly criticized by some opponents during her Supreme Court appointment for once contending in a speech that a "wise Latina," because of her life experiences, would hopefully make better judicial decisions than a White man. Do you agree with Sotomayor that a judge with a lived experience that is not represented on a particular tribunal is preferable to selecting a judge whose background is already well represented on that court?
2. How might you predict previous professional experience to influence the decisions judges make once on the bench? Do you support appointing judges with public defense experience to sit alongside the many with prosecutorial experience? Do you share the regrets expressed by many longtime Supreme Court watchers that candidates with extensive political experience are no longer tapped for appointment? Are there other legal professions that you would argue should be better represented on the federal courts?
3. In leading to the 2020 presidential election, then–Senate Judiciary Committee Chair Lindsey Graham publicly urged conservative judges to consider taking

senior status to ensure their seats would be filled by President Trump. Should members of the elective branches pressure judges to leave the bench for partisan reasons, or is that kind of pressure contrary to the spirit of judicial independence?

4. Before leaving office, President Biden announced his support for ethics reform and term limits for Supreme Court justices. Do you agree with such measures, or do you share the concerns expressed by some, including Justice Neil Gorsuch, that such plans may imperil judicial independence? Given the results of the 2024 elections, do you think such reforms are likely to be enacted?

SUGGESTED RESOURCES

Abraham, Henry J. *Justices, Presidents, and Senators: A History of the U.S. Supreme Court Appointments from Washington to Clinton*. Lanham, MD: Rowman and Littlefield, 1999. A very well-researched and readable history of how presidents have attempted to influence the national political scene through their appointments to the nation's highest court.

Atkinson, David N. *Leaving the Bench: Supreme Court Justices at the End*. Lawrence, KS: University Press of Kansas, 1999. An interesting and accessible history of how every Supreme Court justice left the bench between 1789 and 1999.

Boyd, Christina L., Paul M. Collins Jr., and Lori A. Ringhand. *Supreme Bias: Gender and Race in U.S. Supreme Court Confirmation Hearings*. Stanford, CA: Stanford University Press, 2023. An excellent analysis of the role of race and gender in the confirmation hearings for Supreme Court justices.

Cramton, Roger C., and Paul D. Carrington, eds. *Reforming the Court: Term Limits for Supreme Court Justices*. Durham, NC: Carolina Academic Press, 2005. An excellent collection of articles that presents the pros and cons of term limits for Supreme Court justices, along with a discussion of the legal and constitutional problems inherent in making such changes.

Federal Judicial Center Website. Available at: www.fjc.gov. Provides information about the background of federal judges and ongoing research on the operation of the federal judiciary.

Goldman, Sheldon. *Picking Federal Judges: Lower Court Selection from Roosevelt through Reagan*. New Haven, CT: Yale University Press, 1997. The definitive book on the modern history of lower court appointments, focusing on the selection process used by the president.

Justice System Journal 28 (2007). The entire issue is devoted to the topics of judicial ethics and the formal and informal means of disciplining jurists who depart from established codes of conduct.

Nemacheck, Christine L. *Strategic Selection: Presidential Nomination of Supreme Court Justices from Herbert Hoover through George W. Bush.* Charlottesville, VA: University of Virginia Press, 2007. A scholarly yet accessible political and historical analysis of the Supreme Court appointment process for the previous eight decades.

KEY TERMS

blue slip
conservative
impeachment
liberal
recess appointment
rule of eighty
senatorial courtesy
senior status
socialization

7 POLICY LINKS AMONG THE CITIZENRY, THE PRESIDENT, AND THE FEDERAL JUDICIARY

CHAPTER GOALS AND OBJECTIVES

In this chapter, readers will learn that . . .

- The ability of a president to make an impact upon the decision-making output of the federal courts rests upon four key factors.
- The president's values and policy references are often manifested via their judicial appointees' decisions.
- Presidents Biden and Trump were, in differing ways, positioned to have significant influences upon the federal judiciary.

Because this book is about judicial policymaking, it is appropriate to examine the links between the policy values of the elected chief executive and the decisional propensities of federal judges. If in electing one presidential candidate rather than another, the citizenry expresses its policy choices, do such choices spill over into the kinds of judges presidents appoint and the way those judges decide policy-relevant cases? For instance, if the people decide in an election that they want a president who will reduce the size and powers of the federal bureaucracy, does that president subsequently appoint judges who share that philosophy? And equally important, when those judges hear cases that give them the opportunity either to expand or to reduce the extent of a bureaucrat's power, do they opt for the reduction of authority? Recent evidence, while incomplete, suggests the existence of some policy links.

This phenomenon will be examined by means of two questions. First, what critical factors must exist to enable presidents to obtain a judiciary that reflects their own political philosophy? Second, what empirical evidence is there to suggest that judges' decisions to some degree carry the imprint of the presidents who selected them?

Zahid Quraishi is sworn in during a Senate Judiciary Committee confirmation hearing on April 28, 2021. A former US Army captain and federal prosecutor, he was nominated by President Biden for a position as a US District Court judge for the District of New Jersey. Quraishi was confirmed by the Senate by a vote of 81–16 on June 10, 2021.

Kevin Lamarque/Reuters/Bloomberg via Getty Images

THE PRESIDENT AND THE COMPOSITION OF THE JUDICIARY

Four general factors determine whether chief executives can obtain a federal judiciary that is sympathetic to their political values and attitudes. These are ideology, the number of vacancies to be filled, the president's political clout, and the judicial climate the new judges enter.

Presidential Support for Ideologically Based Appointments

One key aspect of the success of chief executives in appointing a federal judiciary that mirrors their own political beliefs is the depth of their commitment to do so. Some presidents may be content merely to fill the federal bench with party loyalists and pay little attention to their nominees' specific ideologies. Some may consider ideological factors when appointing Supreme Court justices but may not regard them as important for trial and appellate judges. Other presidents may discount ideologically grounded appointments because they themselves tend to be nonideological. Still others may place factors such as past political loyalty ahead of ideology in selecting judges.

Harry Truman and Bill Clinton were chief executives in the first category. As president, Truman had strong political views, but when selecting judges, he placed political loyalty to himself ahead of the judicial candidate's overall ideological orientation. Indeed, though Truman personally had a somewhat liberal stance on civil rights and equal opportunity, he appointed only one Black and just one woman to the bench. And at least three of Truman's key southern district court appointees were identified as being very unfriendly to the cause of civil rights.[1]

In the 1990s, President Bill Clinton—who fashioned himself as a moderate "New Democrat"—often distanced himself from the more liberal image that characterized the Democratic Party during much of the twentieth century. Throughout his administration, Clinton sought to establish a judicial cohort that *looks like America*—a team reflective of the nation's diverse ethnicity and gender instead of a cohort characterized by any singular ideological perspective. As for ideology, one key member of the president's judicial selection team, who worked in both the Justice Department and the White House, put it this way: "Neither side is running an ideology shop. Neither of us consider ourselves to be the guardians of flame. [T]his is not a do or die fight for American Culture. This is an attempt to get highly competent lawyers on the federal bench so they can resolve disputes."[2]

If Clinton and Truman exemplify presidents who eschewed ideological criteria, George W. Bush and Ronald Reagan provide good examples of chief executives who selected their judicial nominees with a clear eye toward compatibility with their own conservative philosophy. Virtually all the W. Bush and Reagan judges had established records as political conservatives. Indeed, Reagan's communications director, Pat Buchanan, made it very clear that ideology was a top concern in picking judges when he stated, "[Our conservative appointment strategy] could do more to advance the social agenda—school prayer, antipornography, anti-busing, right-to-life and quotas in employment—than anything Congress can accomplish in 20 years."[3] George W. Bush and Reagan were not the only presidents to pack the bench with those who shared their political and legal philosophies. Presidents Barack Obama, Jimmy Carter, and Lyndon B. Johnson successfully appointed reliably liberal judges, a fact that demonstrates that both political parties have attempted to use the courts to further their political ideologies.

The Number of Vacancies to Be Filled

A second element affecting the capacity of chief executives to establish a policy link between themselves and the judiciary is the number of appointments available to them. The more judges a president can select, the greater the potential of the White House to put its stamp on the judicial branch. For example, George Washington's influence on the Supreme Court was significant because he was able to nominate ten individuals to the high court. Donald Trump was able to have a substantial impact by appointing three justices to the Supreme Court during his first term in office, whereas Jimmy Carter's imprint on the Court was nil because no vacancies occurred during his tenure as president.

The number of appointment opportunities depends on several factors: how many judicial vacancies are inherited from the previous administration, how many judges and justices die or resign during the president's term, how long the president serves, and whether Congress passes legislation that significantly increases the number of judgeships. Historically, the last factor seems to have been especially important in influencing the number of judgeships available, and politics in its most basic form permeates this process. A study of proposals for new-judges bills in thirteen Congresses tested the following two hypotheses: (1) "proposals to add new federal judges are more likely to pass if the party controls the Presidency and Congress than if different parties are in power," and (2) "proposals to add new federal judges are more likely to pass during the first two years of the President's term than during the second two years." The author of this study concluded that his "data support both hypotheses—proposals to add new judges are about five times more likely to pass if the same party controls the Presidency and Congress than if different parties' control, and about four times more likely to pass during the first two years of the President's term than during the second two years." He then noted that these findings serve "to remind us that not only is judicial selection a political process, but so is the creation of judicial posts."[4] In recent decades, however, both political parties have generally been loath to allow the incumbent president to fill new judicial vacancies, and the minority party has generally opposed such efforts by either refusing to move legislation creating significant numbers of new judgeships or using their power in the Senate minority to filibuster and block such bills. Still, there's no question that the number of vacancies that a president can fill—a function of politics, fate, and the size of the judicial workloads—is another variable that helps determine a chief executive's impact on the composition of the federal judiciary.

The recent two-term Democratic administrations provide good cases in point. President Obama entered the presidency with fifty-four district and trial court vacancies left by his predecessor, George W. Bush. On the other hand, President Clinton inherited a whopping one hundred district and trial court vacancies—14 percent of the total at the time—from his predecessor, George H. W. Bush. As a result, Clinton had a significant advantage over Obama in terms of raw numbers of judgeships to fill. In neither instance did these Democrats have a Congress eager to enact any type of omnibus judgeship bill that might have enhanced their capacity to pack the judiciary. In the end, Obama appointed a total of 324 Article III judges while Clinton tapped 372. The difference of 48 is almost entirely explained by the different number of vacancies they each inherited.

The President's Political Clout

Another factor determining whether the president can get a sympathetic federal judiciary is the scope and degree of presidential skill in overcoming any political obstacles. One such obstacle is the US Senate. If the Senate is controlled by the president's political party, the White House may find it easier to secure confirmation than if opposition forces are in control, although nothing is ever guaranteed. For example, even though the Republicans were firmly in control of the Senate at the time, in 2006, the George W. Bush White House was obliged to negotiate a three-judge nomination deal with two Democratic senators from Michigan. In exchange for Bush's nomination of a moderate candidate for a district court vacancy in their state, the senators agreed not to oppose two more conservative nominees for judgeships in other states selected by the

Bush administration.[5] Of course, when the opposition is in power in the Senate, presidents may have little choice but to engage in a sort of political horse trading to get their nominees approved. An example of this occurred in 2013, when Obama nominated Michael P. Boggs to fill a US district court vacancy in Georgia as part of a bipartisan deal brokered between the White House and Republican senators as a means for moving forward on a group of stalled judicial nominations. Boggs's background was hardly that of the stereotypical progressive Democrat. During his stint as a Georgia state lawmaker, Boggs had sponsored legislation that sought to restrict access to abortion rights, and he had voted to retain the state flag that contained the Confederate battle emblem. Liberal interests were deeply unsettled by the Boggs nomination. "It breaks my heart that this is the first African-American president who is doing something like this," said US Representative David Scott (D-GA). Though the Boggs nomination was ultimately unsuccessful, it stands as an example of the type of compromises that presidents sometimes make.[6] In 1999, President Clinton was obliged to make a similar deal with the conservative chair of the Senate Judiciary Committee, Orrin Hatch. To ensure smooth sailing for at least ten of Clinton's judicial nominations that had been blocked in the Senate, the president agreed to nominate for a federal judgeship a conservative Utah Republican, Ted Stewart, who was backed by Hatch but vigorously opposed by liberals and environmental groups. "Administration officials defended the deal, saying they would get more than an acceptable amount in return for nominating Stewart, whom they acknowledged would not be chosen for the Federal bench by a Democratic President under ordinary circumstances,"[7] reported the *New York Times*.

The Senate Judiciary Committee is also a potential roadblock that may prevent presidents from placing their chosen men and women on the federal bench. Some chief executives have been more adept than others at maneuvering their candidates through the jagged rocks of the Judiciary Committee rapids. Both Presidents John F. Kennedy and Lyndon B. Johnson, for example, had to deal with the formidable committee chair James Eastland of Mississippi, a southern segregationist who often worked to oppose pro–civil rights Democrats. Alas, Johnson seemed to have had the political adroitness to get most of his liberal nominees approved. Kennedy lacked this skill. Under the Obama and Clinton administrations, despite these presidents' considerable political skills, they were never able to parlay those abilities into much clout with the conservative and often hostile Senate Judiciary Committee when it was controlled by Republicans.

The president's personal popularity is another element in the political power formula. Chief executives who are well liked by the public and command the respect of opinion makers in the news media, the regular members of their political party, and the leaders of the nation's major interest groups are much more likely to prevail over any forces that seek to thwart their judicial nominees. Personal popularity is not a stable factor and is sometimes hard to gauge, but presidents' standing with the electorate clearly helps determine the success of their efforts to influence the composition of the American judiciary. For example, in 1930, President Herbert Hoover's choice for a seat on the Supreme Court, John J. Parker, was defeated in the Senate by a two-vote margin. Some historians believe if the nomination had been made a year or so earlier, before the onset of the Great Depression took Hoover's popularity by the throat, Parker might have gotten on the Supreme Court. Likewise, in 1968, President Johnson's low esteem among voters and the powers-that-be may have been partially responsible for the Senate's rejection of his candidate for chief justice, Abe Fortas, and for the Senate's refusal to replace Fortas with Johnson's old pal Homer Thornberry. As one observer commented, "Johnson failed largely because most members of the Senate 'had had it' with the lame-duck President's nominations."[8] In 2005, President George W. Bush saw the failure of his nomination of Harriet Miers to serve on the Supreme Court. Miers never received a vote in the Senate; she was effectively withdrawn from consideration after conservatives lambasted the choice. At the time, Bush—who was in his final term in office and whose administration faced increasing difficulties in the Iraq war—had an anemic approval rating of 41 percent, with 56 percent of the public disapproving of him. This political weakness undoubtedly contributed to the failure of the Miers nomination.[9]

On the other hand, Clinton's approval ratings varied significantly during his years in office, but he showed little desire to expend political muscle in pushing through controversial candidates over Judiciary Committee and Senate objections. This was confirmed by a top Clinton adviser who was key in overseeing Clinton's judicial selections. "There are a couple of cases," she said, "in which we decided that even if we thought we tried winning a fight . . . that it was not worth the time and resources . . . because these fights go for months and months, and during that period it is difficult to concentrate."[10]

The Judicial Climate the New Judges Enter

A final matter affects the capacity of chief executives to secure a federal judiciary that reflects their own political values: the current philosophical orientations of the sitting district and appellate court judges with whom the new appointees would interact. Because federal judges have lifetime appointments during good behavior, presidents must accept the composition and value structure of the judiciary as it exists when they first take office. If the existing judiciary already reflects the president's political and legal orientation, the impact of new judicial appointees will be immediate and substantial. However, if the trial and appellate judiciary has values that are radically different from those of the new chief executive, the impact of subsequent judicial appointments will be weaker and slower to materialize. New judges must respect the controlling legal precedents and the constitutional interpretations that prevail in the judiciary at the time they enter it, or they risk having their decisions overturned by a higher court. Such a reality may limit the capacity of a new set of judges to get in there and do their own thing—at least in the short run.

When Franklin D. Roosevelt (FDR) became president in 1933, he was confronted with a Supreme Court and a lower federal judiciary that had been solidly packed with conservative Republican jurists by his three GOP predecessors in the White House. Much of the high court and most lower court judges viewed most of Roosevelt's New Deal legislation as unconstitutional, and it was not until 1937 that the Supreme Court began to stop overturning much of FDR's major legislative programs.

To make matters worse, his first opportunity to fill a Supreme Court vacancy did not come until the fall of 1937. Thus, despite the ideological screening that went into the selection of FDR's judges, it seems fair to assume that, at least between 1933 and 1938, Roosevelt's trial and appellate judges had to restrain their liberal propensities in the myriad of cases that came before them. This may explain in part why the voting record of the Roosevelt court appointees is not much more liberal than that of the conservative judges selected by Roosevelt's three Republican predecessors; the Roosevelt team just did not have much room to maneuver in a judiciary dominated by staunch conservatives.

President Reagan's impact on the judicial branch was substantial and long-lasting. By the end of his second term, he had appointed an unprecedented 368 federal judges, 50 percent of those on the bench at the time. When he entered the White House, the Supreme Court was already teetering to the right because of Richard Nixon's and Gerald Ford's conservative appointments. Although Carter's liberal appointees still had places on the trial and appellate court benches, Reagan found a good many conservative Nixon and Ford judges on the bench when he took office. Thus, he played a significant role in shaping the entire federal judiciary in his own conservative image, which continued many years after he left office. The judges appointed by George H. W. Bush had a much easier time making their impact felt because well over half of the judiciary already professed conservative, Republican values. After ousting incumbent George H. W. Bush, President Clinton's impact on the judiciary was slower to manifest itself because his nominees entered an environment that was not conducive to liberal decision-making after twelve years of Republican presidential leadership. When Clinton's jurists took their seats on the federal bench, about three-quarters of the sitting judges—including the supervisory appellate panels—were conservative Republicans appointed primarily by Presidents Reagan and George H. W. Bush. Even if the Clinton judges had been closet liberals, they would have had little opportunity to express these values in a judiciary so dominated by more conservative jurists. By comparison, when George W. Bush entered the White House in 2001, a slim majority—51 percent—of federal judges had been appointed by Democratic presidents. This relative balance provided Bush with the opportunity to tilt the ideological direction of the judiciary in a conservative direction.

The example of President Obama provides a slightly different case in point. At the end of the George W. Bush administration, roughly 60 percent of lower federal judges bore the Republican label. Thus, when Obama assumed office, the judiciary was clearly dominated by those who did not share his Democratic values. But as President Obama completed his eighth and final year in office, his administration had effectively flipped the table—around 60 percent of active federal judges at the time had been appointed by Democratic presidents, while approximately 40 percent had been selected by Republican chief executives.[11] Thus, the data indicate that Obama was able to move the ideological balance of the courts in a leftward direction, but the overall picture was one of a federal bench that was not especially far from the political center. Regarding the Supreme Court, however, Obama's inability to overcome staunch GOP opposition to replacing the late Antonin Scalia with a new, presumably more liberal justice in 2016 had a huge limiting impact upon the 44th president's ability to shift the overall ideological direction of the federal bench. So, while Obama moved the ideological split of the overall judiciary in a direction more favorable to Democrats, the administration's failure to tilt the Supreme Court in a liberal direction stands out as a monumental, missed opportunity.

PRESIDENTS' VALUES AND THEIR APPOINTEES' DECISIONS

What evidence is there that presidents have been able to secure a judiciary in tune with their own policy values and goals? When the people elect a particular president, is there reason to believe that their choice will be expressed in the kinds of judges that are appointed and the kinds of decisions they render?

To answer these questions, we examined the liberal–conservative voting patterns of the teams of district court judges appointed by fifteen presidents during the twentieth century and the first twenty years of the twenty-first century. This comprehensive study is the only one that covers enough presidents, judges, and cases to allow for some meaningful generalizations. In essence, the focus is on whether liberal presidents appointed trial judges who decided cases in a more liberal manner and whether conservative chief executives were able to obtain district court jurists who followed their policy views.

We analyzed cases in three broad categories. In the realm of civil rights and civil liberties, liberal judges would generally take a broadening position—that is, their rulings would seek to extend these freedoms. Conservative jurists, by contrast, would prefer to limit such rights. For example, in a case in which a government agency wanted to prevent a controversial person from speaking in a public park or at a state university, a liberal judge would be more inclined than a conservative to uphold the right of the would-be speaker. Or in a case concerning alleged racial bias by an employer, a liberal judge would be more likely to rule for the person who claimed they were discriminated against. In the area of government regulation of the economy, liberal judges would probably uphold legislation that benefited working people or the economic underdog. Thus, if the secretary of labor sought an injunction against an employer for paying less than the minimum wage, a liberal judge would be more disposed to endorse the labor secretary's arguments, whereas a conservative judge would tend to side with business, especially big business. Another broad category of cases often studied by judicial scholars is criminal justice. Liberal judges are, in general, more sympathetic to the motions made by criminal defendants. For instance, in a case in which the accused claimed to have been coerced by the government to make an illegal confession, liberal judges would be more likely than their conservative counterparts to agree that the government had acted improperly.

Figure 7.1 indicates the percentage of liberal decisions rendered by the district court appointees of Presidents Franklin D. Roosevelt through Joe Biden. Forty-seven percent of the decisions of the FDR judges are liberal, which puts these jurists on par with those of Barack Obama, Lyndon Johnson, and Jimmy Carter for having the most liberal voting records. Franklin Roosevelt used ideological criteria to pick his judges, and he put the full weight of his political skills behind that endeavor. He once instructed his dispenser of political patronage, James A. Farley, to use the judicial appointment power, in effect, as a weapon against senators and representatives who were balking at New Deal legislation: "First off, we must hold up judicial appointments in States where the [congressional] delegation is not going along [with our liberal economic proposals]. We must make appointments promptly where the delegation is with us. Second, this must apply to other appointments. I'll keep in close contact with the leaders."[12]

FIGURE 7.1 ■ Percentage of Liberal Decisions Rendered by District Court Appointees of Presidents Franklin D. Roosevelt through Donald Trump

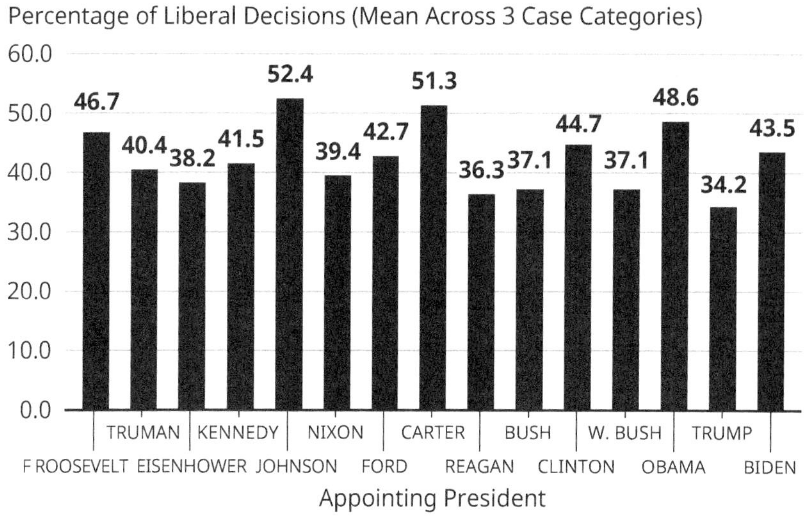

Source: Data collected by Robert A. Carp, Kenneth L. Manning, and Ronald Stidham.

At first, the comparatively conservative voting record of the Truman judges seems a bit strange in view of Truman's personal commitment to liberal economic and social policy goals. Only 40 percent of the Truman judges' decisions were liberal, a full seven percentage points less than those of Roosevelt's jurists. However, Truman counted personal loyalty much more heavily than ideological standards when selecting judges, and as a result, many conservatives found their way into the ranks of Truman jurists.

Because of Truman's lack of interest in making policy-based appointments, coupled with strong opposition in the Senate and lack of popular support throughout much of his administration, his personal liberalism was generally not reflected in the policy values of his judges. Eisenhower's judges were more conservative than Truman's, as expected, but the difference is not great. This resulted in part because Eisenhower paid little attention to purely ideological criteria in making appointments and because his judges had to work in the company of an overwhelming Democratic majority throughout the federal judiciary. These factors must have curbed many of the conservative inclinations of the Eisenhower jurists.

The 42 percent liberalism score of the judges appointed by Kennedy represents a swing to the left. This is to be expected, and at first, it may appear strange that Kennedy's team on the bench was not more left of center. However, Kennedy had problems dealing with the conservative, southern-dominated Senate Judiciary Committee; he lacked political clout in the Senate, which often made him a pawn of senatorial courtesy; and he was unable to overcome the stranglehold of local Democratic bosses, who often prized partisan loyalty over ideological purity—or even, sometimes, competence—when it came to appointing judges.

Johnson's judges moved impressively toward the left and were more liberal than FDR's, and much more so than Kennedy's. This can be accounted for based on the four criteria that predict a correspondence between the values of chief executives and the orientation of their judges. Johnson knew how to bargain with individual senators and was second to none in his ability to manipulate and cajole those who were initially indifferent or hostile to the issues (or candidates) he supported. His impressive victories in Congress—for example, the passage of notable antipoverty measures including Medicare and Medicaid, the Civil Rights Act of 1964, and the Voting Rights Act of 1965—are monuments to his skill. Undoubtedly, too, he used his political prowess to secure a judicial team that reflected his liberal policy values. In addition, Johnson was able to fill many vacancies on the bench, and his liberal appointees must have felt at home ideologically in a judiciary headed by the liberal Chief Justice Earl Warren.

If the leftward swing of the Johnson team is dramatic, it is no less so than the shift to the right made by the Nixon judges. Only 39 percent of the decisions of Nixon's jurists were liberal. Nixon placed enormous emphasis on getting conservatives nominated to judgeships at all levels. He possessed the political clout to secure Senate confirmation for most lower court appointees—at least until the Watergate scandal, when the Nixon wine turned into vinegar—and the rightist policy values of the Nixon judges must have been prodded by a Supreme Court that was growing increasingly conservative.

The 43 percent liberalism score of the Ford judges puts them right between the Johnson and Nixon jurists in terms of ideology. That Ford's jurists were less conservative than Nixon's is not hard to explain. First, Ford himself was much less of a political ideologue than his predecessor, as reflected in the way he screened his nominees and the types of individuals he chose. (Ford's appointment of the moderate John Paul Stevens to the Supreme Court, as compared with Nixon's selection of the highly conservative William H. Rehnquist, illustrates the point.) Also, because Ford's circuitous route to the presidency did not enhance his political effectiveness with the Senate, he would not have had the clout to force highly conservative Republican nominees through a liberal, Democratic Senate, even if he had wished to. (Recall that Ford was not elected to the presidency or vice presidency, having become VP after the resignation of Spiro Agnew and chief executive after Nixon stepped down.)

With a score of 51 percent, Jimmy Carter is close to Lyndon Johnson's record for having appointed judges with the most liberal voting records of the thirteen presidents under consideration. Despite Carter's call for an "independent" federal judiciary based on "merit selection," his judges were selected with a keen eye toward their potential liberal voting tendencies.[13] That some correspondence exists between the values of President Carter and the liberal decisional patterns of his judges should come as no surprise. Carter was clearly identified with liberal social and political values, and although his economic policies were perhaps more conservative than those of other recent Democratic presidents, Carter's commitment to liberal values in the areas of civil rights and liberties and of criminal justice was not in doubt. Carter, too, had a chance to pack the bench. The Omnibus Judgeship Act of 1978, passed by a friendly Democratic Congress, created a record 152 new federal judicial openings for Carter to fill. He also possessed a fair degree of political clout with a Judiciary Committee and Senate controlled by Democrats. Finally, the Carter judicial team found many friendly liberals (appointed by Presidents Kennedy and Johnson) already sitting on the bench.

Reagan's judicial team has one of the most conservative voting records of all the judicial cohorts in our study. Only 36 percent of their decisions bear the liberal stamp. Reagan's conservative values and his commitment to reshaping the federal judiciary were well known. Early in his first presidential campaign, he had inveighed against left-leaning activist judges and promised a dramatic change. Like his predecessor Carter, Reagan had the opportunity, through attrition and newly created judgeships, to fill the judiciary with persons reflecting his own inclinations. (At the end of his second term, about half of the federal judiciary bore the Reagan label.) This phenomenon was aided by Reagan's great personal popularity throughout most of his administration and a Senate that his party controlled during six of his eight years in office. Finally, the Reagan cohort entered the judicial realm with conservative greetings from quite a few right-of-center Nixon and Ford judges. The data also indicate that the overall ideology of judges appointed by Reagan's vice president and successor, George H. W. Bush, is virtually identical to that of Reagan.

President Bill Clinton's judges were heavily criticized in the 1990s by Republican senators and representatives, some of whom even called for the impeachment of his so-called liberal-activist judges.[14] However, the data have not supported these GOP condemnations. Clinton's judges have handed down liberal decisions 45 percent of the time. While this is certainly more progressive than the 36 percent or so for Reagan and

George H. W. Bush jurists, it is decidedly more conservative than the 53 and 51 percent liberal decisions handed down by Johnson and Carter appointees, respectively. The record indicates that Clinton's judges have been akin to those appointed by Republican Gerald Ford. They have, in a word, been moderate.

The judicial cohort appointed by President George W. Bush is consistent with the Reagan and Bush Sr. jurists—the W. Bush judges are among the most conservative in our study. With a score of 37 percent, his judges have shown themselves to be reliable conservatives. The George W. Bush administration made judicial nominations a priority and sought to leave a clear ideological mark on the federal bench. In 2003, Bush's assistant attorney general, Viet Dinh, made it clear that Bush's judges would adhere to the president's conservative philosophy when Dinh said in an interview, "we want to ensure that the President's mandate to us that the people who are nominated by him to be on the bench have his vision of the proper role of the judiciary. That is, a judiciary that will follow the law, not make the law."[15]

The data indicate that President Barack Obama appointed judges who, unsurprisingly, have moved in a different ideological direction from their Republican colleagues. Forty-nine percent of the Obama judge decisions have been liberal. This places them somewhat to the left of the judges appointed by Clinton and comparable to (but not quite as liberal as) the jurists selected by Presidents Johnson and Carter. Some on the right accused Obama of harboring far-left "socialist" goals for the judiciary, but the facts simply don't back up such hysteria.[16] The data show that the judges appointed by Obama are more left of center than the jurists appointed by Republican presidents, but his judicial cohort is comprised of mainstream liberals largely in line with the judges appointed by previous Democratic presidents.

Presidents Joe Biden, Donald Trump, and the Federal Judiciary

As this book went to press, Republican Donald Trump had won election to a second term and was poised to retake the Oval Office in January 2025. Facing questions about his advanced age and ability to carry the heavy burden of another four years in office, President Joe Biden announced in July 2024 that he would not seek a second term. Democrats quickly rallied behind Harris, Biden's vice president, as their party's standard bearer to face off against Trump, who was seeking a return to the White House after losing his reelection bid to Biden in 2020. As a result, in 2024 the nation faced a somewhat unusual situation of back-to-back one-term presidents. Of course, Harris lost her White House bid and Trump was positioned to become only the second president in US history to serve two nonconsecutive terms (the first being Grover Cleveland in the late 1800s). What kinds of people did Biden and Trump select for service on the federal bench during their four years in office, and what has been the ideological direction of their judges' decision-making? We will compare and contrast their approaches to judicial selection by applying our four-part model, which addresses whether chief executives can obtain a federal judiciary that is sympathetic to their political values and attitudes.

Commitment to Making Ideological Appointments. Having served two terms as vice president under President Obama from 2009 to 2017, Joe Biden had a front-row seat in the executive branch for the judicial confirmation battles during that presidency. Additionally, as a US senator, Biden had served as chair of the Senate Judiciary Committee from 1987 to 1995, giving him years of involvement with judicial confirmations on Capitol Hill. Biden had thus participated in the judicial selection process at both ends of Pennsylvania Avenue. As reporters noted at the time, "[Biden] and his senior advisers have a deep understanding of the importance of the lifetime appointments and the need to move swiftly."[17] Another observer remarked that "few politicians understand the federal judiciary like President Joe Biden."[18] That said, throughout this long career Biden was known as a mainstream liberal Democrat, neither embracing the left wing occupied by the likes of Representative Alexandria Ocasio-Cortez of New York nor finding home in the moderate faction of the party with politicians like President Bill Clinton. Consider that when Justice Stephen Breyer announced in early 2022 his intention to retire from the Supreme Court, President Biden told an NBC News interviewer that in filling the resulting vacancy he was "not looking to make an ideological choice" and said his nominee would have a "mainstream interpretation of the Constitution."[19] Still, Biden could have been expected to place an emphasis upon shifting the ideology of the judiciary toward the center-left via the appointment of his fellow Democrats, though how much of an ideological shift was an open question.

The process of picking judges and the importance it plays in a presidential administration had been a salient issue during the 2020 election. When Biden won the presidency, there was sentiment in some Democratic circles that they had been "out-hustled" by their Republican opponents with regards to judicial appointments. Liberals were seething about the rushed replacement of the late Ruth Bader Ginsburg with Amy Coney Barrett just seven days before the 2020 election (a move that Democrats saw as profoundly hypocritical), while still being upset about Mitch McConnell's power plays stonewalling the nomination of Merrick Garland in 2016 and ending the filibuster for Supreme Court nominees in 2017. There were also lingering regrets about missed opportunities and, according to some critics, a lackadaisical approach to selecting judges during the early Obama years. Explaining that the Obama administration had its hands full with economic revitalization in his first term, then–Chief of Staff Rahm Emanuel was quoted by one observer as claiming, "I don't give a f— about judicial appointments."[20] Veterans of the Obama administration would undoubtedly dispute this coarse description of their priorities. Still, it is indisputable that the Obama White House was not initially aggressive in filling judgeships. With Biden stepping into the Oval Office in January 2021, there was a strong desire among Democrats for his administration to act differently and take a more assertive posture toward picking judges.

President Biden's White House was thus determined not to repeat past mistakes and his administration took an aggressive, proactive posture with regard to appointing judges. Just days after the new president was sworn in, the *Washington Post* reported that "President Biden's top advisers have spent months building an extensive pipeline of judicial nominees to fill court vacancies throughout the country, attempting to swiftly remake portions of the judiciary and undo one of his predecessor's most significant achievements."[21] It was also reported that Biden administration officials were placing far more emphasis on judicial nominations and planned to fill slots faster than Democrats had in the past. The Biden White House reportedly viewed judicial nominees as an area where the president would invest early political capital. "People are approaching this with a different sense of urgency," said senior White House counsel Paige Herwig, "And they understand. They saw what the Trump administration did for four years."[22] President Biden also continued the Trump administration's practice of not submitting judicial nominees' names to the American Bar Association for that group's prior assessment of the candidate's qualifications, a process that usually delayed nominations by a few weeks. ABA ratings would still be sought, but they would not hold up a nomination.[23]

Donald Trump's approach to selecting judges occurred in a different context but concluded in a similarly robust posture. Candidate Trump ran in 2016 as a combative Republican, though at one point in his adult life he had aligned with Democrats and his positions on several issues did not always hew closely to GOP orthodoxy. This led some to speculate that Trump might not govern from a consistent ideological position. Noted conservative columnist Charles Krauthammer observed during the 2016 campaign that "Trump doesn't even pretend to have [principles], conservative or otherwise."[24]

As president, however, Trump governed from a hard-right perspective. Furthermore, there was clear indication that the Trump White House pursued a coordinated and well-planned strategy regarding filling judicial positions. One news organization reported at the time:

> In the weeks before Donald J. Trump took office [in 2017], lawyers joining his administration gathered at a law firm near the Capitol, where Donald F. McGahn II, the soon-to-be White House counsel, filled a white board with a secret battle plan to fill the federal appeals courts with young and deeply conservative judges. Mr. McGahn, instructed by Mr. Trump to maximize the opportunity to reshape the judiciary, mapped out potential nominees and a strategy, according to two people familiar with the effort. . . .[25]

Many of President Trump's judicial nominees had ties to the Federalist Society, a nationwide group of conservative lawyers and legal thinkers. This group has served as a professional and intellectual incubator for right-leaning attorneys, academics, and Republican jurists. A noted Supreme Court watcher called the Federalist Society the "conservative pipeline to the Supreme Court."[26] One of the key leaders of that group, Leonard Leo, took a leave from the organization to work with the Trump team to compile a list of potential Supreme Court nominees and he continued to advise the administration on judicial nominations. One professor who studies the courts identified Leo as a judicial nominee "gatekeeper" who "has a lot of power and influence" in the Trump administration.[27] A team of news reporters called Leo "President Trump's unofficial judicial adviser."[28]

Trump's commitment to a clear judicial appointment strategy was also reflected in his tendency to select younger people for positions on the bench. Appointing jurists of a younger age will generally enable the judge to serve in the position longer and further enhance the appointing president's long-term impact on the judiciary. The average age of Trump's circuit court nominees was younger than the average nominees of Presidents Obama, George W. Bush, and Bill Clinton.[29] As the *Washington Post* noted at the time, Trump "picked the youngest judges to sit on the federal bench."[30] In what could be considered an indicator of the Trump administration's priority placed upon ideology, an independent analysis by Bloomberg Law in 2018 found that "more of Donald Trump's judicial picks have received 'not qualified' ratings from the American Bar Association than did those nominated by his four most-recent predecessors in the first two years of their presidencies."[31]

With this evidence from these two administrations, it seems clear that at least to some extent, both Presidents Biden and Trump pursued a strategy of making ideologically based appointments to the federal bench, though Trump did so more than Biden. However, with regard to gender and racial/ethnic diversity, the Biden and Trump teams took starkly different approaches.

As a candidate, Biden vowed to appoint a diverse slate of jurists, and there's no question that he fulfilled that promise. His administration had a particular focus on addressing racial imbalance on various US courts of appeals around the country, especially where traditional (i.e., White male) jurists were in a clear majority. As the *New York Times* reported:

> Mr. Biden's first round of judicial picks was an effort to begin addressing such imbalances while the Senate is under Democratic control. Where Mr. Trump emphasized white male conservatives, Mr. Biden is diversifying not only the ethnic backgrounds of his candidates but their professional ones as well, seeking out nominees with varied legal careers. . . . Allies say Mr. Biden, a former longtime chairperson of the Senate Judiciary Committee with a deep background in judicial nominations, is determined to install judges with different sets of experiences from the mainly white corporate law partners and prosecutors who have been tapped for decades by presidents of both parties. Mr. Biden has also promised to appoint the first African American woman to the Supreme Court.[32]

By the summer of 2024, Biden had appointed the most diverse slate of federal judges in American history.[33] Women accounted for around 63 percent of Biden's judges, going a long way to shifting the gender imbalance that has existed on the federal bench for generations. An almost identical percentage of his nominees (62 percent) were from underrepresented racial/ethnic minority groups.[34] As the nonpartisan Pew Research Center noted, before Biden "no president [had] ever appointed a slate of judges consisting mostly of women or racial and ethnic minorities."[35] Biden's White House also tied the Obama record in appointing LGBTQ judges.[36] Like Trump, Biden tended to seek out younger jurists, suggesting that the Biden administration made a strategic consideration in aiming for a lasting impact on the federal bench. As of May 2024, 49 percent of Biden's judicial picks had been under the age of fifty, the same percentage as that of his predecessor.[37]

Biden reportedly saw diversity as key to strengthening the legitimacy of the judicial branch. "We need the country, and lawyers, to look at the judiciary and see themselves, see the full range of faces and backgrounds," said Dana Remus, the White House counsel and Biden's top legal adviser. "Over time, we hope and expect it does mean there's greater trust and faith that judicial decisions reflect the full range of the country's values."[38] Indeed, scholars recognize that diversity on the bench is important for the perceived legitimacy—and therefore authority and power—of the courts. As Carl Tobias, a professor at the University of Richmond School of Law, noted, "it's valuable for citizens to have confidence in the courts. So, it's valuable for the courts to reflect the people who come into court and the people who live in the country."[39]

The record indicates, too, that the Biden administration was not willing to sacrifice professional qualifications for diversity. Biden's judicial nominees possessed strong legal credentials and backgrounds. The American Bar Association rated 86 percent of his judicial nominees as "well qualified" and 13 percent as "qualified."[40] Senate Judiciary Chair Dick Durbin claimed that "The number's important, but the quality of the nominee is even more important."[41]

President Trump's approach to diversity on the bench stood in stark contrast to that of Biden. Indeed, Biden nominated as many minority women to be judges in four months as Trump had confirmed in four years.[42] Of the 226 jurists that Trump selected for the Article III courts, 24 percent were women. Only 16 percent of the Trump judges were of a non-White racial/ethnic background. Overall, 64 percent of the Trump judicial cohort were what we identify as "traditional" (i.e., White male) nominees. This is comparable to that of Republican President George W. Bush, who appointed a judicial team that was 67 percent traditional.[43]

How might we understand these sharply different approaches to judicial selection? The answer probably lies in core differences between the political parties. Political science scholars Matt Grossman and David A. Hopkins argued in a 2016 book that the Democratic Party is a coalition of different social groups that act as voting blocs for candidates, whereas the Republican Party serves more as a vehicle for conservative ideology.[44] As one academic put it, "Democratic leaders see themselves as responsible to particular voting blocs and delivering on their policy demands, while Republican leaders see themselves as beholden to symbolic ideological commitments."[45] Relatedly, this gap in diversity is likely explained, too, by the differences in the party membershipas one scholar noted, "The Republican Party is basically a white party."[46] This, in turn, results in a contrast between the parties in prioritizing diversity in the appointment process.

What does empirical evidence suggest regarding Biden's and Trump's attempts to move the judiciary's ideological center of gravity? Figure 7.1 and Table 7.1 provide a look at the decision-making patterns of numerous presidents' district court appointees.

TABLE 7.1 ■ Percentage of Liberal Decisions in Three Categories of Cases Rendered by District Court Appointees of Presidents Lyndon B. Johnson through Donald Trump

Appointing President	Criminal Justice	Civil Rights and Liberties	Economic and Labor Regulation
Johnson	36.9	57.3	63.4
Nixon	26.8	37.6	51.1
Ford	33.0	38.7	53.0
Carter	37.7	50.0	61.9
Reagan	25.4	32.7	49.6
George H. W. Bush	26.8	33.7	50.2
Clinton	37.7	41.6	55.7
George W. Bush	29.1	33.0	51.0
Obama	36.1	43.5	61.8
Trump	40.0	25.5	44.1
Biden	28.0	41.8	59.9

Source: Data collected by Robert A. Carp, Kenneth L. Manning, and Ronald Stidham.

The data previously reported in Figure 7.1 indicate that Biden's judicial cohort has exhibited a liberalism rate of 44 percent, placing his jurists to the right of Obama's and Carter's and comparable to the judges appointed by Bill Clinton. The data indicate that Biden's judges appear to be center-left, in line with judges selected by previous Democratic presidents. On the other hand, 34 percent of the Trump judge decisions have been liberal. This places his judges to the right of all appointees—Democrats *and* Republicans—stretching back to FDR in the 1930s.

Even more intriguing are the numbers reported in Table 7.1, which look at the decision-making of judges selected by the eleven most recent presidents, divided into three extensive categories. The first column in Table 7.1 provides data on judges' voting on criminal justice issues, such as habeas corpus petitions, motions made before and during a criminal trial, and forfeiture of property in a criminal case. In this realm, Biden's judges are significantly less liberal in criminal justice cases than any prior Democratic president, handing down left-leaning decisions only 28 percent of the time. In fact, the data indicate that Biden's judges approach criminal justice cases in a manner that is similar to that of George W. Bush's jurists, who are quite conservative. Compare this to the decision-making record of the Trump team, which at 40 percent liberal is actually *more liberal* than all prior presidents in our analysis, both Democrat and Republican. His judges stand in stark contrast to the conservatism rate of judges appointed by Republican presidents George W. Bush, George Bush Sr., and Ronald Reagan.

How might we account for these surprising results in criminal justice cases? One might hypothesize that the Trump jurists could be reflecting a distinctly antigovernment streak in their criminal justice rulings that Trump himself frequently voiced. The list of Trump's run-ins with the law is lengthy. After leaving office in 2021, Trump faced multiple criminal cases and was charged with eighty-eight offensesmany of them feloniesin four separate indictments, two of them federal.[47] In one of these cases, a New York jury found Trump guilty in May 2024 on thirty-four charges in a scheme to illegally influence the 2016 election through a hush money payment to an adult film actress, making Trump the first former president to be a convicted felon.[48] Even during his presidency Trump was often highly critical of federal law enforcement, referencing a "criminal deep state" and engaging in what one reporter called a "war on the FBI."[49] Not coincidentally, a 2018 survey by Gallup indicated that perceptions of federal law enforcement fell sharply among many Republicans during the Trump years, and "the partisan shift in views [of the FBI] suggests Trump's and other Republicans' efforts to cast doubt on the FBI's professionalism and portray it as a partisan agency have been somewhat successful among their supporters."[50] It is known, too, that former White House counsel Don McGahn, who had a key hand in the administration's selection of judges, was identified by one reporter as "almost militantly libertarian" (i.e., antigovernment) in his background and ideology.[51]

On the other hand, the lower liberalism rate among Biden judges could reflect a mirror opposite effect within the other major party. That same Gallup poll found that approval of the FBI was up nine points from 2014 to 2018 among Democrats.[52] And the trend only appears to have increased after Trump left office. A September 2022 survey by Gallup identified a whopping 50 point gap in FBI approval79 percent of Democrats said the agency was doing a good job but only 29 percent of Republicans held the same view. A separate poll in November 2022 conducted by Penn State University found very similar results, reporting that "a much higher proportion of Democrats than Republicans say that they trust the Federal Bureau of Investigation and that they believe FBI agents are fair."[53]

Some caveats about this are in order. We are engaging in speculation about behavioral motives here, and more data are needed before firm conclusions can be drawn. This is the first look at one set of data, and it should be kept in mind that the legacy a judicial cohort leaves is developed over many years. Still, there is some evidence to suggest that partisanship increasingly infuses people's views of law enforcement, and there are signs here suggesting that the Trump jurists might share in some measure Republicans' increasingly dim views about prosecutors and suspicion of law enforcement. Conversely, it may be that the Biden appointees are reflecting more confidence in prosecutors that Democrats these days are more likely to share.

The second column in Table 7.1 contains data on the dimension of civil rights and liberties; that is, it examines judges' decisions on issues such as freedom of speech and religion, the right to privacy and LGBTQ rights, discrimination against racial/ethnic minorities, and so on. In this realm, the results are truly remarkable.

Around 42 percent of the Biden cohort's decisions in civil liberties and rights have been liberal in nature. This is slightly less liberal than the Obama judges and on par with the Clinton cohort. In fact, Biden's judges are the most centrist of all Democratic presidents and significantly further from the left than the Carter and Johnson judges. In contrast, only 26 percent of the Trump cohort's decisions have been liberal in nature. Like criminal justice cases, this percentage is not in line with the cohorts of the most recent Republican presidents, W. Bush (33), Bush (33.7), and Reagan (32.7). Interestingly, the data indicate that Trump's judges are the most extreme in terms of conservatism in civil rights and liberties issue that we have ever analyzed.

We present data on the judges' decisional patterns in economic and labor regulation in the third column in Table 7.1. A typical case in this category might be a dispute between a labor union and a company, a worker alleging a violation of the Fair Labor Standards Act, or a case involving a governmental effort to regulate business. On this composite variable, around 60 percent of the decisions of the Biden appointees have been on the liberal side. The Obama, Carter, and Johnson judges are more liberal in these cases, but the Clinton judges are a bit more conservative. Overall, Biden judges are pretty comparable to other Democrats in this case type area. Compare that to the 44 percent of rulings by Trump appointees that have been on the liberal side—his judges are, again, more conservative than any recent president we have studied. The numbers for W. Bush, Bush, and Reagan are 51, 50.2, and 49.6 percent, respectively. We find once more that the Trump jurists exhibit distinctly different decision-making behavior: they are more conservative on economic matters than judges selected by any prior Democrat *or* Republican.

Taken altogether, the data provide us with a discernable picture of the ideology of the Biden and Trump judges. Biden's jurists are center-left Democrats, well within the mainstream of the ideology of prior presidents' judges. A conservative activist claimed in 2023 that "[Biden's] nominees . . . will be some of the most radical judges in the country."[54] But the facts do not support that contention. Indeed, the Biden judges are exhibiting a conservative tilt when it comes to criminal justice matters. President Biden clearly made the appointment of judges a priority in his administration, with a key emphasis upon diversity and a preference for mainstream liberals. On the other hand, the Trump administration appears to have placed a singular priority in selecting judges with an eye on ideology. Whether President Trump's judges are "extreme" or not is a normative question that this statistical analysis is unable to adequately answer. Indeed, reactions can be found on both sides of the question. In 2018, David Fontana, a law professor at George Washington University, suggested that Trump's judges were in the mainstream when he observed, "what we are seeing are fairly conventional Republican picks so far."[55] Conversely, some media critics suggested that the president's nominees are "shocking extremist judges."[56] What is clear, however, is that Trump appointed judges who are exhibiting a decision-making pattern that is distinctly different than previous presidents. Overall, his judges are further to the right in civil liberties and rights cases and economic and labor regulation matters than those of any recent Republican president (not to mention Democrats). But with regards to criminal justice issues, the Trump judges have been uncommonly liberal in their decision-making approach.

Considering the sum of the evidence, there is unmistakable indication that President Trump meets the first element of our four-part test. The Trump administration aggressively pursued a strategy of making ideologically based appointments to the federal judiciary. President Biden, on the other hand, appears to have prioritized diversity in his judicial nominees with an eye on appointing mainstream, center-left liberals.

The Number of Judicial Vacancies. The second factor affecting a president's capacity to influence the ideological direction of the judiciary is the number of vacancies he can fill. This is, of course, impacted by the number of vacancies inherited from the president's predecessor, how long the president serves in office, and whether Congress enacts legislation creating new judgeship positions that the president may fill.

Since Biden was a one-term president, the overall number of Article III judges appointed by him falls well below the totals of two-term presidents, including Barack Obama (324), George W. Bush (324), and Bill Clinton (372). After Trump lost his reelection bid in 2020, he ended up leaving the White House having appointed a total of 226 Article III judges. However, his victory in the 2024 election means that Trump's final imprint will likely be comparable to that of other two-term presidents. By comparison, Biden was on track to appoint over 200 judges during his four years in office, including at least 43 court of appeals jurists, according to a July 2024 report by the Brookings Institution.[57] Indeed, an August 2024 news report noted that a bit of a race was on among some Democrats who "have made a priority to eclipse" Trump's number, though other issues competing for limited time on the Senate's legislative calendar left that to be determined.[58] Suffice it to say that both the Biden and first Trump administrations placed a priority on selecting judges and their rapid rate of filling judgeships put them on pace to outrank most one-term presidents. Consider, for example, the fact that the last one-term president before BidenGeorge H. W. Bushfilled 187 positions on the Article III courts.[59] In contrast, as of November 13, 2025, the Senate had confirmed 215 of Biden's judicial nominees, with Democrats racing to confirm more nominees in the final weeks of his presidency.[60]

However, there is no question that when it comes to inherited vacancies, Donald Trump was given an extraordinary opportunity to leave a substantial impact upon the courts that eclipsed that of Joe Biden. When President Obama left office in early 2017, there were 105 judicial vacancies waiting for the Trump administration. Trump thus inherited the second-largest number of vacancies of his recent predecessors (second only to Bill Clinton).[61] The considerable number of open positions waiting for Trump was due mostly to the bitter partisan politics that occurred during the Obama administration and Republican efforts to slow-walk, block, and/or otherwise impede that administration from making appointments to the bench. The resulting vacancies afforded the Trump administration the chance to leave a substantial and lasting imprint upon the federal court system.

The Trump White House put a particular priority on filling vacancies on the courts of appeals. Since district court judge decisions are usually subject to appellate review, and very few cases are ever accepted by the US Supreme Court for review on appeal (fewer than 1 percent of requests for certiorari are granted), the appellate bench represents the de facto "court of last resort" in most federal cases. As such, appellate judges are particularly important in terms of their influence in judicial policymaking, and the Trump administration correspondingly emphasized filling positions on the courts of appeals. Indeed, Trump appointed fifty-four federal appellate judges in four years, one short of the total fifty-five that Obama appointed over twice as much time.[62]

Trump's judicial appointment strategy certainly benefitted by having a key ally in Senate Majority Leader Mitch McConnell (R-KY). Though Trump and McConnell intensely disliked one another on a personal level,[63] the senator considered judicial appointments to be extremely important for the GOP. Indeed, Senator Josh Hawley (R-MO) told one reporter that "Sen. McConnell, when he was majority leader, [confirming judges] was arguably I think his top priority."[64] McConnell worked tirelessly to achieve Senate confirmation of Trump's judges, including reversing a practice of not confirming presidential election-year nominees after the president's party lost the election. In a particularly audacious move that broke from long-standing tradition, the Senate Majority Leader led his party to confirm thirty-three district court judges after Trump lost his reelection bid but before Biden took office on January 20, 2024.[65] McConnell was reported to have said that he would "leave no vacancy behind,"[66] and he lived up to that pledge.

As a consequence, the number of vacancies handed down to Joe Biden was relatively modest. The forty-sixth president inherited forty-six judicial vacancies from Trump, though only two of them were on the courts of appeals.[67] This was not an especially high number by historical standards, and it was less than half the number that were open to Trump when he took office. Still, it was a start, and as previously mentioned in this chapter, the Biden team made a concerted effort of showing that they would prioritize the selection of judges. President Biden also got a bit of a boost during his first week on the job when more than a dozen judges, nominated by presidents of both parties, announced plans to retire or take senior status.[68] By the end of Biden's term, he could point to a sizable number of vacancies that enabled him to successfully leave a mark on the judiciary.

A special point should be made about the opportunity to fill Supreme Court vacancies, since these are both relatively rare and extremely important. On this front Trump, again, had an edge over Biden.

President Trump was afforded the exceptional opportunity to fill three Supreme Court vacancies during his four years in office. Since Senate Republicans held Scalia's seat open for the incoming administration, the new president wasted no time in 2021 in nominating Neil Gorsuch to fill the vacant position. An appellate judge with sterling credentials and a former Federalist Society member, Gorsuch was opposed by Democrats, who filibustered his nomination (recall that Democrats had ended the filibuster for lower court and executive branch nominees but retained the power of the minority party to filibuster a Supreme Court pick). Senate Republicans, led by McConnell, countered the Democrats' filibuster of Gorsuch by changing the Senate rules and ending the filibuster for *all* nominations. With that procedural hurdle removed, and outnumbered Democrats powerless to stop the nomination, Gorsuch was confirmed on April 7, 2017, less than four months after Trump assumed office.[69] Just over one year later, Justice Anthony Kennedy announced his retirement from the high court in June 2018, handing another opportunity to President Trump to leave a major imprint upon the judiciary. Trump nominated Brett Kavanaugh, a DC Court of Appeals judge widely regarded as a staunch conservative, to replace Kennedy. The Kavanaugh nomination turned out to be much more contentious than that of Gorsuch, in large part because of allegations of sexual misconduct during Kavanaugh's younger years by Christine Blasey Ford, a professor of psychology at Palo Alto University. After a very bitter committee hearing process, which included riveting testimony by Dr. Ford and an angry response by the nominee who denied the allegations, the Senate ultimately confirmed Kavanaugh on a close, nearly party-line vote of 50–48.[70]

President Trump was presented with his third, and arguably most momentous, opportunity to fill a Supreme Court vacancy with the death of Ruth Bader Ginsburg at age eighty-seven on September 18, 2020. Ginsburg's passing after a drawn-out battle with cancer was an especially bitter pill for Democrats. The champion of women's rights had resisted hints in 2013 to retire, which would have enabled then-President Obama to keep the seat in liberal hands.[71] Furthermore, Ginsburg's death came just weeks before the 2020 election, and thus presented Trump with an enormous opportunity to tilt the ideology of the Court by replacing the left-leaning justice with a younger conservative stalwart just a few months before leaving office.

Given the timing, Republicans moved quickly to replace Ginsburg before the election. Democrats justly cried hypocrisy, noting that Senate Majority Leader Mitch McConnell had refused even to consider President Obama's nomination of Merrick Garland to replace Justice Scalia after his death in February 2016, citing the election year as an excuse for inaction. But the confirmation of a justice to the Supreme Court often boils down to raw political power, and the fact is that in both instances the Republicans had the upper hand. Eight days after Ginsburg's death, the White House nominated Amy Coney Barrett, a judge on the seventh circuit court of appeals with strong credentials and a clearly conservative background, to fill the seat. Democrats, reeling from the loss of Ginsburg and focused on the upcoming election, were unable to muster much opposition and Barrett's solid professional qualifications gave them little to criticize. Some liberals questioned Barrett's affiliation as a "handmaid" in a small private Christian group called the "People of Praise,"[72] but this issue gained no traction. In the Senate minority and stripped of the ability to filibuster the nominee, Democrats were powerless to block the effort. On October 26, 2020—just eight days before the 2020 election—Barrett was confirmed by the Senate in a 52–48 vote, becoming the fifth woman in US history to serve on the Supreme Court. It was the first time since 1869 that a justice was confirmed with no support from the minority party.[73] And it was a towering victory for the political right as they had flipped a Supreme Court position from a liberal stalwart to a reliable conservative.

President Biden had the opportunity to appoint just one justice to the nation's highest court. While campaigning, Biden had promised that should he be given the chance, "I will appoint the first Black woman to the [Supreme] Court. It's required that they have representation now. It's long overdue."[74] Some Republicans complained that prioritizing gender and race in the nominee constituted de facto discrimination. Republican Senator Ted Cruz of Texas criticized Biden: "He's saying, 'if you're a white guy, tough luck'" (though reporters pointed out that Cruz and other Republicans had been silent when President Trump promised in 2020 to appoint a woman to replace Justice Ginsburg on the bench).[75]

On January 27, 2022, almost exactly one year after President Biden took office, eighty-two-year-old Justice Stephen Breyer, who had been appointed in 1994 by President Clinton, announced that he would step down from the Supreme Court. Liberals breathed a sigh of relief, worried that Breyer might miss the opportunity to allow his seat to be filled by a fellow Democrat in the White House, as Ruther Bader Ginsburg had so famously done during the Obama years. Erwin Chemerinsky, the dean of the law school at the University of California–Berkeley, had suggested in 2021 that Breyer should "learn from Justice Ginsburg's mistake" and step down. "Breyer's best chance at protecting his legacy and impact on the law is to resign now, clearing the way for a younger justice who shares his judicial outlook."[76]

In February 2022, Biden fulfilled his campaign promise and nominated Ketanji Brown Jackson to the Supreme Court.[77] Jackson possessed sterling credentials and in some ways her path to the Court was similar to that of other successful nominees: Harvard Law School, a prestigious Supreme Court clerkship, experience as a federal appeals court and district court judge. But Jackson possessed notable additional experience that made her exceptional. She had previously worked as a public defender and was the only justice with experience on the US Sentencing Commission—a bipartisan agency created by Congress to reduce disparity and promote transparency and proportionality in criminal justice sentencing.[78] Jackson had also spent almost nine years working as a federal district and appeals court judge—more hands-on bench experience than Chief Justice John G. Roberts Jr. and Justices Clarence Thomas and Amy Coney Barrett, who each served less than three years before being nominated. Stephen Vladeck, a law professor at the University of Texas School of Law, observed that "Ketanji Brown Jackson brings more experience as a judge than four of the current justices did combined at the time they joined the court."[79]

Republicans attempted to paint Jackson as a liberal extremist who had been too lenient toward criminals, but her opponents were ultimately unsuccessful.[80] In the Senate minority and having ended the filibuster for Supreme Court nominations in 2017, Republicans now found themselves powerless to block the nominee. In a historic moment of victory for the Biden administration, on April 7, 2022, Ketanji Brown Jackson was confirmed by the Senate in a 53–47 vote, making her the first Black woman to be elevated to the highest court in the nation.[81]

Returning to the matter of judicial vacancies: what about the possibility of Congress enacting legislation that would create new judgeship positions that Presidents Biden or Trump could fill? As was the case with other recent chief executives, there was no law passed during their presidencies that added significant numbers of new judgeships. Despite a need for additional jurists in various jurisdictions around the United States, in recent decades the creation of new judgeships has proven to be an intractable issue that is closely tied to partisan politics. In particular, the Senate remains a substantial obstacle where sixty votes are typically needed to approve a bill and overcome an inevitable filibuster by the minority party. In 2021, legislation was introduced in the House and Senate to add dozens of new federal judgeships.[82] But the bill, entitled the "Judicial Understaffing Delays Getting Emergencies Solved Act or JUDGES Act," ultimately went nowhere. Both Democrats and Republicans have simply been too opposed to the idea of giving the other party an opportunity to leave an expanded imprint upon the judicial branch.

As a candidate in the 2020 election, Biden had faced pressure from some liberal interest groups to support legislation that would create new positions on the Supreme Court. Angry about Republicans' hardball tactics in filling recent Supreme Court positions, some Democrats discussed the idea of expanding the Supreme Court from nine to thirteen justices.[83] This, of course, echoed the "Court-packing" plan of Franklin Roosevelt and his administration's unhappiness with the Supreme Court during the New Deal of the 1930s. "The Republicans stole two seats on the Supreme Court, and now it is up to us to repair that damage," said Senator Ed Markey (D-MA) when he later backed legislation to change the number of justices on the high court.[84] Alas, the idea gained little traction and not even Joe Biden backed the idea.[85] In October 2020, less than a month before the election, Biden poured cold water on the idea when he stated, "I'm not a fan of court packing, [and] I don't want to get off on that whole issue."[86]

More recently, there has been a glimmer of hope for those who recognize the need for more positions on the federal bench. In August 2024, a new judgeship bill passed the US Senate by a unanimous vote that would create sixty-six new judicial seats.[87] Interestingly, this legislation came with a unique twist and was written in a way that sought to circumvent the partisan divide: per the terms of the bill, the new judgeships would be created and filled incrementally over ten years starting in January 2025. And since the proposed law would open new judicial positions to the next (and subsequent) occupants of the White House, and there was no incumbent running in 2024, it could benefit either political party. Though the fate of this legislation was pending in the US House as of November 2024 and its outlook was dim, if the bill passed it would constitute the first significant expansion of the judiciary since 1990.[88]

In sum, both Presidents Biden and Trump had significant numbers of judicial vacancies during their terms. However, given the enormous number of vacant judgeship positions Trump inherited, his appointment of a total of 226 judges (54 of them to the appellate courts), and the three Supreme Court seats his administration was able to fill, it is fair to say that Trump's influence on the federal judiciary outpaced that of Biden.

The President's Political Clout. The third variable affecting the president's ideological impact is the amount and strength of his political influence. How well is the president able to get the Senate to approve his nominees?

When President Biden moved into the Oval Office, his approval ratings were significantly higher than those of his predecessor. After the January 6, 2021, insurrection and violence at the US Capitol by Trump supporters in the closing days of his term, and the subsequent second impeachment of Trump for his role in fomenting the violence, Trump had departed with a 29 percent approval rating, the lowest rating during his tenure in office.[89] Conversely, 57 percent of the public gave their approval of Biden's job as president, with 37 percent disapproving.[90] President Biden thus began his term with a solid level of public approval.

The nation still faced major challenges presented by the COVID-19 pandemic in 2021, and the health care crisis consumed much of the nation's attention. At the same time, the US economy in 2021 continued to rebound from the lows of 2020—aided in part by popular infusions of federal stimulus money—but many people still struggled. After a steep economic downturn at the peak of the pandemic in 2020, prospects had rebounded during Biden's first year. Economic growth improved and the unemployment rate was declining. However, the economy saw a sharp rise in inflation during the first half of Biden's term, peaking at a 9 percent annualized rate in June 2022.[91] Consumers were battered by rising prices and, not coincidentally, Biden's approval ratings declined precipitously. Though inflation moderated in 2023 and 2024, Biden's approval ratings remained mired around 38 percent for much of the final two years of his term.[92] Despite the initial honeymoon, Biden could not point to soaring popularity as a source of political strength for much of his time in office.

But Biden's fellow Democrats had won crucial control of the US Senate after the 2020 elections, albeit by the slimmest of margins. And this made all the difference. With the legislative chamber evenly split between fifty Democrats[93] and fifty Republicans, the tie-breaking vote by Vice President Kamala Harris gave Biden's political party control of the chamber. The importance of this majority status, however narrow it may have been, cannot be overstated. It meant that the Judiciary Committee was chaired by Dick Durbin, a team-player Democrat who had served with Joe Biden when he was in the Senate. The Judiciary Committee was fully in sync with the Biden judicial agenda and shared his urgency to fill judgeships. In June 2021, Durbin encouraged his fellow Democrats to "move our judges as quickly as possible."[94] Senator Richard

Blumenthal (D-CT), a Judiciary panel member, concurred. "We're moving very quickly," he said. "We will fill as many vacancies as possible that there are. You can't displace the Trump appointees, but we'll fill all the vacancies."[95] After the 2022 midterm elections, Democrats got a tiny bit of breathing room when they outperformed expectations and expanded their majority to 51–49.

The Democratic majority also meant that Senate Majority Leader Chuck Schumer, a Democrat from New York, was in charge of the Senate's calendar and thus had the power to bring up Biden's judicial nominees for votes and get them approved. A skilled and personable politician, Schumer had a good working relationship with the White House.[96] Of course, the narrow spilt meant that Democratic leaders could not afford party defections and had to be careful to keep all of their party members together for crucial votes. This was particularly true with regard to Senators Joe Manchin of West Virginia and Kirsten Sinema of Arizona, two moderates who had shown willingness to buck their party at times. That said, Schumer's focused yet gregarious, easygoing style worked effectively in keeping his caucus together, and Democratic senators generally backed the White House on judicial picks.

It is not hard to see, therefore, that the narrow Democratic majority was absolutely crucial to giving Biden the political clout necessary to confirm his judicial choices. Few doubted that had Mitch McConnell and the GOP been in charge, they would have slow-walked and obstructed Biden's judicial picks, just as they had often done with Obama. Without that slim Senate margin, President Biden's prospects for confirming judges would have been much different.

That said, there were a few Biden nominations that met with failure. A federal prosecutor tapped by President Biden to become a district judge in Kansas, Jabari Wamble, withdrew from consideration after waiting nearly two years for action on his nomination. No official explanation was provided for the withdrawal, but an insider familiar with the situation said the candidate was expected to receive a "not qualified" designation from the American Bar Association.[97] The nomination of Sarah Netburn, a US magistrate judge tapped for a district court position in New York, failed to advance out of the Senate Judiciary Committee in July 2024 after Senator Jon Ossoff, a Georgia Democrat, joined unanimous Republicans in voting against the nominee. In a 2022 case, Netburn had granted a transexual inmate's request to move to a women's prison from a men's facility. The person was serving a sentence for distributing child pornography, after they'd previously been convicted of sexual abuse of two minors.[98] Republicans raised fierce objections to Netburn, though Democrats noted that Netburn was simply "applying the facts and the law before her to the best of her ability" and the presiding district court judge for the case affirmed Netburn's decision.[99] Carl Tobias, a professor at the University of Richmond Law School, noted that Ossoff's vote was the only "no" vote cast against a judicial nominee by a Democratic senator on the Judiciary Committee since Biden became president.[100] There were a few other nomination mishaps for the Biden administration, but with an over 95 percent success rate, President Biden's record of getting his judges confirmed was strong.

How did the Trump influence factor compare to Biden? Having lost the popular vote in the 2016 election, President Trump began his presidency with an anemic 45 percent approval rating. It didn't get much better for the forty-fifth president. Indeed, Trump's approval ratings throughout his four years were generally low to an unprecedented level. In the jargon of pollsters, Trump was "underwater" during his entire term in office—there was a greater percentage of people who disapproved of him than approved throughout his four years in the Oval Office.[101] In a clear indication of what a polarizing figure he was, at no point during Trump's presidency did his approval rating ever top 49 percent. In fact, Biden was a more popular president than Trump. But neither of them could draw upon a deep well of public support in battling for their judicial nominees.

Nevertheless, though he was unpopular among the general public, President Trump enjoyed outsized support among loyal Republicans. Over the course of his presidency, an average of 87 percent of Republicans approved of Trump's handling of the job.[102] What's more, though many Republicans grumbled about how Trump comported himself in office, many of those same Republicans strongly agreed with the president's agenda of appointing staunch conservatives to the federal bench. Most Americans do not pay a lot of attention to nominations to the federal courts. But as one researcher noted, "a strong part of the Republican Party base, more so than the Democratic base, are tuned into judges."[103]

Furthermore, just like Biden, Trump's party held majority control in the Senate at the time. President Trump therefore had the benefit of a majority Republican Party that shared his administration's judicial ambitions and a minority party in the Senate largely unable to block the president.

As previously mentioned in this chapter, the White House found a willing partner in Senate Republican leader Mitch McConnell. They were able to set aside their differences for the purposes of judicial nominations and moved judicial nominations forward at a rapid clip. Republicans took advantage of the Democrats' 2013 decision to end filibusters for lower court judicial nominees, and the GOP engaged in some rule changes of their own. As noted above, they ended filibusters for Supreme Court nominations in 2017. Republicans also changed the Senate rules in 2019 regarding the number of hours allowed to debate district court nominees, cutting down the time from thirty hours to two hours for district court judges, allowing the majority to move substantially faster on confirmations.[104] The GOP majority also altered the blue slip tradition. Senator Charles Grassley, the Republican chair of the Senate Judiciary Committee, sharply curtailed home state senator influence by deciding to recognize blue slips only selectively.[105] Democrats, recalling that the GOP aggressively used blue slips to stall or block several of Obama's nominees, were incensed by the Republican flip-flop. But lacking the votes, and with the filibuster gone and the blue slip process in tatters, there was truly little that the minority party in the Senate could do to block Trump's judicial nominees. Ironically, many of these same changes would later help pave the way for Biden to fill judgeships.

That is not to say that President Trump saw all his judicial nominees approved. The White House was forced to withdraw the nomination of Ryan Bounds to a position on the Ninth Circuit Court of Appeals in July 2018. Bounds had ridiculed multiculturalism and groups concerned with racial issues while an undergraduate at Stanford University. Faced with this evidence, two key GOP senators—Tim Scott of South Carolina and Marco Rubio of Florida—withdrew their support for the nominee, and Republicans found themselves without enough votes to confirm Bounds.[106] Another Trump nominee, Matthew Petersen, withdrew his name from consideration for a position as a judge on the DC district court after video surfaced of Peterson at a congressional hearing being unable to answer basic questions about the law and judicial procedure. A staff lawyer with the Federal Election Commission, Peterson admitted that he had no trial court experience.[107] Two other district court nominees, Brett Talley and Jeff Mateer, were pulled after Senator Grassley told the White House to "reconsider" the nominations. Talley later received a *not qualified* rating from the American Bar Association, due in large part to his lack of courtroom experience. Mateer ran into trouble over comments describing transgender youth as part of "Satan's plan" and labeling as "disgusting" the Supreme Court's 2015 decision in *Obergefell v. Hodges*, which legalized gay marriage.[108] The Trump administration had ended the practice of prior submission of judicial nominees' names to the American Bar Association for that group's assessment of the candidate's qualifications, and it appears that in a few situations, this decision might have backfired.

These instances aside, President Trump held substantial political sway when it came to pushing his judicial nominations during his four years in office. Given the polarized nature of contemporary US politics, Trump's influence rested mostly upon his support by Republicans on Capitol Hill and the party's ability to hold on to the levers of power. Russell Wheeler, a Brookings Institution researcher, has noted that the confirmation process has become hardball politics and is less about cooperation between the parties. Voicing the thoughts of some partisans, he observed, "It's just dog-eat-dog for the moment, and we'll worry about what happens when the tables get turned later. I don't see how you ratchet it back."[109] Ultimately, despite their relatively low levels of approval among the general public, both Presidents Biden and Trump had the political clout to get most of their nominees through the US Senate's confirmation process.

The Judicial Environment That New Judges Enter. The final ingredient in the president's capacity to make an ideological mark on the federal judiciary is the judicial environment that new judges enter. If it is unfavorable because the judiciary is packed with jurists whose ideologies are opposed to that of the appointing president, the chief executive may have a long wait before the new appointees can fully express their judicial values. On the other hand, if the judiciary is evenly divided, or even somewhat disposed to the president's ideological values, the fruits of the appointments will be much more readily seen.

How did this impact President Biden's potential to leave his stamp on the courts? When Biden became president, 51 percent of federal judges had been appointed by Republican presidents while 49 percent had been tapped by Democrats. This would suggest a balanced ideology on the federal bench. By comparison, when Trump became president in early 2017, around 60 percent of active federal judges at the time had been appointed by Democratic presidents, while approximately 40 percent had been selected by Republican chief executives.[110] When Trump vacated the Oval Office in January 2021, the tilt of the federal bench had shifted. Trump ended up appointing 28 percent of the 816 active judges serving at the time. Thus, the data indicate that Trump was able to move the overall ideological balance of the federal judiciary from one that favored Democrats to one that appeared rather evenly balanced.

But a deeper look into the numbers reveals a picture much more favorable to conservatives. Trump successfully nominated 30 percent of the appeals court bench, and in the process he "flipped" the balance of several appeals courts from many Democratic appointees to many Republican appointees.[111] Nowhere was this more apparent than in the Fifth Circuit Court of Appeals, which was a particularly activist bench during the Biden years and named by a reporter at the *USA Today* as "the most right-wing appeals court" in the United States.[112] In fact, Trump ended up appointing 30 percent of the courts of appeals jurists serving on the bench when President Biden took over in January 2021—a substantial accomplishment for a one-term president. With Trump poised to take office again in 2025, his final impact will undoubtedly be greater.

The Trump administration's impact upon the Supreme Court was similarly significant. With three newly seated right-leaning justices, including the replacement of a consistent liberal (Ruth Bader Ginsburg) with a conservative (Amy Coney Barrett), Trump solidified a high court conservative majority. And since the Supreme Court tends to set the ideological tone for the federal courts overall, and the Court in the past few years has been particularly activist in its decision-making, there is little question that conservatives were pleased with what Trump accomplished regarding the ideological environment of the judiciary.

Add it all up and it is clear that the Biden cohort faced serious ideological headwinds. Trump took a federal judiciary that had a tilt that was fairly even, even leaning in a liberal direction among the lower courts, and transformed it into a conservative judicial powerhouse.

After four years of concerted effort to fill judgeships, Biden and his liberal supporters could rightfully point to a record of success. But the climate that the Biden judges entered was a particularly challenging one for liberals. President Biden's final imprint upon the judiciary remains to be seen, but with Trump set to being a second term, Biden and his fellow Democrats certainly have a long road ahead of themselves if they wished to tilt the judiciary away from conservatives.

SUMMARY

At the national level, the judicial selection process includes a variety of participants, despite the constitutional mandate that the president shall do the appointing with the advice and consent of the Senate. If presidents are to dominate this process and name to the bench individuals with similar policy values, several conditions must be met. Chief executives must want to make ideologically based appointments; they must have an ample number of vacancies to fill; they must be adroit leaders with political clout; and the existing judiciary must be attuned to their policy goals. If most of these conditions are met, presidents tend to get the kinds of judges they want. In other words, an identifiable policy link exists among the popular election of the president, the appointment of judges, and the substantive content of the judges' decisions.

FURTHER THOUGHT AND DISCUSSION QUESTIONS

1. When presidents make judicial appointments, should they anticipate how their nominees are going to rule on important policy decisions, or should they consider only the quality of their formal credentials and/or the relative prestige of their professional accomplishments?
2. Over time, the judicial appointees of Republican presidents have had decidedly more conservative decision-making records on the bench than those of judges selected by Democratic chief executives. Is this evidence that our judicial system has been *tainted* by politics, or is it proof that the democratic process prevails throughout our political system? What does this suggest about judicial independence?
3. Since large numbers of people do not pay close attention to most judicial nominations and confirmations, to what extent do you think the process is influenced by special interest groups and/or political partisans who have distinct ideological agendas?

SUGGESTED RESOURCES

Binder, Sarah A., and Forrest Maltzman. *Advice and Dissent: The Struggle to Shape the Federal Judiciary.* Washington, DC: Brookings Institution Press, 2009. A well-researched discussion of the sources on conflict in the judicial confirmation process, with a particular focus on the lower federal courts.

Epstein, Lee, and Jeffrey Segal. *Advice and Consent: The Politics of Judicial Appointments.* Oxford: Oxford University Press, 2007. A thorough discussion of the politics of the judicial selection process and how this process does—and does not—reflect the democratic process.

Goldman, Sheldon. *Picking Federal Judges: Lower Court Selection from Roosevelt through Reagan*. New Haven, CT: Yale University Press, 1997. Based on thorough, careful scholarship, Goldman writes in easy-to-follow prose about the judicial selection process between 1933 and 1989.

Slotnick, Elliot, Sara Schiavoni, and Sheldon Goldman. "Obama's Judicial Legacy: The Final Chapter." *Journal of Law and Courts* 5 (2017): 363–422. A review of the judges appointed by President Barack Obama and the confirmation battles during his years in office.

Yalof, David A. *Pursuit of Justices: Presidential Politics and the Selection of Supreme Court Nominees*. Chicago, IL: University of Chicago Press, 2001. A thorough discussion of the political pressures upon presidents as they select people to nominate for a position on the US Supreme Court.

8 LAWYERS, LITIGANTS, AND INTEREST GROUPS IN THE JUDICIAL PROCESS

CHAPTER GOALS AND OBJECTIVES

In this chapter, students will learn that . . .

- The legal profession has changed dramatically across US history and can be affected by widespread challenges such as economic recession.
- The twenty-first century has so far been a time of flux in the legal profession, with challenges brought about by economic uncertainty, the student debt crisis, and issues related to providing greater access for those from groups historically excluded from the profession.
- The legal profession is stratified, and various legal careers are not considered to be equally as lucrative or prestigious.
- In the legal process, not all litigants are expected to be equally as successful, whether their goals are more ordinary and compensation-oriented or more policy-oriented and political in nature.
- Interest groups are now routinely involved in litigation, especially at the appellate level. Mounting test cases and filing amicus curiae briefs are two principal tactics used by interest groups in the contemporary legal process.

In this chapter, we lay the foundation for a detailed examination of the courts in action by focusing on three crucial actors in the judicial process: lawyers, litigants, and interest groups. Judges in the United States make decisions only in the context of cases brought to the courts by individuals or organizations that have some sort of disagreement or dispute with one another. These adversaries, commonly called litigants, sometimes argue their own cases in such minor forums as small-claims courts, but they are almost always represented by lawyers in the more important judicial arenas.

Given the prominent role of lawyers in the US system of justice, the first part of our discussion is devoted to an examination of legal training and the legal profession. Next, the role of individual litigants and interest groups in the judicial process is examined. Although our discussion applies generally to both the federal and state judicial systems, it is necessary in some instances to distinguish between the two levels.

Elizabeth Prelogar became only the second woman in US history to serve as solicitor general when she was appointed to the post by President Joe Biden. Based on the experiences of other recent solicitors general, Prelogar will likely return to her career in the private sector as an elite Supreme Court litigator at the conclusion of her time with the US Department of Justice.

Sipa USA/Alamy Stock Photo

LAWYERS AND THE LEGAL PROFESSION

Our examination of lawyers focuses on the training and work of attorneys in the United States, first putting lawyers and the legal profession in a historical context.[1]

Development of the Legal Profession

The Colonial Period

Lawyers were not popular during the early colonial years, and there were few of them among the early settlers. Eventually, however, lawyers became necessary to a growing society facing problems that required their skills. Some who rendered legal services had been trained in England; others were laypeople who had only a smattering of legal knowledge. According to renowned legal historian Lawrence M. Freidman, "a competent, professional bar, dominated by brilliant and successful lawyers . . . existed in all major communities by 1750."[2]

The colonies had no law schools during this period to train those interested in the legal profession. Some young men—especially those who lived in the South, which had no colleges—went to England for their education and attended the Inns of Court in London. The Inns were not formal law schools; however, they were part of the English legal culture and enabled students to become familiar with English law.

Americans who aspired to the law during this period generally went through some form of clerkship or apprenticeship with an established lawyer. In other words, the student paid a fee to the lawyer, who promised to train him in the law. Some found this to be a fruitful experience, whereas others complained that it was of little or no value.

Each colony established its own standards for admission to the bar (the entire group of lawyers permitted to practice law in the courts of that colony). In some instances, the colony's highest court was given control over licensing and admission to the bar. In Massachusetts, for example, each court admitted its own lawyers; in Rhode Island, any court could admit lawyers, and admission by one court automatically conferred admission to all the courts in the colony.

The impact of lawyers on the American political system was evident during this preliminary period. Of the fifty-six signers of the Declaration of Independence, twenty-five were lawyers, and thirty-one of the fifty-five delegates to the Constitutional Convention were lawyers.[3]

From the Revolution to the Mid-Nineteenth Century

Friedman notes that after the Revolution, the number of lawyers increased rapidly because neither legal education nor admission to the bar was strict. During the first half of the nineteenth century there were no large law firms. However, some lawyers garnered wealth by representing rich clients and prosperous merchants. Other lawyers simply eked out a living by handling petty claims in minor courts.

The right social background appears to have been important. According to Friedman, more than half of lawyers admitted to the bar in Massachusetts between 1810 and 1840 were sons of lawyers and judges, up from about 38 percent prior to 1810.[4]

The apprenticeship method continued to be the trendiest way to receive legal training, but law schools were coming into existence. The first law schools grew out of law offices that had begun to specialize in training clerks or apprentices. The earliest such school was the Litchfield School in Connecticut, founded by Judge Tapping Reeve in 1784. This school, which used the lecture method, placed primary emphasis on commercial law.

Eventually, a few colleges began to teach law as part of their general curriculum. The College of William and Mary in Virginia was the first to establish a chair of law and appointed George Wythe, a legal mentor to Thomas Jefferson, to the professorship. Professorships were also established at the University of Virginia, the University of Pennsylvania, and the University of Maryland during the late eighteenth and early nineteenth centuries.

A chair of law was established at Harvard in 1816, and the first professor, Isaac Parker, worked to bring about a professional, independent law school. A major gift from Nathan Dane in 1826 helped to realize this goal. He gave Harvard $10,000 to support a professorship and suggested that Joseph Story be appointed the first Dane professor. Story was an associate justice of the US Supreme Court when he accepted the position in 1829.[5] Harvard, which awarded an LL.B. (*Bachelor of Laws*) degree to students who completed the law school course, was to become the model for all the newer schools.

The Second Half of the Nineteenth Century

During this period, the number of law schools increased dramatically. In 1850, only 15 law schools were operating, but by 1900 there were 102.[6]

The law schools of that time differed from those of today in two major ways. First, law schools then did not usually require any previous college work. Second, in 1850, the standard law school curriculum could be completed in one year. Later in the 1800s, many law schools instituted two-year programs.

In 1870, major changes were initiated at Harvard that have had a lasting impact on legal training. Christopher Columbus Langdell was appointed dean of the law school, and as a start, he instituted stiffer entrance requirements. A student without a college degree was required to pass an entrance test. Langdell also made it more difficult to graduate. The law school course was increased to two years in 1871 and to three years in 1876. Another hurdle was the requirement that a student pass first-year final examinations before proceeding to the second-year courses.

Undoubtedly, the most lasting change attributed to Langdell was the introduction of the case method of teaching. In place of lectures and textbooks, the method used casebooks (collections of actual case reports), which were designed to explain the principles of law, what they meant, and how they developed. Teachers then used the Socratic method to guide the students to a discovery of legal concepts found in the cases. Students initially resisted this new method of teaching law, but other schools eventually adopted the Harvard approach. It remains the accepted method in many law schools today.

As the demand for lawyers increased during the late 1800s, there was a corresponding acceleration in the creation of new law schools. Establishing a law school was not expensive, and a few night schools, using lawyers and judges as part-time faculty members, sprang into existence. Standards were often lax, and the curriculum tended to emphasize local practice. The major contribution of these schools was to make legal training more readily available to poor, immigrant, and working-class students.

The legal profession itself changed dramatically during this time. Lawyers no longer came solely from the upper rungs of society. Bar associations became interested in legal education as a way of controlling entry into the profession. Around the turn of the twentieth century, the Association of American Law Schools was created, and along with the American Bar Association (ABA), the organization became involved in the accreditation of law schools.

The Twentieth Century

The twentieth century saw some major changes in legal education and the legal profession. For one thing, the number of people wanting to study law increased dramatically.

By the 1960s, the number of applicants to law schools had grown so large that nearly all schools became more selective, with the more prestigious schools accepting only the best students.

In response to social pressure and litigation, many law schools began actively recruiting female and minority applicants, although law school faculty and classmates were often reluctant or even hostile to such diversification efforts. Throughout her career, Justice Ruth Bader Ginsburg was often asked about her experience as a law student, beginning at Harvard in 1956 before transferring to Columbia. (Harvard only began admitting women to their law school in 1950.) One well-known anecdote is that the small number of female students in attendance at a dinner party hosted by Harvard Law Dean Erwin Griswold were asked by the dean why they were taking a seat that could be held by a man.[7]

Ginsburg and the other eight women in her incoming cohort at Harvard also spoke about the practice among some faculty at the time of holding a "ladies' day," when the very few women in a particular class were lined up in the first row to answer questions and even be required to sing on demand. Flora Schnall, one of Ginsburg's Harvard classmates and another attendee at the dean's 1956 dinner party, characterized being questioned in front of the rest of the class as "a chance to be humiliated."[8] Both Schnall and Ginsburg recalled Schnall's response to the notorious dinner party question, where she quipped "What better place to find a man?" given how few women were enrolled alongside more than five hundred male classmates.

With respect to the form and content of legal education in the United States, the case method of instruction continued to dominate the legal education process. By the 1920s, however, the legal realist movement, predicated on the idea that understanding how law works requires observing how officials choose to navigate the formal rules at their disposal,[9] began to have an impact on the law school curriculum. New courses in areas such as administrative law and taxation found their way into the curriculum. Some schools also began to add clinical training.

By the 1960s, the curriculum in some law schools had been expanded to include social concerns such as civil rights law and law-and-poverty issues. Courses in intellectual property law and foreign law also became available. Another development was the increasing number of courses in alternative dispute resolution and negotiation. This is attributed to the fact that full-blown trials have become more of a rarity in settling disputes in today's courts.[10]

Apart from the curriculum, another key change came about through the evolution away from the undergraduate LL.B. (*Legum Baccalaureus*) degree to the professional J.D. (*Juris Doctor*) as the dominant legal degree in the United States. As the 1900s progressed, more and more students were coming to study law after already earning a bachelor's degree. Although many law schools (including the University of Chicago) mounted postgraduate J.D. programs earlier in the 1900s, the reputational juggernauts of Yale, Columbia, and especially Harvard derailed those earlier efforts to break fully from the history of providing legal training through an undergraduate degree rather than a postgraduate doctorate.[11]

By the 1960s, however, the groundswell of demand for change from students and alumni caused even the most recalcitrant of programs to make the shift, in part due to the perception that graduates with professional doctorates (J.D.s) from lower-tiered schools may have a competitive advantage over graduates with the undergraduate LL.B. from the most prestigious law schools in the nation. The ABA and the Association of American Law Schools also supported the change. The shift to the J.D. being the dominant degree for lawyers in the United States happened quickly. In 1965, ABA-approved law schools awarded roughly four times as many LL.B. degrees compared to J.D.s. Just three years later, more than three times as many J.D.s than LL.B.s were conferred.[12] Unlike the United States, many countries around the world have retained the undergraduate approach to legal education through LL.B. degrees.

Finally, the increasing use of advertising by lawyers in the 1900s has had a profound impact on the legal profession. In a 1977 decision, the US Supreme Court struck down Arizona's ban on such advertising.[13] On television stations and billboards across the country one can now see lawyers making appeals to attract new clients. Furthermore, legal clinics, established to handle the business generated by the increased use of advertising, have spread rapidly.

The Early Twenty-First Century

American law schools annually produce far more attorneys than any other country. According to a 1996 study, for instance, "Japan produces approximately 350 new lawyers each year, fewer than Harvard Law School alone."[14] According to the ABA, the number of lawyers in the United States reached 1,331,290 by 2023.[15] Even so, legal education and the legal profession in the early decades of the twenty-first century have been challenged to respond to a fast-changing world. These challenges include reacting to economic recession, technological changes, the student debt crisis, and increased considerations of issues related to diversity in the legal profession.

We begin by considering where attorneys in the United States work today. The National Association for Law Placement (NALP) provides information. Of law school graduates in 2023 who were employed as of March 15, 2024, some 58.2 percent were in private practice, 11.1 percent worked for the government, 10.4 percent held judicial clerkships, 9.7 percent were employed in the public interest area, 8.1 percent were in the business field, 1.4 percent were educators, and 1.0 percent were in the military.[16] Note that these numbers for 2023 graduates exclude those who were unemployed, although the Class of 2023 saw the highest overall employment rate (at a remarkable 92.6 percent) that NALP has ever recorded.

The employment success achieved for those coming out of law school in 2023 is especially notable given how badly the legal profession was hit by the Great Recession, starting in late 2007. The employment rate for newly minted law school graduates was as low as 84.5 percent in 2013, and although the employment rate has been slowly ticking up since 2016, some of the increase has been due to a recent decline in the number of people graduating from law school. In other words, the employment rate has recently increased even as the number of legal jobs found by graduates has yet to recover fully since the Great Recession. Similarly, the employment numbers presented here do not account for recent law school graduates who may be underemployed (such as in part-time positions or those that do not require bar passage), although the trend has shown improvement since the darkest days of the Great Recession as well. For the Class of 2023, 81.1 percent reported employment that was full-time, long-term, and required bar passage, which is a remarkable 23-point improvement compared to the job placement rate for those who graduated in 2011.[17]

With respect to the numbers of students in law school, the ABA reported a substantial drop in the number of students matriculating in ABA-accredited law schools during the recent recession, with more than 47,500 students entering J.D. programs in 2011 (early in the Great Recession), but just over 37,000 students in 2016.[18] In 2018, 2019, and 2020, the numbers of matriculating law school students hovered at just over 38,000 per year. Nearly 43,000 students entered J.D. programs in American law schools in 2021,[19] although matriculation numbers for incoming classes in 2022 and 2023 have returned to the recent norm of approximately 38,000 across the country.[20]

What should we make of this information? On the one hand, these statistics indicate a legal profession that has steadily been rebounding from the Great Recession, in terms of job placements for those entering legal practice in recent years. On the other hand, concerns linger in the wake of the disruption caused by that financial crisis, as well as by the even more recent COVID-19 pandemic. Law school enrollments are still down compared to the pre–Great Recession years, and there is evidence that the job market for newly minted lawyers may not be able to accommodate any significant increase in new graduates all that comfortably if enrollments were to increase more dramatically and consistently in the coming years. Although data will not be collected until after this book is published, the employment rate (especially in full-time, long-term positions requiring bar passage) for the larger Class of 2024 (roughly five thousand more students enrolled in J.D. programs in 2021 than in 2020) may provide a useful counterpoint to the rosy employment prospects of those graduating just one year earlier.

Matriculation statistics and employment rates are not the only factors to consider when assessing the state of legal education in the United States today. The cost of a legal education is of particular concern. A 2021 survey of more than 1,300 new lawyers (most in their twenties and thirties) found that more than 90 percent had taken out law school loans, with more than half of respondents reporting that law school debt caused them to consider salary more heavily in selecting a job than anticipated when they began law school. Many also reported that law school debt affected other major life decisions, such as whether to buy a house or have children. The 2021 report found that less than half (47 percent) agreed that their degree was worth the cost, although 55 percent said they would have attended the same law school if they had the choice.[21]

In 2024, the Center on Education and the Workforce (CEW) at Georgetown University calculated that the return on investment (measured as median earnings minus median debt payments four years after graduation) of a law degree varied greatly from school to school. The best returns on investment were concentrated among a small number of highly selective law schools. "By comparison, graduates of the 33 lowest-ranking law schools earn less than $55,000 net of debt four years after graduation and have a lower bar passage rate."[22]

It is clear that the opening decades of the twenty-first century have been very challenging to navigate for students and for young lawyers. As a result, law school enrollments have dropped compared to the very early years of this century. For those students who have made the choice to earn a J.D., doing so requires thoughtful consideration of the return on investment.

The recent decline in the numbers of students attending law school has also caused serious financial problems for many law schools themselves. Some have had to respond by reducing the size of their faculty, with some of the hardest hit schools having to merge campuses or close entirely. In 2017, Whittier Law School in Southern California became what is believed to be the first ABA-accredited law school in the country to make the decision to shut down.[23] Others have recently closed as well, but those schools were typically either unaccredited or only provisionally accredited by the ABA.[24] Although the closing of a law school is surely tremendously disruptive to the students, faculty, and staff on campus, not to mention the surrounding community, the closing of some of the poorest performing law schools in the country is not necessarily a bad thing, especially given recent challenges in the legal job market. A 2016 survey of admissions officers at ABA-accredited law schools across the country found that 65 percent agreed that "it would be a good idea if at least a few law schools closed."[25]

Beyond the few schools that have not been able to find a viable path through these unpredictable times, law schools across the country have had to work harder to fill their classrooms. In an effort to attract a sufficient number of students without decreasing the quality of incoming classes, schools have restructured their programs and curriculum to appeal to students in today's global and fast-moving world. Experiential learning opportunities have expanded on many campuses. In 2014, the ABA began mandating that every student complete a minimum of six credits of experiential coursework through opportunities such as law clinics, courses that include simulation experiences, or externships.[26] The ABA has subsequently considered expanding the experiential learning requirement even further. Schools have likewise begun developing online and part-time options, although the ABA regulates the extent to which a law school can move its curriculum to an online format.[27] Law schools have also looked to attract students by mounting accelerated, interdisciplinary, and non-J.D. programs.[28] Independent law schools that are not part of a larger university institutional setting may find it particularly difficult to respond successfully to these recent challenges.[29]

Just as some schools have found it harder to navigate this upheaval smoothly, not all law students or young lawyers have been affected in the same way by concerns over student debt, job placement, and return on investment in a J.D. Another factor that has dominated the world of legal education and the practice of law early in the twenty-first century has been the challenge inherent in fostering more diversity in the profession. In 2016, women made up a majority of all law students for the first time in American history. Their ranks in the classroom have only increased since then, and by 2022, women held 55.7 percent of the seats in ABA-accredited law school classrooms.[30] Law schools have also gradually increased their racial and ethnic diversity in recent years. Between 2012 and 2022, the percentage of students of color at ABA-accredited law schools increased six points, from 27 percent in 2012 to one-third in 2022.[31]

Even considering such gains, law students from more marginalized backgrounds still face adversity in the legal profession, compared to some of their classmates. According to Georgetown's Center on Education and the Workforce, the median return on investment of a law degree is lower for women and members of marginalized racial or ethnic groups, and especially so for Black women and Hispanic/Latina women.[32] Student debt loads are also higher for students from more marginalized racial and ethnic backgrounds.[33]

In 2023, an assessment of diversity in US law firms found that women constituted the majority of all associates for the first time in history.[34] Their representation at the partnership level still lags, with women comprising just 27.76 percent of all partners. People of color represent 30.15 percent of associates, but only 12.01 percent of all partners. The numbers of associates and partners identifying as members of the LGBTQ community have also increased over time. As of 2023, 6.79 percent of associates and 2.57 percent of partners identified as LGBTQ, compared to 1.33 percent of associates and 0.79 percent of partners in 2004.

The tension between supporting efforts at truly diversifying a professional field that has historically been hostile to those from underrepresented backgrounds and navigating the economic realities of legal education and the legal profession today has proven difficult. With respect to diversity, clear gains have been made, but students and young lawyers from marginalized backgrounds have, as a general rule, experienced a lower return on investment from a J.D., compared to their classmates.

The American Bar Foundation recently published the results of a major study tracking the lives of more than 4,500 lawyers for twenty years after passing the bar.[35] This "After the JD" (AJD) study confirmed that stratification across different professional "hemispheres" remains connected to race, gender, and law school status and prestige. Although the students entering law school today are more diverse than ever, the challenges faced by those from traditionally excluded groups still influence their lives, deep into their careers. These durable connections between personal background and professional opportunity and status should be kept in mind as we turn our attention to what we mean by "stratification" in the legal profession.

Stratification in the Legal Profession

Within the legal field, some environments have historically proven more profitable and prestigious than others. This situation has led to what is known as professional stratification. Because of increased diversification within the legal field and increased specialization within the profession, America's lawyers have become a less homogeneous group. The result is a profession stratified into "two hemispheres divided by backgrounds, clients, functions, structures, rewards, and associations."[36]

One of the major factors influencing the prestige rating is the type of legal specialty and type of clientele served. Lawyers with specialties geared toward big business and large institutions occupy the top hemisphere; those who represent individual interests are in the bottom hemisphere.

At the top of the prestige ladder are the elite law firms. These include the law practices originally (or still) situated on New York City's Wall Street and other large national firms. The basic pattern followed by the large national firms was established early in the twentieth century by the Wall Street firm Cravath, Swaine & Moore. The ideal candidate for the firm was an editor of the *Law Review* at a top-ranked law school. Those recruited served a kind of internship during which they performed general work for a few of the firm's partners. Later, they moved into an area of specialization, and by the tenth year, they were evaluated for a partnership in the firm. Some lawyers were rewarded with partnerships; others left for another job.

This approach, used by most large firms, stresses that attorneys must be dedicated to the interests of their clients and work long hours on their behalf. They have traditionally been known less for court appearances than for the counseling they provide their clients. The clients must be able to pay for this high-powered legal talent, and thus, they tend to be major corporations rather than individuals. However, many of these large national firms often provide pro bono (free) legal services to further civil rights, civil liberties, consumer interests, and environmental causes.

The large national firms consist of partners and associates. The associates are paid salaries, and in essence, they work for the partners. These firms compete for the top-ranking law school graduates, tempting first-year associates with large beginning salaries, annual salary increases, and in some instances, opportunities for bonuses. The most prestigious firms have five hundred or more lawyers and employ hundreds of other people as paralegals (nonlawyers who are specifically trained to handle many of the routine aspects of legal work), administrators, librarians, and secretaries. In addition to New York City, prestigious firms are found in other major cities, such as Chicago, Houston, Los Angeles, San Francisco, and Washington, DC. Many of these firms have branches in several US cities and even abroad.

Occupying a notch below attorneys working in large national firms are those employed by large corporations. Many corporations use national law firms as outside counsel but also hire their own salaried attorneys. The legal staffs of some corporations rival in size those of private firms. These corporations now compete with the major law firms for the best law school graduates.

The legal division of a typical large corporation is headed by a senior-level official known as the general counsel, who often also holds a title such as vice president or secretary. Instead of representing the corporation in court (a task usually handled by outside counsel when necessary), the legal division handles the multitude of legal problems faced by the modern corporation. For example, the legal division monitors the company's personnel practices to ensure compliance with federal and state regulations concerning hiring and removal procedures. The corporation's attorneys may help in strategic planning by advising the board of directors about such matters as contractual agreements, mergers, stock sales, and other business practices. The company lawyers may also help educate other employees about the laws that apply to their specific jobs and make sure that they are following them. The legal division of a large company also serves as a liaison with outside counsel.

Most of the nation's lawyers toil in the lowest hemisphere of the legal profession in terms of prestige. One classic study aptly noted that "the Manhattan megafirm with scores of highly paid associates may command headlines for the moment, but the truth is that most lawyers . . . work in firms of fewer than 20 lawyers."[37] Even today, NALP reports that more recent graduates work at firms with fewer than twenty-five lawyers, rather than at a huge firm of five hundred or more members.[38]

Whereas the attorneys in the upper hemisphere are primarily involved in representing corporate clients, the lawyers who work in the lower hemisphere are engaged in a wide range of activities. They are much more likely to be found, day in and day out, in the courtrooms of the United States. These are the attorneys who represent clients in personal injury suits, who prosecute and defend persons accused of crimes, who represent spouses in divorce proceedings, who help people conduct real estate transactions, and who help people prepare wills, to name just a few of their activities.

Many attorneys, especially those in solo practice, handle distinct types of cases instead of specializing in one or two areas. Some charge a flat hourly rate for their services; those representing plaintiffs in a personal injury suit often work under a contingency fee arrangement. Under this arrangement, the attorney receives no compensation in advance. Instead, if the suit is successful and the plaintiff is awarded monetary damages, the lawyer receives a certain percentage for their services.

A popular image of lawyers conveyed on television is that they are primarily engaged in litigation.[39] In truth, many lawyers rarely, if ever, argue cases in a courtroom. Instead, they perform a few other significant services for their clients. Notable among these is counseling. One study notes that lawyers "spend about one-third of their time advising their clients about the proper course of action in anticipation of the reactions of courts, agencies, or third parties."[40]

A second important service is negotiating, in both civil and criminal cases. Plea bargaining, a dominant feature of criminal case processing, is an example of negotiation between prosecutors and defense attorneys. In civil cases, pretrial hearings and conferences provide opportunities for lawyers to negotiate with one another to reach a settlement and avoid costly and time-consuming trials.

Drafting documents is a third important service provided by attorneys. Many clients hire lawyers to write and/or revise important documents such as contracts, wills, deeds, and leases.

A fourth function in certain types of cases is investigating. In a criminal case, for example, the defense attorney may engage in, or hire a private investigator to engage in, a search for facts, witnesses, medical or other records, and physical evidence to support a defendant's plea.

Finally, lawyers engage in research—that is, they search for precedents that support their cases and adapt legal doctrines to specific cases. Much of the research activity is carried out in larger firms and those that specialize in handling appeals of trial court decisions.

Attorneys who work for the government are generally included in the lower hemisphere. Some, such as the US attorney general and the solicitor general, occupy prestigious positions, but many others toil in rather obscure and poorly paid positions. Some attorneys seek careers as judges at the federal or state level.

Government Attorneys in the Judicial Process

Given that so many cases involve the government in some capacity, it is appropriate to look more extensively at the lawyers who handle the legal work of the government at the state or federal level. Government attorneys work at all levels of the judicial process, from trial courts to the highest state and federal appellate courts. However, the bulk of the cases never move beyond the trial courts, so we begin by looking at the government attorneys whose work occurs predominantly at the trial court level.

Federal Prosecutors

Although the exact origins of the public prosecutor are uncertain, the prosecution of criminal cases in colonial America became the responsibility of a district attorney (or a person with an equivalent title), who was appointed by the governor and assigned to a specific region. The practice persisted, and by the end of the American Revolution every state had passed legislation creating a public prosecutor. In most instances, the public prosecutor was an elected county official. The Judiciary Act of 1789 also provided for a US attorney to be appointed by the president for each federal district court. Since these beginnings, "the prosecutor has become the most powerful figure in the criminal justice system."[41]

Today, each federal judicial district has a US attorney (a "USA") and one or more assistant US attorneys ("AUSAs"). As characterized by political scientists Banks Miller and Brett Curry, USAs "implement federal criminal policy in localized contexts and thus represent the primary conduits for the US government's application of force against its citizens."[42] US attorneys and their assistants prosecute defendants in the federal district courts and defend the United States when it is sued in a federal trial court. Primarily, then, they function as prosecutors for the federal government, with considerable discretion in deciding which criminal cases to prosecute. The US attorneys have the authority to determine which civil cases to attempt to settle out of court and which ones to take to trial.

US attorneys are appointed by the president and confirmed by the Senate. Nominees must reside in the district to which they are appointed and must be lawyers in practice. They serve a formal term of four years but can be reappointed indefinitely or removed at the president's discretion.[43] The appointment of a US attorney can be a political reward.[44] Overwhelmingly, only lawyers who belong to the president's party are considered; it has become customary for US attorneys to resign their positions when the opposition party wins the presidency. Because each nominee must be confirmed by the Senate, the senator or senators who are of the president's party and represent the state where the vacancy exists become important actors in the appointment process.

The discretion granted to US attorneys in doing their work does afford the executive and legislative branches the ability to exert influence over how USAs exercise this discretion. In part, this is due to the ambitions of individual USAs, who understand the short-term nature of their current job and may be looking ahead to future opportunities (such as a federal judgeship or other appointive position within the executive branch) held at the discretion of the political branches.[45]

The assistant US attorneys are formally appointed by the US attorney general, although in practice, they are chosen by the US attorney, who forwards the selection to the attorney general for ratification. Assistant US attorneys may be fired by the attorney general.

Prosecutors at the State Level

Those who prosecute persons accused of violating state criminal statutes are commonly known as district attorneys. In most states, they are elected county officials, but in a few states, they are appointed. The district attorney's office usually employs several assistants who do the bulk of the trial work. Many of these assistant district attorneys are recent graduates of law school and are using the position to gain trial experience. Some will later enter private practice, often as criminal defense attorneys. Others will seek to become district attorneys or perhaps judges after a few years.

The district attorney's office has a great deal of discretion in the handling of cases. Given budget and personnel constraints, not all cases can be afforded the same amount of time and attention. Therefore, some cases are dismissed, others are not prosecuted, and still others are prosecuted vigorously in court. Most cases, however, are subject to plea bargaining. As discussed further in Chapter 9, this means that the district attorney's office agrees to accept the defendant's plea of guilty on a reduced charge or to drop some charges against the defendant in exchange for pleas of guilty on others.

Public Defenders

Often, the person charged with violating a state or federal criminal statute is unable to pay for the services of a defense attorney. In some areas, a government official known as a public defender bears the responsibility for representing indigent defendants. Thus, the public defender is a counterpart of the prosecutor. Unlike the district attorney, however, the public defender is usually appointed rather than elected.

Some parts of the country have statewide public defender systems; in other regions, the public defender is a local official, usually associated with a county government. In New York City, an independent organization known as the Legal Aid Society serves as the primary public defender for the city. New York's Legal Aid Society also has a civil division. Like the district attorney, the public defender employs assistants and investigative personnel.

Other Government Lawyers

At both the state and federal levels, some government attorneys are better known for their work in appellate courts than in trial courts. For example, each state has an attorney general who supervises a staff of attorneys charged with the responsibility of handling the legal affairs of the state. At the federal level, the Department of Justice has similar responsibilities on behalf of the United States.

The US Department of Justice

Although the Justice Department is an agency of the executive branch of the government, it has a natural association with the judicial branch. Many of the cases heard in federal courts involve the national government in one capacity or another. Sometimes the government is sued; in other instances, the government initiates the lawsuit. In either case, an attorney must represent the government. Most of the litigation involving the federal government is handled by the Justice Department, although several other government agencies have attorneys on their payrolls.

The Justice Department has several key divisions, offices, agencies, and bureaus. The Office of the Solicitor General is extremely important in cases argued before the Supreme Court. The Justice Department also has several legal divisions, each headed by an assistant attorney general and staffed by specialized lawyers. These legal divisions supervise the handling of litigation by the US attorneys, take cases to the courts of appeals, and aid the solicitor general's office in cases argued before the Supreme Court.

US Attorney General

The US attorney general, a cabinet official, is the head of the Department of Justice (DOJ). As such, some of their duties might best be described as bureaucratic or managerial. Unlike the solicitor general, the US attorney general does not regularly appear before the US Supreme Court, or any other court, for that matter. However, they do supervise the work of the US attorneys in each district and may use that power to influence the scope of legal activity aimed at pursuing the administration's policy goals.

At times, the attorney general's role supervising the Justice Department can be fraught, which is of particular consequence when the tension is over the handling of prosecutorial decisions within the DOJ. In September 2020, for example, the Justice Department's inspector general opened an investigation into Attorney General William Barr's intervention in the criminal case against President Donald Trump's longtime adviser and ally Roger Stone.[46] In February of that year, Barr intervened to seek a lighter sentence recommendation for Stone, after AUSAs and an acting USA handpicked by Barr had submitted a harsher recommendation. Stone was convicted in 2019 of multiple charges related to obstruction, witness tampering, and making false statements in connection to the House investigation into the Trump campaign's coordination with Russia during the 2016 election. Stone's sentence would eventually be commuted by President Trump, but not before an assistant US attorney testified before the House Judiciary Committee that he had "never seen political influence play any role in prosecutorial decision-making," until the Roger Stone case.[47] Barr responded by noting that all prosecutorial power is vested in the attorney general, and that "the notion that line prosecutors should make the final decisions at the Department of Justice is completely crazy."[48]

US Solicitor General

The solicitor general of the United States is assisted by several deputies and several assistant solicitors general. The solicitor general's primary function is to decide on behalf of the United States which cases will and will not be presented to the US Supreme Court for review. Whenever an executive branch department or agency loses a case in one of the courts of appeals and wishes a Supreme Court review, that department or agency will formally request that the Justice Department seek certiorari. The solicitor general will determine whether to appeal the lower court decision.[49]

Many factors must be considered when making this decision. Perhaps the most important consideration is that the Supreme Court is limited in the number of cases it hears in each term. Thus, the solicitor general must determine whether a particular case is one of the seventy or so cases that deserve extensive consideration by the Court during that term. How successful have solicitors general been in this assessment? One extensive study says that:

> the advantage that the solicitor general enjoys in his capacity as a petitioner is clear. The solicitor general sought certiorari in 1,294 cases between 1959

and 1989 and was successful in obtaining the Court's review 69.78 percent of the time. Certiorari requests were granted in only 4.9 percent of the private litigation.[50]

A more recent study examining the influence of solicitor general recommendations at the certiorari stage found that even justices who are likely to be against the solicitor general's recommendation based on things such as ideology or policy preferences were still willing to follow his or her recommendation.[51] However, the solicitor general's influence is limited by legal factors in that justices are less likely to follow the solicitor general's recommendation when that advice contradicts legal cues indicating whether or not the justices should take up the case.[52]

In addition to deciding whether to seek Supreme Court review of a particular lower court decision, the solicitor general and assistant solicitors general personally argue most of the government's cases heard by the high court. Former Solicitor General Rex E. Lee pointed out that the "tradition has been that the hardest cases—the most important cases—usually are argued by the Solicitor General."[53]

A recent book on the Office of the Solicitor General (OSG) has provided further evidence of the influence of these attorneys on the justices of the Supreme Court.[54] This study found that attorneys working for the OSG are more likely to win their cases, even controlling for other factors that influence the outcome of Supreme Court cases. They are more likely to prevail even when facing attorneys who are equally experienced, including those who used to work for the OSG. Furthermore, the arguments brought up in briefs filed by the solicitor general influence the content of Supreme Court opinions, both in terms of the language used in the opinion and how the Court interprets precedent.

The influence and experience of the solicitor general before the US Supreme Court is also seen in the postgovernment careers of many of those who have recently held that position. Any simple Internet search of names such as Noel Francisco, Paul Clement, Seth Waxman, Don Verrilli, or Neal Katyal (all recent solicitors general or acting solicitors general)[55] will find that they are all well positioned in high-profile DC law firms, with their previous experience as solicitor general listed prominently in their professional biographies. Elena Kagan, another recent solicitor general, would of course go on to become one of President Obama's appointees to the US Supreme Court.

Although the solicitor general works for the attorney general and serves at the pleasure of the president, it has traditionally been argued that this official "must have the independence to exercise his craft as a lawyer on behalf of the institution of government without being a mouthpiece for the President."[56] In recent years, however, some scholars have suggested that the solicitor general's office has become more politicized and thus more likely to press for adoption of the president's agenda.[57] There is some evidence that "a solicitor general perceived as politically biased . . . stands to jeopardize success when defending positions" on behalf of the federal government.[58]

State Attorneys General

Each state has an attorney general who serves as its chief legal official. In most states, this official is elected on a partisan statewide ballot. The attorney general oversees a staff of attorneys who primarily handle civil cases involving the state. Although the prosecution of criminal defendants is generally handled by the local district attorneys, the attorney general's office often plays a significant role in investigating statewide criminal activities. Thus, the attorney general and their staff may work closely with the local district attorney in preparing a case against a particular defendant.

The state attorneys general also perform the important function of issuing advisory opinions to state and local agencies. Many of these agencies cannot afford their own legal staff. The attorney general's opinion will often interpret an aspect of state law not yet ruled on by the courts. Although the advisory opinion might eventually be overruled in a case brought before the courts, the attorney general's opinion is important in determining the behavior of state and local agencies.

Although state attorneys general are often seen simply as bureaucrats or managers of a state's Department of Justice, Mississippi Attorney General Michael Moore showed that they also can be innovative legal strategists. Moore became quite well known for the lawsuit he spearheaded in 1994 against the tobacco industry. He focused on the cost to the state of treating smoking-related illnesses. Within a year, similar suits were filed by Florida, Minnesota, and West Virginia. By the end of 1998, forty-one state attorneys general had filed individual lawsuits against the tobacco industry. In the resulting settlement, the tobacco companies agreed to distribute $206 billion over twenty-five years to forty-six states, five commonwealths and territories, and the District of Columbia.[59]

Today, state attorneys general of both political parties play a regular and high-profile role in challenging federal policies to which they are opposed. In May 2024, for example, Texas Attorney General Ken Paxton (a Republican) issued a press release touting the seventy-fifth legal action he had taken against the Biden administration to date.[60] For their part, Democratic attorneys general challenged many of President Trump's policies, suing the Trump administration over immigration, the environment, birth control, and Internet regulations, among other issues.[61] During the Obama administration, Republican attorneys general around the country filed suit against the president's policies on issues such as health care, environmental regulation, and gay rights.[62]

Private Lawyers in the Judicial Process

In criminal cases in the United States, the defendant has a constitutional right to be represented by an attorney. Some jurisdictions have established public defender's offices to represent indigent defendants, as noted previously. In other areas, there is some method of assigning a private attorney to represent a defendant who cannot afford to hire one. Those defendants who can afford to hire their own lawyers will do so.

Assigned Defense Counsel

In many jurisdictions throughout the country, especially rural areas, the standard procedure is to appoint a private lawyer to represent an indigent defendant. Usually, the assignment is made by an individual judge on an ad hoc basis. Local bar associations or lawyers themselves often provide the courts with a list of attorneys who are willing to provide such services. Compensation for representing an indigent defendant is generally based on a flat rate for hours spent in and out of court. The fee varies from area to area and often according to the case's complexity. It is usually a good deal less than an attorney would earn for providing services to a private client. One recent study found that indigent defendants fared better with public defenders compared to assigned defense counsel.[63] Defendants represented by assigned counsel were particularly disadvantaged when outside labor market options induced less qualified attorneys to take on assigned counsel work.[64] In other words, the pool of attorneys available as assigned counsel varies as the market changes, and when that pool is relatively heavy in lower-quality attorneys, indigent defendants should expect less favorable outcomes in their criminal cases.

Private Defense Counsel

Some attorneys in private practice specialize in criminal defense work. Such lawyers are more often found in solo practices or in small rather than large law firms. One of the major worries of the criminal defense attorney is getting paid. The criminal defense lawyer generally requires advance payment of part of the fee. The average criminal defense attorney must therefore handle many cases to survive, and thus must spend a great deal of time in court and in the office juggling cases. All told, the lawyer who specializes in criminal defense work typically leads a hectic life.

Legal Services for the Poor

Although criminal defendants are constitutionally entitled to be represented by a lawyer, those who are defendants in a civil case or who wish to initiate a civil case do not have the right to representation. This means that **pro se litigants** who cannot afford to hire a lawyer may find it difficult to obtain justice.

To deal with this problem, legal aid services of one sort or another are now found in many areas. Legal aid societies were established in New York and Chicago as early as the late 1880s, and many other major cities followed suit in the twentieth century. Although some legal aid societies are sponsored by bar associations, most are supported by private contributions. Legal aid bureaus also are associated with charitable organizations in some areas. In addition, many law schools operate legal aid clinics to provide assistance for the poor as well as valuable training for law students. Critics contend, however, that the civil legal needs of poor and even middle-income individuals are unmet, a particularly ironic situation given the enormous number of attorneys in the United States.[65] Another source of legal help for indigent clients deserves mention.

Many lawyers provide legal services **pro bono publico** (for the public good) because they consider this free assistance a professional obligation or an opportunity to work on issues they may be passionate about.

The "unbundling" of legal services is yet another avenue, whereby a lawyer and a client agree that the lawyer will provide some but not all the services necessary to usher a case through the litigation process. Compared to a "soup-to-nuts" approach to legal representation as a full-service expense, unbundling provides more of an "a la carte" experience, in terms of the legal services provided, and the resulting fees.[66]

LITIGANTS

The previous discussion of pro se litigants highlights that lawyers, critical to how many cases are resolved, are not involved in every legal dispute in the country. However, all cases involve litigants. In some cases taken before the courts, the litigants are individuals, whereas in other cases one or more of the litigants may be a government agency, corporation, union, interest group, or university.

In short, almost any individual or organization has the potential to become a litigant in the courts. Marc Galanter's classic assessment of the American legal system advanced the idea that not all litigants are likely to be equally as successful.[67] Some litigants, due to increased resources or opportunities to litigate, for example, are advantaged in our legal system. Questions concerning the advantages favoring the "haves" over the "have nots" have continued to be addressed with respect to litigant success before state and federal courts.[68]

What motivates a person or group to take a grievance to court? In criminal cases, the answer to this question is relatively simple. A state or federal criminal statute has allegedly been violated, and the government prosecutes the party charged with violating the statute. In civil cases, the answer is not so easy. Although some persons readily take their grievances to court, many others avoid this route because of the time and expense involved. Still, enough cases are filed annually to cause concern about how the federal and state courts can manage their dockets.

One way to categorize cases is distinguishing between private law cases and public law controversies. Private law disputes are those in which one private citizen or organization sues another. Public law controversies involve the government more directly. In these situations, a citizen or organization contends that a government agency or official has violated a right established by a constitution or statute. For both public and private law actions, litigation may be compensatory or policy oriented.[69]

A classic example of private, or ordinary, compensation-oriented litigation is when a person injured in an automobile accident sues the driver of the other car to win monetary damages to compensate for the medical bills they had to pay. This type of litigation is personal and is not aimed at changing governmental or business policies.

Some private law cases, however, are policy oriented or political in nature. Personal injury suits and product liability suits may appear, on the surface, to be simply compensatory in nature but may also be used to change the manufacturing or business practices of the private firms being sued. Climate scientists, for example, have called for a wave of private lawsuits against fossil fuel companies for delaying action on policy related to climate change.[70]

Most political or policy-oriented lawsuits are public law controversies. That is, they are suits brought against the government primarily to stop allegedly illegal policies or practices. They may also seek damages or some other specific form of relief. A case decided in 2014 by the US Supreme Court, *Burwell v. Hobby Lobby Stores, Inc.*, provides a good example.[71] After the passage of the Patient Protection and Affordable Care Act of 2010, federal regulations required that employers provide no-cost access to twenty distinct kinds of contraceptive devices for female employees. The owners of Hobby Lobby, along with the owners of two additional corporations (each was similar to Hobby Lobby in that they were for-profit corporations closely held and controlled by members of a single family), argued that this regulation violated their religious liberty as dictated by the Religious Freedom Restoration Act (passed by Congress in 1993), because four of the required twenty contraceptive devices may result in the destruction of an embryo. The Supreme Court ruled in Hobby Lobby's favor, finding that the regulation requiring that employer insurance cover these four contraceptives violated the sincere religious beliefs of those family members who owned and closely controlled for-profit corporations.

Political or policy-oriented litigation is more prevalent in the appellate courts than in the trial courts and is most common in the US Supreme Court. Ordinary compensatory litigation is often terminated early in the judicial process because the litigants find it more profitable to settle their dispute or accept the verdict of a trial court. However, litigants in political cases generally do little to advance their policy goals by gaining victories at the lower levels of the judiciary. Instead, they prefer the more widespread reach and publicity attached to a decision by an appellate tribunal. Pursuing cases in the appellate courts is expensive. Therefore, many lawsuits that reach this level are supported in one way or another by interested groups and organizations.

INTEREST GROUPS IN THE JUDICIAL PROCESS

Although interest groups are probably better known for their attempts to influence legislative and executive branch decisions, they also pursue their policy goals in the courts. Some groups have found the judicial branch to be far more receptive to their efforts than either of the other two branches of government. Interest groups lacking the economic resources to mount an intensive lobbying effort in Congress or a state legislature may find it much easier to hire a lawyer and locate some constitutional or statutory provision on which to base a court case. Likewise, a small group with few registered voters among its members may lack the political clout to exert much influence on legislators and executive branch officials. Large memberships and political clout are not prerequisites for filing suits in the courts, however.

Interest groups may also turn to the courts because they find the judicial branch more sympathetic to their policy goals than the other two branches. The National Association for the Advancement of Colored People (NAACP) provides an excellent example. This group, which dates from the early twentieth century, soon realized that Congress and the executive branch were not generally sympathetic to the struggle for civil rights of Black citizens. Seeing the courts as potentially more sympathetic, the NAACP started to focus its efforts on litigation as a means for achieving its goals. As the Supreme Court became more favorable to civil rights after 1937, the NAACP began to realize the value of the judiciary as a forum for its activities and eventually established the Legal Defense Fund, a separate organization composed of lawyers who represented them in litigation.

Following the pattern established by the NAACP, other minority and marginalized group organizations began to use the courts. In 1972, for example, Ruth Bader Ginsburg cofounded the American Civil Liberties Union's (ACLU) Women's Rights Project. Between 1973 and 1976, Ginsburg argued six women's rights cases before the Supreme Court, winning five of them, shaping not only legal strategy but constitutional law via her advocacy of women's rights issues.[72]

At the same time that Ginsburg was beginning her work with the ACLU, the Lambda Legal Defense and Education Fund was created in an effort to advance gay civil rights in the mold of the NAACP.[73] Lambda remains "the oldest and the largest organization dedicated to litigating gay rights claims."[74] Similarly, cases dealing with the rights of Hispanics and women have been pursued vigorously by groups such as the Mexican American Legal Defense and Educational Fund and the National Organization for Women.

Throughout the 1960s and 1970s, interest groups with liberal policy goals fared especially well in the federal courts. In addition, the concept of the public interest law firm, attributed to consumer advocate Ralph Nader, gained prominence during this period. These law firms pursue cases that serve the public interest in general—including cases in the areas of consumer rights, employment discrimination, occupational safety, civil liberties, and environmental concerns.

Organizations on the liberal side of the American ideological continuum are not the only ones interested in pushing for policy change via the judiciary; conservative groups have also turned their attention to legal advocacy work. For example, several Christian conservative legal organizations (or CCLOs) rose to prominence in the 1980s and 1990s.[75] One of the most significant has been the Alliance Defending Freedom (ADF). Founded in 1994, the ADF advocates and litigates on a variety of issues of importance to many evangelical Christian conservatives, including religious freedom, ending abortion, and prohibiting same-sex marriage. The ADF reports having directly represented parties in fifteen victories at the US Supreme Court between 2011 and 2024,[76] including *Trinity Lutheran Church of Columbia, Inc. v. Comer*, where the Supreme Court ruled that a Missouri policy denying a church or other religious entity from applying for state-funded grants to reimburse the costs associated with repaving a playground violates the First Amendment's Free Exercise of Religion Clause.[77] The ADF also recently litigated the case of Jack Phillips, the Colorado baker whose refusal to create a wedding cake for a same-sex couple was at the center of the *Masterpiece Cakeshop, Ltd. v. Colorado Civil Rights Commission* case.[78] Since 2016, the Southern Poverty Law Center has designated the ADF as an anti-LGBTQ hate group due to its litigation and legislative practices and priorities.[79]

Beyond the US Supreme Court, liberal and conservative interest groups are also involved in appellate litigation at the federal courts of appeals and at the state level. Such interest group involvement in the judicial process may take several different forms, depending on the goals of the group. However, two principal tactics stand out: involvement in test cases and presentation of information before the courts through amicus curiae briefs.

Test Cases

Because the judiciary engages in policymaking only by rendering decisions in specific cases, one favorite tactic of interest groups is to make sure that a case appropriate for obtaining its policy goals is brought before the judiciary. In some instances, this means that the interest group will initiate and sponsor the case by providing all the necessary resources.

Undoubtedly the best-known historic example of this type of sponsorship may be found in *Brown v. Board of Education* in 1954.[80] Although the suit against the Board of Education of Topeka, Kansas, was filed by the parents of Linda Brown, the NAACP supplied the legal help and money necessary to pursue the case all the way to the Supreme Court, where Thurgood Marshall (who later became a US Supreme Court justice) argued the suit on behalf of the plaintiffs and the NAACP. As a result, the NAACP gained a victory through the Supreme Court's decision that segregation in the public schools violates the Equal Protection Clause of the Fourteenth Amendment. (Recall that Brown was denied admission to a public school in Topeka, Kansas, based on her race.)

How extensive is interest group sponsorship of cases? If one is referring to those cases that constitute ordinary litigation, the answer is that a ridiculously small proportion of them involve group sponsorship. However, group sponsorship is far more common in cases that have the potential to be heard by the Supreme Court and to produce a major legal ruling.[81]

The American Civil Liberties Union (ACLU), an organization dedicated to defending the Bill of Rights, is probably the interest group best known for sponsorship of cases in the nation's courts.[82] On the occasion of its seventieth anniversary in 1990, the ACLU touted that the organization "had been involved in 80 percent of the post-1920 'landmark' cases regularly cited in constitutional law texts."[83]

Amicus Curiae Briefs

Submission of **amicus curiae** (friend of the court) briefs is the easiest method by which interest groups can become involved in cases. Consequently, it is also the most usual form of group involvement, and these briefs are used far more often in appellate rather than trial courts. This method allows a group to get its message before the court even though it does not control the case. Provided it has the permission of the parties to the case or the permission of the court, an interest group may submit an amicus brief to supplement the arguments of the parties.

The frequency of amicus curiae participation has increased over the years. Judicial scholars Lee Epstein and Thomas Walker noted that "on average, organized interests filed at least one amicus brief in over 85 percent of all cases decided by full opinion between 1986 and 2002."[84] The growth in amicus curiae briefs "is symbolized by the record-breaking eighty-five that were submitted in the Court's 2003 case on affirmative action in law school admissions."[85] Since 2003, subsequent cases have seen even more amicus curiae participation, with the 2013 challenge to the Affordable Care Act attracting 136 briefs, the 2015 challenge to same-sex marriage bans resulting in the submission of 148 amicus briefs,[86] and the 2022 case overturning *Roe v. Wade* attracting more than 140 amicus briefs.[87]

Typically, an amicus brief is submitted on behalf of one side or the other in a case, although sometimes the brief is submitted in support of neither party in the case. In high-profile and particularly salient cases, both sides will attract amicus briefs in support. For example, approximately one hundred groups and individuals participated as amici curiae in *Lucas v. South Carolina Coastal Council.* Decided in 1992, *Lucas* involved a state law that prevented a landowner from building any permanent habitable structure on his property. The Supreme Court ruled that the ban violated Lucas's rights under the Takings Clause of the Fifth Amendment. A close examination reveals that "supporters of Lucas and the state matched constituency for constituency, at least in the areas of government, environment/public interest, and land use."[88]

Recent scholarship has provided useful insight into questions concerning the use and influence of amicus curiae briefs by interest groups. For example, one study found that justices are more likely to vote in favor of the arguments raised in the amicus briefs of interest groups that "are more connected with other interest groups and collaborate with other well-connected groups" compared to briefs submitted by groups that are less central.[89] Another found that many groups collaborate with other groups in submitting amicus briefs to be able to participate and claim credit with their supporters without expending the resources required to write and submit an amicus brief alone.[90]

Scholars have begun to pay more attention to the fact that amicus curiae briefs are often filed to persuade an appellate court either to grant or deny review of a lower court decision. A study of the US Supreme Court found, for instance, that the presence of amicus briefs significantly increased the chances that the Court would give full treatment to the case and concluded that "interested parties can have a significant and positive impact on the Court's agenda by participating as amici curiae prior to the Court's decision on certiorari or jurisdiction."[91]

Although the literature on friend-of-the-court participation deals most extensively with the US Supreme Court, some scholars have more recently turned their attention to amicus curiae briefs filed in federal courts of appeals. One recent study by Paul M. Collins Jr. and Wendy L. Martinek focused on amicus curiae briefs filed in the circuits from 1997 to 2002, concluding that amici "can help level the playing field between appellants and appellees by serving to counter the propensity to affirm in the US Courts of Appeals."[92] Other scholars have analyzed amicus curiae participation in state appellate courts. An examination of litigation activity in sixteen state supreme courts indicates that there is not only a heightened presence of organized interests but also a wider range of groups participating as amici curiae.[93] Furthermore, findings indicate that "business groups, other organizational players, and even individual amici appear to be quite successful."[94] One specific way that amici curiae can be helpful in state supreme court cases is to intervene in support of a position advocated by an individual with a relatively low level of resources.[95] Interest groups may also rely on amicus briefs in state or federal court as an avenue to advocate for their policy goals, while simultaneously pursuing the important maintenance goal of appealing to the current or potential members critical to the group's future.

Participation by amici curiae may also be found in courts in other parts of the world. One study of the European Court of Justice says that "member states, institutions of the European Union, and in some cases, interested individuals may participate in cases to which they are not a party as a sort of amicus curiae."[96]

SUMMARY

In this chapter, we laid the groundwork for later chapters, which deal more extensively with the steps in the judicial process. Our focus was on three important actors in the judicial process: lawyers, litigants, and interest groups.

We traced the development of the legal profession from its beginnings in colonial days to the contemporary practice of law, including recent concerns over the job market associated with the Great Recession and the student debt crisis. Our discussion focused on the stratification of the legal profession and the diverse types of lawyers who practice in the United States, and we have highlighted how the legal profession remains stratified based on things like race, ethnicity, and gender. Singled out for special emphasis were the government lawyers who are primarily involved in handling cases in the state and federal trial and appellate courts.

We next turned our attention to those who become litigants in US courts. In some cases, the adversaries are ordinary litigants who are primarily concerned with being compensated for their losses. At other times, the combatants are involved in political litigation and have as their major goal influencing public or corporate policy. Still other cases feature litigants who are interested in both personal compensation and exerting some influence over public policy.

We concluded with an examination of the role of interest groups in the judicial process. Following a brief look at the reasons why groups across the ideological spectrum become involved in litigation, we discussed the major strategies and tactics used by interest groups in the judicial arena: involvement in test cases and the use of amicus curiae briefs.

FURTHER THOUGHT AND DISCUSSION QUESTIONS

1. Should the American Bar Association be more proactive in sanctioning law schools that admit students with qualifications that call into question whether those students will successfully finish law school and pass the bar exam?
2. Is it appropriate for the attorney general to intervene in prosecutorial decisions being made by prosecutors in the Department of Justice, as William Barr did with respect to the criminal case of Donald Trump ally Roger Stone? Do you find Barr's argument that all federal prosecutorial discretion ultimately resides with the attorney general convincing?
3. Is it concerning that elite lawyers and well-heeled litigants are generally expected to be more successful in the judicial process?
4. Is increased involvement of interest groups in litigation before the US Supreme Court a sign that the judiciary is weighing in on too many issues of significant, national importance?

SUGGESTED RESOURCES

American Bar Association. Available online at www.americanbar.org. Useful information for lawyers, students, and the public.

Biskupic, Joan, Janet Roberts, and John Shiffman. "The Echo Chamber: A Reuters Special Report." December 8, 2014. Available online at https://www.reuters.com/investigates/special-report/scotus/ (accessed August 1, 2024). A recent assessment of the small number of elite attorneys who participate most frequently before the US Supreme Court.

Black, Ryan C., and Ryan J. Owens. *The Solicitor General and the United States Supreme Court: Executive Branch Influence and Judicial Decisions*. New York, NY: Cambridge University Press, 2012. A comprehensive analysis of the solicitor general's influence before the Supreme Court.

Epstein, Lee, and Joseph F. Kobylka. *The Supreme Court and Legal Change: Abortion and the Death Penalty.* Chapel Hill: University of North Carolina Press, 1992. A study of the nature and tactics of interest groups involved in trying to influence decisions of the US Supreme Court in abortion and death penalty cases.

Friedman, Lawrence M. *A History of American Law.* 3rd ed. New York, NY: Simon & Schuster, 2005. An excellent summary of the development of law in the United States.

Ginsburg, Ruth Bader, and Amanda L. Tyler. *Justice, Justice Thou Shalt Pursue: A Life's Work Fighting for a More Perfect Union.* Berkeley, CA: University of California Press, 2021. Inspired by Ginsburg's 2019 delivery of the first annual Herma Hill Kay Memorial Lecture at the University of California at Berkeley, Ginsburg reflects on her life and career in this book.

Law & Society Review. In 1999 (vol. 33, no. 4), the journal published a special issue on litigant status, based on Marc Galanter's classic work on the subject.

Law School Admission Council. Available online at www.lsac.org. Vital information for anyone considering law school and a career in the legal profession.

Miller, Banks, and Brett Curry. *U.S. Attorneys, Political Control, and Career Ambition.* New York, NY: Oxford University Press, 2019. An interesting recent analysis of how US attorney discretion may be influenced by the political branches of the federal government.

NALP—The National Association for Law Placement. Available online at www.nalp.org (accessed August 2, 2024). Provides useful information and statistics about careers for lawyers and other legal professionals.

Nelson, Robert L., Ronit Dinovitzer, Bryant G. Garth, Joyce S. Sterling, David B. Wilkins, Meghan Dawe, and Ethan Michelson. *The Making of Lawyers' Careers: Inequality and Opportunity in the American Legal Profession*. Chicago: The University of Chicago Press, 2023. An ambitious recent study tracking the lives of roughly 4,500 lawyers for twenty years after passing the bar exam.

Strohl, Jeff, Catherine Morris, and Ban Cheah. "A Law Degree Is No Sure Thing: Some Law School Graduates Earn Top Dollar, but Many Do Not." Press release, Georgetown University Center on Education and the Workforce, 2024.

Available at https://cew.georgetown.edu/cew-reports/law/#resources (accessed July 31, 2024). Includes a "Find Your School" option for school-specific data on median monthly debt payments, annual earnings, and annual earnings net of debt payments for recent graduates.

Walker, Samuel E. *In Defence of American Liberties: A History of the ACLU.* New York, NY: Oxford University Press, 1991. A detailed historical analysis of one of the interest groups most frequently involved in the American judicial system.

KEY TERMS

Amicus curiae
Pro bono publico
pro se litigants

9 CRIME AND PROCEDURES PRIOR TO A CRIMINAL TRIAL

CHAPTER GOALS AND OBJECTIVES

In this chapter, readers will learn that . . .

- It is important to understand the nature and categories of crime in the United States.
- Under US law there are, in theory, five critical elements to a crime.
- There are key stages in the criminal process: the arrest, the subsequent appearance before a magistrate, and the activities of either a grand jury or a preliminary hearing.
- Plea bargaining is a key element of our judicial system at both the state and federal levels.

This is the first of three chapters that examine US courts from a courtroom procedure perspective. This chapter analyzes the criminal process—from the stage when a law is first broken to subsequent stages such as arrest and indictment. Chapter 10 focuses on the criminal trial itself and its aftermath, such as sentencing and the appeals process. Finally, Chapter 11 examines the civil process in the same manner to provide a sense of how the system looks and feels to a litigant or observer. Keep in mind that there is no such thing as a single criminal or civil court process in the United States. Instead, the federal system has a court process at the national level, and each state and territory has its own set of rules and regulations that affect the judicial process. Norms and similarities do exist among all these governmental entities, and our discussion will focus primarily on them, but we wish to emphasize that no two states have identical judicial process systems, and no state's system mirrors that of the national government.

THE NATURE AND SUBSTANCE OF CRIME

"It's a crime the way you never clean up after yourself," a friend scolds her messy roommate, who has failed to tidy up for the umpteenth time that month. Anyone who has had roommates knows comments such as this are heard with some frequency. Although it is clear what the friend is getting at, in the literal sense no crime has been committed. Being a messy roommate may be wrong, but in the United States, at least, it is not a crime because it does not violate any specific law. The nature of criminality can be understood by this example. An act is not automatically a crime because it is hurtful, sinful, or even neglectful. (Only about half of the Ten Commandments are enforced by criminal law.) An action constitutes a true crime only if it specifically violates a criminal statute duly enacted by Congress, a state legislature, or some other public authority.

Bryan Kohberger, the Idaho college murder suspect, pleads not guilty at his arraignment.

Zach Wilkinson-Pool/Getty Images

We should also keep in mind that the notion of what is considered a crime varies markedly from one nation and culture to another. For example, on April 3, 2015, the French parliament passed a law criminalizing the use of advertisements with "anorexic models:"[1]

> Modeling agencies would have to produce a medical report showing that their models have maintained a healthy mass-to-height ratio. . . . A second change in the law would make it a crime to glorify "excessive thinness," which would target those who run pro-anorexia websites, punishable by up to one year in prison and 10,000 euros in fines.[2]

Or in the country of Malawi, a person convicted of being gay can be sentenced to fourteen years in prison with hard labor.[3] Take a more extreme example, in North Korea a person can be executed for listening to South Korean music and distributing films.[4]

A good working definition of a crime, then, is that it is an offense against the state, punishable by fine, imprisonment, or death. A crime is a violation of obligations due the community as a whole and can be punished only by the state. The sanctions of imprisonment and death cannot be imposed by a civil court or in a civil action (although a fine may be either a civil or a criminal penalty).

In the United States, there are a vast variety of crimes. Most of them are sins of commission (committing an act that is prohibited), such as aggravated assault and embezzlement; a few are sins of omission (failure to act when required to do so), such as failing to stop and render aid after a traffic accident or failing to file an income tax return. The government considers some crimes serious (such as murder and treason), and this seriousness is reflected in the corresponding punishments (such as life imprisonment or the death penalty) and other crimes as less serious (such as double parking or disturbing the peace), with punishments often minor (such as a small fine or a night in the local jail).

Some crimes constitute actions that virtually all citizens regard as outside the sphere of acceptable human conduct (such as kidnapping or sexual assault), whereas others involve actions about which opinion may be divided. Relevant laws include a 1965 Alabama statute where one can be sentenced to jail for up to one year and impose a fine of $500 for fraudulently dressing as a religious leader;[5] a Nebraska statute that forbids bingo games at church suppers;[6] and Florida, Michigan, and Mississippi laws that forbid unmarried couples from living together under the same roof (such living arrangements are regarded as "lewd and lascivious"). Other criminal statutes lamely reflect the standards and mentality of long-gone eras and are no longer enforced, such as an 1883 Florida statute "making it a misdemeanor to question a woman's chastity."[7]

The most serious crimes in the United States are felonies and less serious crimes are considered misdemeanors or infractions. In many of the states, a felony is any offense for which the penalty may be death or imprisonment in a penitentiary (prison; a jail is not a penitentiary or prison). While in other states (and federal law), a felony is an offense for which the penalty is punishable by more than one year in prison. Thus, felonies are differentiated in some states according to the place where the punishment occurs or by the length of the sentence. Examples of common felonies include murder, manslaughter, arson, sexual assault, human trafficking, and armed robbery.

Misdemeanors are regarded as minor crimes by the state, and their punishment usually consists of confinement in a city or county jail for less than a year. Public intoxication, shoplifting, perjury, prostitution, and petty theft are common examples of misdemeanors. Most states have a third category of offenses known as infractions. Some examples include minor traffic offenses (such as parking violations, running a red light, speeding), jaywalking, and littering. The penalty is usually limited to a small fine. Fines may also be part of the penalty for misdemeanors and felonies.

CATEGORIES OF CRIME

A useful way to consider distinct types of crime is to sort them according to their public policy implications.[8] Scholars have classified the types of crimes into five broad categories that constitute the primary offenses against the government in the United States. They include conventional, economic, organized, political, and consensual crime.

Conventional Crimes

Conventional crime is not a legal term; rather, it is a journalistic and scholarly phrase. It refers to those crimes that are most referred to on routine television news, that are found in the daily crime report covered by the news. That is, conventional crimes tend to fall into the category of a thief breaking into a home, someone being mugged in the parking lot of a mall, a murder in a back alley, or a hold-up at a local liquor store. The term tends not to refer to less visible white-collar crimes or to more exotic criminal activity, such as treason or espionage.

Property crimes make up the lion's share of the over 8 million conventional crimes committed annually in the United States. In 2022, the US Department of Justice determined that 42 percent of all offenses (approximately 6.5 million) were property crimes,[9] and 7 percent were violent crimes (1,232,428).[10] While the government differentiates property crime from violent crime, the two often go hand in hand. For instance, the thief who breaks into a home and stabs the occupant is involved in more than just the property crime of burglary.

The less numerous, but more feared, conventional crimes are those against the person. These crimes of violence include murder, manslaughter, sexual assault, robbery, and aggravated assault. In 2022, there occurred 133,294 sexual assaults; 893,980 aggravated assaults; and 220,450 robberies. Homicide was the least frequent violent victimization—21,156 such crimes were committed in 2022.[11] The good news is that violent crime has slowly been on the decline in the United States since 1994. The reasons why are not entirely clear. One study conducted by the Brennan Center for Justice found that income growth and the aging population in the United States have played an important role in reducing crime across the country.[12]

In our discussion of crime numbers and trends, it might be insightful to compare statistics in the United States with those of other nations that have similar traditions and keep good records, such as the European Union (EU). Conventional journalistic accounts claim that America is the most crime-infested nation among the modern industrial democracies. However, as noted above, crime has been declining in the United States, and many Western democracies have crime rates higher than those in the United States. For example, according to Eurostat (the statistical office for the European Union), which records crime statistics for the EU, in 2022, there were just over 5 million reported thefts; approximately 253,000 robberies; and 1,179,600 burglaries. For more violent offenses, in 2022, there were 3,862 reported homicides and just over 231,000 reported sexual assaults. When compared with data from the previous year (2021), crime rates are on the rise in the EU.[13] When comparing crime statistics among the United States and our friends to the north (Canada) and south (Mexico), the United States falls in the middle. For example, according to the United Nations Office on Drugs and Crime, in 2022, the data show that Mexico's murder rate was approximately 33,287 (or a rate of 26.1 per 100,000 people). By contrast, Canada's murder rate in 2022 was approximately 874 (or a rate of 2.3 per 100,000 people). In the middle lies the United States, with a murder rate of 21,594 (or a rate of 6.4 per 100,000 people) in 2022. The murder rate in the United States is approximately three times the rate of Canada; however, Mexico's murder rate is four times that of the United States and nearly eleven times that of Canada.[14]

Economic Crimes

What are economic crimes? They are usually characterized as financially motivated, nonviolent criminal activity that are based on deception and fraud. Economic crimes are often referred to as white-collar crimes. Examples of economic crime include tax evasion, insider trading, bribery, embezzlement, money laundering, and fraud. Economic crimes are a costly business in the United States. Recently, it has been determined that Medicare fraud, waste, and abuse total about $100 billion.[15] For example, in June 2023, the Department of Justice filed charges against seventy-eight defendants across sixteen states for an alleged Medicare fraud scheme totaling $2.5 billion (many of the fraudulent schemes targeted elderly people, disabled people, HIV patients, and pregnant women).[16] Of those charged, twenty-four were doctors, nurses, and health care executives. The Justice Department press release reports that the defendants used the proceeds from "the schemes to purchase luxury items, including exotic automobiles, jewelry, and yachts."[17] In terms of dollars-and-cents, economic crimes are far more costly than conventional crimes. According to the Department of Justice, economic crimes are estimated to cost the United States $400 billion to $1.7 trillion annually, but that number is likely to be higher because such crimes are either unreported or have gone undiscovered.[18]

In addition to being extremely costly to the American people, economic crimes have two other characteristics that make them relevant to some of the broader themes of this chapter. First, economic crimes are harder to detect and more complicated to prove in court than are other, conventional crimes. Convicting a thief who has been caught red-handed running out of a jewelry store with a bag of watches and diamonds is a relatively easy and routine endeavor. Not so with most economic crimes. Second, because most citizens do not regard economic crimes to be as serious as burglary or assault, fewer law enforcement resources are earmarked for these illegalities. Finally, we note sometimes sentencing judges and juries look much kindlier on the stockbroker whose "misjudgment" caused her to engage in a "little" illegal insider trading (after all, she did not hurt anyone, did she?) than on the pickpocket who was caught stealing someone's wallet.

Organized Crimes

Organized crime differs from others addressed so far in that it is engaged in by groups of people organized by a hierarchical basis. It represents an ongoing activity that is inexorably intertwined with fear and corruption. The FBI, for example, defines organized crime as "any group having some manner of a formalized structure and whose primary objective is to obtain money through illegal activities."[19] Organized crime may be manifested in a variety of ways, but it tends to focus on several areas that are particularly lucrative—namely, trafficking in illegal drugs (such as cocaine, heroin, fentanyl, and marijuana), gambling, prostitution, firearms trafficking, human trafficking, and cybercrimes. For example, recently the leader of the Lorenzana drug trafficking organization, one of the largest and most influential drug cartels in Guatemala, was sentenced in US court to thirty-three years in federal prison and ordered to forfeit $27 million in gains obtained from her international drug trafficking enterprise.[20]

Political Crimes

The usual meaning of political crime has been that it constitutes an offense against the government: treason, espionage, armed rebellion, assassination of public officials, and sedition. (Sedition refers to any illegal actions that would promote the overthrow of the lawful government—e.g., a speech calling for the immediate overthrow by force of the duly constituted government.) The January 6, 2021, riots in Washington, DC, provide a vivid example, when thousands of individuals, some of whom were armed, stormed the nation's Capitol to stop the certification of the 2020 presidential election. Political crimes, like economic crimes, can also be hard to prosecute. For example, some time ago a Harris County (Houston), Texas, commissioner was accused of accepting an illegal gift from a contractor. The contractor had paved a mile-long driveway from the commissioner's home to a nearby highway. "It was just an anniversary gift to me and my wife," said the commissioner. It took two juries (one of them was hung), enduring weeks of testimony and deliberation, before the court could finally determine that a crime had been committed.

Consensual Crimes

The final category is known as consensual crimes. Consensual crime is often referred to as "victimless" crime. Examples of consensual crimes include prostitution, gambling, illegal drug use, and unlawful sexual practices between consenting adults. Such crimes are called consensual because both perpetrator and client desire the forbidden activity, but to call them all victimless may not be the most appropriate description. The children whose parents spend their money and time on drugs rather than on properly caring for them may well regard themselves as victims. And homeowners whose streets suddenly become part of a prostitution circuit would not agree that this activity is victimless. Nevertheless, because a vast number of Americans question whether many of these consensual activities should be proscribed by the criminal code, difficult problems are created for law enforcement officials, judges, and juries.

A significant amount of discretion exists at all levels of the judicial process. The way in which decision-makers exercise this discretion is a function of their values and attitudes. Because attitudes about consensualor victimlesscrimes vary significantly among police officers, the public at large (and the potential jurors they represent), and judges, studies not surprisingly reveal great differences in how the judicial system treats participants in consensual criminal activity.

ELEMENTS OF A CRIME

Crimes have several basic but distinct elements. The burden is on the government to demonstrate, in court, the existence of these essential elements; otherwise, there can be no conviction. Although the judicial process in the courtroom may not focus separately and distinctly on each of these elements, they are at least implicit throughout the entire process of convicting someone of a criminal offense.

A Law Defining the Crime and the Punishment

If an act is to be prohibited or required by the law, a duly constituted authority (usually Congress or a state legislature) must properly spell out the matter so that the citizenry can know in advance what conduct is prohibited or required. Lawmakers must also set forth the penalties to be imposed upon the individual who engages in the criminal conduct. If no definition of the illegal act has been provided, and no penalty has been prescribed, there is technically no crime.

Several years ago, one of the coauthors of this book served on a state grand jury, and on a few occasions, a sheriff's deputy presented evidence on a pyramid club scheme that he had been investigating. Persons, often elderly and living alone, were persuaded to buy membership shares in the club and then asked to recruit other members. The original purchaser of the club membership would receive a percentage of the membership fees of all the new members, and so on. Some would make money from this scam, but ultimately most people would be left holding the bag.

Before long, most of the grand jurors were persuaded that an indictment was in order, and the district attorney (DA) was so informed. After a day or so of delay, the DA appeared and said: "What this club is doing is wrong and shameful and people are being victimized, but in this state, there is no law against pyramid schemes. You can do nothing." As the Latin maxim succinctly puts it, *nulled crimen sine lege*—no crime without law.

There are several corollaries related to this general principle. One is that the US Constitution forbids criminal laws that are **ex post facto**—that is, laws that declare certain conduct to be illegal after the conduct has taken place. Past harmful or undesirable actions may not be declared criminal under the US legal system. Likewise, the state may not pass **bills of attainder**, which single out a particular person or group of persons and declare that something is criminal for them but legal for everyone else. In the United States, if an action (or inaction) is to be considered criminal, it must be so for all citizens.

A final corollary is that a law defining a crime must be precise, so that the average person can determine in advance what conduct is prohibited or required. As the US Supreme Court has put it, a statute defining a crime must be "sufficiently explicit to inform those who are subject to it what conduct on their part will render them liable to penalties."[21] A classic example centers on a Jacksonville, Florida, municipal vagrancy ordinance that the Supreme Court, in 1972, struck down because of the vagueness for which it was written. According to the Jacksonville ordinance, criminal penalties were levied against:

> Rogues and vagabonds; dissolute persons who go about begging; common gamblers; persons who use juggling or unlawful games or plays; common drunkards; common night walkers, thieves, pilferers, or pickpockets; traders in stolen property; lewd, wanton, and lascivious persons; keepers of gambling places; common railers and brawlers; persons wandering or strolling around from place to place without any lawful purpose or object; habitual loafers; disorderly persons; persons neglecting all lawful business and habitually spending their time by frequenting houses of ill fame, gaming houses, or places where alcoholic beverages are sold or served; and persons able to work but habitually living on their wives or minor children.[22]

The Court pointed out that the Jacksonville ordinance takes normal activities, such as night walking or frequenting places that serve alcohol, and makes them criminal. Justice William O. Douglas explained in the majority opinion, "Persons 'neglecting all lawful business and habitually spending their time by frequenting places where alcoholic beverages are sold or served' would literally embrace many members of golf clubs and city clubs."[23] In short, the Court declared the ordinance unconstitutional because it "fails to give a person of ordinary intelligence fair notice that his contemplated conduct is forbidden by the statute, it encourages arbitrary and erratic arrests and convictions, it makes criminal activities that by modern standards are normally innocent, and it places almost unfettered discretion in the hands of the police."[24]

But the United States is not the only country that has (or had) laws that were so vague and open-ended that they could be construed in almost any way by legal authorities. For example, in the spring of 2015, five Chinese women activists were arrested for their public campaign against sexual harassment on public transportation and for obtaining more restroom facilities for women. The charge on which they were arrested was "picking quarrels and provoking trouble."[25] Imagine the unbridled discretion that this would give to police officers and judges to arrest and convict someone under a statute such as this!

In addition to defining the crime, the law must have a formal penalty attached to it. Traditional jurisprudence has always held that the punishment is an integral part of the crime. For example, many years ago, the state of Wyoming sought to convict a man for practicing medicine without a license. The accused unquestionably was actively prescribing medicines and even performing operations without a medical license. During his trial, it was noticed that the law forbidding unlicensed medical practice said not a word about the penalty for violating this law. The judge was forced to instruct the jury to bring in a verdict in favor of the accused. The "doctor" promptly decided to leave town, and the Wyoming legislature soon added a penalty clause to the statute.

The Actus Reus

Actus reus is a Latin phrase meaning the criminal action committed by the accused that gives rise to the legal prosecution. The *actus reus* is the material action element of the crime and will vary from one offense to another. This element may be the commission of an action that is forbidden (for instance, arson, murder, assault, or speeding), or it may be the failure to perform an action that is required (for instance, a person's refusal to stop and render aid to the victim of a motor vehicle accident or to pay one's taxes). Actus reus is concerned with distinguishing between the actual infliction of harm and mere evil thoughts. For example, thinking about burning a home down is arguably wrong, but it is not a crime. However, deliberately setting a house on fire is the material action.

The Mens Rea

The **mens rea** is the essential mental element of the crime. An old legal axiom holds that "an act does not make the doer of it guilty, unless the mind be guilty; that is, unless the intention be criminal." The American legal system has always made a distinction between harm that was caused intentionally and harm that was caused by simple negligence or accident. "Even a dog," said Justice Oliver Wendell Holmes, "distinguishes between being stumbled over and being kicked."[26] Thus, *mens rea* is most concerned with one's culpability or blameworthiness. For instance, if a person takes the life of another, the state does not always call it murder. If the killing was premeditated, it will likely be termed "murder in the first degree." But if the killing occurred in the passion of a barroom brawl, it would more likely be called "second-degree murder," which carries a lesser penalty. Reckless driving on the highway that results in someone's death would correspondingly be considered "negligent homicide"—a wrong, to be sure, but less serious in the eyes of the state than the intentional, premeditated killing of another.

Likewise, if a defendant is found to be "incompetent" at the time of the trial, then no trial may take place unless and until the individual is found to be mentally able to undergo it. This phenomenon was demonstrated vividly in 2019 when Dimitrios Pagourtzis, for no understandable reason, savagely killed ten of his fellow high school students in Santa Fe, Texas, and wounded another thirteen. After being examined independently by three psychiatrists, the experts declared that Pagourtzis "was incompetent to stand trial" and that he had "no understanding of the matter and proceedings."[27] Pagourtzis was then transferred to a state mental hospital until such time as he is found to be mentally competent.

Sometimes, the judge or jury's determination of the *mens rea* defines the crime itself. Suppose that a police officer comes across a woman inside a store warehouse on a cold winter's night. An arrest is made, but what crime should be charged: burglary or simple criminal trespass? Burglary is defined as "entering a building without the consent of the owner with the intent to commit theft," whereas trespass means "to enter a building or habitation without the effective consent of the owner." Did the woman break into that warehouse to steal merchandise or to keep warm on a particularly cold evening? The determination of the *mens rea* will influence how the crime is charged and ultimately the punishment at stake.

An Injury or Result

Except for regulatory crimes in which a definition of the injury is abstract (e.g., an illegal merger of two large airlines), a crime consists of a specific injury or a wrong perpetrated by one person against another. The crime may harm society at large, such as selling military secrets to a foreign government, or the injury may be inflicted on an individual, and because of its nature, it is considered to offend society. The nature of the injury, as with the *mens rea*, often determines the nature of the crime itself. For example, consider the following road rage example where two individuals have been cutting each other off in traffic. They both stop their cars and a fight ensues. Suppose one of them hits the other so hard that he dies. The crime may be murder (of some degree). If the person does not die but suffers serious bodily harm, the crime is aggravated assault. If the injury is minor, the charge may be simple assault. Because the nature of the injury often determines the offense, it is frequently asserted that the nature of the injury is the key legal element of the crime. Take a more concrete example. When Kentucky Senator Rand Paul was assaulted by his neighbor in the fall of 2017, charges against his assailant were not immediately filed—not because there was much doubt about the facts in question but because the police wanted to see how badly Paul was injured; the worse the injuries appeared to be, the more serious a charge could be filed. As Kentucky State Trooper Jeremy Hodges put it, "If it is found there was a serious physical injury that occurred, then the original assault charge, which was a misdemeanor, can be bumped up to the felonious charge of assault in the second degree."[28]

A Causal Relationship between the Action and the Resultant Injury

Before there can be a conviction for a criminal offense, the state must prove that the conduct of the accused was the proximate cause of the injury or result. This means that the defendant, acting in a natural and continuous sequence, produced the harmful situation. In other words, without the defendant's conduct, there clearly would have been no harm or injury. Proving a causal relationship is usually not difficult. Suppose Jane stabs Jack with a knife and inflicts a minor wound; Jane has committed assault with a deadly weapon. But what if Jack does not obtain proper medical care for the wound, develops an infection, and subsequently dies? Has Jane now committed manslaughter or murder? Or what if after being stabbed, Jack stumbles into another person, causing serious injury to them? Is Jane to blame for this, too?

Resolution of questions such as these is often difficult for judges and juries. The law requires that all circumstances be considered. The accused can be convicted only if the state can prove that their conduct is the direct, immediate, or determining cause of the resultant harm to the victim. If other circumstances have come into play, the question becomes: was the injury inflicted by the defendant sufficient to cause the result had the intervening factor(s) not occurred? Only if the harmful consequences were beyond the control of the accused or were not a natural or probable consequence of their actions is the defendant free from criminal liability.

PROCEDURES PRIOR TO A CRIMINAL TRIAL

Before a criminal trial can be held, federal and state laws require a series of procedures and events. Some of these stages are mandated by the US Constitution and state constitutions, some by court decisions, and others by legislative statutes. Although the exact nature of these procedural events varies from federal to state practice—and from one state to another—some basic similarities exist throughout the country. The focus in this discussion will be on the common patterns, but differences will be indicated whenever possible. Furthermore, note that several procedures are not as automatic or routine as they might appear. At all stages, the decision-makers exercise ample discretion according to their values, attitudes, and views of the world.

The Arrest

In 2022, there were approximately 708,001 law enforcement officials in the United States[29] (not counting some 1.5 million private security guards). These personnel, along with corrections and judicial activities, cost the American taxpayer more than $274 billion annually.[30] In 2022, officers made some 7,364,553 arrests (not counting traffic offenses).[31] The arrest is significant because it represents the first substantial contact between the state and the accused. The US legal system provides for two basic types of arrest—those with a warrant and those without.

Once law enforcement has established probable cause that someone has committed a crime they can seek out an arrest **warrant**. To obtain a warrant, law enforcement presents to a magistrate judge an affidavit that lays out the factual information that establishes probable cause. If, upon review of the warrant application, the judge believes probable cause has been met they will issue a warrant. However, while arrest warrants are constitutionally preferred, the Supreme Court has carved out several exceptions to the warrant requirement, which recognizes that because of the surrounding circumstances obtaining a warrant beforehand may not be possible (for instance, if law enforcement is in hot pursuit of a suspect, requiring a warrant beforehand could mean the suspect escapes). If a crime has been committed in the presence of law enforcement, police may make an arrest without first obtaining a warrant from a neutral magistrate. After the arrest, law enforcement will have to show the court that they had probable cause to make the arrest. This is done by providing a sworn statement to the court, often called an affidavit, or providing testimony. In the United States, up to 95 percent of all arrests are made without a warrant.

An officer's decision to make an arrest is far from simple or automatic. Generally, the officer who witnesses a crime will make an arrest on the spot, if possible. But most lawbreaking incidents are not that simple or clear-cut, and police officials possess—and exercise—wide discretion about whether to take someone into custody. The police simply do not have sufficient resources to enable them to proceed against all activities that Congress and state legislatures have forbidden. Consequently, discretion must be exercised in determining how to allocate the time and resources that do exist.

Criminal justice scholars have identified several areas in which police discretion is at a maximum: (1) minor or trivial offenses; (2) situations in which the victim will not seek prosecution; (3) cases in which the victim is also involved in misconduct; and (4) criminal conduct thought to reflect the mores of a community subgroup.

Trivial Offenses

Many police manuals advise officers that when minor violations of the law are concerned, a warning is a more appropriate response than a formal arrest. This not only makes common sense for borderline, trivial offenses but also reserves law enforcement resources for more serious conduct. Traffic violations, misconduct by juveniles, drunkenness, gambling, vagrancy, and use of the services of a prostitute all constitute less serious crimes and entail many close judgment calls by police.

The use of a warning instead of making an arrest or issuing a ticket is common for minor traffic violations. The following interview with Police Sergeant Rita Peerenboom of the Milwaukee Police Department is instructive about police discretion. Sergeant Peerenboom was asked, "How did you decide who to arrest?" She responded with the following:

> You arrest people who are wanted or you arrest people who just have an attitude, you know. If they are disruptive and they are hampering your investigation, then you give them a disorderly conduct charge. If they are cooperative with things, and a lot of times even if you have something against them, we'll let them go, depending on what it is, if it's not something major.[32]

Another illustration of police discretion is the handling of juvenile offenses. Juvenile crime investigator Detective Michelle Reichenbach of the Denver Police Department explains how discretion comes into play when handling an intervention. She explains:

> When I use the term intervention I'm referring to the decisions I make about what to do with a juvenile offender. In other words, do I write him a summons or file charges in district court? Do I not charge him with anything and, instead, give him a warning talk or talk to his parents? Do I get the school involved, or do I let the school handle the whole incident? Within my area of discretion I have choices for what to do with a particular juvenile. I use the term intervention to describe the decision I make for the juvenile to hopefully get him on the right track.[33]

The overarching point of these various examples is to show that law enforcement possesses ample discretion in the decision to arrest for trivial offenses.

Victim Will Not Seek Prosecution

Nonenforcement of the law is also the rule in situations where the victim of a crime will not expend their own time to help the state in the successful prosecution of a case. A crime victim may not cooperate with the police in making an arrest for a variety of reasons. In the instance of minor property crimes, the victim is often interested only in restitution; if that occurs, the victim may be satisfied. For example, when a person is caught shoplifting, the merchant may be unwilling to prosecute, asserting that they cannot afford the time away from the store to testify in court or they worry about bad publicity. Typically, unless the police have already expended considerable resources in investigating a particular property crime, they generally abide by the victim's wishes.

While police may defer to a victim's wishes in whether an arrest is made, domestic violence incidents are an area where police have far less discretion than they once had. Since the 1990s, almost all states (forty-seven plus the District of Columbia) have passed mandatory arrest laws when responding to domestic violence calls.[34] However, research has been mixed on the effectiveness of the mandatory arrest policy. Some scholars have found the policy has helped protect victims and deter repeat batterers; however, other studies found no deterrent effect.[35]

Victim Also Involved in Misconduct

When police officers perceive that the victim of a crime is also involved in some type of improper or questionable conduct, the officers may not to make an arrest. Suppose Mike Venmo's his drug dealer and the dealer fails to deliver the drugs but keeps the money Mike paid. If Mike filed a complaint to his local police department an arrest is unlikely to be made. In situations where the victim does not have clean hands, and officers know that even if they do make an arrest, such cases are usually dropped by the prosecution, the officer will generally elect not to make an arrest.

Criminal Conduct Thought to Reflect the Mores of a Community Subgroup

A final area of maximum police discretion in making an arrest deals with lawbreaking that officers ignore because they regard it as normal and acceptable for members of racial minorities or economically disadvantaged persons. While it is generally agreed that this is not an acceptable reason to utilize discretion, it is, however, the reality in which many live. One study found that race and socioeconomic status played a role in how officers utilize their discretion. For example, the scholars found that race and the economic status of the neighborhood predicted arrests and that police tend to be more responsive to White victims of crime than to other racial categories.[36] Other studies have shown that officers are more likely to use discretion to arrest in poor and socially disorganized neighborhoods.[37]

In short, it is important to understand that police are confronted with a variety of incidents and situations on a daily basis and have discretion in how they respond. What is clear is, "The choices available to officers enable them to determine when, how, and where to enforce laws and maintain order, rendering police use of discretion a key decision point in the criminal justice process."[38]

Appearance before a Magistrate

After a suspect is arrested for a crime, they are booked at the police station—that is, the facts surrounding the arrest are recorded and the accused fingerprinted and photographed. The next major step is for the accused to appear before a lower-level judicial official whose title may be judge, magistrate, or commissioner. Such an appearance is supposed to occur "without unnecessary delay." Although the meaning of this phrase varies from state to state, the maximum delay permitted by law has traditionally been twenty-four hours. However, in 1991, the more conservative US Supreme Court ruled, 5–4, that police may now detain an individual arrested without a warrant for up to forty-eight hours without a court hearing on whether the arrest was justified.[39] (In China, by contrast, defendants can be held for up to one month without being charged. In Mexico, the waiting time is eighty days!) However, in 2009, the high court seemed to reinforce the importance of getting suspects to their first court appearance as soon as possible (at least for those in federal custody). The Court ruled that even some voluntary confessions might not be admissible in federal court if authorities waited too long to get suspects to appear before a magistrate. Without such a rule, Justice David Souter wrote for the majority, "federal agents would be free to question suspects for extended periods before bringing them out in the open, and we have always known what custodial secrecy leads to."[40]

This court appearance is the occasion for several momentous events in the criminal justice process. First, the accused must be informed of the precise charges and must be informed of all constitutional rights and guarantees. Among these rights is the now famous *Miranda v. Arizona* decision handed down in 1966 by the US Supreme Court under Chief Justice Earl Warren. The accused "must be warned prior to any questioning that he has the right to remain silent, that anything he says can be used against him in a court of law, that he has the right to the presence of an attorney, and that if he cannot afford an attorney one will be appointed for him prior to any questioning."[41] Before this important Court ruling, it was common for persons arrested for a crime to unwittingly make incriminating statements to the police that subsequently undermined their criminal cases. Also, before *Miranda*, the right to an attorney during police interrogation was available only to those who could afford one, which meant that this important legal protection was unavailable to the indigent. (Such warnings must also be given by the arresting officer if they question the suspect about the crime.)[42] In some states, the accused must be informed about other rights that are provided for in the state's Bill of Rights, such as the right to a speedy trial and the right to confront witnesses.

Second in the series of notable events in the criminal justice process, the magistrate will determine whether the accused is to be released on bail, and if so, they will set the amount of bail. The only constitutional requirement for the amount is that it should not be "excessive." When making bail determinations, the judge will consider the seriousness of the offense, whether the accused is a flight risk, the accused's prior criminal history, and whether the accused has any community ties. However, if the magistrate believes that the accused will appear for any future trial proceedings, no bail may be required, and the accused may be released on their own recognizance. Bail is considered a privilege—not a right—and it may be denied altogether in cases that indicate compelling evidence of guilt or if the magistrate believes that the accused will flee from prosecution, no matter what the amount of bail.

The subject of bail has been riddled with controversy for a variety of reasons. It is often used as a form of preventive detention when a judge intentionally sets bail at a level that is impossible for the defendant to meet. A decision to set a high amount of bail can be based on factors such as the defendant's prior criminal record, publicity the case may have generated, the recommendation of the prosecutor, and the defendant's previous conduct while out on bail. If a defendant cannot make bail, they must remain in jail. This subjects legally innocent persons to punishment; it separates them from their family, friends, and jobs; it hinders their efforts to prepare for their defense in court; and it adds to the overcrowding that already bedevils most county jails. One report noted,

> The Bureau of Justice Statistics shows that 71 percent of inmates had jobs when they were arrested. There is no way to calculate how many of those people will lose their jobs because they can't afford to bail out and will fail to come to work, or how many will lose their housing because of the downward spiral.[43]

An alternative to bail is to release the defendant on recognizance, basically on a pledge by the defendant to return to court on the appointed date for trial. Some jurisdictions have special programs designed to maximize the number of persons eligible for release on recognizance. Perhaps the best known and most often copied is the Manhattan Bail Project, which arranges for defendants to be interviewed by pretrial investigators according to a special point system that takes into consideration such factors as the defendant's prior record, ties to the local community, and employment.

Another alternative is a newly developed system in Harris County (Houston), Texas, in the summer of 2020. The county hired a team of experts to determine whether someone arrested for a crime should be released on only "their own recognizance," or be retained in jail. After a six-month study, the monitor of this new system determined that "People's jail stays are [now] far shorter. Hearings are far more robust and fairer. And we see no change in repeat offending. . . . Gone are the days when a poor person would be locked up solely due to an inability to pay."[44] In 2020, New York prohibited cash bail for misdemeanor and nonviolent felonies. Under the bail reform provision judges must release defendants on their own recognizance or release them with specific conditions aimed at ensuring the defendant returns to court.[45] Recently, in New Jersey, courts have turned to utilizing a standardized assessment of whether one presents a flight risk or poses a danger to the community.[46]

In minor cases, the accused may be asked to plead guilty or not guilty. If the plea is guilty, a sentence may be pronounced on the spot. If the defendant pleads not guilty, a trial date is scheduled. However, in the typical serious (felony) case, the next primary duty of the magistrate is to determine whether the defendant requires a preliminary hearing. If such a hearing is appropriate, the matter is adjourned by the prosecution and a subsequent stage of the criminal justice process begins.

The Grand Jury Process or the Preliminary Hearing

At the federal level, all persons accused of a crime are guaranteed by the Fifth Amendment to have their cases considered by a grand jury. However, the Supreme Court has refused to make this right binding on the states. Today, only about half of the states use grand juries; in some states, they are used only for special types of cases. For example, in Florida only first-degree murder cases require the use of grand juries. Those states that do not use grand juries employ a preliminary hearing or an examining trial. (A few states use both procedures.) Regardless of which method is used, the primary purpose of this stage in the criminal justice process is to determine whether there is probable cause for the accused to be subjected to a formal trial. This is the widespread practice in the United States, but it is not necessarily the case in all countries. For instance, the criminal justice system in Iraq provides for a formal indictment only after the prosecution's evidence has been tested in court.

The Grand Jury

Grand juries consist of sixteen to twenty-three citizens, usually selected at random from the voter registration lists, who render decisions by a majority vote.[47] Their terms may last from one month to one year, and some may hear more than a thousand cases during their term. The prosecutor alone presents evidence to the grand jury. Grand jury proceedings are secret, meaning they are not open to the public and even the accused and their attorney are not permitted. If a majority of the grand jurors believes probable cause exists, then an indictment, or true bill, is brought. Otherwise, the result is a no bill.

Historically, two arguments have been made in favor of grand juries. One is that grand juries serve as a check on a prosecutor by protecting people from harassing, baseless, and malicious prosecutions. Ideally, an unbiased group of citizens would interpose themselves between an unethical prosecutor and the defendant.

A second justification for grand juries is to make sure that the DA has done some homework and has secured enough evidence to warrant the trouble and expense—for both the state and the accused—of a full-fledged trial. Sometimes in the haste and tedious routine of the criminal justice process, persons are brought to trial when insufficient evidence has been gathered to justify it. The following is an account of how a state grand jury served to prevent this from happening (albeit by accident):

> We had one case where the prosecutor tells us that several witnesses claim they saw this guy driving a stolen vehicle. So, we vote a true bill—no questions asked. Then later in the day when we were eating our sandwiches during lunch, one lady [also on the grand jury] was leafing through the files just for something to do. She says to us: "Hey, you know that guy we indicted this morning for auto theft? He claims he was on National Guard duty at the time a thousand miles away."
>
> Now we figured that that wasn't the sort of defense you'd lie about because it could be checked out so easily, so we called the DA back in. We asked him if he had called the guy's commanding officer on the WATS line to check out his story. The DA told us we weren't supposed to be trying this case and that there was probable cause because of the witnesses. But we made him call anyway, and sure enough there was a record that the guy was on guard duty the day the car was stolen. That day we did what a grand jury was supposed to be doing but, my God, it was only because that lady was bored with her baloney sandwich.

Substantial evidence is available that the prosecutor tends to dominate the grand jury process and that the jury's utility as a check on the motives and thoroughness of the government is minimal.[48] In recent years, the grand jury system has come under ever-increasing criticism for the great reluctance of such juries to indict police officers accused of taking the life of suspected criminals—and more specifically of persons of color. For example, a recent study in Houston, Texas, found that "police have been nearly immune from criminal charges in shootings" in Houston and in other large cities. In Harris County, Texas, "[Houston] grand juries haven't indicted a Houston police officer since 2004; in Dallas, grand juries reviewed 81 shootings between 2008 and 2012 and returned just one indictment. Separate research by Bowling Green State University [in Ohio] criminologist Philip Stinson has found that officers are rarely charged in on-duty killings."[49] One policing expert noted that because the public has demanded more accountability in police shootings, there have been incremental shifts in bringing charges against officers. For example, in 2020, sixteen officers were charged in fatal shootings and in 2021, twenty-one police officers were charged with murder or manslaughter.[50]

The Preliminary Hearing

States that do not use the grand jury system instead hold a preliminary hearing to determine whether there is enough evidence to move forward to the trial. Like the grand jury, the judge in a preliminary hearing determines if there is probable cause for the accused to be bound over for trial. However, the preliminary hearing is different from the grand jury in that it is a public hearing (not held in secret), the accused and their attorney are present, and it is overseen by a judge (rather than the prosecutor). At this hearing, the prosecution presents its case, and the accused has the right to cross-examine witnesses and to produce favorable evidence. Sometimes as a strategy, the defense will elect not to fight at this stage of the criminal process. When this happens the accused will waive the preliminary hearing.

If the examining judge determines that there is probable cause for a trial or if the preliminary examination is waived, the prosecutor must file a **bill of information** with the court where the trial will be held. A bill of information, like an indictment, outlines precisely the charges that will be adjudicated in the new legal setting.

The Arraignment

Arraignment is the process in which the defendant is brought before the judge in the court where they are to be tried to respond to the grand jury indictment or the prosecutor's bill of information. The prosecutor or a clerk usually reads in open court the charges that have been brought against the accused. The defendant is informed that they have a constitutional right to be represented by an attorney and that one will be appointed without charge if necessary.

The defendant has several options about how to plead to the charges. The most common pleas are guilty and not guilty. But the accused may also plead not guilty by reason of insanity, former jeopardy (having been tried on the same charge at another time), or **nolo contendere** (no contest). Nolo contendere means, in effect, that the accused does not deny the facts of the case but denies that they have not committed any crime, or it may mean that the defendant does not understand the charges. The *nolo contendere* plea can be entered only with the consent of the judge (and sometimes the prosecutor as well). The main advantage of pleading no contest is that it allows the defendant to avoid admitting guilt. It may help the accused save face vis-à-vis the public because they can later claim that technically no guilty verdict was reached even though a sentence or a fine may have been imposed.

If the accused pleads not guilty, the judge will schedule a date for a trial. If the plea is guilty, the defendant may be sentenced on the spot or at a later date set by the judge. Before the court will accept a guilty plea, the judge must certify that the plea was made voluntarily, and that the defendant was aware of the implications of the plea. A guilty plea is, for all intents and purposes, equivalent to a formal verdict of guilty.

The Possibility of a Plea Bargain

At both the state and federal levels most of all criminal cases never go to trial. That is because before the trial date the prosecutor and the defendant's attorney have struck a bargain concerning the official charges to be brought and the nature of the sentence that the state will recommend to the court. In effect, some form of leniency is promised in exchange for a guilty plea. For instance, a recent study found that 98 percent of criminal cases in federal court resulted in guilty pleas; at the state level, the figure is 95 percent.[51] The Supreme Court has even recognized that **plea bargaining** has become the norm rather than the exception in the US criminal justice system. In a 2012 case, *Missouri v. Frye*, Justice Anthony M. Kennedy, writing for the majority, stated, "The reality is that plea bargains have become so central to the administration of the criminal justice system . . . ours is for the most part a system of pleas, not a system of trials. . . ."[52] One chief assistant prosecuting attorney in Harrison County, West Virginia, explained that in her experience, "more than ninety percent of cases end up in a plea, if not higher. It might even be like ninety-eight percent. It's that predominant."[53] Similar trends occur at the federal level, as one Assistant US Attorney (federal prosecutor) noted, "The big majority of our cases are settled by plea bargaining."[54]

Under plea bargaining, the role of the judges in the criminal justice system is much smaller than is generally assumed. In federal cases, the Federal Rules of Criminal Procedure preclude a judge from participating in plea negotiations.[55] The federal rule states, "An attorney for the government and the defendant's attorney, or the defendant when proceeding pro se, may discuss and reach a plea agreement. The court must not participate in these discussions."[56] However, in the states, judge involvement in the plea bargaining process varies across jurisdictions from prohibiting participation (like the federal system) to encouraging an active role. For example, in Arkansas, Colorado, Georgia, Mississippi, New Mexico, North Dakota, Pennsylvania, South Dakota, Tennessee, Virginia, and West Virginia judges are prohibited from participation.[57] On the other end of the spectrum, judicial participation is either allowed or encouraged in states such as Arizona, Idaho, New York, North Carolina, Massachusetts, Minnesota, Montana, Oregon, and Vermont.[58] And in the middle, the following states take a neutral approach: Alabama, Connecticut, Florida, Indiana, and Oklahoma.[59] Whatever the judicial involvement, judges also ensure that the proper legal and constitutional procedures have been followed.

Judicial scholars are not unanimous on why plea bargaining has become the norm instead of the exception, and some have argued that some form of plea bargaining has always existed. (But for whatever reasons, the ever-increasing caseloads of the past several decades have made the judicial system more dependent on the quick and simple plea bargain.) There are three (not mutually exclusive) basic types of plea bargains.

Reduction of Charges

The most usual form of agreement between a prosecutor and a defendant is a reduction of the charge to one less serious than that supported by the evidence. The defendant is thereby subject to a lower maximum sentence and is likely to receive a lighter sentence than would have been the case with a guilty verdict on the original charge. In many states a common plea bargain for an individual accused of theft is to plead guilty to burglary with the intent to commit theft. This results in a substantially reduced range of sentence possibilities.

A second reason for a defendant to plead guilty to a reduced charge is to avoid a felony record altogether. For example, in March 2015, David Petraeus, "the best-known military commander of his generation, reached a plea deal with the Justice Department and admitted providing his highly classified journals to a mistress when he was director of the CIA." Under the terms of the plea bargain, Petraeus agreed "to plead guilty to one count of unauthorized removal and retention of classified material"—only a misdemeanor rather than a felony.[60]

Deletion of Tangent Charges

A second form of plea bargain is the agreement of the government to drop other charges pending against an individual. There are two variations on this theme. One is an agreement not to prosecute "vertically"—that is, not to prosecute more serious charges filed against the individual. For example, it is common in many jurisdictions for individuals using credit cards illegally to be charged simultaneously with forgery and possession of a stolen credit card. A bargain may be made to drop the forgery indictment in exchange for a plea of guilty on the lesser charge. The second type of agreement is to dismiss "horizontal" charges—that is, to dismiss additional indictments for the same crime pending against the accused. It is not unusual for several counts of burglary to be dropped following a confession to one other burglary charge in the indictment. (For a charge to be dropped, most jurisdictions require the prosecutor to file with the court a motion of **nolle prosequi**—"I refuse to prosecute"—but such motions are usually granted as a matter of course.)

Another variation of the type of plea bargaining concerned with dropping charges is the agreement in which a repeater clause is dropped from an indictment. At the federal level, and in many states, a person is considered a habitual offender on the third conviction for a violent felony anywhere in the United States. Often under these "Three Strikes You're Out" laws the mandatory sentence for the habitual criminal can be life imprisonment. In state courts, the habitual violent criminal charge is often dropped in exchange for a plea of guilty. For example, one San Diego, California, public defender recalled a case where the prosecutor offered to ignore one of the strikes in exchange for a guilty plea:

> I had one petty theft where the guy was a third striker. They [district attorney] wanted to put him away for life because he stole a binder and some other stuffa set of pans worth eight dollars. He had two prior residential burglary convictions about fifteen years old. He was technically a third-striker looking at twenty-five to life. The D.A. was willing to give him six yearsto ignore one of the strikes and give him six years. He [the defendant] did not want to take it. Absolutely noteven six years. We pushed forward. I said we were going to trial. Eventually they [district attorney] offered him a year with probation. That case got played out over two or three months because of the three-strikes law, where before it would not have made it past the initial hearing stage because it wouldn't have [been] that big a deal.[61]

More often than not the difference between the two punishments often is enough to convince one to accept this type of plea deal.

Sentence Bargaining

A third form of plea bargaining concerns a plea of guilty from the defendant in exchange for a prosecutor's agreement to ask the judge for a lighter sentence.[62] At first blush, it might seem that this type of plea negotiation is a weak substitute for either the reduction-of-charge or the dropping-of-charge form. After all, under sentence bargaining the state can make only a nonbinding recommendation to the court regarding the sentence, whereas under the other two types of plea bargains (reduction of charges and deletion of tangent charges) the state's concessions are clearer and more concrete.

The strength of the sentence negotiation, however, is based on the realities of the limited resources of the judicial system and the idea of the courtroom workgroup discussed in Chapter 3. At the state level, at least, prosecutors can promise the defendant a specific sentence with confidence that the judge will accept the recommendation. If the judge were not to do so, the prosecutor's credibility would quickly begin to wane, and many of the defendants who had been pleading guilty would begin to plead not guilty and take their chances in court. The result would be a gigantic increase in court dockets that would overwhelm the judicial system and bring it to a standstill. Prosecutors and judges understand this reality, and so do the defense attorneys.

A variation on this theme was witnessed by one of the coauthors of this book, who recently served as a juror in a criminal court case. Before the trial, the prosecutor had offered the defendant a plea bargain of seven years for a drug-related offense.

The defendant's girlfriend persuaded him that he could do better if he asked for a jury trial—which might find him innocent or, if found guilty, might give him a lighter sentence. In this instance, the jury not only convicted the defendant but gave him a fourteen-year sentence (under Texas law a defendant can elect before trial to have the jury decide the sentence rather than the judge). After the trial, the presiding judge, Marc Carter, met with the jurors to discuss the case. In part, the dialogue went as follows:

> *Judge:* The district attorney was happy with your sentence of fourteen years.
>
> *Juror:* Sir, do you mean the district attorney wanted a real long sentence?
>
> *Judge:* No, not particularly. It's just that she wanted a sentence longer than her [plea bargain] offer of seven years. If you [the jurors] would have given him five years or something, the word would have gotten out to every prisoner in the jail, and they would all be asking for jury trials. That would just overwhelm our system. A defendant needs to know that he is getting a good deal when the DA offers him a plea.[63]

Constitutional and Statutory Restrictions on Plea Bargaining

At both the state and federal levels, the requirements of due process of law dictate that plea bargains must be made voluntarily and with comprehension. This means that the defendant must be admonished by the court of the consequences of a guilty plea (e.g., the defendant waives all opportunities to change his or her mind at a later date); that the accused must be sane; and that, as one typical state puts it, "It must plainly appear that the defendant is uninfluenced by any consideration of fear, or by any persuasion, or delusive hope of pardon, prompting him to confess his guilt."[64] According to these requirements, the prosecutor's promise of a lighter sentence in exchange for a guilty plea seems to violate the letter, if not the spirit, of the Due Process Clause. Not so, the courts have ruled. If judges tell the defendants that, at least in principle, they are subject to any sentence that is pronounced and the accused acknowledge this, the requirement of due process has been met.

For the first two types of plea bargains, some stricter standards govern the federal courts. One, as discussed, is that the judge may not participate in the process of plea bargaining, whereas at the state level judges may play an active role. Likewise, if a plea bargain has been made between the US attorney and the defendant, the government may not renege on the agreement. If the federal government does so, the federal district judge must withdraw the guilty plea. Finally, the Federal Rules of Criminal Procedure require that "the court shall not enter a judgment upon a plea of guilty unless it is satisfied that there is a factual basis for the plea."[65] This means that before a guilty plea may be accepted, the prosecution must present a summary of the evidence against the accused, and the judge must agree that there is compelling evidence of the defendant's guilt.

On March 21, 2012, the Supreme Court handed down a pair of decisions that vastly expanded lower court judges' supervision of the criminal justice system.[66] The decisions mean that what was formerly unregulated and highly informal deal-making is now subject to new restrictions when bad legal advice leads defendants to reject favorable plea offers. To highlight one of the cases, in *Missouri v. Frye*, the defendant, Galin Frye, was charged with driving with a revoked license. Due to his previous three convictions for the same act, he was charged, under Missouri law, with a felony, which carries a maximum prison term of four years. In a letter to Frye's legal counsel, the prosecution offered two potential plea agreements including an offer to reduce the charge to a misdemeanor and to recommend, with a guilty plea, a ninety-day sentence.[67] Frye's attorney failed to tell him about the plea bargain offers and they expired. Just a few days before the preliminary hearing in the case, Frye was arrested again for driving with a revoked license. He ended up pleading guilty without any sort of plea agreement and was sentenced to three years in prison.

The Court held that defense counsel has an obligation to communicate the formal offers from the prosecution to the defendant. Writing for the majority in a 5–4 decision, Justice Kennedy said that "The right to adequate assistance of counsel cannot be defined or enforced without taking account of the central role plea bargaining takes in securing convictions and determining sentences."[68] One law professor commented that "The Supreme Court's decision in these two cases constitute the single greatest revolution in the criminal justice system since *Gideon v. Wainwright* provided indigents with the right to counsel," referring to the Court's 1963 landmark decision.[69]

Arguments for and Against Plea Bargaining

For the defendant, the obvious advantage of the bargain is that they are treated less harshly than would be the case if convicted and sentenced under maximum conditions. Also, the absence of a trial often lessens publicity on the case, and because of personal interests or simple social pressures, the accused may wish to avoid the length and publicity of a formal trial. Finally, some penologists (professionals in the field of punishment and rehabilitation) argue that the first step toward rehabilitation is for a criminal to admit guilt and recognize their problem. The belief is that a guilty plea is at least nominally the first step toward a successful return to society.

Plea bargaining also offers some distinct advantages for the state and for society. The most obvious is the certainty of conviction because no matter how strong the evidence may appear, an acquittal is always a possibility so long as a trial is pending. (Evidence may be stolen or lost; important witnesses may die or drop out of sight; the prosecutor may make a key error in court that results in a mistrial.) Also, the DA's office (and arguably the defense attorney) and judges are saved an enormous amount of time and effort by not having to prepare and preside over cases in which there is no real contention of innocence or that are not suited to the trial process. Finally, when police officers are not required to be in court testifying in criminal trials, they arguably have more time to devote to preventing and solving crimes.

Plea bargains do have their critics. The most frequent objection to plea bargaining is that the defendant's sentence may be based on nonpenological grounds. With the large volume of cases making plea bargaining the rule, the sentence often bears no relation to the specific facts of the case, to the correctional needs of the criminal, or to society's legitimate interest in vigorous prosecution of the case. A second defect is that if plea bargaining becomes the norm of a particular system, undue pressure may be placed on even innocent persons to plead guilty. Studies have shown that in some jurisdictions, the less chance there is for conviction, the harder the bargaining may be because the prosecutor wants to get at least some form of minimal confession out of the accused. Thus, defendants may be enticed into pleading guilty to crimes they did not commit. As one despondent public defender in Washington, DC, recently wrote: "you tell your client that they would *probably* win at trial, but if they lose, they will go to prison. The plea promises some meaningful benefit: getting out of jail sooner, avoiding deportation, not losing a job, seeing a daughter before her next birthday. But your client would have to accept responsibility for a crime they may not have committed."[70]

A third disadvantage of plea bargaining is the possibility of the abuse called **overcharging**, whereby the prosecutor brings charges against the accused that are more severe than the evidence warrants, with the hope that this will strengthen their hand in subsequent negotiations with the defense attorney. Thus, there is often an incentive for the government to initially overcharge the case. One coauthor of this book who served on a state grand jury had this exchange with a representative of the district attorney's office:

> *Grand Juror:* In this case where one person killed another in that barroom fight, why do you want us to indict on a first-degree murder charge? There doesn't seem to be any premeditation here. You'll never get a conviction on that.
>
> *DA:* Oh, I know. But it will strengthen our hand at the time when we talk with his attorney.

The grand jury in question chose to indict on a lesser and more appropriate charge.

Another flaw with the plea-bargaining system is its extremely low level of visibility. Bargains between prosecutor and DA are not made in open court, presided over by a neutral jurist, and for all to observe. While it is true that the negotiation process is handled behind closed doors, there is an on-the-record overview of the deal in court, called the allocution, where the judge, through a series of questions of the defendant, ensures the agreement was made voluntarily and that the defendant understands the terms and consequences of the plea deal.[71]

Another criticism of plea bargains is that the victim's perspective or wishes may not be taken into account during the negotiation. For instance, one former US Attorney for the District of Nevada made the following reflection about a case he pled out:

> I can recall accepting a plea in a white-collar, Ponzi-scheme sort of casea Madoff type case on a much smaller leveland hearing from the victims who lost their life savings, in some cases. And the plea was absolutely the right thing. I think we were getting a twenty-year sentence, if I recall. But from the victims' perspectivesand I heard this from more than one victimthe question was, "Well, I think that the defendant should get the death penalty." And it's a tough thing to respond to as a prosecutor. And, of course, I would say something like, "Well, you know, we don't do that. The system doesn't allow for executing fraud defendants. And the response routinely would be, 'Why not? That was my life savings.'"[72]

Finally, the system has the potential to circumvent key procedural and constitutional rules of evidence. Critics have pointed out that plea bargains force defendants to waive their Fifth and Sixth Amendment rights. For example, when a defendant accepts a plea bargain they ultimately waive their right to a jury trial (Sixth Amendment), right to confront witnesses (Sixth Amendment), and right against self-incrimination (Fifth Amendment). Thus, the plea bargain may deprive the accused of basic constitutional rights.

Finally, a recent study concludes that "plea bargaining is spreading into an increasing number of countries in spite of criticisms of scholars around the world." The author of this article also suggests that "the International Criminal Court (ICC) should [with some reservations] follow the example of other international criminal tribunals and implement a plea-bargaining policy."[73]

The Adversarial Process as Contrasted with the Inquisitorial Method

The principles of the **adversarial process** as it exists in American criminal courts are largely true of civil trials as well. The adversarial model assumes that there are two sides to every case or controversy. In criminal cases, the government claims a defendant is guilty while the defendant contends innocence; in civil cases, the plaintiff asserts that the person they are suing has caused some injury, while the respondent denies responsibility. In the courtroom, each party vies against the other; each provides their side of the story as they see it. The theory (or hope) underlying this model is that the truth will emerge if each party is given unbridled opportunity to present the full panoply of evidence, facts, and arguments before a neutral and attentive judge (and jury).

The lawyers representing each side are the major players in this courtroom drama. The judge acts more as a passive, disinterested referee whose primary role is to keep both sides within the accepted rules of legal procedure and courtroom decorum. The judge eventually determines which side has won in accordance with the rules of evidence, but only after both sides have had a full opportunity to fight it out.

The adversarial process is the norm in the United States, but it is not in most other countries, including almost all the Western industrial democracies and Latin America. Most use a version of what legal scholars call the **inquisitorial method**, in which the judge (or judges) is the primary actor in the courtroom and the attorneys passively defend their clients' interests. Under this method the judge(s) actively and aggressively conducts an inquiry into the truth of the charges that the state or a plaintiff has lodged against a defendant. The French model is representative of that used in most countries employing the inquisitorial method. In a typical case, a panel of perhaps three judges presides. They are joined by several laypersons—ordinary citizens—who participate in overseeing the proceedings and help decide on innocence or guilt. But these ordinary citizens are not jurors in the American sense of the term. They merely sit with the professional judges on an elevated bench, and they all deliberate together. French courtrooms exhibit less drama because the lawyers for each side make many of their arguments in writing rather than orally, so that few verbal duels between the attorneys take place. Likewise, there are fewer skirmishes over evidence because virtually all evidence that the French judges deem relevant is allowed.

Although most countries prefer the judicial system that they have acquired by custom and tradition, there are still some transformations in the making. For example, with our neighbor to the south, in June 2008, Mexico threw open the doors to its judicial system, allowing US-style public trials and creating a presumption of innocence. Under the long-awaited constitutional amendment signed by former President Felipe Calderón, guilt or innocence would no longer be decided behind closed doors by a judge relying on written evidence. Prosecutors and defense lawyers would now argue their case in court, and judges must explain their decisions to defendants. "This is perhaps the most important reform to the criminal system that Mexicans have had in a long time," Calderón said after signing the amendment.[74]

SUMMARY

We began this chapter with a discussion of the nature and substance of crime—at least as it is currently understood. We then reviewed myriad procedures that constitute the judicial process at the federal and state levels. We analyzed the various aspects of crime that lead to an arrest, the subsequent appearance before a magistrate, and the activity of the grand jury or the preliminary hearing. We also observed how plea bargaining enormously tempers the criminal court process, and finally, we outlined the key differences between the adversarial process used in the American courtroom and the inquisitorial methods that are the choice of most other nations. Throughout the chapter, we stressed that the backgrounds and attitudes of the criminal justice participants have as much to do with the nature and quality of justice as do the formal rules of the game.

FURTHER THOUGHT AND DISCUSSION QUESTIONS

1. Would the United States be better served to remove from the criminal statute books all laws that are not enforced, such as laws against small-time gambling and laws forbidding sexual activity between certain consenting adults? Does the refusal to carry out some laws while others are strictly enforced undermine respect for law in general?
2. The United States is on par with Russia in having more persons per capita in prison than is the case in any other nation. Is that a sign that the United States is a nation that enforces its laws, or is it an indication that something is inherently wrong with its criminal justice system?
3. Should America follow the example of many other countries when faced with terrorism or excessive domestic violence by simply suspending the constitutional rights of those accused of crimes? If so, who should make the decision to take this course of action, and how long should the suspension of rights be allowed to continue?
4. Should we abolish plea bargains entirely and instead have a full-blown trial for everyone accused of a crime? What if the defendant wanted to plead guilty and declined a trial? Should lower sentences be promised to defendants who acknowledge their guilt and cooperate with the police?

SUGGESTED RESOURCES

American Bar Association Resources on Criminal Justice website. Available online at https://www.americanbar.org/groups/criminal_justice/resources/. An excellent source of information about the criminal justice system.

Cole, George F., Christopher E. Smith, and Christina De Jong. *Criminal Justice in America*, 10th ed. Boston, MA: Cengage Learning, 2022. A well-written textbook on all the key aspects of the criminal justice system in the United States.

Fisher, George. *Plea Bargaining's Triumph: A History of Plea Bargaining in America*. Stanford, CA: Stanford University Press, 2004. An excellent history of plea bargaining along with an in-depth explanation of why it has become the norm in the modern judicial system.

Hessick, Carissa Byrne. *Punishment Without Trial: Why Pleas Bargaining Is a Bad Deal*. New York, NY: Abrams Press, 2021. This is a well-done book that covers the consequences of plea bargaining.

Messner, Steven F., and Richard Rosenfeld. *Crime and the American Dream*, 5th ed. Belmont, CA: Wadsworth, 2013. A short but well-written text that expands on the causes and social consequences of crime as outlined in this chapter.

Neubauer, David W., and Henry F. Fradella. *America's Courts and the Criminal Justice System*, 13th ed. Boston, MA: Cengage Learning, 2018. A classic political science textbook on all the major stages present in the criminal justice process.

Reichel, Philip L. *Comparative Criminal Justice Systems: A Topical Approach*, 7th ed. New York, NY: Pearson, 2018. An excellent text that compares pretrial criminal procedures in the United States and several other countries.

Stevenson, Bryan. *Just Mercy: A Story of Justice and Redemption*. New York, NY: Spiegel & Grau, 2014. An excellent account of one man's journey in defending the poor and the wrongly condemned. This book highlights many issues with our criminal justice system.

Walker, Samuel. *Sense and Nonsense about Crime, Drugs, and Communities: A Policy Guide*, 8th ed. Boston, MA: Cengage Learning, 2015. A discussion of the pros and cons of both liberal and conservative approaches to preventing and punishing criminal behavior.

KEY TERMS

Actus reus
adversarial process
Arraignment
bills of attainder
bill of information
ex post facto
inquisitorial method
mens rea
nolo contendere
nolle prosequi
overcharging
plea bargaining
warrant

10 THE CRIMINAL TRIAL AND ITS AFTERMATH

CHAPTER GOALS AND OBJECTIVES

In this chapter, students will learn that . . .

- Key procedures in a criminal trial are dictated by the US Supreme Court's interpretation of important provisions in the US Constitution.
- The attorneys prosecuting the case and providing defense for the accused are key actors in the criminal trial, in terms of developing legal strategy and presenting their case to the judge or jury.
- The role of the judge in a criminal trial is typically considered to be passive, although the rulings a judge makes throughout the trial often represent the main grounds for appeal of a conviction.
- While the US Constitution requires trial by impartial juries, it can be challenging to select a jury that represents the community and can assess the case against the defendant without bias.
- The victims' rights movement of the 1970s ushered in a greater opportunity for victims of crime to inform courts of how the defendant's actions affected them.
- The appeals process provides an important role in protecting the rights of those accused of crimes, but it is rare for an appeal to result in someone convicted of a crime being released from prison.

In the previous chapter, we outlined the steps that lead up to a criminal trial in the United States. This chapter focuses on the trial itself. In New York City in 2024, the first criminal trial of a former president was held, when Donald Trump[1] was tried and found guilty on thirty-four counts of falsifying business records in the first degree, in connection to a scheme in the lead-up to the 2016 presidential election to pay off adult film actress Stormy Daniels to stay quiet about allegedly having sex with Trump in 2006.[2] Given Trump's status as this case has evolved (from a former president to Republican nominee for and eventual winner of the 2024 president election), Trump's criminal trial was surely atypical of most, in terms of its social relevance and the attention given to it. In other ways, though, the Trump trial illustrated many of the typical steps in how criminal cases proceed in the United States, and we reference that recent trial (and a few other high-profile criminal trials) throughout this chapter. The chapter begins with a brief discussion of the most significant constitutional rights that apply in criminal trials, before examining key steps in the trial, sentencing, and appeals process. We give particular attention to the roles played by key actors in a criminal trial, including the attorneys, the judge, and the jury.

PROCEDURES DURING A CRIMINAL TRIAL

Assuming that no plea bargain has been struck and that the accused maintains their innocence, a formal trial will take place. This is a right that the Sixth Amendment guarantees to all Americans charged with federal crimes and a right guaranteed by the various state constitutions—and by the Fourteenth Amendment—to people charged with state offenses. The accused has many constitutional and statutory rights during the trial. The following is a summary of the primary rights that are binding on both the federal and state courts.

In 2024, Donald Trump became the first former president in US history to be tried on criminal charges when he was found guilty of thirty-four counts of falsifying business records. Even with its historic nature and its complicated resolution, the Trump trial followed the typical steps dictating how criminal trials proceed in the United States.

Spencer Platt/Getty Images

Basic Rights Guaranteed during the Trial Process

The Sixth Amendment says, "In all criminal prosecutions, the accused shall enjoy the right to a speedy and public trial." The founders emphasized the word *speedy*, so that an accused would not languish in prison for a long time prior to the trial or must wait an unduly long time before their fate is determined. But how soon is speedy? Although the Supreme Court has defined this word in several ways, Congress gave new meaning to the term when it passed the Speedy Trial Act of 1974. The act mandated time limits, ultimately reaching one hundred days, within which criminal charges must be either brought to trial or dismissed. Most states have similar measures on the statute books, although the precise period varies from one jurisdiction to another. By "public trial," the founders meant to discourage the notion of secret proceedings whereby an accused could be tried without public knowledge and whisked off to some unknown detention camp—a situation typical of totalitarian regimes.

The Sixth Amendment also guarantees the right to an impartial jury. At a minimum, this has meant that prospective jurors must not be prejudiced in any way before the trial begins. What the concept of an impartial jury of one's peers has come to mean in practice is that jurors are to be selected randomly from voter registration lists—supplemented in an increasing number of jurisdictions by lists based on automobile registrations, driver's licenses, welfare rolls, and so on.[3] Although this does not provide a perfect representation of the community because not all persons are registered to vote or possess a driver's license, the Supreme Court has said that this method is good enough. The legal requirement is that the jury pool be drawn from a "fair cross section" of the community.[4]

Besides being guaranteed the right to be tried in the same locale where the crime was committed and to be informed of the charges, Americans have the right to be confronted with the witnesses against them. They have the right to know who their accusers are and what they are charging so that a proper defense may be formulated. The accused is also guaranteed per the Sixth Amendment to the US Constitution the opportunity "to have the Assistance of Counsel for his defense." Before the 1960s, this meant that one had this right (at the state level) only for serious crimes and only if one could pay for an attorney. However, because of a series of Supreme Court decisions, the law of the land guarantees the accused an attorney if tried for any crime that may result in a prison term, and the government must provide the legal defense for an indigent defendant. This is the rule at both the national and state levels.

As discussed in Chapter 8, indigent defense comes in the form of attorneys working for state or county public defender offices or with the assignment of private attorneys who supplement their practice by representing indigent defendants. Criticisms of how indigent defendants are represented focus on the unmanageable caseloads and low compensation of those tasked with providing adequate defense.[5] One study found that when all other relevant variables were held constant, there was virtually no difference in the outcome whether the defendant used a public defender or retained counsel, perhaps due to the positive working relationship that public defenders have within the courtroom workgroup.[6]

The Fifth Amendment to the US Constitution declares that no person shall "be subject for the same offence to be twice put in jeopardy of life and limb." This is the famous Double Jeopardy Clause, which means in effect that no one may be tried twice for the same crime by any state government or by the federal government. It does not mean, however, that a person may not be tried twice for the same action if that action has violated both national and state laws. For example, someone who robs a federally chartered bank in New Jersey runs afoul of both federal and state laws. That person could legally be tried and acquitted for the offense in a New Jersey court and subsequently be tried for that same action in federal court. Again, this clause means that the same level of government may not try a person twice for the same crime.

Nor does it mean that a crime victim cannot bring a civil suit against an alleged perpetrator. This famously occurred in the 1997 case involving former football star O. J. Simpson, who had been acquitted in 1995 of criminal charges in the deaths of his ex-wife, Nicole Brown, and her friend, Ronald Goldman. The victims' families later brought a civil suit against Simpson, and in 1997, a jury found Simpson liable for the wrongful deaths of Brown and Goldman. The jury ordered Simpson to pay more than $33 million to the families.[7] Cases of this type are unusual, however, because most criminal defendants, unlike Simpson, do not have much money, so crime victims can rarely justify the considerable expense of suing the wrongdoer.

Even with these important considerations, the constitutional provision against double jeopardy is a critical protection against overreach by both federal and state governments. In 2024, for example, the US Supreme Court unanimously ruled that the double jeopardy rights of Damian McElrath had been violated by the Supreme Court of the state of Georgia.[8] McElrath had been tried for three charges—malice murder, felony murder, and aggravated assault—connected to the 2012 death of McElrath's mother when McElrath was eighteen years old. At trial, McElrath did not dispute that he had killed his mother, but he asserted an insanity defense, based on his history of mental illness, including a diagnosis of schizophrenia. The jury rendered a split verdict where McElrath was found not guilty by reason of insanity on the malice-murder charge but was found guilty but mentally ill on the other two charges. On appeal, the Georgia Supreme Court vacated and remanded *both* the malice-murder and felony-murder verdicts because verdicts relying on irreconcilable mental states were "repugnant" under Georgia state law. In a unanimous decision written by Justice Ketanji Brown Jackson, the US Supreme Court reiterated that "[o]nce rendered, a jury's verdict of acquittal is inviolate" and that the "Double Jeopardy Clause prohibits second-guessing the reason for a jury's acquittal" on the malice-murder charge.[9] One legal analyst summarized *McElrath* by noting that although few scholars would remember the Court's brief and unanimous opinion written by the Court's most junior justice, the value of the ruling was in the justices' willingness to review the case in order to prevent Georgia from a "rather contemptuous violation of McElrath's constitutional rights."[10]

Another important right guaranteed to the accused at both the state and federal levels by the Fifth Amendment is not to "be compelled in any criminal case to be a witness against himself." This has been interpreted to mean that if the accused elects not to testify on their own behalf in court, this may not be used against the person by judge and jury. This guarantee serves to reinforce the principle that under the US judicial system the burden of proof is on the state; the accused is presumed innocent unless and until the government proves otherwise beyond a reasonable doubt.

Finally, the Supreme Court has interpreted the guarantee of due process of law to mean that evidence procured in an illegal search and seizure may not be used against the accused at trial. The source of this so-called exclusionary rule is the Fourth Amendment to the US Constitution; the Supreme Court has made its strictures binding on the states as well. The Court's purpose was to eliminate any incentive the police might have to illegally obtain evidence against the accused. Civil libertarians have argued that this rule is a key element in the basic concepts of due process and fair play. Others have countered that this right does not discourage improper police behavior and that it serves only as a technical loophole to free the guilty. Subsequent Supreme Court rulings have taken steps to narrow the effect of the exclusionary rule. In 2006, for example, the Supreme Court allowed evidence that was seized in a raid in which police officers violated their department's "knock and announce" rule before entering a home.[11] In 2013, furthermore, the Court ruled that the collection of DNA evidence as a routine part of the booking process for serious crimes was, like fingerprinting, reasonable under the Fourth Amendment.[12]

Selection of Jurors

If the accused elects not to have a bench trial—that is, not to be tried and sentenced by a judge alone—their fate will be determined by a jury. At the federal level, twelve persons must render a unanimous verdict. Until recently, a small number of states allowed nonunanimous convictions. In 1972, the US Supreme Court ruled that the Sixth Amendment only guaranteed a right to a unanimous jury conviction in federal, but not state, court. In 2020, the Court ruled in *Ramos v. Louisiana* that the unanimous jury requirement "applies to state and federal criminal trials equally," requiring the two states that allowed nonunanimous verdicts (Louisiana and Oregon) to change course.[13]

A group of potential jurors is summoned to appear in court. This group is known as a **venire** (sometimes known as an array). The venire is then questioned in open court (and perhaps in written questionnaires) about their general qualifications for jury service in a process known as **voir dire**. The prosecutor and the defense attorney ask general and specific questions of the potential jurors. Are they citizens of the state? Have they or anyone in their family ever been tried for a criminal offense? Have they read about or formed any opinions about the case at hand?

In conducting the voir dire, the state and the defense have two general goals. The first is to eliminate all members of the panel who might have an obvious reason for not rendering an impartial decision in the case. For example, relatives or friends of a participant in the trial, or someone openly admitting a strong bias in the case are generally grounds for elimination of a potential juror. Objections to jurors in this category are known as challenges for cause, and the number of such challenges is unlimited. The judge determines whether these challenges are valid.

The second goal of the opposing attorneys in questioning the array of potential jurors is to eliminate those whom they believe would be unfavorable to their side even though no overt reason for bias is apparent. This can be done because each side is given **peremptory challenges**—requests to the court to exclude a prospective juror with no reason given. Long ago, attorneys were able to exclude potential jurors by using the peremptory challenge for virtually any reason. However, in 1986, the Supreme Court interpreted the Fourteenth Amendment's Equal Protection Clause to restrict this unbridled discretion. The high court ruled in the case of *Batson v. Kentucky* that prosecutors may not use their challenges to exclude African Americans from serving on a criminal jury solely based on race.[14] Out of this case came the *Batson* rule, which bars the racially discriminatory use of peremptory challenges. In 1994, the Court extended the rule to prohibit the exclusion of women.[15] Since then, some courts have expanded the *Batson* rule to include other groups—for example, ethnic groups such as Italian Americans and Jews—and have barred exclusions based on sexual orientation.[16] Expressing continued concern about bias in the peremptory challenge process, the Supreme Court ruled in 2005 that defense attorneys could point to statistical analysis of the venire, side-by-side comparison of struck and impaneled jurors, differences in questions asked, and evidence of historical discrimination in proving bias in the peremptory challenge process. This ruling arose out of a Texas case in which the prosecution had used its peremptory challenges to strike ten of the eleven African Americans who were eligible to serve on the jury.[17]

The process of questioning and challenging prospective jurors continues until all those duly challenged for cause are eliminated, the peremptory challenges are either used up or waived, and a jury of twelve (six in some states, particularly in misdemeanor cases) has been assembled. In some states, alternate jurors are also chosen. They attend the trial but participate in deliberations only if one of the original jurors is unable to continue in the proceedings. Once the panel has been selected, the jurors are sworn in by the judge or the clerk of the court and the trial usually begins immediately.

During the week-long jury selection process for Donald Trump's criminal trial in New York City, each side was allowed ten peremptory challenges, with the defense using all ten. The jury selection process whittled two separate pools of roughly one hundred potential jurors each down to the twelve jurors and six alternates required for a felony case in New York State.[18] Voir dire included questions related to whether potential jurors had attended Trump rallies, were supporters of far-right or far-left leaning groups (such as the Proud Boys or antifa), and whether they followed Trump on social media.

In highly publicized criminal trials, the Sixth Amendment's protection of a right to a trial by "an impartial jury" can be difficult to secure, particularly given that criminal trials are to be held "in the State where the said Crimes shall have been committed."[19] As asked by Justice Ruth Bader Ginsburg in a case concerning the conviction of Enron executive Jeffrey Skilling, "When does the publicity attending conduct charged as criminal dim prospects that the trier can judge a case as due process requires, unswayed by outside influence?"[20]

Efforts by Donald Trump's legal team to change the venue of his case out of Manhattan were rejected by courts in New York. The defense argued that the influence of local media attention to this and other pending criminal cases against Trump made selecting an unbiased jury impossible. The prosecution countered by arguing that Manhattan jurors were no less able to act as fair and impartial jurors given the worldwide media attention to Trump's legal challenges, as well as by noting that Trump himself was responsible for much of the media attention due to his drawing attention to the trial on social media and at campaign rallies.[21]

Opening Statements

At the beginning of the formal trial, both the prosecution and the defense make their opening statements, although the defense is not technically required to do so. Long and detailed statements are more likely to be made in jury trials than in bench trials. The purpose of opening statements is to provide members of the jury—who lack familiarity with the law and with procedures of criminal investigation—with an outline of the major objectives of each side's case, the evidence to be presented, the witnesses to be called, and what each side seeks to prove from the evidence of the witnesses. If the opening statements are well presented, the jurors will find it easier to grasp the meaning and significance of the evidence and testimony, and ideally, they will be less likely to get confused and bogged down in the complexities and technicalities of the case. The usual procedure is for the state to make its opening statement first and for the defense to follow with a statement about how it will refute that case.

In the opening statement in the Trump hush money trial, the prosecuting attorney endeavored to give an overview of how "the defendant, Donald Trump, orchestrated a criminal scheme to corrupt the 2016 presidential election. Then he covered up that criminal conspiracy by lying in his New York business records over and over and over again."[22] The defense attorney countered by arguing that the charges against Trump were baseless and preemptively attacking the credibility of Michael Cohen, a key prosecution witness who had previously pled guilty to charges related to the same hush money scheme.

The Prosecution's Case

After the opening statements, the prosecutor presents the evidence amassed by the state against the accused. Evidence is generally of two types—physical evidence and the testimony of witnesses. The physical evidence may include such things as weapons, ballistics tests, fingerprints, handwriting samples, blood or urine tests, and other documents or items that serve as physical aids. The defense may object to the admission of any of these tangible items, and if successful, they will have the item excluded from consideration. If unsuccessful, the physical evidence is labeled by one of the courtroom personnel and becomes part of the official record.

Most evidence at criminal trials takes the form of testimony of witnesses. The format is a question-and-answer procedure that may appear a bit stilted, but its purpose is to elicit specific information in an orderly fashion. The goal is to present only evidence that is relevant to the case at hand and not to give confusing or irrelevant information or illegal evidence that might result in a mistrial.

After each witness, the defense attorney has the right to cross-examine. The goal of the defense will be to impeach the testimony of the prosecution witness—that is, to discredit it. The attorney may attempt to confuse, fluster, or anger the witness, causing them to lose self-control and begin providing confusing or conflicting testimony. The testimony of the witness for the prosecution may also be impeached if defense witnesses who contradict the version of events suggested by the state are subsequently presented. On completion of the **cross-examination**, the prosecutor may conduct a redirect examination, which serves to clarify or correct some telling point made during the cross-examination. After the state has presented all its evidence and witnesses, it rests its case.

The prosecution's case against Donald Trump lasted for about four weeks. The prosecution's case relied extensively on witness testimony, including testimony from Stormy Daniels (who testified about her alleged sexual encounter with Trump in 2006) and multiple former Trump aides and associates.[23] Most notable was the testimony of Michael Cohen, Trump's former attorney who pled guilty in 2018 to multiple counts related to his role in orchestrating payments to two women (including Daniels) in the months leading up to the 2016 presidential election. During cross-examination, the defense focused on calling the credibility of key prosecution witnesses, Cohen and Daniels in particular, into question.

The Case for the Defense

The presentation of the case for the defense is similar in style and format to that of the prosecution. Tangible evidence is less common in the defense's case, and most of the evidence will be that of witnesses who are prepared to rebut or contradict the prosecution's arguments. The witnesses are questioned by the defense attorney in the same style as those in the prosecution case. Each defense witness may in turn be cross-examined by the prosecution, and then a redirect examination is in order.

The real difference between the case for the prosecution and the case for the defense lies in their obligation before the law. The defense is not required by law to present any new or additional evidence or any witnesses at all. The defense may consist merely of challenging the credibility or the legality of the state's evidence and witnesses. The defense is not obligated to prove the innocence of the accused; it need show only that the state's case is not beyond a reasonable doubt. The defendant need not even take the stand. However, if they elect to do so, the accused faces the same risks of cross-examination as any other witness.

The defense's case in the Trump trial was very much in line with the general approach described here. Compared to the twenty witnesses and two hundred pieces of evidence relied upon by the prosecution, the defense called only two witnesses to the stand. The first was a paralegal called to enter into evidence phone records used by the defense to suggest that Michael Cohen had perjured himself during his previous testimony in the case. The second was Robert Costello, an attorney brought forth to discredit Cohen's testimony further.[24] Although Trump had publicly teased for weeks that he might testify, the defense rested its case without Trump taking the stand. If he had chosen to testify, he surely would have undergone intensive cross-examination by the prosecution.

After the defense has rested its case, the prosecution has the right to go back on the attack and present rebuttal evidence. In turn, the defense may offer a rejoinder known as a surrebuttal. After that, each side is ready for the closing arguments. This is often one of the more dramatic episodes in the trial because each side seeks to sum up its case, condense its strongest arguments, and make one last appeal to the jury. New evidence may not be presented at this stage, and the arguments of both sides tend to ring with emotion and appeals to values that transcend the immediate case.

In the Trump trial, the defense used closing arguments to continue hammering the credibility of the prosecution's key witnesses, especially Cohen, whom Trump attorney Todd Blanche referred to as "the human embodiment of reasonable doubt" during his closing. The prosecution's closing was somewhat more extensive, walking the jury through the testimony and other evidence (including texts and emails) connecting the falsification of the business records to the scheme to influence the 2016 election by preventing Daniels from making her allegations of a sexual encounter with Trump public.[25]

Role of the Judge during the Trial

The judge's role in the trial, although important, is a relatively passive one. Judges do not present any evidence or take an active part in the examination of the witnesses. The judge is called on to rule on the many motions of the prosecutor and of the defense attorney regarding the types of evidence that may be presented and the kinds of questions that may be asked of the witnesses. In some jurisdictions, the judge is permitted to ask substantive questions of the witnesses and to comment to the jury about the credibility of the evidence that is presented; in other states, the judge is constrained from such activity. Still, the American legal tradition has room for a variety of judicial styles that depend on the personality, training, and wisdom of individual judges.

This is vividly demonstrated when comparing how New York County Supreme Court Justice Juan Manuel Merchan presided over the Trump trial to the job done by Los Angeles Superior Court Judge Lance Ito in presiding over the O. J. Simpson trial in 1995. Although both judges had previous experience presiding over high-profile criminal trials, the Trump trial quickly exemplified Justice Merchan's "tough and no-nonsense but fair" reputation for being "always in control of the courtroom."[26] This played out during the Trump trial through such examples as managing voir dire efficiently with the use of a forty-two-point questionnaire and a clear time limit for lawyers from both sides to question prospective jurors.

In the Simpson trial, on the other hand, Judge Ito made the controversial decision to allow cameras in the courtroom and to many observers did not appear to be in strong control of the courtroom proceedings, which lasted for eight long months.[27] He allowed an inordinately considerable number of peremptory challenges, which greatly delayed jury selection; he permitted the attorneys to bicker endlessly, both inside and outside of the courtroom; and he refused to restrict lengthy excursions on the witness stand (for example, allowing nine days of testimony by police criminalist Dennis Fung).

While judicial styles vary from one courtroom to another, all American jurists are expected to manifest some similar traits. For example, the judge is expected to play the part of a disinterested party whose primary job is to ensure that both sides are allowed to present their cases as fully as possible within the confines of the law. If judges depart from the appearance or practice of being fair and neutral parties, they run counter to fundamental tenets of American jurisprudence and risk having their decisions overturned by an appellate court. Although judges do, for the most part, play an independent role, their backgrounds and values may affect their decisions in close calls—when they must rule on a motion for which the arguments are equally strong or on a point of law that is open to a variety of interpretations. These potentially close calls, in turn, may be at the center of any defense appeal of a conviction.

Role of the Jury during the Trial

Passive is the word that generally characterizes the jurors' role during the trial. Their job is to listen attentively to the cases presented by the two opposing attorneys and then come to a decision based solely on the evidence that is set forth. They are ordinarily not permitted to ask questions either of the witnesses or of the judge and they may not be allowed to take notes during the proceedings. This is not necessarily because of constitutional or statutory prohibitions but primarily because it has been the traditional practice of courts in America. The adversarial form of justice requires lawyers to play the primary role during the trial; the judge and jury are generally to behave as dispassionate observers.

Not all trial courts in the United States strictly follow this norm, however, and some judges have allowed jurors to become more involved in the judicial arena. One

2003 study of "mock jurors" in an experimental design found that allowing jurors to take notes during complex cases improved their performance in deciding the case, regardless of whether or not the jurors were able to access the notes during the verdict deliberations.[28] In the Trump trial, jurors were allowed to take notes, but were instructed to use them only for refreshing the individual note-taking juror's recollection and were not to substitute for personal recollection, the judge's explanation of law governing the case, or the recorded trial transcript.[29]

Instructions to the Jury

A particularly important function of the judge during the trial is to charge the jury after the prosecution and defense have rested their cases. Although the jury's job is to weigh and assess the facts of the case, the judge must instruct the jurors about the meaning of the law and how the law is to be applied. The judge's instructions conceivably could be drafted in a way that favors one side or the other. For example, if someone were accused of embezzlement and the judge favored acquittal, it might be possible to give the jury such a narrow legal definition of the word *embezzlement* that it would be difficult to bring in a guilty verdict. Likewise, if the judge were disposed toward conviction, a broader discussion of the laws on embezzlement might facilitate a conviction.

Both the prosecutor and the defense attorney know that the nature of the instructions can nudge the jury in one direction or another. Consequently, each side in the case often submits its own set of instructions to the judge, asking that its version be the official one read to the jury. The judge may then select either of the two sets of instructions, or as often as not, the judge may develop one of their own (perhaps based on selected parts of those offered or on a previously used set of instructions).

Because many appeals are based on claims of faulty jury instructions, judges tend to take great care that the wording be technically and legally correct, and jury instructions tend to share some basic elements. One is to define for the jurors the crime with which the accused is charged. This may involve giving the jurors a variety of options about what kind of verdict to bring.

The judge also must remind the jury that the burden of proof is on the state and that the accused is presumed to be innocent. If, after considering all the evidence, the jury still has a reasonable doubt as to the guilt of the accused, it must bring in a verdict of not guilty. Jurors are often troubled by what this means. "How sure do we have to be?" they may ask themselves, "75 percent, 90 percent, 99 percent?" What is reasonable, and how strong may the doubt be? Jury instructions in Trump's trial defined "reasonable doubt" as:

> an honest doubt of the defendant's guilt for which a reason exists based upon the nature and quality of the evidence. It is an actual doubt, not an imaginary doubt. It is a doubt that a reasonable person, acting in a matter of this importance, would be likely to entertain because of the evidence that was presented or because of the lack of convincing evidence.[30]

Finally, the judge usually acquaints the jurors with a variety of procedural matters: how to contact the judge if they have questions, the order in which they must consider the charges if there are more than one, and who must sign the official documents that express the verdict of the jury. After the instructions are read to the jury (and the attorneys for each side have been given an opportunity to offer objections), the jurors retreat to a deliberation room to decide the fate of the accused.

The Jury's Decisions

The jury deliberates in complete privacy; no outsiders observe or participate in its debate. During their deliberation, jurors may request clarification of legal questions from the judge, and they may look at items of evidence or selected segments of the case transcript, but they may consult nothing else—no law dictionaries, no legal writings, no opinions from experts. The consequences when a juror consults other information can be serious. In Vermont, Donald Fell was convicted and sentenced to death under federal law (the state of Vermont does not have the death penalty) in 2005 for a murder that occurred in 2000. In 2014, the conviction and sentence were overturned, and Fell was granted a new trial after evidence of juror misconduct surfaced.[31] Fell's lawyers contended that a juror in the initial trial secretly traveled to the crime scene and talked with the other jurors about what he observed there.[32] Fell's subsequent trial was initially set for 2016, but it was delayed until 2018, at which time a plea deal was reached, allowing Fell to plead guilty in exchange for the withdrawal of the government's intention to seek the death penalty.[33] Nearly eighteen years after the murder, on September 28, 2018, Fell was sentenced to life in prison without the possibility of parole.

When a decision has been reached by a vote of its members, the jury returns to the courtroom to announce its verdict. If a decision has not been reached by nightfall, the jurors are typically sent home with firm instructions not to discuss the case with others or to follow it in news reports. In unusually high-profile cases, the judge might order **sequestration** of the jury, which means that its members will spend the night in a local hotel away from the public eye. In 2001, the state of New York loosened its jury sequestration law by allowing judges to decide on a case-by-case basis whether a jury should be sequestered.[34] The jury in Trump's case was not sequestered at any stage of the trial, including jury deliberations.

The jury in Trump's trial deliberated for nearly ten hours over two days before delivering a unanimous verdict of guilty on all thirty-four counts.[35] Had the jury become deadlocked and unable to reach a verdict, it may have reported that fact to the judge. In such an event, the judge may have insisted that the jury continue its effort to reach a verdict. Or if the judge is convinced that the jury is hopelessly deadlocked, they may dismiss the jury and call for a new trial.

In Massachusetts in 2024, Karen Read was tried on multiple charges, including second-degree murder, in the 2022 death of her boyfriend, Boston police officer John O'Keefe. The jury deliberated in this case for nearly a full week, reporting back to the judge three times that they were unable to reach a verdict. The first time the jury communicated to the judge that they were at an impasse after four days of deliberation, Judge Beverly Cannone simply sent them back to deliberate further, indicating that she was not yet "prepared to find that there have been due and thorough deliberations."[36] When the jury indicated a second time that they were unable to reach a unanimous verdict, Judge Cannone pressed the jurors to "reexamine their positions in light of the position of those with opposite positions."[37] Under Massachusetts law, it is within the judge's discretion whether and when to give a struggling jury this kind of charge, but such pressure to resolve a case has been "characterized as approaching the limit of allowable pressure the judge may place on the jury" to reach a verdict.[38] Law in the state of Massachusetts requires that once this "dynamite" charge is issued, the judge must declare a mistrial if the jurors come back again without a unanimous verdict. When the jurors came back deadlocked a third time in Read's case, the judge was therefore required to declare a mistrial. Read may be tried again before another jury. There is no issue with double jeopardy, given that the original jury did not agree on a verdict.

Jurors, like police officers, prosecutors, grand jurors, and judges, reflect their personal values and backgrounds in their decision-making process. Earlier studies have shown that men speak up more than women in the jury deliberation process and have more influence on the outcome, and well-educated people play a more significant role than those with lesser educational backgrounds. Some evidence also suggests that during the jury deliberation process, ethnic or racial minorities may draw on their firsthand experiences as members of a disadvantaged group and may be more likely to favor the accused. In a more recent study assessing how actual jurors reported their own participation on juries, researchers found that while jurors with more education and who are wealthier reported participating more on juries, they found less support than seen in previous studies for the conclusion that men participate more than women or that White jurors participate more than non-White jurors.[39]

When the members of the jury do finally reach a decision, they return to the courtroom and their verdict is announced in open court, often by the jury foreperson. At this time, either the prosecutor or the defense attorney often asks that the jury be polled—that is, that each juror is asked individually if the verdict reflects their own opinion. The purpose is to determine whether each juror supports the overall verdict or whether they have given in to group pressure. The polling of the jury in the Trump hush money case revealed that all jurors were of the same mind on all thirty-four guilty verdicts in the case, with the jurors reportedly remaining "expressionless as they were individually polled to confirm the verdict, even as Mr. Trump looked at them."[40]

PROCEDURES AFTER A CRIMINAL TRIAL

At the close of the criminal trial, two stages generally remain for the defendant if they have been found guilty: sentencing and an appeal.

Sentencing

Sentencing is the court's formal pronouncement of judgment on the defendant, at which time the punishment or penalty is set forth.

Penologists have traditionally given four justifications for punishing those who break the laws of society: retribution, incapacitation, deterrence, and rehabilitation. Each one contains separate, although not mutually exclusive, philosophies about why the state should punish offenders. Some emphasize past actions, while others focus on the future behavior of the criminal. Some place their primary focus on the rights and needs of society, while others are more oriented toward the criminal as a human being. While all four philosophies of sentencing have some compelling elements, each contains some inconsistencies and shortcomings, and none seems to address all the complex aspects of this important but complicated societal issue.[41]

At the federal level and in most states, only judges impose sentences.[42] Some states have a bifurcated procedure for determining innocence or guilt and then imposing a sentence for the guilty; after reaching a guilty verdict, the jury deliberates a second time to determine the sentence. At this time, the rules of evidence are more relaxed, and the jury may be permitted to hear evidence that was excluded during the trial (for example, the previous criminal record of the accused). In the Trump hush money case in New York, sentencing was initially scheduled for July 11, 2024, but was rescheduled by Judge Merchen until September, due to the US Supreme Court's decision regarding presidential immunity from criminal prosecution in *Trump v. United States*.[43] Although the criminal charges against Trump in the hush money case do not implicate any official conduct as president on Trump's part, some of the evidence shown to jurors during the trial may now be inadmissible due to its connection to Trump's official duties.[44]

As of the writing of this edition, sentencing had not occurred in Trump's case, and sentencing may never happen, depending on how Judge Merchen rules on the defense's requests that Trump's conviction be overturned and the charges against him dismissed in the wake of the Supreme Court's presidential immunity ruling.[45] In the wake of Trump's victory in the 2024 presidential election, Judge Merchen delayed sentencing further in order to consider Trump's argument that the case be dismissed entirely, given his status as the next president of the United States.[46]

In virtually all fifty states and in federal cases, crime victims are allowed the right to give a **victim impact statement**, in some form or another, at sentencing.[47] These statements, as written or oral statements to the court, provide victims an opportunity to describe the impact of the crime on their lives. The rise of victim impact statements came about as part of the victims' rights movement of the 1970s. Their widespread adoption, however, has run counter to objections to their use expressed by some in the legal community. Opponents have raised concerns that the information contained in an impact statement is not related to the purposes of punishment and that they can be so emotional as to have an inappropriate influence on sentencing decisions.[48] However, in an article entitled "In Defense of Victim Impact Statements" published in 2009, law professor and former US District Court Judge Paul Cassell argued that impact statements can provide an important role in informing the sentencing jury or judge about the true harm of the crime, helping victims deal with the crimes committed against them, educating defendants of the full consequences of their actions, and creating a perception of fairness at sentencing.[49]

In 1987, the US Supreme Court abolished the use of impact statements in death penalty cases, arguing that the formal presentation of a victim impact statement at sentencing in these cases

> can serve no other purpose than to inflame the jury and divert it from deciding the case on the relevant evidence concerning the crime and the defendant. The admission of these emotionally charged opinions as to what conclusions the jury should draw from the evidence clearly is inconsistent with the reasoned decision-making we require in capital cases.[50]

However, four years later, the Supreme Court overturned the key holding in the earlier case in deciding that

> a State may properly conclude that, for the jury to assess meaningfully the defendant's moral culpability and blameworthiness, it should have before it at the sentencing phase [in a capital case] evidence of the specific harm caused by the defendant.[51]

Victim impact statements are now a regular part of the criminal sentencing process across the country. In 2018, victim impact statements were highlighted extensively on the national news when Ingham County (Michigan) Circuit Judge Rosemarie Aquilina allowed more than 150 victims of Dr. Larry Nassar to provide statements in court at Nassar's sentencing hearing after he pled guilty to seven counts of first-degree criminal sexual conduct. Nassar, a former team doctor for USA Gymnastics and Michigan State University, was accused by at least 265 women and girls of sexual assault.[52] Prior to the marathon sentencing hearing, Nassar submitted a letter in which he stated that he was not sure he could handle days of listening to impact statements. In responding to this letter, Judge Aquilina noted that Nassar "spent thousands of hours perpetrating sexual assault on minors," and that he should be able to handle a few days of hearing from his victims.

The lengthy sentencing hearing helped bring Nassar's crimes, and the possible culpability of others associated with USA Gymnastics and the Michigan State athletic program, to the nation's consciousness. For example, one-time US Olympic women's gymnastics coach John Geddert was suspended from USA Gymnastics while Nassar's sentencing hearing was being held, and Michigan State University President Lou Anna Simon resigned hours after Nassar was sentenced.[53] Judge Aquilina sentenced Nassar to 40–175 years in prison, on top of his 60-year sentence on federal child pornography charges and an additional 40–125 year sentence after pleading guilty to three counts of first-degree criminal sexual conduct in Eaton County (Michigan) Circuit Court.[54]

In the wake of the seven-day sentencing hearing, Olympic gold medalist Alexandra "Aly" Raisman released a statement thanking, among others, Judge Aquilina:

> To Judge Aquilina, thank you sincerely. Your leadership, your professionalism, your compassion, and your commitment to allow each ONE of us survivors the opportunity to share our impact statements in open court was extremely important and meaningful. As I shared in court, I wasn't planning to speak, but thanks to the army of survivors and you, I am forever grateful that all our voices are finally heard. Thank you for listening to us all.[55]

Paul Cassell highlighted the Nassar trial and the lengthy attention to victim impact statements at Nassar's sentencing hearing as "a pivotal moment in our country's history regarding victim's rights. The whole country began to appreciate how important victims are in the sentencing process."[56] Even so, concerns are still expressed that impact statements, and the complicated and emotional information contained in them, may have problematic effects on criminal sentencing. In addition to the ongoing concern that emotionally charged victim impact statements may improperly increase criminal sentences, other researchers have contended that judges or jurors may interpret some impact statements in ways that discredit or punish the victim (for example, for meeting an assailant in a bar) or in ways that treat the impact on Black victims' loss and grief as being less important than that experienced by White victims.[57]

Victim impact statements do not necessarily have to be read in court prior to the decision on sentencing. For example, victims of the 2013 Boston Marathon bombing were allowed to give statements in court but only after the jury reached a decision on the death sentence for defendant Dzhokhar Tsarnaev.[58] The timing of these statements, of course, meant that they had no bearing on the jury's sentencing decision but would still have the possible effect of providing some sense of justice or closure to the victims and their families. For example, Rebekah Gregory, who lost a leg due to the bombing, wrote to Tsarnaev that "I realized that sitting across from you was somehow the crazy kind of step forward that I needed all along."[59]

In terms of the sentences that can be imposed, one of the lightest punishments that a judge can hand down is **probation**. Probation tends to be the penalty if the crime is regarded as relatively minor or if the judge believes that the guilty person is not likely to engage in future criminal activity. If a probated sentence is handed down, the criminal may not spend any time in prison, provided that the conditions of the probation are met. These might include staying away from bars or convicted criminals, not committing other crimes, or performing some type of community service. For example, in 2009, R&B singer Chris Brown pled guilty to physically assaulting his former girlfriend, pop star Rihanna. As part of his sentence, he was required to do six months of community service, much of which he completed by doing a variety of menial tasks for law enforcement authorities in Richmond, Virginia.[60]

If the judge is not disposed toward probation and feels that tough time is in order, they must impose a prison sentence that is within a range prescribed by law. For example, in a certain state, the penalty for aggravated assault may be a prison term of "no less than five but no more than fifteen years in the state penitentiary." The reason for a range of years instead of an automatically assigned number is that the law recognizes that not all crimes and criminals are alike and that, in principle, the punishment should fit the crime. Thus, a criminal with a prior record who held up a liquor store might be given a longer sentence than the person with no record who embezzled some money to pay for his child's life-or-death surgery. Although the government is not allowed to appeal a verdict of not guilty, either side in a criminal case may appeal with respect to the sentence.

To eliminate gross disparities in sentencing for basically the same set of circumstances, the federal government and many states have developed precise guidelines to ensure greater consistency among judges. At the national level, this effort led to the Sentencing Reform Act of 1984, which established the United States Sentencing Commission as an independent agency within the judicial branch directed by Congress to promulgate and amend federal sentencing guidelines.[61] In 1987, the Commission put into effect the first set of guidelines to structure the sentencing process:

> The guidelines contain a Sentencing Table with 43 offense levels on the vertical axis and six categories of criminal history on the horizontal axis. Offenders in criminal history category 1 would likely have little or no criminal record, while those in category 6 would likely have extensive criminal histories.
>
> The judge would find the applicable guideline sentencing range, which the table expresses in months of imprisonment, by determining the offense level and then reading across the axis to the proper criminal history category. Offense level 4, for example, which could apply to an offender convicted of theft of $100 or less, prescribes a sentencing range of 0 to 4 months for an offender in criminal history category 1, and 6 to 12 months for an offender in criminal history category 6. Offense level 38, which could apply to an offender convicted of aircraft hijacking, prescribes a sentencing range of 235–293 months for offenders in criminal history category 1, and 360 months to life for offenders in both the 5th and 6th criminal history categories.[62]

Although the US Sentencing Commission has amended the sentencing table many times since the 1980s, the guidelines currently in use retain the approach of relying on a grid of forty-three offense levels across six categories of criminal history.

The original act by Congress stated that judges could depart from the guidelines only if they found an aggravating or mitigating circumstance. Although the congressional guidelines did not specify the kinds of factors that could constitute grounds for disregarding the sentencing guidelines, Congress did state that the grounds could not include race, gender, national origin, creed, religion, socioeconomic status, drug dependence, or alcohol abuse.[63] In 2005, however, the Supreme Court ruled in the case of *United States v. Booker* that the mandatory sentencing guidelines violated the constitutional right to a trial by jury, since the rules required that sentences be based on facts found by judges after the jury had issued a conviction.[64] The Court's decision effectively meant that the sentencing guidelines could be considered advisory, not mandatory.

What effects have the federal guidelines had? Besides stirring up a storm of controversy among some US judges who resent restrictions on their traditionally broad sentencing authority, two observations now appear warranted. First, prior to the *Booker* decision, many federal judges were adhering to the guidelines, and thus aggregate disparities among judges declined after the guidelines were introduced in the 1980s. However, some data suggest that adherence to the guidelines has declined somewhat since *Booker*—69 percent of sentences were within the guidelines in 2003, but only 61 percent were in 2005.[65] Moving forward, the adherence to the guidelines declined further. According to the US Sentencing Commission, from December 2007 through September 2011, only 54 percent of sentences were within the guidelines.[66]

The US Sentencing Commission has continued to track sentencing behavior in the wake of the *Booker* decision. In a 2017 report that examined sentencing results from 2012 through 2016, the Commission noted that demographic factors continued to be associated with sentence length, with Black male offenders receiving average sentences more than 19 percent longer than similarly situated White male offenders. (Female offenders of all racial or ethnic backgrounds received shorter sentences than White male offenders during the same time frame.)[67] Even more recently, the Commission reported in 2020 that although the influence of the guidelines had decreased in general after *Booker* rendered them advisory, the guidelines' influence may have stabilized over the post-*Booker* years.[68]

Second, there is recent movement within the federal government (and in some states) to reduce the lengthy sentences that some nonviolent offenders are given under this system. In April 2014, the United States Sentencing Commission voted unanimously to reduce the base sentencing guidelines for most drug trafficking offenders.[69] The Commission estimated that this change would affect 70 percent of federal drug offenders, reducing sentences by an average of eleven months (down to fifty-one months from the previous sixty-two on average).[70] In July 2014, the Commission again voted unanimously, this time to make these sentence reductions apply retroactively to eligible prisoners.[71]

These efforts, to some extent, continued into the first Trump administration with the bipartisan passage of the First Step Act in 2018. With respect to sentencing in federal cases, the First Step Act shortened federal prison sentences and gave defendants more opportunity to avoid mandatory minimum penalties by broadening the judge's discretion to impose a sentence lower than the statutory minimum in some cases. According to an analysis conducted by the Brennan Center for Justice one year after the act's passage, its sentencing reforms were "off to a strong start," with judges "immediately [beginning to sentence] people to shorter prison terms."[72] That said, in

2022, the Brennan Center issued a report indicating that for "all its successes, the First Step Act continues to fall short of its promise" in urging further correctional reforms to be taken by the legislative and executive branches.[73]

Following the lead of the federal government over the decades, states created a variety of programs for avoiding vast disparities in judges' sentences. Guidelines of some sort were in effect in twenty-one states by 2008.[74] Most states have enacted **mandatory sentencing laws** that require an automatic specific sentence upon conviction of certain crimes—particularly violent crimes, crimes in which a gun was used, or crimes perpetrated by habitual offenders. While some analysts concluded that these state guidelines served to reduce sentencing disparity,[75] as with their federal counterparts, many states have reconsidered sentencing practices that resulted in exceptionally long sentences, especially for nonviolent offenders. In California, for example, voters easily approved Proposition 36 in 2012, which revised the state's Three Strikes Law and limited the circumstances under which a life sentence could be imposed.[76]

Despite their enormous impact on the sentence, judges do not necessarily have the final say on the matter. Whenever a judge sets a prison term, it is still subject to the parole laws of the states. There is no parole system at the federal level—Congress abolished parole when it passed the Sentencing Reform Act in 1984. However, many federal prisoners can earn an advance release for "good behavior." By law, federal prisoners serving more than one year in prison and engaging in "satisfactory behavior" are eligible for up to fifty-four days a year off their sentence for every year they serve.[77] Parole boards (and sometimes governors, who may grant pardons or commute sentences) have the final say about how long an inmate stays in state prison.

The Death Sentence

Some specific attention to the death penalty as the "ultimate punishment" is warranted. In 1976, after a five-year pause, the US Supreme Court reinstated the death penalty. In 1976, fewer than 500 persons were awaiting execution, but in 2015, nearly 2,900 were on death row either at the federal penitentiary in Terre Haute, Indiana, or in its counterparts in the states with capital punishment. In 1991, the Supreme Court made it harder for convicted criminals, especially those on death row, to repeatedly challenge the constitutionality of their convictions. The high court ruled that when a prisoner files a second habeas corpus petition in federal court, the prosecutor must specify which claims are being made for the first time.[78] The prisoner is then obliged to provide compelling reasons as to why these current issues, such as the unavailability of factual or legal information, were not raised in the initial petition. The prisoner must demonstrate that their case was prejudiced by the alleged constitutional violations.[79]

In 2021, eight inmates were executed in five states in the United States, with another three executions conducted by the federal government.[80] After increasing throughout the 1980s and 1990s, the annual number of executions in the United States has declined fairly steadily since 1999, when ninety-eight inmates were executed.[81] As was the case in 2021, Texas often tops the list of states with the most executions.[82] A recent study found that while reliance on the death penalty is declining in the United States, its current use is being driven largely by a smattering of counties scattered across a handful of states. These "outlier counties" in Alabama, Arizona, California, Florida, Louisiana, Nevada, and Texas each imposed five or more death sentences between 2010 and 2015.[83] The study's authors pointed to issues such as inadequate defense, overzealous prosecutors, and racial bias in explaining why these counties have unusually large numbers of death sentences imposed.

Despite the willingness of Congress and state legislatures to enact death sentence statutes and the willingness of judges and juries to hand down the ultimate penalty, America seems to be troubled about the fairness of the laws and by the increasing evidence that innocent persons have been, and are being, executed. In terms of the fairness issue, it has long been recognized that minorities are more likely than Whites to receive a death sentence. For example, even though Black people and White people commit the crime of murder at roughly the same rate, of persons on death row in 2021, around 41 percent were Black.[84] Another issue is the indication that innocent persons, often represented by attorneys of questionable ability, are being sentenced to death. Some observers have noted that "in the last decade DNA tests have provided stone-cold proof that sixty-nine people were sent to prison and death row in North America for crimes they did not commit," and the "number has been rising at a rate of more than one a month."[85]

Between 2018 and 2023, four states (Colorado, New Hampshire, Virginia, and Washington) abolished the death penalty. In addition, as of 2023, six states (Arizona, California, Ohio, Oregon, Pennsylvania, and Tennessee) had governor-imposed moratoriums on executions.[86] Governors in these states noted multiple ongoing concerns about the death penalty, including racial bias, expense, and concern over the execution of innocent people.

Americans have long supported the death penalty. As recently as the mid-1990s, upwards of 80 percent of Americans were in favor of the death penalty. However, support for the ultimate punishment has been waning in the United States in recent decades. The Gallup polling organization reports that as of 2023, 53 percent of Americans favored the death penalty for convicted murderers, with 50 percent of Americans expressing concern that the death penalty is applied unfairly.[87] This represents the lowest support for the death penalty in approximately half a century.

In recent decades, justices on the US Supreme Court have reconsidered aspects of the death penalty, most notably with respect to the question of who may be executed in the United States. In its 2002 decision in *Atkins v. Virginia*,[88] the Supreme Court ruled that intellectually disabled persons could not be legally executed in the United States because their intellectual disability affects their *mens rea*, or mental culpability for the crime. Similarly, in the 2005 case of *Roper v. Simmons*,[89] the Supreme Court held that individuals who were minors when they committed their crimes could not be executed because scientific research has shown that the intellectual development of those under the age of eighteen is such that many are not fully able to understand the implications of their actions. In 2001, moderately conservative Supreme Court Justice Sandra Day O'Connor stated publicly that

> after 20 years on the high court, I must acknowledge that earnest questions are being raised about whether the death penalty is being fairly administered in this country. . . . Perhaps most alarming . . . is the fact that if statistics are any indication, the system may well be allowing some innocent defendants to be executed.[90]

Even with the quite clear trend of flagging support for the death penalty among the public and some (even more conservative) states, President Donald Trump's administration reignited this issue during his first term in office, when the federal government resumed federal executions. Prior to 2020, the last federal execution occurred in 2003. From July 14, 2020, through January 16, 2021 (four days before the inauguration of President Joe Biden), thirteen people were executed by the federal government, with six of the executions occurring after the November 2020 election during Trump's lame-duck period.[91] These executions often occurred soon after fractured Supreme Court decisions handed down on their **shadow docket**, meaning that the Court handled the final decision through an emergency order or summary decision, outside of the Court's main docket of argued cases.[92] In 2021, the Biden administration issued a moratorium on federal executions pending a review of policies related to capital publishment.[93]

One last point about the use of the death penalty in the United States is warranted. Even with the decreased use of the death penalty in the United States in recent decades, the country remains an outlier on the world stage, especially compared to other Western nations. According to Amnesty International, recent statistics on death sentences and executions are dominated by countries like China, Iran, and Saudi Arabia. However, in 2023 more people were executed in America than all but a handful of the most death penalty–active countries around the world. In that same year, the United States led all countries in North and South America with respect to executions, death sentences, and the number of people known to be under a sentence of death.[94]

An Appeal

At both the state and federal levels, everyone has the right to at least one appeal after being convicted of a felony, but few criminals avail themselves of this privilege. An appeal is based on the contention that an error of law was made during the trial process. Such an error must be reversible, as opposed to harmless. An error is considered harmless if it had no effect on the outcome of the trial. A **reversible error**, however, is a serious one that might have affected the verdict of the judge or jury. For example, a successful appeal might be based on the argument that evidence was improperly admitted at trial, that the judge's instructions to the jury were flawed, or that a guilty plea was not voluntarily made. However, appeals must be based on questions of procedure and legal interpretations, not on factual determinations of the defendant's guilt or innocence.

Criminal defendants do have some degree of success on appeal less than 20 percent of the time, but this does not mean that the defendant goes free.[95] The usual practice is for the appellate court to remand the case (send it back) to the lower court for a new trial. At that point, the prosecution must determine whether the procedural errors in the original trial can be overcome in a second trial and whether it is worth the time and effort to do so. A second trial is not considered double jeopardy because the defendant has chosen to appeal the original conviction.

One final observation about the appellate process in general is appropriate. The media and champions of law and order often make much of appellate courts that turn loose obviously guilty criminals and reverse convictions on technicalities. This undoubtedly happens from time to time, but many in the public have the false impression that it is a frequent occurrence. Some basic data reveal the reality of the situation. First, about 90 percent of all defendants plead guilty, and this plea virtually excludes the possibility of an appeal. Of the remaining group, roughly two-thirds are found guilty at trial, and only a small percentage of these appeal. Of those who do appeal, less than 20 percent have any measurable degree of success. Furthermore, of those whose convictions are reversed, many are found guilty at a subsequent trial. (For example, in the famous case of *Miranda v. Arizona*, which spearheaded the criminal rights emphasis of the Warren Court, Ernesto Miranda's conviction was overturned by the high court because tainted evidence had been used to convict him. Nevertheless, at a subsequent trial—minus the tainted evidence—he was again convicted of the same crime.)[96] The oft-held perception that legions of criminals are freed due to minor errors is simply not accurate. In fact, well under 1 percent of persons convicted of crimes are subsequently freed because of reversible court errors. Most people would likely consider that an acceptable risk in a free society, and one might argue that it is inevitable in a democratic country whose legal system is based on fair play and the presumption of the innocence of the accused.

SUMMARY

We began this chapter by outlining the basic rights of the accused in a criminal trial and looked at the jury selection process. We then examined the key stages in the criminal trial process, highlighting the critical players at the trial—the prosecutor, the defense attorney, the judge, and the jury. For reference, we used the recent high-profile trial of Donald Trump in New York City to illustrate relevant stages in the criminal trial process. We also examined the posttrial procedures of sentencing and appeal. Throughout the chapter, we have highlighted the tension between norms and rules dictating criminal procedure and the backgrounds and attitudes of the people responsible for the administration of justice in our criminal courts. We have also emphasized the importance of actions taken by other actors, particularly legislators, in defining criminal offenses and setting sentencing expectations.

FURTHER THOUGHTS AND DISCUSSION QUESTIONS

1. Although the nationally relevant nature of the trial against Donald Trump was atypical of many criminal trials in the United States, it is common for certain crimes to garner a good deal of local interest and attention. Do the procedural steps described in this chapter adequately balance the defendant's right to a fair trial with the expectation that a trial be held where the alleged crime occurred?
2. Is it appropriate to allow victim impact statements to be submitted at the sentencing phase of a criminal trial? Is it more appropriate to have them read in open court prior to the sentencing decision, or should they be held until the sentence has already been determined? Does the use of these statements make a difference to you in terms of whether it is a judge or a jury that determines the sentence?
3. What place, if any, should the death penalty hold in the criminal justice system in the United States? How relevant, if at all, should global trends on the use of the death penalty be to its use in the United States?

SUGGESTED RESOURCES

Cassell, Paul G., and Edna Erez. "Army of Survivors: How Victim Impact Statements in the Larry Nassar Sentencing Promoted Justice." *Marquette Lawyer*, Summer 2024. Available at https://law.marquette.edu/assets/marquette-lawyers/pdf/marquette-lawyer/2024-summer/2024-summer-p14.pdf (accessed July 9, 2024). Provides a thematic content analysis of the 168 victim impact statements issued by victims in Larry Nassar's 2018 criminal trial.

Dammer, Harry R., and Erika Fairchild. *Comparative Criminal Justice Systems*. Belmont, CA: Wadsworth, 2005. An introduction to the judicial and corrections systems around the world.

Jonakait, Randolph N. *The American Jury System*. New Haven, CT: Yale University Press, 2003. A comprehensive discussion of US juries, including the jury selection and decision-making processes.

Judicature 83 (May–June 2000). The entire issue of this journal is dedicated to an examination of the twenty-first-century American jury.

Neubauer, David W. *America's Courts and the Criminal Justice System*. 9th ed. Belmont, CA: Wadsworth, 2007. A classic political science textbook on all the major stages present in the criminal justice process.

United States Sentencing Commission. Various reports on the influence of *Booker v. United States* on federal sentencing practices. Available at https://www.ussc.gov/topic/us-v-booker (accessed July 9, 2024).

Useem, Bert, and Anne Morrison. *Prison State: The Challenge of Mass Incarceration*. Cambridge, MA: Cambridge University Press, 2008. A rigorous analysis of the causes and consequences of the increase in imprisonment in the United States.

KEY TERMS

cross-examination
mandatory sentencing laws
peremptory challenges
probation
reversible error
shadow docket
venire
victim impact statement
voir dire

11 THE CIVIL COURT PROCESS

CHAPTER GOALS AND OBJECTIVES

In this chapter, students will learn that . . .

- There are many similarities and differences with respect to the substance and process of civil disputes, compared to those in criminal court. Civil courts do not need to adhere to many of the due process rights associated with criminal court, although as with criminal cases, most civil cases are heard in state courts.
- Civil law encompasses multiple kinds of cases, including torts and issues associated with family law.
- There are many reasons why potential disputes do not reach the status of a full-fledged civil trial. The costs and time required to litigate create challenges for access to the civil justice system, especially for lower-income litigants.
- The Alternative Dispute Resolution (ADR) Movement, which began to flourish in the 1970s, focused on reforms intended to ease workload pressure and access to justice concerns by providing opportunities to resolve civil cases outside the time-consuming and expensive structure of the civil court system. These reforms, however, have raised other concerns, including that litigants may be coerced into waiving access to civil courts.
- For those civil disputes that go through a full trial, there are many time-consuming procedural steps involved in seeing a complicated civil case through to its final resolution.

This chapter continues our examination of courts from a judicial process perspective, focusing on the civil courts. After discussing how civil law differs from criminal law and describing the most important categories of civil law, we consider alternatives to trials and then proceed step by step through the civil trial process.

THE NATURE AND SUBSTANCE OF CIVIL LAW

The American legal system observes several important distinctions between criminal and civil law. Criminal law is concerned with conduct that is offensive to society. Civil law pertains primarily to the duties of private citizens to one another. In civil cases, the disputes are usually between private individuals, although the government may sometimes be a party in a civil suit. Criminal cases always involve government prosecution of an individual for an alleged offense against society.

Members of the family of George Floyd (seen here at the March on Washington in August 2020) filed a lawsuit against the city of Minneapolis and four former Minneapolis police officers for the wrongful death of Floyd while he was in police custody in May 2020. In March 2021, Minneapolis agreed to the largest civil settlement of its kind in the city's history.

Olivier DOULIERY/POOL/AFP) (Photo by OLIVIER DOULIERY/POOL/AFP via Getty Images

Civil actions are separate and distinct from criminal proceedings. In a civil case, the court attempts to settle a particular dispute between the parties by determining their legal rights. The court then decides on an appropriate remedy, such as awarding monetary damages to the injured party or issuing an order that directs one party to perform or refrain from a specific act. In a criminal case, the court decides whether the defendant is guilty or not guilty. A guilty defendant may be punished by a fine, imprisonment, or both.

In some instances, the same act may give rise to both a criminal proceeding and a civil suit. Suppose that Alex and Pete, two political scientists attending a convention in Atlanta, are sharing a taxi from the airport to their downtown hotel. During the ride, they become involved in a heated discussion over the president's appointees to the federal courts. By the time the taxi stops at their hotel, the discussion has become so heated that Alex suggests they settle their differences without delay. If Pete strikes Alex in the ribs with his briefcase as he gets out of the taxi, Pete may be charged with criminal assault. In addition, Alex might file a civil suit against Pete to obtain a monetary award against him.

Civil cases outnumber criminal cases in both the federal and state courts, although they generally attract less media attention. Nonetheless, they often raise important policy questions and cover a broad range of disagreements in society. One leading judicial scholar summarizes the breadth of the civil law field as follows:

> Every broken agreement, every sale that leaves a dissatisfied customer, every uncollected debt, every dispute with a government agency, every libel and slander, every accidental injury, every marital breakup, and every death may give rise to a civil proceeding.[1]

As virtually any dispute between two or more persons may provide the basis for a civil suit, the number of suits is huge. However, most of them fall into one of five basic categories, which we explore in the next section.[2]

The Main Categories of Civil Law

The five main categories are contract law, property law, the law of succession, family law, and tort law. We turn our attention to these various kinds of civil cases, giving particular attention to the latter two categories.

Contract Law

Contract law is primarily concerned with voluntary agreements between two or more people. Basic to such agreements are a promise by one party and a counter promise by the other party, usually a promise by one party to pay money for the other party's goods or services. Pertinent examples include insurance contracts, credit card agreements, and cellular telephone contracts, among many others.

Property Law

A distinction traditionally has existed between real property and movable property. The former normally refers to real estate—land, houses, and buildings—and has included growing crops. Basically, everything else is considered private property, including money, jewelry, automobiles, furniture, and bank deposits.

Most adults in America have some involvement with both real estate and movable property. Most are renters or homeowners, or they live with someone who is. No special field of law is devoted to movable property. Instead, it is generally considered under the rubric of contract law, commercial law, and bankruptcy law.

The Law of Succession

The law of succession considers how property is passed from one generation to another. The American legal system recognizes a property owner's right to dispose of it as they wish. One common way to do this is to execute a will. If a valid will exists, the courts enforce it. However, if no will was written—or if it was improperly drawn up—the person has died intestate (without a valid will), and the state must dispose of the property.

The state's disposition of the property is then carried out according to the fixed procedure set forth in its statutes. By law, intestate property passes to the deceased person's heirs—that is, to the nearest relatives. Occasionally, a person who dies intestate has no living relatives, in which case the property escheats, or passes, to the state in which the deceased resided.

Many Americans prepare wills to ensure that their property is disposed of according to their wishes, not according to a scheme determined by the state. A will is a formal document. It must be carefully drafted, and in most states, it must be witnessed by at least two persons.

Family Law

Family law clearly touches the lives of a great many Americans each year. It concerns such things as marriage, divorce, child custody, and children's rights.

Although the US Supreme Court has upheld the right of same-sex couples to marry, other conditions necessary for entering a marriage have traditionally been spelled out by state law. These laws typically cover the minimum age of the parties, required blood tests or physical examinations, mental condition of the parties, license and fee requirements, and waiting periods. Some states have recently reconsidered their laws concerning the age of consent for marriage.[3] Delaware became the first state to ban child marriage when the state legislature raised the minimum age to marry to eighteen in 2018.[4] Between 2018 and 2024, another twelve states passed laws banning marriage for those under the age of eighteen. (Laws prohibiting marriage for those under eighteen years old have also been enacted in American Samoa, Puerto Rico, and the US Virgin Islands.) In the remaining thirty-seven states, child marriage is allowed in at least some circumstances, such as with parental or judicial approval or if a minor is pregnant. As of 2024, there is no minimum age requirement at all for marriage in California, Mississippi, New Mexico, and Oklahoma. In all four of these states, bills have been introduced in recent years to limit or ban child marriage, but none have yet been successful. Some opposing these bills have argued that child marriage limitations or bans violate parental rights and religious freedom. Still other, more progressive interests have argued that banning child marriage will not stop coercive relationships from forming and might harm young women (who are often the victims of coercive marriages involving children) in particular by pushing them further from the reach of social services or eliminating a viable pathway out of the foster care system.[5]

The termination of a marriage was once rare. In the early nineteenth century, some states granted divorces only through special acts of the legislature. South Carolina simply did not allow divorce. In the other states, divorces were granted only when one party proved some grounds for divorce. In other words, divorces were available only to "innocent" parties whose spouses were engaged in such actions as adultery, desertion, or cruelty.

The twentieth century saw an enormous change in divorce laws, moving away from restrictive laws and toward a concept known as no-fault divorce. This trend was the result of two factors. First, for many years there was an increasing demand for divorces. Second, the stigma once attached to divorced persons all but disappeared.

The no-fault divorce system means that the traditional grounds for divorce have been eliminated. Basically, the parties simply explain that irreconcilable differences exist between them, and that the marriage is no longer viable. In some states, the defendant is not even required to appear in court. In short, in some instances, the no-fault divorce system has put an end to the adversarial nature of divorce proceedings.

Not so easily solved are some of the other problems that may result from an ended marriage. Child custody battles, disputes over child support payments, and disagreements over visitation rights still find their way into court on a regular basis. Custody disputes are probably more common and contentious today than they were before no-fault divorce. The child's needs come first, and courts no longer automatically assume that this means granting custody to the mother. Fathers are increasingly being granted custody, and it is also now common for courts to grant joint legal custody to the divorced parents.

Tort Law

Tort law may generally be described as the law of civil wrongs. It concerns conduct that causes injury and fails to measure up to some standard set by society.

Several subfields of tort law serve to illustrate the importance of this category of civil law. One common subfield involves personal injury or bodily injury claims. Automobile accidents have traditionally been responsible for many of these types of claims. A second important subfield of tort law, product liability, is often seen as an effective way to hold corporations accountable for injuries caused by defective foods, toys, appliances, automobiles, drugs, and a host of other products. A third important subfield of tort law is medical malpractice. Courts generally use a traditional negligence standard when resolving medical malpractice suits. This means that the law does not attempt to make doctors guarantee successful treatment, but it instead makes the doctor liable if the patient can prove that the physician failed to perform in a manner consistent with accepted methods of medical practice.

Jury awards for damages may be of two types: compensatory and punitive. Compensatory damages are intended to cover the plaintiff's actual loss. Examples include repair costs, doctor bills, and hospital expenses. Punitive (or exemplary) damages are designed to punish the defendant or serve as a warning to refrain from such behavior in the future. Data from a 2005 survey of civil bench and jury trials in state courts provide some context.[6] When all general civil cases were considered, the authors found that about 60 percent of the trials involved a tort claim and about one-third involved contractual issues. Plaintiffs won in about 60 percent of the trials, and the median damage award for plaintiffs who won monetary damages was $28,000. The median punitive damage awarded to those who won punitive damages was $64,000. Furthermore, 16 percent of the punitive damage awards were more than $250,000 and 13 percent were $1 million or more.

Some have argued that the potential for large awards in tort cases encourages plaintiffs to file suits that are not strong or that lack merit altogether. As a result of concern over large jury awards and the increasing number of so-called frivolous cases, some government officials, corporate executives, interest groups, and members of the legal community have called for legislation aimed at tort reform. In 1986, the American Tort Reform Association (ATRA) was founded. ATRA serves as an advocate of such reform and reports that states have limited awards for noneconomic damages, modified their laws governing punitive damages, and enacted statutes penalizing plaintiffs who file frivolous lawsuits.[7]

ATRA's influence on the civil justice system has not occurred without notice or controversy, however. Perhaps most notable is ATRA's connection to corporate interests. For example, in 1995, half of ATRA's budget came from the tobacco lobby, funneled through the Covington and Burling law firm, headquartered in Washington, DC.[8] Although ATRA characterizes itself on its website as a "nationwide network of state-based legal reform coalition organizations backed by 142,000 grassroots supporters,"[9] its close ties to business interests and elite DC firms cannot be overlooked. In fact, in describing the organization in briefs submitted to the US Supreme Court, ATRA commonly refers to itself as "a broad-based coalition of businesses, corporations, municipalities, associations, and professional firms that have pooled their resources to promote reform of the civil justice system with the goal of ensuring fairness, balance, and predictability in civil litigation."[10]

In addition, the very claim that the United States is a particularly litigious society requires attention when discussing tort law. Many scholars have called into question the veracity of the claim that tort litigation has run amok in the United States, or that we are particularly litigious compared to people in other nations. The reality is that researchers have typically refuted the claim of excessive litigiousness in the United States. Law Professor David M. Engel, for example, concluded in a recent study that the tort reformers "got it wrong, with their unfounded tales of trigger-happy plaintiffs," and that their "highly successful public relations campaign exemplifies victim blaming at its worst."[11]

§1983 Suits and Police Violence

One example of tort law that is worthy of added attention is related to excessive force claims against police officers, particularly in cases where excessive force is used against racial minorities. Section 1983 of Title 42 of the United States Code, originally part of the Ku Klux Klan Act of 1871, creates a right to sue any person who, acting under color of state law, deprives someone of their constitutional rights. Such lawsuits may involve, among other issues, use of force. Thus, §1983 suits have become the preferred tool for suing police. Beginning in 1967, however, the US Supreme Court began to develop a legal doctrine called "qualified immunity" that in practice requires that plaintiffs find a previous case that is similar enough to demonstrate that police officers should have known that their conduct was illegal.[12] The qualified immunity doctrine can pose obstacles for mounting a successful §1983 claim by providing immunity for police officers engaging in behavior that does not quite match that of a past case.[13]

A recent example of a §1983 suit culminated in March 2021, when the city of Minneapolis settled with the family of George Floyd, who died in May 2020 after being handcuffed and pinned to the ground by Minneapolis police officers. In July 2020, Floyd's family filed a §1983 lawsuit against four (now former) Minneapolis police officers for violating Floyd's right to be free from the use of excessive force and against the city of Minneapolis for relying on unconstitutional policies, customs, and/or practices.[14]

In what the family's attorneys referred to as the biggest pretrial settlement in a civil rights' wrongful death suit in US history, the city agreed to pay $27 million. Ben Crump, attorney for the Floyd family in this litigation, noted that the settlement "is not just historic because of the $27 million paid out, but for the impact on social justice policy reforms and police reforms."[15] For example, $500,000 of the settlement was allotted to benefit the neighborhood (now widely known as George Floyd Square) where Floyd died. In addition, Minneapolis Mayor Jacob Frey announced at the settlement news conference that the city would go beyond the monetary settlement to implement major policy changes in pursuit of racial justice in the city. Although members of Floyd's family concurred that these changes will hopefully bring about "healing in the way that policing is carried on," Minneapolis had previously settled or lost multiple large dollar-value civil claims against the city for excessive police violence in the years leading up to Floyd's death while in police custody in 2020.[16]

THE COURTS AND OTHER INSTITUTIONS CONCERNED WITH CIVIL LAW

Disagreements are common in the daily lives of Americans. These disagreements can usually be settled outside the legal system. Sometimes they are so serious, however, that one of the parties sees no alternative but to file a lawsuit. The decision of whether to go to court is a significant first step in creating a legal dispute. In this section, that first step is addressed. In addition, the civil justice system has developed multiple alternatives to a full-fledged trial. Those alternatives are discussed in this section as well.

Deciding Whether to Go to Court

Every year, thousands of potential civil cases are resolved without a trial because the would-be litigants settle their problems in another way, or the prospective plaintiff decides not to file suit. When faced with a decision to call on the courts to try to settle differences or simply to forget the problem, many people resort to a simple cost-benefit analysis. That is, they weigh the costs associated with a trial against the benefits likely to be gained if they win. Should a quick calculation indicate that the tangible and intangible costs in terms of such things as time, money, publicity, stress, and anxiety outweigh the benefits, most people will opt for an alternative to a trial. However, if the prospective plaintiff perceives the costs to be low enough, then they might file suit against the defendant.

To get a sense of the magnitude of possible disputes that could result in civil filings, one classic study of civil litigation patterns relied on a telephone survey of approximately one thousand households selected at random in 1980 in each of five federal judicial districts: central California, New Mexico, eastern Pennsylvania, South Carolina, and eastern Wisconsin.[17] The authors of the study found that about 40 percent of the households reported a grievance totaling $1,000 (in 1980 dollars) or more during the previous three years, and approximately 20 percent reported two or more such grievances. Although many grievances were never pursued further, some resulted in the plaintiffs initiating a claim. Once a claim is filed, that claim may be accepted, partially accepted, or rejected.

Claims that are met with a partial or total rejection move on to become disputes. The odds are high that a claim will become a dispute. In the telephone survey under discussion, approximately 63 percent of the claims became disputes (met with partial or total rejection).

The authors of the study next focused on the extent to which disputants hired attorneys and took their cases to court. Overall, they found that attorneys were hired in fewer than one-fourth of the disputes and that only about 11 percent of the disputants reported going to court. This finding should not be seen as minimizing the importance of lawyers and judges, however. Each party's understanding of everyone's legal position is based on the lawyer's advice, which in turn is based on an understanding of previous court decisions.

Alternative Dispute Resolution

In practice, few persons make use of the entire judicial process. Instead, most cases are settled without resort to a full-fledged trial. In civil cases, a trial may be both slow and expensive. As the statistics on judicial workload indicate, most courts are hard-pressed to keep up with their dockets, and these challenges were only exacerbated in recent years by the COVID-19 pandemic.[18] Also, civil trials may be exceedingly complex and can therefore be time-consuming and costly to litigate. Since there is no constitutional right to counsel in civil cases, litigants have to choose between hiring their own attorneys, attempting to access underfunded state or federal civil legal services, or representing themselves *pro bono* in civil court.[19]

In the 1970s, judicial caseload and access to justice concerns created an incentive for developing alternatives to costly and time-consuming civil litigation practices.[20] Alternative dispute resolution (ADR) processes allow people to resolve disputes without holding a formal trial. As such, ADR proponents have long argued that these alternatives provide an opportunity to help reduce caseloads by funneling cases (in part or in full) away from the court system while also providing better access to justice by easing the complexity, time, and cost associated with navigating the formal civil justice system.

The ADR movement is now well established in the United States. New York is a good example of a state that has been using ADR for many years. Since 1981, it has used the Community Dispute Resolution Centers Program (CDRCP) to provide community forums for the resolution of disputes as an alternative to criminal, civil, and family litigation. The CDRCP is available in all sixty-two counties of New York State, through local community nonprofit agencies, to provide a variety of dispute resolution services to individuals, families, organizations, and communities. Now in existence for over forty years, the CDRCP reports that the program serves tens of thousands of New Yorkers annually.[21] Roughly half of the referrals to individual Community Dispute Resolution Centers (CDRCs) are made by courts, with the remaining half coming from other organizations (including law enforcement, legal services, and schools) or self-referrals, including many previous clients.

During the 2022–2023 fiscal year, 37 percent of the 21,610 cases screened or resolved by CDRCs were small claims matters, with another 28 percent involving custody, visitation, or divorce proceedings. The remainder consisted of criminal matters, housing matters, larger civil claims, guardianship and probate concerns, youth matters, public welfare/benefit claims, or criminal cases.[22]

For its *2013–2014 Annual Report*, the CDRCP collaborated with researchers at Stanford University to study mediation services provided by CDRCs, reporting that more than 74 percent of the mediated cases resulted in an agreement. The research team also found that more than 92 percent of participants felt overwhelmingly that the mediation process was fair.[23]

Even so, some scholars and observers continue to voice skepticism that the ADR movement has met the goals of reducing caseloads and providing better access to justice for litigants. Fordham Law Professor and ADR expert Jacqueline Nolan-Haley has noted an array of possible concerns about ADR procedures, including lack of guidance for the litigants, overly rushed processes, and lack of true consent among litigants involved in ADR.[24] These issues may be most disadvantageous to the less affluent litigants and those navigating the process on their own without an attorney. Potential concerns regarding the coercive use of ADR and unequal power of those involved are addressed in further detail in the coming discussion, but some explanation of how ADR works is useful to address first. Although the broad term *alternative dispute resolution* incorporates an array of various procedures, the two best known are *mediation* and *arbitration*, and we focus on those two methods as particularly relevant examples of how ADR works in practice.

Mediation

Mediation is a private, confidential process in which an impartial person helps the disputing parties identify and clarify issues of concern and reach their own agreement. The mediator does not act as a judge. Instead, the parties themselves maintain control of the final settlement.

Although almost any type of dispute may be resolved through mediation, it is especially appropriate for situations in which the disputants have an ongoing relationship.[25] Examples include disputes between family members, neighbors, employers and employees, and property owners and tenants. Mediation may also be useful in divorce cases because it can assist in changing the procedure from one of confrontation to one of cooperation. Child custody and visitation rights are frequently resolved through mediation as well. And in many areas, personal injury and property claims involving insurance companies are settled through mediation. In short, a wide variety of disputes that once found their way into courts are now being settled through mediation.

Arbitration

The arbitration process is like going to court. After listening to both parties in a dispute, an impartial person, called an arbitrator, decides how the controversy should be resolved. There is no judge or jury. Instead, the arbitrator makes the final decision. Disputants may choose arbitration because it saves time and money and is more informal than a court hearing.

Arbitration is used privately to resolve a variety of consumer complaints. Business, commercial, and employment disputes are examples of issues that are now often resolved by arbitration.

While participants in the CDRCP in New York are generally satisfied with how alternate dispute resolution assists in the resolution of civil disputes in that state, one aspect of modern-day ADR that has become controversial is the growing use of mandatory arbitration clauses in business contracts. Corporate America is interested in avoiding prolonged and costly court battles to settle business disputes. Thus, many consumer agreements one signs, whether for a credit card, a cell phone, cable television service, Internet service, or buying or selling stock, require that a dispute between the consumer and the provider will be resolved through binding arbitration. This means that the consumer waives their right to sue the provider in a court of law and perhaps gives up the right to participate in a class action claim against the service provider.

Consider the following example. Recently, one of this book's coauthors received an email from a popular streaming service with an update to their Terms of Use. In the introductory paragraph of the updated policy, the service provider noted that:

> In the unlikely event that an issue between us remains unresolved [after communication with their Help Center], please note that these terms require arbitration on an individual basis, rather than jury trials or class action.

Later in the lengthy updated policy, the streaming provider clarified that:

> You and _____agree to arbitrate in each of our individual capacities only, not as a representative or member of a class, and each of us expressly waives any right to file a class action or seek relief on a class basis.
>
> Rather than force everyone to visit us in California, if you can demonstrate that arbitration in California would create an undue burden to you, you are free to initiate the arbitration in your home state. Otherwise, the arbitration hearings will be held in Los Angeles County, California.

This provider does provide one exception to the arbitration agreement, in that:

> [The company] is happy to give you the right to pursue in small claims court any claim that is within that court's jurisdiction if you proceed only on an individual basis.

These, and all the other updated policies included in the communication, went into effect automatically thirty days after the revised Terms were posted by the streaming provider. Included in the short excerpts listed above are policy changes not only requiring arbitration (with the sole exception of individual small claims filings), but a ban on class action litigation or arbitration, and the default rule that arbitration will occur in Los Angeles County. Although absent in this mandatory arbitration clause example, such clauses may include information on the specific arbitration firms to be used, confidentiality of the arbitration resolution, and/or language requiring the losing party to pay all the arbitration fees, including the other side's attorney fees, among other possible provisions.

Whether or not consumers are aware of the importance of these contractual agreements and updates, binding arbitration clauses such as the one included here have become a routine part of the day-to-day lives of most every American. According to a recent report issued by the pro-labor Economic Policy Institute (EPI),[26] a distinction should be made between mandatory arbitration clauses in consumer and employment contracts compared to those in contracts between two businesses or between a business and a union. In the latter cases, according to the EPI, "the parties have voluntarily negotiated as equals and knowingly agreed to arbitrate disputes between them."[27]

Average Americans, in the context of signing (or otherwise agreeing to) consumer or employment contracts, on the other hand, often have no opportunity to negotiate the mandatory arbitration clause in the contract, having to either take it or leave it. The streaming service example, furthermore, highlights how these clauses may be added to the terms of agreement after a consumer has already gotten accustomed to using a particular service. Note that although this discussion has focused specifically on addressing concerns over the evolution of arbitration practices in the United States, similar concerns over consent and unequal power have been expressed regarding other forms of ADR in the United States, as well as to practices in other countries, especially with respect to the use of alternative civil justice procedures in developing countries.[28]

Although mandatory arbitration clauses are not a new part of our contractual landscape, their growth in recent decades, especially in consumer and employment contracts, has drawn a good amount of criticism and litigation. The US Supreme Court has played an especially significant role in interpreting relevant statutes in this area of law. According to the EPI, in the last few decades "the Supreme Court has engineered a massive shift in the civil justice system that is having dire consequences for consumers and employees."[29] In many recent cases, the Supreme Court has ruled to uphold the enforcement of mandatory arbitration clauses over concerns that they restrict the legal rights protecting employees or consumers. In 2018, for example, the Supreme Court ruled that an employment contract requiring individualized arbitration to resolve employment disputes was to be enforced over the employee's argument that the clause violated a provision in the National Labor Relations Act (NLRA) of 1935 that protects the right of workers to organize unions and bargain collectively.[30] In the majority opinion written by Justice Neil Gorsuch, the Court ruled that the Federal Arbitration Act (FAA), passed by Congress in 1925, required that courts treat arbitration agreements as valid, irrevocable, and enforceable.

In a dissenting opinion she read from the bench, Justice Ruth Bader Ginsburg characterized Gorsuch's opinion as "egregiously wrong." In the dissent, Ginsburg highlighted how the power imbalance in the employer–employee relationship means that the NLRA's worker protections should not be reduced by generally non-negotiable arbitration clauses, enforceable by the FAA. Ginsburg concluded that the problems she anticipated coming from this decision were not due to the laws passed by Congress decades ago, but by the way these laws are being interpreted by the Supreme Court today.

With the Supreme Court's recent rulings in this area, then, it is fair to presume that most arbitration clauses in consumer and employment contracts would be deemed enforceable by a court of law. One last recent high-profile example perhaps demonstrates the lengths to which consumers sometimes must go to have the ability to file suit in civil court rather than go through private arbitration. In May 2018, the ride-sharing company Uber announced that anyone bringing a sexual assault or harassment claim against the company would not be forced into arbitration and could pursue their claim in court. Uber as well announced the removal of a clause requiring people with such claims to sign a nondisclosure agreement. This reversal of policy came about after a concerted effort on the part of more than a dozen women who went public with their allegations of sexual harassment and assault while using Uber.[31] In the face of mounting public pressure (including a campaign urging riders to #DeleteUber), the company announced the changes to its policy. It is worth noting, however, that Uber policy continued to bar customers from banding together to bring class action lawsuits against the company for sexual assault, and the company has not lifted the nondisclosure requirement for those who settled disputes with the company prior to the policy change.[32]

Specialized Courts

For civil cases that do enter the court system, most are filed at the state level, and as discussed in Chapter 3, the civil caseload in state court is immense. Therefore, states generally rely on several specialized courts that are set up to handle different types of civil cases. Domestic relations courts are often established to deal with such matters as divorce, child custody, and child support. In many jurisdictions, probate courts handle the settlement of estates and the contesting of wills.

Perhaps the best known of the specialized courts are small-claims courts. These courts have jurisdiction to handle cases in which the money being sued for is not above a certain amount. The amount varies by jurisdiction, but in many states the maximum is roughly $10,000. The first small-claims court, established in Cleveland in 1913, had a simplified process, a nominal filing fee, and no requirement that the parties be represented by a lawyer. By 1920, other major cities, including Chicago, Minneapolis, New York, and Philadelphia, as well as the state of Massachusetts, had set up small-claims courts based on the Cleveland model.[33] Today, small-claims courts enable less complex cases to be resolved more informally than in most other trial courts. Filing fees are low, and the summons to the other party to appear in court can often be served by certified mail. Pleadings are often not required, and the use of attorneys may be discouraged.

These courts are not without problems, however. One complaint prevalent in several large cities is that collection agencies use these courts as a relatively cheap and efficient way to collect small debts. New York has enacted legislation to prohibit this use of small-claims courts.[34] And because lawyers are often not used in small-claims court, persons who are not familiar with their legal rights and do not know much about preparing their cases may be at a disadvantage, especially when the other party is experienced in such courts.

Administrative Bodies

Several government agencies have also established administrative bodies with quasi-judicial authority to handle certain types of cases. At the state level, a common example of an administrative body that aids in the resolution of civil claims is a workers' compensation board. This board determines whether an employee's injury is job-related and thus whether the person is entitled to workers' compensation. Many state motor vehicle departments have hearing boards to make determinations about revoking drivers' licenses. Another type of administrative board commonly found in the states rules on civil rights matters and cases of alleged discrimination.

At the federal level, on the other hand, agencies such as the Federal Trade Commission and the Federal Communications Commission carry out adjudications of sorts within their respective spheres of authority. An appeal of the ruling of one of these agencies may be taken to a federal court of appeals. In a 2024 decision, however, the US Supreme Court ruled that the Securities and Exchange Commission (SEC) violated the Seventh Amendment's right to a trial by jury in civil cases when an SEC administrative law judge imposed a civil penalty of $300,000 against investment adviser George Jarkesy Jr. and his investment firm for committing securities violations.[35] Although the SEC was acting with the approval of Congress in handling such securities violations in-house, the majority opinion written by Chief Justice John Roberts determined that securities violations were not within the area of exceptions where Congress was constitutionally allowed to assign matters for resolution within the administrative agency and without a jury.

In her dissenting opinion, Justice Sonia Sotomayor highlighted the far-reaching effect this decision was going to have on the ability of many administrative agencies (including the Food and Drug Administration, the Environmental Protection Agency, and the Consumer Financial Protection Bureau) to pursue civil penalties for wrongdoers, especially for those agencies (like the Federal Energy Regulatory Commission and the Department of Agriculture, among other "countless agencies") that are empowered under federal law to pursue civil penalties only in administrative proceedings and not in federal court.[36]

Although this 2024 decision signifies a potentially major change in how federal administrative agencies are able to seek penalties from those who violate the law, it does not extend to how administrative decision-making occurs at the state level. The Seventh Amendment's right to a trial by jury does not apply to civil adjudication at the state level.

THE CIVIL TRIAL PROCESS

Although many disputes are resolved through some method of ADR, in a specialized court, or by an administrative body, many cases each year still find their way into one of the nation's civil courts.

The adversarial process used in criminal trials is also used in civil trials, with a few crucial differences. First, a litigant must have standing. This concept means simply that the person initiating the suit must have a personal stake in the outcome of the controversy. Otherwise, there is no real controversy between the parties and thus no actual case for the court to decide.

A second major difference is that the standard of proof used in civil cases is a preponderance of evidence, not the more stringent beyond-a-reasonable-doubt standard used in criminal cases. A preponderance of evidence is generally taken to mean that the evidence is sufficient to overcome doubt or speculation. It clearly means that less proof is required in civil cases than in criminal cases.

A third major difference is that many of the extensive due process guarantees that a defendant has in a criminal trial do not apply in a civil proceeding. For example, neither party is constitutionally entitled to counsel. The Seventh Amendment does guarantee the right to a jury trial in lawsuits "where the value in controversy shall exceed twenty dollars." Although this amendment has not been made applicable to the states, most states have similar constitutional guarantees.[37]

For the remainder of this section, we address the typical steps involved in bringing a civil case through the trial process, for the (relatively unusual) cases that do go through the civil trial process in full.[38]

Filing a Civil Suit

The person initiating the civil suit is known as the **plaintiff**, and the person being sued is the defendant or the respondent. A civil action is known by the names of the plaintiff and the defendant, such as *Jones v. Miller*. The plaintiff's name appears first. In a typical situation, the plaintiff's attorney pays a fee and files a complaint or petition with the clerk of the proper court. The complaint states the facts on which the action is based, the damages alleged, and the judgment or relief being sought.

It is useful to understand how a decision is made as to which court should hear the case. The decision involves the concepts of jurisdiction and **venue**. Jurisdiction deals with a court's authority to exercise judicial power, and venue means the place where that power should be exercised.

Jurisdictional requirements are satisfied when the court has legal authority over both the subject matter and the person of the defendant. This means that more than one court may have jurisdiction over the same case. Suppose, for example, that you are a resident of Dayton, Ohio, and are seriously injured in an automobile accident in Tennessee, when the car you are driving is struck from the rear by a car driven by a resident of Kingsport, Tennessee. Total damages to you and your car run about $80,000. A state trial court in Tennessee has subject matter jurisdiction and jurisdiction over the defendant as well. Also, because diversity of citizenship exists and the amount in controversy is more than $75,000, a federal district court in Tennessee would have jurisdiction. Assuming that jurisdiction is your only concern, you, as plaintiff, may sue in either of these courts.

This hypothetical example raises several questions: Which of these courts is the proper one to handle the case? Which is the best place for the case to be tried?

Venue is often a matter of convenience, given that improper venue can be waived. In other words, if a court has proper jurisdiction, and the parties do not object to venue, the court can render a valid judgment. Or the determination of proper venue may be prescribed by statute, based on avoiding possible prejudice. The federal law states that proper venue is the district in which either the plaintiff or the defendant resides, or the district where the injury occurred. State venue statutes vary somewhat, but they usually stipulate that when land is involved, proper venue is the county where the land is located. In most other instances, venue is the county where the defendant resides.

Venue issues may also be related to the perceived or feared prejudice of either the judge or the prospective jury. For this reason, attorneys sometimes object to holding the trial in a particular area and may move for a change of venue. Although this type of objection is perhaps more commonly associated with highly publicized criminal trials, it also occurs in civil trials.

Once the appropriate court has been determined and the complaint has been filed, the court clerk will attach a copy of the complaint to a summons, which is then issued to the defendant. The summons may be served by personnel from the sheriff's office, a US marshal, or a private process-service agency.

The summons directs the defendant to file a response, known as a pleading, within a certain period (usually thirty days). If the defendant does not do so, they may be subject to a default judgment.

Pretrial Activities

These simple actions by the plaintiff, the clerk of the court, and a process server set the civil case in motion. What happens next is a flurry of activities that precede a trial and may last for several months. Most cases are resolved without a trial during this time, however.

Motions

Once the summons has been served on the defendant, several motions can be made by the defense attorney. A motion to quash asks the court to void the summons on the grounds that it was not properly served. For example, a defendant might contend that the summons was never personally delivered to them, as required by state law.

Two types of motions are meant to clarify or to object to the plaintiff's petition. A motion to strike asks the court to excise, or strike, certain parts of the petition because they are prejudicial, improper, or irrelevant. Sometimes the defense attorney will file a motion asking the court to require the plaintiff to be more specific about the complaint. For instance, the defendant's attorney may ask that the alleged injuries be described in greater detail.

Another type of motion often filed in a civil case is a motion to dismiss, which may argue, for example, that the court lacks jurisdiction. Or it may insist that the plaintiff has not presented a legally sound basis for action against the defendant, even if the allegations are true. This action is called a demurrer in many state courts.

The Answer

If the complaint survives the judge's rulings on the motions, the defendant then submits an **answer** to the complaint. The response may contain admissions, denials, defenses, and counterclaims. When an admission is contained in an answer, there is no need to prove that fact during the trial. A denial, however, brings up a factual issue to be proved during the trial. A defense says that certain facts set forth in the answer may bar the plaintiff from recovery.

The defendant may also create a separate action by seeking relief against the plaintiff. This is known as a counterclaim. In other words, if the defendant thinks that a cause of action against the plaintiff arises from the same set of events, they must present the claim to the court in response to the plaintiff's claim. The plaintiff may want to file a reply to the defendant's answer. In that reply, the plaintiff may admit, deny, or defend against the allegations of fact contained in the answer.

Discovery

Although surprise was once a legitimate trial tactic, the present legal system provides **discovery** procedures that "take the sporting aspect out of litigation and make certain that legal results are based on the true facts of the case—not on the skill of the attorneys."[39] In other words, to prevent surprise at the trial and to encourage settlement, each party is entitled to information in the possession of the other. The term *discovery* "encompasses the methods by which a party or potential party to a lawsuit obtains and preserves information regarding the action."[40]

There are several tools of discovery. A **deposition** is the testimony of a witness taken under oath outside the court. As in the courtroom, the question-and-answer format is used. All parties to the case must be notified that the deposition is to be taken, so that their attorneys may be present to cross-examine the witness.

A second tool of discovery is known as **interrogatories**—written questions that must be answered under oath. Interrogatories can be submitted only to the parties in the case, not to witnesses. They are useful in obtaining descriptions of evidence held by the opposing parties in the suit.

The production of documents is a third tool. One of the parties often requests an inspection of documents, writings, drawings, graphs, charts, maps, photographs, or other items held by the other party. Finally, when the physical or mental condition of one of the parties is at issue, the court may order that person to submit to an examination by a physician.

What happens if a party refuses to comply with discovery requests? The judge may compel compliance, deem the facts of the case established, dismiss the cause of action, or enter judgment by default.

The Pretrial Conference

As a result of the discovery phase, as noted earlier, surprise is no longer a major factor in civil cases. Therefore, many cases are settled without going to trial. If the parties do not reach a settlement of their own accord, the judge may try to facilitate such an agreement during a pretrial conference.

Judges call such conferences to discuss the issues in the case informally with the opposing attorneys. The general practice is to allow only the judge and the lawyers to attend the conference, which is normally held in the judge's chambers.

The judge and the attorneys use the conference to come to some agreement on uncontested factual issues, which are known as stipulations. The purpose of stipulations is to make the trial more efficient. The attorneys also share with one another a list of witnesses and documents that are a part of each case. In the words of Judge J. Skelly Wright, "We make each side disgorge completely and absolutely everything about its case. There can't possibly be surprise, if the lawyers know what they are doing."[41] Lawyers and judges may also use the pretrial conference to try to settle the case. Some judges actively work to bring about a settlement to avoid going to trial.

The Civil Trial

The right to a jury trial in a civil suit in a federal court is guaranteed by the Seventh Amendment. State constitutions likewise provide for this right. A jury trial may be waived, in which case the judge decides the matter. Although the jury traditionally consisted of twelve persons, today the number varies. Most of the federal district courts now use juries of fewer than twelve persons in civil cases. Many states also authorize smaller juries in some or all civil trials.

Selection of Jury

Jurors must be selected in a random manner from a cross section of the community. A large panel of jurors is called to the courthouse, and when a case is assigned to a court for trial, a smaller group of prospective jurors is sent to a particular courtroom.

Following the voir dire examination, which may include challenges to certain jurors by the attorneys, a jury to hear the case will be seated. Lawyers may challenge a prospective juror for cause, in which case the judge must determine whether the person challenged is impartial. Each side may also exercise a certain number of peremptory challenges—recall from Chapter 10 that this means excusing a juror without stating any reason. However, as also noted in the earlier chapter, the US Supreme Court has ruled that the equal protection guarantee of the Fourteenth Amendment prohibits the use of such challenges to disqualify jurors from civil trials because of their race or gender.[42] Peremptory challenges are fixed by statute or court rule and normally range from two to six.

Opening Statements

After the jury has been chosen, the attorneys present their opening statements. The plaintiff's attorney begins, explaining to the jury what the case is about and what the plaintiff's side expects to prove. The defendant's lawyer can usually choose either to make an opening statement immediately after the plaintiff's attorney finishes or to wait until the plaintiff's case has been completely presented. If the defendant's attorney waits, they will present the entire case for the defendant continuously, from opening statement onward. Opening statements are valuable because they outline the case and make it easier for the jury to follow the evidence as it is presented.

Presentation of the Plaintiff's Case

In the average civil case, the plaintiff's side is first to present and attempt to prove its case to the jury. In presenting the case, the plaintiff's lawyer will normally call witnesses to testify and produce documents or other exhibits.

On being called, the witness will undergo direct examination by the plaintiff's attorney. Then the defendant's attorney will have the opportunity to ask questions or cross-examine the witness. Several states have taken steps to help jurors do a better job of making decisions in civil cases by allowing them to pose questions to witnesses, either verbally or in writing.[43] Following the cross-examination, the plaintiff's lawyer may conduct a redirect examination, which may be followed by a second cross-examination by the defendant's lawyer.

Witnesses may testify only about matters they have observed; they may not express their opinions. An important exception to this general rule is that expert witnesses are specifically called on to give their opinions in matters within their areas of expertise.

To qualify as an expert witness, a person must possess substantial knowledge about a particular field. Furthermore, this knowledge must normally be established in open court. Both sides often present experts whose opinions are contradictory. When this happens, the jury must ultimately decide which opinion is the more persuasive one.

When the plaintiff's side has presented all its evidence, the attorney rests the case. It is now the defendant's turn.

Motion for Directed Verdict

After the plaintiff's case has been rested, the defendant will often make a motion for a directed verdict. With the filing of this motion, the defendant is saying that the plaintiff has not proved their case and thus should lose. The judge must then decide whether the plaintiff could win at this point if court proceedings were to cease. Should the judge determine that the plaintiff has not presented sufficiently convincing evidence, they will sustain the motion and direct the verdict for the defendant. Thus, the plaintiff will lose the case.

Presentation of the Defendant's Case

Assuming that the motion for a directed verdict is overruled, the defendant then presents evidence. The defendant's case is presented in the same way as the plaintiff's case—that is, employing direct examination of witnesses and presentation of documents and other exhibits. The plaintiff has the right to cross-examine witnesses. Redirect and recross questions may follow.

Rebuttals

After the presentation of the defendant's case, the plaintiff may bring forth rebuttal evidence, which is aimed at refuting the defendant's evidence. Next, the defendant's lawyer may present evidence to counter the rebuttal evidence. This rebuttal-and-answer pattern may continue until the evidence has been exhausted.

Closing Arguments

After all the evidence has been presented, the lawyers make closing arguments, or summations, to the jury. The plaintiff's attorney speaks both first and last. That is, they open the argument and close it, and the defendant's lawyer argues in between. At this stage, each attorney attacks the opponent's evidence for its unreliability and may also attempt to discredit the opponent's witnesses. In doing so, the lawyers often wax eloquent or deliver an emotional appeal to the jury. However, the arguments must be based on facts supported by the evidence and introduced at the trial. In other words, they must stay within the record.

Instructions to the Jury

Assuming that a jury trial has not been waived, the instructions to the jury are given after the closing arguments. The judge informs the jury that the verdict must be based on the evidence presented at the trial. The judge's instructions also inform the jurors about the rules, principles, and standards of the legal concept involved. In civil cases, a finding for the plaintiff is based on a preponderance of the evidence. This means that the jurors must weigh the evidence presented during the trial and be convinced that the greater weight of the evidence, in merit, favors the plaintiff.

The Verdict

The jury retires to the seclusion of the jury room to conduct its deliberations. The members must reach a verdict with no outside contact. In some instances, the deliberations are so long and detailed that the jurors must be provided with meals and sleeping accommodations until they can reach a verdict. The verdict, then, represents the jurors' agreement after detailed discussions and analyses of the evidence. Sometimes the jury deliberates in good faith but still cannot reach a verdict. When this occurs, the judge may declare a mistrial, which means that a new trial may have to be conducted.

After the verdict is reached, the jury returns to open court and delivers its verdict to the judge. The parties are informed of the verdict. It is then customary for the jury to be polled by the judge: the jurors are individually asked whether they agree with the verdict.

Post-Trial Motions

Once the verdict has been reached, a dissatisfied party may pursue a variety of tactics. The losing party may file a motion for judgment notwithstanding the verdict. This type of motion is granted when the judge decides that reasonable persons would not have rendered the verdict the jury reached. Put another way, this decision says that the verdict is unreasonable considering the facts presented at the trial and the legal standards to be applied to the case.

The losing party may also file a motion for a new trial. The usual basis for this motion is that the verdict goes against the weight of the evidence. The judge will grant the motion on this ground if they agree that the evidence presented simply does not support the verdict reached by the jury. A new trial may be granted for several other reasons: excessive damages, grossly inadequate damages, the discovery of new evidence, and errors in the production of evidence, to name a few.

In some cases, the losing party also files a motion for relief from judgment. This type of motion may be granted if the judge finds a clerical error in the judgment, discovers some new evidence, or determines that the judgment was induced by fraud.

Judgment and Execution

A verdict in favor of the defendant ends the trial. However, a verdict for the plaintiff requires yet another stage in the process. There is no sentence in a civil case, but a determination of the remedy or damages to be assessed must be made. This determination is called the judgment.

In situations where the judgment is for monetary damages and the defendant does not voluntarily pay the set amount, the plaintiff can ask the court to execute the judgment. The defendant's property may be seized and sold, with the proceeds then applied to the money owed to the plaintiff. In 2024, for example, far-right radio host and conspiracy theorist Alex Jones was ordered by a bankruptcy judge in Texas to liquidate many of his personal assets to pay a roughly \$1.5 billion judgment for claiming the 2012 Sandy Hook Elementary School shooting was a hoax.[44] Soon thereafter, a court-appointed bankruptcy trustee indicated plans to sell off Jones's "Infowars" media empire as well.[45]

Appeal

If one party maintains that an error of law was made during the trial, and if the judge refuses to grant a post-trial motion for a new trial, the dissatisfied party may appeal to a higher court. Probably the most common grounds for appeal are that the judge allegedly admitted evidence that should have been excluded, refused to admit evidence that should have been introduced, or failed to give proper instructions to the jury.

An attorney lays the groundwork for an appeal by objecting to the alleged error during the trial. This objection goes into the trial record and becomes part of the trial transcript, which may be reviewed by an appellate court. The appellate court decision may call for the lower court to enforce its earlier verdict or to hold a new trial.

SUMMARY

In this chapter, we focused on the handling of civil cases. We began by looking at some of the important categories of civil law: contracts, property, the law of succession, family law, and torts. We gave particular attention to §1983 civil rights suits filed in response to police violence.

We then discussed the ADR movement, which has been in existence for some time but has only recently gained significant attention from the courts. We described the two best-known ADR techniques being used by federal and state courts, recent Supreme Court decisions enforcing the provisions contained in mandatory arbitration clauses, and some of the concerns that have arisen due to the growing use of mandatory arbitration in employment and consumer disputes.

Finally, we examined the procedure followed in resolving civil cases. Once a complaint has been filed in a civil case, a few pretrial motions may narrow the scope of the dispute or lead to a settlement of the case. The discovery process is also useful in narrowing the scope of the case and preventing surprises should the case proceed to trial. However, as in criminal cases, most civil cases never go to trial.

The cases that are not settled prior to trial become part of a standard process, which was discussed step by step. Where appropriate, we pointed out differences between a civil trial and a criminal trial.

FURTHER THOUGHTS AND DISCUSSION QUESTIONS

1. Is the civil litigation process an effective way to hold law enforcement officers accountable for violence committed against members of minority groups?
2. Are jurors qualified to determine the amount of compensatory and punitive damages that should be awarded to a successful plaintiff? Or should that task be handled only by a judge?
3. Does the increased use of ADR to resolve disputes conflict with the often-heard view that every person is entitled to their day in court? Should the enforcement of mandatory arbitration clauses be the same whether they are included in contracts between two corporations, as compared to contracts including employees and/or consumers?

SUGGESTED RESOURCES

American Bar Association. Section of Family Law website. Available at www.abanet.org/groups/family_law.html (accessed July 17, 2024). Provides useful information about family law as well as links to a wide variety of other sources.

American Tort Reform Association (ATRA) website. Available at https://www.atra.org/ (accessed July 17, 2024). Includes information on civil justice reform laws advocated by ATRA across the country.

Carter, Lief, Sarat Austin, Mark Silverstein, and William Weaver. *New Perspectives on American Law*. Durham, NC: Carolina Academic Press, 1997. An excellent discussion of contracts, property, and torts. Also provides a good overview of civil procedure.

Economic Policy Institute. Available at www.epi.org/ (accessed July 17, 2024). Provides information on a variety of issues of relevance to low- and middle-income workers.

Friedman, Lawrence. *A History of American Law*, 4th ed. New York, NY: Oxford University Press, 2019. An excellent review of the development, nature, and substance of civil law in the United States.

Haltom, William, and Michael McCann. *Distorting the Law: Politics, Media, and the Litigation Crisis*. Chicago, IL: University of Chicago Press, 2004. Assessments of the state of the tort reform movement, media coverage of tort law, and concerns over the so-called litigation crisis.

Hames, Joanne Banker, and Yvonne Ekern. *Introduction to Law*, 6th ed. Upper Saddle River, NJ: Pearson Education, Inc., 2019. An introduction to law in the United States, with good discussions of family law, wills, trusts, probate, and alternative dispute resolution.

Jacob, Herbert, Herbert M. Kritzer, Doris Marie Provine, Erhard Blankenburg, and Joseph Sanders. *Courts, Law, and Politics in Comparative Perspective*. New Haven, CT: Yale University Press, 1996. An excellent comparative study of the processing of civil and criminal cases. The countries discussed in the book are France, Germany, Japan, the United Kingdom, and the United States.

Miller, Richard E., and Austin Sarat. "Grievances, Claims, and Disputes: Assessing the Adversary Culture." *Law and Society Review* 15 (1980–1981): 525–66. A study of the evolution of civil cases from grievances to court cases.

Ramseyer, J. Mark, and Eric B. Rasmusen. "Are Americans More Litigious? Some Quantitative Evidence." *The American Illness: Essays on the Rule of Law*. New Haven, CT: Yale University Press, 2013. A good assessment of the litigation crisis that incorporates economic theory in its analysis, while placing the American civil justice system in comparison to that in other Western nations.

Stone, Katherine V. W., and Alexander J. S. Colvin. "The Arbitration Epidemic: Mandatory Arbitration Deprives Workers and Consumers of Their Rights." Economic Policy Institute Briefing Paper #414, December 7, 2015. Available at https://www.epi.org/publication/the-arbitration-epidemic/ (accessed July 17, 2024). Provides a thorough summary of the history of mandatory arbitration in the United States, with a focus on the use of such clauses in consumer and employment contracts.

KEY TERMS

answer
deposition
interrogatories
plaintiff
Tort
venue

12 DECISION-MAKING BY TRIAL COURT JUDGES

CHAPTER GOALS AND OBJECTIVES

In this chapter, readers will learn that . . .

- Trial court judges' rulings are influenced by a wide variety of legal and extralegal factors.
- Decisions by trial court judges are generally guided by law, facts, and precedent. But there are instances when these jurists may have significant discretion, and in those cases, other factors may influence a judge's ruling.

On what basis and for what reasons do judges in the United States rule the way they do on the motions, petitions, and judicial policy questions that require their attention? In this chapter, we respond to this query by summarizing the theories and research findings of many judicial scholars who have tried to find out what makes judges tick. (Chapter 13 then examines the special case of decision-making on the collegial appellate courts at the state and federal levels.) In this chapter, we examine federal and state jurists as a group because, to a substantial extent, the variables that influence judicial decision-making are the same for judges at both levels. For instance, both types of judges tend to be governed strongly by court precedents, and virtually all judges reflect to some degree their political party affiliation. Where differences between federal and state judges can be anticipated, we take note of this. For example, one would expect public opinion to have less effect on federal judges, who are appointed for life, than it has on those state judges who must regularly stand for reelection.

It is useful to begin with a brief discussion of the decision-making environment in which trial judges and their appellate colleagues operate. Because of the differing purposes and organizational frameworks of trial and appellate courts, judges of each type face particular kinds of pressure and expectations. However, all jurists are subject to two major kinds of influence, as described by classic judicial politics scholars: the legal subculture and the democratic subculture.[1] In any given case, it is often difficult to determine the relative impact of a specific influence on a judge. Studies have suggested that when judges, especially trial judges, find no significant precedent to guide them—that is, when the legal subculture cupboard is bare—they tend to turn to the democratic subculture, a combination of determinants that includes their own political inclinations.

Judge Beverly Cannone, a Massachusetts Superior Court judge, presided in the high-profile trial of Karen Read, who was accused of killing her police officer boyfriend in 2022. Judge Cannone declared a mistrial in the case after jurors deadlocked and failed to reach a unanimous verdict.

Pat Greenhouse/The Boston Globe via Getty Images

At the base of the federal and state judicial hierarchies are the trial court judges, who preside over the judicial process and corporately make hundreds of millions of decisions each year. Some decisions pertain to legal points and procedures raised by litigants even before a trial begins, such as a motion by a criminal defendant's lawyer to exclude from trial a piece of illegally obtained evidence. During the trial, a judge must rule on scores of motions made by the attorneys in the case—for example, an objection to a particular question asked of a witness or a request to strike contested testimony from the record. Even after a verdict has been rendered, a trial judge may be confronted with demands for decisions—for instance, a litigant's request to reduce a monetary award made by a civil jury.

Trial judges can and occasionally do take ample time to reflect on the more important decisions and may consult with their staff or other judges about how to handle a particular legal problem. Nevertheless, a huge portion of their decision-making must be done spontaneously, without the luxury of lengthy reflection or discussion with staff or colleagues. As one trial judge told us, "We're where the action is. We often must 'shoot from the hip' and hope you're doing the right thing. You can't ruminate forever every time you have to make a ruling. We'd be spending months on each case if we ever did that." (Virtually all the judges interviewed for this study were promised anonymity.)

Decision-making by the appeals courts and the supreme courts is different in several important respects. By the time a case reaches the appellate level, the record and facts have already been established. The jurists' job is to review dispassionately the transcript of a trial that has already occurred, to search for legal errors that may have been committed by others. Few snap judgments are required. And although the appeals courts and a supreme court may occasionally hear oral arguments by attorneys, they do not examine witnesses, and they are removed from the drama and confrontations of the trial courtroom. Another difference in the decision-making process is that the trial level is largely individualistic, whereas the appellate level is to some degree the product of group deliberation.

Despite the acknowledged differences between trial and appellate judge decision-making, all-American jurists have many values in common. We examine several studies that have sought to explain why judges think and act as they do, using the legal subculture and the democratic subculture analytic framework. The thrust of these scholarly efforts has differed. Some view judges as akin to judicial computers who take in a volume of facts, law, and legal doctrines and spew out "correct" rulings—determinations that are virtually independent of the judges' values and characteristics as human beings. Other researchers tend to explain judicial decision-making in terms of the personal orientations of the judges. A decision is seen not so much as the product of some unbiased, exacting thought process that judges learn in law school but rather as having been affected by the judge's life experiences, prejudices, and overall social values. As with most theories of human behavior, each of these approaches has its fair share of the truth, but none provides the whole story.

THE LEGAL SUBCULTURE

It is useful in examining the legal subculture as a source of trial judge decision-making to focus on several specific questions: What are the basic rules, practices, and norms of this subculture? Where do judges learn these principles, and what groups or institutions keep judges from departing from them? How often and under what circumstances do judges respond to stimuli other than those from the traditional legal realm?

The Nature of Legal Reasoning

In the classic movie set at Harvard Law School, *The Paper Chase*, the formidable Professor Kingsfield promises his budding law students that if they work hard and entrust their mush-filled brains to him, he will instill in them the ability "to think like a lawyer." How do lawyers and judges think when they deliberate in their professional capacities? One classic answer to this question is that "the basic pattern of legal reasoning is reasoning by example. It is a three-step process described by the doctrine of precedent as follows: (1) similarity is seen between cases; (2) the rule of law inherent in the first case is announced; and (3) the rule of law is made applicable to the second case."[2] For example, the cases of *Lane v. Wilson* and *Gomillion v. Lightfoot* had similar arguments and factual situations.[3] In *Lane*, an African American citizen of Oklahoma brought suit in federal court, alleging that he had been deprived of the right to vote. In 1916, the legislature of that state had passed a law, ostensibly designed to give formerly disenfranchised Black citizens the right to vote, which required them to register, but the registration period lasted only twelve days. (White voters were for all practical purposes exempted from this scheme with a "grandfather clause.") If Black people did not sign up within that short interval, never again would they have the right to vote. The Oklahoma legislature clearly realized that a twelve-day period was wholly inadequate for African Americans to mount a voter registration drive and that the vast majority would not exercise their right to vote. The plaintiff in this case did not get on the registration rolls in 1916. When he was thereafter forbidden to vote, he sued, claiming that the Oklahoma registration scheme was unconstitutional. The Supreme Court agreed with the plaintiff. In striking down the statute, it set forth this principle, or rule of law: "The Fifteenth Amendment nullifies sophisticated as well as simple-minded modes of discrimination."[4] Two decades later, another Black citizen, Charles Gomillion, sued in the federal courts, alleging a denial of his right to vote as secured by the Fifteenth Amendment. Here an Alabama statute altered the Tuskegee city boundaries from a square to a twenty-eight-sided figure, allegedly removing "all save only four or five of its 400 Negro voters while not removing a single white voter or resident." Although not denying a legislature's right to alter city boundaries "under normal circumstances," the Court saw through the Alabama legislature's thinly disguised attempt to deny suffrage to the African American citizens of Tuskegee. Reasoning that the situation in *Gomillion* was analogous to that in the Oklahoma case, the Court used the precedent of *Lane v. Wilson* to strike down the Alabama law: "It is difficult to appreciate what stands in the way of adjudging a statute having this inevitable effect invalid in light of the principles of which this Court must judge, and uniformly has judged, statutes that, howsoever speciously defined, obviously discriminate against colored citizens. 'The Fifteenth Amendment nullifies sophisticated as well as simple-minded modes of discrimination.' *Lane v. Wilson*."[5] This is one example of the judicial reasoning process—of thinking like Professor Kingsfield's lawyer. Two cases are compared because the facts or principles are similar; a rule of law gleaned from the first case is applied to the second. This step-by-step process is the essence of proper and traditional legal reasoning.

Adherence to Precedent

A related value held by trial and appellate judges is a commitment to follow precedents—decisions rendered on similar subjects by judges in the past. The doctrine of *stare decisis* ("stand by what has been decided") is a cardinal principle of the common law tradition. In a national survey of more than one thousand trial court judges in the United States, the jurists were asked about how important precedent was in their decision-making—especially when the precedent was "clear and directly relevant." Ninety-one percent replied that it was "very important." By contrast, when these same jurists were asked to rate the importance of their own personal "view of justice in the case," only 28 percent said that was "very important."[6] As for appellate court judges, a 2010 study focused on a random sample of five hundred Supreme Court cases, yielding over ten thousand subsequent treatments in the US courts of appeals. The authors concluded that "hierarchical control [that is, the appellate courts generally following the decisions of the Supreme Court] appears strong and effective."[7] The US Supreme Court, although technically free to depart from its own precedents, does not ordinarily do so, for when "the Court reverses itself or makes new law out of whole cloth—reveals its policy-making role for all to see—the holy rite of judges consulting a higher law loses some of its mysterious power."[8] Indeed, one study of the Supreme Court found that "in any given decade, the Court overturns less than .002 percent of its previous decisions."[9] Consider, for example, the fact that despite the Court being divided, 6–3, on divergent political lines, in its 2023–2024 term the justices decided 41 percent of their cases unanimously.[10] A sophisticated study of this phenomenon published in 2008 further concluded that "legal factors play an important role in Supreme Court decision making."[11] Ideally, adherence to past rulings endows the law with predictability and continuity and reduces the dangerous possibility that judges will decide cases on a momentary whim or with an individualistic sense of right and wrong.

Not all legal systems have placed such emphasis on *stare decisis*. In ancient Greek times, for example, the judge-kings decided each case based on what appeared fair and just to them at the time. When a judge-king resolved a dispute, the judgment was assumed to be the result of direct divine inspiration.[12] The early Greek model is thus the antithesis of the common law tradition. However, strict adherence to past precedent may be something of a legal fiction. Judges can and do distinguish among various precedents in creating new law. This helps to keep the law flexible and reflective of changing societal values and practices. Many scholars have argued that the readiness of common law judges to occasionally discard or ignore precedents that no longer serve the public has contributed to the survival of the common law tradition.

Constraints on Trial Judge Decision-Making

Another significant element of the legal subculture is found under the heading of what one prominent scholar called the "great maxims of judicial self-restraint."[13] These maxims derive from a variety of sources—the common law, statutory law, legal tradition—but each serves to limit and channel the decision-making of state and federal judges. Because these various principles have already been discussed in detail, we merely reiterate a few of the major themes of judicial self-restraint.

Before a judge will agree to consider a lawsuit, a definite case or controversy at law or in equity must exist between bona fide adversaries under the Constitution. The case must concern the protection or enforcement of valuable legal rights, or the punishment, prevention, or redress of wrongs related to the litigants. Allied with this maxim is the principle that US judges may not render advisory opinions—that is, rulings on abstract, hypothetical questions. (This rule is not followed as strictly in many state systems.) Also, all parties to a lawsuit must have standing or a substantial personal interest infringed on by the statute or action in question.

The rules of the game also forbid jurists to hear a case unless all other legal remedies have been exhausted. In addition, the legal culture discourages the judiciary from deciding political questions or matters that ought to be resolved by one of the other branches of government, by another level of government, or by the voters. Judges are also obliged to give the benefit of the doubt to statutes and official actions when their constitutionality is being questioned. A law or an executive action is presumed to be constitutional until proven otherwise. (Some judges adhere to this principle on economic issues but not on matters of civil rights and civil liberties, believing that in these matters the burden of proof is on the government.) In this same realm, judges feel bound by the norm that if a law must be invalidated, they will do so on as narrow a ground as possible or will void only that portion of the statute that is unconstitutional.

Finally, American jurists may not throw out a law or an official action simply because they personally believe it is unfair, stupid, or undemocratic. For a statute or an official deed to be invalidated, it must clearly be unconstitutional. Judges do not always agree about what is a clearly unconstitutional act, but most acknowledge that broad matters of public policy should be determined by the people through their elected representatives—not by the judiciary.

The Impact of the Legal Subculture: An Example

Because the principles that make up the legal subculture—reasoning, precedent, and restraint—tend to be abstract, it is useful to illustrate them with a real-life example. *Evers v. Jackson Municipal Separate School District* was an uncomplicated 1964 school integration case in which a group of African American children and their parents sought to prevent the "district and its officials from operating a compulsory biracial school system."[14] The facts and controlling precedents were clear: (1) Jackson, Mississippi, was overtly maintaining a segregated public school system; (2) the US Supreme Court had ruled a decade earlier, in *Brown v. Board of Education*, that such segregation was unconstitutional; and (3) the US Court of Appeals for the Fifth Circuit, which has jurisdiction over Mississippi, had handed down a string of rulings ordering the integration process to go forward.

The federal trial judge in *Evers*, Sidney Mize, did not like the commands he heard from the legal subculture. Appointed to the federal bench in 1937, Mize was an unabashed segregationist, as his written opinion in this case clearly shows. After discussing a score of alleged physical and mental differences between Black people and Whites, Mize claimed that Whites were intellectually superior to non-Whites and segregated schools were good because, in his view, "separate classes allow greater adaptation to the differing educational traits of Negro and white pupils, and actually result in greater scholastic accomplishments for both."[15] Given Judge Mize's prejudiced views, it would seem clear where this decision was headed. But then entered the legal subculture. After fourteen single-spaced printed pages of racially biased argument against the integration of the Jackson schools, Mize yielded to the requirements of legal reasoning, respect for precedent, and judicial self-restraint. Almost sheepishly he concluded his decision with these unexpected words:

> Nevertheless, this Court feels that it is bound by what appears to be the obvious holding of the United States Court of Appeals for the Fifth Circuit that if disparities and differences such as that reflected in this record are to constitute a proper basis for the maintenance of separate schools for the white and Negro races it is the function of the United States Supreme Court to make such a decision and no inferior federal court can do so.[16]

Mize then meekly blocked the school district and its officials from operating a compulsory segregated school system. The legal subculture prevailed.

Wellsprings of the Legal Subculture

The institutions that instill and maintain the legal values in the United States are "the law schools, the bar associations, the judicial councils, and other groups that spring from the institutionalization of the 'bench and the bar.'"[17] "The purpose of law school," a scholar wrote, "is to change people; to turn them into novice lawyers; and to instill in them a nascent self-concept as a professional, a commitment to the value of the calling, and a claim to that elusive and esoteric style of reasoning called 'thinking like a lawyer.'"[18] The world just does not look the same to someone on whom law school has worked its indoctrinating magic. Facts and relationships in the human arena that formerly went unnoticed suddenly become *compelling* and *controlling* to the fledgling advocate. Likewise, other facets of reality that previously had been important in one's worldview are now dismissed as *irrelevant and immaterial.*

Besides the teaching that occurs in law school, the values of the legal subculture are maintained by the state and national bar associations and by a variety of professional–social groups whose members are from both bench and bar—for example, the honorary Order of the Coif.[19] The values and practices of jurists are handed down from one generation to another. Thus, the traditions and tenets of the American legal subculture are well tended by powerful support groups. They are rightly accorded ample deference if one is to understand judicial decision-making in America.

The Limits of the Legal Subculture

Despite the taut nature of judicial reasoning and the importance of *stare decisis* and judicial self-restraint, the legal subculture does not totally explain the behavior of

American jurists. If objective facts and obvious controlling precedents were the only stimuli to which jurists responded, the judicial decision-making process would be largely mechanical, and all judicial outcomes would be predictable. Yet even the legal subculture's most loyal supporters would concede that judges often distinguish between precedents and that some judges are more inclined than others toward self-restraint.

To understand the thinking of judicial decision-makers and the evolution of the law, it is necessary to consider more than law school curricula and the canons of the bar associations. One of the first great minds to realize this was Justice Oliver Wendell Holmes Jr., who almost 150 years ago wrote that:

> the life of the law has not been logic; it has been experience. The felt necessities of the time, the prevalent moral and political theories, intuitions of public policy, avowed or unconscious, even the prejudices which judges share with their fellowmen have had a good deal more to do than syllogism in determining the rules by which men should be governed. The law embodies the story of a nation's development through many centuries, and it cannot be dealt with as if it contained only the axioms and corollaries of a book of mathematics. To know what it is, we must know what it has been, and what it tends to become. The very considerations which judge most rarely mention, and always with an apology, are the secret root from which the law draws all the juices of life. I mean, of course, considerations of what is expedient for the community concerned.[20]

By about the 1920s, an entire school of thought had developed that argued that judicial decision-making is as much the product of human, extralegal stimuli as it is of some sort of mechanical legal thought process. Adherents of this view, who were known as **judicial realists**, insisted that judges, like other human beings, are influenced by the values and attitudes learned in childhood. As one of these realists once put it, a judge's background "may have created plus or minus reactions to women, or blonde women, or men with beards, or southerners, or Italians, or Englishmen, or plumbers, or ministers, or college graduates, or Democrats. A certain facial twitch or cough or gesture may start up memories, painful or pleasant."[21]

Over the ensuing decades, the study of the personal, extralegal influences on decision-making has become more rigorous. Often calling themselves judicial behavioralists, modern-day advocates of the realist approach have improved on it in two ways. First, they have tried to test empirically many of the theories and propositions advanced by the realist school. Second, they have attempted to relate their findings to more scientifically grounded theories of human behavior. Thus, whereas a realist might have asserted that a Democratic judge would probably be more supportive of labor unions than would a Republican jurist, a judicial behavioralist might go a step further by taking a generous random sample of labor union versus management decisions and statistically determining whether Democratic judges are significantly more likely than their GOP counterparts to back the union. It is one thing to intuitively ascribe a cause for human behavior; it is another to subject an assertion to careful empirical analysis.

THE DEMOCRATIC SUBCULTURE

The legal subculture has an impact on American jurists. Evidence shows that popular democratic values—manifested in a variety of ways through many different mediums—have an influence as well. Some scholars have argued that the only reason courts have maintained their significant role in the American political system is that they have learned to bend when the democratic winds have blown. That is, judges have tempered rigid legalisms with commonsense popular values and have maintained "extensive linkages with the democratic subculture":

> Very often, legal elites such as bar associations and judicial councils are more noticeable spokespeople for the federal judiciary than are the spokespeople of the democratic subculture. However, representatives of the democratic subculture, such as members of political parties, members of social and economic groups, and local state political elites, can also be observed commenting on controversial questions. In matters like staffing the courts, determining their structure and organization, and fixing federal jurisdiction, democratic representatives have access through Congress and other institutions that are influential in establishing judicial policy. Although Congress provides a main channel to the federal courts, access for democratic values is also obtained through the President, the attorney general, and nonlegal officials who deal with the judiciary. In addition, the location of federal courts throughout the states and regions renders them unusually susceptible to local and regional democratic forces.[22]

In discussing the democratic subculture, we focus on the influences most often observed by students of the American court system—political party affiliation, localism, public opinion, and the legislative and executive branches of government.

The Influence of Political Party Affiliation

Do the political party affiliations of judges affect the way they decide certain cases? The question is straightforward enough, but the responses are by no means in unanimous agreement. To most attorneys, judges, and court watchers among the public, the question rings with outright impertinence, and their answer is usually something like this: after taking the judicial oath and donning the black robe, a judge is no longer ostensibly a Republican or a Democrat. Former affiliations are (or at least certainly should be) put aside as the judge enters a realm in which decisions are the product of evidence, sound judicial reasoning, and precedent, as opposed to such a base factor as political identification. As one author once quipped, "Most judges would sooner admit to grand larceny than confess a political interest or motivation."[23] Indeed, during his 2017 confirmation hearings before the Senate Judiciary Committee, then–US Court of Appeals Judge, and future Supreme Court Justice Neil Gorsuch proclaimed, "There is no such thing as a Republican judge or Democratic judge. We just have judges."

The data, however, tell a different story. Despite the cries of indignation from those who contend that the legal subculture explains virtually all judicial decision-making, evidence compiled over many years of research clearly indicates that judges' political identification does impact their behavior on the bench.[24] Studies have shown that other personal factors—such as religion, gender, race, and prejudicial career—may also play a role. Indeed, political party affiliation seems to have a significant and consistent capacity to explain and predict the outcome of judicial decisions in many instances.[25] One prominent student of American politics explained why there may be a cause-and-effect relationship between judges' party allegiance and their decisional patterns:

> If judges are party identifiers before reaching the bench, there would be a basis for believing that they—like legislators—are affected in their issue orientations by party. Furthermore, judges are generally well educated and the vote studies show that the more educated tend to be stronger party identifiers, to cast policy preferences in ideological terms, to have clearer perceptions of issues and of party positions on those issues, to have issue attitudes consistent with the positions of the party with which they identify, and to be more interested and involved in politics. For judges, even more than for the general population, party may therefore be a significant reference group on issues.[26]

Federal District Court Judges. Given the relationship between party affiliation and court decision-making, the following observation should come as no surprise: as a whole, Democratic trial judges on the US district courts are more liberal than their Republican colleagues. In an analysis of more than 118,000 published district court decisions reached between 1932 and 2024, Democratic judges took the liberal position 47 percent of the time, whereas Republican jurists did so in only 38 percent of the cases.[27] Thus, for our eighty-eight-year time frame, the Democrats' ratio of liberal-to-conservative opinions has been around 1.45 times greater (more liberal) than the Republican ratio.[28] Although the overall differences cannot be called overwhelming, neither can they be dismissed as inconsequential.

As the data in Table 12.1 suggest, differences between Republican and Democratic judges depend considerably on the type of case. An analysis of partisan voting patterns in twenty-eight separate case categories indicates that differences between judges from the two parties were greatest for cases concerning affirmative action, in which preferential treatment was given to members of racial and ethnic minority groups and to women (referred to negatively by its opponents as "reverse discrimination"); the right to privacy (for example, abortion, gay and lesbian rights); race discrimination; and deviations in sentencing guidelines (in which judges use their discretion to call for upward or downward variations in sentencing guidelines). Partisan differences were very modest or virtually nonexistent in cases involving rent control and excess profits, in disputes between union members and their union hierarchy, and in cases where the federal government was regulating labor unions or the employer.

TABLE 12.1 ■ Liberal Decisions of Federal District Court Judges in Order of Magnitude of Partisan Differences for Twenty-Eight Types of Cases, 1932–2024

	Overall	Democrat	Republican	Partisan Difference	Odds Ratio (α)
Affirmative action/reverse discrimination	57	69	47	23	2.60
Right to privacy	50	60	40	20	2.25
Racial discrimination	40	48	30	17	2.10
Sentencing guidelines deviation	47	55	38	18	2.04
Local economic regulation	65	72	60	13	1.79
Criminal convictions	34	40	28	12	1.73
Freedom of religion	50	56	43	13	1.68
Gender equality/ women's rights	46	53	40	13	1.68
Fourteenth Amendment	35	41	30	11	1.62
NLRB v. employer	58	64	53	10	1.53
US habeas corpus pleas	27	31	23	8	1.52
Rights of the disabled	38	44	34	10	1.52
Criminal court motions	31	36	27	9	1.48
Alien petitions	39	44	34	9	1.48
Voting rights	47	52	43	10	1.47
Native American rights	49	54	45	10	1.47

(Continued)

TABLE 12.1 ■ Liberal Decisions of Federal District Court Judges in Order of Magnitude of Partisan Differences for Twenty-Eight Types of Cases, 1932–2024 (*Continued*)

	Overall	Democrat	Republican	Partisan Difference	Odds Ratio (α)
Freedom of expression	57	62	53	9	1.44
Environmental protection	60	64	56	8	1.42
US commercial regulation	71	74	67	7	1.38
State habeas corpus pleas	26	28	23	6	1.36
Social Security cases	61	64	57	7	1.33
NLRB v. union	66	70	63	6	1.32
Union v. company	53	56	50	6	1.29
Age discrimination	31	34	29	5	1.26
Employee v. employer	38	41	35	6	1.27
Union member v. union	39	41	38	3	1.15
Rent control/excess profits	59	61	57	4	1.16
Government v. union/ employer	57	57	57	0	1.00

Notes: NLRB = National Labor Relations Board. The odds ratio (a), also called the cross-product ratio, is a measure of the relationship between two dichotomous variables. Specifically, it is a measure of the relative odds of respondents from each independent variable category being placed in a single dependent variable category. Percentages may not total to 100 due to rounding.

Source: Data collected by Robert A. Carp and Kenneth L. Manning.

Excerpts of interviews with two jurists who were lifelong members of each of the two parties are revealing about the impact of partisanship. Sitting in the same city and on the same day, they discussed a subject that in recent decades has divided Republican and Democratic judges—their philosophy of criminal justice and, more specifically, their views about sentencing convicted felons. The rank-and-file Democrat said, in part:

> Most of the people who appear before me for sentencing come from the poorer classes and have had few of the advantages of life. They've had an uphill fight

> all the way and life has constantly stepped on them. I come from a humble background myself, and I know what it's like. I think I take all this into consideration when I must sentence someone, and it inclines me towards handing down lighter sentences, I think.

One hour later, a lifelong Republican addressed the same issue but with a different twist at the end:

> When I was first appointed, I was one of those big law-and-order types. You know—just put all those crooks and hippies in jail and all will be right with the world. But I've changed a lot. I never realized what poor, pathetic people there are who come before us for sentencing. My God, the terrible childhoods and horrendous backgrounds that some of them come from! Mistreated when they were kids and kicked around by everybody in the world for most of their lives. Society has clearly failed them. As a judge there's only one thing you can do: send them to prison for as long as the law allows because when they're in that bad a state there's nothing anyone can do with them. All you can do is protect society from these poor souls for as long as you can.

Although we would not contend that all Republican and all Democratic trial judges think precisely in those terms, we believe that something of the spirit of partisan differences is captured in these two quotations.

A 2011 study reaffirmed the importance of partisan, ideological differences among US district court judges, which the author concluded are "modest, but not unsubstantial. During the recent era of independent executive-vetting practices, the likelihood of a conservative decision is approximately 78–85 percent for Democratic appointees, and 85–90 percent for Republican appointees."[29] Furthermore, there is at least some evidence that partisan differences may be increasing. Research published in 2017 suggests that the increasing partisan polarization seen in recent decades in Congress may be occurring in the federal district courts as well.[30]

Federal Appeals Court Judges. As for partisan variations in the voting patterns of US appeals court judges, here, too, evidence shows that their (prior) party affiliation tempers their decision-making to some degree.[31] A study conducted in the 1960s concluded that "on balance, the findings underscore the absence of a sharp ideological party cleavage in the United States but also give support to the contention that the center of gravity of the Democratic party is more 'liberal' than that of the Republican party."[32] This finding has stood the test of time. In subsequent decades, other research has also found that Democratic judges on the whole tend to be more supportive of the rights of criminal defendants and of those seeking to expand First and Fourteenth Amendment freedoms.[33] And a major 2006 study by a research team headed by Harvard Law professor Cass Sunstein found that the partisanship of federal appeals court judges predicts their decision-making in the aggregate and that "Republican appointees vote very differently from Democratic appointees."[34]

Another study of voting patterns among appellate court judges was conducted on decisions made en banc—by all or a specified number of the judges in a circuit court of appeals instead of by the usual three-judge panels. This research focused primarily on partisan differences in cases dealing with criminal justice and civil liberties issues. The scholars found that support for criminal appellants by the Democrats was 59 percent, whereas for Republican appointees the figures were significantly lower—around 21 percent. Likewise, Democrats supported civil liberties petitioners approximately 67 percent of the time, whereas Republicans did so only around 35 percent of the time.[35]

US Supreme Court Justices. Does political party affiliation affect the way members of the US Supreme Court decide their cases? Scholars have found this to be a difficult subject to investigate. There is a common perception that the Supreme Court has usually decided cases in a partisan way, with voting splits often falling exactly along party lines. While this is true in some instances, the overall picture is not nearly that simple. The Supreme Court decides dozens of cases in any given term, and some of those disputes are more politically salient than others. In numerous cases, the justices are unanimous in their rulings.[36] In the 2020–2021 term, for example, the Supreme Court was unanimous in 43 percent of the cases it granted full review and decided.[37] In other instances, the jurists do not split neatly along party or ideological lines. Consider the fact that in the 2020–2021 Supreme Court term, conservative Justice Clarence Thomas (an appointee of Republican President George H. W. Bush) agreed with liberal Justice Sonia Sotomayor (who was selected by Democrat Barack Obama) in 30 percent of the Court's decisions that year. The agreement rate between Chief Justice John Roberts (appointed by George W. Bush) and Obama nominee Elana Kagan was even higher: 63 percent. In other words, Justices Thomas and Sotomayor agreed nearly one-third of the time, while Justices Roberts and Kagan agreed *most* of the time.[38] To suggest that partisanship is usually the overwhelming motivator of Supreme Court rulings is to ignore basic facts such as this.

Still, researchers have looked past the political spin and have engaged in rigorous, painstaking research on this question, and they have found reliable evidence indicating that partisanship may be a factor in some instances. The research hurdle on this question stems, in part, from the fact that the Court has nine justices, and generalizing about the behavior of groups this small is incredibly challenging. Moreover, the conventional wisdom that party is influential in Supreme Court decision-making often takes a very limited-time view of the Court, sometimes applying contemporary political understandings to an institution that has a more than two-century history. Numerous political parties have been represented on the Court over the decades, and the definitions of Federalist, Democrat, Whig, Republican, liberal, and conservative have varied so much over time that generalizations often become problematic. For example, before the 1920s, most mainstream Democrats opposed civil rights for African Americans. Since that era, most champions of the civil rights movement have been Democrats. In the jargon of the trade, the variables are so numerous, and the *n*s (number of justices) are so small that statistically significant observations are extremely difficult to make.

Despite the methodological problems involved, judicial scholars have sought to explore this subject. In a comprehensive study of the relationship between party affiliation and the liberal–conservative voting patterns of justices in the early part of the twentieth century, one scholar found that party identification was "clearly a good cue for selecting judicial decision-makers with the proper values."[39] This research indicated that on matters of support for the economic underdog, Democratic Supreme Court justices were more liberal than their Republican colleagues. It also found that greater liberalism of Democratic Court members extended to matters of civil rights and liberties, thereby reaffirming "the concept that judges are not random samples of their group." But even this scholar conceded, as did those who studied partisan voting by appeals court and trial court judges, that the relationships were not huge:

> The inability to predict at high rates of probability is not surprising when one considers the assumptions that must be made and the variety of other influences on the Court, such as political and environmental pressures, social change, precedent, reasoned argument, intra-court social influences and idiosyncrasy.[40]

One major study of partisan voting patterns on the Supreme Court focused on criminal justice cases. Among other things, the researchers concluded, "Democratic control of the Court and the White House, coupled with a high proportion of the Court's docket devoted to criminal issues, results in significantly higher support levels for criminal defendants than under the condition of the Republicans occupying the presidency and a majority of the Supreme Court seats with a relatively low priority placed on criminal justice appeals."[41] Nonetheless, some scholars urge caution before making a flat-out pronouncement about the relationship between the justices' backgrounds and their subsequent voting patterns. For example, one prominent researcher has argued that previous studies may be time bound—that is, during some time periods, decisional differences among the justices might be explained by background characteristics, whereas during others, background is only a modest predictor of behavior.[42] When one is faced with such conflicting and tentative studies, it is clear that the final chapter of a book on this subject is yet to be written.

More recently, however, there is evidence that the contemporary Supreme Court has tended to exhibit increasingly partisan differences. Those who assert that partisanship is frequently paramount in Supreme Court decision-making might point to the epic 2000 case of *Bush v. Gore*, the controversial 5–4 ruling that fell perfectly along party lines and effectively handed the disputed presidential election that year to George W. Bush. At the same time, there is indisputable data that Congress has become more polarized along party and ideological lines in recent years,[43] and it would be logical to speculate that something similar could also be happening on the Supreme Court. A 2011 article by scholars Lawrence Baum and Neal Devins argued that "for the first time in our political lifetimes, each of the four Democratic appointees has a strong tendency to favor liberal outcomes, while the five Republicans typically take conservative positions."[44] Baum also noted in 2014 that "the [Supreme] Court is now divided along partisan lines in a way that hasn't been true" in the past.[45] Still, this must be tempered with the understanding that many cases—even highly political ones—do not always reveal consistent partisan trends. Consider that in the landmark 2015 same-sex marriage case of *Obergefell v. Hodges*, a five-vote majority of four Democrats and one Republican ruled in favor of marriage rights for gay couples.[46] In another blockbuster case during that same term, *King v. Burwell*, the Court upheld a key provision of the Affordable Care Act (aka "Obamacare") in a 6–3 ruling, in which the majority included two Republican appointees along with four Democrats.[47] Had partisanship been the sole predictor of the voting in those two high-profile cases, the rulings—and American history—would have been very different.

Finally, it is interesting to note that while the overall data are somewhat mixed, the American public often seems to believe that partisan politics influences the vote of Supreme Court justices. For example, prior to the Court's first ruling on the Affordable Care Act in the summer of 2012, a Bloomberg News poll in March of that year revealed that a full 75 percent of the American public thought "the [C]ourt's decision will be based more on politics than on constitutional merit."[48]

Partisanship in State Courts. The federal courts are not the only arena in which Republican and Democratic jurists sometimes square off against one another. Partisan voting patterns often occur as well among the people who sit on the trial and appellate court benches. However, the evidence at the state level is weaker, for three general reasons. First, the state courts have not been studied as extensively and systematically as have the federal courts. This may be because some political scientists have held the (mistaken) view that state judiciaries are less important than their federal counterparts or because many state court decisions are unpublished and therefore much more difficult to obtain and study. Second, partisanship among state jurists is not strongly uniform across the country. In some states, for instance, judicial selection is truly bipartisan (or nonpartisan), and both political parties may support the same candidates. Also, many state judges do not have extensive relationships with a political party. Although they may have partisan identifications, they may not view judicial questions as being reflective of their party's ideology. Finally, the United States has several states in which one party dominates and in which most judges bear one same party label. For example, it would make little sense to study partisan variations among appellate judges in Texas because they are virtually all now Republicans. Nonetheless, keen levels of partisanship have been documented in some jurisdictions—particularly in states with big cities. One study revealed that the intensity of partisan rhetoric has increased in campaigns for judicial office ever since the Supreme Court ruled in *Republican Party of Minnesota v. White* that free speech rights extend "to candidates for judicial office, allowing them the freedom to announce their views on a variety of political and legal issues."[49,50]

There is quite a bit of recent anecdotal evidence that suggests that partisanship is influential at times in state supreme court decision-making. In Florida, for example, after Republican Ron DeSantis won election in 2018, he quickly moved to fill three vacancies on the state's supreme court. DeSantis appointed staunch conservatives to the bench who had extensive records working for various Republican officeholders.[51] That he would tap fellow members of the GOP was neither surprising nor improper. After all, chief executives of both parties have long appointed their party colleagues to positions of authority. But political observers noted that the new political tilt of the Florida Supreme Court meant that at least when it came to the highly political process of redrawing congressional district lines, the litigation deck would be stacked in favor of the GOP. The nonpartisan Center for Politics at the University of Virginia observed that "With a new jurisprudence dominating the [Florida Supreme] court, Democrats will find a less sympathetic audience for any redistricting challenges. . . ."[52]

From 2019 to 2021, a power struggle with clear partisan overtones played out in Wisconsin between that state's conservative-controlled Supreme Court and Democratic Governor Tony Evers. After former Republican Governor Scott Walker narrowly lost his reelection bid to Evers in 2018, Walker supported legislation in his final days in office that significantly limited the powers of the incoming governor. This led Evers to several legal clashes with the state's high court, which counted four Walker loyalists as members. The court upheld Walker's late-term power shuffle curtailing Evers's authority,[53] and it sided with Republicans in a dispute over eighty-two political appointments made by Walker in the last four weeks of his tenure.[54] The court also struck down face mask and lockdown orders that Evers instituted during the COVID-19 pandemic.[55] But in 2023, the partisan tables turned. In that year liberal judge Janet Protasiewicz was elected to the Wisconsin Supreme Court, flipping the body's ideological majority. Among other issues, it was widely anticipated that the new majority on that state's high court would end the use of highly gerrymandered legislative maps that favored the GOP in Wisconsin.[56]

Of course, these are just examples. What does the empirical research show? A study in Michigan of partisan voting patterns among that state's judges is noteworthy. Research showed that on labor–management issues, for example, Democrats on the bench were significantly more likely to support the side of the worker in unemployment compensation cases and in issues dealing with workers' compensation (on-the-job injuries). Democratic judges were also more likely to support criminal defendants seeking a new trial, to favor government efforts to regulate business, and to side with persons who sue business enterprises—all consistent with the voting behavior of Democrats on the federal bench.[57] Another study that focused on Michigan reaffirmed the high level of judicial partisanship in that state.[58] In a study of partisan conflict on a California intermediate court of appeals, significant differences were found between Democrats and Republicans in both criminal and civil cases.[59] Studying issues such as votes in criminal justice cases, labor–management disputes, debtor–creditor disagreements, and consumerism, the author concluded that "as previous research . . . would have predicted, the results are in the expected direction, with Republican panels significantly more likely to reach conservative outcomes than Democratic panels."[60]

Illinois, Iowa, Maryland, New York, and Pennsylvania are examples of other states where researchers have found meaningful partisan differences between Republican and Democratic judges.[61] Finally, a comprehensive study of state supreme court chief justices in 2005 found that there has been "a significant relationship between citizen ideology and the ideology of the chief justice"—that is to say, the partisan values of a majority of a state's voters is often reflected in corresponding partisan behavior by the state's supreme court chief justice.[62]

An Appraisal. The political party affiliation of the judges and justices can make a difference in the way they decide cases. Of all the background variables studied, it seems to be the most compelling and consistent. But a word of caution is in order. Although evidence of partisan influence on judicial behavior is convincing, it by no means suggests that Democrats always take the liberal position on all issues, whereas Republicans always opt for the conservative side. Rather, it is a matter of tendencies—that is, when the decision is a close call, a Democrat on the bench tends to be more liberal than a Republican judge. When controlling precedents are absent or ambiguous, or when the evidence in the case is about evenly divided, Democrats are more inclined than Republicans to be supportive of civil rights and liberties, to support government regulation that favors the worker or the economic underdog, and to turn a sympathetic ear toward the pleas of criminal defendants.

The Impact of Localism

A wide range of influences are included in the term *localism*, and we regard it as a broad second category of factors that affect federal and state judicial decision-making. A substantial body of literature suggests that federal judges are influenced by the traditions and mores of the region in which their courts are located, or in the case of Supreme Court justices, it varies by the geographic area in which they were reared. For trial and appeals court judges, geographic differences define both the legal and the democratic subcultures as well as the nature of the questions they must decide. Historically, such judges have had strong ties to the state and the circuit in which their courts are situated, and on many issues, judicial decision-making reflects the parochial values and attitudes of the region. As two leading students of the subject noted:

> A persistent factor in the molding of lower court organization has been the preservation of state and regional boundaries. The feeling that the judiciary should reflect the local features of the federal system has often been expressed by state officials most explicitly. Mississippi Congressman John Sharp Williams declared that he was "frankly opposed to a perambulatory judiciary, to carpetbagging Nebraska with a Louisianian, certainly to carpetbagging Mississippi or Louisiana with somebody north of Mason and Dixon's line."[63]

Why should judges in one district or circuit decide cases differently from their colleagues in other localities? Why should a Supreme Court justice make decisions differently from colleagues who hail from other parts of the United States?[64] Noted scholars Richard Richardson and Kenneth Vines put the matter succinctly:

> Since both district and appeals judges frequently receive legal training in the state or circuit they serve, the significance of legal education is important. If a federal judge is trained at a state university, they are exposed to and may assimilate state and sectional political viewpoints, especially since state law schools are training grounds for local political elites. Other than education, different local environments provide different reactions to policy issues, such as civil rights or labor relations. Indeed, throughout the history of the lower court judiciary there is evidence that various persons involved in judicial organization and selection have perceived that local, state, or regional factors make a difference and have behaved accordingly.[65]

Moreover, trial and appellate judges tend to come from the district or state in which their courts are located, and the vast majority were educated in law schools of the state or circuit in which they work. (For example, two-thirds of all district judges in one study were born in the state where their court is located, and 86 percent of all circuit judges attended a law school in their respective circuits.)[66] Also, the strong local ties of many judges tend to develop and mature even after their appointment to the bench.[67] In identifying with their regional base, judges are similar to other political decisionmakers. Public attitudes and voting patterns on a wide range of issues vary from one section of America to another.[68] As for national political officials, there is evidence that regionalism affects the voting patterns of members of Congress on many prominent issues—for example, civil rights, conservation, price controls for farmers, and labor legislation.[69]

Regionalism at the Three Judicial Levels

When President George Washington appointed the first Supreme Court, half of its members were northerners and half were southerners. Washington's choices were surely more than just a symbolic gesture to give a superficial balance to the Court. Having successfully led a group of squabbling former colonies during the Revolutionary War, Washington understood that the attitudes and mores of his fellow citizens differed widely from one locale to another and that justices would not be immune to these parochial influences. Studies of the early history of the high court reveal that sectionalism did creep into its decision-making patterns—particularly along North–South lines.

For example, a study of Supreme Court voting patterns in the sectional crisis that preceded the Civil War noted that the four justices who were most supportive of southern regional interests were all from the South, whereas jurists from the northern states usually favored the litigants from that region.[70] In the twentieth century, evidence also supported the belief that where the justices came from tempered their decision-making to some degree.[71] In the 1970s, President Richard Nixon sought to use a Supreme Court appointment as part of his "Southern Strategy" to appeal to White voters in Dixie. Nixon pursued this tactic as a means of aligning himself with White southerners who felt maligned by the Supreme Court's 1960s liberalism on racial and criminal justice matters. Though Nixon eventually settled on Warren Burger of Minnesota after the failed nominations of Clement Haynsworth Jr. of South Carolina and G. Harrold Carswell of Florida, the nomination of the two southerners was seen as a way for Nixon to "satisfy southern aspirations."[72]

Although political leaders and much of the public believe that a relationship exists between the justices' regional backgrounds and their judicial decisions, scholars have had difficulty documenting this phenomenon. First, links between the justices' regional heritage and their subsequent voting behavior are difficult to pinpoint, and they exist at most for probably a few regionally sensitive issues. Also, after Supreme Court justices are appointed and move to Washington, DC, they may, over time, take on a more national perspective, loosening to a significant degree the attitudes and narrow purview of the regions in which they were reared and educated. For example, in his early days in Alabama, Hugo Black had been a member of the Ku Klux Klan, but after his judicial appointment in 1937, he became one of the most articulate advocates of civil rights ever to sit on the Supreme Court.

Some evidence indicates that regionalism pervades the federal judicial system at the appeals court level as well.[73] One study noted regional differences on such prominent issues as rights of the consumer, pleas by criminal defendants, petitions by workers and by Black people, public rights in patent cases, and immigration litigation. The author of this research concluded that "regionalism is an inescapable adjunct of adjudicating appeals in one of the oldest regional operations of federal power in existence." He observed that although the appeals courts may adhere to national standards, such norms are nevertheless "regionally enforced. In the crosswinds of office and constituencies, Courts of Appeals may mediate cultural values—national and local, professional and political—in federal appeals."[74] In a study of regional variations in the voting of court of appeals judges, judicial politics scholar Susan Haire noted, for example, that "in search and seizure cases, Western judges were more liberal than their counterparts in the East (including the South). But in race-based employment discrimination cases Western judges adopted positions that were more conservative than their colleagues in the East."[75] In studies of federal district judges, East–West differences have never been found to be great. However, significant variations have traditionally existed between judges living in nonsouthern states and those holding court in the South. Between 1932 and 1979, just over 39 percent of the southern judges' decisions were liberal, whereas the figure was around 45 percent for jurists in the nonsouthern states. However, the data in Table 12.2 indicate that in the past four decades, these differences have declined to only 2.2 percent, although on some specific issues, southern jurists may still manifest strongly conservative sentiments. For example, a 1990 study showed that federal district judges in the more conservative South were almost 70 percent more likely to take an antiabortion stance than their colleagues in the North. This was found to be consistent with the values of the region as measured by public opinion polls and other data.[76] Also recall that in the 2016 and 2020 presidential elections, some of the strongest support for the conservative Republican ticket was in the southern states.

TABLE 12.2 ■ Liberal and Conservative Decisions by Nonsouthern and Southern Judges in Two Time Periods

		Nonsoutherners	*Southerners*
		%	%
1932–1979	Liberal	45.2	39.6
	Conservative	54.8	60.4
	Odds ratio (α) = 1.26		
1980–2024	Liberal	43.0	40.8
	Conservative	57.0	59.2
	Odds ratio (α) = 1.09		

Note: The odds ratio (α), also called the cross-product ratio, is a measure of the relationship between two dichotomous variables. Specifically, it is a measure of the relative odds of respondents from each independent variable category being placed in a single dependent variable category.

Source: Data collected by Robert A. Carp and Kenneth L. Manning.

Regional influences on judges' voting behavior are by no means a uniquely American phenomenon. For example, even in a small country such as Norway, the way judges vote in certain types of cases is often influenced by the regions they come from. One early study found that for violations of the conscientious objector laws, the likelihood of being convicted varied from a low of 3 percent if the judge was in the Western Military District (Vestlandet) to a high of 54 percent if the jurist was from the Northern District (Nordland).[77]

Variances in Judicial Behavior among the Circuits. Not only may judicial decision-making vary from one region of the country to another, but each of the circuits, according to studies, has its own way of administering the law and making decisions.[78] One reason is that circuits tend to follow sectional lines that mark off historical, social, and political differences. Another reason is that the circuit courts of appeals tend to be idiosyncratic, and thus the standards and guidelines they provide to the trial judges will reflect their own approach.[79] In a study of variations in the behavior of appellate judges from one circuit to another, scholar Susan Haire observed that the "findings . . . strongly suggest judges' decisional tendencies are shaped by the circuit." In her analysis, Haire found "meaningful policy differences" in such fields as search-and-seizure cases, obscenity rulings, and employment discrimination lawsuits.[80] Likewise, a study published in 2002 indicates that there were significant circuit-by-circuit variations in the degree to which these entities adhered to Supreme Court precedents.[81] Similarly, the behavior of US trial judges has been observed to vary on a circuit-by-circuit basis. Between 1980 and 2014, for example, in the US Ninth Circuit 49.7 percent of district court judges' decisions were liberal. (The Ninth Circuit covers many of the western states, including the traditionally liberal states of California, Hawaii, Oregon, and Washington.) At the other end of the scale was the Fourth Circuit (Maryland, North and South Carolina, Virginia, and West Virginia), whose trial jurists rendered liberal decisions only 36.8 percent of the time.[82] Such circuit-by-circuit differences among trial judges are also manifested in variations in sentencing behavior. An article in the *Wall Street Journal* noted, "Government researchers did find wide disparities in sentencing across the country's 12 regional judicial circuits. In drug cases, for example, district judges in San Francisco's Ninth Circuit were 19 times as likely to mete out sentences below the guidelines of the U.S. Sentencing Commission—to make what are called 'downward departures'—as those in the Fourth Circuit, based in Richmond, Va."[83]

Variances in Trial Judge Behavior among the States. At first blush, it may appear strange to argue that US judicial decisions vary significantly from one state to another because the state is not an official level of the federal judicial hierarchy, which advances from district to circuit to nationwide system. Nonetheless, direct and indirect evidence suggests that each state is unique in the way its federal judges administer justice. There are several explanations for this. First, a state, like a circuit or a region, is often synonymous with a particular set of policy-relevant values, attitudes, and orientations. One would automatically expect, for instance, that on some issues, US trial and appellate judges in Texas would act differently from Massachusetts jurists, not so much because they are from different states but because they are from different political, economic, legal, and cultural milieus. Second, many judges regard their states as meaningful boundaries and behave accordingly. For example, a US trial judge in Louisiana once noted, "One thing I frequently discuss with the other judges here is sentencing matters. Judge X has been a tremendous help with this. I wouldn't want to hand down a sentence which is way out of line with what the other judges are doing here in this state for the same crime."[84] Another example occurred in 2002, when South Carolina's active federal trial judges voted "to ban secret legal settlements, stating that such agreements have made the courts complicit in hiding the truth about hazardous products, inept doctors and sexually abusive priests. Mary Squiers, who tracks individual federal courts' rules for the U.S. Judicial Conference, said only Michigan had a similar rule, which unseals secret settlements after two years."[85] Third, note the impact on federal judicial behavior of diversity of citizenship cases. These are disputes that involve litigants from two (or more) different states. These suits constitute almost a quarter of the district courts' civil business and about one in ten civil appeals to circuit courts. Because the Supreme Court requires the lower courts to apply state instead of federal law in such cases, it behooves US trial judges to keep abreast of and be sensitive to the latest developments in state law. The effect may be the same for circuit judges. For example, when three-judge appellate panels are appointed for diversity of citizenship cases, the tendency is to name circuit judges from states whose law governs. As one scholar observed, "A 'slight local tinge' thus colored diversity opinions as part of a general tendency of members to defer to colleagues most knowledgeable about the subject."[86] Quantitative studies of federal trial judges' voting behavior substantiate the proposition that meaningful differences are evident on a state-by-state basis. Also, both circuits that cross North–South boundaries (the Sixth and the Eighth) and the district courts in the border and southern states have tended to be more conservative than those in the other states.[87] This suggests that local and regional values—as personified by the state—may have a greater influence on trial judge decision-making than do those of the circuit.

Localism and the Behavior of State Judges. If regional factors leaven the bread of federal judicial decisions, this phenomenon is even more pervasive for state jurists. State judges, even more than their federal counterparts, tend to be local folks—born, bred, educated, and socialized in the locale in which they preside. Whether they have been elected directly by the people or appointed because of their political connections with the governor or the local political machine, state judges are likely to mirror the values and attitudes of their environment. A study that compared and contrasted judges and justices in Minneapolis and Pittsburgh provides a fitting example.[88] The researcher reported that in Minneapolis the state trial judges were elected on a nonpartisan ballot, and in practice, the political parties had almost no role in the selection of judges. "The socialization and recruitment of [the] . . . judges reflect this pattern of selection. Most of these judges [like much of the local population] have Northern European–Protestant and middle-class backgrounds, and their pre-judicial careers have been predominantly in private legal practice. Such career experiences seem to have stimulated these judges to be interested more in 'society' than in the defendant."[89] Minneapolis' traditionalistic, middle-class environment, from which its judges come, is reflected in the law-and-order, no-nonsense grist of the judicial mill:

> This pre-judicial experience, reinforced by their lack of party or policy-oriented experiences and their middle-class backgrounds, seems to have contributed to the legalistic and universalistic character of their decision-making and their eschewal of policy and personal considerations. In their milieu, rules were generally emphasized, especially legal ones, and these rules had been used to maintain and protect societal institutions. Learning to "get around" involved skill in operating in a context of rules. The judges' success seems to have depended more on their objective achievements and skills than on personal relationships.[90]

The environment of the Pittsburgh jurists stood in stark contrast. The highly partisan (Democratic) judges there reflected the working-class, ethnic group–based values of the political machine that put them on the bench. They were likely to have held public office before becoming judges, and as a result, they were much more people-oriented than their counterparts in Minneapolis. They often felt that their own "minority ethnic and lower-income backgrounds and these government and party experiences had developed their general attachment to the problems of the 'underdog' and the 'oppressed.'" The author makes the following conclusion about the impact of the local environment and recruitment process on judicial behavior:

> Their political experiences and lack of much legalistic experience apparently contributed to the highly particularistic and nonlegal character of their decision-making, their emphasis on policy considerations, and their use of pragmatic criteria. Personal relationships, especially with constituents, were emphasized, and focused on particular and tangible entities. Success depended largely on the ability to operate within personal relationships. It depended on whom one knew, rather than on what one knew. Abstractions such as "the good of society as a whole" seem to have been of little concern.[91]

Although social science still needs to develop more systematic empirical evidence for the relationship between the local environment and the output of state courts, these brief case studies are indicative of the kinds of phenomena we are describing.

The Impact of Public Opinion

If one were to approach a typical federal judge or justice and ask whether public opinion affected the decisions made from the bench, the jurist might respond with a fair measure of indignation. The answer might be something like this: "Look, as a judge with a lifetime appointment, I'm expected to be free from the pressures of public opinion. That's part of what we mean when we say that we're a 'government of laws—not of men.' When I decide a case, I look at the law and the facts. I don't go out into the streets and take some sort of public opinion poll to tell me what to do."

Yet to some degree and on certain issues, American judges do seem to temper their decision-making with public opinion. There are several intuitive reasons for this. First, judges—as human beings, as parents, as consumers, and as residents of the community—are themselves part of public opinion. Putting on a black robe may stimulate a greater concern for responsible, objective decision-making, but it does not void a judge's membership in humanity. As one judicial scholar has noted, "Since judges, both appointed and elected, usually have been born and reared locally and recruited from a local political system, it seems likely that public opinion would have an effect, especially in issues that are locally visible and controversial. In addition . . . many judges seem to consider themselves independent judicial officials who represent local populations in the courts. Consequently, judges may feel that they ought to take local values into account."[92] Even a conservative and strict constructionist such as former Supreme Court Chief Justice William H. Rehnquist acknowledged this in a revealing statement:

> Judges, so long as they are relatively normal human beings, can no more escape being influenced by public opinion overall than can people working at other jobs. And, if a judge on coming to the bench were to decide to hermetically seal himself off from all manifestations of public opinion, he would accomplish truly little; he would not be influenced by current public opinion, but instead would be influenced by the state of public opinion at the time he came to the bench.[93]

There is anecdotal evidence that public opinion may influence some judicial decisions. In June 2003, when the Supreme Court handed down its decision in *Lawrence v. Texas* that overturned Texas' antisodomy law, much of the Court indicated that it wished to keep in step with world public opinion. The decision had the effect of overturning all the other state laws that criminalized gay sex. In *Lawrence*, Houston police had entered the petitioner's apartment after responding to a "reported weapons disturbance" (the sound of gunfire) and observed the petitioner and another adult man engaging in a consensual sexual act. The two men were arrested and charged with "deviate, sexual intercourse, namely anal sex, with a member of the same sex (a man)."[94] The applicable state law prohibited two persons of the same sex from engaging in "deviate sexual intercourse." (The law permitted the same sexual acts between straight individuals.) The *Lawrence* decision overruled the decision of *Bowers v. Hardwick*,[95] which had affirmed a similar law in the state of Georgia. In a televised interview on the ABC show *This Week*, Justices Sandra Day O'Connor and Stephen Breyer recalled that in deciding the case the justices discussed

> whether the court should consider the legal opinions of other world courts, such as the European Court of Human Rights. Breyer agreed with [Justice Anthony M.] Kennedy's view that the foreign courts' views that gays and lesbians had a right to privacy in their sexual behavior showed that the U.S. Supreme Court's prior decision to the contrary was not in keeping with Western tradition. . . . "We see this all the time, Justice O'Connor and I, and the others, how the world really—it's trite but it's true—is growing together," Breyer said.[96]

The following is another example of judges' keen sensitivity to local public opinion. It was previously noted that the federal district judges in South Carolina unanimously voted to abolish the use of secret settlements in their state. Why? The justification for this decision, as stated by Chief Judge Joseph F. Anderson Jr., clearly reveals that he and the other trial judges were responding to the public mood: "Here is a rare opportunity for our court to do the right thing and take the lead nationally in a time when the Arthur Andersen/Enron/Catholic priest controversies are undermining public confidence in our institutions and causing a growing suspicion of things that are kept secret by public bodies."[97]

In some instances, public opinion is supposed to be an official factor in the decision-making process. For example, in the implementation of the famous *Brown v. Board of Education* school desegregation ruling, the Supreme Court refused to set strict national guidelines for how its decision was to be carried out. Instead, individual federal district judges were to implement the high court decision, based on the judges' determination of local moods, conditions, and traditions.[98] Likewise, when the Supreme Court ruled that federal courts could hear cases concerning malapportionment of state legislatures, it refused to indicate how its decision was to be carried out. It was, in effect, left to the lower federal courts to implement the ruling in accordance with the way they viewed local needs, conditions, and the state political climate.[99] Another example may be found in the obscenity rulings of the Burger Court, in which the justices determined that the courts should use community values and attitudes in determining what materials are obscene.[100] Yet another example: the Supreme Court ruled in the case of *Trop v. Dulles* that when seeking to determine what constitutes "cruel and unusual punishment" that is prohibited by the Constitution, "The [Eighth] Amendment must draw its meaning from the evolving standards of decency that mark the progress of a maturing society."[101] In other words, it's the ever-changing beliefs and values of society that will impact our understanding of the law. Thus, not only is it impossible for judges to rid themselves of the influence of public opinion, but in many important types of cases, they may be obliged to consider the attitudes and values of the public. This does not mean that judges go out and take opinion polls whenever they face a tough decision, but public opinion is often one ingredient in the decision-making calculus.

It should also be noted that both federal and state judges are aware that ultimately their decisions cannot be carried out unless there is a reasonable degree of public support. As scholar Lawrence Baum has noted, "Justices care about public regard for the Court, because high regard can help the Court in conflicts with the other branches of government and increase people's willingness to carry out its decisions."[102] It has been an open secret for a long time that when the Court is about to hand down a major decision likely to be unpopular among many groups of Americans, the author of the majority opinion may take pains to word the decision so as to generate popular support for it—or at least to salve the wounds of those potentially offended by it. Examples of high court decisions in which the author is thought to have written as much for the public at large as for the usual narrow audience of lawyers and lower court judges include *Marbury v. Madison*, in which the Court claimed for itself the right to declare acts of Congress unconstitutional; *Brown v. Board of Education*, which called for an end to racial segregation in the public schools; *Roe v. Wade*, in which the Court upheld a woman's right to an abortion; and *Lawrence v. Texas*, the case in which the justices struck down state laws that discriminate against LGBTQ persons by criminalizing gay sex.[103]

The empirical evidence for the impact of public opinion is suggestive but hardly conclusive, in part because relatively few comprehensive studies of the phenomenon have been conducted and the proposition is difficult to prove. While many of the earliest studies of this subject produced conflicting conclusions, more recent and exhaustive investigations have begun to map a real, albeit imperfect, relationship between public opinion and jurists' decisional patterns.[104] A 2010 study found that public opinion may influence decision-making on the Supreme Court, but the authors state, "we're not sure why."[105] In 1993, two Supreme Court researchers concluded that popular sentiment "exercises important influence on the decisions of the Court even in the absence of changes in the composition of the Court or in the partisan and ideological make up of Congress and the presidency."[106] However, they qualified their findings by noting that there was a fairly lengthy interval—three to seven years—between a change in the public mood and a corresponding alteration in justices' voting behavior.[107] Moreover, these voting changes tended to be concentrated among only a handful of justices.[108]

Another team of researchers led by a scholar at Emory University addressed this matter and came up with a set of conclusions that are more emphatic and contain fewer qualifications about the link between public mood changes and Supreme Court decisional patterns. Their analysis "provides partial support for the idea that justices' preferences shift in response to the same social forces that shape the opinions of the general public." They further concluded that "even in the absence of membership change . . . public opinion may provide a mechanism by which the preferences of the Court can be aligned with those of the public."[109] Research that has looked at the question of public opinion influence on the lower federal courts has been less conclusive.[110] Further studies will have to resolve this apparent enigma about why lower federal court jurists may be immune to shifts in the public mood, while US Supreme Court justices are not. Research is also being done to determine whether shifts in public opinion affect the decision-making of federal appeals court judges as well as US trial jurists.

Researchers have also explored this phenomenon at the state level. For example, a study of California state courts found that the severity of sentencing in marijuana cases often changed soon after a popular referendum was held on reducing criminal penalties for personal use of the drug. For example, judges who had given light sentences before the referendum sometimes gave harsher sentences if the local vote was in favor of maintaining criminal penalties. Conversely, harsh-sentencing jurists sometimes became more lenient when the vote indicated that the public favored reducing the penalties.[111] Given that in many states judges must periodically run for election, they probably are more attuned to public opinion than are federal judges, who have lifetime tenure. One study of elected state supreme court justices found that "to appease their constituencies, justices who have views contrary to those of the voters and the court majority, and who face competitive electoral conditions will vote with the court majority instead of casting unpopular dissents on politically volatile issues."[112] Likewise, another study involving state supreme court justices' voting behavior in death penalty cases found a clear link between their voting patterns and voter sentiment about capital punishment. The authors noted that "on the highly salient issue of the death penalty, mass opinion and the institution of electing judges systematically influence composition and judge behavior."[113]

The following more down-to-earth example illustrates a state judge's stronger grassroots political awareness and the greater degree to which elected jurists interact with the local environment. On November 28, 1988, Jack Hampton, a conservative Republican state district court judge in Dallas, Texas, gave a thirty-year prison sentence to a defendant who had been convicted of murdering two gay men. The killer, Richard Bednarski, had testified in court that he and some friends went to a central Dallas park to "pester homosexuals" and ended up killing two of them in what authorities called an execution-style slaying. (Bednarski placed a gun in one victim's mouth and pulled the trigger; he then shot the other man several times.) Because of the heinous and unprovoked nature of the crime and because Hampton was known as a "hanging judge" who usually gave life sentences for murder, the *Dallas Times Herald* decided to interview the judge about his lighter-than-usual sentence. During the interview, Judge Hampton stated that the murder victims got what they asked for because they were "queers" who "wouldn't have been killed if they hadn't been cruising the streets picking up teenage boys."[114] "I put prostitutes and gays at about the same level," Hampton said. "And I'd be hard put to give someone life for killing a prostitute."[115] Immediately after the interview was published, public protests were staged by human rights groups, local church leaders, and various gay rights organizations. Protest rallies were held, including one attended by five hundred people at the City Hall Plaza, where letters of support were read from Senator Edward M. Kennedy of Massachusetts and Texas State Treasurer Ann Richards. Also, formal complaints were filed with the Texas Commission on Judicial Conduct, calling for Hampton to be disciplined (and the Commission eventually censured the judge for his statements).[116] In response to the outcry about his remarks, this elected judicial official issued a four-paragraph letter to a group of eight Methodist ministers. Judge Hampton said he wished "to apologize" for his "poor choice of words that appeared in a recent newspaper story." He promised that in his court "everyone is entitled to and will receive equal protection."[117]

Was the judge's public apology a response, at least in part, to his perception of public opinion and its possible effect on his bid for reelection? This might be surmised from the judge's later statement, responding to a question about the possible political fallout from the incident: "If it makes anybody mad, they'll forget it by 1990" (when Judge Hampton was up for reelection and was, in fact, reelected).[118] This particular incident is not typical of the behavior of state judges, but it demonstrates the degree to which locally elected judicial officials may respond to the tides of public opinion.

Very rarely do lifetime judicial appointees, such as federal judges, feel the need to justify their sentencing behavior in interviews with the local press or to issue public apologies when public opinion turns critical of their behavior. For better or worse, public opinion does affect judicial behavior at some level, and this is particularly true when judges must be accountable directly to the electorate.

Finally, a study of state supreme court justices found that jurists who served in states where they were elected to office (as opposed to being appointed) were more responsive to public opinion on the matter of whether they dissented from the courts' majority opinions. The study found that "within elective courts, justices respond to elections by pursuing a *consensual approach* [emphasis added] regardless of their seniority."[119] Thus, despite the traditional notion of the blindfolded justice weighing only the facts in a case and the relevant law, common sense and statistical evidence support the assertion that jurists do keep their eyes (and ears) open to public opinion.

The Influence of the Legislative and Executive Branches

The executive and legislative branches are the final set of stimuli that the democratic subculture may bring to bear on the behavior of American judges.

Congress and the President. Perhaps the most obvious link between the values of the democratic subculture and the output of the federal courts is that the people elect the president and members of the Senate, and the president appoints judges and justices, with the advice and consent of the Senate. The chief executive and certain key senators greatly influence what kinds of people will sit on the bench, but even after judges have been appointed, the president and Congress may have an impact on the content and direction of judicial decision-making.

First, to a large degree, the jurisdiction of the federal trial and appellate courts is set by the Congress of the United States, which has the authority to determine the types of issues that may become appropriate for judges to resolve. For example, when Congress passed the Civil Rights Act of 1964, Title VII and its subsequent amendments greatly expanded the rights of women to be free from gender discrimination in the workplace. In doing so, Congress in effect expanded the jurisdiction of the federal courts to hear many disputes that previously had been outside the purview of the federal judiciary. And the evidence suggests that the courts have not been idle in expanding the power Congress gave them.[120] Conversely, Congress may restrict the jurisdiction of the federal courts. For example, in fall 2004, many members of Congress feared that the federal courts would strike the words "under God" from the Pledge of Allegiance on the ground that they violated the Establishment Clause of the First Amendment. As a result, the US House of Representatives, by a 247–173 vote, passed a bill that would prevent the federal courts, including the Supreme Court, from hearing cases challenging the words "under God" in the pledge.[121] (The bill died in the Senate and thus did not become law.)[122] Even if Congress does not pass such legislation, the threat to do so may cause the federal courts to pull in their horns when it comes to deciding cases in ways that are not in accord with the will of the president or Congress. Indeed, a 2009 study found that historically, during time periods when Congress appeared to be hostile to the Supreme Court, the justices exercised greater self-restraint in overturning acts of Congress.[123]

Second, judicial decision-making is likely to be bolder and more effective if it has the active support of at least one other branch of the federal government, and ideally of both.[124] School integration is a case in point. When the federal courts began to order desegregation of the public schools after 1954, they met with considerable opposition—primarily from those parts of the country most affected by the Supreme Court ruling in the *Brown* case. It is doubtful whether the federal courts could have overcome this resistance without the support given them (sometimes reluctantly) by the president and Congress. For example, in 1957, Arkansas Governor Orville Faubus sought to obstruct a district judge's order to integrate Little Rock's Central High School. President Dwight D. Eisenhower then mobilized the National Guard, and in effect, he used federal bayonets to implement the judge's ruling. President John F. Kennedy likewise used federal might to support a judge's decision to admit a Black student to the University of Mississippi in the face of massive local resistance. Congress also gave its support to federal desegregation rulings. For instance, it voted to withhold federal aid to school districts that refused to comply with district court desegregation decisions. Surely, White House and congressional support emboldened the Supreme Court and the lower judiciary to carry on with their efforts to end segregation in the public schools.

Presidential and congressional actions may sometimes lead rather than just implement judicial decision-making. One study analyzed the impact on trial judge behavior of the 1937 Supreme Court decisions that permitted much greater government regulation of the economy.[125] As expected, federal district judges' support for government regulation increased markedly after the Supreme Court gave its official blessing to the government's new powers. However, it was also learned that district court backing for labor and economic regulation had been building before the Supreme Court's decisions. Proregulation decisions by US trial judges increased from 44 percent in 1936 to 67 percent in 1937. The authors attributed this change at least in part to the fact that before 1937, the president and Congress, in response to public opinion, were strongly pushing legislation that favored an expanded federal role in labor and economic regulation.[126]

Thus, the Supreme Court and the lower courts are not, and cannot be, immune to the will of Congress and the chief executive as they go about their judicial business. Not only does the president, with the advice and consent of the Senate, select all members of the federal judiciary, but to a large degree, Congress also prescribes the jurisdiction of the federal courts and often the qualifications of those who have standing to sue in these tribunals. Moreover, many court decisions cannot be meaningfully implemented without the support of the other two branches of government—a fact not lost on the judges and justices. Sometimes, too, the courts appear to follow the lead of the president and Congress on various public policy matters. Whatever the circumstances, the legislative and executive branches of government clearly constitute an important source of nonjudicial influence on court behavior.

The State Legislature and the Governor. Just as the legislative and executive branches affect judicial decision-making at the national level, their counterparts at the state and local levels also have profound influence. In almost half of the jurisdictions, the popularly elected governor (or the state legislature) selects the state judges, and a policy link is likely to exist among the value sets of the voters, the appointing officials, and the judges who render subsequent decisions. For example, when Texas Governor Rick Perry met privately with a group of Dallas school officials in 1994, he candidly "predicted . . . that a lawsuit challenging the state school finance law [would] fail because his appointees to the Texas Supreme Court [would not] force changes on the Legislature." As the former president of the Highland Park (Dallas) school board said in response to the governor's comments, "He didn't say he had spoken to them [the justices], but I just couldn't believe it, and a lot of other people couldn't believe it either. They were stunned that a governor would say something like that."[127] (As it happened, the governor's prediction was accurate because the state supreme court did not overturn the law in question.)

More specifically, the authors of one study found three major ways in which the political branches affect the role of the state courts.[128] First, legislation sponsored by the governor or passed by the legislature regulates the types of claims that can be adjudicated in state courts and brought to the state appellate courts. For example, class action suits may be easily brought in state judicial tribunals. (Such suits facilitate access to the courts by allowing large numbers of potential litigants with small individual claims to band together, thereby reducing or eliminating entirely the financial costs of seeking redress.) Actions by the legislature determine who may bring such suits and under what circumstances. The evidence suggests that the states vary greatly in this area. Some states make it extremely easy to initiate such suits, whereas in others, access to the courts is difficult.[129]

Second, actions by the legislature (which may or may not be part of the governor's political agenda) determine the authority of the state supreme court to regulate its workload and focus on important cases. For example, it is generally accepted that for most cases litigants should have the right to appeal trial court decisions. In states that have an ample number of intermediate appellate courts, this right to appeal is readily available. However, in states without enough intermediate appeals courts or in states where the supreme court is forced by law to deal with a succession of relatively minor disputes, the chances are slim that litigants will have their cases heard by the supreme court. This fact is significant in terms of the distribution of justice, and it is also important for another reason: in states where the legislature forces the supreme court to overwork on judicial trivia, the court does not have time to devote much attention to cases that raise important policy questions. For instance, after the legislature in North Carolina created intermediate courts of appeals, a study concluded that this action enabled the state high court to assume "a position of true leadership in the legal development of the state."[130] Thus, actions by the legislature (supported or opposed by the governor) may determine whether the Supreme Court plays a major or a minor role in policy questions important to the state.

Finally, because a prime function of courts is to enforce existing legal norms, the sorts of issues that state courts address depend to a large degree on the substantive law of the state. For instance, seventeen state constitutions contain "little ERAs" (equal rights amendments); ten states specifically protect the right to privacy; and some states guarantee a right to quality of the environment.[131] Thus, a judge in a state where good air quality is guaranteed will have a much greater opportunity and right to issue an injunction against a polluter than will the judge in a state where such a right is not legally provided. An example of legislatures taking an issue out of the hands of state judges has taken place in the realm of gay and lesbian rights. After the courts began to hand down decisions favoring such rights (for example, *Lawrence v. Texas*,[132] discussed earlier), numerous state legislatures adopted state constitutional amendments that defined marriage as being between a man and a woman.[133] This in effect precluded judges in those states from handing down a ruling in favor of same-sex marriage that was based on these states' laws or constitutions. All these state limits were rendered moot by the Supreme Court's 2015 ruling in *Obergefell v. Hodges*, in which the Court announced a federal right for same-sex marriage that trumped state limitations.[134] Still, the point is that state judges often render decisions within the existing constitutional and legal environment of their respective states. Such an environment is largely the product of political decisions made by the governor and the legislature as representatives of the electorate.

In sum, the output of the state courts, like that of federal tribunals, is to a significant degree the result of the political values and policy goals of the chief executive and the legislative branch of government.

THE SUBCULTURES AS PREDICTORS

Scholarly opinion differs on whether judicial decision-making is essentially the product of facts, laws, and precedent (the legal subculture model) or whether the various extralegal factors carry more weight (the realist-behavioralist view). In other words, are court decisions better explained by understanding the facts and laws that impinge on a given case, or by knowing which newspaper the judge reads in the morning, or how the judge voted in the last election?

The clue to answering the question lies in knowing what kind of case the judge is being asked to decide. Many federal trial judges' cases and much appellate judicial business involve routine norm enforcement decisions. In cases in which the law and the controlling precedents are clear, the victor will be the side that is able to marshal better evidence to show that its factual case is stronger. In other words, in the lion's share of cases, the legal subculture model best explains and predicts judicial decision-making. When traditional legal cues are ambiguous or absent, however, judges are obliged to look to the democratic subculture for guidance in their decision-making. We think that then-Illinois Senator

Barack Obama got close to the truth in a 2005 speech dealing with judicial appointments. Obama argued that 95 percent of court cases are easily settled since the law and precedent. But in "those 5 percent of rigid cases the legal process alone will not lead you to a rule of decision and the critical ingredient is supplied by what is in the judge's heart."[135]

When the Legal Evidence Is Contradictory

It is probably fair to say that in many cases, the facts, evidence, and controlling precedents distinctly favor one side. In such instances, the judge is clearly obliged to decide for the party with the stronger case. Not to do so would violate the judge's legal training and mores; subject a trial or appeals court judge to reversal by a higher court, an event most jurists find embarrassing; and render the Supreme Court vulnerable to the charge that it was making up the law as it went along—an impression not flattering to the high court justices. However, judges often find themselves in situations in which the facts and evidence are about equally compelling on both sides or in which a roughly equal number of precedents sustain a finding for either party. As one US trial judge in Houston said:

> There are days when you want to say to the litigants, "I wish you guys would've settled this out of court because I don't know what to do with you." If I grant the petition's request, I can often modify the relief requested [to even out the decision], but still one side has got to win and one side has got to lose. I could cite good precedents on either side, and it's no good worrying about the appeals court because there's no telling what they would do with it should the judge's decision be appealed.

The following is an example in which a US trial judge was forced to decide a case by his own lights (that is, using his democratic subculture values) because the cues from the legal subculture were clearly contradictory or nonexistent. Judge Robert E. Coyle, who held court in the Eastern District of California (Fresno), was presented with a case that stemmed from an employment discrimination complaint filed with the Equal Employment Opportunity Commission (EEOC). Alicia Castrejon had been employed by the Tortilleria La Mejor of Farmersville, California, and claimed in her suit that she had been dismissed from her job because of previous complaints filed with the EEOC against her employer.

The legal issue was whether Castrejon had the right to file a suit in the first place because she was an undocumented immigrant. When Congress passed the Immigration Reform and Control Act of 1986, which prohibits employment of undocumented workers, it did not specify whether immigrants who have applied for amnesty are protected during the period when their applications are being processed. Castrejon had filed for amnesty, but her application had not been acted on at the time she filed her employment discrimination complaint.

The judge looked to the Department of Labor and to the EEOC for some legal guidance on the matter of the interim rights of undocumented residents. Both federal agencies maintained that workers are covered by federal labor and antidiscrimination laws even if they are here illegally. But the judge learned that many employers had been interpreting the Immigration Reform and Control Act to mean that undocumented immigrants are not protected, and they were able to point to a 1987 ruling by a federal district judge in Alabama. That decision dismissed an undocumented immigrant's claim for minimum wages and overtime pay because, the judge said, that would conflict with the congressional act of 1986. The legal subculture was giving Judge Coyle few cues as to the "right" answer, and the existing cues were contradictory. Furthermore, in deciding this case, the judge had to tap attitudes and values derived from his democratic subculture and to put much of his legal subculture orientation on hold.

After sitting on the case for more than two years, the judge finally issued a ruling that had a significant immediate impact on hundreds of thousands of immigrants. For reasons known fully only to Judge Coyle, he ruled that undocumented workers do have the right to pursue discrimination suits against an employer—regardless of legal residency status. In his decision, the judge acknowledged the seeming incongruity of discouraging illegal immigration, while at the same time allowing undocumented workers to seek legal recourse against discrimination on the job: "We doubt, however, that many undocumented immigrants come to this country to gain the protection of our labor laws. Rather it is the hope of getting a job—at any wage—that prompts most undocumented immigrants to cross our borders."[136] In situations such as this, judges have little choice but to turn to their personal value sets to determine how to resolve the cases. Decision-making is affected by local attitudes and traditions or by the judge's perception of the public mood or the will of the current Congress or state legislature or administration.

Since the 1970s, a significant number of the Supreme Court's decisions have been regarded as "ideologically imprecise and inconsistent," often sustained by weak 5–4 majorities. This has increased the likelihood that trial and appellate judges will respond to stimuli from the democratic rather than the legal subculture. That is, the potential confusion created by the Court in setting forth ambiguous or contradictory guidelines has meant that judges in the lower federal and state courts—and perhaps even members of the Supreme Court—have been forced to rely on (or have felt free to give vent to) their personal ideas about how the law should read. As one study concluded, "With the decline of the fact-law congruence after 1968 the . . . [lower courts] became freer to take their decision-making cues from personal-partisan values rather than from guidelines set forth by the Higher Court."[137] The problem caused by Supreme Court ambiguity is still very much alive in the Roberts Court. For example, in June 2006, "a splintered Supreme Court rolled back coverage of the Clean Water Act, ruling the federal regulators had gone too far in protecting wetlands lying more than 10 miles from navigable waters."[138] This ambiguous, multipronged ruling prompted the new chief justice, John G. Roberts Jr., to lament in his opinion that "it is unfortunate that no opinion commands a majority of the Court on precisely how to read Congress' limits on the reach of the Clean Water Act. Lower courts and regulated entities will now have to feel their way on a case-by-case basis."[139]

When a Case Concerns New Areas of the Law

Researchers also set aside the legal subculture model and turn to the democratic subculture approach when jurists are asked to resolve new types of policy questions for which statutory law and appellate court guidelines are virtually absent. Since about 1937, most new and uncharted areas of the law (at least at the federal level) have been in the realms of civil liberties and criminal justice rather than in labor and economic regulation. Meanwhile, the federal courts have generally leaned toward self-restraint and deference to the elected branches when it comes to ordering the economic lives of the American people.[140] Moreover, in recent decades, Congress has legislated, often with precision, in the areas of economic regulation and labor relations, and this has further restricted the discretion of judges in these fields. As a result, the noose of the legal subculture has been drawn tightly around the trial judge's neck, leaving little room for creative decision-making or responding to the tug of the heart instead of the clear command of the law. Since the days of the New Deal, the legal subculture, not the democratic subculture, has often been the better predictor of trial and appellate judge decision-making in labor and economic regulation cases.

Since the 1930s, the opposite trend has been observable for many issues of criminal justice and civil rights and liberties:

> The "great" and controversial decisions of the Stone, Vinson, Warren, and Burger Courts [as well as the Rehnquist Court] focused primarily on issues of civil liberties and of the rights of criminal defendants, and it is precisely those sorts of issues which evoked the greatest partisan schisms among the justices. Research has shown that . . . [the lower courts] were by no means immune to the debates and divisions which racked the nation's High Court; they, too, seem to have split along "political" lines more often on criminal justice and on civil rights matters than they did with other sorts of cases.[141]

The ambiguity (or perhaps the constant state of flux) of the law on such matters as the rights of criminal defendants, First Amendment freedoms, and equal protection of the law has given the federal jurists greater opportunity to respond than they have had in the labor and economic realms, where their freedom of action has been more circumscribed. Put another way, since the 1930s, the democratic subculture model has become increasingly important as a predictor of judicial behavior on issues pertaining to the Bill of Rights.[142]

A series of interviews with a wide range of district and appellate court judges lends further credence to this notion. In William Kitchin's study, trial judges were asked about their willingness to "innovate"—that is, to make new law in areas where appellate court or congressional guidelines were ambiguous or nonexistent. After asking why judges create new law through judicial innovation, Kitchin offered one possible explanation: courts innovate because other branches of government ignore certain significant problems that, to individual judges, cry out for attention. Accordingly, the individual district judge innovates to fill a legal vacuum. As one judge commented, "The theory is that judges should not be legal innovators, but there are some areas in which they have to innovate because legislatures won't do the job. Race relations is one of these areas." Other areas identified as needing judicial innovation because of legislative inaction were housing, equal accommodations, and criminal law (especially habeas corpus).[143] Another study of decisional patterns and variations in US district judges' decision-making showed that "the subjects that [the Kitchin study] found to represent the greatest areas of freedom in judicial decision making are the very same subjects that we find to maximize partisan voting differences among the district judges. In situations where judges are freer to take their decision-making cues from sources other than appellate court decisions and statutes, they are more likely to rely on their personal-partisan orientations."[144]

Ambiguity was a key problem for courts in the 1960s and 70s, when judges struggled mightily in search of a legal definition of obscenity. In 1957, the Supreme Court ruled that sexually explicit materials that are "obscene" are not protected by the First Amendment, and it said that obscenity could be defined as material that dealt with sex "in a manner appealing to prurient interest."[145] Webster's dictionary defines "prurient" as something that arouses an immoderate or unwholesome interest or desire.[146] Seven years later, the Supreme Court said that hypothetical "national standards" should be used in determining what appealed to the prurient interest of the average person.[147] However, nine years after that, the Court changed its mind and ruled that "state community standards" could be employed.[148] But what is obscenity? No one seems to know today with any greater certainty than Justice Potter Stewart did in 1964, when he confessed that he could not intelligibly define obscenity, but "I do know it when I see it."[149] As US District Judge José Gonzalez wrote in 1990, in determining that an album by controversial Miami-based hip-hop group "2 Live Crew" was obscene and thus illegal to sell, "It is an appeal to 'dirty' thoughts and the loins, not to the intellect and mind." (2 Live Crew's attorney defended the album as "art" and said, "Put in its historical context, it is a novel and creative use of sound and lyrics.")[150] The Eleventh Circuit Court of Appeals later overturned the obscenity conviction.[151] Given the reluctance or the inability of Congress and the Supreme Court to precisely define obscenity, America's trial and appellate judges had little choice but to look to their personal values and perceptions of the local public need to determine what kinds of music, books, films, art, and plays the First Amendment protects in their respective jurisdictions. Today, the legal dispute about defining obscenity has largely become a back-burner issue due to rapidly changing technology and evolving public attitudes regarding sexual matters. But it's not entirely gone from the public landscape. In 2023, a federal judge in Arkansas wrestled with this question while ruling on a state law that would create criminal liability for librarians who distribute content that could be considered "obscene" or "harmful to minors." The Arkansas law said that library employees who knowingly distribute obscene material would risk conviction of a felony. But the age-old question remained: what, exactly, is "obscene"? The judge eventually put a temporary halt to the law pending a full trial, ruling that the law could lead to arbitrary interpretation and "content-based restrictions" that violate the First Amendment right to freedom of expression.[152]

Another active area of the law that is potentially vexing to federal judges is the subject of sexual harassment. This issue has received much attention in recent years given disturbing revelations about major media figures such as movie producer Harvey Weinstein and others. Ever since Congress added sexual harassment to the list of items prohibited in the workplace by Title VII of the Civil Rights Act of 1964, federal jurists have had a challenging time defining what sexual harassment means. Obvious examples are clear enough (a boss explicitly telling an employee that sexual favors are required for a pay raise), but the legal gray areas have taxed judges' minds because while an act may be widely deemed inappropriate, it does not mean that it automatically rises to the level of a federal civil rights violation under the law. For example, a US trial judge in Los Angeles was asked to rule that there was sexual harassment in an office because the breasts of female workers were being compared and sexual toys were being given as presents. The judge ruled that while the office in question had been turned into a "bawdy sorority," federal law did not provide a "cause of action for embarrassment."[153] Another example of a federal judge having to resolve an issue never examined by a court occurred in 2010. The previous year, Quinnipiac University had eliminated the women's volleyball team for budgetary reasons. But the school knew it needed to comply with Title IX of a 1972 federal law that mandated equal opportunities for people in education and athletics. So, Quinnipiac established a much less expensive "sport" called "competitive cheerleading." Students did not buy it and sued in federal court. As a consequence, U.S. District Judge Stefan Underhill had to address the novel question, is cheerleading a sport? Obviously, it would have done him no good to have asked, how would the Founding Fathers have answered this question? Nor did he have any reason to believe that the authors of the 1972 law had pondered this query. With the legal subculture silent in this realm, the jurist was obliged to rely on the democratic subculture to find an answer. Relying upon his own perspectives and understandings, Judge Underhill ruled: "Competitive cheer [*sic*] may, sometime in the future, qualify as a sport under Title IX. Today, however, the activity is still too underdeveloped and disorganized to be treated as offering genuine varsity athletics participation opportunities for students."[154]

Judicial innovation in new legal realms or in the absence of appellate court or legislative guidelines is by no means confined to federal jurists; it is just as significant an occurrence at the state court level. For example, in 2001, the New Jersey Supreme Court was asked to decide a novel question: can a man have the frozen embryos he and his ex-wife created implanted in the body of the man's new wife? The case involved Mr. "M. B." and Mrs. "J. B.," who created seven embryos during their marriage and had them frozen by a company specializing in that activity. (The couple had struggled with infertility and used in vitro fertilization to enable them to have children.) The couple divorced in 1998, but the divorce settlement left open the question of custody of the embryos. Mr. "M. B." remarried and wished to have the frozen embryos implanted in his new wife, but the first wife objected, stating that she "did not want to become a parent against her will." The New Jersey Supreme Court ruled that Mr. "M. B." could retain the embryos or have them destroyed, but he could not have them implanted in his new wife. As one Atlanta attorney who has handled several cases involving disputed embryos said of this case: "There is really no guiding principle nationwide in these cases. There are very few states that have looked at the issue."[155] This case is a vivid reminder that judicial policymaking in new legal realms is by no means the exclusive activity of the federal courts.

The Judge's Role Conception

In the discussion of which better explains judicial decision-making—the rules of the legal subculture or stimuli from the democratic subculture—one additional factor must be considered: how judges conceive of their judicial role. Judicial scholars often talk about three basic decision-making categories regarding whether judges should make law when they decide cases. Lawmakers are those who take a broad view of the judicial role. Often referred to as activists or innovators, these jurists contend that they can and must make law in their decisions because the statutory law and appellate or Supreme Court guidelines are often ambiguous or do not cover all situations, and in addition, legislative intent is frequently impossible to determine. In Kitchin's study of federal district judges, 14 percent were classified in this category, whereas in an investigation of appeals court judges, 15 percent were associated with this role.[156] At the other end of the continuum are the law interpreters, who take a narrow, traditional view of the judicial function. Sometimes called strict constructionists, they do not believe that judges should substitute judicial wisdom for the rightful power of the elected branches of government to make policy. They tend to eschew making innovative decisions that may depart from the literal meaning of controlling precedents. In the Kitchin study, 52 percent of the US trial judges were found to be law interpreters, whereas only 26 percent of the appeals court judges were so designated.[157] This finding is consistent with the fact that federal district judges are more concerned with routine norm enforcement, whereas the appellate judges' involvement—and their perception of it—is with broader questions of judicial policy.

Midway between the law interpreters and the lawmakers are judges known as pragmatists or realists, who believe that on occasion they are obliged to make law, but that for most cases, a decision can be made by consulting the controlling law or appellate court precedents. Studies have indicated that a third of federal district judges assume this moderate role, whereas a full 59 percent of their appellate court colleagues do so.[158] Comparing federal jurists with state judges, one scholar has noted, "A slightly greater number of federal than state judges take the pragmatist or realist views, possibly because they have more opportunities to make innovative decisions."[159]

A study of the importance of judicial roles in thirty-five states reaffirmed the value of such investigations. The researcher concluded, "Regardless of the particular dynamics that are discovered . . . no model of state high court decision making is complete without the essential variable of judicial role."[160]

Thus, whether judicial decisions are better explained by the legal model or by the democratic model depends not only on the nature of the cases and the state of the controlling law and precedents but also to some degree on how the individual judges evaluate these factors. In virtually every case that comes before them, judges must determine how much discretion they have and how they wish to exercise it. This is a subjective process, and as one research team put it, "activist judges will find more discretion in a given fact situation than will their more restrained colleagues."[161]

SUMMARY

Federal and state judges make millions of decisions each year, and scholars have sought to explain the thinking behind them. Two schools of thought provide explanations. One theory is based on the rules and procedures of the legal subculture. Judges' decisions, according to this model, are the product of traditional legal reasoning and adherence to precedent and judicial self-restraint. Another school of thought, the realist-behavioralist approach, holds that judges are influenced in their decision-making by such factors as party affiliation, local values and attitudes, public opinion, and pressures from the legislative and executive branches. In most cases, the legal subculture model is the more accurate predictor of judicial decision-making. However, stimuli from the democratic subculture often become useful in accounting for judges' decisions when (1) the legal evidence is contradictory or equally compelling on both sides; (2) the situation concerns new areas of the law and significant precedents are absent; and/or (3) judges are inclined to view themselves more as activist lawmakers than as law interpreters.

FURTHER THOUGHT AND DISCUSSION QUESTIONS

1. Should a judge's political party affiliation affect the way they make decisions on the bench? Most Americans would say "no," although they prefer to elect their judges and sometimes do this on a party basis. Is there an inherent inconsistency in these preferences?

2. Should judges' decisions reflect public opinion? Many Americans might find that idea offensive. However, even former Chief Justice William H. Rehnquist said it is inevitable and unavoidable that judges reflect public opinion in their decision-making at times. Sometimes, for example, trial judges are encouraged by the appellate courts to reflect the public mood in their decision-making.

3. Judges are much more likely in some situations than others to hand down decisions that reflect their personal values. What are the circumstances that allow one to predict whether a judge will render a decision "in accordance with the law" or in accordance with their personal attitudes?

SUGGESTED RESOURCES

Burton, Steven J. *An Introduction to Law and Legal Reasoning*, 3rd ed. New York, NY: Aspen Publishers, 2007. Explains what it has traditionally meant to "think like a judge"; explores the judicial reasoning process.

Carter, Lief H., and Thomas F. Burke. *Reason in Law*, 8th ed. New York, NY: Longman, 2009. A short, excellent discussion of how judges think and reason, and a good explication of the legal subculture.

Epstein, Lee, William M. Landes, and Richard Posner. *The Behavior of Federal Judges*. Cambridge, MA: Harvard University Press, 2013. A major empirical study of decision-making by judges in the federal courts.

O'Brien, David M. *Judges on Judging: Views from the Bench*, 5th ed. Washington, DC: CQ Press, 2016. A presentation of the judicial philosophies and political views of those on the bench. This volume includes "off-the-bench" writings and speeches in which judges discuss the judicial process, constitutional and statutory interpretation, and the role of the judiciary.

Posner, Richard A. *How Judges Think*. Cambridge, MA: Harvard University Press, 2008. A distinguished federal judge and judicial scholar explains the processes and calculations that judges employ in arriving at their judicial decisions.

Richardson, Richard J., and Kenneth N. Vines. *The Politics of Federal Courts: Lower Courts in the United States*. Boston, MA: Little, Brown, 1970. A classic discussion of the influences of both the legal subculture and the democratic subculture on judicial decision-making.

Rowland, C. K., and Robert A. Carp. *Politics and Judgment in Federal District Courts*. Lawrence: University Press of Kansas, 1996. A comprehensive study of decision-making at the federal district court level, based on a large data sample.

Tanenhaus, Joseph, and Walter F. Murphy. *The Study of Public Law*. New York, NY: Random House, 1972. Systematically discusses the history of public law and examines the various approaches to its study.

KEY TERM

judicial realists

13 DECISION-MAKING IN COLLEGIAL COURTS

CHAPTER GOALS AND OBJECTIVES

In this chapter, readers will learn that . . .

- Decision-making by multimember appellate courts has different dynamics than decision-making by trial court judges.
- The rulings of collegial courts are often influenced by the interactions among the judges on the bench.
- Scholars have developed a variety of effective empirical approaches to better understand decision-making by multimember courts.

Until now, we have treated decision-making by American judges at all levels as if it were essentially the product of the same two influences—the legal and the democratic subcultures. To a substantial degree, this is a valid approach. Jurists on multijudge appellate courts adhere to the same legal reasoning process as do their colleagues on the trial court bench. Lower court judges may be influenced in close cases by their political party affiliation, just as members of the appeals courts are. But before an analysis of judicial decision-making can be complete, one vital difference between trial courts and the state and federal appellate courts must be recognized. The former render decisions that are largely the product of a single individual, whereas the latter, as **collegial courts**, make decisions through group interaction. As one former trial judge, and subsequently a member of an appellate court, said,

> The transition between a district judge and circuit judge is not an easy one, primarily because of, shall I say, the autocratic position occupied by the district court judge. He is the sole decider. He decides as he sees fit, and files the decision in a form as he sees fit. A Court of Appeals decides by committee. One of the first traumas I had was when opinions were sent back by the other judges asking me to add this sentence, change that, etc., to get concurrence. I admit at the beginning I resisted that. It was pride. I learned it was a joint project, but it was a tricky thing. I see the same in others.[1]

What are the extra ingredients that go into a decision made by the nine-member Supreme Court or by a three-judge state appellate panel? What is the essence of the

The nine members of the US Supreme Court do much of their work—and debating—in their private conference room. The justices typically gather twice a week, and their meeting is completely private: only the nine jurists are present. No public notes or transcripts of the conference are made available, thus enabling the justices to be candid with one another.

Steve Petteway, Collection of the Supreme Court of the United States

dynamics of multijudge decision-making that distinguishes it from a judgment made by a single jurist? We discuss several theoretical approaches that have attempted to get a handle on this slippery subject. Although we continue to address these phenomena as they affect both state and federal judges, the several judicial systems will not be treated as separate entities. There is no reason to believe that the variables and forces being explored affect state jurists and federal judges in separate ways. For example, when we contend that the group decision of a collegial court is often the product of personal interaction, there is no reason to believe that such interpersonal variables would be significantly different for the US Supreme Court or the highest tribunal of a given state.[2] An increasing amount of comparative data about appellate jurists in other countries reveal that some patterns of collegial court behavior may be international in nature.

CUE THEORY

If trial and appeals courts have jurisdiction over a case, the judges must render some type of decision on the merits. They have little discretion about the composition of their dockets. If the judges view a particular case as presenting a trivial question, they will not spend time agonizing over it, but they are still obliged to provide a formal ruling on the substance of the matter. Not so with the Supreme Court. Of the approximately seven thousand to eight thousand petitions presented to the Court each year,[3] the justices typically grant and hear oral argument on only around seventy-five to eighty cases. In the 2020–2021 term, the number was even lower: just sixty-seven decisions handed down that constituted formal opinions of the Court.[4] Since the enactment of legislation in 1988, which limited the mandatory jurisdiction of the Supreme Court,[5] the Court has exercised almost complete control over its own docket. That is, the justices decide which issues they want to tackle in each term and which ones are not ripe for adjudication or must be summarily dismissed for "want of a substantial federal question." This has importance because the issues on which the Supreme Court decides not to rule are often as significant as those it does choose to scrutinize. (The state supreme courts vary greatly in the amount of control they have over their dockets.[6])

Judicial scholars have sought to identify the reasons for giving special attention to some petitions while the rest never receive those important four votes needed to grant certiorari and decide the case. A pioneering study of this question was conducted by a research team during the 1960s.[7] Analysts began by examining the Court's official reasons for granting certiorari, as set forth in US Supreme Court Rule 17, which specifies that the Court may hear a case if (1) an appeals court has decided a point of local law in conflict with local decisions; (2) a court of appeals has departed from "the usual course of judicial proceedings"; (3) a conflict is perceived between a lower court decision and a Supreme Court precedent; (4) a conflict exists on a point of law among the various federal circuits; or (5) the Court feels it must have the final word on a particularly important question.

The research team tested these official reasons by comparing the cases for which certiorari was granted with those in which review was denied. The official reasons did not prove to be an accurate or useful guide to the Court's decision-making. For example, in more than 50 percent of the cases selected for review, the Court's official reason for its actions was that the cases were "important"—however that was defined. The researchers thought they could do better. They set out to identify certain key characteristics of the cases granted review as well as those denied it. They hoped to develop some predictive statements that were more precise and reliable than Rule 17. The result was **cue theory**.

Cue theory assumes that the Supreme Court justices have neither the time nor the desire to wade through myriad pages in the thousands of petitions presented to them each year. Therefore, they presumably must have developed some sort of shortcut to help them select the petitions. The researchers hypothesized that the justices must look for cues in each petition—readily identifiable characteristics that trigger a positive response as they skim through the cumbersome piles of legal documents. After all, people have their own cue theories as they go about their daily lives. People often keep a close eye out for key messages in their email "inbox," quickly sifting through the spam messages that frequently flood in. The research team reasoned that just as people look for cues in sorting through their daily mail, justices on the Supreme Court do likewise as they sort through the petitions for certiorari that arrive daily.

Of the several possible cues that the research team tested, three were found to be highly relevant. In order of importance, they were: (1) whether the US government was a party to a case and was asking for Court review; (2) whether a civil rights or civil liberties issue was debated; and (3) whether there was dissension among the judges in the court that had previously heard the case (or disagreement between two or more courts and government agencies). If a case contained all three cues, there was an 80 percent chance that certiorari would be granted; if none were present, the chance dropped to a mere 7 percent. Clearly, the researchers had developed a useful model to explain this one aspect of Supreme Court behavior.

Over the subsequent decades, judicial scholars have further tested, elaborated on, and revised cue theory. Some studies have found a relationship between the way the justices voted on a grant of certiorari and their eventual vote on the merits of the case at conference.[8] Additional studies have suggested that a fourth cue has considerable weight—the ideological direction of the lower court decision.[9] Justices may be more inclined to hear a case if the lower court decision is inconsistent with the justice's own ideological preferences. Why? Because they may be particularly keen on overturning the lower court's ruling, seeing it as being decided in error.[10] But note that these trends are just that: trends, and they may not always hold. For example, one study of the Rehnquist Court found that the justices in the late 1980s did not engage in much "error correction" activity—that is, overturning lower court decisions with which it disagreed. Instead, the Court at that time chose to affirm a tremendous percentage of conservative lower court decisions with which it was in ideological harmony, thereby underscoring the values inherent in these cases.[11] No studies have been done yet on the application of cue theory to the Roberts Court, but there is nothing to suggest that the current Court is markedly different from previous ones in this respect.

Cue theory, then, may be one predictor of high court voting behavior. One judicial scholar effectively summarized the certiorari behavior of the Court during the past several decades:

> When the civil rights movement was building in importance (1950s), the Supreme Court, under the leadership of Chief Justice Earl Warren, paid special attention to cases involving civil liberties violations, and during the 1960s various underdog appellants, such as aliens, minorities, criminal defendants, laborers, and other have-nots, were more successful than others in getting certiorari. However, as the Supreme Court has shifted toward the conservatives, upperdogs such as governments at all levels and businesses have received more attention by the Supreme Court.[12]

SMALL-GROUP ANALYSIS

As applied to the judiciary, most **small-group analysis** is based on the thesis that judges want to influence the judgments of their colleagues and to be on the winning side as often as possible. This school of thought assumes that judges' positions are not written in stone from the start but are susceptible to moderation or even to a 180-degree turn on occasion. More specifically, scholars believe that a good deal of interaction and conflict takes place among justices from the time a case is first discussed in conference to the moment the final decision is rendered in open court some weeks or months later.[13] One researcher has referred to the appellate judges' openness to change as **fluidity**.[14]

The way judges relate to one another affects their behavior on the court. This, in turn, has led many to argue that the inclusion of diverse viewpoints and perspectives on the bench will inevitably have a positive impact upon the nature of judicial decision-making. The Brennan Center, a liberal but nonpartisan law and policy institute, puts it succinctly in their claim that "diversity on the bench is an essential component of a fair and impartial judiciary. Bringing a range of experiences and perspectives to bear allows judges to make better informed decisions and increases public confidence in their rulings."[15] Most scholars agree and multiple studies have been published that demonstrate that the presence of judges on the bench who are "nontraditional" (i.e., women and/or members of racial or ethnic minority groups) can significantly impact the judicial decision-making process.[16]

Examination of the personal papers of members of the Supreme Court, interviews with appellate court jurists, and reminiscences of former law clerks all reveal the impact of group dynamics on voting behavior and the content of written opinions.[17] Two characteristics in particular seem to carry weight when justices seek to influence their colleagues: personality and intellect. Judges who are viewed as warm, good-hearted, fair-minded, and so on seem able to put together winning coalitions and hammer out compromises a bit more effectively than colleagues with a reputation for condescension, self-righteousness, hostility, or vindictiveness.[18] As one researcher put it after interviewing state supreme court justices in Louisiana, Massachusetts, New Jersey, and Pennsylvania:

> Generally, the judges believed it is important for court members to moderate their own personal idiosyncrasies to maintain as much harmony in the group as possible. Such things as arrogance, pride, sense of superiority, and loss of temper were condemned. A pleasing personality . . . can be particularly important on collegial courts because the judges interact on a continuous basis: they operate as a small, permanent committee.[19]

This reflection on human nature should come as no surprise. A student who had served on his university's multimember student court provided an illustration of this phenomenon, and although a student tribunal is certainly not a state or federal appellate court, the interpersonal dynamics are similar:

> We had this guy on the court who was one of these people that you just kind of naturally take to. I mean, he had a good sense of humor and was decent and outgoing. I don't think he was that much of a "brain" or anything, but you always felt that he honestly wanted to do the right thing. Well, when we were split on some case—especially on matters of what punishment to hand

down—and he suggested a way out, I think we all listened carefully to what he thought was fair. He was just that sort of person.

The other personal attribute that is part of small-group dynamics is the knowledge and intellectual capacity of the individual judge.[20] A justice with a superior intellect or wide experience in a particular area of the law has a good deal more clout than a jurist who is seen as an intellectual lightweight. As one appeals court judge observed:

> Personality doesn't amount to so much as opinion-writing ability. Some judges are simply better than others. Some know more, think better. It would be strange if among nine [persons] all had the same ability. Some simply have more respect than others. That's bound to be so in any group. The first thing, is the judge particularly broad and experienced in the field? A couple of judges are acknowledged masters in admiralty. What they think carries more weight. I don't have much trouble being heard on criminal law or state government. I've been there. Ex-district judges on Courts of Appeals certainly carry more weight in discussion of trial procedures, instructions to juries, etc. Every judge is recognized for a particular proficiency obtained before or after his appointment. It saves enormous spadework and drudgery [to assign opinions accordingly]. No one could develop an expertise in all these fields.[21]

In 2020, judicial interactions faced a virtually unprecedented challenge when the COVID-19 pandemic affected tribunals throughout the United States. Most courts, including the US Supreme Court, halted in-person meetings and courthouse gatherings. But by necessity much of their work continued, with judges often meeting virtually, utilizing online video-conferencing technology such as Zoom, Skype, and/or Microsoft Teams, and sometimes, as in the case of the US Supreme Court, via conference telephone call. This inevitably had an impact upon how judges worked together. Appellate court panels were able to function reasonably well via this technology, though at least some adaptation was necessary. For example, instead of the talkative back-and-forth discussions that typically mark US Supreme Court oral arguments—interactions that Justice Clarence Thomas previously likened to a boisterous TV game show ("We look like *Family Feud*," the reserved jurist once noted)—oral arguments during the pandemic were a staider series of one-at-a-time questions individually posed to and answered by counsel.[22]

Trial courts, on the other hand, faced bigger challenges presented by the pandemic. Most jury trials were restricted or delayed, in-person proceedings were suspended, and deadlines were extended. A court official in one state noted that "The court system in Texas has responded really well in everything except jury trials. It's not really possible or feasible to have a lot of people in a room."[23] At the same time, some judges viewed the pandemic as a jolt that could spur positive change and reform. Michigan Chief Justice Bridget Mary McCormack said that "the pandemic was not the disruption we wanted, but the disruption we needed."[24] How these various COVID-19–based changes impacted the working of the courts will likely be studied by scholars in the future. But all signs indicate that small-group interactions adapted to, but did not end with, the pandemic.

Regardless, the fact remains that techniques or strategies that judges use in their conscious (or even unconscious) efforts to maximize their impact on multijudge courts can be grouped in three broad categories: persuasion on the merits, bargaining, and threat of sanctions. Although the tactics overlap and are inherently interrelated, each has a different focus.

Persuasion on the Merits

The strategy of persuasion on the merits means that, because of their training and values, judges are open to persuasion based on sound legal reasoning bolstered by legal precedents. Unless judges have taken a fixed position from the start, most can be swayed by an articulate and well-reasoned argument from a colleague with a differing opinion.

One study of the Supreme Court concluded that the justices

> can be persuaded to change their minds about specific cases as well as about broad public policies, and intellectual persuasion can play a significant role in such shifts.... Repeatedly positions first taken at conference are changed as other Justices bring up new arguments. Perhaps most convincing in demonstrating the impact of intellectual factors are the numerous instances on record in which the Justice assigned the opinion of the Court has reported back to the conference that additional study had convinced him that he and the rest of the majority had been in error.[25]

For example, Justice Robert Jackson, hardly shy when it came to holding fast to a judicial point of view, once commented, "I have changed my opinion after reading the opinions of the other members of this Court. And I am as stubborn as most. But I sometimes wind up not voting the way I voted in conference because the reasons of the majority didn't satisfy me."[26] Judges on state appellate courts appear to be just as willing to have their positions altered by arguments seasoned by precedent and sound judicial reasoning. After interviews with supreme court justices in four states, one scholar observed:

> When differences become evident, members of the court may attempt to persuade other judges to adopt their view by vigorously presenting their position or arguing the merits of their way of analyzing the case. Because of different amounts of influence exerted by the chief justice or by judges who have special personal status on the court, certain members of the court may be "persuaded" to abandon their own position and adopt the views of others.[27]

The persuasion on merits strategy has its limits, however. If the facts and legal arguments are straightforward, a justice may not be open to change. And judges who are deeply committed to a specific point of view or whose egos are sufficiently great will probably be impervious to legal arguments inconsistent with their own views. For instance, Thurgood Marshall and (later in his career) Harry A. Blackmun were profoundly and morally opposed to the principle of capital punishment and often said so in their opinions. It is doubtful that any amount of legal reasoning or any calling up of "sacred precedents" could have altered their belief that executions constitute "cruel and unusual punishment" by contemporary standards.

Bargaining

Bargaining may be a strange word to use in talking about the personal interactions of judges on collegial courts. When students first hear the term, they often think of the vote-trading technique called logrolling that legislators sometimes use. For example, one lawmaker might say to another, "If you vote for a new federally funded transportation project in my district, I'll vote to increase spending on the federal research center in yours." Is this what happens with judges as well? Is there evidence that they sometimes say to one another, "If you vote for me in this case, I'll decide with you in one of your 'pet cases'"? No, there is virtually no such evidence. Bargaining does take place, but it is subtle and does not involve vote-swapping. Although some bargaining occurs in the give-and-take that goes on in conference, when the initial votes are taken, attention is largely focused on the scope and contents of the majority (or even the dissenting) opinion. One study of bargaining concluded that "in 58.8% of [the cases studied] members of the majority conference coalition bargained with the opinion author" and that, in the authors' opinion, "our results therefore suggest that justices are indeed rational actors—systematically making judgments about the most efficacious tactic to secure favored outcomes."[28] A study published in 2007 concluded that opinion assignment is "a critical element of judicial strategy" with regard to how the Supreme Court hands down decisions.[29] More to the point, it is hard to overstate how important bargaining is in the decision-making process on collegial courts.

To understand how the bargaining process works, it is important to realize that usually much more is at stake in the outcome of a decision than merely whether party A or party B wins. Judges also must discuss such questions as these: How broad should the decision be? Should they suggest in their written opinion that this case is unique, or should they open the gates and encourage other suits of this nature? Should they overturn what appears to be the controlling precedent, or should they "distinguish around" it and let the precedent stand? Should they base their decision on constitutional grounds, or should they allow the victor to win on more technical and restrictive grounds? In other words, most decisions at the appellate level are not zero-sum games in which the winner automatically takes all. Important supplementary issues almost always must be discussed or bargained for.

The landmark 1973 abortion rights cases provide a good example. In its famous *Roe v. Wade* ruling, along with the companion case *Doe v. Bolton*, the Supreme Court handed down a joint decision on the matter of abortion.[30] To most citizens, the only issue the Court had to decide was whether abortion is legal. Although that may have been the bottom-line issue, many others were at stake, and the bargaining over them among the majority justices was intense.[31] What is human life, and when does it begin? Should the decision rest on the Ninth Amendment, or should it be based on the Due Process Clause of the Fourteenth Amendment? Does a fetus have any constitutional rights? Does a woman face a greater health risk in having an abortion than in delivering a child after carrying it to full term? Can a woman decide to have an abortion on her own, or does a physician have to concur? If the latter, how many doctors must concur? And this by no means completes the list.

The justices spent more than a year trying to hammer out a decision on the abortion cases that would be acceptable to a majority. Draft opinions were sent around, altered, and changed again, as the official opinion writer, Justice Blackmun, tried to accommodate all views—or at least not offend someone in the majority so strongly that he would join the dissenters. Bob Woodward and Scott Armstrong noted in their book, *The Brethren: Inside the Supreme Court,* that the law clerks "in most chambers were surprised to see the Justices, particularly Blackmun, so openly brokering their decision like a group of legislators."[32] But the law clerks themselves were not immune to the bargaining process. In the Supreme Court's cafeteria, law library, and gymnasium, the clerks asked one another whether "your Justice" could go along with this or that compromise or related that "my Justice" would never support an opinion containing such and such offensive clause.

Bargaining of this nature is just as common on state collegial courts as it is at the national level. This statement by one state supreme court justice is quoted by a scholar who regards it as typical:

> You might say to another judge that if you take this line out, I'll go along with your opinion. You engage in a degree of compromise and if it doesn't hurt the point you're trying to make in an opinion, you ought to agree to take it out. The men will write an opinion and circulate it. And then the other judges will write a letter or say at conference, can you change this or that, adjust the language here, etc. Your object is to get a unanimous court. That's always best.[33]

In a massive portion of appellate court cases, then, bargaining is the name of the game; it is one way in which a group of jurists, in a unanimous or majority opinion, can present a united front. The author of one classic study focusing on the Supreme Court observed,

> For Justices, bargaining is a simple fact. Despite conflicting views on literary style, relevant precedents, procedural rules, and substantive policy, cases must be settled, and opinions written, and no opinion may carry the institutional label of the court unless five Justices agree to sign it. In the process of judicial decision-making, much bargaining may be tacit, but the pattern is still one of negotiation

> and accommodation to secure consensus. Thus, how to bargain wisely—not necessarily sharply—is a prime consideration for a Justice who is anxious to see his policy adopted by the Court. A Justice must learn not only how to put pressure on his colleagues but how to gauge what amounts of pressure are sufficient to be "effective" and what amounts will overshoot the mark and alienate another judge. In many situations a Justice must be willing to settle for less than he wants if he is to get anything at all. As [Louis] Brandeis once remarked, the "great difficulty of all group action, of course, is when and what concession to make."[34]

Appellate judges do most of their face-to-face bargaining at the three-judge conferences and then iron out the details of the opinion later, using the telephone and short memos. As with Supreme Court decision-making, a threat to dissent can often result in changes in the way the majority opinion is drafted:

> When a conservative minority sought to amend a middle-of-the-road compromise by which the 5th circuit achieved unanimity in the Mississippi school case, for example, a former legislator reportedly threatened to bolt to the left. "They came back into the fold in a hurry," a colleague remarked. "So, you see, the judicial process is like legislation. All decisions are compromises."[35]

Of course, some judges are better at bargaining than others. When Supreme Court Justice Antonin Scalia died in 2016, he was praised for his intellectual leadership in promoting the originalist approach to interpreting the Constitution. But Scalia wasn't especially effective in building coalitions on the bench. As one observer noted:

> The great shapers of law are the justices who excel at building majorities in support of their opinions. This involves a lot of strategy, a fair amount of give-and-take, a knack for compromise. Scalia served for 20 years with one of the masters of this approach, retired Justice Sandra Day O'Connor . . . Scalia was nothing like [O'Connor]. Fiercely committed to his "originalist" philosophy, in which the meaning of the Constitution never changes with changing times, Scalia was allergic to compromise. He stuck fast to even his most awkward positions . . . He preferred writing a pure and knife-edged dissent, no matter how lonely, to the sort of pureed mumbo-jumbo that sometimes results from blending competing ideas into a single majority opinion. . . .[36]

The current chief justice, John G. Roberts, certainly seems to understand the dynamics of bargaining well. In a 2009 decision involving the Voting Rights Act,[37] the Supreme Court surprised many observers when the majority upheld challenged provisions of the voter law. Conservatives had hoped for a win that would have scaled back the law but were disappointed when the Court failed to do so. Based on a reading of the opinions, Court followers were able to infer that swing justice Anthony Kennedy was reluctant to join Roberts in agreeing to a major overturning of the law. This, they concluded, led the chief justice to hand down a narrower ruling that avoided a conservative defeat but was able to command a sizable majority. Most scholars had little doubt that if Roberts had had Kennedy's vote, he would have gone further in trying to overturn the law. Constitutional law scholar Doug Kmiec observed that "[w]hen [Chief Justice Roberts] can get five justices, when he can persuade Justice Kennedy in particular to come to the conservative side, he takes that victory as far as he can."[38] Indeed, since this 2009 ruling, Roberts seems to have acted much as Kmiec suggested. Justice Kennedy retired in 2017 and was replaced by Neil Gorsuch, who has proven to be more reliably conservative on voting rights cases. In 2021, the Court handed down a conservative ruling in the case of *Brnovich v. Democratic National Committee*,[39] which "gutted most of what remains of the landmark Voting Rights Act. The Court's decision, while leaving some protections involving redistricting in place, left close to a dead letter the law once hailed as the most effective civil rights legislation in the nation's history."[40] With a reliably conservative majority under his control, Roberts could shift sharply to the right and no longer had to bargain to compose a majority opinion.

Threat of Sanctions

In addition to persuasion on the merits and bargaining, there is one other tactic that jurists use in their efforts to maximize their impact on multimember appellate tribunals—the threat of sanctions. Basically, three sanctions against colleagues can be invoked: the vote, the willingness to write a strong dissenting opinion, and the threat to "go public."

The Judge's Vote. The threat to withdraw one's vote from the majority, and thus dissent, may cause the majority to alter its views. For example, in 1889, Justice Horace Gray sent this message to Justice Samuel Miller:

> After a careful reading of your opinion in *Shotwell v. Moore*, I am deeply sorry to be compelled to say that the first part of it . . . is so contrary to my conviction, that I fear, unless it can be a good deal tempered, I shall have to deliver a separate opinion on the lines of the enclosed memorandum. I am particularly troubled about this, because, if my scruples are not removed, and Justices Field, Bradley and Lamar adhere to their dissent, your opinion will represent only four judges, half of those who took part in the case.[41]

His back against the wall because of the narrow majority, Justice Miller was obliged to yield to his colleague's costly "scruples."

For the most part, the potential effect of a threat to dissent from the majority depends on how small that majority is. If the initial vote of a three-judge appellate panel was 3–0, one member's threat to dissent would not be all that serious; there would still be a 2–1 majority. Conversely, if at a preliminary Supreme Court conference, the vote was 5–4, the threat to defect by one of those five would be of concern to the remaining four. If one jurist occupies a pivotal position on a closely divided Court, that judge has the potential to exert an especially outsized influence via their vote.

Consider, for example, the pivotal role that Justice Anthony Kennedy played for many years on the Supreme Court. During the Court's 2017–2018 term, Kennedy voted with the majority in divided cases more than 92 percent of the time, the most of any justice on the Court.[42] Such influence was not unusual for the justice; in the 2006–2007 term, Kennedy joined the majority in *all* its 5–4 decisions. In the important Second Amendment case of *DC v. Heller* in 2008, Kennedy insisted upon including language in the majority opinion that the decision "should not be taken to cast doubt" on many kinds of existing gun control laws. With a narrow 5–4 majority on his side, gun control opponent Justice Antonin Scalia, who wrote the opinion, was obliged to accommodate Kennedy's request lest the majority in the case flip and the outcome change.[43] One law professor once called Kennedy "The Decider" because his vote was often pivotal to the outcome of so many cases.[44] Indeed, Justice Kennedy's role on the Court was considered so important that one research team who studied the Court's rulings suggested that Justice Kennedy acted as a "supermedian justice" in whose hands often sat the judicial balance of the nation's highest court.[45] There is some indication that Justice Brett Kavanaugh, who was appointed to the Court in 2018 by Republican President Donald Trump, may be following in Kennedy's swing-vote footsteps. In the 2020–2021 term, Justice Kavanaugh was likely to join the Democratic appointees to the Court 85 percent of the time.[46] In fact, Kavanaugh joined the majority—on either the liberal or conservative side—in 97 percent of the cases decided that year.[47] In the 2022–2023 term he was in the majority in 96 percent of cases, leading the *Wall Street Journal* to declare that Kavanaugh had become a "swing justice" on the Court.[48]

The judicial papers of Thurgood Marshall also provide a colorful example of how pivotal one justice's vote can be. In 1989, the Court decided to take the case of *Webster v. Reproductive Health Services*, which dealt with the constitutionality of a Missouri law severely restricting abortions.[49] Many Court observers believed that a viable conservative majority on the Court could strike down the 1973 *Roe v. Wade* and *Doe v. Bolton* decisions, which established the constitutional right to an abortion. Justice Marshall's informal tally sheet, dated April 28, indicated five tentative initial votes to uphold the Missouri law: Justices William H. Rehnquist, Byron White, Antonin Scalia, Kennedy, and Sandra Day O'Connor. Rehnquist assigned the majority opinion to himself, and Justice Blackmun penned a bitter dissent in which he said, in part, that the right to abortion "no longer survives."

> Over the course of two months, in flurries of court memos, the justices traded views and language. Throughout, O'Connor remained the pivotal swing vote. But she couldn't bring herself to join Rehnquist. Within days of the end of the term, O'Connor changed her mind. She signaled her switch when she wrote that *Roe* was "problematic," rather than "outmoded," as she had said in an earlier draft.[50]
>
> Nonetheless,

on June 27, Rehnquist circulated his fourth draft. The document still said, "Chief Justice Rehnquist delivered the opinion of the Court," traditional wording indicating that he had not given up his hopes of getting O'Connor's support. Then something definitive happened to the Rehnquist majority. On June 28, O'Connor and Blackmun submitted drafts referring to the Rehnquist opinion as a "plurality," rather than a majority.[51]

The next day, Rehnquist circulated his final draft, in which, for the first time, he called his opinion the "judgment" of the Court instead of the majority opinion—meaning, in effect, that the Missouri law would be upheld but there would be no reversal of *Roe v. Wade* at that time. This illustration shows vividly how important a single justice's vote can be when the Court is split evenly between two ideological camps.

And the justices certainly may follow through on their threats to withdraw their votes. For example, Court insiders leaked the news that during the 2023–2024 term, Justice Samuel Alito lost the votes of two of his fellow justices in a key, high-profile case. After prevailing in a vote at conference, Alito's "hardline" approach to writing the majority opinion backfired and alienated two of his colleagues. This ultimately left him on the losing side of a 6–3 ruling in a case involving the First Amendment rights of social media companies.[52]

Sometimes, however, the impact of one's vote is not merely a function of how divided the Court is. On occasion, the perceived need for unanimity may be so strong that any justice's threat to vote against the prevailing view may have a disproportionate effect. For example, before the 1954 *Brown v. Board of Education* decision, a majority on the Supreme Court opposed segregation in the schools. Chief Justice Earl Warren and the other liberal justices believed, however, that a simple majority was not enough to confront the backlash expected if segregation were struck down. Only a unanimous Court, they felt, would have any chance of seeing its will prevail throughout the nation. Therefore, the liberal majority bided its time during the early 1950s until the moment came when all nine justices were willing to take on the malignant giant of racial segregation.

Another example occurred in the 1990s when President Bill Clinton, the former governor of Arkansas, wished to postpone the sexual harassment suit brought against him by former Arkansas state employee Paula Jones. He argued that presidents should be immune to such troublesome and time-consuming litigation during their tenure in the White House. But the Supreme Court disagreed, handing down a unanimous decision that went against the president. Speaking for the majority, Justice John Paul Stevens said, in part:

> We think the District Court may have given undue weight to the concern that a trial might generate unrelated civil actions that could conceivably hamper the President in conducting the duties of his office. When that should occur, the court's discretion would permit it to manage those actions in such fashion

> (including deferral of trial) that interference with the President's duties would not occur. But no such impingement upon the President's conduct of his office was shown here.[53]

The decision was important not only for the opinion it expressed but also because the vote was unanimous; even the president's two Supreme Court appointees (Ruth Bader Ginsburg and Stephen G. Breyer) voted against him. A unanimous vote coming from the ideologically divided Rehnquist Court underscored the legal principle involved in the case, and it quashed any notion that partisan politics was a variable in the decision. The defection of just a single vote, while not changing the outcome, would have detracted from the decisive impact of a totally unified Court.

State judges, too, may feel the need for unanimity in certain types of cases. For example, one New Jersey Supreme Court justice told a researcher: "We did have a case where we felt a unanimous opinion was necessary. No one felt strongly about a dissent, so no dissents were made. A religious case, for example, needs a unanimous decision. Courts don't try to be divisive on this."[54] Although the impact of the threat to abandon the majority is usually in direct proportion to the closeness of the vote, occasions arise when a majority will pay top dollar to keep any judge or justice from breaking ranks. That is, the majority may accommodate the contents and scope of its majority opinion to suit the demands of the minority justices to get them to join the final opinion and make it unanimous.

The Willingness to Write a Strong Dissent. There are dissents, and there are dissents. Appellate court jurists who intend to vote against the majority must decide whether to write a lengthy, assertive dissenting opinion or merely dissent without opinion. If jurists are not regarded by other justices—or by the public at large—as being prestigious or articulate, their threat to write a dissenting opinion may be taken with the proverbial grain of salt. If, however, potential dissenters are respected jurists with a reputation for a keen intellect or for often being right overall, the situation is different. The other judges may be willing to alter their views to accommodate potential dissenters' positions or at least dissuade them from attacking the majority position. As one Court observer has noted:

> There are factors which push the majority Justices, especially the opinion writer, to accept accommodation. An eloquent, tightly reasoned dissent can be an upsetting force. [Harlan Fiske] Stone's separate opinions during the thirties pointed up more sharply the folly of the conservative Justices than did any of the attacks on the Court by elected politicians. The majority may thus find it profitable to mute criticism from within the Court by giving in on some issues.[55]

Thus, the second sanction—the threat to write a dissenting opinion—depends on the circumstances for its effectiveness. Sometimes it may be regarded as no more than a nuisance or the fruit of judicial egomania. On other occasions, it may be viewed as likely to weaken the impact of the majority opinion.

In the latter years of his extensive career, conservative Justice Antonin Scalia became well known for using colorful and combative language in some of his blistering opinions disagreeing with the Court majority. In *King v. Burwell*, Scalia's dissent in that key 2015 case concerning the Affordable Care Act suggested that the majority's ruling upholding the law was "jiggery-pokery" (an old-fashioned term for something that is dishonest manipulation or nonsense) and called it "pure applesauce."[56] Scalia was especially blistering when it came to cases involving gay and lesbian rights. In *Lawrence v. Texas*,[57] a 2003 case that overturned a Texas law that criminalized gay sex, Scalia wrote angrily:

> the [Supreme] Court has taken sides in the culture war, departing from its role of assuring, as neutral observer, that the democratic rules of engagement are observed. Many Americans do not want persons who openly engage in gay conduct as partners in their business, as scoutmasters for their children, as teachers in their children's schools, or as boarders in their home. They view this as protecting themselves and their families from a lifestyle that they believe to be immoral and destructive.

And in *Obergefell v. Hodges*, the landmark case in which the Court upheld gay marriage rights, Scalia warned apocalyptically in his dissent that "I write separately to call attention to this Court's threat to American democracy."[58]

In state courts, the power of the threat to write a strong dissent differs significantly from state to state because the dissent rate varies highly. A 2009 study found that in state supreme courts with substantial discretionary jurisdiction, the percentage of cases with at least one dissent ranged from about 81 percent in Mississippi to only about 4 percent in Nebraska and Massachusetts. In state supreme courts with substantial mandatory jurisdiction, dissent rates ranged from 60 percent in Mississippi to less than 2 percent in Kansas.[59] This research reported that nationally, around 27 percent of cases heard on discretionary review by state supreme courts generated at least one dissenting opinion.[60] Logic would suggest that in states and situations where dissenting opinions are less common, the threat to write a stinging contradictory opinion would carry greater weight than in instances where dissents and disagreements are routine.

Of course, there are limits to how far a dissenting judge can take it. Overly harsh dissents may alienate peers and may prove to be counterproductive. For example, regarding outspoken Justice Scalia, a former law school dean observed:

> [Scalia's] ability to build coalitions is hampered by his snarky, one-liner, Borscht-Belt approach to writing judicial opinions. No one that has served with him approaches their job that way . . . If you have a crazy uncle pounding on the table when you are looking for nuanced middle ground, after a while you may stop listening entirely.[61]

The Threat to "Go Public." On rare occasions an appellate judge may use the ultimate weapon against colleagues—public exposure. Such strong medicine is usually administered only when a jurist believes a colleague (or a group of judges) has violated the basic rules of the game. The judge then threatens to hang out the dirty linen for all to see. For example, one appeals court judge told how, as a newcomer to the bench, he had threatened public exposure to force a senior colleague to withdraw an opinion filed without obtaining the permission of the new judge to include him in the opinion—a possibility he had been warned of by another judge on the court: "It was my first sitting as a circuit judge," he recalled. "It was not a major case. But there was strong give and take!"[62]

Consider, too, this example. When the vote was taken at conference on the landmark 1973 abortion cases (*Roe v. Wade*, considered jointly with *Doe v. Bolton*), Chief Justice Warren Burger was in the minority. According to Supreme Court practice, this meant that the senior member of the majority—in this case William O. Douglas—would have been assigned to speak for the Court. Ignoring Court protocol, Burger assigned the official opinion writing to his alter ego, Justice Blackmun. This enraged Douglas. But the pot did not boil over until several months later, when Burger lobbied from his minority status to have the case postponed until the next term. (Douglas wanted the decision to be handed down immediately.) These extracts from *The Brethren* capture something of the drama of the confrontation:

> This time Douglas threatened to play his ace. If the conference insisted on putting the cases over for reargument, he would dissent from such an order, and he would publish the full text of his dissent. Douglas reiterated the protest he had made in December about the Chief's assigning the case to Blackmun, Burger's response and his subsequent intransigence. . . . Douglas . . . continued: "When, however, the minority seeks to control the assignment, there is a destructive force at work in the Court. When a Chief Justice tries to bend the Court to his will by manipulating assignments, the integrity of the institution is imperiled."
>
> Douglas's pen then became more acid:
>
> Borrowing a line from a speech he had given in September in Portland, Douglas then made it clear that, despite what he had said earlier, he did in fact view the Chief and Blackmun as Nixon's Minnesota Twins. "Russia once gave its Chief Justice two votes; but that was too strong even for the Russians."[63]

Douglas was ultimately prevailed on to refrain from publishing this petulant opinion.

Sometimes judges can even "go public" anonymously via the press. Consider the 2012 example when the Supreme Court handed down its landmark ruling in *NFIB v. Sebelius* upholding by a 5–4 vote President Barack Obama's signature health care law.[64] A reporter for *CBS News* obtained a major "scoop" when she reported from reliable sources inside the Court, just days after the decision was announced, that Chief Justice

John Roberts had switched his vote in the case.[65] Revelations to the press of "behind-the-scenes" ruminations on the Court are virtually unheard of, especially so soon after the handing down of a ruling. The effect of this leak was viewed by some as an attempt by conservatives on the Court to discredit Roberts and to mete out a form of punishment to him for what many felt was a huge betrayal.[66]

The threat to go public is probably a less potent weapon at the state level than it is for federal judges—particularly Supreme Court justices—because state appellate courts are generally much less visible to the public except in the most unusual and controversial cases. If a judge on a typical state appellate court were to threaten to go public and reveal some irregularity to which they had been subjected, the jurist might be told, "So, who cares?"

Despite the availability of several sanctions, they are usually invoked with varying degrees of hesitation, lest a judge or justice acquire a reputation for intransigence. For example, regarding a justice's willingness to write a dissenting opinion, one perceptive scholar has noted:

> Although dissent is a cherished part of the common law tradition, a Justice who persistently refuses to accommodate his views to those of his colleagues may come to be regarded as an obstructionist. A Justice whose dissents become levers for legislative or administrative action reversing judicial policies may come to be regarded as disloyal to the bench.[67]

Putting it in more human terms, one appeals court judge observed that "you have to keep on living with each other. In the next case the situations may be reversed."[68] This sentiment was expressed bluntly by the well-respected conservative federal appeals court judge Richard Posner, who revealed dismay about the attack-via-leaks against Chief Justice Roberts in 2012:

> I think these right-wingers who are blasting Roberts are making a serious mistake. Because if you put [yourself] in his position . . . what's he supposed to think? That he finds his allies to be a bunch of crackpots? Does that help the conservative movement? I mean, what would you do if you were Roberts? All the sudden you find out that the people you thought where your friends have turned against you, they despise you, they mistreat you, they leak to the press. What do you do? Do you become more conservative? Or do you say, "What am I doing with this crowd of lunatics?" Right? Maybe you must re-examine your position.[69]

The Special Roles of the US Chief Justice, the US Chief Judges, and the State Supreme Court Chief Justices

The heads of the multijudge federal and state appellate tribunals have several special duties and responsibilities. Their respective roles constitute one more ingredient in the recipe for small-group interaction.

The Chief Justice of the United States. The Constitution makes only passing reference to the chief justice of the United States, whose stature has come to loom so large in the eyes of Court observers. Despite the constitutional slight, the chief justice can have considerable impact on the decision-making process. The key seems to be whether the chief justice possesses the capacity and the will to use the formal and informal powers that have accrued to the office during the past two centuries.

The chief justice's greatest potential for leadership is at the conference, where the cases are discussed, and the justices' initial votes are taken. Because the chief has the primary responsibility for setting the agenda of the conference and traditionally is the first to offer an opinion about each case, the potential for influencing both the format and the tone of the deliberation is significant. Scholar David J. Danelski identified two roles for justices at conference: **social leader** and **task leader**. The social leader "attends to the emotional needs of his associates by affirming their values as individuals and as Court members, especially when their views are rejected by the majority. Ordinarily he is the best liked member of the Court. In terms of personality, he is apt to be warm, receptive and responsive." The task leader, however, is the intellectual force behind the conference deliberations, focusing on the final decision and trying to keep the Court consistent with itself. Danelski describes how the two roles complement each other:

> As presiding officer of the conference, the Chief Justice is in a favorable position to assert task and social leadership. His presentation of cases is an important task function. His control of the conference's process makes it easy for him to invite suggestions and opinions, seek compromises, and cut off debate that appears to be getting out of hand, all important social functions.[70]

One observer, commenting on the transition from the Burger to the Rehnquist Court, noted the contrasts in leadership style:

> Differences are already apparent during oral arguments. Rehnquist is sharper, more thoughtful, more commanding and wittier than his predecessor in the center chair. And from the far right of the bench, Scalia almost bubbles over with energy and questions for counsel. No less revealing is that in the week before the start of the 1986–87 term on the first Monday in October, Rehnquist managed to get the justices to dispose of over 1,000 cases (granting 22 and denying or otherwise disposing of the rest). He did so in only two days, whereas it usually took Burger more than twice as long to get through about the same number.[71]

In addition to his task leadership abilities, Rehnquist was known for his social leadership skills. One scholar noted that Rehnquist was recognized as being "agreeable, affable, [and] well-liked."[72] His combination of administrative efficiency, friendly style, and powerful intellect made him an effective chief who skillfully presided over an often-divided Court.[73]

Chief Justice Roberts joined the Court in 2005, and initial reviews of his term in the center seat suggested that the chief "presid[ed] over the court with grace, wit, and meticulous preparation."[74] And after nearly twenty years on the Court, indications are that the chief justice remains well regarded by his peers. Early on, Roberts claimed that he wished to use his leadership position to forge consensus as much as possible, telling one reporter that he believed that most successful chief justices in American history have been able to persuade their colleagues to speak with one voice and avoid the deeply polarized 5–4 split decisions that make it hard for the Court to overcome the public perception that it is a politicized institution.[75]

However, more recently Roberts's claim has been tested and his leadership has come under some criticism. At the end of the 2020–2021 term, a prominent lawyer who argued cases frequently before the Court, Lisa S. Blatt, suggested that Roberts's leadership may have slipped a bit. Blatt observed that "the loss of control by the chief justice felt palpable" at the end of that term, suggesting that the Chief Justice Roberts may no longer be in the driver's seat.[76] Some recent developments hint that Blatt may be correct.

Roberts's declared desire at the start of his tenure to avoid sharp ideological divisions has, for the most part, not been realized. Throughout Roberts's tenure as chief, the Court has often exhibited significant rates of sharp disagreement.[77] And with a current majority of six justices appointed by Republican presidents, the Court has taken an activist stance toward jurisprudence. In a number of high-profile cases, the Supreme Court has handed down sharply divided conservative decisions overturning precedent on issues such as gun control, government regulation, presidential power, voting rights, andmost notablyabortion rights. Foremost among these polarized rulings was the Court's divided decision in *Dobbs v. Jackson Women's Health Organization* in 2022, which overturned *Roe v. Wade*. One respected Court observer noted that "[Roberts] is inevitably raising tensions by a series of polarized decisions, largely along ideological 6–3, conservative-liberal lines and his 'nothing to see here' mantra in the face of the court's unpopularity and ethics controversy. . . ."[78]

Even the release of the decision in *Dobbs* indirectly brought criticism upon the chief. Seven weeks prior to the ruling's announcement, in an event unprecedented in modern Court history, the draft language of the *Dobbs* majority opinion was leaked to the press. Chief Justice Roberts ordered an investigation to find the source of the leak, but the inquiry was criticized for not being independentit was conducted by the Marshal of the Court, who is answerable to and appointed by the Court itself. What's more, the investigation employed a double standard: unlike others working at the Court who were intensively interrogated, the justices themselves were not asked to sign sworn affidavits or have their personal cell phones scrutinized.[79] The inquiry ultimately failed to identify the perpetrator and the matter was closed. In an indirect swipe at Roberts's leadership, a former Justice Department official and scholar at the Brookings Institution said:

> the leak investigation [the Supreme Court] conducted demonstrates how not to conduct a leak investigation. It also illustrates, again, the need for internal

> oversight at the Court, which should have a better permanent capacity to police itself by more credibly investigating alleged misconduct and by identifying faulty procedures proactively. . . . It was an Alice in Wonderland investigation: The conclusion seemed to come first—let's focus on the clerks and employees, not the justices, as the likely source of the leak—rather than result from a consistent investigation focusing on all potential leakers.[80]

Roberts has also come under criticism for his less-than-aggressive stance toward ethics questions swirling around the Court. Justice Clarence Thomas has been questioned for, among other things, failing to disclose costly trips sponsored by a billionaire Republican megadonor and allegations that the justice did not pay back a $267,000 loan from a wealthy health insurance executive that Thomas used to purchase a deluxe motor home.[81] Justice Samuel Alito was also criticized for flying ideological flags outside of his Virginia home and New Jersey beach house, flags that were associated with the January 6 insurrection and efforts to overturn the 2020 election. Many experts called for the justices to voluntarily be bound by the mandatory Judicial Ethics Code, which applies to lower federal court judges and would prohibit the aforementioned actions. But Roberts refused and sidestepped the issue by having the Court release a statement in which the justices "reaffirm and restate" their commitment to ethical principles and signed on to nonbinding ethics guidelines. This fell short on several fronts, legal ethics experts said. They faulted the court for its decision not to adopt a formal code of conduct when public trust in the institution has dropped after such high-profile ethical concerns, as well as a public backlash to some of the Court's rulings on hot-button issues like abortion and guns.[82] "It's reflecting kind of a startling level of intransigence given the problems the court's confronted," said one law professor, noting that public support for the Court had plunged.[83]

Indeed, during Roberts's leadership public approval of the institution has taken a hit. In October 2023 an *ABC News* survey found that only 38 percent of Americans approved of the job the Court was doing, a result that was termed "dismal."[84] Gallup, a major polling organization that has tracked the question since 2000, reported in 2023 that Supreme Court approval was "at record low."[85] The number ticked up a bit in 2024,[86] but there's no question that, overall, the Court's approval has trended downward during much of Roberts's stewardship. An Associated PressNORC poll released at the end of June 2024 crystallized the issue: nearly four in ten respondents said they have hardly any confidence in the Court, and seven in ten said they believe the justices' decisions are motivated by ideology, not fairness and impartiality.[87] Similarly, a July 2024 *Fox News* poll also found Supreme Court approval at a record low, down twenty points since 2017.[88] Not coincidentally, in July 2024 President Joe Biden announced support for changes to the Court, including term limits for the justices and a mandatory ethics code.[89] Though the chances of these proposals passing in a deeply divided Congress were slim, it's hard to envision a president calling for significant institutional reform if the Court were in a stronger position vis-à-vis the public.

Of course, the justices have lifetime tenure and are largely immune from the ebbs and flows of electoral politics. But scholars have long noted that public approval of the Court is directly tied to the perceived legitimacy of the institution, upon which its authority ultimately rests. And as chief justice, John Roberts has a special responsibility in protecting the Supreme Court's position in the constitutional order. To be sure, the high court is not required to hand down decisions that are always popular. But it's a delicate balance, and losing the support of the public may ultimately be harmful to the institution. "They've got a potential legitimacy problem," said Charles Geyh, an Indiana University law professor and expert on judicial ethics. "The traditional notion that we will accept the results of the court whether we agree with it or not . . . is decreasingly the case. A lot of the ethics problems the court confronts fuel the perception that it is an organization more political than legal."[90] Indeed, in announcing his support for Court reform, President Biden claimed that the Court's "extremism is undermining the public confidence in the court's decisions."[91] In 2023, Erwin Chemerinsky, one the nation's foremost constitutional scholars and dean of the UC Berkeley Law School, criticized the chief justice in no uncertain terms, claiming that "time is running out for John Roberts and the Supreme Court."[92]

The chief justice may also have a key role in setting up what is called the discuss list—special petitions selected out of the many to which the Court will give full consideration. Chief Justice William Rehnquist described it this way:

> Shortly before each [conference of the justices], the Chief Justice sends out a list of the petitions he wishes to have discussed. After the Chief's "discuss list" has come around, each of the Associate Justices may ask to have additional cases put on this list. . . . The petitions . . . that are not discussed at conference are denied without any recorded vote. . . . [The] great majority of petitions . . . are never even discussed at conference and are simply denied without being taken up by the justices as a group.[93]

The chief's law clerks helped with this task, but the chief guided their judgment. Recent practice has seen most of the justices pool their law clerks and give a single clerk the authority to summarize a particular petition for all the justices participating in the pool. However, not all members of the Court may participate in this practice—for example, Justice Samuel A. Alito and former Justice John Paul Stevens had their individual law clerks screen all petitions and write memos only on those they deemed important enough for the justice to consider. Whether the chief justice chooses to play a major or minor role in this process, the activity is important because it helps to determine which cases the Court will consider as a group and which are to be summarily dismissed.[94] That said, since it is part of the Court's private internal deliberations, the discuss list is not made public and there is much that is unknown about the process. One source suggests that the number of cases that make it to the discuss list has shrunk considerably during the Roberts Court era.[95]

The final power of the chief justice is the assignment of opinions—that is, designation of who will write the official decision of the Court.[96] This task falls to the chief justice only if he is in the majority when the vote on a case is taken at conference; otherwise, the most senior justice in the majority selects the opinion writer. The chief justice has the greatest control over an opinion when he assigns it to himself, and traditionally, he has retained many important cases for that reason.[97] In such cases as *Marbury v. Madison, Brown v. Board of Education*, and *United States v. Nixon*, the chief justice used his option to speak as the official voice of the Court. The chief justice may assign himself the opinion more often in highly salient cases, and particularly those in which the Court is closely divided. Noted Supreme Court expert Linda Greenhouse observed that this is a strategy that Chief Justice Roberts, like many chief justices before him, has pursued.[98] For example, Roberts assigned himself the majority opinions in the highly salient Affordable Care Act (aka "Obamacare") cases *King v. Burwel*[99] and *NFIB v. Sebelius*.[100] When the chief justice chooses not to write the opinion, he may assign it to that member of the majority whose views are closest to the dissenters', with the hope that some of the minority may subsequently switch their votes to the majority view.[101] Or, as has most often been the case in recent decades, the chief justice may assign the opinion to an ideological alter ego so that the grounds for the decision will be favorable to his own. Because opinion assignment potentially involves a significant amount of strategic calculus, it is a subject that scholars have done much work investigating.[102] One study of opinion assignments made by Chief Justice Rehnquist indicated that he used this power for institutional rather than policy reasons. For example, he had an eye for evenly distributing the workload and assigning opinions to justices who had expertise in the subject matter of the case.[103] Chief Justice Roberts has reportedly also used his power to assign opinions to encourage his colleagues to write narrow decisions that justices on both sides can accept. Fellow Justice Antonin Scalia noted in 2008 that "the chief may say, 'Why don't you come along with a very narrow opinion? We can get seven votes for that, and it will look a lot better.' You want to go along with the Chief Justice because . . . you want to make the institution work. So, he has."[104]

Despite the considerable influence a chief justice may have on the Court's small group, the crucial factor seems to be whether the chief has both the capacity and the desire to exert such potential authority. For example, Chief Justice John Marshall, who is widely considered to be one of the greatest chiefs in the Court's history, possessed both these traits, which helped fill the intellectual vacuum on the Court during the early 1800s:

> Marshall, like many justices in the court's history, was an experienced politician. He guided the Court in a series of sweeping decisions through force of personality and a talent for negotiation. Justice William Johnson, a Jefferson appointee, grumbled to his patron about Marshall's dominance. Wondering why Marshall invariably wrote the Court's opinions, Johnson reported to Jefferson that he had "found out the real cause. [William] Cushing was

> incompetent. [Samuel] Chase could not be got to think or write. [William] Paterson was a slow man and willingly declined trouble, and the other two judges [Marshall and Bushrod Washington] you know are commonly estimated as one judge."[105]

Although John Marshall had the skill and the desire to influence the Court, not all his successors possessed these traits. For example, the nation's chief justice between 1941 and 1946, Chief Justice Harlan Fiske Stone, had neither the talent nor the will for task leadership and social leadership. As his biographer sadly wrote of him, "He was totally unprepared to cope with the petty bickering and personal conflict in which his court became engulfed."[106]

The Chief Judges of the US Appeals Courts. As with the chief justice, the leadership potential of the administrative circuit heads is determined, in part, by their intellectual and negotiating skills and their desire to put them to use.[107] In reality, however, their potential effect on their respective circuits is probably smaller than is the potential impact of the chief justice of the Supreme Court. First, because most appellate court decisions are made by three-judge panels on a rotating basis, the chief judge is not likely to be part of most circuit decision-making. Second, the circuits are more decentralized than the Supreme Court. Third, the chief judge is not nearly so prominent a figure in the eyes of the public or of other government decision-makers. As one former chief judge said about the job: "The only advantage is that the title sounds more imposing if you are speaking in public or writing an article. Otherwise, it's a pain in the ass."[108] Much of a chief judge's work is administrative (such as docketing cases, keeping financial records, adjusting caseloads), but administration and policymaking are not mutually exclusive endeavors. A chief judge of the US Fifth Circuit once acknowledged, "So many times judicial problems slop over into administrative problems and vice versa" that the real questions are when and where this effect occurs. Commenting on the influence of the chief judges, one observer said:

> As with strong presidents [or strong chief justices, he might have added] . . . the spillover depends on the personality of the chief and the countervailing force of experienced colleagues. The impact of chief judges was most noticeable on first-year students and the composition of three-judge district courts. ("If all the judges are new, he'll pack a wallop out of proportion to one vote.") Southern judges made no bones about packing three-judge district courts in race relations cases. ([The liberal] "[Elbert P.] Tuttle was not about to set up a three-judge court with [segregationists such as Benjamin F.] Cameron and [William H.] Cox on it; this occurs no more.") Of all administrative powers, plainly the most potent instruments of policy leadership involve the assignment of work.[109]

The State Supreme Court Chief Justices. To some extent, the powers and leadership potential of state chief justices mirror those of the US chief justice, but significant differences exist, not only between the federal and state levels but also from one state to another. At the national level, the chief justice is appointed by the president with the advice and consent of the Senate. In some states—Michigan, for example—the chief justice is chosen by fellow associate justices; in Ohio and Texas the chief justices are elected directly by the people.[110] In some other states, the chief is simply the justice with the most seniority. This issue became politicized in 2015 when Republicans led by Governor Scott Walker in Wisconsin pushed a ballot initiative in that state asking voters to change the way the chief was selected, from a seniority-based system to one in which the chief would be chosen by the court members. The incumbent chief at the time, Shirley Abrahamson, was widely viewed as a liberal, but many of the justices on the court were considered conservatives. Soon after the initiative was approved by the public, justices on the Wisconsin Supreme Court voted to wrest control of the center seat away from Abrahamson and handed the chief's gavel to a right-leaning justice.[111]

The states also differ regarding whether the chief justice has the most power in the assignment of opinions. Only four states, including Hawaii, closely follow the practice of the US Supreme Court in assigning opinions. In more than a quarter of the states the chief justice assigns opinions in all cases, whether they are in the majority.[112] Well over half of the states use an automatic method of opinion assignment, whereby a justice either draws cases by lot or, more often, receives them by rotation. In less than half of the twenty states that use the rotation system, the assignments hold only if the justice to whom the case is assigned is in the majority.

On the effectiveness of the chief justice under the different methods of opinion assignment, one scholar concluded:

> A chief justice who is an extraordinary leader can make the court perform more effectively and efficiently by using selective opinion assignment. A court without an extraordinary leader may be better served by a rotational method of assignment. Nondiscretionary methods best maintain social cohesion, but the chief justice's discretion in assigning opinions can best accomplish the efficient disposition of the workload.[113]

As with the US chief justice, however, nothing inherent in the office guarantees that a state supreme court chief justice will be an active and effective leader. Intellect, personality, political skills, and a fair degree of happenstance still interact and blend in mysterious ways to create chief justices whom court watchers' term either "great" or "ineffectual." On the positive side, there have been people such as Arthur Vanderbilt, who became chief justice of the New Jersey Supreme Court in 1948. As one scholar observed of him:

> Once installed as chief justice he had to contend with a set of judges who had served under the old constitution and did not fully share either his vision or his aims. Nevertheless, Vanderbilt provided impetus and direction to the

> movement for judicial reform in the state, and, as chief justice, he secured the gains of the reform movement, gave the court stature, and ensured it the independence it needed to play a significant role in the governance of the state. Despite the obvious differences, the comparison that springs to mind is with John Marshall, who—like Vanderbilt—assumed the leadership of a relatively moribund court and transformed it.[114]

On the negative side, examples can be cited of persons who came to the state high court bench with enormous potential but lacked the ability or the political savvy (and perhaps the luck) to provide leadership when confronted with opposition or political lethargy. For instance, when Frank D. Celebrezze headed the Ohio Supreme Court during the early 1980s, he blatantly politicized the court until he was driven from office by the voters in the 1986 election. One observer summarized the unhappy period of his chief justiceship:

> Squabbles on the Celebrezze court were important because, owing to the Celebrezze agenda, the court was important. The irony of Celebrezze's stewardship is that as his court attained prominence, his actions, so visible on so many fronts, brought the court as an institution into disrepute. During [Celebrezze's term as chief justice] Ohioans perceived their court as a "circus."[115]

Evidence of Small-Group Interaction

We have argued that small-group dynamics include persuasion on the merits between individual judges, bargaining among the appellate jurists, and the threat of sanctions—a judge changing their vote, a willingness to write a strong dissent, and (at least for federal judges) the threat to go public. We have also contended that US Supreme Court chief justices and chief judges of the appeals courts can potentially affect the decision-making of their respective small judicial groups. The evidence for this cited thus far has largely been anecdotal or subjective, but more rigorous empirical data are available to back up our arguments.

One study compared US Supreme Court justices' initial votes at conference with the final votes as they appeared in the published reports.[116] Any change in the two sets of votes was attributed to small-group interaction. The findings reveal several things. First, there were vote changes in about 60 percent of all cases. Most of these changes occurred when a justice who had not participated in the first vote or who had been a dissenter opted to join the majority position.

But when one considers all votes for all cases, the justices changed positions only 9 percent of the time. In such instances of vote change, the initial majority position lost out in only 14 percent of the cases. A study of conference and final votes underestimates the extent of small-group interaction because plenty of such interaction takes place prior to the initial conference vote.[117] Another study of fluidity on the Supreme Court not only confirms that it is an ongoing phenomenon but also reveals that most of the vote changes stem from justices who move from the minority to the majority positions rather than vice versa. The authors of the study suggested that:

> the majority opinion author has little incentive to be responsive to the suggestions of a dissenter. Since the majority opinion becomes the law of the land, justices who wish to shape the law have an incentive to be part of the majority. Consistent with this theory is the fact that justices who initially voted with the majority switched only 4.6% of the time, and justices who initially dissented switched 18.1% of the time.[118]

Many other empirical studies dealing with the federal appeals courts and state supreme courts likewise suggest the importance of small-group dynamics as a factor in judicial decision-making.[119] For example, a 2007 study found that voting fluidity "is widespread" on state supreme courts. This research found that roughly 90 percent of judges that they surveyed throughout the United States claimed that other jurists have a significant impact in their decision-making process.[120]

Although it is unclear how many final outcomes are determined by small-group dynamics, it is a major factor in the drawing up of the majority opinion and in setting forth its parameters and corollaries. Scholars still lack a precise measure of the impact of small-group interaction, but it seems fair to say that it is considerable. Attempts to be more precise—both theoretically and empirically—about the output of appellate court decision-making have resulted in the development of several analytic approaches that seek to explain and analyze this phenomenon with greater and more quantifiable precision. The first and primary of these approaches is attitude theory; the others are variations of what is called the rational choice model.

ATTITUDE THEORY

Many judicial scholars have been dissatisfied with small-group analysis, arguing that the fruits of such exploration are barely worth their efforts. Although not denying that personal interactions make a difference in some cases and perhaps play a key role in a handful of decisions, they contend that the richest ore for explaining judicial behavior can be found in other mines. A decision-making model that claims greater explanatory power deals with discovery of the justices' basic, judicially relevant attitudes and with the coalitions, or blocs, formed by jurists who share similar attitudes.[121] This approach rests on the assumption that judges—particularly appellate jurists—view cases primarily in terms of the broad political and socioeconomic issues they raise, and that they generally respond to these issues in accordance with their personal values, attitudes, and policy preferences. The justices' official reasons for their decisions (found in their published opinions) are regarded as mere rationalizations. For example, suppose that Judge X strongly believes that the government should never tamper with freedom of the press. If a case comes before the court in which censorship is the central issue,

Judge X will follow his convictions and vote on the side of the news media. His written opinion may be full of impressive legal citations, quotations from eminent law reviews, or lofty discussions of the importance of maximum freedom of expression in a democracy. But all of this, the scholars of attitude theory contend, is only a rationalization after the fact. The real reason for Judge X's vote is his strong dislike for the concept of government censorship.

The attitude theorists do not claim that their decision-making models explain everything, and they do not deny that judges must often decide cases against the grain of their personal values. For instance, a justice may be a strong environmentalist, but if a pro-environment petitioner has absolutely no standing to sue, the justice is unlikely to yield to the tug of the heart. Nevertheless, supporters of the judicial attitude approach contend that it can explain a massive portion of judicial behavior and is well worth the research time and effort that such studies require.

Specific questions about this approach arise: Where do judicial attitudes originate? How does one learn about a judge's attitudes? What are some of the limitations of the attitudinal model?

Appellate jurists acquire their relevant attitudes from the same sources that people in general do—from family and friends, educational institutions, the media, political activities, and so on. Thus, attitude theorists and those who study judicial background characteristics clearly have overlapping interests. The difference is that the latter want to know from what sources the justices acquire their values, whereas the former concentrate on measuring the effects of judges' values—regardless of their origin—on collegial decision-making. The attitude scholars acknowledge that some beliefs change during a jurist's tenure on the bench, but they postulate "that attitudes are 'relatively enduring.'"[122] Learning about judges' true attitudes, however, can be a challenge. Jurists are generally unwilling to answer the sort of in-depth questionnaires that might reveal judicially significant attitudes—particularly on matters that relate to issues that may come before them in court. While many judges are happy to discuss judicial and legal matters in a broad sense, they are generally very reluctant to give speeches, grant interviews, or author articles that truly bare their judicial souls. They consider such behavior inappropriate, a violation of their role as neutral arbiters of the law. Therefore, judges do not make it easy for reporters and social scientists to suggest a link between their personal values and the way they decide cases.

The **attitudinal model** (as it is often called by scholars) does have its limitations. One criticism of the attitude theory approach has focused on the source of the corresponding data: the contents of the written opinions that are used to categorize judges' primary values. A justice who writes a strong opinion attacking government interference with the free operation of the marketplace is said to have a conservative economic attitude. This sort of approach has opened researchers to the charge that they have created a tautology: a justice writes several conservative economic opinions, is classified as an economic conservative, and lo and behold, aggregate analysis of their voting patterns concludes that the judge is a conservative on economic issues. Such theorists respond that this criticism is unfair because the patterns they have uncovered have proved to be consistent over time and susceptible to duplication by other researchers using similar methodologies. Furthermore, an important study based on attitude theory successfully formulated and applied three separate and independent ways to eliminate the circular reasoning problem: using facts derived from lower court records of cases decided by the US Supreme Court, conducting content analysis of editorials appearing in publications before a justice's confirmation, and employing the justice's previous voting behavior as a predictor of votes in subsequent cases.[123] Another shortcoming is that the attitudinal model has not been used as successfully to explain and predict lower court behavior, and some scholars have even argued that the model is inherently not applicable to trial judge decision-making.[124] As one of the biggest supporters of the attitudinal model, Professor Harold Spaeth, once acknowledged:

> Lower courts do operate in an environment distinctly different from that of the Supreme Court. These differences may cause lower-court judges to decide on bases other than their personal policy preferences. They may be electorally accountable and as a result render decisions that enhance their reelection. Others may seek higher positions—either inside or outside the judiciary—and color their decisions accordingly. Most courts are subject to appellate review. Judges thereon may decide according to their superiors' dictates rather than their own preferences. And except for some state supreme courts, judges do not have control of their dockets as the [US Supreme Court] justices do. Hence, their decision making may involve run-of-the-mill litigation in which policy matters are either absent or not amenable to discretion because a jury decides or because matters are open and shut.[125]

The fact that attitude theory may be time-bound is another criticism that its supporters concede. Virtually all research has focused on recent decades instead of the more distant past, and during many periods in the Supreme Court's history, many decisions were unanimous, so that there would be no variance to measure or explain. Finally, critics of attitude theory note that it has been applied only to the justice's final vote—the one specified in the reports of the Court's decisions. Its thrust thus misses the important matters of coalition formation and opinion writing.

Despite these limitations, attitude theory is still regarded by most judicial behavioralists as perhaps the most elegant and persuasive model for predicting appellate judge behavior. In large part, this is because there is ample high-quality research that supports attitude theory. A major 2013 work involving respected judicial politics scholar Lee Epstein examined over forty thousand votes by forty-four Supreme Court justices between the years 1946 and 2009. Using sophisticated statistical methods analyzing votes in thousands of cases, Epstein and her colleagues concluded that a judge's personal ideology figures into decision-making, at least to some extent, at *all* levels of the federal judiciary.[126] Cass Sunstein, a leading professor at Harvard Law School, led a research team that studied thousands of US courts of appeals cases handed down over a decade and concluded in a 2006 book titled *Are Judges Political?* that "judges do adhere to the law, but where the law is not plain, political convictions clearly play a role. And when like-minded judges sit together, they may well go to extremes."[127] And a study published in 2006 by Spaeth presented convincing numerical data strongly indicating that the US Supreme Court under the leadership of Rehnquist was a "poster child for the attitudinal model."[128] Students of foreign collegial court systems have also used the attitudinal model effectively to explain decision-making on these tribunals. A study of voting on search-and-seizure cases by justices on the Canadian Supreme Court found that the attitudinal model "correctly predicts 77 percent of the judicial decisions." Other studies using the attitudinal model have found it highly instructive in explaining the voting patterns of justices in countries as diverse as Australia, Canada, India, Japan, and the Philippines.[129]

RATIONAL CHOICE THEORY

The **rational choice theory** by no means rejects the basic assumptions of attitude theory. Rational choice theorists generally agree that appellate court jurists are primarily motivated by their personal, deeply felt attitudes about public policy and vote accordingly in their judicial decisions. But the rational choice school contends that there is more to it than that, and that the attitudinal position is somewhat simplistic and short-sighted. These theorists contend that goal-directed justices operate in what they term "strategic" or "inter-dependent decision-making contexts." The justices realize that the fate of their policy goals often depends on the values of other decision-makers, such as their colleagues on the bench, the president, and members of Congress. The justices must often include in their calculus not only what they personally want as a case outcome but also how such an outcome might be affected by the decisions of these other actors. As two key scholars associated with the **strategic behavior** approach put it:

> If justices are "single-minded seekers of legal policy" [as the attitude theorists contend], would those justices not care about the ultimate state of that policy? To rephrase the question, why would justices who are policy maximizers take a position they know Congress would overturn? To argue that justices would do this—merely vote their attitudes—is to argue that the Court is full of myopic thinkers, who consider only the shape of policy in the short term. It is also to argue that justices do not consider the preferences of other political actors and the actions they expect others to take when they make their decisions and simply respond to stimuli before them. Such a picture does not square with much important writing about the Court . . . or with the way many social scientists now believe that political actors make decisions.[130]

These and other scholars have found empirical evidence to support the basic tenets of the rational choice approach.[131] One study found that the small-group interactions of Supreme Court justices are often greatly influenced by rational choice considerations.[132] Scholars have also effectively used the strategic approach to gain an understanding of the various stages of the internal workings of the Supreme Court decision-making process.[133] Furthermore, research suggests that the rational choice approach is not limited to US courts and thus may provide a good model for understanding behavior in other countries. For example, a study of the Indian Supreme Court during the 1990s found that "that tribunal acted strategically in its relations to other political actors."[134]

As with all explanatory models, there are variations on a theme, and rational choice is no exception. Some exponents of this model argue, for example, that when it comes to congressional responses to Supreme Court decisions, the justices do more than act to minimize the possibility of a conflict with Congress (which might result in a congressional override of the Court's decision). These theorists note that the Court often calls for and invites congressional action to help secure the policy goals that the justices desire. One study found unmistakable evidence of this phenomenon and concluded:

> Our most striking finding concerned the ideological position of the justices who joined in the Court's majority opinion. The strong statistical impact of this variable suggests that one motivation for invitations to override is a concern with achieving both good law and good policy. More specifically, one response to a perceived conflict between the two is for justices to follow the law as they see it while asking Congress to supplant their choice with good policy as they see it.[135]

Rational choice theory, then, is not a rejection of the attitudinal model but argues that attitude theorists are too narrow in their approach. The rational choice school suggests that justices often consider in their decision-making the possible responses of other political actors—sometimes even going so far as to invite some of these other actors to modify or supplement the high court's decisions.

PRACTICAL APPLICATIONS OF THESE FOUR APPROACHES

Sometimes these theoretical approaches are a bit difficult to appreciate in the abstract. This can be remedied by studying an example that explores how theorists in each of these four categories might examine and evaluate judicial phenomena. In the following section, we look at the 2012 Supreme Court decision on health care reform as a vehicle to demonstrate the approaches of theorists in all four categories.

Following passage of major health care reform in 2010, opponents of the law, mostly conservative Republicans, filed legal challenges to key provisions of the statute. These cases were heard in federal courts in a number of different judicial circuits and were eventually consolidated into two separate but connected cases that landed at the US

Supreme Court: *National Federation of Independent Business (NFIB) v. Sebelius*[136] and *Florida v. Department of Health and Human Services*.[137] The health care reform law—officially called the Patient Protection and Affordable Care Act, but typically referred to in the press as the "Affordable Care Act" (ACA), "health care reform," or (usually by its opponents) "Obamacare"—contained numerous wide-ranging provisions: new regulations on the private health insurance market, which increased coverage and ended some controversial insurance practices; expanded prescription drug coverage for Medicare recipients; a new federal mandate that individuals would be required to obtain health insurance; and a major expansion of Medicaid to provide health care for greater numbers of low-income and working-class Americans. Ultimately, the health care cases offer insight on how scholars might utilize a variety of models to develop a better understanding of decision-making in multimember courts.

Cue Theory

A few factors suggest that cue theory may have provided some predictive ability in the health care cases. There's no question that health care is a major public policy issue facing governmental leaders at both the state and federal levels. It is also an issue that is often highly salient to many voters. What's more, the ACA was considered by many observers to be the most wide-ranging legislative effort passed by Congress since the 1960s.

The monumental nature of this issue alone might have given the justices reason to pay especially close attention to the matter. Yet, a review of the amicus curiae briefs filed at the appellate level may also have indicated to the justices the importance of the issue. A record number of amicus briefs—136—were filed in the health care cases. This figure completely shattered the previous record of 102.[138] What's more, the filed briefs were notable for their prominence, and the groups and individuals behind the briefs constituted a veritable "who's who" of American politics: many state attorneys general, governors, and members of Congress; dozens of national interest groups, including AARP, the single largest interest group in the United States; leading health care groups; major business organizations, such as the National Association of Manufacturers; and prominent academics from the nation's top universities and think tanks. Also distinguishing the health care cases was the fact that courts in the Fourth, Sixth, and District of Columbia Circuits had all handed down rulings on the health care law, and some of these decisions had been against one another (intercircuit conflict has been shown likely to lead to Supreme Court action). In sum, the legal history of these cases leading up to the high court provided the justices with ample cues that the cases were exceptional, and hence worthy of particular attention.

Small-Group Analysis

Judges who work together in small groups typically cultivate a sense of professional collegiality as a means for maintaining an effective working environment. Supreme Court

Justice O'Connor once noted, "When you work in a small group of that size, you have to get along, and so you're not going to let some harsh language, some dissenting opinion, affect a personal relationship. You can't do that." Her colleague Justice Stephen Breyer concurred: "I have never heard one member of the court say something insulting about another, even as a kind of joke. It's professional. We conduct our discussions in what I would call a very civilized way."[139] However, while jurists who work in small groups often maintain a certain level of civility in their interactions, this does not mean that sharp differences do not emerge or that justices do not find themselves bridging differences within a small cohort.

One Supreme Court justice who exemplified the importance of such small-group interaction was Anthony Kennedy. The Reagan appointee was widely viewed as a critical swing vote on the Court in some cases. Analysis of the voting patterns of the Court during much of his tenure revealed a rather consistent trend. On the right, Justices Antonin Scalia, Clarence Thomas, Samuel Alito, and Chief Justice John Roberts were generally considered reliable conservatives. Justices Ruth Bader Ginsburg, Stephen Breyer, Sonia Sotomayor, and Elena Kagan frequently cast liberal votes. This sometimes left Justice Kennedy as the deciding vote in some key cases. Although Kennedy was appointed by Ronald Reagan and often sided with the conservatives, research showed that in some case types Kennedy revealed a very clear tendency to act as a "swing vote."[140] Numerous legal experts predicted that the health care ruling could result in a 5–4 vote, and many eyes were focused on Kennedy as the deciding vote. One scholar echoed the sentiment of many when he predicted, "It comes down to Kennedy, of course, and during the oral arguments, his position appeared ambiguous. If forced to choose, I'd say the court will vote 5–4 to strike the [health care] mandate."[141]

The experts' 5–4 forecast was correct, but their prediction of who would be the swing vote missed the mark. As it turns out, Kennedy sided with the reliably conservative bloc on the Court, while the liberal cohort held firm on the other side. It was Chief Justice Roberts who was the "swing vote" on health care. Did Roberts's action of siding with the liberals in this instance result in a "falling out" among the justices? Not according to Justice Scalia, a staunch conservative who voted to strike down the health care law. Soon after the ruling, he told a reporter: "No, I haven't had a falling out with Justice Roberts." The reporter asked: "Were there loud words or slammed doors?" Again, Scalia rejected the notion: "No, no, nothing like that. There are clashes on legal questions but not personally. The press likes to paint us as nine scorpions in a bottle, and that's just not the case at all."[142]

Attitudinal Model

One can readily hypothesize that the attitudinal model may have been applicable in the 2012 health care cases. As previously mentioned, the ideological preferences of the justices on both the left and the right were rather powerful in predicting most of the jurists' votes in the health care decisions, and most legal observers accurately predicted how most of the justices would vote in these cases. More to the point, all four liberals on the Court voted for the liberal policy outcome (i.e., in favor of the health care law) and four of the five conservatives voted for a conservative policy outcome. Yet, the health care cases also provided a key instance in which a justice's attitude about their role on the Court may have been crucial in guiding the justice's decision.

Chief Justice John Roberts's position as the swing vote in the health care cases surprised many. It certainly angered a lot of conservative political pundits. But a closer reading of the matter suggests that much of the shock may have been unwarranted. How could the conservative chief justice, who was appointed by Republican George W. Bush, rule to uphold a health care overhaul championed by President Obama and his fellow Democrats?

In many ways, the answer to this question depends on the view of "conservative." Roberts's vote in the cases was not conservative in the sense that it sided with the policy preferences of the Republican Party on the health care law (the GOP had, of course, strenuously opposed "Obamacare"). The chief justice's decision on the Affordable Care Act was, however, deeply conservative in other ways.

Contained within the opinion written by Roberts, upholding the law is legal doctrine that conservatives have long sought as a means for constricting Congress' power under the Commerce Clause of Article I, Section 8, of the US Constitution. "The commerce clause is not a general license to regulate an individual from cradle to grave," Justice Roberts wrote.[143] Said one Yale Law School professor:

> This opinion reinvigorates a stricter understanding of all the powers of government. There's a renewed interest in limits to federal power. The language about inactivity suggests that any laws that purport to order conduct, including existing laws, have the potential to be challenged. This could become a powerful tool to achieve a more limited federal government.[144]

Given that paring back the size of government is one of the stated goals of modern American conservatism, in this way Roberts's opinion can be viewed as furthering one of the long-term interests of his fellow travelers on the political right.

Chief Justice Roberts's opinion is also conservative in the sense that he showed deference to the elected branches of government and displayed an unwillingness to engage in "judicial activism"—that is, working aggressively to overturn laws passed by the duly elected branches of government, the branches chosen by and closest to the people. One reporter noted that "Roberts' decision was conservative but not nakedly partisan. He adhered to the court's traditional deference to the legislative branch, citing the 1895 opinion in *Hooper v. California*, which states that 'every reasonable construction must be resorted to, in order to save a statute from unconstitutionality.'"[145] Well-known Harvard law professor Lawrence Tribe echoed this sentiment when he observed that "as a modest guy and someone who did not want the court to shatter an historic piece of legislation even though he didn't like it, John Roberts was bound to take a step that would ultimately be modest."[146] Indeed, research unveiled during the Roberts confirmation struggle in 2005 suggested that the judge had a tendency toward judicial modesty. The *Washington Post* noted that the study found that Roberts "showed a liberal streak on economic regulation and labor issues," suggesting that Roberts tended to give general deference to regulators.[147]

Rational Choice

One may also identify shades of strategic decision-making in the health care cases. Indeed, it may be argued that the Court came close to striking the optimal strategic position in its decisions in both cases.

Like so many other profound debates in American political life, the health care dispute gave rise to differing opposing ideological positions. But taken in context, the law passed by Congress was in many ways a classic compromise between left and right. There's no doubt that the law contained elements that pleased liberals, most notably a major step toward their long-sought goal of health care coverage for all. But some on the left were disappointed that the idea of a Canadian-style single payer system—in which government ensures truly universal coverage and foots the bill for the entire nation's health care—was never under serious consideration by President Obama.

Conservatives decried the health care law for its new taxes and increased regulations. But their leaders surely recognized that the Affordable Care Act was based on a plan originally proposed by a conservative think tank, the Heritage Foundation, in 1993 in response to the health care reform effort rolled out by President Bill Clinton. The proposal, which conservatives at the time embraced, contained the central pillars of the plan they later decried as "Obamacare."[148] What's more, the national health care law was modeled on the plan that was enthusiastically embraced by a Republican governor, Mitt Romney, in his successful effort to expand coverage in Massachusetts.

Public opinion polls on the Affordable Care Act were mixed. A Gallup poll in June 2012 found that 45 percent said the passage of the health care law was a good thing, while 44 percent said it was a terrible thing.[149] Another poll found that when asked about "Obamacare" overall, Americans opposed it by a twelve-point margin. However, the same poll found that many of the specific provisions within the law were exceedingly popular by large margins.[150] It was against this political backdrop that the health care cases were debated. Liberals hoped that the Court would uphold the law, while conservatives sought just the opposite. Ultimately, the Court's decisions on the Affordable Care Act handed a victory to liberals, but it was not an unqualified one. Within the decisions were provisions that both liberals and conservatives could support and that also left neither side entirely satisfied. In this way, it was arguably optimal for the Court from a strategic perspective.

In upholding the ACA based upon Congress' taxing authority, the Supreme Court handed a clear victory to President Obama and the Democrats. However, as previously discussed, the Court gave a key win to conservatives in the opinion by limiting the expansiveness of Congress' power to regulate economic activity under the Commerce

Clause. What's more, the Court struck down Congress' attempt to link the states' existing Medicaid dollars to an embrace of the expanded Medicaid requirement contained in the new law. This provision was hailed by conservatives as a victory for state sovereignty, a position generally championed by those on the right.

It was, in sum, a decision in which the Court brought some resolution to a contentious issue while cautiously avoiding the adoption of an absolutist position that might do major damage to its popularity—hence, its legitimacy—among large segments of the population. Indeed, the ruling likely bolstered the Supreme Court's long-term institutional legitimacy. A poll found that over time support for the ACA increased significantly, with 59 percent of US adults having a favorable view of the law in 2024.[151] Furthermore, it was a decision that was not far from corresponding to the views held by significant numbers of Americans at the time. Rational choice scholars examining the health care rulings could easily conclude that the Court engaged in strategic behavior and, given the political circumstances in which the Court faced a potential no-win situation, handed down the optimal decision.

SUMMARY

We began this chapter with the observation that decision-making by judges on collegial appellate courts is in some key ways different from decision-making by judges acting alone on trial benches. Because of these differences, scholars have devised theories and research techniques to capture the special reality of decision-making by jurists on federal and state multijudge appellate courts. We took a close look at the discretionary review process of the Supreme Court and noted that the issues on which it decides not to rule are often as substantively important as those cases it selects for full review. In this context, we discussed the importance of cue theory—the attempt by scholars to learn the characteristics of those few cases chosen from the many for Supreme Court consideration.

We then focused on several separate theoretical approaches to explain the decision-making of multijudge courts: small-group analysis, attitude theory, and the rational choice model. In our discussion, we often noted the similarity of patterns in US courts and those of other countries and those instances in which the American experiences seem to be unique.

Each of these theoretical models has its own working assumptions and research techniques that are used to glean the explanatory data. Although it is tempting to speculate on which of these several approaches provides the best insights into appellate court behavior, it is probably fairest to say that the jury of judicial scholars is still out. A growing belief in recent years is that models representing a combination of these and other approaches provide much greater explanatory power than any of them taken alone.[152] Finally, using the example of the Supreme Court's 2012 health care decisions, we indicated how theorists in all four categories might select and evaluate relevant data.

FURTHER THOUGHT AND DISCUSSION QUESTIONS

1. In the distant past, Congress largely mandated which cases would be heard by the US Supreme Court, but today, the high court justices have almost complete control over their own docket. Is it a good idea for the Supreme Court to control its own agenda—without being required to explain refusing to hear almost 99 percent of the cases appealed to it?
2. When appellate court justices get together to discuss a case and decide its outcome, are their deliberations on a high and lofty plane, or are their motivations and actions no different from those of any group of ordinary citizens acting as an organized committee?
3. Using the health care reform law as a point of reference, do you think any of the four theories—cue, small-group analysis, attitude, and rational choice—yield more, or better, insight into collegial courts' decision-making? Or is each approach equally helpful in its own way? Might one theory be more, or less, relevant to different cases?
4. Are patterns of appellate judge behavior similar throughout the world, or are the decision-making patterns of America's collegial court jurists unique?

SUGGESTED RESOURCES

Epstein, Lee, and Jack Knight. *The Choices Justices Make*. Washington, DC: CQ Press, 1998. An excellent summary of the several theoretical approaches to the study of appellate court decision-making with an emphasis upon strategic behavior.

Howard, J. Woodford, Jr. *Courts of Appeals in the Federal Judicial System*. Princeton, NJ: Princeton University Press, 1981. A well-written study of decision-making at the level of the US appellate courts, containing both quantitative and anecdotal information.

Langer, Laura. *Judicial Review in State Supreme Courts: A Comparative Study*. Albany, NY: SUNY Press, 2012. A study of decision-making in the state supreme courts. The author views judges as forward-thinking individuals who pursue both policy and electoral goals.

Lazarus, Edward. *Closed Chambers: The Rise, Fall, and Future of the Modern Supreme Court*. New York, NY: Penguin Group, 2005. A former Supreme Court law clerk provides a behind-the-scenes glimpse of the ideological and personal battles on the Court.

Maltzman, Forrest, James F. Spriggs, and Paul J. Wahlbeck. *Crafting Law on the Supreme Court: The Collegial Game.* New York, NY: Cambridge University Press, 2000. A study of how majorities are built on the Supreme Court. The authors conclude that the process is a highly strategic one in which the justices' behavior is influenced by their peers.

Murphy, Walter F. *Elements of Judicial Strategy.* Chicago, IL: University of Chicago Press, 1964. This classic emphasizes the importance of personal interactions on the outcome of collegial court decision-making.

Perry, H. W., Jr. *Deciding to Decide: Agenda Setting in the United States Supreme Court.* Cambridge, MA: Harvard University Press, 1991. Emphasizes the importance of the Supreme Court's decisions with respect to the types of cases it agrees or declines to hear. The author argues that these decisions are as important as the ultimate disposition of the cases the Court does consider.

Segal, Jeffrey A., and Harold J. Spaeth. *The Supreme Court and the Attitudinal Model Revisited.* New York, NY: Cambridge University Press, 2002. Two well-known scholars in the field provide an excellent analysis of the predominant model for analyzing the decision-making of the Supreme Court.

Segal, Jeffrey A., Harold J. Spaeth, and Sara C. Benesh. *The Supreme Court in the American Legal System.* New York, NY: Cambridge University Press, 2005. A thorough examination of judicial decision-making in the American legal system.

Sunstein, Cass, David Schkade, Lisa M. Ellman, and Andres Sawicki. *Are Judges Political? An Empirical Analysis of the Federal Judiciary.* Washington, DC: Brookings Institution Press, 2006. A comprehensive, quantitative study of decision-making on the US courts of appeals.

Toobin, Jeffrey. *The Nine: Inside the Secret World of the Supreme Court.* New York, NY: Anchor Books, 2008. A journalistic account of behind-the-scenes personal interactions on the Supreme Court.

KEY TERMS

attitudinal model
collegial courts
cue theory
rational choice theory
small-group analysis
strategic behavior

14 IMPLEMENTATION AND IMPACT OF JUDICIAL POLICIES

CHAPTER GOALS AND OBJECTIVES

In this chapter, readers will learn that . . .

- Though lower court judges are bound by precedent, in many instances, they also have significant discretion in their decision-making and are often key actors in implementing higher court decisions.
- The legislative branch, executive branch, and other actors frequently play important roles in influencing the implementation of judicial decisions.
- Judges' decisions can have a wide-ranging impact upon the lives of individuals, the political system, and society.

In the previous two chapters, we focused on decision-making by judges. In this chapter, we extend the discussion to examine what happens after a decision has been reached. Decisions made by judges are not self-executing, and a wide variety of individuals—other judges, public officials, even private citizens—may be called on to implement a court's decisions. In this chapter, we look at the various actors involved in the implementation process, their reactions to judicial policies, and the methods they may use to respond to a court's decision.

Depending on the nature of the court's decision, the judicial policy may have a narrow or a broad impact. A suit for damages incurred in an automobile accident would directly affect only the persons involved and perhaps their immediate families. But the famous *Miranda v. Arizona* decision has directly affected millions of people in one way or another for generations.[1] In *Miranda*, the Supreme Court held that prior to a custodial interrogation law enforcement must warn a person of their right to remain silent along with other constitutional rights and procedural safeguards. Scores of people—defendants, judges, lawyers, and especially law enforcement—have felt the effects of that judicial policy. In the 2012 case of *National Federation of Independent Business v. Sebelius*, the Supreme Court ruled on the constitutionality of the Affordable Care Act (ACA), a case with potentially life or death implications for virtually everyone in the United States since it touched upon the financial foundation of American health care. And in 2022, in the case of *Dobbs v. Jackson Women's Health Organization*, the Court overruled an earlier precedent that gave women the right to terminate one's pregnancy and ruled that the Constitution does not provide a right to abortion.[2] Whether cases are narrow or broad, implementing those rulings shapes the impact of judicial policymaking on society.

Protesters gather outside the US Supreme Court building in 2022 following the *Dobbs v. Jackson Women's Health Organization* decision in which the Supreme Court overturned *Roe v. Wade*.

Brandon Bell/Getty Images

THE IMPACT OF HIGHER COURT DECISIONS ON LOWER COURTS

Americans often view the appellate courts, notably the US Supreme Court, as most likely to be involved in policymaking. The trial courts are frequently seen as norm enforcers rather than policymakers. Given this traditional view, the picture that often emerges portrays the Supreme Court as making a decision that is then implemented by a lower court. In short, some envision a judicial bureaucracy with a hierarchy of courts much like superiors and subordinates.[3] But studies have cast doubt on this bureaucracy theory, arguing that "most of the work of the lower courts seems less dependent on the Supreme Court than . . . bureaucracy [theory] would indicate."[4] In other words, lower court judges have a great deal of independence from the appellate courts and may be viewed as "independent actors . . . who will not follow the lead of higher courts unless conditions are favorable for their doing so."[5] For example, not all federal district judges immediately enforced the Supreme Court's public school desegregation decision.[6]

Some judges allowed school districts to engage in a variety of tactics ranging from evasion to postponement of the Supreme Court mandate.[7]

Lower Court Discretion

Why do the lower court judges have so much discretion when implementing a higher court's policy? In part, the answer may be found in the structure of the US judicial system. The judiciary has always been characterized by independence, decentralization, and individualism. Federal judges are protected by life tenure and traditionally have been able to run their courts as they see fit. Disciplinary measures are not at all common, and federal judges have historically had little fear of impeachment. As some scholars suggest, the main stick higher courts have in inducing compliance with its rulings is reversal, but even the threat of reversal may not be enough given the decentralized structure of the American judiciary.[8] At the state level, to retain their positions, the state trial court judges often do not have to worry about the appellate courts in their system. In many states, they simply must keep the electorate satisfied to keep their judicial seat. In short, lower court judges have a good deal of freedom to make their own decisions and respond to upper court rulings in their own way.

The discretion exercised by a lower court judge may also be a product of the higher court's decision, itself. For example, following the famous school desegregation decision in 1954, the Supreme Court heard further arguments on the best way to implement its new policy. In 1955, it handed down its decision in *Brown v. Board of Education of Topeka II*.[9] In that case, the Court was faced with two major questions: (1) How soon are the public schools to start desegregating? (2) How much time should they be given to complete the process? Federal district judges given the task of enforcing the high court's ruling were told, in the decision, that the public schools should make a prompt and reasonable start and then proceed with all deliberate speed to bring about desegregation. What constituted a prompt and reasonable start? How rapidly did a school district need to proceed to be moving "with all deliberate speed"? Because the Supreme Court justices did not provide specific answers to these questions, many lower court judges were faced with school districts that dragged their feet, while at the same time claiming they were acting within the high court's guidelines.

Another example of lower court discretion may be found in how a recent US district court judge distinguished a US court of appeals precedent in his ruling. One way a judge can use their discretion is by differentiating their case from precedent by showing that the facts are distinctive or an issue was not addressed. For instance, in 2022, Alabama passed a law that prohibited minors from using puberty blockers and gender-affirming hormone treatments. The law was challenged in the federal courts, and the Eleventh Circuit US Court of Appeals upheld the ban in the *Eknes-Tucker v. Governor of Alabama* decision.[10]

Not long afterward, in May 2023, Florida passed a similar ban on gender-affirming treatment. The new law was immediately challenged in federal court. In his decision,

US District Court Judge Hinkle noted that *Eknes-Tucker* was a binding precedent in the Eleventh Circuit, and he is obligated to follow it. However, he also explained that the *Eknes-Tucker* decision did not raise or resolve the animus issue presented in the current case (plaintiffs in the case argued that Florida legislators were motivated by hate [animus] when passing the law). In *Doe v. Ladapo* (2024), Judge Hinkle wrote, "*Eknes-Tucker* did *not* address the issue of animus—no claim of animus was presented on the appeal in the case—so the animus issue is open here."[11] Judge Hinkle ruled that the Florida law was unconstitutional because he found significant evidence that animus (the intent to harm) motivated many Florida legislators to pass the law. Judge Hinkle explained, "There is substantial evidence of animus in the adoption of the statute and rules at issue here."[12] He went on to find that the Florida legislature was motivated by animus when they passed the antitransgender legislation. The judge held that the ban on gender-affirming treatment violated the Equal Protection and Due Process Clauses of the Fourteenth Amendment because the regulation was unrelated to a legitimate state interest in safeguarding health.[13]

Therefore, federal district judges implementing court of appeals rulings, like the one described above, may exercise a high degree of freedom and still legitimately say that they followed the precedent of the circuit. Although not all appellate court decisions allow such discretion, a suitable number of them do. Higher court opinions that are ambiguous or poorly written are almost certain to encounter problems during the implementation process.

A court's decision may be unclear for several reasons. Sometimes the issue or subject matter may be so complex that it is difficult to fashion a clear policy. In obscenity cases, for instance, the Supreme Court had little difficulty deciding that pornographic material is not entitled to constitutional protection. But defining "obscenity" proved to be another matter. Phrases such as "prurient interest," "patently offensive," "contemporary community standards," and "lacks serious literary, artistic, political, or scientific value" became commonplace in obscenity opinions. However, these terms leave considerable room for subjective interpretation, and thus defining what is "obscene" became exceedingly difficult for courts and prosecutors. It is little wonder that one Supreme Court justice admitted that he could not define obscenity but added that "I know it when I see it."[14] Today, obscene (e.g., pornographic) materials remain technically illegal in most jurisdictions around the United States. But because defining what is actually "obscene" is so ambiguous and difficult, prosecutions for possession of obscene materials are now rare.

Policies established by collegial courts are often ambiguous because the majority opinion is written to accommodate several judges. At times, such opinions read more like committee reports than forceful, decisive statements. The majority opinion may also be accompanied by several concurring opinions. When this happens, lower court judges may lack a clear-cut precedent to follow. A 1972 death penalty case serves as a good example. In *Furman v. Georgia*, the Supreme Court struck down the death penalty in several states, but for a variety of reasons. There were five concurring majority opinions authored in the 5–4 ruling and four dissenting opinions. Some justices opposed the death penalty, per se, on the ground that it constitutes cruel and unusual punishment in violation of the Eighth Amendment to the Constitution. Others voted to strike down the state laws because they were applied in a discriminatory manner.[15] The *Furman* decision affected not only lower court judges but also state legislatures. The states passed a rash of widely divergent death penalty statutes and caused a considerable amount of new litigation. Just four years later, in *Gregg v. Georgia*, the Supreme Court upheld the death penalty for the crime of murder.[16]

Opinions of the Supreme Court, lower federal courts, and state appellate courts are available in many courthouses, law schools, and university libraries, and they are also typically available on the Internet (either for free or via subscription services such as Westlaw or LexisNexis). Many court opinions can now be read on the same day they are handed down or within just a few days. Typically when a new US Supreme Court opinion along with any new circuit decisions are issued, research staff of each circuit court of appeals email new court opinions to the judges, along with their law clerks and staff attorneys. However, for some judges and courts this widespread availability does not guarantee that they will be read and clearly understood. One complication is that some lower-level state judges, such as justices of the peace and juvenile court judges, are nonlawyers with little interest or skill in reading complex judicial decisions.[17] Finally, even those judges who have an interest in higher court decisions and the ability to understand them may find they do not have adequate time to keep abreast of all the new opinions.

Given these problems, how do judges become aware of upper court decisions? One way is to hear of them from lawyers presenting cases in the lower courts. It is generally assumed that the opposing attorneys will present relevant precedents in their written and oral arguments before the judge. Those judges who are fortunate enough to have law clerks may also rely on them to search out recent decisions from higher courts. Judges may also learn of new developments in the law via continuing legal education, which is required of many lawyers and some judges in certain jurisdictions around the United States.

While rare, some higher court policies are not quickly and strictly enforced because sometimes lower court judges are not aware of them. Even those of which they are aware may not be as clear as a lower court judge might like. Either reason contributes to the discretion exercised by lower court judges placed in the position of having to implement judicial policies.

Interpretation by Lower Courts

One study noted that "important policy announcements almost always require interpretation by someone other than the policy maker."[18] This is certainly true in the case of judicial policies established by appellate courts. One important way that lower court judges exercise discretion is interpreting what the higher court's decision means.

Consider the extraordinary case of *Flowers v. Mississippi* where, over the course of twenty-three years, Curtis Giovanni Flowers was tried six times by the same local prosecutor for a quadruple murder in Mississippi. In 2019, the US Supreme Court granted review to address whether the Mississippi Supreme Court erred in how it applied the *Batson v. Kentucky* precedent to this case. As you may recall from Chapter 10, *Batson v. Kentucky* prohibits attorneys from discriminating based on race when using their peremptory challenges during the jury selection process. In a 7–2 vote, the Supreme Court reversed Flowers's death sentence because the prosecutor had a long history of using his peremptory challenges in a racially discriminatory manner by removing Black prospective jurors in all six trials Flowers faced. Justice Kavanaugh, who wrote the majority opinion, stated the "numbers spoke loudly" because in all six trials, the prosecutor persistently used its peremptory challenges to strike Black prospective jurors from the jury.[19] The majority opinion highlighted that "In the six trials combined, the State struck 41 of the 42 Black prospective jurors it could have struck."[20] The majority noted that the prosecutor's goal was to remove as many Black prospective jurors as possible. Justice Kavanaugh remarked, "The State appeared to proceed as if *Batson* had never been decided."[21] The Court made clear that per the *Batson* decision, the "Constitution forbids striking even a single prospective juror for a discriminatory purpose."[22]

At the close of its opinion, the Supreme Court noted that it reversed the Mississippi Supreme Court's decision and remanded the case for "further proceedings not inconsistent with this opinion."[23] A few months later, on August 29, 2019, the Mississippi Supreme Court reversed Flowers's conviction. Justice Coleman, writing for the Mississippi Supreme Court, stated, "In accordance with the Supreme Court's opinion, we reverse the circuit court's judgment of conviction and sentence and remand the case to the circuit court for a new trial consistent with the Supreme Court's opinion."[24]

After the case was remanded back to the trial court, Flowers was removed from death row, following the reversal of his sentence, and placed into county jail. On September 19, 2019, Flowers's lawyers filed a motion to dismiss all the charges in the case, and on December 16, 2019, after spending twenty-three years behind bars, Curtis Flowers was released on bail. Shortly thereafter, the state attorney general took over the prosecution of the case. Seven months later, on September 4, 2020, the Mississippi attorney general's office filed a motion to dismiss charges with prejudice (which means the case cannot be brought back to court) and the trial court judge issued an order dismissing the case. Flowers became a free man, and on March 2, 2021, Curtis Flowers was awarded $500,000 in compensation for his wrongful imprisonment, the maximum amount allowed under Mississippi law.[25]

The way a lower court judge interprets a policy established by a higher court depends on a few factors. Among them is the fact that many policies are not clearly stated. Thus, reasonable people may disagree over the proper interpretation. Even policy pronouncements that do not suffer from ambiguity are sometimes interpreted differently by different judges.

A judge's personal policy preferences may also affect the interpretation they give to a higher court policy. Judges come to the courts with their own unique background characteristics. Some are Republicans, others are Democrats; one judge may be liberal, another conservative. They come from different regions of the country. Some have been prosecutors; others have been defense or corporate lawyers. A policy enthusiastically embraced by some judges may be totally rejected by others.

Strategies Used by Lower Courts

Appellate court policies are open to different interpretations. Those who favor and accept a higher court's policy will naturally try to enforce it and perhaps even expand on it. Those who dislike a higher court's policy decision may implement it sparingly or only under duress.

A judge who basically disagrees with a policy established by a higher court can use several strategies. One rarely used strategy—defiance—came into play in a standoff between a federal court and the state of Alabama in 2015. The case involved two women, Cari D. Searcy and Kimberly McKean, who were legally married in California in 2008. Searcy wished to adopt McKean's biological son and filed a petition to do so in a probate court in Mobile, Alabama. But their petition was denied because Searcy did not qualify under Alabama law as a spouse, as gay marriage was prohibited in the state at the time by the Alabama Marriage Protection Act and an amendment that enshrined that law in the state constitution. On appeal, US District Court Judge Callie V. S. Granade overruled the state court and declared that the Alabama provisions were unconstitutional, allowing the adoption to proceed.[26] But soon after Judge Granade's decision, Chief Justice Roy Moore of the Alabama Supreme Court issued a letter stating that probate judges should not issue or recognize marriage licenses inconsistent with the Alabama Constitution. Judge Moore effectively blocked the probate judge from following the federal court's order.[27]

This was quickly appealed to the US Supreme Court, which ruled against Alabama and upheld the federal court's decision—the marriage must be recognized as Judge Grenade had initially ruled. Judge Moore then raised a dubious legal argument that the federal court order was not binding on probate judges because it had been addressed to the state's attorney general, not its judiciary. The Alabama Supreme Court ordered on March 3, 2015, that probate judges around the state must stop issuing marriage licenses to same-sex couples, again in direct opposition to Judge Granade's order. But three months later, the US Supreme Court would effectively put an end to this standoff in its June 2015 decision in *Obergefell v. Hodges*, unequivocally upholding the right for same-sex couples to marry throughout the United States. Alabama's defiance was quashed.

Research suggests that outright defiance by lower courts as that seen in the above scenario is unusual. A study of the libel decisions of the US courts of appeals between 1964 and 1974 did not find a sole case of noncompliance with Supreme Court mandates.[28] Another study, focusing on compliance with the Supreme Court's *Miranda v. Arizona*[29] decision, found only one instance of possible noncompliance and twelve decisions that could be classified as narrow compliance among the 250 cases studied.[30] However, more recent scholarship shows that as the Court has become more polarized, implementers can take advantage and overtly resist Court rulings. For example, one 2021 study found that resistance to the *Obergefell v. Hodges* decision by county clerks affected how the media covered same-sex marriage. The authors show that disobedience to the *Obergefell* decision changed the media's coverage from one of equal rights to one of anti-same-sex marriage that centered on religious freedom.[31]

Another strategy often used by judges not favorably inclined toward a higher court policy is to avoid having to apply the policy. Sometimes a case may be disposed of on technical or procedural grounds so that the judge does not have to rule on the merits of the case. It may be determined, for example, that the plaintiff does not have standing to sue or that the case has become moot because the issue was resolved before the trial commenced. Lower court judges sometimes avoid accepting a policy by declaring a portion of the higher court decision to be dicta. **Dicta** refers to the part of the opinion that does not contribute to the central logic of the decision. It may be useful as guidance, but it is not seen as binding. However, what constitutes dicta is open to interpretation.

Yet another tactic often used is to apply the policy as narrowly as possible. One method is for the lower court judge to rule that a precedent is not controlling because of factual differences between the higher court case and the one before the lower courts. Therefore, precedent does not have to be followed. Consider the following example that illustrates this strategy.

Under the Fourth Amendment, obtaining a warrant before conducting a search is constitutionally preferred. However, over the years, the Supreme Court has carved out several exceptions to the warrant requirement based on exigent circumstances, such as officer safety, public safety, and loss of evidence. One of the exceptions to the warrant requirement is known as a search incident to a lawful arrest (or valid arrest). Under this exception, law enforcement can conduct a warrantless search of a lawfully arrested person and the area within their immediate control. However, in 2009, the Court in *Arizona v. Gant* placed an important restriction on this long-standing exception.[32] In *Gant*, five police officers handcuffed and placed Rodney Gant in the back of a squad car and then conducted a warrantless search of Gant's vehicle. The Court struck down this warrantless search and held that a search incident to a lawful arrest may only be conducted without a warrant if the suspect is unsecured and within reaching distance to the area to be searched (meaning the suspect can gain access). Because Gant was handcuffed and placed in the back of a squad car, the Court reasoned that the justifications (officer safety and loss of evidence) that allow for a warrantless search incident to a lawful arrest are not valid when the suspect is secured.[33]

In 2020, the Fourth Circuit US Courts of Appeals applied the *Gant* precedent narrowly in *United States v. Ferebee*.[34] In March 2017, Quentin Ferebee was visiting his friend Shana Dunbar, who, unbeknownst to him, was on probation. As luck would have it, Dunbar's probation officer arrived unannounced to conduct a warrantless search per the terms of her probation. Upon arrival, the probation officer found Ferebee sitting on Dunbar's couch with a marijuana blunt in his hand and a backpack positioned nearby. Ferebee was placed under arrest for marijuana possession, handcuffed, and brought outside the residence. Without a warrant, officers searched the backpack, and they found a gun, drug paraphernalia, marijuana, and Ferebee's identification card. On appeal, Ferebee's attorney argued that based on the *Gant* precedent, the officers conducted an unlawful search of Ferebee's backpack because, at the time of the search, he was standing outside the residence and in handcuffs.[35] However, the court of appeals upheld the warrantless search and explained that this situation was distinguishable from the *Gant* precedent. They reasoned,

> Thus, the situation here is quite different from *Gant*. Whereas the defendant in *Gant* was handcuffed and locked in the back of a police car, Ferebee was only a few steps away from the backpack. He was handcuffed, but he still could walk around somewhat freely and could easily have made a break for the backpack inside the house. Under these circumstances, we do not believe that Ferebee was "secured" within the meaning of *Gant*. . . . We therefore conclude that, despite the fact that Ferebee was handcuffed, the police reasonably could have believed that Ferebee could have accessed the backpack.[36]

As the decision above shows, this is a classic example of a lower court taking a narrow application of a Supreme Court precedent based on factual differences.

As noted in Chapter 3, state court judges faced with interpreting or implementing policies on civil liberties may rely on what is termed *new judicial federalism*, an idea that originated in the early 1970s. Many civil libertarians, fearful that the Warren Burger Court would erode or overturn major Warren Court decisions of the 1960s, began to look to state bills of rights as alternative bases for their court claims. The Burger Court encouraged a return to state constitutions by pointing out that the states could offer greater protection under their own bills of rights than was available under the federal Bill of Rights.

Initially, courts used this approach to circumvent some Supreme Court decisions. However, since that time "state courts have undertaken major initiatives involving school finance, exclusionary zoning, the rights of defendants, and the right to privacy."[37] Some studies have cautioned against too much optimism among those who advocate reliance on state constitutions to avoid conservative precedents espoused by the Burger, Rehnquist, and Roberts Courts. In separate examinations of criminal justice decisions from all fifty state high courts, one research team concluded that state supreme courts continue to rely on federal law in many of their decisions.[38] Not all lower court judges are opposed to a policy announced by a higher court. Some judges have risked social ostracism and various kinds of harassment to implement policies they believed in even when those policies were not popular in their communities.[39] Typically, a judge who is in basic agreement with a higher court policy is likely to give that policy as broad an application as possible. The precedent might be expanded to apply to other areas as well.

For example, in *Griswold v. Connecticut*, the Supreme Court held that a Connecticut statute forbidding the use of birth control devices was unconstitutional because it infringed on a married couple's constitutional right to privacy.[40] In other words, the Court said that the use of birth control devices is a personal decision to be made without interference from the state. Five years later, a three-judge federal district court expanded the *Griswold* precedent to justify its finding that the Texas abortion statute was unconstitutional.[41] The three-judge panel ruled that the law infringed on an unmarried woman's right of privacy to decide, at least during the first trimester of pregnancy, whether to obtain an abortion. Thus, the lower court went further than the Supreme Court in striking down state involvement in such matters.

Influences on Lower Court Judges

Lower courts are not mere subordinates of the higher courts when implementing judicial policies. They have a great degree of independence and discretion. At times, the lower courts must decide cases for which the higher courts have not provided precise standards. Whenever this occurs, lower court judges must turn elsewhere for guidance in deciding a case before them.

One study notes that in such a position lower court judges "may take their cues on how to decide a particular case from a wide variety of factors including their party affiliation, their ideology, or their regional norms."[42] Several analysts point out that differences between Democratic and Republican lower court judges are especially pronounced when Supreme Court rulings are ambiguous, when there is a transition from one Supreme Court era to another, or when the issue area is so new and controversial that more definite standards have not yet been formulated.[43] Regional norms have also been mentioned prominently in the literature as having an influence on lower court judges when they interpret and apply higher court decisions.[44] One study found, for example, that "federal judges tend to be more vigilant in enforcing national desegregation standards in remote areas than when similar issues arise within the judge's immediate work/residence locale." The prevailing local norms may mean that "when faced with desegregating his own community a judge may be more concerned with public reaction than when dealing with an outlying area."[45]

Scholars have recently begun focusing on lower court compliance with Supreme Court summary decisions. A series of studies that analyze the most common type of summary decision, the GVR (grant, vacate, and remand), have found significant compliance with Supreme Court precedent. Because the Supreme Court has limited resources and cannot hear oral arguments in every case, it may grant certiorari and issue a summary decision without an oral argument. In other words, a GVR decision occurs when "the Court grants the petition for certiorari, vacates the lower-court decision, and remands the case to the court below with directions to reconsider the case 'in light of' a specific precedent announced by the Supreme Court."[46] In a 2019 study, political scientists Ali Masood, Benjamin Kassow, and Donald Songer analyzed lower court compliance with summary decisions at both the federal and state levels and found significant compliance with Supreme Court precedent. The trio of authors concluded that there is "clear and incontrovertible evidence that there is a causal relationship between the Supreme Court's summary decisions and the frequency with which lower courts adopt the Supreme Court's precedent."[47] As recent trends have shown, justices may increasingly rely on summary decisions as an effective tool to maintain compliance within the courts.

CONGRESSIONAL INFLUENCES ON THE IMPLEMENTATION PROCESS

Once a federal judicial decision is made, Congress can offer a variety of responses. It may aid or hinder the implementation of a decision and can also alter a court's interpretation of the law. For instance, Congress may choose to pass a new statute in response to a Court decision, or work to pass a constitutional amendment to overturn a Court decision based on constitutional interpretation. Members of Congress can mount an attack on individual judges and/or the opinion itself. Alternatively, Congress may try to remove the Court's jurisdiction to hear certain types of cases. Finally, members of Congress can use the confirmation process to praise or attack the judiciary. Naturally, the actions of individual members of Congress will be influenced by their partisan and ideological leanings.

While deciding cases, the courts are often called on to interpret federal statutes. On occasion, the judicial interpretation may differ from what a majority in Congress intended. When that situation occurs, the statute can be changed by new legislation that, in effect, overrules the court's initial interpretation.[48] A good example of this occurred in 2009 when Congress passed, and President Barack Obama signed into law, the Lilly Ledbetter Fair Pay Act.[49] This law effectively overturned the 2007 US Supreme Court case of *Ledbetter v. Goodyear Tire & Rubber*.[50] That case involved a woman who spent her career working at a Goodyear tire plant in Alabama. Lilly Ledbetter, who was hired in 1979, was paid less than her male colleagues in the same position throughout her career with Goodyear. However, she only became aware of this discriminatory action soon before she retired in 1998. She filed a lawsuit against the company and a jury awarded her $3.3 million (though this was later reduced to $300,000).[51] Goodyear appealed to the Supreme Court, which ruled in a 5–4 decision in favor of the company and against Ledbetter. The Court decided that Ledbetter could not sue for a violation of Title VII (which prohibits employment discrimination based on race, color, religion, sex, and national origin) of the Civil Rights Act of 1964 or the Equal Pay Act of 1963. The reason? The conservative majority on the Court interpreted the 180-day statute of limitations written into the law to mean that Ledbetter should have filed her claim years before, when the initial discriminatory wage decision was made by Goodyear in 1979, and not at the date of her most recent paycheck in the 1990s. Outraged by the majority's opinion, Justice Ruth Bader Ginsburg took the unusual step of reading her dissent from the bench. She concluded her dissent by stating, "Once again, the ball is in Congress' court . . . the Legislature may act to correct this Court's parsimonious reading of Title VII."[52] Congress did just that. In response to this controversial ruling, Congress changed the law in 2009. The new law clarified that the 180-day statute of limitations for filing an equal-pay lawsuit regarding pay discrimination resets with each new paycheck affected by a discriminatory action. Though it could not address Lilly Ledbetter's case, the 2009 law effectively negated the Supreme Court's 2007 decision in *Ledbetter v. Goodyear Tire & Rubber*.

In addition to ruling on statutes, the federal courts interpret the Constitution. Congress has two methods to reverse or alter the effects of a constitutional interpretation it does not like.

First, it can respond with another statute. In *Texas v. Johnson*, the Supreme Court overturned a Texas flag desecration statute that made it illegal to "cast contempt" on the flag by "publicly mutilating, defacing, burning, or trampling" on it. Gregory Lee Johnson had been found guilty of violating the law when he burned an American flag at the 1984 Republican National Convention in Dallas.[53] Although President George H. W. Bush and some legislators argued in favor of a constitutional amendment to overturn the Court's decision, others preferred not to tinker with the Constitution. Instead, Congress enacted a statute designed to avoid the constitutional problems of the Texas law by eliminating any reference to the motives of a person who damages an American flag. The Flag Protection Act was passed by Congress in October 1989 and became effective after President Bush allowed it to become law without his signature.[54] The new law was immediately challenged in several flag-burning demonstrations that were held in various parts of the country soon thereafter. In one of these exhibitions, held on the steps of the Capitol, Gregory Lee Johnson joined several others in again igniting an American flag. However, he was not among those charged with violating the new federal statute. In 1990, the Supreme Court declared the Flag Protection Act unconstitutional.[55]

Second, a constitutional decision can be overturned directly by an amendment to the US Constitution. Although many such amendments have been introduced over the years, it is difficult to obtain the necessary two-thirds vote in each house of Congress to propose the amendment and then achieve ratification by three-fourths of the states. In fact, only four Supreme Court decisions in the history of the Court have been overturned by constitutional amendments. The Eleventh Amendment overturned *Chisholm v. Georgia* (dealing with suits against a state in federal court); the Thirteenth Amendment overturned *Scott v. Sandford* (dealing with the legality of slavery); the Sixteenth Amendment overturned *Pollock v. Farmers' Loan and Trust Co.* (pertaining to the constitutionality of the income tax); and the Twenty-Sixth Amendment overturned *Oregon v. Mitchell* (giving eighteen-year-olds the right to vote in state elections).[56]

Congressional attacks on the federal courts in general and on certain judges are another method of responding to judicial decisions. These attacks are sometimes in the form of verbal denouncements that allow a member of Congress to let off steam over a decision or series of decisions. A recent example centers on the *Garland v. Cargill* case, where the Supreme Court struck down a ban on bump stocks, devices that allow a shooter to convert a semiautomatic rifle into operating like a machine gun. In 2017, in response to the Las Vegas mass shooting where fifty-eight people were killed and over five hundred injured, then-President Trump signed an executive order prohibiting bump stocks. Michael Cargill challenged the executive action. In 2024, the Supreme Court held that the executive branch exceeded its authority to classify a bump stock as a machine gun.[57] Justice Alito, in his concurring opinion, noted that "There is a simple remedy for the disparate treatment of bump stocks and machineguns. Congress can amend the law. . . ."[58] Many members of Congress were outraged by the Court's ruling. To illustrate, Representative Steve Cohen (D-TN) issued a press release stating, "Today's Supreme Court decision is out-of-touch with the reality of gun violence in America";[59] Representative Rosa DeLauro (D-CT) said, "This decision is outrageous, dangerous, and will have deadly consequences";[60] and Senator Dick Durbin (D-IL) expressed, "This ruling is deeply disappointing."[61] Other members of Congress praised the ruling. For instance, Representative Matt Gaetz (R-FL) stated the ruling "vindicates the rights of gun owners,"[62] and Senator Pete Ricketts (R-NE) declared, "The Supreme Court made the right decision."[63]

At other times, bills may be introduced to limit or remove the courts' jurisdiction in certain types of cases. For example, to prevent the courts from ruling in favor of same-sex marriage, a bill passed in the House of Representatives in 2004 would have limited the federal courts' jurisdiction over questions related to the definition of marriage. The bill ultimately failed in the Senate.[64] Keep in mind, too, that federal judges may be impeached and removed from office by Congress. In 2010, after an investigation found that he had committed perjury and lied about receiving money and gifts from lawyers, Judge G. Thomas Porteous Jr. of the Eastern District Court in Louisiana was found guilty on four articles of impeachment and removed from the bench.[65] Although the congressional bark may be worse than its bite in the use of this weapon, it is still part of its overall arsenal, and the impeachment of several federal judges serves as a reminder of that fact.

Finally, the confirmation process offers a chance for an attack on the courts. As a new federal judicial appointee goes through hearings in the Senate, individual senators sometimes use the opportunity to denounce individual judges or specific decisions and perhaps to gain insight into how the nominee would rule on specific issues. Sonia Sotomayor, a current Supreme Court justice and former federal trial and appeals court judge, was grilled extensively by members of the Senate Judiciary Committee about her views on controversial legal issues and her opinions in specific cases.[66] In 2018, Justice Brett Kavanaugh faced a particularly grueling confirmation hearing in light of the sexual misconduct allegations that arose, but he was eventually confirmed. In the most recent Supreme Court confirmation hearing, Justice Ketanji Brown Jackson also faced harsh questioning by some members of the Senate Judiciary Committee. Political scientists and law scholars Christina L. Boyd, Paul M. Collins, and Lori A. Ringhand described her hearing as heated and often disrespectful.[67] In recent years, attacking the Court and Supreme Court nominees has almost been the norm rather than the exception.

Congress and the federal courts are not always natural adversaries, even though it occasionally may appear that way. Retaliations against the federal judiciary are rare, and the two branches often work in harmony toward similar policy goals. For example, Congress played a key role in implementing the Supreme Court's school desegregation policy by enacting the Civil Rights Act of 1964, which empowered the Justice Department to initiate suits against school districts. Title VI of the Act also provided a potent weapon in the desegregation struggle by threatening the denial of federal funds to schools guilty of segregation. In 1965, Congress further solidified its support for a policy of desegregated public schools by passing the Elementary and Secondary Education Act. This act gave the federal government a much larger role in financing public education and thus made the threat to cut off federal funds a most fundamental problem for many segregated school districts.[68] In short, congressional support is significant because the likelihood of compliance with a Court decision increases when unity prevails among the branches of government.[69]

EXECUTIVE BRANCH INFLUENCES ON THE IMPLEMENTATION PROCESS

At times, the executive branch may be called on directly to implement a judicial decision. A pertinent example is a decision handed down by the Supreme Court in June 2006.[70] By a 5–3 vote, the Court decided that President George W. Bush, as commander in chief, lacked congressional authority to try Guantánamo Bay detainees by means of military commissions. The decision compelled the administration to devise a different method to try Salim Hamdan and some 450 other detainees.

Even when not directly involved in the enforcement of a judicial policy, the president may still be able to influence its impact. Because of the status and visibility of the office, a president, simply by words and actions, may encourage support for, or resistance to, a new judicial policy. For instance, it has been argued that President Dwight D. Eisenhower's lack of enthusiasm for the *Brown v. Board of Education* decision and "his unwillingness to support it in more than a pro forma fashion encouraged southern resistance."[71] As a consequence, Eisenhower later had to send federal troops to Little Rock, Arkansas, to enforce the district court's integration order. Sending in troops made President Eisenhower's participation in the implementation process more direct.

A president can propose legislation aimed at retaliating against the courts. President Franklin D. Roosevelt, for instance, famously urged Congress to increase the size of the Supreme Court to "pack" it with justices who supported New Deal legislation. More recently, President Joe Biden in 2021 created the Presidential Commission on the Supreme Court of the United States to consider potential structural and/or procedural changes to the High Court.[72] Many liberals have called for judicial reform considering recent conservative decisions that severely weakened campaign finance laws, overturned prior precedents on abortion and affirmative action, along with gutting the Voting Rights Act, coupled with the highly partisan appointment processes of Justices Brett Kavanaugh and Amy Coney Barrett. The commission has discussed reducing the Supreme Court's power and could entertain the idea of expanding the Court's membership beyond nine justices.[73] Though this commission does not have policymaking power and can only make recommendations, its very existence is an implicit message that there is substantial displeasure with the way the Court has been operating and fundamental change could be considered by Congress.

The appointment power also gives the president an opportunity to influence federal judicial policies. Although senatorial courtesy is important in the appointment of federal district judges, evidence points to the fact that the president dominates the process at the Supreme Court and courts of appeals.

Presidents have long realized that lower federal judges are also important in the judicial policymaking process. For this reason, many chief executives have shown an interest in appointing lower court judges who share their basic ideologies and values.[74] A president can also influence judicial policymaking through the activities of the Justice Department. The attorney general and staff subordinates can emphasize specific issues according to the overall policy goals of the president. For example, the 1964 Civil Rights Act authorized the Justice Department to file school desegregation suits. This allowed the executive branch to become more actively involved in implementing the policy goal of racial equality. The other side of the coin, however, is that the Justice Department may, at its discretion, deemphasize specific policies by not pursuing them vigorously in the courts. For example, during the first administration of President Donald Trump, the Justice Department sought to pare back civil rights protections for minorities. News reporters noted at the time that it was "a change that would mark one of the most significant shifts in civil rights enforcement in generations."[75]

Another official who can influence judicial policymaking is the solicitor general. Historically, this person has been seen as having dual responsibility, to both the judicial and the executive branches.[76] The solicitor general is often viewed as a counselor who advises the Court about the meaning of federal statutes and the Constitution. The solicitor general also determines which of the cases involving the federal government as a party will be appealed to the Supreme Court. Furthermore, they may file an amicus curiae brief urging the Court to grant or deny another litigant's certiorari petition or supporting or opposing a particular policy being urged on the high court. The solicitor general thus reacts to the policy decisions of the Supreme Court.

Many judicial decisions are implemented by the various departments, agencies, bureaus, and commissions that abound in the executive branch. To mention just one example, the Environmental Protection Agency is responsible for enforcing the various laws relating to clean air and water standards and other aspects of the environment. Administration compliance with court decisions is generally good, albeit sometimes reluctant. Outright defiance is unusual, though not unprecedented. For example, a few federal agencies during the Trump administration were accused of ignoring or defying the courts.[77] One example involved the US Department of Education (ED) under the leadership of Secretary of Education Betsy DeVos. After a court ordered a halt to student loan repayment by former students at a defunct for-profit college chain in May 2018, the Department of Education ignored the judge and continued to seek repayment by the students. The magistrate judge in the case, Sallie Kim, called the action a "flagrant and continuing violation" of her order stopping the collections. The students challenged the action and eventually won after much struggle, and attention was drawn to ED's willful disobedience. In 2020, Secretary of Education DeVos was held in contempt of court and ED was fined $100,000 for defying the court order.[78]

Another instance of defiance occurred on August 8, 2018, in a deportation case involving a daughter and her mother who sought asylum in the United States after she suffered "two decades of horrific sexual abuse by her husband" in El Salvador, according to a lawsuit.[79] The government had assured the court the previous day that the individuals would not be deported while their case was still under review. But the American Civil Liberties Union filed an emergency petition with the judge after the group learned that the women had in fact been placed by the Justice Department on an outbound flight to El Salvador. US District Court Judge Emmet Sullivan threatened to begin contempt of court proceedings against Attorney General Jeff Sessions if the government did not order the turnaround of the airplane carrying the two plaintiffs whose case was still pending before the judge. "This is pretty outrageous," Judge Sullivan said after being told about the removal. "That someone seeking justice in US court is spirited away while her attorneys are arguing for justice for her? I'm not happy about this at all. This is not acceptable."[80] Under pressure by the judge, the women were allowed to remain on the jet and return to the United States, and they were later granted asylum. The Justice Department declined to give any explanation for why the individuals had been placed on the flight.[81]

Fortunately, these examples of noncompliance are the exception rather than the rule. Most administrations realize that disobedience of court orders is often counterproductive and, as these examples demonstrate, likely to be futile.

OTHER IMPLEMENTERS

In addition to lower court judges, Congress, the president, and others in the executive branch, many other actors are involved in the interpretation and implementation of judicial policies.[82]

Although the focus thus far has been primarily on various federal officials, implementation of judicial policies is often performed by state officials.[83] Many of the Supreme Court's criminal due process decisions, such as *Gideon v. Wainwright*[84] and *Miranda v. Arizona*,[85] have been enforced by state court judges and other state officials. State and local police officers, for instance, have played a significant role in implementing the *Miranda* requirement that criminal suspects must be advised of their rights. The *Gideon* ruling that an attorney must be provided at state expense for indigent defendants in felony trials has been implemented by public defenders, local bar associations, and individual court-appointed lawyers.

State legislators and executives are also frequently drawn into the implementation process, often as unwilling participants. A judge who determines that a wrong has been committed may use the power to issue an equitable decree as a way of remedying the wrong. The range of remedies available is broad because cases vary in the issues they raise and the types of relief sought. Among the more common options from which a judge may choose are process remedies, performance standards, and specified remedial actions.[86] Process remedies provide for such things as advisory committees, citizen participation, educational programs, evaluation committees, dispute resolution procedures, and special masters. The remedies do not specify a particular form of action. Performance standards call for specific remedies—a certain number of housing units or schools or a certain level of staffing in a prison or mental health facility. The specific means for attaining these goals are left to the discretion of the officials named in the suit. Examples of specified remedial actions are school busing, altered school attendance zones, and changes in the size and condition of prison cells or hospital rooms. This type of remedy gives the defendant no flexibility concerning the specific remedy or the means for attaining it.

Implementation of these remedial decrees often devolves, at least partially, to the state legislatures. An order calling for a certain number of prison cells or a certain number of guards in the prison system might require new state expenditures, which the legislature would have to fund. Similarly, an order to construct more modern mental health facilities or provide more modern equipment would mean an increase in state expenditures. Governors would also naturally participate in carrying out these kinds of remedial decrees because they typically are heavily involved in state budgeting procedures. Also, governors may sign or veto laws. Some even have an item veto power, which permits them to veto certain budget items while approving others.

Sometimes judges appoint certain individuals to assist in carrying out the remedial decree. Special heads are usually given some decision-making authority.

Court-appointed monitors are also used in some situations, but they do not relieve the judge of decision-making responsibilities. Instead, the monitor is an information gatherer who reports on the defendant's progress in complying with the remedial decree.

THE IMPACT OF JUDICIAL POLICIES

Thus far, the focus has primarily been on the implementation of judicial policies by various government officials, which is entirely appropriate because court decisions are often specifically directed at other public policymakers. Such decisions typically place courts in the middle of political controversies, as three high-profile cases illustrate. All focused on immigration, health care, and abortion, and all were decided by the US Supreme Court during the 2011–2012 and 2021–2022 terms.

On June 25, 2012, the Court announced its decision in *Arizona v. United States*, a case dealing with the highly politicized issue of illegal immigration.[87] This dispute began when the Arizona legislature passed, and Governor Jan Brewer signed, a controversial law aimed at cracking down on undocumented immigrants in that state. The federal government sought to stop enforcement of the law in US district court before it could take effect, arguing that federal immigration laws preempted the Arizona statute. The federal trial court blocked provisions of the Arizona law that (1) created a state-law crime for being unlawfully present in the United States, (2) created a state-law crime for working or seeking work while not being authorized to do so, (3) required state and local officers to verify the citizenship or alien status of anyone who was lawfully arrested or detained, and (4) authorized warrantless arrests of aliens believed to be removable from the United States.

Arizona appealed the decision to the Ninth Circuit Court of Appeals, which affirmed the district court's decision. Arizona then sought review by the US Supreme Court. Justice Anthony Kennedy, writing for the majority, upheld the lower court decisions blocking provisions 1, 2, and 4. The Court held Provision 1 to conflict with federal immigration registration requirements and enforcement provisions already in place. Provision 2 was preempted because its method of enforcement interfered with federal law. Provision 4 was also preempted because it usurped the federal government's authority to use discretion in the process of removing undocumented persons.

However, the Court upheld the constitutionality of Provision 3, stating that it simply allowed state law enforcement officials to communicate with federal immigration and customs enforcement officers during otherwise lawful arrests. Furthermore, limitations were already in place to protect individual rights. Justice Kennedy did note, however, that the Court's decision did not foreclose future constitutional challenges to the law on an applied basis.

On June 28, 2012—the last day of its October 2011 term—the Supreme Court announced its highly anticipated decision in *National Federation of Independent Business v. Sebelius*,[88] one of the cases that challenged the constitutionality of the ACA (aka "Obamacare").[89] One of the key parts of the law that was challenged was a provision for expanding Medicaid, the federal—state cooperative program that provides health care coverage for low-income people. The ACA stipulated those states were required to accept an expansion of Medicaid coverage to continue to receive federal funds for the Medicaid program. Other important provisions in the law required individuals to have health insurance coverage or they would have to pay a fine and an employer mandate that required certain businesses to provide health insurance coverage for their employees. Several states challenged the law and sought a declaration that the ACA was unconstitutional. The plaintiffs argued that (1) the individual mandate exceeded Congress's enumerated power under the Commerce Clause, (2) the Medicaid expansions were unconstitutionally coercive, and (3) the employer mandate impermissibly interfered with state sovereignty.

After mixed rulings by lower courts, the ACA case eventually landed at the US Supreme Court. Following six hours of oral argument, which featured sharp exchanges between the justices and attorneys, political and legal commentators offered various opinions about what the Court might do.

On the morning of Thursday, June 28, 2012, Chief Justice Roberts announced to a packed Court the close decision. Speaking for a five-member majority that consisted of himself and Justices Ginsburg, Breyer, Sotomayor, and Kagan, the Court upheld the individual mandate tax penalty as a valid exercise of Congress's power to tax and spend, and they ruled in favor of the employer mandate. The same five-member majority also held that the Medicaid expansion provision, minus the unconstitutional threat to completely withdraw Medicaid funding, could stand as a valid exercise of Congress's power under the Taxing and Spending Clause.

Reaction to both decisions was swift. Republican leaders in Congress vowed to repeal the ACA, while Democrats and the Obama administration, of course, praised the Court's ruling.

Two subsequent cases—*King v. Burwell*[90] and *California v. Texas*[91]—again saw the courts wrestling with the ACA and health care policy. In the 2015 *King* case, the Court was asked to rule on the permissibility of tax credits available to individuals who buy their health plans through the ACA "exchanges," online websites where low-income to middle-income individuals can access subsidized health insurance. Some states had established these exchanges themselves, while others had chosen to allow the federal government, through the Department of Health and Human Services (HHS), to run them. Conservative opponents of the ACA had argued that specific language of the law meant that individuals could not receive health care plan tax credits in states that allowed the HHS to run their exchanges. These tax credits effectively subsidized the health plans, and without them most would not be able to afford to buy health insurance and the exchange system would effectively collapse. But the Court ruled against the ACA opponents and upheld the exchanges. In a 6–3 ruling, the majority held that the ACA's tax credits are available to individuals in all states with exchanges, regardless of whether the state or HHS operated them. Chief Justice John Roberts wrote, "Those credits are necessary for the Federal Exchanges to function like their State Exchange counterparts, and to avoid the type of calamitous result that Congress plainly meant to avoid."[92] Roberts went on to write, "Congress passed the Affordable Care Act to improve health insurance markets, not to destroy them. If at all possible, we must interpret the Act in a way that is consistent with the former, and avoids the latter."[93]

In the case of *California v. Texas*, the Supreme Court in 2021 dismissed another challenge to the ACA. This case involved litigants who argued that since the tax penalty for not having health insurance had been reduced by Congress in 2017 to zero, the penalty was no longer a "tax" as the Court had held in *NFIB v. Sebelius*. And because the tax was central to the overall design of the ACA, the whole law should be held unconstitutional. Most legal observers believed the reasoning in the lawsuit challenging the ACA was dubious and gave the plaintiffs little chance of succeeding. They were proven correct when the Supreme Court, in a June 2021 ruling, dismissed the case and effectively ruled again in favor of the ACA.

Finally, the most high-profile example where the Court has placed itself front and center in American politics is the *Dobbs v. Jackson Women's Health Organization* decision that ended the constitutionally protected right to abortion. Previously, under *Roe v. Wade* and *Planned Parenthood v. Casey*, women possessed a constitutionally protected right to terminate their pregnancies. However, the *Dobbs* decision overturned these two precedents. Since the decision in 2022, fourteen states have passed laws that have entirely banned abortion, three states have placed a six-week ban, two states have put a twelve-week ban, and two states have bans in the fifteen-to-eighteen-week range.[94] Abortion remains legal in twenty-seven states, and twenty-one of the twenty-seven states have added new legal protections since *Dobbs*. For example, states such as California, Illinois, Massachusetts, Michigan, Minnesota, New Jersey, and Vermont have either had voter-led initiatives enshrining the right to abortion in their state constitution or the state supreme court has recognized a right to abortion under their state constitution.[95] Additionally, Kansas rejected a ballot measure that would remove the right to abortion from the state Constitution. As a result, in Kansas, women are still able to terminate their pregnancy up to twenty-two weeks.

In January 2024, the Supreme Court agreed to take up a case where the US district court halted enforcement of an Idaho law that criminalized health care providers from providing abortions. However, in June 2024, the Supreme Court reversed course and dismissed *Idaho v. United States* and *Moyle v. United States* as improvidently granted (this means that the court mistakenly granted review).[96] The central issue in the case revolves around an Idaho law that makes it a criminal offense for health care providers to perform an abortion. The law provided a narrow exception to save the life of the mother. The Biden administration, however, argued that the federal Emergency Medical Treatment and Labor Act of 1986 (EMTALA) preempts Idaho's law and requires hospital ERs that receive Medicare funding to provide an abortion in emergencies even if the procedure is not necessary to save the life of the mother.[97] In August

2022, the US District Court for the District of Idaho issued a preliminary injunction to stop the enforcement of Idaho's law. Justice Kagan, who wrote a concurring opinion to the Supreme Court order, explained the conflict between the two laws this way:

EMTALA requires a Medicare-funded hospital to offer an abortion when needed to stabilize a medical condition that seriously threatens a pregnant woman's life or health. Idaho allows abortions only when "necessary to prevent" a pregnant woman's "death." By their terms, the two laws differ. What falls in the gap between them are cases in which continuing a pregnancy does not put a woman's life in danger, but still places her risk of grave health consequences, including loss of fertility. In that situation, federal law requires a hospital to offer an abortion, whereas Idaho law prohibits that emergency care.[98]

The 2024 Supreme Court order leaves in place the preliminary injunction issued by the District Court. Thus, for now, emergency abortions will be permitted in Idaho.

These decisions, which delve into the intricacies of tax policy, health insurance regulation, abortion rights, and the like, highlight arguments that American courts are sometimes too heavily engaged in making decisions that affect society and too involved in policymaking. This is not the case in all countries. For example, political scientist Susan W. Johnson in her study of Canadian judges finds significant evidence that "justices are not as polarized, nor perhaps, as overtly policy driven, as the US Supreme Court."[99]

Nonetheless, policies developed by the US Supreme Court have had significant effects on society. Notable examples can be found in the areas of racial equality and criminal due process.

Racial Equality

Many point to the Supreme Court's *Brown* decision as the impetus for the drive for racial equality in the United States. Congress and the executive branch were also involved in the process of ensuring implementation of the decision's desegregation policy, but the courts took the lead in pursuing a national policy of racial equality. Thus, one of the most important ways the federal judiciary can influence policy is to place issues on the national political agenda.

In the beginning, the court decisions were often vague, leading to evasion of the new policy. The Supreme Court justices and many lower federal judges were persistent in decisions following *Brown*, and in this way, they kept the policy of racial equality on the national political agenda. Their persistence paid off with passage of the 1964 Civil Rights Act, ten years after *Brown*. That act, which had the dedicated support of Presidents John F. Kennedy and Lyndon B. Johnson, squarely placed Congress and the president on record as advocating racial equality in America.

One other aspect of the federal judiciary's importance in the policymaking process is illustrated by *Brown* and the cases that followed it. Although the courts stood virtually alone in the quest for racial equality for several years, their decisions did not go unnoticed. The *Brown* decision, as one team of scholars of judicial impact stated:

> was a highly visible Court decision, a judicial attempt to generate one of the greatest social reforms in American history. And certainly, in the years that followed, African Americans and their allies brought considerable pressures on other governmental bodies to desegregate the schools. Indeed, the pressures soon went far beyond schools to demand integration of all aspects of American life.[100]

Some debate has arisen, however, over whether *Brown* was a major cause of this mobilization of effort. One scholar empirically examined the causal link between *Brown* and civil rights mobilization by studying the coverage of civil rights in periodicals dating from 1940 to 1965.[101] He concluded that no evidence exists that *Brown*'s "influence was widespread or of much importance to the battle for civil rights."[102] Other scholars, however, attribute much greater influence on *Brown* in the mobilization process.[103]

Although gains have been made, the battle over racial equality and equal opportunity for racial minorities is far from over. According to legal expert Linda Greenhouse, the Roberts Court has actively limited programs and practices that promote race consciousness.[104] Consider two cases: one involving the Voting Rights Act and the other concerning affirmative action in college admissions. The Supreme Court in the case of *Shelby County v. Holder* (2013) invalidated a key provision of the Voting Rights Act of 1965 (VRA). Congress enacted the VRA to prevent states and localities from passing laws denying citizens equal voting rights.[105] Specifically, the VRA included a preclearance provision that required states and localities "with histories of obstructing minority voters to get federal approval before changing any election procedure."[106] In the 5–4 decision, written by Chief Justice Roberts, the Court ruled that the methodology used to determine whether a state or locality needs to obtain preclearance from the federal government is unconstitutional. Justice Roberts wrote, "Our country has changed, and while any racial discrimination in voting is too much, Congress must ensure that the legislation it passes to remedy that problem speaks to current conditions."[107] The decision put the ball back in Congress's court to update the preclearance formula, but to date, Congress has not done so.

More recently, in 2023, the Court overturned college and university affirmation action programs in *Students for Fair Admissions, Inc. v. President and Fellows of Harvard College*.[108] In this case, the Court addressed whether colleges could consider an applicant's race as part of the admissions process. The Supreme Court ruled that colleges could no longer consider race as one of the many factors in their admissions process, which effectively overturned earlier Court precedents. In the 6–2 decision (Justice Jackson did not participate in the case), the Court held that affirmative action programs that consider race in the admissions process violate the Equal Protection Clause of the Fourteenth Amendment. While the Court held that race can no longer play a role in the admissions process, Chief Justice Roberts was quick to clarify that "nothing in this opinion should be construed as prohibiting universities from considering an applicant's discussion of how race affected his or her life, be it through discrimination, inspiration, or otherwise."[109] As colleges and universities adjust their admissions guidelines, it remains to be seen how this momentous decision will impact the college admissions landscape. And the true impact of this decision won't be realized for some time. However, one study found that in the aftermath of the *Student for Fair Admissions* decision there were no changes in the ethnic and racial composition of the applicant pool across the United States or how students discuss both in their college essays.[110]

Criminal Due Process

Judicial policymaking around criminal due process is most associated with the era of the Warren Court. As a former solicitor general said, "Never has there been such a thorough-going reform of criminal procedure within so short a time."[111] The Warren Court decisions were aimed primarily at changing the procedures followed by the states in dealing with criminal defendants. By the time Chief Justice Earl Warren left the Supreme Court, new policies had been established to deal with a wide range of activities. Among the most far-reaching decisions of the Warren Court were *Mapp v. Ohio, Gideon v. Wainwright*, and *Miranda v. Arizona*.[112]

The *Mapp* decision extended to the states the exclusionary rule, which had applied to the national government for several years. This rule required state courts to exclude from trial evidence that had been illegally seized by the police. Although some police departments, especially in major urban areas, have tried to establish specific guidelines for their officers to follow in obtaining evidence, such efforts have not been universal. Because of variations in police practices and differing lower court interpretations of what constitutes a valid search and seizure, implementation of *Mapp* has not been consistent throughout the country.

Perhaps even more important in reducing the originally perceived impact of *Mapp* has been the lack of solid support for the exclusionary rule among the Supreme Court justices. To begin with, this was not a unanimous decision, and over the years, some of the justices have been openly critical of the exclusionary rule. Not surprisingly, as the Court has become more conservative there have been decisions that have limited the scope of the exclusionary rule. In 1984, the Court adopted a limited good-faith exception to the exclusionary rule, which allows officers to seize evidence in good faith, relying on search warrants that may later prove to be defective.[113] This good-faith exception was reaffirmed in 1995 in *Arizona v. Evans* and 2008 in *Herring v. United States*.[114] Decisions of the Burger and Rehnquist Courts broadened the scope of legal searches, thus limiting the applicability of the rule.[115] The Roberts Court has follow suit. In *Hudson v. Michigan*, decided by a 5–4 vote in June 2006, the Court ruled that the exclusionary rule is not an appropriate remedy when law enforcement officers have a valid search warrant but fail to knock and announce themselves before entering a suspect's home.[116]

The *Gideon v. Wainwright*[117] decision held that attorneys must be provided for indigent defendants when they go to trial in a felony case in state courts. After the Court's decision public defender programs were established in many regions. Additionally, local bar associations cooperated with states courts to implement indigent defense programs.

The impact of *Gideon* is clearer and more consistent than that of *Mapp*. One reason, no doubt, is that many states had already implemented the policy called for by *Gideon*. It was simply more widely accepted than the policy established by *Mapp*. The policy announced in *Gideon* was also more sharply defined than the one in *Mapp*. Although the Court did not specify whether a public defender or a court-appointed lawyer must be provided, it is still clear that the indigent defendant must have the help of an attorney. The Burger Court did not retreat from the Warren Court's policy of providing an attorney for indigent defendants, as it did on the search-and-seizure issue addressed by *Mapp*. All these factors add up to a more recognizable impact for the policy announced in *Gideon*.[118]

In *Miranda v. Arizona*,[119] the Supreme Court went a step further, ruling that police officers must advise suspects taken into custody of their constitutional rights, one of which is to have an attorney present during questioning. These rights are so clearly stated that police departments have had the ruling printed on cards for officers to carry in their shirt pockets; when suspects are subjected to a custodial interrogation, the officers read the suspects their rights.

If measured simply in terms of police officers reading the *Miranda* rights to persons they arrest, compliance with the Supreme Court policy reaches a prominent level. Some researchers, however, have questioned the impact of *Miranda* because of the method used to advise suspects of their rights. It is one thing to read to a person from a card; it is another to explain what is meant by the high court's requirements and then try to make the suspect understand them. Viewed from this standpoint, the impact of the policy announced in *Miranda* is not as clear.

Two years after the decision, Congress reacted to *Miranda* by enacting a statute that, in essence, made the admissibility of a suspect's statements turn solely on whether they were made voluntarily. The statute received little attention until 1999, when the US Court of Appeals for the Fourth Circuit ruled on a case involving an alleged bank robber who moved to suppress a statement made to the FBI on the ground that he had not received "*Miranda* warnings" before being interrogated. The court of appeals held that the statute was satisfied because the suspect's statement was voluntary. The decision raised the question of whether the congressional act or the high court's *Miranda* decision should be followed. In the 2000 case of *Dickerson v. United States*, the Supreme Court held that *Miranda*, being a constitutional decision of the Court, could not, in effect, be overruled by an act of Congress.[120] In other words, *Miranda* still governs the admissibility of statements made during custodial interrogation in state and federal courts.

In sum, the impact of the Supreme Court's criminal justice policies has been mixed, for several reasons. In some instances, ambiguity is a problem. In other cases, less than solid support for the policy may be evident among justices, or support erodes when some members of the Court are replaced by others. All these variables translate into greater discretion for the implementers.

Concluding Comments on the Impact of Judicial Policies

Some judicial policies have a more significant impact on society than others. The judiciary plays a greater role in developing the nation's policies than the framers of the Constitution envisioned. However:

> American courts are not all-powerful institutions. They were designed with severe limitations and placed in a political system of divided powers. To ask them to produce significant social reforms is to forget their history and ignore their constraints.[121]

Within this complex framework of competing political and social demands and expectations is a policymaking role for the courts. Because the other two branches of government are sometimes not receptive to the demands of certain segments of society, their only alternative is to turn to the courts. Civil rights organizations, for example, made no real headway until they found the Supreme Court to be a supportive forum for their school desegregation efforts. They were then able to use *Brown* and other decisions as a springboard to attack a variety of areas of discrimination. Thus, a champion at a high government level may offer hope to individuals and interest groups.

As civil rights groups attained some success in the federal courts, others were encouraged to use litigation as a strategy. For example, as several scholars have found, supporters of women's rights followed a pattern established by minority groups when they began taking their grievances to the courts.[122] What began as a narrow pursuit for racial equality was broadened to a quest for equality for other disadvantaged groups in society.

A good example may be found in the most highly anticipated decision reached in the Supreme Court's October 2014 term. The case concerned the issue of same-sex marriage. As noted earlier in this chapter, the number of states allowing members of the same sex to lawfully marry increased dramatically over the years. However, a few states refused to permit same-sex marriages or to honor a same-sex marriage performed in a state where it was legal. Kentucky, Michigan, Ohio, and Tennessee—states located in the Sixth Circuit—were examples of states that did not permit marriages between same-sex couples. Fourteen petitioners filed suits in federal district courts in their home states, claiming that state officials violated the Fourteenth Amendment by denying them the right to marry or to have marriages lawfully performed in another state given full recognition. Each district court ruled in favor of the petitioners, but the Sixth Circuit Court of Appeals consolidated the cases and reversed the decisions of the district courts.

As discussed previously, the 2015 case of *Obergefell v. Hodges*[123] effectively put an end to the debate about the legality of gay marriage. In a 5–4 decision, the Court held that the Fourteenth Amendment requires a state to license a marriage between two people of the same sex and to recognize a marriage between two people of the same sex when their marriage was lawfully licensed and performed out of state. To deny such rights is a violation of the Due Process and Equal Protection Clauses of the Fourteenth Amendment.

Legal scholar Erwin Chemerinsky, in discussing the Court's decision, says that "the difference between the majority and dissents, and between the liberal and conservative commentators, is about the appropriate role of the Supreme Court in a democratic society." He takes the position, however, that protecting the rights of minorities, especially fundamental rights, is not left to the political process for protection. The Supreme Court performed exactly its proper role in the constitutional system by protecting the rights of individuals when it struck down the laws prohibiting same-sex marriage.[124]

Clearly, the courts can announce policy decisions that attract national attention and perhaps emphasize that other policymakers have failed to act. In this way, the judiciary may invite the other branches to exercise their policymaking powers. Follow-up decisions indicate the judiciary's determination to pursue a particular policy and help keep alive the invitation for other policymakers to participate in the endeavor.

Given the circumstances, the courts seem best equipped to develop and implement narrow policies that are less controversial in nature. The policy established in the *Gideon* case provides a good example. The decision that indigent defendants in state criminal trials must be provided with an attorney did not elicit any strong protests. Furthermore, it was a policy that primarily required the support of judges and lawyers; action by Congress and the president was not necessary. A policy of equality for all segments of society, however, is one that must sometimes involve the judicial branch. Thus, June 26, 2015—the date that the Court announced its decision in *Obergefell*—will be remembered like dates such as May 17, 1954, when the Court decided *Brown v. Board of Education*, as the Court taking a historic step forward in advancing liberty and equality.[125]

SUMMARY

We began this chapter by pointing out that judicial decisions are not self-executing. The courts depend on a variety of individuals, both inside and outside the judicial branch, to carry out their rulings.

Lower court judges are prominent in the implementation process. Our discussion of their role in carrying out decisions of higher courts emphasized the discretion they exercise. Factors that account for the flexibility that rests with the lower court judge include the decentralization of the judicial system and the ambiguity of higher court rulings. We also examined the strategies that lower court judges may use in resisting appellate court decisions they dislike.

Congress and the president may also be involved in the implementation process. Each of these branches can react either positively or negatively to a court decision. As described in some detail, they may exert a wide range of influences in enforcing a judicial decision.

We also noted that some policies call on state officials to take part in the implementation process. State court judges, for example, played the significant role in enforcing the Warren Court's decisions on criminal due process. Local school boards have also been called on to carry out Supreme Court policies.

We concluded the chapter with a discussion of the impact on society of several important federal court policies. Explanations were offered as to why some policies have a greater impact on society than others. Most important, perhaps, is that if a ruling faces strong opposition, Congress and other implementers are likely to drag their feet. The last section of the chapter offered some thoughts on the role of courts in bringing about changes in society. It was noted that the judiciary can act as a kind of beacon for traditionally underrepresented groups seeking to achieve their goals.

FURTHER THOUGHTS AND DISCUSSION QUESTIONS

1. What arguments can you make for the level of discretion lower court judges should have when implementing decisions of appellate courts? How does this level of individual discretion affect the application of justice in society?
2. Should the judicial branch develop and implement public policy, or should that power belong exclusively to the executive and legislative branches? One of our assumptions in this book is that judges routinely engage in policymaking, but what would judicial decisions look like if they were completely divorced from the context of public policy?
3. Should overturning acts of Congress require a supermajority vote of the Court?
4. What are the major strengths and weaknesses of the US Supreme Court in influencing social policies in the United States?

SUGGESTED RESOURCES

Banks, Christopher P., and David M. O'Brien. *Courts and Judicial Policymaking.* New York, NY: Pearson, 2006. A thorough overview of the role of courts and judges in the policymaking process.

Braman, Eileen. *Constitutional Powers and Politics.* Charlottesville, VA: University of Virginia Press, 2023. An impressive examination of how citizens think about government action and constitutional change.

Canon, Bradley C., and Charles A. Johnson. *Judicial Policies: Implementation and Impact*, 2nd ed. Washington, DC: CQ Press, 1999. A good study of the processes and actors involved in carrying out and enforcing judicial decisions.

Daugherity, Brian J., and Charles C. Bolton, eds. *With All Deliberate Speed: Implementing Brown v. Board of Education.* Fayetteville, AR: University of Arkansas Press, 2008. Essays by various scholars on the challenges and political conflicts involved in the implementation of the landmark *Brown* decision.

Hitt, Matthew P. *Inconsistency and Indecision in the United States Supreme Court.* Ann Arbor, MI: University of Michigan Press, 2019. An examination of inconsistent Supreme Court decisions and what happens when the Court does not issue a clear precedent.

Peltason, Jack W. *Fifty-Eight Lonely Men.* New York, NY: Harcourt, Brace and World, 1961. An excellent study of the southern federal judges who were given the task of implementing the US Supreme Court's *Brown v. Board of Education* decision.

Rosenberg, Gerald N. *The Hollow Hope: Can Courts Bring About Social Change?* 2nd ed. Chicago, IL: University of Chicago Press, 2008. This book focuses on the ability of courts to effect social change.

Supreme Court of the United States website. Available online at www.suprem e-cour-tus.gov. The official site of the US Supreme Court; provides information about all aspects of the nation's highest court.

Ziegler, Mary. *Abortion and the Law in America: Roe v. Wade to the Present.* New York, NY: Cambridge University Press. 2020. An excellent book on the Supreme Court's abortion decisions.

KEY TERM

Dicta

15 POLICYMAKING BY AMERICAN JUDGES: A SYNTHESIS

As the saying goes, "An education is what you have left after you've forgotten what you've learned." This book has presented many facts, theories, statistics, and examples about the federal and state court systems. But as time goes on and myriad details are largely forgotten, what knowledge should you retain about the operation and policymaking of American courts? It is the purpose of this chapter to extract from the preceding fourteen chapters certain key ideas and significant themes that we would like you to remember long after most of the factual tidbits have faded from memory.

This small courthouse in Inverness, Florida, is typical of thousands across America. Much of the day-to-day administration of justice is rendered in these less ostentatious citadels of justice.

iStockPhoto/Aneese

The decisions of federal and state judges and justices affect the lives of all Americans. Whether one is referring to the norm enforcement rulings or to broader policymaking decisions, the output of federal and state courts permeates the warp and woof of the body politic in the United States. To have a full and accurate understanding of the American political system, it is necessary to be cognizant of the work of the people who wear the black robe. In examining decision-making by the judiciary, we must consider two basic questions: First, what are the conditions that cause judges to engage in policymaking and to do it so boldly? Second, does the literature give any clues about the substantive direction of this policymaking—that is, will it be conservative or liberal, supportive of or antagonistic toward the status quo? In seeking answers to these two basic questions, we have synthesized four sets of variables that shed some light in this area: (1) the nature of the case or issue presented to the court, (2) the values and orientations of the judges, (3) the nature of the judicial decision-making process, and (4) extraneous influences that serve to implement and sustain judicial decisions.

THE NATURE OF THE CASE OR ISSUE

One critical variable that clearly affects the degree to which (and sometimes the direction in which) American jurists influence citizens' lives is the type of controversy that might serve as grist for the judicial mills. If it is the sort of issue that judges can resolve with room for significant maneuvering, the impact of the case on public policy may be impressive. Conversely, if American jurists are forbidden to enter a certain decision-making realm or enter with only limited options, the policy impact will be nil. This general proposition has several aspects.

Jurisdiction

In Chapter 4, we outlined the jurisdiction of the three levels of the federal and state judiciaries. Knowledge of this topic is inherently important, but it takes on a second meaning in the context of this discussion—namely, that judges may not make policy in subject areas over which they have no legal authority. The controversy between the United States and Iran over whether Iran should be permitted to develop nuclear weapons is of major significance to the American people, as well as for world security. However, US judges are unlikely to have an impact on that controversy because they have no jurisdiction over Iranian nuclear policy or over disputes between the United States and other nations. Conversely, the courts will have considerable impact in matters concerning affirmative action policies of public universities and the prosecution of corporate executives accused of accounting irregularities because such disputes fall squarely within the legal jurisdiction of the US judiciary.

Although the courts do have some leeway in determining whether they have jurisdiction over a particular subject, for the most part, jurisdictional boundaries are set forth in the US and state constitutions and by acts of Congress and the state legislatures. In the same context, a legislative body's power to create and restrict the courts' jurisdiction can often greatly affect the direction of judicial decision-making. For example, Congress, by virtue of the Voting Rights Act, has granted citizens the right to sue local governments in federal courts if those governments alter the boundaries of electoral districts to significantly dilute the voting strength of minorities. By giving courts jurisdiction in this area and telling judges, in effect, how to decide the cases (by establishing the decision-making goals), Congress has had a major impact on judicial policymaking.

Judicial Self-Restraint

The nature-of-the-case variable is also related to whether a controversy falls into one of those forbidden realms where the "good judge" should not set foot. One judge might like to rule on a particular matter that is crying for adjudication, but if the litigant has not yet exhausted all legal or administrative remedies, the jurist will have to stay his hand. Another judge might want to overturn a particular presidential action because she thinks it "smacks of fascism," but if no specific part of the Constitution has been violated, she will have to express her displeasure in the voting booth, not in the courtroom. The enormous emphasis that the judicial system places on respecting past precedents (the doctrine of *stare decisis*) further deters jurists from impulsive decision-making. The various maxims of judicial self-restraint come from a variety of sources, including the Constitution, tradition, and acts of Congress and state legislatures; some have been imposed by the judges themselves. But whatever the source, they serve to channel the potential areas of judicial policymaking. Judges would have little success in attempting to adjudicate matters if doing so would soon bring reversal, censure, or organized opposition from those in a position to "correct" a judge who has strayed from the accepted pathway of judicial behavior.

Norm Enforcement versus Policymaking

Throughout this book, we have discussed judicial behavior as including both norm enforcement and significant policymaking. Most cases fall into the former category, particularly for the lower judiciary. That is, in most cases, judges routinely cite the applicable precedents, yield to the side with the weightiest evidence, and apply the statutes that clearly control the given situation. Discretion is at a minimum. In these routine cases, judges are not so much making policy as they are applying and enforcing existing norms and policy. In addition to norm enforcement, however, judges are presented with cases in which the room to maneuver—the potential to make policy—is much greater. Such opportunities exist at all levels of the judiciary, but appellate judges and justices probably have more options for significant policymaking than do their colleagues on the trial court bench. Since the late 1930s, Bill of Rights issues, not labor and economic questions, have provided judges with the greatest opportunities for significant policymaking.

In exploring this subject, we identified several situations (or case characteristics) that greatly enhance the judge's capacity to make policy rather than merely enforce existing policy. One such opportunity occurs when the legal evidence is contradictory or is equally strong on both sides. It is not uncommon for judges to preside over a case in which the facts and evidence for both sides are about equally compelling, or cases in which there is an equal number of precedents that would sustain a finding for either party. Being pulled in several directions at once may not be an entirely comfortable position, but it does allow the jurists freer rein to strike out on their own than would be possible if prevailing facts and law impelled them toward one position.

Likewise, judicial policymaking can flower when jurists are asked to resolve new types of controversies for which statutory law and past judicial precedents are virtually absent. For example, when the federal courts were asked whether artificially created life forms could be patented, they could not avoid making policy. (Even the refusal to decide is a decision, as the existentialists have long argued.) Thus, some cases by their very nature invite judicial policymaking, whereas others carry with them no such invitation. Judges differ in their perceptions of whether a given case offers an opportunity for creative, innovative decision-making. To some extent such differences are a function of the judges themselves. But our contention here is that the nature of the controversy itself determines to a substantial extent whether a case calls for garden-variety norm enforcement or invites major judicial policymaking.

Concluding Remarks about the Nature of the Case or Issue

In considering whether and in what direction judges' decisions will significantly affect people's lives, we can say this: the nature of the case is a vital component in this line of inquiry. Judges can make policy only in those areas over which the US and state constitutions and the legislative branches have granted them jurisdiction and only in a manner consistent with the norms of judicial self-restraint. Also, if the controversies presented to the judges provide some room to maneuver—as do many current civil rights and liberties issues—more policymaking is likely to occur than it would if the cases were circumscribed by clearly controlling precedents and law.

THE VALUES AND ORIENTATIONS OF THE JUDGES

A second set of variables to be considered in reaching an understanding of judicial policymaking and the direction it will take concern the judges themselves. What are their backgrounds? How were they appointed (or elected), and by whom? How do they conceive of their judicial role? By learning something about the values and orientations of the people who are tapped for judicial service, researchers are better able to explain and predict what they will do on the bench. (Also recall from Chapters 8, 9, 10, and 11 that the attitudes and values of other actors in the judicial process—for example, police officers, prosecutors, and the solicitor general—affect the content and direction of their important duties.)

We have looked at judicial background characteristics in a variety of contexts in this book. Here we examine several that have relevance vis-à-vis judicial policymaking and its direction.

Judges as a Socioeconomic Elite

In Chapters 5 and 6, we pointed out that America's jurists come from a narrow segment of the social and economic strata. To an overwhelming degree, they are offspring of upper- and upper-middle-class parents and come from families with a tradition of political, and often judicial, service. They are the people to whom the US system has been good, who fit in, and who have succeeded. The mavericks, malcontents, and ideological extremists are—by and large—discreetly weeded out by the judicial recruitment process.

What does all of this suggest about judicial policymaking and its direction? Given the striking similarity of the jurists and their backgrounds, their overall policymaking is generally going to be modest, conventional, and ideologically moderate. Although many judges are committed to reform and will use their policymaking opportunities to achieve this end, it is to adjust and enhance a way of life in which they basically believe. Seldom bitten is the hand of the socioeconomic system that feeds them. Although an occasional maverick may slip in or develop within the judicial ranks, most judges are basically conservative, in that they hold dear the traditional institutions and rules of the game that have brought success to them and their families. America's elite has its fair share of both liberals and conservatives, but it does not have many who would use their discretionary opportunities to alter radically the basic social and political system.

Judges as Representatives of Their Political Parties

Although the nature of the judicial recruitment process gives virtually all US judges a similar and conventional cast, there are differences. The prior political party affiliation of jurists does alter the way they exercise their policymaking discretion when the circumstances of a case offer room to maneuver. Judges and justices who come from the membership of the Democratic Party have been somewhat more liberal than their colleagues from Republican ranks. This has meant, for one thing, that Democrats on the bench are more likely to favor government regulation of the economy—particularly when such rulemaking appears to benefit the underdog or the worker in disputes with management. In criminal justice matters, Democratic jurists are more disposed toward the motions made by defendants. In questions concerning civil rights and liberties, the Democrat on the bench tends to establish policies that favor a broadening position.

In the same context, we emphasize the important policy link between the partisan choice made by voters in a presidential election, the judges whom the chief executive appoints, and the subsequent policy decisions of these jurists. When voters make a policy choice in electing a conservative or a liberal to the presidency, they have a discernible impact on the judiciary as well. We have noted that this phenomenon occurs not only in the United States but also in many other nations, including Canada, Germany, and Japan. Despite the many participants in the judicial selection process and the variety of forces that would thwart policy-oriented presidents (and governors) from getting "their kind of people" on the bench, it is still fair to say that, to an impressive degree, chief executives tend to get the type of people they want in the judiciary.

In a speech made just before the 1984 presidential election, conservative Supreme Court Justice William H. Rehnquist discussed this phenomenon with unusual candor. Although he was speaking primarily about the Supreme Court, his remarks pertain to the entire US judiciary. There is "no reason in the world," said Rehnquist, "why President Ronald Reagan should not attempt to *pack* the federal courts. The institution has been constructed in such a way that the public will, in the person of the president, have something to say about the membership of the Court and thereby indirectly about its decisions." Thus, Rehnquist felt, presidents may seek to appoint people who are sympathetic to their political and philosophical principles. After calling new judicial appointments "indirect infusions of the popular will," Rehnquist added that it "should come as no surprise" that presidents attempt to pack the courts with people of similar policy values, but "like murder suspects in a detective novel, they must have motive and opportunity."[1]

Judges as Manifestations of Localism

Another aspect of the values and orientations of judges affects their policymaking process: the attributes and mores they carry with them from the region where they grew up or hold court. We have documented a wide variety of geographic variations in the way both trial and appellate jurists view the world and react to its demands. For example, we noted that on many policy issues northern jurists have been more liberal than their colleagues in the South. We also noted that regional variations in judicial decision-making are not unique to the United States. For example, conscientious objector cases in Norway were decided differently depending on the region of the country in which the case was heard (see Chapter 12).

Not only does judicial policymaking vary from one region to another, but studies reveal that each of the circuits tends to be unique in the way its appellate and trial court judges administer the law and make decisions. The presence of significant state-by-state differences in the behavior of US trial judges is additional evidence that judges bring to the bench certain local values and orientations that subsequently affect their policymaking patterns.

Judges' Conceptions of Their Role

We noted three basic ways in which judges conceive of their role vis-à-vis the policymaking process. At one end of the spectrum are the lawmakers, who take a broad view of the judicial role. These jurists, often referred to as activists or innovators, contend that they can and sometimes must make significant public policy when rendering many of their decisions. At the other end of the spectrum are the law interpreters, who take a narrow view of the judicial function. Sometimes called strict constructionists, they believe that norm enforcement is the only proper role of the judge. In between are the pragmatists, or realists, who contend that judging is primarily a matter of enforcing norms but that on occasion they can and must formulate new judicial policy.

Understanding the conception of the role that a judge brings to the bench (or develops on the bench) will not reveal much about the substantive direction of their policymaking. It is possible to be an activist either as a conservative or as a liberal. One can go out on a judicial limb and give the benefit of the doubt to the economic giant or to the underdog, to the criminal defendant claiming police brutality, or to the police officer urging renewed emphasis on law and order. But knowledge of the way judges conceive of their role will provide a good indication of whether they are more inclined to defer to the norms and policies set by others or to strike out occasionally and make policy on their own.

Concluding Remarks on the Values and Orientations of the Judges

In attempting to learn about judicial policymaking and its substantive direction, we have set forth a second factor that helps channel our thinking—the values and orientations that the judges bring with them to the bench. Four factors are particularly relevant: (1) America's judges come from the establishment's elite, which serves to discourage radical policymaking; (2) judges' policymaking is reflective of their partisan orientations and of the executive who nominated them; (3) policy decisions manifest the local values and attitudes that judges possess when they first put on the black robe; and (4) judges will engage in more policymaking if they bring to the bench a belief that it is right and proper for judges to act in this manner.

THE NATURE OF THE JUDICIAL DECISION-MAKING PROCESS

Knowing how judges think and reason, how they are influenced in their decision-making, provides a good clue about judicial policymaking. Although this factor is outlined in this chapter and in Chapter 9, it is distinct enough to warrant a separate discussion. In the section about the legal subculture in Chapter 12, we examined the nature of the legal reasoning process that is at the heart of the system of jurisprudence in America. We noted that this is essentially a three-step process described by the doctrine of *stare decisis*: (1) similarity is seen between cases; (2) the rule of law inherent in the first case is announced; and (3) the rule of law is made applicable to the second case. Adherence to past precedents is also part of the legal reasoning process. Skillfully shaping and crafting the wisdom of the past, as found in previous court rulings, and applying it to contemporary problems are what this time-honored process is all about.

Decision-making by collegial courts has some dimensions not inherent in the behavior of trial judges sitting alone. In Chapter 13, we examined several approaches used by judicial scholars to get a theoretical handle on the way appellate court judges and justices think and act. One of these approaches is small-group dynamics, which views the output of the appellate judiciary as being strongly influenced by three general phenomena: persuasion on the merits, bargaining, and the threat of sanctions.

Persuasion lies at the heart of small-group dynamics. It means that judges, because of their training and values, are receptive to arguments based on sound legal reasoning, often seasoned with relevant legal precedents. Both hard evidence and anecdotal evidence indicate that judicial policies are influenced in the refining furnace of the judicial conference room.

Bargaining, too, molds the content and direction of judicial policy outputs. The compromises made among jurists—during the decision-making conference and while an opinion is being drafted—to satisfy the majority judges are almost always the product of bargaining. It is not that judges say to one another, "If you vote for my favorite judicial policy position, I'll vote for yours." Instead, a justice might phrase a bargaining offer—say, in a case dealing with the right of students to appeal to the federal court adverse disciplinary rulings from a state university—more like this: "I don't agree with your opinion as it now stands permitting students to appeal all adverse disciplinary decisions to the local federal district court. That's just too liberal for me, and I don't approve of interfering in university affairs to that degree. However, I could go along with a majority opinion that permitted appeals in really serious disciplinary matters that might result in the permanent suspension of a student." The first justice must then decide how badly the colleague's vote is needed: badly enough to water down the opinion to include only cases dealing with permanent suspension instead of all cases, as in the original opinion? This is how judicial policies are generated through bargaining.

The sanctions previously discussed include a variety of items in the genteel arsenal of judicial weaponry. A judge's threat to take a vote away from the majority and to dissent may cause the majority judges to alter the content of a policy decision. A judge's willingness to write a strong, biting dissent is another sanction that occasionally causes a unity-conscious majority to consider policy changes in an opinion. The threat to "go public" is a third tactic used by judges in collegial courts to alter the policy course of other jurists. Public exposure of an objectionable internal court practice or stance is probably the least pleasant of the sanctions. Finally, we noted that chief justices of the US and state supreme courts and their counterparts at the appellate and trial court levels all have singular opportunities to guide and shape the policy decisions of the courts. The status and options that are part of their unique leadership positions offer an opportunity to craft court policy if they have the desire and innate ability to make the most of it.

In addition to small-group dynamics, we looked at an approach to appellate court decision-making known as attitude theory. This school of thought views judges as possessing a stable set of attitudes that guide their policy choices. Such attitudes exist on issues involving civil rights and liberties, social matters (such as voting and ethnic status), and economic questions dealing with the equal distribution of wealth. Justices with similar attitudes on these matters tend to vote on cases in a comparable manner and thus form voting blocs. Research has demonstrated impressively that members of the appellate judiciary do decide cases in accordance with consistent underlying values and that voting blocs do behave according to predictable patterns. Attitude theory has been used successfully to explain and predict the voting patterns of appellate court jurists in many other nations, such as Australia, Canada, India, Japan, and the Philippines.

An approach that has been gaining many new adherents in recent years is rational choice theory. This model does not reject the assumptions of attitude theory, but it contends that the attitudinal model is simplistic and short-sighted. Rational choice theorists argue that goal-directed justices operate in what they call strategic or interdependent decision-making contexts. The justices understand that the outcome of their policy goals depends on the values of other decision-makers, such as Congress, the president, and other judges in the federal judiciary. When making decisions, the justices must consider not only how they want the case to be decided but also how such an outcome might be affected by the decisions of these other actors. Rational choice theorists have been able to marshal some impressive data to sustain their theoretical contentions.

What does this third general factor—the nature of the judicial decision-making process—say about judicial policymaking and its substantive direction? We offer two observations. First, most policymaking by judges is likely to be slow and incremental. This is exactly what one would expect from a reasoning process that relies so heavily on respecting precedents and places such emphasis on stability and continuity. The decision-making process of American judges does not lend itself to radical and abrupt departures from precedents and past behavior. Yet change does occur, and new policies are made. But legal history suggests that American jurists have often "reformed to preserve," and that is a principle often associated with conservatism.

Second, an understanding of the judicial thought process and of the small-group dynamics of collegial courts does not in itself reveal anything about the substantive direction of a court's policymaking. However, knowing which judges and justices are experts at persuasion, bargaining, and the use of sanctions does provide some insight into explaining and predicting the content of judicial policy decisions. If, on a given court, the conservatives have developed an understanding of these tactics, the bettor would do well to wager a few dollars on more conservative judicial decisions.

THE IMPACT OF EXTRANEOUS INFLUENCES

The making and implementation of judicial policy decisions undoubtedly are influenced by a variety of actors and forces outside the courtroom. It is not just the judges and the law clerks with leather-bound casebooks and arguments by silver-tongued lawyers that affect the shaping and carrying out of judicial decisions. Into the calculus must also go such unwieldy variables as the values and ability of the chief executive, the will of Congress or the legislature, the temper of public opinion, the strength and ideological orientation of key interest groups, and the attitudes and goodwill of those called on to implement judicial decisions in the real world.

The chief executive's input into the making and implementation of key judicial decisions is considerable. As the policymaking choice of the citizenry in the past election, the chief executive could fill the courts with people who share the basic political and judicial philosophies of the administration. Once on the court, judges may be encouraged or discouraged in their policymaking by the words and deeds emanating from the White House or the governor's mansion. For instance, the willingness of Presidents Dwight D. Eisenhower and John F. Kennedy to use federal troops to help enforce judicial integration orders must have encouraged subsequent policy decisions regarding the presidents' use of armed force to achieve this goal. Conversely, when President Donald Trump referred to illegal immigrants as murderers and terrorists, this perhaps reduced the likelihood that some judges would be willing to give such persons their full day in court when they requested vindication of their rights. The overall role of the chief executive in implementing judicial policy decisions was examined in Chapter 14.

Congress has an impact on creating and nurturing judicial policy decisions, just as the legislature does at the state level. In its power to establish most of the original and appellate jurisdiction of the federal judiciary, Congress has the capacity to determine the subject matter arenas where judicial policy battles are fought. In its capacity to establish the number of courts and determine the financial support they will have, Congress can show its approval or displeasure regarding the third branch of government. By accepting or rejecting presidential nominees to the courts, the Senate helps to determine who the judicial decision-makers will be and hence their value orientations. Finally, the implementation of many key judicial policy decisions is dependent on legislation that Congress must pass to make the ruling a meaningful reality for those affected by it. Had Congress not passed several key bills to implement the courts' desegregation orders (discussed in Chapter 14), integration of the public schools would be little more than a nice idea for those whom the rulings were intended to benefit.

Public opinion also has a role to play in this policymaking process—not an outrageous prospect for a nation that calls itself a democracy. In rendering key policy decisions, judges can hardly be oblivious to the mood and values of the citizenry of which they are a part. The Supreme Court's recent decision on gay marriage may well have been determined, at least in part, by the general public's increasing acceptance and approval of the concept during the past two decades. In many policy areas (such as obscenity, desegregation, and legislative apportionment), the Supreme Court has ordered judges to take the local political and social climate into consideration when tendering their rulings. The support or opposition of the public is often a key variable in determining whether a judge's orders are carried out in the spirit as well as the letter of the law.

Interest group activity is another thread in the tapestry of judicial policymaking. Such organizations often provide the president (or a state governor) with the names of individuals whom they support for judicial office, and they lobby against those whose judicial values they consider suspect. They often provide the vehicle for key judicial decisions by instigating legislation, sponsoring test cases, and giving legal and financial aid to those litigants whose cases they favor. They can thwart implementation of judicial decisions or help carry them out more effectively (see Chapter 14).

The final group of extraneous forces consists of those individuals and organizations that are expected to implement the judicial policy decision on a daily basis out on the street; the police officer who is asked to be sure that the accused understand their legal rights; the physician who must certify that a requested abortion is truly in the interest of a pregnant woman's mental and physical health; the personnel officer at a state institution who could readily find some technicality for refusing to hire a minority applicant; or the censor on the town's movie review board who is told that nudity and obscenity are not synonymous but who does not want to believe it. The values, motivations, and actions of such individuals must be considered to fully understand the judicial policymaking process. Their good-faith support of a judicial policy decision is vital to making it work; their indifference or opposition may cause the judge's ruling to die aborning.

Our intention in this chapter is to get a grip on the slippery handle of policymaking by American judges. Although many more questions have been raised than answered, perhaps this discussion has provided a better understanding of where to search for some of the answers. To learn the conditions that allow for bold policymaking, and to predict the direction that policymaking will take, attention must be focused on the nature of the case or controversy that can properly be brought into court; on the values and orientations of the jurists who preside over these courts; on the precise nature of the decision-making process of American judges; and finally, on a variety of extraneous actors and forces whose values and effects filter into the American judicial process from beginning to end.

APPENDIX

Annotated Constitution

THE CONSTITUTION OF THE UNITED STATES OF AMERICA

[Preamble]

We, the People of the United States, in Order to form a more perfect Union, establish Justice, ensure domestic Tranquility, provide for the common defense, promote the general Welfare, and secure the Blessings of Liberty to ourselves and our Posterity, do ordain and establish this Constitution for the United States of America.

> *The preamble does not confer any governmental power, but the Supreme Court has referred to it as a source of legal direction. See* McCulloch v. Maryland, *17 U.S. 316 (1819)*; Martin v. Hunter's Lessee, *14 U.S. 304 (1816).*

ARTICLE 1

Section 1

All legislative Powers herein granted shall be vested in a Congress of the United States, which shall consist of a Senate and House of Representatives.

> *The recognition of "legislative powers" implies that there are separate and distinct governmental powers: legislative, executive, and judicial.*

Section 2

The House of Representatives shall be composed of Members chosen every second Year by the People of the several States, and the Electors in each State shall have the Qualifications requisite for Electors of the most numerous Branch of the State Legislature.

The Constitution sets the qualifications for federal elective office. The Supreme Court has ruled that states may not impose their own restrictions, such as term limits. See U.S. Term Limits, Inc. v. Thornton, *514 U.S. 779 (1995).*

No Person shall be a Representative who shall not have attained to the age of twenty-five Years and been seven Years a Citizen of the United States, and who shall not, when elected, be an Inhabitant of that State in which he shall be chosen.

Representatives and direct Taxes shall be apportioned among the several States which may be included within this Union, according to their respective Numbers, which shall be determined by adding to the whole Number of free Persons, including those bound to Service for a Term of Years, and excluding Indians not taxed, three fifths of all other Persons. The actual Enumeration shall be made within three Years after the first Meeting of the Congress of the United States, and within every subsequent Term of ten Years, in such Manner as they shall by Law direct. The Number of Representatives shall not exceed one for every thirty Thousand, but each State shall have at Least one Representative; and until such enumeration shall be made, the State of New Hampshire shall be entitled to choose three, Massachusetts eight, Rhode-Island and Providence Plantations one, Connecticut five, New-York six, New Jersey four, Pennsylvania eight, Delaware one, Maryland six, Virginia ten, North Carolina five, South Carolina five, and Georgia three.

States must apportion congressional districts in such a manner that each district contains an approximately equal number of residents to ensure that each person's vote carries equal political weight—"one person, one vote." See Reynolds v. Sims, *377 U.S. 533 (1964).*

When vacancies happen in the Representation from any State, the Executive Authority thereof shall issue Writs of Election to fill such Vacancies.

Only fifteen judges and three presidents (Pres. Trump was impeached twice) have been impeached in U.S. history. No president was convicted, but eight of the fifteen jurists were removed. This occurred most recently in 2010, when U.S. District Court Judge Thomas Porteous of Louisiana was removed from the bench after he was convicted by the Senate for corruption and perjury.

The House of Representatives shall choose their Speaker and other Officers; and shall have the sole Power of Impeachment.

Section 3

The Senate of the United States shall be composed of two Senators from each State, chosen by the Legislature thereof, for six Years; and each Senator shall have one Vote.

> *The Seventeenth Amendment supersedes this provision and allows for the popular election of senators.*

Immediately after they shall be assembled in Consequence of the first Election, they shall be divided as equally as may be into three Classes. The Seats of the Senators of the first Class shall be vacated at the Expiration of the second Year, of the second Class at the Expiration of the fourth Year, and of the third Class at the Expiration of the sixth Year, so that one third may be chosen every second Year; and if Vacancies happen by Resignation, or otherwise, during the Recess of the Legislature of any State, the Executive thereof may make temporary Appointments until the next Meeting of the Legislature, which shall then fill such Vacancies.

No Person shall be a Senator who shall not have attained to the Age of thirty Years and been nine Years a Citizen of the United States, and who shall not, when elected, be an Inhabitant of that State for which he shall be chosen.

The Vice President of the United States shall be President of the Senate but shall have no Vote unless they be equally divided. The Senate shall choose their other Officers, and a President pro tempore, in the Absence of the Vice President, or when he shall exercise the Office of President of the United States.

> *The Senate may establish its own rules and procedures for handling impeachment cases. See* Nixon v. U.S., *506 U.S. 224 (1993).*

The Senate shall have the sole Power to try all Impeachments. When sitting for that Purpose, they shall be on Oath or Affirmation. When the President of the United States is tried the Chief Justice shall preside: And no Person shall be convicted without the Concurrence of two thirds of the Members present.

Judgment in Cases of Impeachment shall not extend further than to removal from Office, and disqualification to hold and enjoy any Office of honor, Trust or Profit under the United States: but the Party convicted shall nevertheless be liable and subject to Indictment, Trial, Judgment and Punishment, according to Law.

Section 4

The Times, Places and Manner of holding Elections for Senators and Representatives, shall be prescribed in each State by the Legislature thereof; but the Congress may at any time by Law make or alter such Regulations, except as to the Places of choosing Senators.

> *The Constitution vests in Congress, not the courts, the power to determine the legitimacy of congressional elections—an inherently political question.*

The Congress shall assemble at least once in every Year, and such Meeting shall be on the first Monday in December, unless they shall by Law appoint a different Day.

> *The Twentieth Amendment changed the date of congressional assembly to January 3, and it set January 20 as the beginning and ending date of a presidential term.*

Section 5

Each House shall be the Judge of the Elections, Returns and Qualifications of its own Members, and a Majority of each shall constitute a Quorum to do Business; but a smaller Number may adjourn from day to day, and may be authorized to compel the Attendance of absent Members, in such Manner, and under such Penalties as each House may provide.

Each House may determine the Rules of its Proceedings, punish its members for disorderly Behaviour, and, with the Concurrence of two thirds, expel a member.

Each House shall keep a Journal of its Proceedings, and from time to time publish the same, excepting such Parts as may in their Judgment require Secrecy; and the Yeas and Nays of the Members of either House on any question shall, at the Desire of one fifth of those Present, be entered on the Journal.

> *The* Congressional Record *is the official journal of the proceedings of Congress. It is available online at* www.congress.gov/congressional-record.

Neither House, during the Session of Congress, shall, without the Consent of the other, adjourn for more than three days, nor to any other Place than that in which the two Houses shall be sitting.

Section 6

The Senators and Representatives shall receive a Compensation for their Services, to be ascertained by Law, and paid out of the Treasury of the United States. They shall in all Cases, except Treason, Felony and Breach of the Peace, be privileged from Arrest during their Attendance at the Session of their respective Houses, and in going to and returning from the same; and for any Speech or Debate in either House, they shall not be questioned in any other Place.

No Senator or Representative shall, during the Time for which he was elected, be appointed to any civil Office under the Authority of the United States, which shall have been created, or the Emoluments whereof shall have been increased during such time; and no Person holding any Office under the United States, shall be a Member of either House during his Continuance in Office.

> *This provision, which is one of many that separate governmental powers, prohibits members of Congress from simultaneously serving in the judicial branch.*

Section 7

All Bills for raising Revenue shall originate in the House of Representatives; but the Senate may propose or concur with amendments as on other Bills.

> *Bills must be approved or rejected in their entirety. The line-item veto, which allows executives to veto specific provisions of a spending bill while leaving the remainder of the legislation intact, was ruled unconstitutional. See* Clinton v. City of New York, *524 U.S. 417 (1998).*

Every Bill which shall have passed the House of Representatives and the Senate, shall, before it become a law, be presented to the President of the United States: If he approve he shall sign it, but if not he shall return it, with his Objections to that House in which it shall have originated, who shall enter the Objections at large on their Journal, and proceed to reconsider it. If after such Reconsideration two thirds of that House shall agree to pass the Bill, it shall be sent, together with the Objections, to the other House, by which it shall likewise be reconsidered, and if approved by two thirds of that House, it shall become a Law. But in all such Cases the Votes of both Houses shall be determined by Yeas and Nays, and the Names of the Persons voting for and against the Bill shall be entered on the Journal of each House respectively. If any Bill shall not be returned by the President within ten Days (Sundays excepted) after it shall have been presented to him, the Same shall be a Law, in like Manner as if he had signed it, unless the Congress by their Adjournment prevent its Return, in which Case it shall not be a Law.

Every Order, Resolution, or Vote to which the Concurrence of the Senate and House of Representatives may be necessary (except on a question of Adjournment) shall be presented to the President of the United States; and before the Same shall take Effect, shall be approved by him, or being disapproved by him, shall be repassed by two thirds of the Senate and House of Representatives, according to the Rules and Limitations prescribed in the Case of a Bill.

Section 8

The Congress shall have Power To lay and collect Taxes, Duties, Imposts and Excises, to pay the Debts and provide for the common Defense and general Welfare of the United States; but all Duties, Imposts and Excises shall be uniform throughout the United States.

Courts have ruled that the federal power to tax is broad and that judges should generally defer to the legislative branch on the question of what constitutes proper taxation. See McCray v. U.S., *195 U.S. 27 (1904). This reasoning was the basis for the Supreme Court decision upholding the landmark Affordable Care Act in 2012. See* National Federation of Independent Business v. Sebelius, *567 U.S. 519 (2012).*

To borrow Money on the credit of the United States.

To regulate Commerce with foreign Nations, and among the several States, and with the Indian Tribes.

*The ability to regulate interstate economic activity is a major source of congressional authority. The Commerce Clause has been at the center of many important Supreme Court cases, and courts have generally allowed Congress to exercise broad regulatory power (*Gibbons v. Ogden, *22 U.S. 1 [1824];* U.S. v. Darby, *312 U.S. 100 [1941]); exercise federal police powers (*Champion v. Ames, *188 U.S. 321 [1903]); even promote civil rights (Heart of Atlanta Motel v. U.S., 379 U.S. 241 [1964]). However, recent decades have witnessed instances of the Court's reluctance to defer to Congress's use of the Commerce Clause. See U.S. v. Morrison, 529 U.S. 598 (2000); U.S. v. Lopez, 514 U.S. 549 (1995).*

To establish a uniform Rule of Naturalization, and uniform Laws about Bankruptcies throughout the United States.

To coin Money, regulate the Value thereof, and of foreign Coin, and fix the Standard of Weights and Measures.

To provide for the Punishment of counterfeiting the Securities and current Coin of the United States.

To establish Post Offices and post Roads.

To promote the Progress of Science and useful Arts, by securing for limited Times to Authors and Inventors the exclusive Right to their respective Writings and Discoveries.

The Constitution leaves the structure of the lower federal courts up to Congress. This is an oft-overlooked power balance between the legislative and judicial branches.

To constitute Tribunal's inferior to the supreme Court.

To define and punish Piracies and Felonies committed on the high Seas, and Offences against the Law of Nations.

> *A* letter of marque *is a document from a government that grants a private person the power to seize the subjects of a foreign state. A* letter of reprisal *provides for an act of retaliation against someone for injuries received.*

To declare War, grant Letters of Marque and Reprisal, and make Rules concerning Captures on Land and Water.

To raise and support Armies, but no Appropriation of Money to that Use shall be for a longer Term than two Years.

To provide and maintain a Navy.

To make Rules for the Government and Regulation of the land and naval Forces.

To provide for calling forth the Militia to execute the Laws of the Union, suppress Insurrections and repeal Invasions.

To provide for organizing, arming, and disciplining, the Militia, and for governing such Part of them as may be employed in the Service of the United States, reserving to the States respectively, the Appointment of the Officers, and the Authority of training the Militia according to the discipline prescribed by Congress.

To exercise exclusive Legislation in all Cases whatsoever, over such District (not exceeding ten Miles square) as may, by Cession of Particular States, and the Acceptance of Congress, become the Seat of the Government of the United States, and to exercise like Authority over all Places purchased by the Consent of the Legislature of the State in which the Same shall be, for the Erection of Forts, Magazines, Arsenals, dock-Yards and other needful Buildings;—And

> *The Necessary and Proper Clause—also known as the Elastic Clause—is the source of the* implied powers *doctrine. Implied powers expand Congress's authority beyond the enumerated powers listed in Article 1, Section 8, to include the goals and objectives associated with such powers. See* McCulloch v. Maryland, *17 U.S. 316 (1819).*

To make all Laws which shall be necessary and proper for carrying into Execution the foregoing Powers and all other Powers vested by this Constitution in the Government of the United States, or in any Department or Officer thereof.

Section 9

The Migration or Importation of such Persons as any of the States now existing shall think proper to admit, shall not be prohibited by the Congress prior to the Year one thousand eight hundred and eight, but a Tax or duty may be imposed on such Importation, not exceeding ten dollars for each Person.

> *Habeas corpus is the procedure by which a court inquires into the legality of a person's detention. Should the detention be found improper, the court may issue an order directing authorities to release the petitioner.*

The Privilege of the Writ of Habeas Corpus shall not be suspended, unless when in Cases of Rebellion or Invasion the public Safety may require it.

No Bill of Attainder or ex post facto Law shall be passed.

> *There are three types of ex post facto laws: those "which punish as a crime an act previously committed, which was innocent when done; which make more burdensome the punishment for a crime, after its commission; or which deprive one charged with crime of any defense available according to law at the time when the act was committed." See* Collins v. Youngblood, *497 U.S. 37 (1990).*

No Capitation, or other direct, Tax shall be laid, unless in Proportion to the Census of Enumeration herein before directed to be taken.

No Tax or Duty shall be laid on Articles exported from any State.

No Preference shall be given by any Regulation of Commerce or Revenue to the Ports of one State over those of another: nor shall Vessels bound to, or from, one State, be obliged to enter, clear or pay Duties in another.

No Money shall be drawn from the Treasury, but in Consequence of Appropriations made by Law; and a regular Statement and Account of the Receipts and Expenditures of all public Money shall be published from time to time.

No Title of Nobility shall be granted by the United States: And no Person holding any Office of Profit or Trust under them, shall, without the Consent of the Congress, accept of any present, Emolument, Office, or Title, of any kind whatever, from any King, Prince or foreign State.

Section 10

No State shall enter any Treaty, Alliance, or Confederation; grant Letters of Marque and Reprisal; coin Money; emit Bills of Credit; make any Thing but gold and silver

Coin a Tender in Payment of Debts; pass any Bill of Attainder, ex post facto Law, or Law impairing the Obligation of Contracts, or grant any Title of Nobility.

> *A bill of attainder is a legislative act that declares a person or group of persons guilty of some crime and punishes them without benefit of a trial.*

No State shall, without the Consent of the Congress, lay any Imposts or Duties on Imports or Exports, except what may be necessary for executing its inspection Laws: and the net Produce of all Duties and Imposts, laid by any State on Imports or Exports, shall be for the Use of the Treasury of the United States; and all such Laws shall be subject to the Revision and Control of the Congress.

No State shall, without the Consent of Congress, lay any Duty of Tonnage, keep Troops, or Ships of War in time of Peace, enter into any Agreement or Compact with another State, or with a foreign Power, or engage in War, unless invaded, or in such imminent Danger as will not admit of delay.

ARTICLE 2

Section 1

The executive Power shall be vested in a President of the United States of America. He shall hold his Office during the Term of four Years, and, together with the Vice President, chosen for the same Term, be elected, as follows:

> *Compare the language of Article 1, Section 1 ("All legislative Powers herein granted . . . "), to Article 2, Section 1 ("The executive Power shall be vested . . . ").*
>
> *The Constitution is quite specific about legislative powers, but it is less clear about what constitutes executive power.*

Each State shall appoint, in such Manner as the Legislature thereof may direct, several Electors, equal to the whole Number of Senators and Representatives to which the State may be entitled in the Congress: but no Senator or Representative, or Person holding an Office of Trust or Profit under the United States, shall be appointed an Elector.

> *The presidential election methodology and term of office have been the most revisited issues in the Constitution. They are the subject of five amendments: the Twelfth (changes*

to the election of the president via the Electoral College); the Twentieth (changes to the commencement of the terms of the president, vice president, and members of Congress); the Twenty-second (imposing a limit of two terms for a president); the Twenty-third (provision for presidential electors from the District of Columbia); and the Twenty-fifth (provisions for instances of presidential and vice-presidential vacancy of office and disability).

The Electors shall meet in their respective States, and vote by Ballot for two Persons, of whom one at least shall not be an Inhabitant of the same State with themselves. And they shall make a List of all the Persons voted for, and of the Number of Votes for each, which List they shall sign and certify, and transmit sealed to the Seat of the Government of the United States, directed to the President of the Senate. The President of the Senate shall, in the Presence of the Senate and House of Representatives, open all the Certificates, and the Votes shall then be counted. The Person having the greatest Number of Votes shall be the President, if such Number be a Majority of the whole Number of Electors appointed; and if there be more than one who have such Majority, and have an equal Number of Votes, then the House of Representatives shall immediately choose by Ballot one of them for President; and if no Person have a Majority, then from the five highest on the List the said House shall in like Manner choose the President. But in choosing the President, the Votes shall be taken by States, the Representatives from each State having one Vote; a quorum for this Purpose shall consist of a Member or Members from two thirds of the States, and a Majority of all the States shall be necessary to a Choice. In every Case, after the Choice of the President, the Person having the greatest Number of Votes of the Electors shall be the Vice President. But if there should remain two or more who have equal Votes, the Senate shall choose from them by Ballot the Vice President.

The Congress may determine the Time of choosing the Electors, and the Day on which they shall give their Votes, which Day shall be the same throughout the United States.

No Person except a natural born Citizen, or a Citizen of the United States, at the time of the Adoption of this Constitution, shall be eligible to the Office of President; neither shall any person be eligible to that Office who shall not have attained to the Age of thirty-five Years, and been fourteen Years a Resident within the United States.

In Case of the Removal of the President from Office, or of his Death, Resignation, or Inability to discharge the Powers and Duties of the said Office, the Same shall devolve on the Vice President, and the Congress may by Law provide for the Case of Removal, Death, Resignation or Inability, both of the President and Vice President, declaring what Officer shall then act as President, and such Officer shall act accordingly, until the Disability be removed, or a President shall be elected.

The President shall, at stated Times, receive for his Services, a Compensation, which shall neither be increased nor diminished during the Period for which he shall have been elected, and he shall not receive within that Period any other Emolument from the United States, or any of them.

> *The current annual salary for the president is $400,000. The president also receives a $50,000 per year expense account for official purposes, though he must pay for his own meals and personal expenses, as well as those of his family, while living in the White House.*

Before he enters on the Execution of his Office, he shall take the following Oath or Affirmation:—"I do solemnly swear (or affirm) that I will faithfully execute the Office of President of the United States, and will to the best of my Ability, preserve, protect and defend the Constitution of the United States."

> *Regarding the presidential oath of office, note that the Constitution does not require the words "so help me God," which are customarily uttered after the mandated language. Tradition has the chief justice administering the oath of office with the president holding his hand on a Bible. However, the Constitution does not mandate a copy of scripture, nor does it dictate who shall deliver the oath.*

Section 2

The President shall be Commander in Chief of the Army and Navy of the United States, and of the Militia of the several States, when called into the actual Service of the United States; he may require the Opinion, in writing, of the principal Officer in each of the executive Departments, upon any Subject relating to the Duties of their respective Offices, and he shall have Power to Grant Reprieves and Pardons for Offences against the United States, except in Cases of Impeachment.

> *The president has especially broad powers around foreign affairs: "the President alone has the power to speak or listen as a representative of the nation." See* U.S. v. Curtiss-Wright, *299 U.S. 304 (1936).*
>
> *The president's authority to* hire *also includes the power to* fire, *except in instances where the Constitution or statute specifically limits the president's removal authority. See* Myers v. U.S., *272 U.S. 52 (1926).*

He shall have Power, by and with the Advice and Consent of the Senate, to make Treaties, provided two thirds of the Senators present concur; and he shall nominate, and by and with the Advice and Consent of the Senate, shall appoint Ambassadors, other public Ministers and Consuls, Judges of the supreme Court, and all other Officers of the United States, whose Appointments are not herein otherwise provided for, and which shall be established by Law: but the Congress may by Law vest the Appointment of such inferior Officers, as they think proper, in the President alone, in the Courts of Law, or in the Heads of Departments.

> *Presidents may appoint federal judges through the recess appointment process, but their commissions are not permanent unless they are approved by the Senate after it reconvenes.*

The President shall have Power to fill up all Vacancies that may happen during the Recess of the Senate, by granting Commissions which shall expire at the End of their next Session.

> *The Supreme Court held in 2014 that recess appointments are generally permissible if they are made during Senate breaks of ten or more days. But such appointments are not allowed when the Senate adjourns and then holds so-called* pro forma *sessions every three days. See* NLRB v. Noel Canning, *573 U.S. (2014).*

Section 3

He shall from time to time give to the Congress Information on the State of the Union, and recommend to their Consideration such Measures as he shall judge necessary and expedient; he may, on extraordinary Occasions, convene both Houses, or either of them, and in Case of Disagreement between them, with Respect to the Time of Adjournment, he may adjourn them to such Time as he shall think proper; he shall receive Ambassadors and other public Ministers; he shall take Care that the Laws be faithfully executed, and shall Commission all the Officers of the United States.

> *The president is chief law enforcement officer, and "Congress [cannot] transfer from the President to the courts the Chief Executive's most important constitutional duty, to 'take Care that the Laws be faithfully executed.'" See* Lujan v. Defenders of Wildlife, *504 U.S. 555 (1992). However, in 2024 the Supreme Court overturned a long-established precedent and imposed new constraints on the executive branch's power to*

interpret and apply regulations. In doing so, the Court empowered the judiciary's role in the process. See Loper Bright Enterprises v. Raimondo, *___U.S.___ (2024).*

Section 4

The President, Vice President and all Civil Officers of the United States, shall be removed from Office on Impeachment for and Conviction of Treason, Bribery, or other high Crimes and Misdemeanors.

ARTICLE 3

Section 1

The judicial Power of the United States shall be vested in one supreme Court, and in such inferior Courts as the Congress may from time to time ordain and establish. The Judges, both supreme and inferior Courts, shall hold their Offices during good behaviour, and shall, at stated Times, receive for their Services, a Compensation, which shall not be diminished during their Continuance in Office.

The Supreme Court is the only court specifically mentioned in the Constitution, which leaves the structure of the federal court system entirely up to Congress. "During good behaviour" is understood to mean lifetime tenure, with removal only in cases of impeachment for improper professional conduct. The annual salary for a US district court judge as of 2024 was $243,300; appellate court jurists were paid $257,900; and Supreme Court justices earned $298,500.

Section 2

The judicial Power shall extend to all Cases, in Law and Equity, arising under this Constitution, the Laws of the United States, and Treaties made, or which shall be made, under their Authority;—to all Cases affecting Ambassadors, other public ministers and Consuls;—to all Cases of admiralty and maritime Jurisdiction;—to Controversies to which the United States shall be a Party;—to Controversies between two or more States;—between a State and Citizens of another State; —between Citizens of different States;—between Citizens of the same State claiming Lands under Grants of different States, and between a State, or the Citizens thereof, and foreign States, Citizens or Subjects.

Judicial power is "the right to determine actual controversies arising between diverse litigants, duly instituted in courts of proper jurisdiction." See Muskrat v. U.S., *219 U.S. 346 (1911). As an extension of their power to decide cases, courts have the authority to do such things as punish those in contempt of their authority* (Michaelson v. U.S., *266 U.S. 42 [1924]); issue writs and orders* (McIntire v. Wood, *11 U.S. 504 [1813]), Ex parte Bollman, 8 U.S. 75 [1807]); and admit and disbar attorneys (Ex parte Garland, 71 U.S. 333 [1867]). The power of judicial review is not specifically enumerated in the Constitution, but it is implicit in the Supreme Court's appellate authority. See* Marbury v. Madison, *5 U.S. 137 (1803).*

In all Cases affecting Ambassadors, other public Ministers and Consuls, and those in which a State shall be Party, the supreme Court shall have original Jurisdiction. In all the other Cases before mentioned, the supreme Court shall have appellate Jurisdiction, both as to Law and Fact, with such Exceptions, and under such Regulations as the Congress shall make.

The Trial of all Crimes, except in Cases of Impeachment, shall be by Jury; and such Trial shall be held in the State where the said Crimes shall have been committed; but when not committed within any State, the Trial shall be at such Place or Places as the Congress may by Law have directed.

The Constitution guarantees the right to a trial by jury in two places: here and in the Sixth Amendment.

Section 3

Treason against the United States shall consist only in levying War against them, or in adhering to their Enemies, giving them Aid and Comfort. No Person shall be convicted of Treason unless on the Testimony of two Witnesses to the same overt Act, or on Confession in open Court.

The founders were fearful that the charge of treason might be used to punish political enemies, as this had been done in England. Therefore, they restricted the definition of the charge and limited how someone might be convicted of treason to instances involving multiple witnesses or outright confession.

The Congress shall have Power to declare the Punishment of Treason, but no Attainder of Treason shall work Corruption of Blood, or Forfeiture except during the Life of the Person attainted.

ARTICLE 4

Section 1

Full Faith and Credit shall be given in each State to the public Acts, Records, and judicial Proceedings of every other State. And the Congress may by general Laws prescribe the Manner in which such Acts, Records and Proceedings shall be proved, and the Effect thereof.

> *This section of the Constitution generally deals with the principle of* comity. *This consists of a body of rules and practices that essentially establish that the courts in one jurisdiction will extend recognition and enforcement of rights claimed by individuals by virtue of the laws of another jurisdiction.*

Section 2

The Citizens of each State shall be entitled to all Privileges and Immunities of Citizens in the several States.

A Person charged in any State with Treason, Felony, or other Crime, who shall flee from Justice, and be found in another State, shall on Demand of the executive Authority of the State from which he fled, be delivered up, to be removed to the State having Jurisdiction of the Crime.

No Person held to Service or Labour in one State, under the Laws thereof, escaping into another, shall, in Consequence of any Law or Regulation therein, be discharged from such Service or Labour, but shall be delivered up on Claim of the Party to whom such Service or Labour may be due.

> *This clause was a pillar of the injustice of slavery. It enabled slave owners to seize and return to slavery those who fled to free states while also prohibiting free states from granting release to those who escaped from bondage.*

Section 3

New States may be admitted by the Congress into this Union; but no new State shall be formed or erected within the Jurisdiction of any other State; nor any State be formed by the Junction of two or more States, or Parts of States, without the Consent of the Legislatures of the States concerned as well as of the Congress.

> *The Supreme Court has held that states enjoy "equal footing" and that "equality of constitutional right and power is the condition of all the States of the Union, old and new." See* Escanaba Co. v. Chicago, *107 U.S. 678 (1883).*

The Congress shall have Power to dispose of and make all needful Rules and Regulations respecting the Territory or other Property belonging to the United States; and nothing in this Constitution shall be so construed as to Prejudice any Claims of the United States, or of any State.

Section 4

The United States shall guarantee to every State in this Union a Republican Form of Government and shall protect each of them against Invasion; and on Application of the Legislature, or of the Executive (when the Legislature cannot be convened) against domestic Violence.

> *What constitutes "a Republican Form of Government" is a political question, according to the Supreme Court: "[I]t rests with Congress to decide what government is the established one in a State . . . as well as its republican character." See* Luther v. Borden, *48 U.S. 1 (1849).*

ARTICLE 5

The Congress, whenever two thirds of both Houses shall deem it necessary, shall propose Amendments to this Constitution, or, on the Application of the Legislatures of two thirds of the several States, shall call a Convention for proposing Amendments, which, in either Case, shall be valid to all Intents and Purposes, as Part of this Constitution, when ratified by the Legislatures of three fourths of the several States, or by Conventions in three fourths thereof, as the one or the other Mode of Ratification may be proposed by the Congress; Provided that no Amendment which may be made prior to the Year One thousand eight hundred and eight shall in any Manner affect the first and fourth Clauses in the Ninth Section of the first Article; and that no State, without its Consent, shall be deprived of its equal Suffrage in the Senate.

> *The amendment process is how the Constitution may be formally modified. However, the most common way the document has been effectively changed is through evolving judicial interpretation.*

ARTICLE 6

All Debts contracted and Engagements entered, before the Adoption of this Constitution, shall be as valid against the United States under this Constitution, as under the Confederation.

> *The Supremacy Clause asserts that "the States have no power, by taxation or otherwise, to retard, impede, burden, or in any manner control, the operations of the constitutional laws enacted by Congress." See* McCulloch v. Maryland, *17 U.S. 316 (1819).*

This Constitution, and the Laws of the United States which shall be made in Pursuance thereof; and all Treaties made, or which shall be made, under the Authority of the United States, shall be the supreme Law of the Land; and the Judges in every State shall be bound thereby, any Thing in the Constitution or Laws of any state to the Contrary notwithstanding.

The Senators and Representatives before mentioned, and the Members of the several State Legislatures, and all executive and judicial Officers, both United States and of the several States, shall be bound by Oath or Affirmation, to support this Constitution; but no religious Test shall ever be required as a Qualification to any Office or public Trust under the United States.

ARTICLE 7

The Ratification of the Conventions of nine States, shall be sufficient for the Establishment of this Constitution between the States so ratifying the same.

> *The Constitution was ultimately ratified by all thirteen states. The document did not provide for a means to address any potential political crises that might have resulted had one or more states refused to join the Union.*

AMENDMENTS TO THE CONSTITUTION OF THE UNITED STATES OF AMERICA

Amendment 1 (The first ten amendments were ratified December 15, 1791.)

> *At its base, the First Amendment guarantees spiritual and intellectual liberty. As such, it affords what are arguably the most important protections in the Constitution. Justice Harlan Fiske Stone suggested that First Amendment freedoms should be accorded a*

"preferred position" in interpreting the Constitution. See U.S. v. Carolene Products Co., *304 U.S. 144 (1938).*

Congress shall make no law respecting an establishment of religion or prohibiting the free exercise thereof; or abridging the freedom of speech, or of the press; or the right of the people peaceably to assemble, and to petition the Government for a redress of grievances.

Amendment 2

A well-regulated Militia, being necessary to the security of a free State, the right of the people to keep and bear Arms, shall not be infringed.

Despite the heated political debate surrounding gun control, the Second Amendment has been the source of remarkably little Supreme Court litigation. In a major 2008 decision, the Court struck down a ban on handguns in the District of Columbia, ruling that the Second Amendment protects an individual right to possess a firearm unconnected with service in a militia and to use that arm for traditionally lawful purposes such as self-defense. See District of Columbia v. Heller, *554 U.S. 570 (2008); New York State Rifle & Pistol Association v. Bruen, 597 U.S. 1 (2022). Previously, the Court had suggested that the key purpose of the amendment was to protect states' authority to maintain a militia. See* U.S. v. Miller, *307 U.S. 174 (1939).*

Amendment 3

No Soldier shall, in time of peace be quartered in any house, without the consent of the Owner, nor in time of war, but in a manner to be prescribed by law.

There has never been a Supreme Court case that directly addressed the Third Amendment. However, the Supreme Court referred to this amendment as part of the constitutional underpinning of the right to privacy. See Griswold v. Connecticut, *381 U.S. 479 (1965).*

Amendment 4

The right of the people to be secure in their persons, houses, papers, and effects, against unreasonable searches and seizures, shall not be violated, and no Warrants shall issue, but upon probable cause, supported by Oath or affirmation, and particularly describing the place to be searched, and the persons or things to be seized.

The Fourth Amendment does not prohibit governmental searches—only "unreasonable" ones. The amendment's protections would be virtually meaningless without the exclusionary rule, which prohibits prosecutorial use of evidence obtained via improper searches. See Mapp v. Ohio, *367 U.S. 643 (1961).*

Amendment 5

No person shall be held to answer for a capital, or otherwise infamous crime, unless on a presentment or indictment of a Grand Jury, except in cases arising in the land or naval forces, or in the Militia, when in actual service in time of War or public danger; nor shall any person be subject for the same offence to be twice put in jeopardy of life or limb; nor shall be compelled in any criminal case to be a witness against himself, nor be deprived of life, liberty, or property, without due process of law; nor shall private property be taken for public use, without just compensation.

The Fifth Amendment deals primarily with criminal justice rights, one of the most important of which is the guarantee of due process—the principle that legal procedure must not conflict with the Constitution or the law and that the law must be equally applied. Note that the Fifth Amendment implicitly authorizes the death penalty by allowing the government, if it follows due process, to deprive a person of life. The Takings Clause, found at the end of the Fifth Amendment, protects individuals from arbitrary property seizures. Government is constitutionally allowed to take private property (a power known as eminent domain) if it meets two requirements: the owner must receive "just compensation" for the property and the action must be for some "public use." This issue was the subject of much debate in the Supreme Court case of Kelo v. New London, *545 U.S. 469 (2005).*

Amendment 6

In all criminal prosecutions, the accused shall enjoy the right to a speedy and public trial, by an impartial jury of the State and district wherein the crime shall have been committed, which district shall have been previously ascertained by law, and to be informed of the nature and cause of the accusation; to be confronted with the witnesses against him; to have compulsory process for obtaining witnesses in his favor, and to have the Assistance of Counsel for his defense.

The Sixth Amendment is another amendment that confers criminal justice guarantees. This is the second place in the Constitution where one finds the guarantee of a right to a jury trial (the first is in Article 3, Section 2). The Supreme Court has ruled that the Constitution prohibits nonunanimous jury verdicts for serious crimes. See Ramos v. Louisiana, *590 U.S. 83 (2020). But the Sixth Amendment does not require that a jury must consist of twelve jurors. See* Williams v. Florida, *399 U.S. 78 (1970); a criminal jury can be as small as six, but no smaller. See* Ballew v. Georgia, *435 U.S. 223 (1978). The right to a lawyer is also guaranteed in the Sixth Amendment. The right to retain an attorney is, in essence, the right to protect one's rights. See* Gideon v. Wainwright, *372 U.S. 335 (1963).*

Amendment 7

In Suits at common law, where the value in controversy shall exceed twenty dollars, the right of trial by jury shall be preserved, and no fact tried by a jury, shall be otherwise re-examined in any Court of the United States, then according to the rules of the common law.

Although the Seventh Amendment guarantees the right to a jury trial in federal civil cases, such a right has not been held to apply to state courts. See Alexander v. Virginia, *413 U.S. 836 (1973).*

Amendment 8

Excessive bail shall not be required, nor excessive fines imposed, nor cruel and unusual punishments inflicted.

The Supreme Court has resisted giving an exact definition of what constitutes "cruel and unusual": "Difficulty would attend the effort to define with exactness the extent of the constitutional provision. . . ." See Wilkerson v. Utah, *99 U.S. 130 (1878).*

Amendment 9

The enumeration in the Constitution, of certain rights, shall not be construed to deny or disparage others retained by the people.

Federalists such as James Madison were concerned that a bill of rights could be interpreted as listing all the rights of citizens, and thus deny more liberties than it protected (see The Federalist, No. 84). *To guard against such an interpretation, the Ninth Amendment was adopted.*

Amendment 10

The powers not delegated to the United States by the Constitution, nor prohibited by it to the States, are reserved to the States respectively, or to the people.

> *The Tenth Amendment has become a popular rallying point for those who seek to limit federal legislative authority and expand states' rights.*

Amendment 11 (Ratified February 7, 1795)

The Judicial power of the United States shall not be construed to extend to any suit in law or equity, commenced or prosecuted against one of the United States by Citizens of another State, or by Citizens or Subjects of any Foreign State.

> *The Eleventh Amendment was adopted to overturn the unpopular Supreme Court decision* Chisholm v. Georgia, *2 U.S. 419 (1793). The justices ruled in* Chisholm *that citizens of another state could sue states in federal court. At that time, many people feared that allowing such suits would interfere with states' rights.*

Amendment 12 (Ratified June 15, 1804)

The Electors shall meet in their respective states and vote by ballot for President and Vice-President, one of whom, at least, shall not be an inhabitant of the same state with themselves; they shall name in their ballots the person voted for as President, and in distinct ballots the person voted for as Vice-President, and they shall make distinct lists of all persons voted for as President, and of all persons voted for as Vice-President, and of the number of votes for each, which lists they shall sign and certify, and transmit sealed to the seat of the government of the United States, directed to the President of the Senate;—The President of the Senate shall, in the presence of the Senate and House of Representatives, open all the certificates and the votes shall then be counted;—The person having the greatest Number of votes for President, shall be the President, if such number be a majority of the whole number of Electors appointed; and if no person have such majority, then from the persons having the highest numbers not exceeding three on the list of those voted for as President, the House of Representatives shall choose immediately, by ballot, the President. But in choosing the President, the votes shall be taken by states, the representation from each state having one vote; a quorum for this purpose shall consist of a member or members from two-thirds of the states, and a majority of all the states shall be necessary to a choice. And if the House of Representatives shall not choose a President whenever the right of choice shall devolve upon them, before the fourth day of March next following, then the Vice-President shall act as President, as in the case of the death or other constitutional disability of the President—The person having the greatest number of votes as Vice-President, shall be the Vice-President, if such number be a majority of the whole number of Electors appointed, and if no person have a majority, then from the two highest numbers on the list, the Senate shall choose the Vice-President; a quorum for the purpose shall consist of two-thirds of the whole number of Senators, and a majority of the whole number shall be necessary to a choice. But no person constitutionally ineligible to the office of President shall be eligible to that of Vice-President of the United States.

> *The Twelfth Amendment modifies Article 2, Section 1, and it was adopted to prevent the recurrence of a tie vote, as occurred in the election of 1800, when Thomas Jefferson and Aaron Burr received an equal number of votes in the Electoral College. Exposing flaws of the Electoral College, the close election was ultimately decided in the House of Representatives, even though the electors had intended Jefferson to be president and Burr to be vice president.*

Amendment 13 (Ratified December 6, 1865)

Section 1. Neither slavery nor involuntary servitude, except as a punishment for crime whereof the party shall have been duly convicted, shall exist within the United States, or any place subject to their jurisdiction.

> *The first of the three Civil War amendments, the Thirteenth effectively codified President Abraham Lincoln's 1863 proclamation freeing the slaves.*

Section 2. Congress shall have power to enforce this article by appropriate legislation.

Amendment 14 (Ratified July 9, 1868)

Section 1. All persons born or naturalized in the United States and subject to the jurisdiction thereof, are citizens of the United States and of the State wherein they reside. No State shall make or enforce any law which shall abridge the privileges or immunities of citizens of the United States; nor shall any State deprive any person of life, liberty, or property, without due process of law; nor deny to any person within its jurisdiction the equal protection of the laws.

Section 2. Representatives shall be apportioned among the several States according to their respective numbers, counting the whole number of persons in each State, excluding Indians not taxed. But when the right to vote at any election for the choice of electors for President and Vice President of the United States, Representatives in Congress, the Executive and Judicial officers of a State, or the members of the Legislature thereof, is denied to any of the male inhabitants of such State, being twenty-one years of age, and citizens of the United States, or in any way abridged, except for participation in rebellion, or other crime, the basis of representation therein shall be reduced in the proportion which the number of such male citizens shall bear to the whole number of male citizens twenty-one years of age in such State.

The Fourteenth Amendment is profoundly important on several fronts. The Citizenship Clause overturned the Supreme Court's decision in Dred Scott v. Sanford, *60 U.S. 393 (1857) and conferred citizenship—and thus legal rights—on former slaves. This amendment also enshrines the citizenship principle of jus soli, in which citizenship is determined by place of birth. The Privileges and Immunities Clause was effectively undermined in the* Slaughterhouse Cases, *83 U.S. 36 (1873). However, the Fourteenth's Equal Protection and Due Process Clauses have been the means by which the Supreme Court has applied to the states most of the provisions of the Bill of Rights, and the clauses are frequently the basis for legal challenges to laws that are alleged to be discriminatory.*

Section 3. No person shall be a Senator or Representative in Congress, or elector of President and Vice President, or hold any office, civil or military, under the United States, or under any State, who, having previously taken an oath, as a member of Congress, or as an officer of the United States, or as a member of any State legislature, or as an executive or judicial officer of any State, to support the Constitution of the United States, shall have engaged in insurrection or rebellion against the same, or given aid or comfort to the enemies thereof. But Congress may by a vote of two-thirds of each House, remove such disability.

Section 4. The validity of the public debt of the United States, authorized by law, including debts incurred for payment of pensions and bounties for services in suppressing insurrection or rebellion, shall not be questioned. But neither the United States nor any State shall assume or pay any debt or obligation incurred in aid of insurrection or rebellion against the United States, or any claim for the loss or emancipation of any slave; but all such debts, obligations and claims shall be held illegal and void.

Section 5. The Congress shall have power to enforce, by appropriate legislation, the provisions of this article.

Amendment 15 (Ratified February 3, 1870)

Section 1. The right of citizens of the United States to vote shall not be denied or abridged by the United States or by any State on account of race, color, or previous condition of servitude.

Section 2. The Congress shall have power to enforce this article by appropriate legislation.

Although the Fifteenth Amendment has prohibited racial discrimination in voting since its ratification in 1870, in the period after its approval, states adopted several voting hurdles. Among these were poll taxes, White primaries (intraparty elections in which only Whites could vote), literacy tests, racial gerrymanders (the drawing of electoral district boundaries to maximize the advantage of Whites), and grandfather clauses. These impediments had profoundly discriminatory effects and ran directly counter to the spirit of the Fifteenth Amendment.

Amendment 16 (Ratified February 3, 1913)

The Congress shall have power to lay and collect taxes on incomes, from whatever source derived, without apportionment among the several States, and without regard to any census or enumeration.

The Sixteenth Amendment is another amendment that negated a Supreme Court decision. The Court initially overturned the federal income tax in its ruling in Pollock v. Farmers' Loan & Trust Co., *157 U.S. 429 (1895), 158 U.S. 601 (1895).*

Amendment 17 (Ratified April 8, 1913)

The Senate of the United States shall be composed of two Senators from each State, elected by the people thereof, for six years; and each Senator shall have one vote. The electors in each State shall have the qualifications requisite for electors of the most numerous branches of the State legislatures.

When vacancies happen in the representation of any State in the Senate, the executive authority of such State shall issue writs of election to fill such vacancies: Provided, That the legislature of any State may empower the executive thereof to make temporary appointments until the people fill the vacancies by election as the legislature may direct.

This amendment shall not be so construed as to affect the election or term of any Senator chosen before it becomes valid as part of the Constitution.

Amendment 18 (Ratified January 16, 1919)

Section 1. After one year from the ratification of this article the manufacture, sale, or transportation of intoxicating liquors within, the importation thereof into, or the exportation thereof from the United States and all territory subject to the jurisdiction thereof for beverage purposes is hereby prohibited.

The Eighteenth Amendment, the nation's disastrous experiment with writing public policy into the Constitution, was later overturned by the Twenty-first Amendment.

Section 2. The Congress and the several States shall have concurrent power to enforce this article by appropriate legislation.

Section 3. This article shall be inoperative unless it shall have been ratified as an amendment to the Constitution by the legislatures of the several States, as provided in the Constitution, within seven years from the date of the submission hereof to the States by the Congress.

Amendment 19 (Ratified August 18, 1920)

The right of citizens of the United States to vote shall not be denied or abridged by the United States or by any State on account of sex. Congress shall have power to enforce this article by appropriate legislation.

In 1914, women in only eleven states enjoyed some voting rights, although Wyoming had famously accorded universal suffrage to women as early as 1869.

Amendment 20 (Ratified January 23, 1933)

Section 1. The terms of the President and Vice President shall end at noon on the 20th day of January, and the terms of Senators and Representatives at noon on the 3rd day of January, of the years in which such terms would have ended if this article had not been ratified; and the terms of their successors shall then begin.

Section 2. The Congress shall assemble at least once in every year, and such meeting shall begin at noon on the 3rd day of January, unless they shall by law appoint a different day.

Section 3. If, at the time fixed for the beginning of the term of the President, the President elect shall have died, the Vice President elect shall become President. If a President shall not have been chosen before the time fixed for the beginning of his term, or if the President elect shall have failed to qualify, then the Vice President elect shall act as President until a President shall have qualified; and the Congress may by law provide for the case wherein neither a President elect nor a Vice President elect shall have qualified, declaring who shall then act as President, or the manner in which one who is to act shall be selected, and such person shall act accordingly until a President or Vice President shall have qualified.

Section 4. The Congress may by law provide for the case of the death of any of the persons from whom the House of Representatives may choose a President whenever the right of choice shall have devolved upon them, and for the case of the death of any of the persons from whom the Senate may choose a Vice President whenever the right of choice shall have devolved upon them.

Section 5. Sections 1 and 2 shall take effect on the 15th day of October following the ratification of this article.

Section 6. This article shall be inoperative unless it shall have been ratified as an amendment to the Constitution by the legislatures of three-fourths of the several States within seven years from the date of its submission.

Amendment 21 (Ratified December 5, 1933)

Section 1. The eighteenth article of amendment to the Constitution of the United States is hereby repealed.

The Twenty-first is the only amendment adopted by ratifying conventions in three-fourths of the states. All other amendments have been approved by state legislatures.

Section 2. The transportation or importation into any State, Territory, or possession of the United States for delivery or use therein of intoxicating liquors, in violation of the laws thereof, is hereby prohibited.

Section 3. This article shall be inoperative unless it shall have been ratified as an amendment to the Constitution by conventions in the several States, as provided in the Constitution, within seven years from the date of the submission hereof to the States by the Congress.

Amendment 22 (Ratified February 27, 1951)

Section 1. No person shall be elected to the office of the President more than twice, and no person who has held the office of President, or acted as President, for more than two years of a term to which some other person was elected President shall be elected to the office of the President more than once. But this Article shall not apply to any person holding the office of President, when this Article was proposed by the Congress, and shall not prevent any person who may be holding the office of President, or acting as President, during the term within which this Article becomes operative from holding the office of President or acting as President during the remainder of such term.

Presidents prior to Franklin D. Roosevelt followed a long-standing tradition, established by George Washington, of serving for no more than two terms. Breaking the unwritten rule, FDR was elected four times. The Twenty-second Amendment was adopted to formalize the two-term tradition.

Section 2. This article shall be inoperative unless it shall have been ratified as an amendment to the Constitution by the legislatures of three-fourths of the several States within seven years from the date of its submission to the States by the Congress.

Amendment 23 (Ratified March 29, 1961)

Section 1. The District constituting the seat of Government of the United States shall appoint in such manner as the Congress may direct: A number of electors of President and Vice President equal to the whole number of Senators and Representatives in Congress to which the District would be entitled if it were a State, but in no event more than the least populous State; they shall be in addition to those appointed by the States, but they shall be considered, for the purposes of the election of President and Vice President, to be electors appointed by a State; and they shall meet in the District and perform such duties as provided by the twelfth article of amendment.

> *In recent decades, proposals have been made to pass a constitutional amendment that would remove the District of Columbia from the control of Congress and grant it status as a state. However, the issue of District of Columbia statehood gets entangled with party politics, and the idea has gained little traction. Because the District of Columbia is a bastion of Democratic Party support, Republicans have generally resisted the idea of establishing it as the fifty-first state.*

Section 2. The Congress shall have power to enforce this article by appropriate legislation.

Amendment 24 (Ratified January 23, 1964)

Section 1. The right of citizens of the United States to vote in any primary or other election for President or Vice President, for electors for President or Vice President, or for Senator or Representative in Congress, shall not be denied or abridged by the United States or any State by reason of failure to pay any poll tax or other tax.

> *The poll tax was adopted by several southern states as a means of discouraging the poor—and especially African Americans—from voting. The Twenty-fourth Amendment was ratified in 1964 to force these states to end the discriminatory policy.*

Section 2. The Congress shall have power to enforce this article by appropriate legislation.

Amendment 25 (Ratified February 10, 1967)

Section 1. In case of the removal of the President from office or of his death or resignation, the Vice President shall become President.

Section 2. Whenever there is a vacancy in the office of the Vice President, the President shall nominate a Vice President who shall take office upon confirmation by a majority vote of both Houses of Congress.

Section 3. Whenever the President transmits to the President pro tempore of the Senate and the Speaker of the House of Representatives his written declaration that he is unable to discharge the powers and duties of his office, and until he transmits to them a written declaration to the contrary, such powers and duties shall be discharged by the Vice President as Acting President.

Section 4. Whenever the Vice President and a majority of either the principal officers of the executive departments or of such other body as Congress may by law provide, transmit to the President pro tempore of the Senate and the Speaker of the House of Representatives their written declaration that the President is unable to discharge the powers and duties of his office, the Vice President shall immediately assume the powers and duties of the office as Acting President.

Thereafter, when the President transmits to the President pro tempore of the Senate and the Speaker of the House of Representatives his written declaration that no inability exists, he shall resume the powers and duties of his office unless the Vice President and a majority of either the principal officers of the executive department or of such other body as Congress may by law provide, transmit within four days to the President pro tempore of the Senate and the Speaker of the House of Representatives their written declaration that the President is unable to discharge the powers and duties of his office. Thereupon Congress shall decide the issue, assembling within forty-eight hours for that purpose if not in session. If the Congress, within twenty-one days after receipt of the latter written declaration, or, if Congress is not in session, within twenty-one days after Congress is required to assemble, determines by two-thirds vote of both Houses that the President is unable to discharge the powers and duties of his office, the Vice President shall continue to discharge the same as Acting President; otherwise, the President shall resume the powers and duties of his office.

Amendment 26 (Ratified July 1, 1971)

Section 1. The right of citizens of the United States, who are eighteen years of age or older, to vote shall not be denied or abridged by the United States or by any State on account of age.

Section 2. The Congress shall have power to enforce this article by appropriate legislation.

The Voting Rights Act of 1965 extended the right to vote in federal, state, and local elections to those aged eighteen and older. However, in Oregon v. Mitchell, *400 U.S. 112 (1970), the Supreme Court determined that Congress did not have the authority to set age requirements for state and local elections. The Twenty-sixth Amendment was quickly passed, circumventing the Court's ruling.*

Amendment 27 (Ratified May 7, 1992)

No law varying the compensation for the services of the Senators and Representatives shall take effect, until an election of Representatives shall have intervened.

This amendment was initially proposed in 1789, but it received scant support at the time. It was revisited and approved by the Ohio legislature eighty-four years later, in 1873. After research by an enterprising legislative staff person in Texas, it was revisited once again and finally approved in 1992. Thus, 203 years elapsed between the initial proposal and final ratification. See Richard Bernstein, "The Sleeper Wakes: The History and Legacy of the Twenty-seventh Amendment," Fordham Law Review *61 (1992): 497.*

GLOSSARY

Activism (judicial). The willingness of a judge to inject into a case their own personal values about what is good and bad public policy.

Actus reus. The material element of the crime, which may be the commission of a forbidden action (for example, robbery) or the failure to perform a required action (for example, to stop and render aid to a motor vehicle accident victim).

Adversarial process. The process used in American courtrooms, where the trial is seen as a battle between two opposing sides, and the role of the judge is to act as a sort of passive referee. See also *inquisitorial method.*

Advisory opinions. Rendering a decision on an abstract or hypothetical question (something that American courts are generally not supposed to do).

Alternative dispute resolution (ADR). Methods of resolving disputes (often with the help of neutral third parties) without a trial. Mediation and arbitration are two well-known ADR techniques.

Amicus curiae ("friend of the court"). A person (or group), not a party to a case, who submits views (usually in the form of written briefs) about how the case should be decided.

Answer. The formal written statement by a defendant responding to a civil complaint and setting forth the grounds for their defense.

Appellate jurisdiction. The authority of a higher court to review the decision of a lower court.

Arraignment. The process in which the defendant is brought before the judge in the court where they are to be tried to respond to the grand jury indictment or the prosecutor's bill of information.

Attitudinal model. The theory of appellate judge behavior that holds that once the researcher learns the judges' basic set of attitudes, they can explain and predict how those judges will vote in the cases that come before them.

Bail. A sum of money put up with the court by the defendant to ensure that they will appear at the time of trial.

Bench trials. Trials without a jury in which the judge decides which party prevails.

Bill of attainder. A law, forbidden by the US Constitution, that makes conduct illegal for one person (or class of persons) but not for the population in general.

Bill of information. A statement of the charges against the accused prepared by the prosecutor, which, if approved by a judge, will require the accused to stand trial for the alleged crimes. This is used in states that do not employ a grand jury.

Blue slip. The device that senators use to invoke the practice of senatorial courtesy when they are objecting to a president's nomination to a lower federal court judgeship.

Certification. The procedure by which one of the US appeals courts asks the US Supreme Court for instructions or clarification about a particular legal matter. The justices may either choose to honor this request or not, or they may request that the entire record of the case be sent to the Supreme Court for review and final judgment.

Cert petition. A cert petition, or petition for a writ of certiorari, is a request to the Supreme Court to review a lower court's decision.

Civil law. The law that pertains to the relationship between one private citizen and another, between a private citizen and a corporation, or between one corporation and another.

Class actions. Suits brought by persons having similar grievances against a common entity—for example, a group of smokers with lung cancer suing a tobacco company.

Collegial courts. Courts having more than one judge, which are almost always appellate courts.

Common law. A system of law inherited from England based on legal precedents or tradition instead of statutory law or systematic legal codes.

Complaint. A written statement filed by the plaintiff who initiates a civil case. It states the wrongs allegedly committed by the defendant and requests relief from the court.

Concurrent jurisdiction. A situation in which two courts have a legal right to hear the same case. For example, both the US Supreme Court and US trial courts have concurrent jurisdiction in certain cases brought by or against ambassadors or consuls.

Concurring opinion. An opinion by a member of a court that agrees with the result reached in the case but offers its own rationale for the decision.

Conservatives. For judges, this means support for the prosecution in criminal cases, support for the government in its attempts to restrict freedom of expression, and support for the individual (or corporation) that is being regulated by the government.

Corpus juris. The entire body of law for a particular legal entity.

Court of appeals. A court that is higher than an ordinary trial court and has the function of reviewing or correcting the decisions of trial judges.

Courtroom work group. The regular participants in the day-to-day activities of a particular courtroom. The most visible members of this group are judges, prosecutors, and defense attorneys.

Crimes. Offenses against the state, punishable by fine, imprisonment, or death.

Criminal law. The law that pertains to offenses against the state itself, actions that may be directed against a person but that are deemed to be offensive to society as a whole—for example, armed robbery or rape.

Cross-examination. During a trial, the questions posed to a witness who has been called to the stand by the opposing attorney.

Cue theory. The theory that Supreme Court justices do not have the time to carefully review all cases that are appealed to them, so they develop shorthand methods of seeking out easy-to-find cues to help them determine whether they want to review a particular case.

Damages. Money paid by defendants to successful plaintiffs in civil cases to compensate the plaintiffs for their injuries. Compensatory damages are designed to cover the plaintiff's actual loss; punitive damages are designed to punish the defendant.

Declaratory judgments. When a court outlines the rights of the parties under a statute, a will, or a contract.

Defendant. In a civil case, the person or organization against whom the plaintiff sues; in a criminal case, the person accused of the crime.

Deposition. An oral statement made before an officer authorized by law to administer oaths. Such statements are often taken to examine potential witnesses in the discovery process.

Dicta. Short for obiter *dictum,* Latin for "something said in passing." The part of a court opinion that does not contribute to the central logic of the decision. May be the opinion(s) expressed by the judge(s) on points that do not necessarily arise in the case.

Discovery. The process by which lawyers learn about their opponent's case in preparation for trial. Typical tools of discovery include depositions, interrogatories, and requests for documents.

Dissenting opinion. An opinion by a member of a court that disagrees with the result reached in the case by the court.

Diversity of citizenship matters. Suits between individuals who are citizens of different states.

Diversity of citizenship suit. A civil legal proceeding brought by a citizen of one state against a citizen of another state.

En banc ("in the bench" or "as a full bench"). Court sessions with the entire membership of a court participating, not just a smaller panel of judges.

Equity. That realm of the law in which the judge can issue a remedy that will either prevent or cure the wrong that is about to happen—for example, an injunction against an illegal strike by a union.

Ex post facto. Forbidden by the US Constitution, this law declares conduct to be illegal after the conduct takes place.

Federal question. If a court case centers around the interpretation of a federal law, the US Constitution, or a treaty, then it contains a federal question, and the case may be heard by a US court.

Felony. Any offense for which the penalty may be death or imprisonment in a penitentiary more than one year.

Fluidity. The degree that appellate court judges change their opinions between the time a conference vote is taken, and the vote is announced in open court.

Forum shopping. The practice of filing a case in the court expected to be most sympathetic to the plaintiff, when more than one court has jurisdiction over the dispute.

Grand jury. A body of sixteen to twenty-three citizens who listen to evidence of criminal allegations, which is presented by the prosecutors, and determine whether probable cause exists to believe an individual committed an offense. See also *indictment.*

Habeas corpus. A writ (court order) that is usually used to bring a prisoner before the court to determine the legality of their imprisonment.

Impeachment. The only way in which a federal judge or other high-ranking federal official may be removed from office. The House of Representatives brings the charge(s), and the Senate, following trial, convicts by a two-thirds vote of the membership.

Indictment. The decision of a grand jury to order a defendant to stand trial because the jury believes that probable cause exists to warrant a trial.

Inquisitorial method. The procedure used in most European and Latin American courtrooms in which the judge and jury take an active role in the trial, and the attorneys act only to aid and supplement the judicial inquiry. See also *adversarial process.*

Interrogatories. Written questions sent by one party in a lawsuit to an opposing party as part of pretrial discovery in civil cases. The party receiving the interrogatories is required to answer them in writing under oath.

Judgments. The official decisions of a court finally resolving the dispute between the parties to the lawsuit.

Judicial realists. Those who believe that judges, like other human beings, are influenced by the values and attitudes learned in childhood.

Judicial review. The power of the judicial branch to declare acts of the executive and legislative branches unconstitutional.

Jurisdiction. The authority of a court to hear and decide legal disputes and to enforce its rulings.

Justiciability. Whether a judge ought to hear or refrain from hearing certain types of cases. It differs from jurisdiction, which pertains to the technical right of a judge to hear a case. For example, lawsuits dealing with political questions are considered nonjusticiable.

Law. A social norm that is sanctioned in threat or in fact by the application of physical force. The party that exercises such physical force is recognized by society as legitimately having this kind of authority, such as a police officer.

Liberals. For judges, this means support for the defendant in criminal cases, support for a broadening position for freedom of expression, and support for the government in its attempt to economically regulate individuals and corporations.

Magistrate. A lower-level judicial official to whom the accused is brought after the arrest. A magistrate has the obligation to inform the accused of the charges against them and to explain their legal rights.

Mandatory sentencing laws. Statutes that require automatic jail time for a convicted criminal, usually for a minimum period. This is often for violent crimes in which a gun was used and for habitual offenders.

Mens rea. The mental element of the crime; that is, what was intended by the perpetrator of the crime. Usually, the more intentional and willful the mental state, the more serious the crime.

Merit selection. A method of selecting state judges that requires the governor to make the appointment from a brief list of names submitted by a special commission established for that purpose. After serving for a brief period, the judge must run in a retention election. Voters thus determine whether the judge should be retained for a full term.

Misdemeanors. Minor crimes for which the punishment is generally no longer than six months in jail.

Moot. Describes a case when the basic facts or the status of the parties have significantly changed between the time the suit was filed to when it comes before the judge.

National security. The protection of a nation's stability and well-being from various threats, including military, economic, social, and environmental factors that can significantly impact the quality of life and choices available to the government and its people.

Nolle prosequi ("I refuse to prosecute"). A motion filed by a prosecutor before a judge, in which the prosecutor sets forth specific and justifiable reasons for not wishing to press charges against a criminal defendant.

Nolo contendere ("no contest"). A plea by a criminal defendant in which they do not deny the facts of the case but claims not to have committed any crime, or it may mean that the defendant does not understand the charges.

Opinion of the court. A judge's written explanation of the court's decision. Because the case may be heard by a panel of judges in an appellate court, the opinion can take two forms. If all the judges completely agree with the result, one judge will write the opinion for all. If all the judges do not agree, the formal decision will be based on the view of the majority, and one member of the majority will write the decision.

Oral argument. An opportunity for lawyers to summarize their position before the court and to answer the judges' questions.

Ordinance-making power. The power of state governors to fill in the details of legislation passed by state legislatures.

Original jurisdiction. The court that by law must be the first to hear a particular type of case. For example, in suits with alleged damages more than $75,000 between citizens from different states, the federal district courts are the courts of original jurisdiction.

Overcharging. The process whereby a prosecutor charges a criminal defendant with crimes more serious than the facts warrant to obtain a more favorable plea bargain from the defendant's attorney.

Per curiam ("by the court"). An unsigned opinion of the court, often brief.

Peremptory challenge. An objection that an attorney might have to a prospective juror. The juror may be eliminated from the array without the attorney having to give a public reason for the objection. The number of such challenges is limited by law.

Petit juries (or trial juries). A group of citizens who hear the evidence presented by both sides at trial and determine the facts in dispute.

Plaintiff. The person who files the complaint in a civil lawsuit.

Plea bargain. A bargain or deal that has been struck between the prosecutor and the defendant's attorney whereby some form of leniency is promised in exchange for a guilty plea.

Political question. When the courts refuse to rule because they believe that under the US Constitution, the founders meant that the matter at hand should be dealt with by Congress or the president, the courts are refusing to rule on a political question.

Private law. This deals with the rights and obligations that private individuals and institutions have when they relate to one another.

Probation. Punishment for a crime that allows the offender to remain in the community and out of jail so long as they follow court-ordered guidelines about their behavior.

Pro bono publico ("for the public good"). Usually refers to legal representation undertaken without fee for some charitable or public purpose.

Pro se litigants. Litigants or parties representing themselves in court without the assistance of counsel.

Public law. The relationships that individuals have with the state as a sovereign entity—for example, the tax code, criminal laws, and Social Security legislation.

Rational choice theory. The theory that appellate judges' votes may be explained by knowing more than just their basic attitudes. Judges realize that the fate of their policy goals often depends on the values of other decision-makers, such as their colleagues on the bench, the president, and members of Congress. Judges will thus act in deliberate ways to maximize the likelihood of success in achieving their goals.

Recess appointment. An appointment made by the president when Congress is in recess. A recess appointment must be confirmed by the Senate by the end of the next session of Congress, or the appointment expires.

Reversible error. An error committed at the trial court level that is so serious that it requires the appellate court to reverse the decision of the trial judge.

Role (judicial). How judges view themselves as jurists and the degree to which they believe in judicial activism or judicial self-restraint.

Rule of eighty. When the sum of a judge's age and number of years on the bench is eighty, Congress permits the individual to retire with full pay and benefits.

Rule of four. On the Supreme Court, at least four justices must agree to take a case before the Court will consider it.

Senatorial courtesy. Under this practice, senators of the president's political party who object to a candidate that the president wishes to appoint to a district judgeship in their home state have a virtual veto over the nomination.

Senior status. An option created by Congress for federal judges who have reached retirement age. Senior status judges have not fully retired but are allowed a reduced workload compared to their previous status as full-time "active" judges.

Sequestration (of jury). In particularly important or notorious cases, the jury may be kept away from the public eye by the judge, and this usually means that the jury is housed and fed as a group at taxpayers' expense.

Shadow docket. The cases a court resolves through emergency orders and summary decisions, apart from the cases decided through that court's normal process.

Small-group analysis. The theory that appellate court behavior may be explained in part by what social scientists know generally about the decision-making process of small groups of any kind.

Socialization (judicial). The process by which a new judge is formally and informally trained to perform the specific tasks of the judgeship.

Social leader (on appellate courts). A judge performing this role attends to the emotional needs of their associates by affirming their values as individuals and as court members, especially when their views are rejected by the majority.

Standing. The status of someone who wishes to bring a lawsuit. To have standing the person must have suffered (or be immediately about to suffer) a direct and significant injury.

Stare decisis, doctrine of ("stand by what has been decided"). In effect, the tradition of honoring and following previous decisions of the courts and established points of law.

Statutory law. The type of law enacted by a legislative body, such as Congress, a state legislature, or a city council.

Strategic behavior. Judges engage in this behavior when they make decisions based upon a consideration of the actions of other judicial and political decision-makers.

Task leader (on appellate courts). A judge performing this role is the intellectual force behind the conference deliberations, focusing on the actual decision and trying to keep the court consistent with itself.

Three-judge district court. With some types of important cases, Congress has mandated that the case cannot be heard by a US trial judge acting alone but must be decided by a panel of three judges, one of whom must be an appeals court judge.

Three-judge panels (of appellate courts). Most decisions of the US courts of appeals are not made by the entire court sitting together but by three judges, often selected at random to hear any given case.

Tort. A civil wrong or breach of duty to another person.

Trial de novo. A new trial in which the entire case is retried as if no prior trial had occurred.

Venire. A group of people summoned from a panel of potential jurors to appear in each courtroom.

Venue. The geographical location in which a case is tried.

Victim impact statement. A written or spoken statement, typically provided during the sentencing phase of a criminal trial, where the victim describes the harm caused to them by the defendant's criminal actions.

Voir dire. The procedure by which opposing attorneys question potential jurors to determine whether the jurors might be prejudicial to their individual cases.

Warrant. Issued after a complaint, filed by one person against another, has been presented and reviewed by a magistrate who has found probable cause for the arrest.

Writ of certiorari. An order issued by the US Supreme Court directing the lower court to transfer records for a case that it will hear on appeal.

Writ of mandamus. A court order compelling a public official to perform their duty.

ENDNOTES

FRONT MATTER

1. Lee Epstein, "Partisanship 'All the Way Down' on the U.S. Supreme Court," *Pepperdine Law Review* 51 (2024): 489-514, 4923.

2. Ibid., Figure 6.

3. Adam Liptak and Alicia Parlapino, "In a Volatile Term, a Fractured Supreme Court Remade America," *New York Times*, July 2, 2024, https://www.nytimes.com/2024/07/02/us/politics/supreme-court-term-decisions.html (accessed August 13, 2024).

4. *Trump v. United States*, 603 U.S. _____ (2024).

5. *Trump v. Anderson*, 601 U.S. _____ (2024).

6. *Dobbs v. Jackson Women's Health Organization*, 597 U.S. 215 (2022).

7. Kelly Baden, Joerg Dreweke, and Candace Gibson, "Clear and Growing Evidence That Dobbs Is Harming Reproductive Health and Freedom," *Guttmacher* (May 2024): https://www.guttmacher.org/2024/05/clear-and-growing-evidence-dobbs-harming-reproductive-health-and-freedom (accessed August 13, 2024).

8. Diana C. Mutz and Edward D. Mansfield, "Inflation in 2022 Did Not Affect Congressional Voting, but Abortion Did," *PNAS*, forthcoming.

9. See Stephanie Armour
Julie Appleby, Julie Rovner, and KFF Health News, "Kamala Harris's Record on Abortion Rights Shows Strong Support," *Scientific American* (July 22, 2024), https://www.scientificamerican.com/article/kamala-harris-record-on-abortion-rights-shows-strong-support/ (accessed August 13, 2024).

10. Jennifer De Pinto, "Abortion Rights Support Didn't Always Translate into Harris Support – CBS News Exit Poll Analysis," *CBS News* (November 9, 2024), https://www.cbsnews.com/news/abortion-rights-exit-poll-kamala-harris-2024/ (accessed November 17, 2024).

11. Joseph Copeland, "Favorable Views of Supreme Court Near Historic Low," *Pew Research Center* (August 8, 2024), https://www.pewresearch.org/short-reads/2024/08/08/favorable-views-of-supreme-court-remain-near-historic-low/ (accessed August 13, 2024).

12. Nicholas T. Davis and Matthew P. Hitt, "Supreme Court Legitimacy Exhibits New Partisan Sorting," paper presented at the Annual Meeting of the International Society for Political Psychology, Montreal, Canada, July 9–11, 2023.

13. *Food and Drug Administration v. Alliance for Hippocratic Medicine*, 602 U.S. _____ (2024).

14. *303 Creative LLC v. Elenis*, 600 U.S. _____ (2023).

15. *Securities and Exchange Commission v. Jarkesy*, 603 U.S. _____ (2024).

16. *Dobbs v. Jackson Women's Health Organization*, 597 U.S. 215 (2022).

17. *Students for Fair Admissions, Inc. v. President and Fellows of Harvard College*, 600 U.S. 181 (2023).

18. *Garland v. Cargill* (2024), Docket Number 22-976 (2024).

19. *Obergefell v. Hodges*, 576 U.S. 644 (2015).

CHAPTER 1

1. Noam Scheiber and Santul Nerkar, "Supreme Court, in Starbucks Ruling, Curbs Labor Regulator's Authority," *New York Times*, June 13, 2024, https://www.nytimes.com/2024/06/13/business/economy/supreme-court-starbucks-nlrb.html

2. Noam Scheiber, "Starbucks Fires Memphis Workers Involved in Unionization Efforts," *New York Times*, February 8, 2022, https://www.nytimes.com/2022/02/08/business/economy/starbucks-memphis-union-workers-fired.html

3. Ibid.

4. "Supreme Court to Hear Dispute over Starbucks Firing Pro-Union Workers," Reuters via NBC News, January 12, 2024, https://www.nbcnews.com/politics/supreme-court/supreme-court-hear-dispute-starbucks-firing-union-workers-rcna133790

5. See *AZ index of U.S. government departments and agencies* at https://www.usa.gov/agencies/national-labor-relations-board

6. "Supreme Court Agrees to Hear Starbucks Appeal in Memphis Union Case," Associated Press via PBS News, January 12, 2024, https://www.pbs.org/newshour/politics/supreme-court-agrees-to-hear-starbucks-appeal-in-memphis-union-case

7. Ronald Mann, "Court to Mull Injunction in Starbucks Case against Memphis Union Organizers," SCOTUSblog.com, April 22, 2024, https://www.scotusblog.com/2024/04/court-to-mull-injunction-in-starbucks-case-against-memphis-union-organizers/

8. Ibid.

9. Lauren Kaori Gurley, "Supreme Court Sides with Starbucks in Blow to Union Activists," *Washington Post*, June 13, 2024, https://www.washingtonpost.com/business/2024/06/13/starbucks-union-supreme-court-decision/

10. As quoted in TV news report by Kelli Cook, "'It Makes It Harder for Employees Like Me': Memphis 7 Reacts to US Supreme Court Backing Starbucks in Latest Ruling," Action News 5 (Memphis, TN), published June 13, 2024, https://www.actionnews5.com/2024/06/13/it-makes-it-harder-employees-like-me-memphis-7-reacts-us-supreme-court-backing-starbucks-latest-ruling/

11. Emily Peck, "Starbucks Is Softening Its Stance toward Unions," Axios.com, December 15, 2023, https://www.axios.com/2023/12/15/starbucks-union-stance-nlrb

12. Ibid.

13. Stephen D. Ford, *The American Legal System: Its Dynamics and Limits* (St. Paul, MN: West, 1974), 13. Our elaborations on this definition of law are borrowed from Chapter 1 of Ford's text.

14. US Constitution, Amendment XIV, Section 1.

15. See https://www.federalregister.gov/

16. See https://www.ecfr.gov/

17. https://www.usatoday.com/story/news/politics/2021/01/29/all-executive-orders-president-joe-biden-has-signed/4308740001/ (accessed March 20, 2021).

18. Madeline Holcombe, "Pastors Sue California Governor over Coronavirus Restrictions on Church Gatherings," CNN.com, April 14, 2020, https://www.cnn.com/2020/04/14/us/california-pastors-sue-church-restrictions/index.html

19. Ibid.

20. *Youngstown Sheet & Tube Co. v. Sawyer*, 343 U.S. 579 (1952).

21. "Utah OK's 'A Little Bit Gruesome' Firing Squads," *Houston Chronicle*, March 24, 2015, A5.

22. "Prisoners in 2022Statistical Tables." Data collected and reported by the Bureau of Justice Statistics, US Department of Justice. Accessed July 12, 2024, https://bjs.ojp.gov/library/publications/prisoners-2022-statistical-tables#

23. Isaac Mansell, "Behind Bars and Ballots: The Link Between Democracy, Development, and Incarceration," *Harvard International Review*, January 19, 2024, https://hir.harvard.edu/behind-bars-and-ballots-the-link-between-democracy-development-and-incarceration/ ; Andrew Romano, "Jailbreak!" *Newsweek*, April 23 and 30, 2012, 22.

24. Theodore Reed Fehrenbach, *Lone Star: A History of Texas and the Texans* (New York, NY: American Legacy Press, 1968), 336.

25. Martin Luther King Jr., "Letter from Birmingham Jail, April 16, 1963." The full text of the letter may be found in *Why We Can't Wait* (New York, NY: Harper & Row, 1963).

26. Abe Fortas, *Concerning Dissent and Civil Disobedience* (New York, NY: Signet, 1970), 18.

27. "A Former Clerk Who Refused to Issue Marriage Licenses Must Pay $260,000 in Fees and Costs, a Judge Rules," Associated Press, January 2, 2024, https://apnews.com/article/kim-davis-marriage-licenses-rowan-county-b99cdf7b93a1e144fdff2c3b24d96c2c

28. Nicole Winfield, "Pope Says Druggists Have Moral Right," *Houston Chronicle*, October 30, 2007, A10.

29. Andrew Sinclair, "Prohibition: The Era of Excess," in *Law and the Behavioral Sciences*, ed. Lawrence M. Friedman and Stewart Macaulay (New York, NY: Bobbs-Merrill, 1977), 353.

30. Ibid.

31. "Occupy Arrests.com," http://occupyarrests.moonfruit.com/ (accessed March 17, 2015).

32. "Cohabitation in the United States," http://enwikipedia.org/wiki/Cohabitation_in_the_United States (accessed March 17, 2015).

33. Erum Salam, "Michigan Republicans Fight Effort to Repeal Ban on Unmarried Cohabitation," *The Guardian* (UK), April 21, 2023, https://www.theguardian.com/us-news/2023/apr/21/michigan-republicans-repeal-ban-unmarried-cohabitation

34. "N.C. Cohabitation Law Struck Down," CBSNews.com, September 14, 2006, https://www.cbsnews.com/news/nc-cohabitation-law-struck-down/

35. See, for example, Jack W. Peltason, *Fifty-Eight Lonely Men* (New York, NY: Harcourt, Brace and World, 1961); and Jack Bass, *Unlikely Heroes* (New York, NY: Simon & Schuster, 1981).

36. Federal Judicial Caseload Statistics 2022. Accessed July 10, 2024, https://www.uscourts.gov/statistics-reports/federal-judicial-caseload-statistics-2022

37. 2022 data compiled by the Court Statistics Project, an initiative of the Conference of State Court Administrators and the National Center for State Courts. Accessed July 10, 2024, https://www.courtstatistics.org/court-statistics/interactive-caseload-data-displays/csp-stat-nav-cards-first-row/csp-stat-civil

38. "How Many Court Cases Are Filed Every Year?" http://answers.yahoo.

com/question/index?qid (accessed March 17, 2015).

39. "Tort Costs in America: An Empirical Analysis of Costs and Compensation of the U.S. Tort System," a report by the US Chamber of Commerce Institute for Legal Reform. Accessed November 22, 2022, https://institutef orlegalreform.com/research/tort-co sts-in-america-an-empirical-analys is-of-costs-and-compensation-of-th e-u-s-tort-system/

40. American Bar Association, Profile of the Legal Profession. Accessed July 12, 2024, https://www.abalegalprofil e.com/demographics.html

41. Ibid.

42. Jethro K. Lieberman, *The Litigious Society* (New York, NY: Basic Books, 1983), viii.

43. "Global Litigation Rates: The U.S. Is Not the Leader," *doeLegal Journal*, March 29, 2011, http://doelegal.blogs pot.com/2011/03/global-litigation-r ates-us-is-not.html (accessed April 9, 2012).

44. Stuart Taylor Jr. and Evan Thomas, "Civil Wars," *Newsweek*, December 15, 2003, 45.

45. Stephen Wermiel, "High Court Agrees to Hear Case on Segregation at State Colleges," *Wall Street Journal*, April 16, 1991.

46. *Chambers v. U.S. Department of the Army*, 499 U.S. 645 (1991); and *Kunstler v. Britt*, 499 U.S. 969 (1991).

47. The combined cases are: *EPIC Systems Corp. v. Lewis*, No. 16-285 (2018); *Ernst & Young v. Morris*, No. 16-300 (2018); and *NLRB v. Murphy Oil*, No. 16-307 (2018).

48. Robert Barnes, "Supreme Court Rules That Companies Can Require Workers to Accept Individual Arbitration," *Washington Post*, May 22, 2018, https://www.lmtonline.com/news/a rticle/Supreme-Court-rules-that-co mpanies-can-require-12931130.php (accessed May 29, 2018).

49. For example, see the website of the American Tort Reform Association and its state-by-state analysis of tort reform.

50. The American Tort Reform Association, http://www.atra.org/about/ (accessed March 7, 2018).

51. Alexis de Tocqueville, *Democracy in America*, ed. J. P. Mayer and Max Lerner, trans. George Lawrence (New York, NY: Harper & Row, 1966), 248.

52. Lieberman, *The Litigious Society*, 13.

53. Teresa Griffin, Eldin Hasic, Adrienne Busby, Patrick Reilly, and Stephanie A Koltookian, "Class Action Filings on the Rise in Europe," American Bar Association Litigation Newsletter, November 7, 2022, https://www.amer icanbar.org/groups/litigation/resour ces/newsletters/mass-torts/class-a ction-filings-rise-europe/

54. Sameer Yasir, "A Lifelong Nightmare': Seeking Justice in India's Overwhelmed Courts," *New York Times*, January 13, 2024, https://www.nytim es.com/2024/01/13/world/asia/indi a-judicial-backlog.html

55. Edward Wong, "Quake in China Prompts Lawsuit," *Houston Chronicle*, December 23, 2008, A12.

56. Statement of National Public Radio by Anthony Kuhn, December 23, 2008, https://www.npr.org/templates/s tory/story.php?storyId598657422 (accessed July 15, 2012).

CHAPTER 2

1. See https://www.fjc.gov/sites/default /files/2012/Creat3ed.pdf.

2. Charles Evans Hughes, *The Supreme Court of the United States* (New York, NY: Columbia University Press, 1966), 1.

3. Ibid., 2.
4. Charles Warren, *The Supreme Court in United States History*, vol. 1 (Boston, MA: Little, Brown, 1924), 4.
5. See Sheldon Goldman, *Constitutional Law and Supreme Court Decision-Making* (New York, NY: Harper & Row, 1982), 41.
6. *Marbury v. Madison*, 1 Cranch 137 (1803).
7. See Lawrence Baum, *The Supreme Court*, 5th ed. (Washington, DC: CQ Press, 1995), 22.
8. Herbert Jacob, "Conclusion," in Herbert Jacob et al., *Courts, Law, and Politics in Comparative Perspective* (New Haven, CT: Yale University Press, 1996), 394.
9. Ibid.
10. Robert H. Birkby, *The Court and Public Policy* (Washington, DC: CQ Press, 1983), 1.
11. Sally J. Kenney, "The European Court of Justice: Integrating Europe through Law," *Judicature* 81 (1998): 250.
12. Ibid., 251.
13. *Brown v. Board of Education*, 347 U.S. 483 (1954).
14. https://www.uscourts.gov/sites/default/files/data_tables/supcourt_a1_0930.2023.pdf (accessed July 11, 2024).
15. https://www.uscourts.gov/sites/default/files/data_tables/supcourt_a1_0930.2023.pdf (accessed July 10, 2024).
16. See David M. O'Brien, *Storm Center: The Supreme Court in American Politics*, 2nd ed. (New York, NY: W. W. Norton, 1990), 165.
17. Adam Liptak, "Gorsuch, in Sign of Independence, Is out of Supreme Court's Clerical Pool," *New York Times*, https://www.nytimes.com/2017/05/01/us/politics/gorsuch-supreme-court-labor-pool-clerks.html (accessed June 6, 2024).
18. Joan Biskupic, "Ketanji Brown Jackson's First Few Months at the Fractured Supreme Court," *CNN*, https://www.cnn.com/2022/09/30/politics/ketanji-brown-jackson-supreme-court/index.html (accessed June 6, 2024).
19. See Supreme Court Rule 25, https://www.supremecourt.gov/filingandrules/2023RulesoftheCourt.pdf (accessed June 6, 2024).
20. Amy Howe, "Courtroom Access: The Nuts and Bolts of Courtroom Seatingand the Lines for Public Access," *SCOTUSBlog*, https://www.scotusblog.com/2020/04/courtroom-access-the-nuts-and-bolts-of-courtroom-seating-and-the-lines-to-gain-access-to-the-courtroom/ (accessed June 6, 2024).
21. See https://www.supremecourt.gov/casehand/Guide%20for%20Counsel%202023.pdf (accessed July 11, 2024).
22. Ibid., 7–8.
23. *Mahoney Area School District v. B. L.*, 594 U.S. 180 (2021), 185.
24. *Tinker v. Des Moines Independent Community School District*, 393 U.S. 503 (1969), 506.
25. *Mahoney Area School District v. B. L*, Oral Argument Transcript, April 28, 2021, 19–21.The transcript is available here: https://www.supremecourt.gov/oral_arguments/argument_transcripts/2020/20-255_869d.pdf (accessed July 9, 2024). The audio of the oral argument is available here: https://www.oyez.org/cases/2020/20-255 (accessed July 19, 2024).
26. Ruth Bader Ginsburg, *In My Own Words* (New York, NY: Simon and Schuster, 2016), 211.
27. Ibid., 212.
28. *Lee v. Weisman*, 505 U.S. 577 (1992).

29. Jan Crawford Greenburg, *Supreme Conflict: The Inside Story of the Struggle for Control of the United States Supreme Court* (New York, NY: Penguin Books, 2007), 149.
30. Ibid., 150.
31. Pamela C. Corley, Amy Steigerwalt, and Artemus Ward, *When Dissents Matter: Judicial Dialogue through US Supreme Court Opinions* (Charlottesville, VA: University of Virginia Press, 2023), 128.
32. *Lawrence v. Texas*, 539 U.S. 558 (2003).
33. See https://www.supremecourt.gov/opinions/23pdf/23-719_19m2.pdf (accessed July 9, 2024).
34. For an in-depth discussion of this phenomenon, see https://www.abajournal.com/web/article/scotus-shadow-docket-draws-increasing-scrutiny (accessed July 19, 2024).
35. Stephen Vladeck, *The Shadow Docket: How the Supreme Court Uses Stealth Rulings to Amass Power and Undermine the* Republic (New York, NY: Basic Books, 2023).
36. See https://www.npr.org/2023/05/22/1177228505/supreme-court-shadow-docket (accessed June 6, 2024).
37. EmiLee Smart, "A Shadow's Influence? How the Shadow Docket Influences Public Opinion," *American Politics Research* 52 (2024): 24963.
38. Stephen T. Early, Jr., *Constitutional Courts of the United States* (Totowa, NJ: Littlefield, Adams, 1977), 100.
39. Jennifer Barnes Bowie, Donald R. Songer, and John Szmer, *A View from the Bench and Chambers Examining Judicial Process and Decision Making on the U.S. Courts of Appeals* (Charlottesville, VA: University of Virginia Press, 2014), 1.
40. https://www.uscourts.gov/educational-resources/educational-activities/evarts-act-creating-modern-appellate-courts.
41. See Vanessa K. Burrows, "Administrative Law Judges: An Overview," *Congressional Research Service*, http://www.crs.gov.
42. See Donald R. Songer, "The Circuit Courts of Appeals," in *The American Courts: A Critical Assessment*, ed. John B. Gates and Charles A. Johnson (Washington, DC: CQ Press, 1991), 47.
43. *Food and Drug Administration v. Alliance for Hippocratic Medicine* (2024). For decision see https://www.supremecourt.gov/opinions/23pdf/23-235_n7ip.pdf (accessed June 14, 2024).
44. Howard, *Courts of Appeals in the Federal Judicial System*, 79.
45. See: https://www.uscourts.gov/sites/default/files/data_tables/jb_b1_0930.2023.pdf (accessed July 9, 2024).
46. Jennifer Barnes Bowie, Donald R. Songer, and John Szmer, *A View from the Bench and Chambers: Examining Judicial Process and Decision Making on the U.S. Courts of Appeals* (Charlottesville, VA: University of Virginia Press, 2014), 59.
47. Ibid., 6364.
48. Ibid., 8182.
49. Ibid., 94.
50. https://www.uscourts.gov/sites/default/files/data_tables/jb_b12_0930.2023.pdf (accessed July 9, 2024).
51. See https://www.ca4.uscourts.gov/AppellateProcedureGuide/Decision_Post-Decision/APG-opinionandjudgment.html (accessed July 31, 2024).
52. See https://www.casd.uscourts.gov/Jurors/Jurisdiction-Map.aspx.
53. See Herbert Jacob, *Justice in America*, 4th ed. (Boston, MA: Little, Brown, 1984), chap. 2.
54. Ibid., 37.

55. Robert A. Carp and Claude K. Rowland, *Policymaking and Politics in the Federal District Courts* (Knoxville, TN: University of Tennessee Press, 1983), 3.

56. See https://storage.courtlistener.com/recap/gov.uscourts.flnd.460963/gov.uscourts.flnd.460963.223.0.pdf?utm_source=substack&utm_medium=email, 74 (accessed June 14, 2024).

57. Ibid., 71.

58. The decision of the three-judge district court may be found in *Roe v. Wade*, 314 F. Supp. 1217 (1970), and the Supreme Court decision in *Roe v. Wade*, 410 U.S. 113 (1973).

59. See information about the Executive Office for Immigration Review, immigration courts, and the Board of Immigration Appeals at the U.S. Department of Justice website, http://www.usdoj.gov.

60. Frank M. Coffin, *On Appeal: Courts, Lawyering, and Judging* (New York, NY: W. W. Norton, 1994), 72.

61. Quoted in Robert A. Carp and Russell R. Wheeler, "Sink or Swim: The Socialization of a Federal District Judge," *Journal of Public Law* 21 (1972): 379.

62. Howard, *Courts of Appeals in the Federal Judicial System*, 198.

63. Peter G. Fish, *The Politics of Federal Judicial Administration* (Princeton, NJ: Princeton University Press, 1973), 124, 166.

64. For more specific information about the types of civil and criminal cases, see http://www.uscourts.gov/statistics-reports/analysis-reports/federal-court-management-statistics.

65. See the information available online at http://www.uscourts.gov/statistics-reports/analysis-reports/federal-court-management-statistics.

66. Tessa Berenson, *Time*, August 28, 2017, 12. Also see https://cis.org/Report/Massive-Increase-Immigration-Court-Backlog.

67. https://trac.syr.edu/phptools/immigration/court_backlog/apprep_backlog.php (accessed July 9, 2024).

68. Ibid.

CHAPTER 3

1. Henry R. Glick, "Policymaking and State Supreme Courts," in *The American Courts: A Critical Assessment*, ed. John B. Gates and Charles A. Johnson (Washington, DC: CQ Press, 1991), 88.

2. See, for example, the recent decision by the Georgia Supreme Court, striking down a Georgia law making it a felony for anyone who "publicly advertises, offers, or holds himself or herself out as offering that he or she will intentionally and actively assist another person in the commission of suicide and commits any overt act to further that purpose." In *Final Exit Network, Inc. et al. v. State of Georgia*, 290 Ga. 508 (2012), the court unanimously held that the 1994 law restricts speech in violation of the free speech clauses of the state and federal constitutions.

3. Michael E. Solimine and James L. Walker, *Respecting State Courts: The Inevitability of Judicial Federalism* (Westport, CT: Greenwood Press, 1999), 89.

4. William J. Brennan Jr., "State Constitutions and the Protection of Individual Rights," *Harvard Law Review* 90 (1977): 489–504.

5. See G. Alan Tarr, *Understanding State Constitutions* (Princeton, NJ: Princeton University Press, 1998), 165.

6. "N.C. Court Finds Legislative Districts Unconstitutional," *Houston Chronicle*, September 4, 2019, A11.

7. F. Andrew Hanssen, "Learning about Judicial Independence: Institutional Change in the State Courts," *The Journal of Legal Studies* 33 (2004), 444.

8. Ibid., 446.

9. Ibid.

10. David W. Neubauer, *America's Courts and the Criminal Justice System*, 2nd ed. (Monterey, CA: Brooks/Cole, 1984), 37.

11. Ibid., 38.

12. Henry J. Abraham, *The Judicial Process*, 6th ed. (New York, NY: Oxford University Press, 1993), 138; and see R. Lewis Ray, "Justices of the Peace: Judges for Hire," *North Carolina Central Law Review* 12 (1969): 94.

13. See Roscoe Pound, "The Causes of Popular Dissatisfaction with the Administration of Justice," *Journal of the American Judicature Society* 20 (1937): 178–87.

14. Stumpf, *American Judicial Politics*, 75.

15. See the following two websites for Town and Village Court judge qualifications: https://nysma.net/wp-content/uploads/2019/06/126153_NYS_MAGISTRATES.pdf and https://cjc.ny.gov/Policy.Statements/town_&_village_courts.html (accessed June 18, 2024). For more information on Town and Village Courts in New York, see William Glaberson's three-part *New York Times* 2006 series, "In Tiny Courts of N.Y., Abuses of Law and Power," *New York Times*, September 25, 2006, http://www.nytimes.com/2006/09/25/nyregion/25courts.html?_r51&pagewanted5print. The second article in the series is "Small-Town Justice, with Trial and Error," *New York Times*, September 26, 2006, http://www.nytimes.com/2006/09/26/nyregion/26courts.html?pagewanted5print. The third article in the series is "How a Reviled Court System Has Outlasted Critics," *New York Times*, September 27, 2006, http://www.nytimes.com/2006/09/27/nyregion/27courts.html?pagewanted5print.

16. For two examples of duties Justice Courts perform, see https://www.hydeparkny.us/239/Justice-Court and https://www.ardsleyvillage.com/justice-court (accessed June 18, 2024).

17. See https://www.courtstatistics.org/court-statistics/interactive-caseload-data-displays/csp-stat-nav-cards-first-row/csp-stat-overview (accessed June 19, 2024).

18. Virginia Judicial System website: https://www.vacourts.gov/courts/home.html (accessed June 19, 2024).

19. California Judicial Branch website: http://www.courts.ca.gov/2113.htm.

20. See https://www.vacourts.gov/courtadmin/aoc/djs/programs/cpss/csi/stats/scv/scv_caseload_rpt_2022.pdf (accessed June 19, 2024).

21. For a study of the roles of state courts of last resort in these structural settings, see Burton M. Atkins and Henry R. Glick, "Environmental and Structural Variables as Determinants of Issues in State Courts of Last Resort," *American Journal of Political Science* 20 (February 1976): 97–115.

22. See Paul Brace and Melinda Gann Hall, "Comparing Courts Using the American States," *Judicature* 83 (March–April 2000): 264–65.

23. Our discussion of the various approaches to handling juvenile matters in the states is based on material found in National Center for State Courts, *State Court Caseload Statistics, 2007*, http://ncsconline.org.

24. *O. G. v. The Superior Court of Ventura County*, 11 Cal.5th 82 (2021). Opinion available here: https://supreme.courts.ca.gov/sites/default/files/supremecourt/default/2022-08/S259011.pdf (accessed June 19, 2024).

25. All examples listed comes from "Courting Judicial Excellence in

Juvenile Justice: A 50-State Study" (2022), 17. Available at: https://csgjusticecenter.org/wp-content/uploads/2022/04/Courting-Judicial-Excellence-in-Juvenile-Justice-A-50-State-Study-2.pdf.

26. Thad L. Beyle, ed., *State and Local Government, 2002–2003* (Washington, DC: CQ Press, 2003), 141.

27. James Eisenstein, Roy B. Flemming, and Peter F. Nardulli, *The Contours of Justice: Communities and Their Courts* (Boston, MA: Little, Brown, 1988), 3.

28. For an important study of the influence of local legal culture in nine medium-size criminal courts in three states, see ibid.

29. Our discussion of these influences is based on George F. Cole, Marc G. Gertz, and Amy Bunger, *The Criminal Justice System: Politics and Policies*, 9th ed. (Belmont, CA: Wadsworth/Thomson, 2004), 253–54.

30. See James Eisenstein and Herbert Jacob, *Felony Justice* (Boston, MA: Little, Brown, 1977). Our discussion of the concept of the courtroom work group relies heavily on Eisenstein and Jacob's discussion.

31. Elizabeth Webster, Beth M. Huebner, Alessandra Milagros Early, and Luis C. Torres, "Court Can Happen Anywhere: Courtroom Workgroup Members' Perceptions of the Challenges and Opportunities of a Transformed Workplace," *Criminal Justice and Behavior* 50 (2023): 1737.

32. State of Oregon, Office of Administrative Hearings, at http://www.oregon.gov/oah/Pages/about_us.aspx.

33. See the California OAH website: https://www.dgs.ca.gov/OAH.

34. Ibid.

35. See the Maryland Office of Administrative Hearings website: http://www.oah.state.md.us/home.asp.

36. Ibid.; also see http://www.oregon.gov/oah/Pages/about_us.aspx. Our discussion is drawn from these two sources.

37. See Washington's OAH website: https://oah.wa.gov/ and https://oah.wa.gov/sites/default/files/2024-03/OAH%20Overview.pdf (accessed June 19, 2024).

38. Available online at https://doa.alaska.gov/oah/reports/OAH-annual-report-2023.pdf.

39. Ibid.

40. See, for example, the website of the Maryland OAH: https://msa.maryland.gov/msa/mdmanual/25ind/html/01adminf.html; also see the Minnesota OAH: https://mn.gov/oah/lawyers-and-litigants/administrative-law/mediation.jsp.

41. See https://mn.gov/oah/lawyers-and-litigants/administrative-law/mediation.jsp.

42. *San Antonio Independent School District v. Rodriguez*, 411 U.S. 1 (1973).

43. Brian L. Porto, *May It Please the Court* (New York, NY: Longman, 2001), 264. A list of some of the better-known cases and an excerpt from one of them may also be found in this book.

44. "Pennsylvania's High Court Redraws Congressional Districts," *Houston Chronicle*, February 20, 2018, A6.

45. See Tracy Peters, Neal Kauder, Chuck Campbell, and Carol Flango, *Future Trends in State Courts 2005* (Williamsburg, VA: National Center for State Courts, 2005), 121. For an informative summary of rights afforded gay couples in the various states, see *Fact Box: U.S. Laws on Gay Marriage, Civil Unions*, http://www.reuters.com.

46. Supreme Court of Texas, *Pidgeon v. Turner*, 538 S.W.3d 73 (2017).

47. Ibid.

48. *Obergefell v. Hodges*, 576 U.S. 644 (2015).

49. For a review of the current state of these laws and legal challenges, see https://www.aclu.org/documents/legislation-affecting-lgbtq-rights-across-country-2021.

50. See http://www.ncsc.org/Information-and-Resources/Comparing-the-state-courts.aspx.

51. See the National Drug Court's website: http://www.ndci.org. Also see https://nij.ojp.gov/topics/articles/problem-solving-courts.

52. Ibid.

53. Devon Anderson, "Why I Became a Believer in Specialty Courts," *Houston Chronicle*, January 10, 2021, A15.

54. See http://www.nycourts.gov/Courts/problem_solving/index.shtml.

55. See https://www.ncsc.org/__data/assets/pdf_file/0036/99657/AZ-Mohave-Co.pdf.

56. https://www.ncsc.org/__data/assets/pdf_file/0037/99658/FL-17th-Judicial-Circuit.pdf.

57. https://www.ncsc.org/__data/assets/pdf_file/0033/99663/WA-Olympia.pdf.

58. See https://www.ncsc.org/__data/assets/pdf_file/0034/99664/WV.pdf.

59. Ibid.

60. B. Ostrom, J. Douglas, S. Tallarico, and S. Roth, "The Use of Remote Hearings in Texas State Courts: The Impact on Judicial Workload," National Center for State Courts: Court Consulting Division (2021), https://www.ncsc.org/consulting-and-research/areas-of-expertise/access-to-justice/remote-hearings-and-services/resources-docs/TX-Remote-Hearing-Assessment-Report.pdf

61. Elizabeth Webster, Beth M. Huebner, Alessandra Milagros Early, and Luis C. Torres, "Court Can Happen Anywhere: Courtroom Workgroup Members' Perceptions of the Challenges and Opportunities of a Transformed Workplace," *Criminal Justice and Behavior* 50 (2023): 1741.

62. https://www.courtstatistics.org/court-statistics/interactive-caseload-data-displays/csp-stat (accessed June 20, 2024).

63. See https://www.courtstatistics.org/court-statistics (accessed June 20, 2024).

CHAPTER 4

1. A state-by-state breakdown may be found through Cornell Law School's LII Legal Information Institute at https://www.law.cornell.edu/uscode/text/28/part-I/chapter-5 (accessed August 3, 2024).

2. Administrative Office of the US Courts, "Federal Judicial Caseload Statistics 2023," https://www.uscourts.gov/statistics-reports/federal-judicial-caseload-statistics-2023 (accessed August 3, 2024).

3. *United State v. Lopez*, 514 U.S. 549 (1995).

4. Quote taken from the US Constitution, Article III, Section 2, Clause 1.

5. United States Courts' "Federal Judicial Caseload Statistics 2023," available at https://www.uscourts.gov/statistics-reports/federal-judicial-caseload-statistics-2023 (accessed August 3, 2024).

6. The US Supreme Court has become the model for many constitutional reforms throughout the world. For example, following the collapse of communism in Eastern Europe, all newly established democracies created constitutional courts with power to review legislative enactments. For an in-depth discussion of this

development, see Herman Schwartz, *The Struggle for Constitutional Justice in Post-Communist Europe* (Chicago, IL: University of Chicago Press, 2000).

7. Kristin A. Linsley, "Original Intent: Understanding the Supreme Court's Original Jurisdiction in Controversies between States," *Journal of Appellate Practice and* Process 18 (2017): 21-53.

8. Data collected from *SCOTUSblog*'s recent "Stat Pack" analyses, archived at https://www.scotusblog.com/reference/stat-pack/ (accessed August 4, 2024).

9. US Constitution, Article III, Section 2, Clause 2.

10. Patrick Berry, Alicia Bannon, and Douglas Keith, "Legislative Assaults on State CourtsMay 2021 Update," *The Brennan Center for Justice* (May 19, 2021), https://www.brennancenter.org/our-work/research-reports/legislative-assaults-state-courts-may-2021-update (accessed August 11, 2024).

11. Tom S. Clark, "The Separation of Powers, Court Curbing, and Judicial Legitimacy," *American Journal of Political Science* 53 (2009): 971–989.

12. 18 U.S.C.A. § 245.

13. For a recent empirical study of the interaction between congressional legislation and its interaction with Supreme Court agenda setting, see Anna Harvey and Barry Friedman, "Ducking Trouble: Congressionally Induced Selection Bias in the Supreme Court's Agenda," *Journal of Politics* 71 (2009): 574–92.

14. *Ex Parte McCardle*, 74 U.S. (7 Wall.) 506 (1869).

15. "Final Report of the Presidential Commission on the Supreme Court of the United States," December 2021, available at https://www.whitehouse.gov/wp-content/uploads/2021/12/SCOTUS-Report-Final-12.8.21-1.pdf (accessed August 4, 2024).

16. "Final Report of the Presidential Commission on the Supreme Court of the United States," 154. The broader discussion of the current state of argument surrounding jurisdiction stripping is drawn largely from Chapter 4 ("The Court's Role in the Constitutional System") of the Commission's Final Report.

17. See, for example, Lee Epstein, Kevin T. McGuire, and Thomas G. Walker, *Constitutional Law for a Changing America: Institutional Powers and Constraints*, 11th ed. (Thousand Oaks, CA: Sage, 2023), 86-88.

18. Natan Sachs and Fred Dews, "Israel's Supreme Court Reform Crisis," *Brookings*, July 28, 2023, https://www.brookings.edu/articles/israels-supreme-court-reform-crisis/ (accessed August 4, 2024).

19. Richard A. Posner, "The Jurisdiction of the Federal Courts." In *The Federal Courts* (Cambridge, MA: Harvard University Press, 1996), chap. 4.

20. Federal Judicial Center, "U.S. District Courts for the Districts of Texas: Authorized Judgeships," https://www.fjc.gov/history/courts/us-district-courts-districts-texas-authorized-judgeships (accessed August 3, 2024).

21. See the organization's website at https://firstliberty.org/ (accessed August 3, 2024).

22. Matthew Choi, "With An Eye on Amarillo Courthouse, U.S. Senators Push to Stop Federal Judge Shopping," *Texas Tribune* (April 11, 2024), https://www.texastribune.org/2024/04/11/judge-shopping-texas-amarillo-kasmaryk-senate/ (accessed August 3, 2024).

23. Matt Ford, "Republicans Keep Turning to the Same Texas Judges to Block Biden's Policies" (March 15, 2022), https://newrepublic.com/article/16573

0/northern-district-texas-judges-block-biden-policies (accessed August 3, 2024).

24. March 15, 2024, "Memorandum of the Committee on Court Administration and Case Management of the Judicial Conference of the United States," at https://s3.documentcloud.org/documents/24483622/judicial-conference-policy.pdf (accessed August 3, 2024).

25. Matthew Choi, "With an Eye on Amarillo Courthouse, U.S. Senators Push to Stop Federal Judge Shopping."

26. Scott William Dodson, "The Culture of Forum Shopping in the United States," *The International Lawyer* 57 (2024): 307337, 337.

27. For our discussion of the many aspects of judicial self-restraint, we acknowledge our debt to Henry J. Abraham, on whose classic analysis of the subject we largely relied. See Abraham, *The Judicial Process*, 7th ed. (New York, NY: Oxford University Press, 1998), chap. 9.

28. James R. Rogers and Georg Vanberg, "Judicial Advisory Opinions and Legislative Outcomes in Comparative Perspective," *American Journal of Political Science* 46 (2002): 379.

29. *Steffel v. Thompson*, 415 U.S. 452 (1974), at 482.

30. *Food and Drug Administration v. Alliance for Hippocratic Medicine*, 602 U.S. ____ (2024), at 4.

31. Ibid., at 9.

32. Ibid., at 24.

33. *New York State Rifle & Pistol Association v. City of New York,* 140 S. Ct 1525 (2020).

34. Ibid., Alito dissent, at 2.

35. Ibid., Kavanaugh concurrence, at 2.

36. *Roe v. Wade*, 410 U.S. 113 (1973).

37. *303 Creative LLC v. Elenis*, 600 U.S. ____ (2023).

38. Ibid., at 3.

39. Ibid., at 12.

40. Melissa Gira Grant, "The Mysterious Case of the Fake Gay Marriage Website, the Real Straight Man, and the Supreme Court," *The New Republic*, June 29, 2023, https://newrepublic.com/article/173987/mysterious-case-fake-gay-marriage-website-real-straight-man-supreme-court (accessed August 4, 2024).

41. See, for example, David Post, "More on Standing in the 303 Creative Case," *The Volokh Conspiracy*, July 18, 2023, https://reason.com/volokh/2023/07/18/more-on-standing-in-the-303-creative-case/# (accessed August 4, 2024).

42. *Donald J. Trump for President, Inc v. Secretary of the Commonwealth of Pennsylvania*, U.S. Court of Appeals for the Third Circuit, No. 20-3371, November 25, 2020.

43. *Trump v. Secretary Commonwealth of Pennsylvania*, No. 20-3371, November 27, 2020, https://www2.ca3.us courts.gov/opinarch/203371np.pdf (accessed August 4, 2024), 1.

44. *Zelman v. Simmons-Harris*, 536 U.S. (2002).

45. *Marbury v. Madison*, 5 U.S. 137 (1803).

46. *Plessy v. Ferguson*, 163 U.S. 537 (1896).

47. Brian Naylor, "Barrett Says She Does Not Consider *Roe v. Wade* 'Super-Precedent,'" *NPR* (October 13, 2020), https://www.npr.org/sections/live-amy-coney-barrett-supreme-court-confirmation/2020/10/13/923355142/barrett-says-abortion-rights-decision-not-a-super-precedent (accessed August 4, 2024).

48. *Colegrove v. Green*, 328 U.S. 549 (1946).

49. *Goldwater v. Carter*, 444 U.S. 996 (1979).

50. *Masterpiece Cakeshop, Ltd v. Colorado Civil Rights Commission*, 584 U.S.__ (2018).

51. *Tilton v. Richardson*, 403 U.S. 672 (1971).

52. *Griswold v. Connecticut*, 381 U.S. 79 (1965).

CHAPTER 5

1. Tracey E. George and Albert H. Yoon, "Measuring Justice in State Courts: The Demographics of the State Judiciary," *Vanderbilt Law Review* 70, no. 6 (2017): 1091.

2. Ibid.

3. Tracey E. George and Albert H. Yoon, "The Gavel Gap: Who Sits in Judgment on State Courts?" *American Constitution Society for Law and Policy*, https://www.acslaw.org/wp-content/uploads/2018/02/gavel-gap-report.pdf (accessed July 7, 2024).

4. Ibid.

5. Janna Adelstein and Alicia Bannon, "State Supreme Court DiversityMay 2022 Update," *The Brennan Center for Justice*, May 20, 2022, https://www.brennancenter.org/our-work/research-reports/state-supreme-court-diversity-may-2022-update (accessed July 7, 2024).

6. Ibid.

7. Jackie Borchardt, "Gov. Mike DeWine Signs Bill Creating Partisan Races for State's Top Court," *Cincinnati Enquirer*, July 1 2021, https://www.cincinnati.com/story/news/politics/2021/07/01/ohio-gov-mike-dewine-signs-partisan-judicial-election-bill/7831532002/ (accessed July 24, 2024).

8. Greg Goelzhauser, "Diversifying State Supreme Courts," *Law & Society Review* 45 (2011): 761–81.

9. Stephen Choi, G. Mitu Gulati, and Eric A. Posner, "Professionals or Politicians: The Uncertain Empirical Case for an Elected Rather than Appointed Judiciary," *The Journal of Law, Economics, & Organization* 26 (2008): 290–336.

10. Ibid.

11. Laura Langer, *Judicial Review in State Supreme Courts: A Comparative Study* (Albany, NY: SUNY Press, 2002).

12. Owen G. Abbe and Paul S. Herrnson, "How Judicial Election Campaigns Have Changed," *Judicature* 85 (May–June 2002): 287.

13. Roy Schotland, "Elective Judges' Campaign Financing: Are State Judges' Robes the Emperor's Clothes of American Democracy?" *Journal of Law and Policy* 57 (1985): 2.

14. Owen G. Abbe and Paul S. Herrnson, "How Judicial Election Campaigns Have Changed," 287.

15. Douglas Keith, *The Politics of Judicial Elections 20212022* (Brennan Center for Justice at New York University School of Law), January 29, 2024. Available at https://www.brennancenter.org/our-work/research-reports/politics-judicial-elections-2021-2022 (accessed July 10, 2024).

16. Ibid.

17. Ibid.

18. Douglas Keith and Eric Velasco, "The Politics of Judicial Elections, 20192020," *Brennan Center for Justice*, https://www.brennancenter.org/our-work/research-reports/politics-judicial-elections-2019-20 (accessed July 24, 2022), 4. For 20212022 figures, see Douglas Keith, *The Politics of Judicial Elections 20212022* (Brennan Center for Justice at New York University School of Law), January 29, 2024. Available at https://www.brennancenter.org/our-work/research-re

ports/politics-judicial-elections-2021-2022 (accessed July 10, 2024).

19. Douglas Keith, *The Politics of Judicial Elections 20212022* (Brennan Center for Justice at New York University School of Law), January 29, 2024. Available at https://www.brennancenter.org/our-work/research-reports/politics-judicial-elections-2021-2022 (accessed July 10, 2024).

20. Alicia Bannon, Eric Velasco, Linda Casey, Lianna Reagan, Laurie Kinney, and Peter Hardin, *The New Politics of Judicial Elections 2011–2012: How New Waves of Special Interest Spending Raised the Stakes for Fair Courts* (Justice at Stake Campaign, October 2013), 3.

21. Alicia Bannon, Cathleen Lisk, and Peter Hardin, *The Politics of Judicial Elections 2015–2016* (Brennan Center for Justice at New York University School of Law), https://www.brennancenter.org/our-work/research-reports/who-pays-judicial-races-politics-judicial-elections-2015-16 (accessed July 10, 2024), 5.

22. Douglas Keith, *The Politics of Judicial Elections 20212022* (Brennan Center for Justice at New York University School of Law), January 29, 2024. Available at https://www.brennancenter.org/our-work/research-reports/politics-judicial-elections-2021-2022 (accessed July 10, 2024).

23. Melinda Gann Hall and Chris W. Bonneau, "Mobilizing Interest: The Effects of Money on Citizen Participation in State Supreme Court Elections," *American Journal of Political Science* 52 (July 2008): 457–70.

24. Melinda Gann Hall and Chis W. Bonneau, "Attack Advertising, the *White* Decision, and Voter Participation in State Supreme Court Elections," *Political Research Quarterly* 66 (2013): 115–26.

25. *Caperton v. Massey Coal*, 556 U.S. 868 (2009).

26. Adam Liptak, "Justices Tell Judges Not to Rule on Major Backers," *New York Times*, June 8, 2009, http://www.nytimes.com/2009/06/09/us/politics/09scotus.html (accessed August 18, 2021).

27. Ibid.

28. Sue Bell Cobb, "I Was Alabama's Top Judge. I Am Ashamed by What I Had to Do to Get There," *Politico Magazine*, March/April 2015, https://www.politico.com/magazine/story/2015/03/judicial-elections-fundraising-115503/ (accessed July 10, 2024).

29. Ibid.

30. 575 U.S. (2015).

31. Chris W. Bonneau and Shane M. Redman, "Much Ado About Nothing: The Irrelevance of *Williams-Yulee v. The Florida Bar* on the Conduct of Judicial Elections," *Vanderbilt Law Review En Banc* 68 (2015): 31–41.

32. Chris W. Bonneau and Shane M. Redman, "Much Ado About Nothing," 34.

33. Ibid., 40.

34. Ibid., 39–40.

35. Max Brantley, "The Roots of the Nursing Home/Judicial Election Scandal," *Arkansas Times*, January 20, 2015; Max Brantley, "What Maggio Has Wrought," *Arkansas Times*, January 15, 2015; and Benjamin Hardy, "Mike Maggio Pleads Guilty to Federal Bribery Charge," *Arkansas Times*, January 10, 2015 (Westlaw).

36. Ibid.

37. Owen G. Abbe and Paul S. Herrnson, "How Judicial Election Campaigns Have Changed," 295.

38. James L. Gibson, *Electing Judges: The Surprising Effects of Campaigning on Judicial Legitimacy* (Chicago, IL: University of Chicago Press, 2012).

39. Lee Epstein, "Electoral Benefits: The Assault on the Assaulters of Judicial Elections," *Judicature* 96 (March/April 2013): 218–22.
40. Richard A. Watson and Ronald G. Downing, *The Politics of the Bench and the Bar* (New York, NY: Wiley, 1969), 331.
41. Traciel V. Reid, "The Politicization of Retention Elections: Lessons from the Defeat of Justices Lanphier and White," *Judicature* 83 (September/October 1999): 68–77, at 77.
42. Stephen J. Choi, G. Mita Gulati, and Eric A. Posner, "Professionals or Politicians: The Uncertain Empirical Case for an Elected Rather Than Appointed Judiciary."
43. A. G. Sulzberger, "Ouster of Iowa Judges Sends Signal to Bench," *New York Times*, November 3, 2010, https://www.nytimes.com/2010/11/04/us/politics/04judges.html (accessed July 14, 2024).
44. Ibid.
45. Allison P. Harris, "Voter Response to Salient Judicial Decision in Retention Elections," *Law & Social Inquiry* 44 (2019): 181.
46. Skaggs et al., *The New Politics of Judicial Elections 2009–2010*, 9; and Bannon et al., *The New Politics of Judicial Elections 2011–2012*, 30.
47. Ibid.; and Sulzberger, "Ouster of Iowa Judges Sends Signal to Bench."
48. Larry Aspin, "Trends in Judicial Retention Elections, 1964–2006," *Judicature* 90 (2007): 210.
49. Charles Gardner Geyh, "Judicial Selection and the Search for Middle Ground," *DePaul Law Review* 67 (2018): 333–68.
50. Bannon et al., *The New Politics of Judicial Elections 2011–2012*, 30–33.
51. Ibid.
52. Jim Douglas, *The Vermont Way: A Republican Governor Leads America's Most Liberal State* (New Haven, VT: Common Ground, 2014), 155.
53. See Sandra Day O'Connor, "Take Justice Off the Ballot," *New York Times*, May 22, 2010, http://www.nytimes.com/2010/05/23/opinion/23oconnor.html (accessed August 18, 2021).
54. Herbert M. Kritzer, *Judicial Selection in the States: Politics and the Struggle for Reform* (Cambridge: Cambridge University Press, 2020), 356.
55. Ibid., 358.
56. Ibid., 55.
57. Information on selection methods for state supreme court chief justices was collected from the website of the National Center for State Courts' Judicial Selection in the States Project: http://www.judicialselection.us/ (accessed August 18, 2021).
58. Jason Stein, "Wisconsin Assembly Approves Amendment on Chief Justice Selection," *St. Paul Pioneer Press*, January 22, 2015 (Lexis).
59. Ibid.
60. Dee J. Hall, "Groups Spend on High Court Measure," *Wisconsin State Journal*, March 31, 2015 (Lexis).
61. John Nichols, "Scheming to Replace the Chief Justice," *Wisconsin State Journal*, January 11, 2015; and "Roggensack New Chief Justice; Defiant Shirley Abrahamson Plans to Hold onto the Position," *Wisconsin State Journal*, April 30, 2015 (Lexis).
62. "Roggensack New Chief Justice."
63. Ibid.
64. Crocker Stephenson, Cary Spivak, and Patrick Marley, "Justices' Feud Gets Physical," *Milwaukee Journal Sentinel*, June 25, 2011, http://www.jsonline.-com/news/statepolitics/124546064.html (accessed August 18, 2021).

65. Ibid.

66. Brett Neely, "Wisconsin Plans to Vote in Person Tuesday after Law Minute Chaos," *NPR*, April 6, 2020, https://www.npr.org/2020/04/06/828191015/wisconsin-governor-effectively-reschedules-tuesdays-primary-election (accessed August 18, 2021).

67. Reid J. Epstein, "Why Wisconsin Republicans Insisted on an Election in a Pandemic," *New York Times*, April 15, 2020, https://www.nytimes.com/2020/04/07/us/politics/wisconsin-pandemic-primary-republicans.html (accessed August 18, 2021). Also, "Republicans Consider Moving '20 Prez Primary to Help Kelly Retain Supreme Court Seat," *WisPolitics News*, November 16, 2018, https://www.wispolitics.com/2018/republicans-consider-moving-20-prez-primary-to-help-kelly-retain-supreme-court-seat/ (accessed August 18, 2021).

68. *Gregory v. Ashcroft*, 498 U.S. 979 (1991).

69. Henry Redman, "Republicans Ease Off Impeachment Threat after Supreme Court Accepts Redistricting Case," *Wisconsin Examiner*, October 11, 2023, https://wisconsinexaminer.com/2023/10/11/republicans-ease-off-impeachment-threat-after-supreme-court-accepted-redistricting-case/ (accessed July 10, 2024).

70. See https://www.brennancenter.org/our-work/analysis-opinion/impeachment-and-removal-judges-explainer (accessed July 10, 2024). See also https://constitutioncenter.org/blog/state-judges-have-been-impeached-but-very-rarely (accessed July 10, 2024).

71. See https://www.ncsc.org/__data/assets/pdf_file/0017/26612/g-to-g-special-impeachment.pdf (accessed July 10, 2024).

72. Michael Berens and John Shiffman, "The Teflon Robe Embolden by Impunity," *Reuters*, July 9, 2020, https://www.reuters.com/investigates/special-report/usa-judges-deals/ (accessed July 12, 2024).

73. Ibid.

74. Ibid.

75. See https://graphics.thomsonreuters.com/data/judges/1924.pdf (accessed July 12, 2024).

76. John Schwartz, "Ruling Backs Judge Who Rejected Post–5 P.M. Appeal," *New York Times*, January 21, 2010, http://www.nytimes.com/2010/01/21/us/21judge.html (accessed August 18, 2021).

77. Jolie McCullough, "Presiding Judge Sharon Keller Narrowly Wins Texas Court of Appeals Primary Race," *Texas Tribune*, March 7, 2018, https://www.texastribune.org/2018/03/07/sharon-keller-texas-primary-2018-court-criminal-appeals/ (accessed August 18, 2021).

78. Michael Berens and John Shiffman, "The Teflon Robe," *Reuters*, June 30, 2020, https://www.reuters.com/investigates/special-report/usa-judges-misconduct/ (accessed July 10, 2024).

79. Ibid.

80. Sam Levin, "Stanford Sexual Assault: Read the Controversial Decision," *The Guardian*, June 14, 2016, https://www.theguardian.com/us-news/2016/jun/14/stanford-sexual-assault-read-sentence-judge-aaron-persky (accessed August 18, 2021).

81. Maggie Astor, "California Voters Remove Judge Aaron Persky, Who Gave a 6-Month Sentence for Sexual Assault," *New York Times*, June 6, 2018, https://www.nytimes.com/2018/06/06/us/politics/judge-persky-brock-turner-recall.html (accessed August 18, 2021).

82. Richard Gonzales and Camila Domonoske, "Voters Recall Aaron Persky, Judge Who Sentenced Brock Turner," *NPR*, June 5, 2018, https://w

ww.npr.org/sections/thetwo-way/2018/06/05/617071359/voters-are-deciding-whether-to-recall-aaron-persky-judge-who-sentenced-brock-tur (accessed August 18, 2021).

83. NPR Staff, "How Ousting the Judge in the Stanford Sexual Assault Case Could Impact Future Cases," *NPR*, June 11, 2018, https://www.npr.org/2016/06/11/481656710/how-ousting-the-judge-in-the-stanford-sexual-assault-case-could-impact-future-ca (accessed August 18, 2021).

84. Gbemende Johnson, "Executive Power and Judicial Deference: Judicial Decision Making on Executive Power Challenges in American States," *Political Research Quarterly* 68 (2015)a; 13738.

85. Billy Corriher, "The North Carolina Legislature Is Attacking Judges Who Rule Against It," *ABA Journal*, March 22, 2018, http://www.abajournal.com/news/article/the_north_carolina_legislature_is_attacking_judges_who_rule_against_it (accessed August 18, 2021).

86. Ibid.

87. Ibid.

88. Kritzer, *Judicial Selection in the States*, 93–98. Our discussion of recent events in West Virginia draws fully from this source.

89. Chris W. Bonneau, "NC Needs to Stop Messing with Its Judiciary," *The News & Observer*, May 18, 2018, https://www.newsobserver.com/opinion/op-ed/article211422069.html (accessed August 18, 2021).

90. Anne Blythe, "NC Lawmakers Create Partisan Election Process for Courts That Review Their Laws," *The News & Observer*, December 16, 2016, https://www.newsobserver.com/news/politics-government/state-politics/article121449157.html (accessed August 18, 2021).

91. Herbert M. Kritzer, "Judicial Elections in the 2010s," *DePaul Law Review* 67 (2018): 387–423.

92. Ibid.

93. Kritzer, "Judicial Elections in the 2010s," 392.

94. Kritzer, "Judicial Elections in the 2010s," 392–93.

95. Alicia Bannon and Nathaniel Sobel, "Assaults on the Courts: A Legislative Round-Up," *Brennan Center for Justice*, May 8, 2017, https://www.brennancenter.org/analysis/assaults-courts-legislative-round (accessed August 18, 2021).

96. Anne Blythe and Mark Binker, "Cooper Appoints Democrat to Fill NC Appeals Court Seat after GOP Judge Makes Surprise Early Retirement," *The News & Observer*, April 24, 2017, https://www.newsobserver.com/news/politics-government/politics-columns-blogs/under-the-dome/article146378 394.html (accessed August 18, 2021).

97. Craig Jarvis and Anne Blythe, "Veto Override Means Voters Will Know Judges' Party Affiliations," *The News & Observer*, March 23, 2017, https://www.newsobserver.com/news/politics-government/state-politics/arti-cle140327188.html (accessed August 18, 2021).

98. Kritzer, *Judicial Selection in the States*, 55.

99. Meghan E. Leonard, "State Legislatures, State High Courts, and Judicial Independence: An Examination of Court-Curbing Legislation in the States," *Justice System Journal* 37 (2016): 53–62.

100. Leonard, "State Legislatures, State High Courts, and Judicial Independence," 61.

101. Meghan E. Leonard, "New Data on Court Curbing by State Legislatures,"

State Politics & Policy Quarterly 22 (2022): 483–500.

102. Kritzer, *Judicial Selection in the States*, 368–69.

103. Reid, "The Politicization of Retention Elections," 77.

CHAPTER 6

1. The Federal Judicial Center's *Judiciaries Worldwide* website (at https://judiciariesworldwide.fjc.gov/) provides comparative information on many aspects of judicial procedure around the world, including judicial selection.

2. John Richard Schmidhauser, *Judges and Justices: The Federal Appellate Judiciary* (Scott Foresman & Co., 1979), 49.

3. In 2024, the Supreme Court included one Jewish justice (Elena Kagan), six Catholics (John Roberts, Clarence Thomas, Samuel Alito, Sonia Sotomayor, Brett Kavanaugh, and Amy Coney Barrett), and two Protestants (Ketanji Brown Jackson and Neil Gorsuch, who was raised Catholic but now identifies as Episcopalian). See Frank Newport, "The Religion of the Supreme Court Justices," *Gallup* (April 8, 2022), https://news.gallup.com/opinion/polling-matters/391649/religion-supreme-court-justices.aspx (accessed August 16, 2024).

4. Alicia Bannon, A Public Defender on the High Court," *Brennan Center for Justice* (March 1, 2022), https://www.brennancenter.org/our-work/analysis-opinion/public-defender-high-court (accessed August 16, 2024).

5. In this chapter, we exclude judges appointed to specialized courts and territorial courts, and we also exclude judges who were recess appointees, unless they were subsequently confirmed to their seat.

6. As with all of our data on court of appeals judges, this number does not include the two additional judges Biden appointed to the specialized US Court of Appeals for the Federal Circuit.

7. These quotes come from a letter sent by then-incoming White House Counsel Dana Remus to Senate Democrats in December 2020, https://www.democracydocket.com/wp-content/uploads/2022/02/Biden-Harris-Nom-Letter.pdf (accessed August 16, 2024).

8. Ibid.

9. Following the lead of Drew Noble Lanier and Mark S. Hurwitz, "Diversity by Other Means: Professional, Educational, and Life Diversity of U.S. Appellate Judges," presented at the 2016 Annual Meeting of the Western Political Science Association. We categorize "elite" schools as Chicago, Stanford, Michigan, and UCBerkeley.

10. Chief Justice Roberts, *2006 Year-End Report on the Federal Judiciary* (January 1, 2007), https://www.supremecourt.gov/publicinfo/year-end/2006year-endreport.pdf (accessed August 16, 2024), 34.

11. Rorie Solberg and Eric N. Waltenburg, "Trump and McConnell's Mostly White Male Judges Buck 30-Year Trend of Increasing Diversity on the Courts," *The Conversation*, October 8, 2020, https://theconversation.com/trump-and-mcconnells-mostly-white-male-judges-buck-30-year-trend-of-increasing-diversity-on-the-courts-146828 (accessed August 16, 2024).

12. See, for example, Tiana Headley and Caitlin McLean, "Biden Public Defenders Turned Judges Begin to Make Mark on Bench," *Bloomberg Law* (August 12, 2024), https://news.bloomberglaw.com/us-law-week/biden-public-defenders-turned-judges-begin-to-make-mark-on-bench (accessed August 16, 2024).

13. US Constitution, Article II, Section 2.
14. Scott E. Graves and Robert M. Howard, *Justice Takes a Recess: Judicial Appointments from George Washington to George W. Bush* (Lanham, MD: Lexington Books, 2009), 15.
15. *NLRB v. Noel Canning*, 573 U.S. (2014). See also Kali Borkowski, "Political Consequences of *NLRB v. Canning*," *SCOTUSBlog*, July 15, 2014, http://www.scotusblog.com/2014/07/political-consequences-of-nlrb-v-noel-canning/ (accessed August 16, 2024).
16. Goldman, *Picking Federal Judges*, p. 358.
17. Gregory A. Caldeira and John R. Wright, "Lobbying for Justice: Organized Interests, Supreme Court Nominations, and the United States Senate," *American Journal of Political Science* 42 (1998): 521.
18. Nancy Scherer, *Scoring Points: Politicians, Activists, and the Lower Federal Court Appointment Process* (Stanford, CA: Stanford University Press, 2005).
19. Nancy Scherer, Brandon L. Bartels, and Amy Steigerwalt, "Sounding the Fire Alarm: The Role of Interest Groups in the Lower Federal Court Confirmation Process," *Journal of Politics* 70 (2008): 1038.
20. Sheldon Goldman, *Picking Federal Judges*, 86.
21. Ibid., 115.
22. The classic study of the role of the ABA is Joel B. Grossman, *Lawyers and Judges: The ABA and the Politics of Judicial Selection* (New York, NY: Wiley, 1965).
23. Elliot E. Slotnick, "The ABA Standing Committee on Federal Judiciary: A Contemporary Assessment—Part 1," *Judicature* 66 (1983): 349–62, 354.
24. Elliot E. Slotnick, "The ABA Standing Committee on Federal Judiciary: A Contemporary Assessment—Part 2," *Judicature* 66 (1983): 385–93.
25. Ibid., 393.
26. See Susan Brodie Haire, "Rating the Ratings of the American Bar Association Standing Committee on Federal Judiciary," *Justice System Journal* 22 (2001): 1–17; Dustin Koenig, "Bias in the Bar? ABA Ratings and Federal Judicial Nominees from 1976–2000," *Judicature* 95 (2012): 188–95; Maya Sen, "How Judicial Qualification Ratings May Disadvantage Minority and Female Candidates," *Journal of Law and Courts* 2 (2014): 33–65; Maya Sen, "Minority Judicial Candidates Have Changed: The ABA Ratings Gap Has Not," *Judicature* 98 (2014): 46–53.
27. Koenig, "Bias in the Bar?"; see also Susan Navarro Smelcer, Amy Steigerwalt, and Richard L. Vining Jr., "Bias and the Bar: Evaluating the ABA Ratings of Federal Judicial Nominees," *Political Research Quarterly* 65 (2012): 827–40.
28. Susan Navarro Smelcer, Amy Steigerwalt, and Richard L. Vining Jr., "Where One Sits Affects Where Others Stand: Bias, the Bar, and Nominees to the Federal District Courts," *Judicature* 98 (2014): 35–45.
29. Debra Cassens Weiss, "Like Trump, Biden Asks ABA to Start Judicial Ratings Process after Nominations Are Made," *ABA Journal*, February 3, 2021, https://www.abajournal.com/news/article/like-trump-biden-asks-aba-to-start-judicial-ratings-process-after-nominations-are-made (accessed August 15, 2024).
30. Amanda Hollis-Brusky, *Ideas with Consequences: The Federalist Society and the Conservative Counterrevolution* (Oxford, UK: Oxford University Press, 2015).
31. Ibid., 148.
32. Sheldon Goldman, Elliot Slotnick, Gerard Gryski, and Sara Schiavoni,

"W. Bush's Judiciary: The First Term Record," *Judicature* 88 (2005): 244–75, at 252.

33. Ibid., 253.

34. Ibid., 254.

35. Joel Achenbach, "How Trump and Two Lawyers Narrowed the Field for His Supreme Court Choice," *Washington Post*, July 8, 2018, https://www.washingtonpost.com/politics/how-trump-narrowed-the-field-for-his-supreme-court-pick/2018/07/08/b9d3b16a-808c-11e8-b660-4d0f9f0351f1_story.html (accessed August 16, 2024).

36. Kyle Peterson, "The Weekend Interview with Leonard Leo: Trump's Supreme Court Whisperer," *Wall Street Journal*, February 4, 2017, https://www.wsj.com/articles/trumps-supreme-court-whisperer-1486165573 (accessed August 16, 2024).

37. Jeffrey Toobin, "The Conservative Pipeline to the Supreme Court," *The New Yorker*, April 17, 2017, https://www.newyorker.com/magazine/2017/04/17/the-conservative-pipeline-to-the-supreme-court (accessed August 16, 2024).

38. Stephen J. Choi, Mitu Gulati, and Eric A. Posner, "Trump's Lower-Court Judges and Religion: An Initial Appraisal," *Virginia Public Law and Legal Theory Research Paper No. 2023-49* (2023). Available at SSRN: https://ssrn.com/abstract=4488397 (accessed August 16, 2024).

39. Nancy Scherer and Banks Miller, "The Federalist Society's Influence on the Federal Judiciary," *Political Research Quarterly* 62 (2009): 36678.

40. As a standard procedure, the Senate Judiciary Committee sends to the senator(s) of the state in which there is a district court vacancy a request, printed on a blue form, to approve or disapprove the nomination being considered by the committee. If approval is not forthcoming, the senator retains the slip; if there is no objection, the blue form is returned to the committee. For an excellent discussion of the history of the blue slip and its current status, see Brannon P. Denning, "The Judicial Confirmation Process and the Blue Slip," *Judicature* 85 (2002): 218–26.

41. Mitchel A. Sollenberger, "The Blue Slip: A Theory of Unified and Divided Government, 1979–2009," *Congress & the Presidency* 37 (2010): 125–56.

42. Madison Alder, "Senators Can't Veto Biden Circuit Picks, Maintaining GOP Policy," *Bloomberg Law*, February 17, 2021, https://news.bloomberglaw.com/us-law-week/senators-cant-veto-biden-circuit-picks-maintaining-gop-policy (accessed August 15, 2024).

43. Senator Durbin's statement in response to Senator Johnson's decision to withhold his blue slip for Pocan is available at https://www.judiciary.senate.gov/press/dem/releases/durbin-responds-to-senator-johnson-withholding-blue-slip-for-eastern-district-of-wisconsin-nominee. See also Tierney Sneed, "GOP Sen. Ron Johnson Flip-Flops to Block Biden Judicial Nominee," *CNN* (February 16, 2022), https://www.cnn.com/2022/02/16/politics/ron-johnson-pocan-judge-biden/index.html (accessed August 17, 2024).

44. Logan Dancey, Kjersten R. Nelson, and Eve M. Ringsmuth, *It's Not Personal: Politics and Policy in Lower Court Confirmation Hearings* (Ann Arbor: University of Michigan Press, 2021).

45. Ibid.

46. Christina L. Boyd, Paul M. Collins Jr., and Lori A. Ringhand, *Supreme Bias: Gender and Race in U.S. Supreme Court Confirmation Hearings* (Stanford, CA: Stanford University Press, 2023).

47. Ibid., 124.

48. This discussion of Mangi's confirmation hearing is inspired by and draws

extensively on the research and analysis of Robin Olsen (UVM class of 2026).

49. A full video of Mangi hearing is available at https://www.judiciary.senate.gov/committee-activity/hearings/12/13/2023/nominations (accessed August 17, 2024).

50. Sheldon Goldman, "Assessing the Senate Judicial Confirmation Process: The Index of Obstruction and Delay," *Judicature* 86 (2003): 251–57.

51. Ibid.; and Lisa M. Holmes, Salmon A. Shomade, and Roger E. Hartley, "The Confirmation Obstacle Course: Signaling Opposition through Delay," *American Review of Politics* 33 (2012): 23–49.

52. Ibid.

53. Helen Dewar, "President, Senate Reach Pact to Judicial Nominations," *Washington Post*, May 19, 2004.

54. Ibid., 332.

55. Ibid., 16–7. See also Christina L. Boyd, Michael S. Lynch, and Anthony J. Madonna, "Nuclear Fallout: Investigating the Effect of Senate Procedural Reform on Judicial Nominations" (paper presented at the 2014 annual meeting of the American Political Science Association, Washington, DC, August 28–31); Lisa M. Holmes, "'Going Nuclear' over Appointments: The Causes and Consequences of Filibuster Reform" (paper presented at the 2014 annual meeting of the American Political Science Association, Washington, DC, August 28–31).

56. Jeremy W. Peters, "In Landmark Vote, Senate Limits Use of the Filibuster," *New York Times*, November 21, 2013, https://www.nytimes.com/2013/11/22/us/politics/reid-sets-in-motion-steps-to-limit-use-of-filibuster.html (accessed August 16, 2021).

57. Slotnick, Goldman, and Schiavoni, "Writing the Book of Judges: Part 1" (2015), Tables 2 and 3.

58. This phenomenon also appears to occur among US appeals court judges. See, for example, Stephen L. Wasby, "'Into the Soup?' The Acclimation of Ninth Circuit Appellate Judges," *Judicature* 73 (1989): 13. This article provides a good discussion of the socialization process of appeals court judges in general.

59. New federal district judges with prior state court experience have a somewhat easier time of it, particularly in terms of the psychological adjustment to the judgeship and dealing with some of the administrative problems. However, prior state court experience seems to be of little help in the jurist's efforts to become an expert in federal law. See Robert A. Carp and Russell R. Wheeler, "Sink or Swim: The Socialization of a Federal District Judge," *Journal of Public Law* 21 (1972): 367–74.

60. All quoted in Howard, *Courts of Appeals in the Federal Judicial System*, 224.

61. Patty Reinert, "Colleagues Mourn Long-Serving Justice," *Houston Chronicle*, April 16, 2002.

62. Morgan L. W. Hazelton, Rachael K. Hinkle, and Michael J. Nelson, *The Elevator Effect: Contact and Collegiality in the American Judiciary* (Oxford: Oxford University Press, 2023).

63. Allison P. Harris, "Can Racial Diversity among Judges Affect Sentencing Outcomes?" *American Political Science Review* 118 (2024): 94055.

64. Tierney Sneed and Hannah Rabinowitz, "Isolated and Inexperienced: A Portrait of the Judge Overseeing Trump's Documents Case from Veterans of Her Courtroom," *CNN* (June 7, 2024), https://www.cnn.com/2024/06/07/politics/aileen-cannon-judge-tru

mp-classified-documents/index.html (accessed August 17, 2024).

65. Ibid.

66. See Steven Levitsky and Daniel Ziblatt, *Tyranny of the Minority: Why American Democracy Reached the Breaking Point* (New York: Crown Publishing Group, 2023), 216-17.

67. For a good discussion of the impeachment process, including information on what the founders had in mind regarding the terms "High Crimes and Misdemeanors," see "Impeaching Federal Judges: Where Are We and Where Are We Going?" *Judicature* 72 (1989): 359–65. (The article is an edited version of a panel discussion.) See also Mary L. Volcansek, *Judicial Impeachment* (Urbana, IL: University of Illinois Press, 1993).

68. See https://www.fjc.gov/node/7496 (accessed August 16, 2021).

69. Jada F. Smith, "Federal Judge to Quit Post; He Faced Abuse Charges," *New York Times*, May 29, 2015, https://www.nytimes.com/2015/05/30/us/politics/alabama-federal-judge-mark-fuller-to-quit-post-he-faced-abuse-charge.html (accessed August 16, 2024).

70. Diana Reese, "From Ray Rice to a Federal Judge, Is the System Too Lenient in Domestic Violence Cases?" *Washington Post*, September 10, 2014.

71. For a good discussion of this subject, see Collins T. Fitzpatrick, "Misconduct and Disability of Federal Judges: The Unreported Informal Responses," *Judicature* 71 (1988): 282–83.

72. Data on judicial conduct complaints were collected from the Administrative Office of the US Courts at https://www.uscourts.gov/statistics-reports/complaints-against-judges-judicial-business-2023 (accessed August 17, 2024).

73. See the "Judicial Conduct and Disability Complaint Number 22-90121" issued on behalf of the Judicial Council of the Ninth Circuit at https://cdn.ca9.uscourts.gov/datastore/ce9/2024/22-90121%20News%20Release%20&%20Order%20and%20Certification.pdf (accessed August 17, 2024).

74. Judge Henderson's full statement is available at https://www.cadc.uscourts.gov/internet/home.nsf/650f3eec0dfb990fca25692100069854/e19f9990bda5cd2d8525831e00477e3f/$FILE/PressRelease20181006.pdf (accessed August 16, 2024).

75. Steve Denning, "Chief Justice Roberts Requests Tenth Circuit to Investigate Kavanaugh Ethics Questions," *Forbes*, October 11, 2018, https://www.forbes.com/sites/stevedenning/2018/10/11/chief-justice-roberts-requests-tenth-circuit-to-investigate-kavanaugh-ethics-questions/?sh512196ecd1877 (accessed August 16, 2024).

76. Ibid.

77. Chief Justice Roberts's full statement is available at https://www.cadc.uscourts.gov/intranet/home.nsf/Content/Announcement+-+Letter+from+Chief+Justice+Roberts+Transferring+Judicial+Misconduct+Complaints+Filed+Against+Former+Circuit+Judge+Brett+Kavanaugh+to+the+Tenth+Circuit/$FILE/Ltr%20to%20Chief%20Judge%20Tymkovich%20Oct%2010%202018.pdf (accessed August 16, 2024).

78. Joshua Kaplan, Justin Elliott, and Alex Mierjeski, "Clarence Thomas and the Billionaire," *ProPublica* (April 6, 2023), https://www.propublica.org/article/clarence-thomas-scotus-undisclosed-luxury-travel-gifts-crow (accessed August 17, 2024).

79. Whitney K. Novak, "Financial Disclosure and the Supreme Court," *Congressional Research Service*

(November 22, 2023), https://crsreports.congress.gov/product/pdf/LSB/LSB10949 (accessed August 17, 2024).

80. See Alison Durkee, "Clarence Thomas: Here Are All the Ethics Scandals Involving the Supreme Court Justice Amid New Harlan Crow Trips," *Forbes* (August 5, 2024), https://www.forbes.com/sites/alisondurkee/2024/08/05/clarence-thomas-here-are-all-the-ethics-scandals-involving-the-supreme-court-justice-amid-new-harlan-crow-trips/ (accessed August 17, 2024).

81. Justin Elliot, Joshua Kaplan, Alex Mierjeski, "Justice Alito Took Luxury Fishing Vacation with GOP Billionaire Who Later Had Cases before the Court," *ProPublica* (June 20, 2023), https://www.propublica.org/article/samuel-alito-luxury-fishing-trip-paul-singer-scotus-supreme-court (accessed August 17, 2024).

82. Steven Lubet, "All Supreme Court Ethics Lapses Deserve Scrutiny, Including Sotomayor's," *The Hill* (August 22, 2023).

83. John Roberts, "2011 Year-End Report on the Federal Judiciary," at 4.

84. Joe Biden, "My Plan to Reform the Supreme Court and Ensure No President Is Above the Law," *Washington Post* (July 29, 2024).

85. Albert Yoon, "Pensions, Politics, and Judicial Tenure: An Empirical Study of Federal Judges, 1869–2002," *American Law and Economics Review* 8 (2006): 143–80.

86. David Yalof, "Why Justices Retire," *Judicature* 88 (2004): 42–43.

87. Minor Myers III, "The Judicial Service of Retired United States Supreme Court Justices," *Journal of Supreme Court History* 32 (2007): 46–61.

88. For a full transcript of the interview, go to https://hughhewitt.com/senator-lindsey-graham-on-george-floyd-supreme-court-snd-circuit-vacancies-witnesses-for-obamagate-hearings-sanctions-on-the-ccp-over-hong-kong-regulating-big-tech-joe-biden-and-more (accessed August 17, 2024).

89. Ibid.

90. See John Deschler and Maya Sen, "The Role of Judge Ideology in Strategic Retirements in U.S. Federal Courts," *Journal of Law and Empirical Analysis*, https://doi.org/10.1177/2755323X241246849.

91. Jake S. Truscott and Richard L. Vining Jr., "Ideological Congruence and Strategic Departures: Mapping the Present and Future of the Lower Federal Courts" (paper presented at the 2024 annual meeting of the Midwest Political Science Association, Chicago, IL, April 47), 1.

92. Lisa M. Holmes, Rorie L. Spill Solberg, and Susan B. Haire, "Neither Gone Nor Forgotten: Evaluating the Potential Impact of Senior Status Judges on the U.S. Courts of Appeals," *Judicature* 95 (2012): 227–36.

93. Chief Justice John G. Roberts Jr., "2010 Year-End Report on the Federal Judiciary," December 31, 2010, https://www.supremecourt.gov/publicinfo/year-end/2010year-endreport.pdf (accessed August 16, 2024), 8.

94. Ibid.

95. Gail Collins, "The Unsinkable R. B. G.: Ruth Bader Ginsburg Has No Interest in Retiring," *New York Times*, February 20, 2015, https://www.nytimes.com/2015/02/22/opinion/sunday/gail-collins-ruth-bader-ginsburg-has-no-interest-in-retiring.html (accessed August 16, 2024).

96. Jessica Weisberg, "Supreme Court Justice Ruth Bader Ginsburg: I'm Not Going Anywhere," *Elle*, September 23, 2014, https://www.elle.com/culture/career-politics/interviews/a14788/su

preme-court-justice-ruth-bader-ginsburg/ (accessed August 16, 2024).

97. Jeffrey Toobin, "The Obama Brief: The President Considers His Judicial Legacy," *The New Yorker*, October 27, 2014, https://www.newyorker.com/magazine/2014/10/27/obama-brief (accessed August 16, 2024).

98. Joe Biden, "My Plan to Reform the Supreme Court and Ensure No President Is Above the Law."

99. Tom S. Clark, "The Separation of Powers, Court Curbing, and Judicial Legitimacy," *American Journal of Political Science* 53 (2009): 97189.

CHAPTER 7

1. "Judicial Performance in the Fifth Circuit," *Yale Law Review* 73 (1963): 90–133.

2. Sheldon Goldman and Elliot Slotnick, "Clinton's First Term Judiciary," *Judicature* 80 (1997): 256.

3. Jack Nelson, "Courts' Main Hope for Reagan Social Stand," *Houston Chronicle*, March 18, 1986, A6.

4. Jon R. Bond, "The Politics of Court Structure: The Addition of New Federal Judges," *Law and Policy Quarterly* 2 (1980): 182, 183, 187.

5. Sam Hananel, "Judicial Nomination Held Up over Same-Sex Ceremony," *Detroit Free Press*, October 6, 2006, http://www.freep.com/apps/pbcs.dll/article?AID5/20061006NEWS99/310060004.

6. Carl Hulse, "Obama Judicial Choice Is Urged to Withdraw," *New York Times*, September 22, 2014, http://www.nytimes.com/2014/09/23/us/obama-judicial-choice-michael-p-boggs-is-urged-to-withdraw.html.

7. Neil A. Lewis, "Clinton Critic Is Key to Deal to End Tie-up on Judgeships," *New York Times*, July 3, 1999, http://www.nytimes.com.

8. Henry J. Abraham, *The Judicial Process*, 3rd ed. (New York, NY: Oxford University Press, 1975), 77.

9. See *Gallup: Presidential Approval Ratings—George W. Bush*, https://news.-gallup.com/poll/116500/presidential-approval-ratings-george-bush.aspx.

10. Neil A. Lewis, "Clinton Critic Is Key to Deal to End Tie-up on Judgeships," *New York Times*, July 3, 1999, http://www.nytimes.com.

11. It should be emphasized that when one is discussing a president's potential to make an ideological impact on the judiciary, it is not sufficient to count only the number of appointments the chief executive can make. One also has to factor in which cohorts of judges are retiring from the bench. Thus, if Obama appointed a mainstream Democrat to replace a retiring Clinton judge who is also a mainstream Democrat, there is no ideological gain for the administration. However, if Obama appoints a liberal Democrat to replace a retiring conservative Reagan jurist, there is a twofold gain. This enhanced Obama's potential to nudge the judiciary to the left because he was more likely to replace a conservative Republican with a Democrat who was likely to be more liberal.

12. James A. Farley, "Why I Broke with Roosevelt," *Collier's*, June 21, 1947, 13.

13. See Jon Gottschall, "Carter's Judicial Appointments: The Influence of Affirmative Action and Merit Selection on Voting on the U.S. Courts of Appeals," *Judicature* 67 (1983): 165–73.

14. See Jon O. Newman, "The Judge Baer Controversy: Correspondence from the White House, Senator Dole,

Congressmen, and Judges," *Judicature* 80 (1997): 156.

15. As quoted in Sheldon Goldman, Elliot Slotnick, Gerard Gryski, Gary Zuk, and Sara Schiavoni, "W. Bush Remaking the Judiciary: Like Father Like Son?" *Judicature* 86 (2003): 284.

16. Andy Barr, "Right Tries to Make 'Socialist' Tag Stick," *Politico*, October 27, 2008, https://www.politico.com/story/2008/10/right-tries-to-make-socialist-tag-stick-014984.

17. Ann E. Marimow and Matt Viser, "Biden Moves Quickly to Make His Mark on Federal Courts After Trump's Record Judicial Nominations," February 3, 2021, https://www.washingtonpost.com/local/legal-issues/biden-judge-nomi-nations/2021/02/02/e9932f3a-6189-11eb-9430-e7c77b5b0297_story.html.

18. Madeleine Carlisle, "Inside Joe Biden's Plan to Confirm Diverse Federal Judges," *Time.com*, May 11, 2021, https://time.com/6047501/joe-biden-federal-judges/.

19. Tobi Raji, "Biden Said He Won't Make an 'Ideological' Supreme Court Pick. Republicans Do Exactly That," *Washington Post*, May 22, 2024, https://www.washingtonpost.com/politics/2022/02/14/supreme-court-biden-nominee-ideological/; see also https://twitter.com/NBCNightlyNews/status/1491890684202205187

20. Jon Gould, "Judges Are Not 'Neutral Umpires,'" *The Hill*, August 13, 2014, https://thehill.com/blogs/pundits-blog/the-judiciary/214988-judges-are-not-neutral-umpires.

21. Ann E. Marimow and Matt Viser, "Biden Moves Quickly to Make His Mark on Federal Courts After Trump's Record Judicial Nominations," *Washington Post*, February 3, 2021, https://www.washingtonpost.com/local/legal-issues/biden-judge-nominations/2021/02/02/e9932f3a-6189-11eb-9430-e7c 77b5b0297_story.html.

22. Ibid.

23. Carl Hulse and Michael D. Shear, "Biden Names Diverse Nominees for the Federal Bench," *New York Times*, March 30, 2021, https://www.nyti-mes.com/2021/03/30/us/politics/biden-judges.html.

24. Charles Krauthammer, "The GOP's Ideological Earthquake and the Aftermath," *National Review*, May 6, 2016, https://www.nationalreview.com/2016/05/donald-trump-not-conservative-gop-doesnt-care/.

25. Charlie Savage, "Trump Is Rapidly Reshaping the Judiciary. Here's How," *New York Times*, November 11, 2017, https://www.nytimes.com/2017/11/11/us/politics/trump-judiciary-appeals-courts-conservatives.html.

26. Jeffrey Toobin, "The Conservative Pipeline to the Supreme Court," *The New Yorker*, April 17, 2017, https://www.newyorker.com/magazine/2017/04/17/the-conservative-pipeline-to-the-supreme-court.

27. See radio interview by Mary Louise Kelly, "What Is the Federalist Society and How Does It Affect Supreme Court Picks?" *National Public Radio*, June 28, 2018, https://www.npr.org/2018/06/28/624416666/what-is-the-federalist-society-and-how-does-it-affect-supreme-court-picks.

28. Robert O'Harrow Jr. and Shawn Boburg, "A Conservative Activist's Behind-the-Scenes Campaign to Remake the Nation's Court," *Washington Post*, May 21, 2019, https://www.washingtonpost.com/graphics/2019/investigations/leonard-leo-federalists-society-courts/.

29. Thomas Kaplan, "Trump Is Putting Indelible Conservative Stamp on Judiciary," *New York Times*, July 31, 2018, https://www.nytimes.com/2018

/07/31/us/politics/trump-judges.html.

30. Micah Schwartzman and David Fontana, "Trump Picked the Youngest Judges to Sit on the Federal Bench. Your Move, Biden," *Washington Post*, February 16, 2021, https://www.washingtonpost.com/outlook/2021/02/16/court-appointments-age-biden-trump-judges-age/.

31. Patrick L. Gregory, "Trump Picks More 'Not Qualified' Judges," Bloomberg Law, December 17, 2018, https://news.bloomberglaw.com/us-law-week/trump-picks-more-not-qualified-judges-1

32. Carl Hulse and Michael D. Shear, "Biden Names Diverse Nominees for the Federal Bench," *New York Times*, March 30, 2021, https://www.nyti-mes.com/2021/03/30/us/politics/biden-judges.html.

33. Tobi Raji, "Biden Has Appointed 201 Judges, Boosting Diversity of Federal Courts," *Washington Post*, May 22, 2024, https://www.washingtonpost.com/politics/2024/05/22/biden-200-judges-confirmed-diversity/

34. As of August 7, 2024. Data obtained via the Federal Judicial Center, Biographical Directory of Article III Federal Judges, 1789present, https://www.fjc.gov/history/judges.

35. John Gramlich, "Most of Biden's Appointed Judges to Date Are Women, Racial or Ethnic MinoritiesA First for Any President," Pew Research Center, December 4, 2023, https://www.pewresearch.org/short-reads/2023/12/04/most-of-bidens-appointed-judges-to-date-are-women-racial-or-ethnic-minorities-a-first-for-any-president/

36. Nicole Chavez and Annette Choi, "Biden Administration Ties Record for Number of Confirmed LGBTQ Judges in Federal Courts," *CNN.com*, March 19, 2024, https://www.cnn.com/2024/03/19/us/biden-record-lgbtq-judges-reaj/index.html

37. Nick Mourtoupalas, "Biden Has Installed the Most Non-White Judges of Any President," *Washington Post*, May 22, 2024, https://www.washingtonpost.com/politics/2024/05/17/biden-trump-judges-diversity/

38. Ibid.

39. Oma Seddiq and Madison Hall, "Trump's Judicial Appointments Worsened Racial Diversity in the Federal Courts," *Business Insider*, April 8, 2021, https://www.businessinsider.com/trump-federal-judge-appointments-racial-diversity-2021-4.

40. See American Bar Association, "Ratings of Article III and Article IV Judicial Nominees 118th Congress." Report to the Standing Committee on the Federal Judiciary, December 12, 2023, https://www.americanbar.org/content/dam/aba/administrative/government_affairs_office/fjc-chart-118th-congress-dec-2023.pdf; and American Bar Association, "Ratings of Article III and Article IV Judicial Nominees 117th Congress." Report to the Standing Committee on the Federal Judiciary, December 12, 2022, https://www.americanbar.org/content/dam/aba/administrative/government_affairs_office/webratingchart-117.pdf

41. https://www.politico.com/news/2021/06/15/biden-democrats-judges-494292.

42. Adrian Blanco, "Biden Nominated as Many Minority Women to Be Judges in Four Months as Trump Had Confirmed in Four Years," *Washington Post*, June 14, 2021, https://www.washingtonpost.com/politics/interactive/2021/biden-judge-diversity/.

43. John Gramlich, "How Trump Compares with Other Recent Presidents in Appointing Federal Judges," *Pew Research Center*, January 13, 2021, ht

tps://www.pewresearch.org/fact-tank/2021/01/13/how-trump-compares-with-other-recent-presidents-in-appointing-federal-judges/.

44. See Matt Grossman and David A. Hopkins, "Asymmetric Politics: Ideological Republicans and Group Interest Democrats" (London: Oxford University Press, 2016).

45. Amanda Hollis-Brusky, "Biden Said He Won't Make an 'Ideological' Supreme Court Pick. Republicans Do Exactly That," *Washington Post*, February 14, 2022, https://www.washingtonpost.com/politics/2022/02/14/supreme-court-biden-nominee-ideological/

46. Oma Seddiq and Madison Hall, "Trump's Judicial Appointments Worsened Racial Diversity in the Federal Courts," *Business Insider*, April 8, 2021, https://www.businessinsider.com/trump-federal-judge-appointments-racial-diversity-2021-4.

47. From charges of mishandling classified documents and fomenting the January 6, 2021, insurrection on Capitol Hill, to state charges for interfering in the 2020 election in Georgia and a conviction in New York in May 2024 for falsifying business records to hide hush money payments to maintain the silence of an adult film star with whom Trump had an affair, Trump faced major legal problems.

48. Michael R. Sisak, Jennifer Peltz, Eric Tucker, Michelle L. Price, and Jill Colvin, "Guilty: Trump becomes first former US president convicted of felony crimes," Associated Press, May 31, 2024, https://apnews.com/article/trump-trial-deliberations-jury-testimony-verdict-85558c6d08efb434d05b694364470aa0. Trump appealed the verdict and the status of his appeal was pending as this book went to press.

49. Natasha Bertrand, "The Chilling Effect of Trump's War on the FBI," *The Atlantic*, May 25, 2018, https://www.theatlantic.com/politics/archive/2018/05/the-chilling-effect-of-trumps-war-on-the-fbi/561218/.

50. R. J. Reinhart, "In the News: Americans' Views of the FBI," *Gallup.com*, January 30, 2018, https://news.gallup.com/poll/226505/news-americans-views-fbi.aspx.

51. Michael S. Schmidt, *Donald Trump v. The United States: Inside the Struggle to Stop a President* (New York, NY: Random House, 2020), 21.

52. R. J. Reinhart, "In the News: Americans' Views of the FBI," *Gallup.com*, January 30, 2018, https://news.gallup.com/poll/226505/news-americans-views-fbi.aspx.

53. Craig Helmstetter, "Poll: Trust in the FBI Higher among Democrats," American Public MediaAPM Research Lab, January 4, 2023, https://www.apmresearchlab.org/motn-fbi-trust-jan-2023

54. Fred Lucas, "Biden's 'Most Radical' Judges Could 'Deliver the Left's Policy Preferences,' Judicial Watchdogs Warn," FOX News, February 10, 2023, https://www.foxnews.com/politics/bidens-radical-judges-deliver-lefts-policy-preferences-judicial-watchdogs-warn

55. Alexandra Hutzler, "Donald Trump's Federal Judge Selections Have Been the Most Mainstream Thing He's Done, Experts Say," *Newsweek*, June 29, 2018, https://www.newsweek.com/donald-trump-republican-supreme-court-fed-eral-judges-nomination-mainstream-100100824.

56. Jay Michaelson, "Trump's Shocking Extremist Judges," *The Daily Beast*, October 18, 2017, https://www.thedailybeast.com/trumps-shocking-extre-mist-judges.

57. Russell Wheeler, "Can Biden Top Trump's Number of Judicial Appointments?" The Brookings Institution,

July 23, 2024, https://www.brookings.edu/articles/can-biden-top-trumps-number-of-judicial-appointments/

58. Stephen Neukam, "Senate Dems Eye Trump's Tally for Judicial Confirmations," Axios.com, August 4, 2024, https://www.axios.com/2024/08/04/senate-democrats-judicial-confirmations-trump
59. Data obtained via the Federal Judicial Center, Biographical Directory of Article III Federal Judges, 1789present, https://www.fjc.gov/history/judges.
60. Tobi Raji and Clara Ence Morse, "Trump's Victory, GOP Senate Win Have Democrats Racing to Confirm Judges," *Washington Post*, November 13, 2024. https://www.washingtonpost.com/politics/2024/11/13/trump-biden-federal-judge-vacancies-senate-flip/
61. Russell Wheeler, "Can Biden 'Rebalance' the Judiciary?" Brookings Institution, March 18, 2021, https://www.brookings.edu/articles/can-biden-rebalance-the-judiciary/
62. Stephen Neukam, "Senate Dems Eye Trump's Tally for Judicial Confirmations," Axios.com, August 4, 2024, https://www.axios.com/2024/08/04/senate-democrats-judicial-confirmations-trump
63. Alexander Bolton, "McConnellTrump Relationship Icy as Ever," *The Hill*, April 3, 2024, https://thehill.com/homenews/senate/4570720-mcconnell-trump-icy-relationship/
64. Marianne LeVine, "The One Biden Priority Democrats Are Confident They Can Get Done," Politico.com, June 15, 2021, https://www.politico.com/news/2021/06/15/biden-democrats-judges-494292
65. Russell Wheeler, "Can Biden Top Trump's Number of Judicial Appointments?" The Brookings Institution, July 23, 2024, https://www.brookings.edu/articles/can-biden-top-trumps-number-of-judicial-appointments/
66. Carrie Johnson, "Wave of Young Judges Pushed by McConnell Will Be 'Ruling for Decades to Come,'" *National Public Radio*, July 2, 2020, https://www.npr.org/2020/07/02/886285772/trump-and-mcconnell-via-swath-of-judges-will-affect-u-s-law-for-decades
67. Russell Wheeler, "Can Biden 'Rebalance' the Judiciary?" Brooking Institution, March 18, 2021, https://www.brookings.edu/blog/fixgov/2021/03/18/can-biden-rebalance-the-judiciary/. See also "Archive of Judicial Vacancies" maintained by the Administrative Office of the U.S. Courts, https://www.uscourts.gov/judges-judgeships/judicial-vacancies/archive-judicial-vacancies
68. Ann E. Marimow and Matt Viser, "Biden Moves Quickly to Make His Mark on Federal Courts After Trump's Record Judicial Nominations," *Washington Post*, February 3, 2021, https://www.washingtonpost.com/local/legal-issues/biden-judge-nominations/2021/02/02/e9932f3a-6189-11eb-9430-e7c 77b5b0297_story.html.
69. Ed O'Keefe and Robert Barnes, "Senate Confirms Neil Gorsuch to Supreme Court," *Washington Post*, April 17, 2017, https://www.washingtonpost. com/powerpost/senate-set-to-confirm-neil-gorsuch-to-supreme-court/2017/04/07/da3cd738-1b89-11e7-9887-1a5314b56a08_story.html.
70. Seung Min Kim and John Wagner, "Kavanaugh Sworn In as Supreme Court Justice After Divided Senate Votes for Confirmation," *Washington Post*, October 6, 2018, https://www.washingtonpost.com/politics/kavanaugh-vote-divided-senate-poised-to-confirm-trumps-nominee/2018/10/06/64bf69fa-c969-11e8-b2b5-79270f9cce17_story.html.

71. Susan Dominus and Charlie Savage, "The Quiet 2013 Lunch That Could Have Altered Supreme Court History," *New York Times*, September 25, 2020, https://www.nytimes.com/2020/09/25/us/politics/rbg-retirement-obama.html.

72. Emma Brown, Jon Swaine, and Michelle Boorstein, "Amy Coney Barrett Served as a 'Handmaid' in Christian Group People of Praise," *Washington Post*, October 6, 2020, https://www.washingtonpost.com/investigations/amy-coney-barrett-people-of-praise/2020/10/06/5f497d8c-0781-11eb-859b-f9c27abe638d_story.html.

73. Sarah Binder, "Barrett Is the First Supreme Court Justice Confirmed Without Opposition Support Since 1869," *Washington Post*, October 27, 2020, https://www.washingtonpost.com/politics/2020/10/27/barrett-is-first-supreme-court-justice-confirmed-without-opposition-support-since-least-1900/.

74. Danielle Kurtzleben, "Republicans Take Issue with Biden's Pledge to Pick a Black Woman for Supreme Court," *National Public Radio*, February 4, 2022, https://www.npr.org/2022/02/04/1078358077/republicans-take-issue-with-bidens-pledge-to-pick-a-black-woman-for-supreme-cour

75. Ibid.

76. Erwin Chemerinsky, "Justice Breyer Should Learn from Justice Ginsburg's Mistake—And Retire Now," *Washington Post*, May 8, 2021, https://www.washingtonpost.com/outlook/2021/05/08/breyer-ginsburg-biden-trump/.

77. Tyler Pager, Sean Sullivan, Seung Min Kim, and Ann E. Marimow, "Biden Nominates Ketanji Brown Jackson to the Supreme Court," *Washington Post*, February 25, 2022, https://www.washingtonpost.com/politics/2022/02/25/ketanji-brown-jackson-supreme-court/

78. Adrian Blanco and Shelly Tan, "How Ketanji Brown Jackson's Path to the Supreme Court Differs from the Current Justices," *Washington Post*, March 20, 2022, https://www.washingtonpost.com/politics/interactive/2022/ketanji-brown-jackson-school-career/

79. Ibid.

80. Carl Hulse and Annie Karni, "Jackson Confirmed as First Black Woman to Sit on Supreme Court," *New York Times*, April 7, 2022, https://www.nytimes.com/2022/04/07/us/politics/ketanji-brown-jackson-supreme-court.html

81. Ibid.

82. Mike Scarcella, "House Democrats Move to Add 203 U.S. Trial Court Judgeships," *Reuters.com*, July 30, 2021, https://www.reuters.com/legal/government/house-democrats-move-add-203-us-trial-court-judgeships-2021-07-30/.

83. David Savage, "Can Democrats Really Expand the Supreme Court?" *Los Angeles Times*, April 16, 2021, https://www.latimes.com/politics/story/2021-04-16/can-democrats-really-pack-the-supreme-court.

84. Ibid.

85. Carrie Campbell Severino, "Democratic Opposition to Court-Packing Grows," *National Review*, April 22, 2021, https://www.nationalreview.com/bench-memos/democratic-opposition-to-court-packing-grows/.

86. Barbara Sprunt, "Biden Says He's 'Not a Fan' of Expanding the Supreme Court," *National Public Radio*, October 13, 2020, https://www.npr.org/2020/10/13/923213582/biden-says-hes-not-a-fan-of-expanding-the-supreme-court.

87. Daniel Wiessner and Nate Raymond, "US Senate Approves Bill to Create 66 New Federal Judgeships," Reuters,

August 2, 2024, https://www.reuters.com/legal/government/us-senate-approves-bill-create-66-new-federal-judgeships-2024-08-01/

88. Ibid.

89. "Biden Begins Presidency With Positive Ratings; Trump Departs With Lowest-Ever Job Mark," Pew Research Center, January 15, 2021, https://www.pewresearch.org/politics/2021/01/15/biden-begins-presidency-with-positive-ratings-trump-departs-with-lowest-ever-job-mark/

90. Presidential Approval Ratings—Joe Biden, *Gallup.com*, 2021, https://news.gallup.com/poll/329384/presidential-approval-ratings-joe-biden.aspx (accessed August 16, 2021).

91. Olivier J. Blanchard and Ben S. Bernanke, "What Caused the US Pandemic-Era Inflation?" National Bureau of Economic Research, Working Paper 31417, June 2023, https://www.nber.org/papers/w31417

92. Jeffrey M. Jones, "Biden's 13th-Quarter Approval Average Lowest Historically," *Gallup.com*, April 26, 2024, https://news.gallup.com/poll/644252/biden-13th-quarter-approval-average-lowest-historically.aspx

93. Technically, there were forty-eight Democrats and two independents. The independents—Angus King of Maine and Bernie Sanders of Vermont—aligned and caucused with the Democrats.

94. Marianne Levine, "The One Biden Priority Democrats Are Confident They Can Get Done," *Politico.com*, June 15, 2021, https://www.politico.com/news/2021/06/15/biden-democrats-judges-494292.

95. Ibid.

96. Daniel Strauss, "Joe Biden and Chuck Schumer: A Key Relationship to a Successful Presidency," *The Guardian* (UK), March 16, 2021, https://www.theguardian.com/us-news/2021/mar/16/joe-biden-chuck-schumer-presidency-senate

97. Seung Min Kim and Darlene Superville, "Biden Judicial Nominee Wamble Withdraws from Consideration, Cites Nearly 2-Year Wait for Action," Associated Press, May 24, 2023, https://apnews.com/article/biden-judge-nominee-wamble-withdrawal-kansas-d273116abb62e3b15ab002e24ddc91b5

98. Tiana Headley, "New York Federal Court Nominee Rejected by Senate Committee," Bloomberg Law, July 11, 2024, https://news.bloomberglaw.com/us-law-week/biden-nominee-for-new-york-court-falters-in-senate-committee-1

99. Ibid.

100. Alexander Bolton, "Ossoff Votes with Republicans to Block Controversial Biden Nominee," *The Hill*, July 11, 2024, https://thehill.com/homenews/senate/4766255-ossoff-republicans-judicial-nominee-biden/

101. Gallup.com, "Trump Job Approval," 2021, https://news.gallup.com/poll/203207/trumps-jobs%20approval-weekly.aspx (accessed August 1, 2021).

102. Amina Dunn, "Trump's Approval Ratings So Far Are Unusually Stable—And Deeply Partisan," *Pew Research Center*, August 24, 2020, https://www.pewre-search.org/fact-tank/2020/08/24/trumps-approval-ratings-so-far-are-unusu-ally-stable-and-deeply-partisan/.

103. Nina Totenberg, "Three Trump Judicial Nominees Withdraw, Raising Some Questions About Vetting," *National Public Radio*, December 19, 2017, https://www.npr.org/2017/12/19/572046189/three-trump-judicial-nomi-nees-withdraw-raising-some-questions-about-vetting.

104. Marianne Levine, "The One Biden Priority Democrats Are Confident They

Can Get Done," *Politico.com*, June 15, 2021, https://www.politico.com/news/2021/06/15/biden-democrats-judges-494292.

105. Kevin Freking, "GOP Efforts to Disregard 'Blue Slips' and Move Forward with Wisconsin Judge Riles Dems," *Chicago Tribune*, May 9, 2018, http://www.chicagotribune.com/news/nationworld/politics/ct-blue-slips-wisconsin-judge-michael-brennan-20180,509-story.html.

106. Karoun Demirjian, "White House Withdraws Judicial Nominee Ryan Bounds, After GOP Realizes He Didn't Have Votes for Confirmation," *Washington Post*, July 19, 2018, https://www.washingtonpost.com/power-post/senate-gop-withdraws-judicial-nominee-ryan-bounds-delivering-a-blow-to-trumps-court-plans/2018/07/19/0d81ff50-8b83-11e8-8aea-86e88ae760d8_story.html.

107. John Wagner and Karoun Demirjian, "Trump Judicial Nominee Matthew Petersen Pulls Out After Struggling to Answer Basic Questions," *Washington Post*, December 18, 2017, https://www.washingtonpost.com/politics/trump-judicial-nominee-who-struggled-to-answer-basic-questions-pulls-out/2017/12/18/eadf1326-e424-11e7-833f-155031558ff4_story.html.

108. Josh Gerstein and Seung Min Kim, "Two Trump Judge Nominees Out After Criticism," *Politico.com*, December 13, 2017, https://www.politico.com/story/2017/12/13/brett-talley-trump-nominee-withdraws-295322.

109. Sean Sullivan and Mike DeBonis, "With Little Fanfare, Trump and McConnell Reshape the Nation's Circuit Courts," *Washington Post*, August 14, 2018, https://www.washingtonpost.com/powerpost/with-little-fanfare-trump-and-mcconnell-reshape-the-nations-circuit-courts/2018/08/14/10610028-9fcd-11e8-93e3-24d1703d2a7a_story.html.

110. Data obtained via the Federal Judicial Center, Biographical Directory of Article III Federal Judges, 1789present, https://www.fjc.gov/history/judges.

111. John Gramlich, "How Trump Compares with Other Recent Presidents in Appointing Federal Judges," *Pew Research Center*, January 13, 2021, https://www.pewresearch.org/fact-tank/2021/01/13/how-trump-compares-with-other-recent-presidents-in-appointing-federal-judges/.

112. Maureen Groppe, "How the Most Right-Wing Appeals Court Was Reined in by the Supreme Court This Term," *USA Today*, July 25, 2024, https://www.usatoday.com/story/news/politics/2024/07/25/supreme-court-reins-in-right-wing-appeals-court/74379438007/

CHAPTER 8

1. Our discussion of the evolution of the legal profession draws heavily from Lawrence M. Friedman, *A History of American Law*, 3rd ed. (New York, NY: Simon & Schuster, 2005).
2. Ibid., 55.
3. Ibid., 59.
4. Ibid., 228.
5. Ibid., 240–41.
6. Ibid., 464.
7. Dahlia Lithwick, "'It's Amazing to Me How Distinctly I Remember Each of These Women,'" *Slate*, July 21, 2020, https://slate.com/news-and-politics/2020/07/ruth-bader-ginsburg-interview-transcript.html (accessed August 2, 2024). It may be worth noting that Dean Griswold supported admitting women at Harvard and that Ginsburg believed his question to be motivated by a desire to assure opponents that women would not "just waste this

wonderful education they would get" at Harvard. Ginsburg further noted that Griswold had no sense "that he was making the women feel uncomfortable" with the question.

8. Dahlia Lithwick and Molly Olmstead, "The Class of RBG," *Slate*, July 21, 2020, https://slate.com/news-and-politics/2020/07/the-women-of-harvard-law-rbg-1959.html#ladies (accessed August 2, 2024).
9. Karl N. Llewellyn, *The Bramble Bush: The Classic Lectures on the Law and Law School* (Oxford, NY: Oxford University Press, 2008). Introduction by Steve Sheppard, xii.
10. See Shauna M. Strickland, "Beyond the Vanishing Trial: A Look at the Composition of State Court Dispositions," *Future Trends in State Courts 2005*, http://cdm16501.contentdm.oclc.org/cdm/ref/collection/adr/id/41 (accessed August 1, 2024).
11. David Perry, "How Did Lawyers Become 'Doctors'?" *In Practice* (Winter 2013), https://web.archive.org/web/20150909131931/ http://www.mobar.org/uploadedFiles/Home/Publications/Precedent/2013/Winter/doctors.pdf (accessed August 2, 2024).
12. Michael E. Gehringer, "Questions and Answers," *Law Library Journal* 72 (1979): 15259, 153.
13. *Bates v. State Bar*, 433 U.S. 350 (1977).
14. Joseph Sanders, "Courts and Law in Japan," in *Courts, Law, and Politics in Comparative Perspective*, ed. Herbert Jacob, Erhard Blankenburg, Herbert M. Kritzer, Doris Marie Provine, and Joseph Sanders (New Haven, CT: Yale University Press, 1996), 320.
15. The number of lawyers in the United States, by state, may be found at https://www.abalegalprofile.com/demographics.html (accessed August 1, 2024).
16. NALP, "Jobs & JDs: Employment for the Class of 2023, Selected Findings," https://www.nalp.org/uploads/Class_2023_Selected_Findings.pdf (accessed July 30, 2024), 4. Statistics in this paragraph come from this NALP source. Note that although NALP has been collecting data on employment rates for graduating law students since 1982, their methodology changed in 2014, resulting in data from 1982 through 2013 that may undercount employment rates slightly, compared to metrics used since 2014.
17. Ibid., 5.
18. American Bar Association, "Statistics: Comparison of 2011–2016 Matriculants," https://www.americanbar.org/groups/legal_education/resources/statistics.html (accessed August 3, 2018).
19. American Bar Association, "2021 Standard 509 Information Report Data Overview," https://www.americanbar.org/content/dam/aba/administrative/legal_education_and_admissions_to_the_bar/statistics/2021/2021-509-enrollment-summary-report.pdf (accessed July 30, 2024).
20. American Bar Association, "2023 Standard 509 Information Report Data Overview," https://www.americanbar.org/content/dam/aba/administrative/legal_education_and_admissions_to_the_bar/statistics/2023/2023-aba-standard-509-data-overview-final.pdf (accessed July 30, 2024).
21. ABA Profile of the Legal Profession 2023, https://www.abalegalprofile.com/legaled.html (accessed July 31, 2024).
22. This quote comes from the press release to the Georgetown University Center on Education and the Workforce's "A Law Degree Is No Sure Thing: Some Law School Graduates Earn Top Dollar, but Many Do Not,"

written by Jeff Strohl, Catherine Morris, and Ben Cheah (2024), available at https://cew.georgetown.edu/cew-reports/law/#resources (accessed July 31, 2024).

23. Stephanie Russell-Kraft, "Whittier Law School Closing: The First of Many?" *Bloomberg Law: Big Law Business*, April 21, 2017, https://news.bloomberglaw.com/business-and-practice/whittier-law-school-closing-the-first-of-many (accessed August 1, 2024).

24. Since 1952, the Council of the ABA Section of Legal Education and Admission to the Bar of the American Bar Association has been considered the national agency for the accreditation of J.D. programs in the United States. Such accreditation is crucial because admission to the bar is contingent on earning a degree from an ABA-accredited school in most states. After being open for one year, a school may apply for provisional approval from the ABA. If such provisional approval is granted, graduates of that program are entitled to the same recognition that is accorded graduates of fully approved schools. Provisionally approved law schools may remain at that status for three to five years, after which they may apply for full approval. See American Bar Association: Section of Legal Education and Admissions to the Bar, "Guide to Schools Seeking ABA Approval," https://www.americanbar.org/groups/legal_education/accreditation/schools-seeking-aba-approval/ (accessed August 1, 2024).

25. Kathryn Rubino, "Law Schools Agree: There Are Too Many Law Schools," *Above the Law*, October 6, 2016, https://abovethelaw.com/2016/10/law-schools-agree-there-are-too-many-law-schools/ (accessed August 1, 2024).

26. Karen Sloan, "ABA Eyes Increasing Hands-On Learning Requirement for Law Schools," *Reuters* (2023), https://www.reuters.com/legal/legalindustry/aba-eyes-increasing-hands-on-learning-requirement-law-schools-2023-11-21/ (accessed July 31, 2024).

27. David Yellen, "Post-Crisis Legal Education: Some Premature Thoughts," *Syracuse Law Review* 66 (2016): 52329.

28. Nora V. Demleitner, "Higher Education Under Pressure: What Will the Future Hold?" *Syracuse Law Review* 66 (2016): 64987.

29. Liam Knox, "Vermont's Lone Law School Branches Out," *Inside Higher Ed*, September 5, 2022, https://www.insidehighered.com/news/2022/09/06/struggling-law-school-seeks-reinvent-itself (accessed July 31, 2024).

30. ABA Profile of the Legal Profession 2023, at https://www.abalegalprofile.com/legaled.html (accessed July 31, 2024).

31. Ibid.

32. Georgetown University Center on Education and the Workforce, at https://cew.georgetown.edu/wp-content/uploads/GeorgetownCEW_PressRelease_ROI-Law_06-25-24.pdf (accessed July 31, 2024).

33. See results reported by the American Bar Association Young Lawyers Division Student Loan Survey at https://www.accesslex.org/sites/default/files/2021-09/Student%20Debt_The%20Holistic%20Impact%20on%20Todays%20Yound%20Lawyer.pdf (accessed July 31, 2024).

34. NALP, "2023 Report on Diversity in U.S. Law Firms," January 2024, https://www.nalp.org/uploads/Research/2023NALPReportonDiversityFinal.pdf (accessed July 31, 2024). All data presented in this paragraph come from this source.

35. Robert L. Nelson, Ronit Dinovitzer, Bryant G. Garth, Joyce S. Sterling, David B. Wilkins, Meghan Dawe, and

Ethan Michelson, *The Making of Lawyers' Careers: Inequality and Opportunity in the American Legal Profession* (Chicago: The University of Chicago Press, 2023).

36. Richard Abel, "The Transformation of the American Legal Profession," *Law and Society Review* 20 (1986): 6.

37. "Law Poll," *ABA Journal* (September 1, 1986): 44.

38. NALP, "Class of 2023 National Summary Report," at https://www.nalp.org/uploads/Research/Classof2023NationalSummaryReport_final.pdf (accessed August 2, 2024).

39. See Elayne Rapping, *Law and Justice as Seen on TV* (New York, NY: New York University Press, 2004).

40. Steven Vago, *Law and Society*, 8th ed. (Upper Saddle River, NJ: Pearson Prentice Hall, 2006), 369.

41. Howard Abadinsky, *Law and Justice*, 2nd ed. (Chicago, IL: Nelson-Hall, 1991), 187.

42. Banks Miller and Brett Curry, *U.S. Attorneys, Political Control, and Career Ambition* (New York, NY: Oxford University Press, 2019), xi.

43. For a good case study of the firing of a US attorney, see Howard Ball, *Courts and Politics: The Federal Judicial System* (Englewood Cliffs, NJ: Prentice Hall, 1980), 202–6.

44. For an in-depth analysis of the appointment process for US attorneys, see James Eisenstein, *Counsel for the United States: U.S. Attorneys in the Political and Legal Systems* (Baltimore, MD: Johns Hopkins University Press, 1978), chap. 3.

45. Banks Miller and Brett Curry, *U.S. Attorneys, Political Control, and Career Ambition.*

46. Josh Gerstein, "Justice Department Watchdog Is Probing Handling of Roger Stone Case," *Politico*, September 14, 2020, https://www.politico.com/news/2020/09/14/justice-department-watchdog-probing-roger-stone-case-415005 (accessed August 1, 2024).

47. See "Statement for the Record: Assistant United States Attorney Aaron S. J. Zelinsky" before the House Judiciary Committee, June 24, 2020, https://www.congress.gov/116/meeting/house/110836/witnesses/HHRG-116-JU00-Wstate-ZelinskyA-20200624-U7.pdf (accessed August 1, 2024).

48. Carrie Johnson, "Barr Blasts His Own Prosecutors: 'All Power Is Vested in the Attorney General,'" September 17, 2020, *NPR*, https://www.npr.org/2020/09/17/913891515/in-fiery-speech-barr-assails-his-own-prosecutors-for-political-headhunting (accessed August 1, 2024).

49. For an account of how a solicitor general handles these responsibilities, see "A View from the Inside: Interview with Acting Solicitor General of the United States Walter Dellinger (1997), Conducted by Nina Totenberg," in *Inside the Judicial Process: A Contemporary Reader in Law, Politics, and the Courts*, ed. Jennifer Segal Diascro and Gregg Ivers (New York, NY: Houghton Mifflin Company, 2006).

50. Rebecca Mae Salokar, *The Solicitor General: The Politics of Law* (Philadelphia, PA: Temple University Press, 1992), 25.

51. Ryan C. Black and Ryan J. Owens, "Solicitor General Influence and Agenda Setting on the US Supreme Court," *Political Science Quarterly* 64, no. 4 (2011): 765–78.

52. Ibid.

53. For a fuller discussion of this matter, see "Interview with Solicitor General Rex E. Lee," *The Third Branch* 14 (May 1982): 5.

54. Ryan C. Black and Ryan J. Owens, *The Solicitor General and the United*

States Supreme Court: Executive Branch Influence and Judicial Decisions (New York, NY: Cambridge University Press, 2012).

55. An *acting* solicitor general is simply the title for someone who temporarily holds the responsibility of the position of the solicitor general without having been confirmed (or perhaps even nominated) to the position. Some acting solicitors general, such as Neal Katyal, may never be confirmed to the position. Katyal served as acting solicitor general during the period of transition between President Obama's first solicitor general (Elena Kagan) and Kagan's successor Don Verrilli when Kagan was appointed to the Supreme Court in 2010.

56. Lincoln Caplan, "The Tenth Justice," pt. 1, *The New Yorker*, August 1987, 40.

57. See Caplan, "The Tenth Justice," pt. 1, 41–58; and Caplan, "The Tenth Justice," pt. 2, *The New Yorker*, August 17, 1987, 30–62. See also Salokar, *The Solicitor General*, 172–73.

58. Patrick C. Wohlfarth, "The Tenth Justice? Consequences of Politicization in the Solicitor General's Office," *The Journal of Politics* 71 (2009): 224–37, 235.

59. Our brief account is drawn from Rorie J. Spill, Michael J. Licari, and Leonard Ray, "Taking on Tobacco: Policy Entrepreneurship and the Tobacco Litigation," *Political Research Quarterly* 54 (September 2001): 605–22.

60. The press release is available at https://www.texasattorneygeneral.gov/news/releases/75th-legal-action-against-biden-administration-attorney-general-ken-paxton-sues-over-illegal-eeoc (accessed August 1, 2024).

61. Associated Press, "State Attorney General Races Gain Attention in Trump Era," *Los Angeles Times*, June 2, 2018, https://www.latimes.com/politics/la-na-pol-2018-attorneys-general-20180602-story.html (accessed August 1, 2024).

62. Paul Nolette, "State Litigation during the Obama Administration: Diverging Agendas in an Era of Polarized Politics," *Publius* 44 (2014): 451–74.

63. Michael A. Roach, "Indigent Defense Counsel, Attorney Quality, and Defendant Outcomes," *American Law and Economics Review* 16 (2014): 577–619.

64. Ibid.

65. Deborah L. Rhode, "Access to Justice," *Fordham Law Review* 69 (2001): 1785–1819.

66. See Sara Smith and Will Hornsby, "Unbundled Legal Services: At the Tipping-Point?", ABA Standing Committee on the Delivery of Legal Services (April 2018), https://www.americanbar.org/content/dam/aba/administrative/delivery_legal_services/ls_del_unbundling_tipping_point_article.authcheckdam.pdf (accessed August 1, 2024).

67. Marc Galanter, "Why the 'Haves' Come Out Ahead: Speculations on the Limits of Legal Change," *Law & Society Review* 9 (1974): 95–160.

68. See Donald J. Farole Jr., "Reexamining Litigant Success in State Supreme Courts," *Law & Society Review* 33 (1999): 1043–58; Joel B. Grossman, Herbert M. Kritzer, and Stewart Macaulay, "Do the 'Haves' Still Come Out Ahead?" *Law & Society Review* 33 (1999): 803–10; Donald R. Songer, Reginald S. Sheehan, and Susan Brodie Haire, "Do the 'Haves' Come Out Ahead over Time? Applying Galanter's Framework to Decisions of the U.S. Courts of Appeals, 1925–1988," *Law & Society Review* 33 (1999): 811–32.

69. Phillip J. Cooper, *Hard Judicial Choices* (New York, NY: Oxford University Press, 1988), 13.

70. Geetanjali Ganguly, Joana Setzer, and Veerle Heyvaert, "If at First You Don't

Succeed: Suing Corporations for Climate Change," *Oxford Journal of Legal Studies* 38 (2018): 84168.

71. 573 U.S. 682 (2014).

72. See Amy Leigh Campbell, "Raising the Bar: Ruth Bader Ginsburg and the ACLU Women's Rights Project," *Texas Journal of Women and the Law* 11 (2002): 157–243.

73. Ellen Ann Andersen, *Out of the Closets & into the Courts: Legal Opportunity Structure and Gay Rights Litigation* (Ann Arbor: University of Michigan Press, 2006).

74. Ibid., 27.

75. Daniel Bennett, "The Rise of Christian Conservative Legal Organizations," *Religion and Politics*, June 10, 2015, https://religionandpolitics.org/2015/06/10/the-rise-of-christian-conservative-legal-organizations/ (accessed August 1, 2024).

76. See the website of the Alliance Defending Freedom, at https://adflegal.org/us-supreme-court (accessed August 1, 2024).

77. 582 U.S. (2017).

78. Sarah Posner, "The Christian Legal Army Behind 'Masterpiece Cakeshop,'" *The Nation*, November 28, 2017, https://www.thenation.com/article/archive/the-christian-legal-army-behind-masterpiece-cakeshop/ (accessed August 1, 2024).

79. Southern Poverty Law Center, "Why Is Alliance Defending Freedom a Hate Group?" April 10, 2020, https://www.splcenter.org/news/2020/04/10/why-alliance-defending-freedom-hate-group (accessed August 1, 2024).

80. 347 U.S. 483 (1954).

81. See Lawrence Baum, *The Supreme Court*, 9th ed. (Washington, DC: CQ Press, 2007), 78.

82. For a complete history of the American Civil Liberties Union, see Samuel Walker, *In Defense of American Liberties: A History of the ACLU* (New York, NY: Oxford University Press, 1990).

83. Ibid., 371.

84. Lee Epstein and Thomas G. Walker, *Constitutional Law for a Changing America: Rights, Liberties, and Justice*, 5th ed. (Washington, DC: CQ Press, 2004), 43.

85. Baum, *The Supreme Court*, 79. The case is *Grutter v. Bollinger*, 539 U.S. 306 (2003).

86. Nina Totenberg, "Record Number of Amicus Briefs Filed in Same-Sex Marriage Cases," *NPR* (April 28, 2015), www.npr.org/sections/itsall-politics/2015/04/28/402628280/record-number-of-amicus-briefs-filed-in-same-sex-marriage-cases (accessed August 1, 2024).

87. Ellena Erskine, "We Read All the Amicus Briefs in *Dobbs* So You Don't Have To," *SCOTUSblog* (November 30, 2021), https://www.scotusblog.com/2021/11/we-read-all-the-amicus-briefs-in-dobbs-so-you-dont-have-to/ (accessed August 1, 2024).

88. Lee Epstein and Thomas G. Walker, *Constitutional Law for a Changing America: Institutional Powers and Constraints*, 4th ed. (Washington, DC: CQ Press, 2001), 45.

89. Janet M. Box-Steffensmeier, Dino P. Christenson, and Matthew P. Hill, "Quality over Quantity: Amici Influence and Judicial Decision Making," *American Political Science Review* 107 (August 2013): 446–60, at 458.

90. Paul M. Collins Jr., "Friends of the Court: Examining the Influence of Amicus Curiae Participation in US Supreme Court Litigation," *Law & Society Review* 38 (2004): 807–32.

91. Gregory A. Caldeira and John R. Wright, "Organized Interests and Agenda Setting in the US Supreme

Court," *American Political Science Review* 82 (December 1988): 1122.

92. Paul M. Collins Jr. and Wendy L. Martinek, "Friends of the Circuits: Interest Group Influence on Decision Making in the US Courts of Appeals," *Social Science Quarterly* 91 (June 2010): 397.

93. Lee Epstein, "Exploring the Participation of Organized Interests in State Court Litigation," *Political Research Quarterly* 47 (June 1994): 335–51.

94. Donald R. Songer and Ashlyn Kuersten, "The Success of Amici in State Supreme Courts," *Political Research Quarterly* 48 (March 1995): 40.

95. See Donald R. Songer, Ashlyn Kuersten, and Erin Kaheny, "Why the Haves Don't Always Come Out Ahead: Repeat Players Meet Amici Curiae for the Disadvantaged," *Political Research Quarterly* 53 (September 2000): 552.

96. Sally J. Kenney, "The European Court of Justice: Integrating Europe through Law," *Judicature* 81 (May–June 1998): 252.

CHAPTER 9

1. France Bans, "Super-Skinny Models in Anorexia Clampdown," *Reuters*, April 4, 2015, www.reuters.com/article/2015/04/04/us-france-anorexia-idUSKBN0MU0JK20150404 (accessed July 5, 2024).

2. "France to Criminalize Ads Featuring Models Who Have Anorexia," *Houston Chronicle*, March 17, 2015, A2.

3. Raphael Tenthani, "Penalty for Being Gay in Malawi: 14 Years," *Houston Chronicle*, May 21, 2010, A12.

4. Fiona Drury, "North Korea Cracking Down on Wedding Dresses and Slang," *BBC News*, June 28, 2024, https://www.bbc.com/news/articles/c9r3pv1dyg2o (accessed July 4, 2024).

5. See https://law.justia.com/codes/alabama/title-13a/chapter-14/section-13a-14-4/ (accessed July 26, 2024).

6. "Judge Upholds Cursing Law," *Houston Chronicle*, February 9, 1999.

7. "Prosecute Limbaugh, Lawyer Says," *Houston Chronicle*, March 10, 2012, A4.

8. We wish to express our debt to Harold J. Vetter and Leonard Territo, from whom we borrowed this categorization. See Vetter and Territo, *Crime and Justice in America* (St. Paul, MN: West, 1984), chap. 1.

9. See https://www.statista.com/statistics/202714/number-of-committed-crimes-in-the-us-by-type-of-crime/ (accessed June, 26, 2024).

10. Ibid.

11. Ibid.

12. Oliver Roeder, Lauren-Brooke Eisen, and Julia Bowling, "What Caused the Crime Decline," Brennan Center for Justice at New York University School Law Report (2015). Available at https://papers.ssrn.com/sol3/papers.cfm?abstract_id=2566965.

13. See https://ec.europa.eu/eurostat/statistics-explained/index.php?title=Crime_statistics (accessed July 4, 2024).

14. The data on murder rates in the US, Canada, and Mexico are available at https://dataunodc.un.org/dp-intentional-homicide-victims (accessed July 4, 2024).

15. See https://www.cnbc.com/2023/03/09/how-medicare-and-medicaid-fraud-became-a-100b-problem-for-the-us.html.

16. Sarah N. Lynch, "US Announces Charges in $2.5 Billion Healthcare Fraud Takedown", *Reuters*, June 28, 2023, https://www.justice.gov/opa/pr/national-enforcement-action-results-78-individuals-charged-25b-health-care-fraud

17. Ibid.

18. See https://www.ojp.gov/ncjrs/virtual-library/abstracts/how-much-does-white-collar-crime-cost (accessed July 4, 2024).

19. See https://www.fbi.gov/investigate/organized-crime (accessed July 1, 2024).

20. See https://www.justice.gov/opa/pr/leader-drug-trafficking-organization-sentenced-international-cocaine-trafficking-conspiracy

21. *Whitney v. California*, 274 U.S. 357 (1927).

22. *Papachristou v. City of Jacksonville*, 405 U.S. 156 (1972), see footnote 1.

23. Ibid., 164.

24. Ibid., 156.

25. Julie Makinen, "3 Female Activists to Be Freed in China; 2 Others Still Held," *Houston Chronicle*, April 14, 2015, A7.

26. Quotation in David W. Neubauer, *America's Courts and the Criminal Justice System*, 2nd ed. (Monterey, CA: Brooks/Cole, 1984), 64.

27. Nick Powell, "Santa Fe Suspect Not Fit for Trial," *Houston Chronicle*, November 5, 2019, A1; and Nick Powell, "Galveston County DA Won't Fight Incompetency Finding for Suspect," *Houston Chronicle*, November 6, 2019, A9.

28. "Neighbors Reveal What May Have Led to Assault on Rand Paul," *CBS News*, https://www.cbsnews.com/news/rand-paul-tackled-by-neighbor-over-trivial-dispute/ (accessed July 5, 2024).

29. See https://www.statista.com/statistics/191694/number-of-law-enforcement-officers-in-the-us/ (accessed June 30, 2024).

30. See https://www.urban.org/policy-centers/cross-center-initiatives/state-and-local-finance-initiative/state-and-local-backgrounders/criminal-justice-police-corrections-courts-expenditures (accessed July 2, 2024).

31. See https://www.statista.com/statistics/191261/number-of-arrests-for-all-offenses-in-the-us-since-1990/ (accessed June 30, 2024).

32. Richard Brisbin and John Kilwein, *Real Law Stories Inside the American Judicial Process* (New York, NY: Oxford University Press, 2010), 156.

33. Ibid., 17172.

34. Domestic Violence Legislation" (2023), *FindLaw*, http://family.findlaw.com/domestic-violence/state-domestic-violence-legislation.html (accessed July 2, 2024).

35. Lawrence W. Sherman and Ronald A. Berk, "The Specific Deterrent Effects of Arrest for Domestic Assault," *American Sociological Review* 49 (1984): 261–72; and Ronald A. Berk and Lawrence W. Sherman, "Police Responses to Domestic Violence Incidents: An Analysis of an Experimental Design with Incomplete Randomization," *Journal of the American Statistical Association* 83 (1988): 70–76; Ida M. Johnson, "Victims Perceptions of Police Response to Domestic Violence Incidents," *Journal of Criminal Justice* 35 (2007).

36. Douglas A. Smith, Christy A. Visher, and Laura A. Davidson, "Equity and Discretionary Justice: The Influence of race on Police Arrest Decisions", *The Journal of Criminal Law & Criminology* 75 (1984).

37. Cynthia Lum, "The Influence of Places on Police Decision Pathways: From Call for Service to Arrest," *Justice Quarterly* 28 (2011).

38. Jessica Huff, "Understanding Police Decisions to Arrest: The Impact of Situational, Office, and Neighborhood Characteristics on Police Discretion," *Journal of Criminal Justice* 75 (2021): 1.

39. *County of Riverside v. McLaughlin*, 500 U.S. 44 (1991).

40. *Corley v. United States*, 556 U.S. 303 (2009).

41. *Miranda v. Arizona*, 384 U.S. 436 (1966). This decision was undermined somewhat in 1991, when the US Supreme Court ruled that under some circumstances confessions that are coerced from defendants by police can be used as evidence. *Arizona v. Fulminante*, 499 U.S. 279 (1991).

42. Two years after *Miranda* was decided, Congress attempted to subvert its effect by enacting 18 U.S.C. § 3501, which in essence laid down a rule that the admissibility of a custodial suspect's statement should turn only on whether it was made voluntarily. This law was overturned by the Supreme Court in the case of *Dickerson v. United States*, 530 U.S. 428 (2000). The Court said, in effect, that since *Miranda* was a constitutional decision of the Court, it could not be overturned by an act of Congress, and then the Court went on to reiterate its support of the essence of the 1966 ruling. In addition, in May 2009, these *Miranda* rights were watered down somewhat when the Supreme Court decided, 54, to overturn a long-standing rule that stopped police from initiating questions unless a defendant's lawyer was present. This decision will surely make it easier for prosecutors to interrogate suspects. The Court held that the Sixth Amendment's right to counsel could be waived "so long as the relinquishment of the right is voluntary, knowing and intelligent," which could be established by the state's rote recitation of the *Miranda* warnings and the defendant's uncounseled, voluntary waiver of those rights. *Montejo v. Louisiana*, 556 U.S. 07 (2009).

43. "Almost Half a Million People Are in Jail Awaiting Trial," *The Nation*, https://www.thenation.com/article/archive/almost-half-a-million-people-are-in-jail-awaiting-trial/ (accessed July 5, 2024).

44. Gabrielle Banks, "Report: New Bail System Working," *Houston Chronicle*, September 4, 2020, A1.

45. See https://www.brennancenter.org/our-work/analysis-opinion/new-yorks-upcoming-bail-reform-changes-explained (accessed July 2, 2024).

46. Ibid.

47. There are variations of this, however. In Texas, for example, grand juries consist of twelve persons chosen because they are friends or neighbors of judge-appointed jury commissioners. A vote of nine members is required for a decision.

48. See Robert A. Carp, "The Behavior of Grand Juries: Acquiescence or Justice?" *Social Science Quarterly* 55 (1975): 853–70. For some more current discussions of whether the grand jury is worth keeping and what steps might be taken to improve its work, see *Judicature* 81 (1998): 190–200.

49. Ben Casselman, "It's Incredibly Rare for a Grand Jury to Do What Ferguson's Just Did," http://fivethirtyeight.com/datalab/ferguson-michael-brown-indict-ment-darren-wilson/ (accessed July 2, 2024).

50. See https://www.nbcnews.com/news/us-news/officers-charged-fatal-police-shootings-2021-not-everyone-sees-progres-rcna12799 (accessed July 2, 2024).

51. Lucian E. Dervan, "Fourteen Principles and a Path Forward for Plea Bargaining Reform," *Criminal Justice Magazine*, January 22, 2024. See also the recent 2023 ABA Plea Bargaining Task Force Report, available at https://www.americanbar.org/content/dam/aba/publications/criminaljustice/plea-bargain-tf-report.pdf

52. *Missouri v. Frye*, 566 U.S. 134 (2012), 143.
53. Richard Brisbin and John Kilwein, *Real Law Stories Inside the American Judicial Process* (New York, NY: Oxford University Press, 2010), 179.
54. Ibid., 196.
55. See the Federal Rules of Criminal Procedure 11(c)(1), available at https://www.law.cornell.edu/rules/frcrmp (accessed June 30, 2024).
56. Ibid.
57. Rishi Raj Batra, "Judicial Participation in Plea Bargaining: A Dispute Resolution Perspective," *Ohio State Law Journal* 76 (2015): 573–74.
58. Ibid., 578.
59. Ibid., 577.
60. Michael S. Schmidt and Matt Apuzzo, "Petraeus Gets Plea in Classified Data Case," *Houston Chronicle*, March 4, 2015, A4.
61. Richard Brisbin and John Kilwein, *Real Law Stories Inside the American Judicial Process* (New York, NY: Oxford University Press, 2010), 207–8.
62. Bargains on the sentence are primarily conducted at the state, not the federal, level because federal sentences are largely made by the judge, with advice from the probation officer—with both acting under congressional sentencing guidelines that took effect November 1, 1987.
63. This dialogue occurred on June 9, 2004, in the Harris County (Texas) Courthouse in one of the jury deliberation rooms. The jurist quoted here is Texas Criminal District Court Judge Marc Carter.
64. James N. Johnson, "Sentencing in the Criminal District Courts," *Houston Law Review* 9 (1972): 974.
65. See the Federal Rules of Criminal Procedure 11(b)(3), available at https://www.law.cornell.edu/rules/frcrmp (accessed June 30, 2024).
66. *Missouri v. Frye*, 566 U.S. 134 (2012) and *Lafler v. Cooper*, 566 U.S. 166 (2012).
67. *Missouri v. Frye*, 566 U.S. 134 (2012), 138–39.
68. Ibid., 143.
69. Adam Liptak, "Justices' Ruling Expands Rights of Accused in Plea Bargains," *New York Times*, March 21, 2012.
70. Jeffrey D. Stein, "How to Make an Innocent Client Plead Guilty," *Washington Post*, https://www.washingtonpost.com/opinions/why-innocent-people-plead-guilty/2018/01/12/e05d262c-b805-11e7-a908-a3470754bbb9_story.html?noredirect=on&utm_term=.e115451fb752 (accessed July 5, 2024).
71. Stephanos Bibas, Gregory Brower, Carissa Byrne Hessick, and Clark Neily, "The Pros and Cons of Plea Bargaining", *University of Dayton Law Review* 45 (2020): 524.
72. Ibid., 541.
73. Regina E. Rauxloh, "Plea Bargaining—A Necessary Tool for the International Criminal Court Prosecutor," *Judicature* 94 (2011): 178.
74. Julie Watson, "Mexico Reforms Its Courts," *Houston Chronicle*, June 18, 2008, A11.

CHAPTER 10

1. When discussing the stages of his criminal trial in this chapter, we refer to President Donald Trump without reference to title, to avoid any confusion for the reader with respect to Trump's changing status as "president," "former president," "Republican nominee for president," and "president-elect" at various points in the investigation, the trial, and into

the posttrial period. As noted in the text, however, Trump's status as a two-time president is of great potential relevance to the ultimate resolution of this case.

2. David A. Graham, "Guilty on All Counts," *The Atlantic*, May 30, 2024, https://www.theatlantic.com/ideas/archive/2024/05/donald-trump-guilty-all-counts-manhattan/678549/ (accessed June 20, 2024).
3. Also, in many jurisdictions, laws exempt persons in specific occupations (for example, doctors, members of the clergy, police officers) and in specific situations (for example, full-time students, persons over sixty-five years of age, parents with young children at home).
4. See *Taylor v. Louisiana*, 419 U.S. 522 (1975), and the Jury Service and Selection Act (1968), 28 U.S.C. § 1861.
5. See John P. Gross, "*Gideon* at 50: A Three-Part Examination of Indigent Defense in America," report by the National Association of Criminal Defense Lawyers, March 2013, https://www.nacdl.org/getattachment/cf613fe0-8f46-4dc1-b747-82346328522e/gideon-at-50-rationing-justice-the-underfunding- of-assigned-counsel-systems-part-1-.pdf (accessed July 18, 2024); and *Harvard Law Review*, "Gideon's Promise Unfulfilled: The Need for Litigated Reform of Indigent Defense," *Harvard Law Review* 113, no. 8 (2000): 2062–79.
6. Marian R. Williams, "A Comparison of Sentencing Outcomes for Defendants with Public Defenders versus Retained Counsel in a Florida Circuit Court," *Justice System Journal* 23, no. 2 (2002): 249–57.
7. Hannah Fry, "O. J. Simpson Never Paid the Goldmans the Millions He Owed Them. Can They Finally Collect?" *Los Angeles Times*, April 17, 2024, https://www.latimes.com/california/story/2024-04-17/goldman-family-could-see-money-from-o-j-simpson-trust (accessed July 12, 2024).
8. *McElrath v. Georgia*, 601 U.S. ____ (2024).
9. Ibid., p. 6.
10. Ronald Mann, "Double Jeopardy Clause Bars Georgia from Retrying Man Acquitted by Reason of Insanity," *SCOTUSblog*, February 21, 2024, https://www.scotusblog.com/2024/02/double-jeopardy-clause-bars-georgia-from-retrying-man-acquitted-by-reason-of-insanity/ (accessed June 4, 2024).
11. *Hudson v. Michigan*, 547 U.S. 586 (2006).
12. In *Maryland v. King*, 569 U.S. 435 (2013), the DNA cheek swab of Alonzo King taken at his booking for threatening a group with a shotgun matched the DNA sample collected in a rape case six years earlier.
13. *Ramos v. Louisiana*, 140 S. Ct. 1390 (2020) and Amy Howe, "Opinion Analysis: With Debate over Adherence to Precedent, Justices Scrap Nonunanimous Jury Rule," *SCOTUSblog* (April 20), https://www.scotusblog.com/2020/04/opinion-analysis-with-debate-over-adherence-to-precedent-justices-scrap-nonunanimous-jury-rule/ (accessed July 17, 2024).
14. *Batson v. Kentucky*, 476 U.S. 79 (1986).
15. *J. E. B. v. Alabama*, 511 U.S. 127 (1994).
16. Daniel Wise, "'*Batson*' Protection Extended to Jews," *National Law Journal*, April 28, 1997, A10; and Victoria Slind-Flor, "Illegal to Exclude Gays from Jury," *National Law Journal*, August 26, 1996, A11.
17. *Miller-El v. Dretke*, 545 U.S. 231 (2005).
18. Jeremy Herb and Lauren del Valle, "Takeaways from the Final Day of Jury Selection in Trump's Historic Hush Money Trial," *CNN*, April 20,

2024, https://www.cnn.com/2024/04/19/politics/takeaways-final-day-jury-selection-trump-hush-money-trial/index.html (accessed June 19, 2024)

19. Article III, Section 2, Clause 3. The Sixth Amendment as well requires that the impartial jury shall be "of the State . . . wherein the crime shall have been committed."
20. *Skilling v. United States*, 561 U.S. 358 (2010), at 378–79.
21. Kevin Breuninger, "Trump Loses Last-Minute Bid to Halt Hush Money Trial While He Seeks New Venue," *CNBC*, April 8, 2024, https://www.cnbc.com/2024/04/08/trump-hush-money-judge-recusal-bid-aims-to-delay-evade-gag-order-da-.html (accessed June 20, 2024).
22. Michael R. Sisak, Jennifer Peltz, Eric Tucker, and Jake Offenhartz, "Trump Tried to 'Corrupt' the 2016 Election, Prosecutor Alleges as Hush Money Trial Gets Underway," *APNews*, April 22, 2024, https://www.pbs.org/newshour/politics/trump-tried-to-corrupt-the-2016-election-hush-money-prosecutor-alleges-in-opening-statement (accessed June 20, 2024).
23. Aaron Katersky and Peter Charalambous, "Timeline: Manhattan DA's Stormy Daniels Hush Money Case Against Donald Trump," *ABCNews*, June 13, 2024, https://abcnews.go.com/Politics/timeline-manhattan-district-attorney-case-donald-trump/story?id=98389444 (accessed June 20, 2024).
24. Jeremy Herb, Lauren del Valle, and Kara Scannell, "Takeaways from Donald Trump's Defense in the Hush Money Trial," *CNN*, May 21, 2024, https://www.cnn.com/2024/05/21/politics/takeaways-from-donald-trumps-defense-in-the-hush-money-trial/index.html (accessed June 20, 2024).
25. Jesse McKinley and Kate Christobek, "Trump's Case Heads to the Jury: 5 Takeaways from Closing Arguments," *New York Times*, May 28, 2024, https://www.nytimes.com/2024/05/28/nyregion/trump-trial-closing-argument-takeaways.html (accessed June 20, 2024).
26. Robin Levinson-King and Kayla Epstein, "Who Is Judge Merchan, the No-Nonsense Judge Who Oversaw Trump's Hush-Money Case?" *BBC*, May 31, 2024, https://www.bbc.com/news/world-us-canada-65182727 (accessed July 12, 2024).
27. Bill Boyarsky, "Ito's Attempt to Control Brings Chaos to Trial," *Los Angeles Times*, April 22, 1995, https://www.latimes.com/archives/la-xpm-1995-04-22-mn-57465-story.html (accessed July 17, 2024).
28. Lynne Forster Lee and Irwin A. Horowitz, "The Effects of Jury-Aid Innovations on Juror Performance in Complex Civil Trials," *Judicature* 86, no. 4 (2003): 184–90.
29. Jury instructions in the Trump case can be found at https://static01.nyt.com/newsgraphics/documenttools/d458fdbff3cd7a41/84784522-full.pdf (accessed June 20, 2024).
30. Ibid.
31. Elizabeth Murray, "Donald Fell Death-Penalty Retrial Set for 2016," *Burlington Free Press*, April 10, 2015, https://www.burlingtonfreepress.com/story/news/2015/04/10/fell-death-penalty-trial-due-in-us-court/25564925/ (accessed July 17, 2024).
32. Elizabeth Murray, "Donald Fell Case to Be Retried After 15 Years," *Burlington Free Press*, March 8, 2015, http://www.burlingtonfreepress.com/story/news/local/2015/03/08/death-penalty-case-retried-years/24629173/ (accessed July 17, 2024).
33. Alan J. Keays, "Judge Accepts Plea Deal; Fell Sentenced to Life," *VTDigger*, September 28, 2018, https://vtdigger.org/2018/09/28/breaking-judge

-accepts-plea-deal-fell-sentenced-life/ (accessed July 17, 2024).

34. Somini Sengupta, "New Law Releases Juries in New York from Sequestering," *New York Times*, May 31, 2001, https://www.nytimes.com/2001/05/31/nyregion/new-law-releases-juries-in-new-york-from-sequestering.html (accessed June 20, 2024).

35. Associated Press, Michael R. Sisak, Jennifer Peltz, Eric Tucker, and Michelle L. Price, "Guilty: Trump Becomes First Former U.S. President Convicted of Felony Crimes," *WHYY/PBS*, May 30, 2024. Available at https://whyy.org/articles/trump-hush-money-trial-jury-deliberations-testimony-verdict/ (accessed July 1, 2024).

36. Veronica Haynes, "Karen Read Deliberations Will Resume Monday," *WCVB5*, June 29, 2024, https://www.wcvb.com/article/karen-read-trial-live-updates-jury-deliberations-june-28-2024/61449572 (accessed July 1, 2024).

37. David Duncan, "The Jury: Contamination, Instructions, Deliberations, and Verdict." In *Massachusetts Criminal Practice*, 4th ed. (Eric Blumenson, 2012), ed. Eric Blumenson and Arthur B. Leavens. Available at https://www.suffolk.edu/law/faculty-research/faculty/faculty-forms-and-resources/massachusetts-criminal-practice (accessed July 9, 2024), 35.

38. Ibid., ft. 162.

39. Erin York Cornwell and Valerie P. Hans, "Representation through Participation: A Multilevel Analysis of Jury Deliberations," *Law & Society Review* 45, no. 3 (September 2011): 667–98.

40. Kate Christobek, Jesse McKinley, Olivia Bensimon, Anusha Bayya, and Wesley Parnell, "The Jury That Convicted Donald Trump," *New York Times*, May 30, 2024, https://www.nytimes.com/2024/05/30/nyregion/trump-trial-jury.html (accessed July 17, 2024).

41. David W. Neubauer, *America's Courts and the Criminal Justice System*, 9th ed. (Belmont, CA: Wadsworth, 2007).

42. However, according to a 1994 law passed by Congress (18 U.S.C. §§3593 and 3594), in capital cases, only a jury can hand down a death sentence.

43. *Trump v. United States,* 603 U.S. ____ (2024).

44. Ella Lee and Zach Schonfeld, "Supreme Court Immunity Decision Collides with Trump's NY Conviction," *The Hill*, July 7, 2024, https://thehill.com/homenews/4754512-supreme-court-immunity-trump-conviction/ (accessed July 9, 2024).

45. Michael R. Sisak and Jennifer Peltz, "Trump Lawyers Push to Overturn His Felony Conviction after Supreme Court Immunity Ruling," *PBS*, July 11, 2024, https://www.pbs.org/newshour/politics/trump-lawyers-push-to-overturn-his-felony-conviction-after-supreme-court-immunity-ruling (accessed July 12, 2024).

46. Zach Schonfeld and Ella Lee, "Judge Delays Trump Immunity Decision in NY Hush Money Case," *The Hill*, November 11, 2024, https://thehill.com/regulation/court-battles/4985765-trump-immunity-hush-money/ (accessed November 17, 2024).

47. Paul G. Cassell, "In Defense of Victim Impact Statements," *Ohio State Journal of Criminal Law* 6 (2009): 611–48.

48. Ibid.

49. Ibid., 611–12.

50. *Booth v. Maryland*, 482 U.S. 496, at 508–9 (1987).

51. *Payne v. Tennessee*, 501 U.S. 808, at 825 (1991).

52. Tracy Connor, "Larry Nassar Accuser Count Is Up to 265, Judge Says," *NBC News*, January 31, 2018, https://www

.nbcnews.com/news/us-news/larry-nassar-accuser-count-265-judge-says-n843316 (accessed July 17, 2024).

53. *USA Today*, "Who Is Larry Nassar?" https://www.usatoday.com/pages/interactives/larry-nassar-timeline/ (accessed July 17, 2024).

54. Ibid.

55. Abby Gardner, "Aly Raisman Releases Powerful Statement Following Nassar Sentencing: 'Today Was an Important Victory, but There Is Still Work to Be Done,'" *Glamour*, January 25, 2018, https://www.glamour.com/story/aly-raisman-releases-powerful-statement-following-nassar-sentencing (accessed July 17, 2024).

56. Kyle Swenson, "Gymnastics Victims' Champion or Avenger? Nassar Judge Rosemarie Aquilina Stirs Controversy," *Washington Post*, January 26, 2018, https://www.washingtonpost.com/news/morning-mix/wp/2018/01/26/victims-champion-or-vengeful-nassar-judge-rosemarie-aquilina-stirs-controversy/ (accessed July 17, 2024).

57. Susan A. Bandes, "What Are Victim-Impact Statements For?" *The Atlantic*, July 23, 2016, https://www.theatlantic.com/politics/archive/2016/07/what-are-victim-impact-statements-for/492443/ (accessed July 17, 2024).

58. Ibid.

59. Ibid., 7.

60. "Chris Brown: How He Logged His 1,400 Hours of Community Service," *CBS News*, September 28, 2012, https://www.cbsnews.com/news/chris-brown-how-he-logged-his-1400-hours-of-community-service/ (accessed July 17, 2024).

61. See the website of the United States Sentencing Commission, at https://www.ussc.gov/about-page (accessed July 15, 2024).

62. "News from the Sentencing Commission," *The Third Branch* 19 (May 1987): 3–4.

63. Ibid., 5.

64. *U.S. v. Booker*, 543 U.S. 220 (2005); *U.S. v. Fanfan*, 543 U.S. 220 (2005).

65. "A Year after *Booker:* Most Sentences Still within Guidelines," *The Third Branch* 38 (February 2006): 2.

66. United States Sentencing Commission, Report on the Continuing Impact of *United States v. Booker* on Federal Sentencing, December 2012, https://www.ussc.gov/research/congressional-reports/2012-report-congress-continuing-impact-united-states-v-booker-federal-sentencing (accessed July 17, 2024).

67. United States Sentencing Commission, Demographic Differences in Sentencing: An Update to the 2012 *Booker* Report, November 2017, https://www.ussc.gov/sites/default/files/pdf/research-and-publications/research-publications/2017/20171114_Demographics.pdf (accessed July 9, 2024).

68. United States Sentencing Commission, Report on the Influence of the Guidelines on Federal Sentencing, National Sentencing Practices, 2005–2017, December 2020, https://www.ussc.gov/sites/default/files/pdf/research-and-publications/research-publications/2020/20201214_Guidelines-Influence-Report.pdf (accessed July 9, 2024).

69. United States Sentencing Commission News Release, "U.S. Sentencing Commission Votes to Reduce Drug Trafficking Sentences," April 10, 2014, https://www.ussc.gov/about/news/press-releases/april-10-2014 (accessed July 17, 2024).

70. Ibid.

71. United States Sentencing Commission News Release, "U.S. Sentencing Commission Unanimously Votes to

Allow Delayed Retroactive Reduction in Drug Trafficking Sentences," July 18, 2014, https://www.ussc.gov/sites/default/files/pdf/news/press-releases-and-news-advisories/press-releases/20140718_press_release.pdf (accessed July 17, 2024).

72. Ames Grawert, "What Is the First Step ActAnd What's Happening with It?" *Brennan Center for Justice*, June 23, 2020, https://www.brennancenter. org/our-work/research-reports/what-first-step-act-and-whats-happening-it (accessed July 17, 2024).

73. Ames C. Grawert and Patricia L. Richman, "The First Step Act's Prison Reforms: Uneven Implementation and the Path Forward," September 23, 2022, https://www.brennancenter.org/our-work/research-reports/first-step-acts-prison-reforms (accessed July 9, 2024).

74. Neal B. Kauder and Brian J. Ostrom, "State Sentencing Guidelines: Profiles and Continuum," report by the National Center for State Courts, July 2008, https://www.pewtrusts.org/-/media/legacy/uploadedfiles/wwwpewtrustsorg/reports/sentencing_and_corrections/ncsc20sentencing20guidelines20profiles20july202008pdf.pdf (accessed July 17, 2024).

75. Richard S. Frase, "State Sentencing Guidelines: Still Going Strong," *Judicature* 78 (1995): 177.

76. Tracey Kaplan, "Voters Overwhelmingly Ease Three Strikes Law," *San Jose Mercury News*, November 6, 2012, LexisNexis Academic.

77. 18 U.S.C. § 3624.

78. A petition for habeas corpus is a civil petition by either a state or a federal prisoner, usually filed after he or she has been convicted and has had that conviction upheld by an appellate court. The petition does not focus on whether the evidence supported a conviction but instead challenges the constitutionality of various police, lawyer, or judicial practices that supposedly violated the rights of the defendant.

79. *McCleskey v. Zant*, 499 U.S. 467 (1991).

80. U.S. Department of Justice, Bureau of Justice Statistics, *Capital Punishment, 2021*, November 2023, https://bjs.ojp.gov/document/cp21st.pdf (accessed July 9, 2024).

81. U.S. Department of Justice, Bureau of Justice Statistics, *Capital Punishment, 2013—Statistical Tables*, July 2013, https://bjs.ojp.gov/library/publications/capital-punishment-united-states-2013-statistical-tables (accessed July 17, 2024).

82. U.S. Department of Justice, Bureau of Justice Statistics, *Capital Punishment, 2021*.

83. Michelle Mark, "Just 16 Counties Are Fueling America's Use of the Death Penalty," *Business Insider*, August 23, 2016, https://www.businessinsider.com/16-counties-are-outliers-in-declining-us-use-of-death-penalty-2016-8 (accessed July 17, 2024).

84. U.S. Department of Justice, Bureau of Justice Statistics, *Capital Punishment, 2021*.

85. Jim Dwyer, Peter Neufeld, and Barry Scheck, "When Justice Lets Us Down," *Newsweek*, February 14, 2000, 59.

86. Information on state death penalty policy was collected from the Death Penalty Information Center at https://deathpenaltyinfo.org/states-landing (accessed July 9, 2024).

87. Brenan, Megan. 2023. "New 47% Low Say Death Penalty if Fairly Applied in U.S." *Gallup*, November 6, https://news.gallup.com/poll/513806/new-low-say-death-penalty-fairly-applied.aspx (accessed July 9, 2024).

88. 536 U.S. 304 (2002).

89. 543 U.S. 551 (2005).

90. "O'Connor Rethinks Death Penalty Justice," *Houston Chronicle*, July 5, 2001.

91. Data on federal executions over time were collected from the Federal Bureau of Prisons' Capital Punishment tracker, at https://www.bop.gov/about/history/federal_executions.jsp (accessed July 17, 2024).

92. Mark Walsh, "The Supreme Court's 'Shadow Docket' Is Drawing Increasing Scrutiny," *ABA Journal*, August 20, 2020, https://www.abajournal.com/web/article/scotus-shadow-docket-draws-increasing-scrutiny (accessed July 17, 2024).

93. Hailey Fuchs, "A Pause in Federal Executions, but Uncertainty About What's Next," *New York Times*, July 22, 2021, https://www.nytimes.com/2021/07/16/us/politics/biden-death-penalty.html (accessed July 9, 2024); Michael Ruiz, "Trump Execution Restart to Put Boston Marathon Bomber, Charleston Church Shooter, More Killers in Hot Seat," *Fox News*, November 15, 2024, https://www.foxnews.com/us/trump-execution-restart-put-boston-marathon-bomber-charleston-church-shooter-more-killers-hot-seat (accessed November 17, 2024).

94. Amnesty International, "Amnesty International Global Report: Death Sentences and Execution, 2023." Available at https://www.amnesty.org/en/documents/act50/7952/2024/en/, 1516 (accessed July 15, 2024).

95. Nicole Waters, Anne Gallegos, James Green, and Martha Rozsi, "Criminal Appeals in State Courts," *US Department of Justice, Bureau of Justice Statistics*, September 2015. Available at https://bjs.ojp.gov/content/pub/pdf/casc.pdf (accessed July 9, 2024).

96. *Miranda v. Arizona*, 384 U.S. 436 (1966).

CHAPTER 11

1. Herbert Jacob, *Justice in America*, 4th ed. (Boston, MA: Little, Brown, 1984), 210.

2. We are indebted to Lawrence M. Friedman, from whom we borrowed the classifications and on whose work our discussion is based. See Friedman, *American Law* (New York, NY: W. W. Norton, 1984), 141–53. Also see Friedman, *A History of American Law*, 3rd ed. (New York, NY: Simon & Schuster, 2005), 519–23, 576–82.

3. Shanika Gunaratna, "The 'Ugly' Reality of Child Marriage in the U.S.," *CBS News*, May 5, 2017, https://www.cbsnews.com/news/child-marriage-in-the-u-s-surprisingly-widespread/ (accessed July 17, 2024).

4. Alejandra O'Connell-Domenech, "Child Marriage Is Still Legal in Most of the U.S. Here's Why," *The Hill*, October 31, 2023, https://thehill.com/changing-america/respect/equality/4283941-child-marriage-is-still-legal-in-most-of-the-u-s-heres-why/. Also see statistics available from the organization Unchained At Last, a "survivor-led nonprofit organization dedicated to ending forced and child marriage in the United States," at https://www.unchainedatlast.org/ (accessed July 16, 2024).

5. Anjali Tsui, "In Fight Over Child Marriage Laws, States Resist Calls for a Total Ban," *Frontline*, July 6, 2017, https://www.pbs.org/wgbh/frontline/article/in-fight-over-child-marriage-laws-states-resist-calls-for-a-total-ban/ (accessed July 16, 2024).

6. See Thomas H. Cohen and Kyle Harbacek, "Punitive Damage Awards in State Courts, 2005," *Bureau of Justice Statistics Special Report* (March 2011), https://bjs.ojp.gov/content/pub/pdf/pdasc05.pdf (accessed July 17, 2024).

7. See the American Tort Reform Association website: http://www.atra.org (accessed July 17, 2024).
8. William Haltom and Michael McCann, *Distorting the Law: Politics, Media, and the Litigation Crisis* (Chicago, IL: University of Chicago Press, 2004), 46.
9. American Tort Reform Association, http://www.atra.org/about/ (accessed July 16, 2024).
10. See, for example, "Brief for *Amici Curiae* the American Tort Reform Association in Support of Petitioner," *State Farm Fire and Casualty Company v. United States of America Ex Rel. Cori Rigsby*, on Petition for a Writ of Certiorari to the United States Court of Appeals for the Fifth Circuit, November 2015, No. 15-513, http://www.scotusblog.com/wp-content/uploads/2016/05/15-513-ATRA-Amicus-Brief_111915.2_for-Filing.pdf (accessed July 17, 2024).
11. David M. Engel, *The Myth of the Litigious Society: Why We Don't Sue* (Chicago, IL: University of Chicago Press, 2016), chap. 1.
12. See Randy Means, "The History and Dynamics of Section 1983," *The Police Chief: The Professional Voice of Law Enforcement*, https://www.policechiefmagazine.org/the-history-and-dynamics-of-section-1983/ (accessed July 17, 2024).
13. Jordan Rubin, Kimberly Robinson, and Porter Wells, "Qualified Immunity, or How the Law Shields Police," *Bloomberg*, April 21, 2021, https://www.bloomberg.com/news/articles/2020-06-09/qualified-immunity-or-how-the-law-shields-police-quicktake (accessed July 17, 2024).
14. The complaint filed on behalf of George Floyd's family may be found at https://minnesota.cbslocal.com/wp-content/uploads/sites/15909630/2020/07/Filed-Floyd-Complaint.pdf (accessed July 16, 2024).
15. Holly Bailey and Toluse Olorunnipa, "George Floyd's Family to Receive Record $27 Million in Settlement Approved by Minneapolis City Council," *Washington Post*, March 12, 2021, https://www.washingtonpost.com/nation/2021/03/12/derek-chauvin-trial-update/ (accessed July 17, 2024).
16. Ibid. For a list of other recent excessive force payments made by the city of Minneapolis, see Liz Navratil and Maya Rao, "Minneapolis to Pay Record $27 Million to Settle Lawsuit with George Floyd's Family," *Star Tribune*, March 12, 2021, https://www.startribune.com/minneapolis-to-pay-record-27-million-to-settle-lawsuit-with-george-floyd-s-family/600033541/ (accessed July 17, 2024).
17. Richard E. Miller and Austin Sarat, "Grievances, Claims, and Disputes: Assessing the Adversary Culture," *Law and Society Review* 15 (1980–1981): 525–66. This study informs the remainder of the discussion on punitive damages.
18. Gina Jurva, "The Impacts of the COVID-19 Pandemic on State & Local Courts Study 2021: A Look at Remote Hearings, Legal Technology, Case Backlogs, and Access to Justice," *Thomason Reuters Institute* (2021).
19. John G. Levi and David M. Rubenstein, "Introduction" to a special issue on "Access to Justice," *Daedalus* 148, no. 1 (2019): 79, 7.
20. Mauro Cappelletti and Bryant Garth, "Access to Justice: The Newest Wave in the Worldwide Movement to Make Rights Effective," *Buffalo Law Review* 27 (1978): 181-292; Jacqueline Nolan-Haley, "Does ADR's 'Access to Justice' Come at the Expense of Meaningful Consent?" *Ohio State Journal on Dispute Resolution* 33, no. 3 (2018): 373-96.
21. See the *CDRCP Annual Statistical Report for Fiscal Year 2022-2023*, https:

//www.nycourts.gov/LegacyPDFS/ip/adr/2022-2023-CDRC-Annual-Report.pdf (accessed July 17, 2024). Our discussion is drawn from facts and figures found in this report.

22. Ibid., Table 1.

23. *CDRCP Annual Statistical Report for Fiscal Year 2013-2014*, https://ww2.nycourts.gov/sites/default/files/document/files/2018-07/AnnualReport_2013-14.pdf (accessed July 17, 2024).

24. Jacqueline Nolan-Haley, "Mediation, Self-Represented Parties, and Access to Justice: Getting There from Here," *Fordham Law Review Online* 87, no. 1 (2019): 111.

25. Cappelletti and Garth, "Access to Justice: The Newest Wave in the Worldwide Movement to Make Rights Effective," 226.

26. The Economic Policy Institute is a "nonprofit, nonpartisan think tank working for the last 30 years to counter rising inequality, low wages and weak benefits for working people." (See https://www.epi.org/about/, accessed July 17, 2024.)

27. Katherine V. W. Stone and Alexander J. S. Colvin, "The Arbitration Epidemic: Mandatory Arbitration Deprives Workers and Consumers of Their Rights," *EPI Briefing Paper*, December 7, 2015, https://www.epi.org/publication/the-arbitration-epidemic/ (accessed July 17, 2024), 5.

28. Ibid. See also William Davis and Helga Turku, "Access to Justice and Alternative Dispute Resolution," *Journal of Dispute Resolution* 1, no. 4 (2011).

29. Ibid., p. 26.

30. On May 21, 2018, the Supreme Court handed down a decision in three consolidated cases: *Epic Systems Corp. v. Lewis, Ernst & Young LLP et al. v. Morrie et al., and National Labor Relations Board v. Murphy Oil USA, Inc., et al.*, 200 L.Ed. 2d 889 (2018).

31. Daisuke Wakabayaski, "Uber Eliminates Forced Arbitration for Sexual Misconduct Claims," *New York Times*, May 15, 2018, https://www.nytimes.com/2018/05/15/technology/uber-sex-misconduct.html (accessed July 17, 2024).

32. Ibid.

33. See Howard Abadinsky, *Law and Justice*, 2nd ed. (Chicago, IL: Nelson-Hall: 1991), 273; and Christine B. Harrington, *Shadow Justice: The Ideology and Institutionalization of Alternatives to Court* (Westport, CT: Greenwood, 1985).

34. See Abadinsky, *Law and Justice*, 273.

35. *Securities and Exchange Commission v. Jarkesy*, 603 U.S. ____ (2024).

36. *Jarkesy* (Sotomayor, J., dissenting), at 35.

37. See Jack H. Friedenthal, Mary Kay Kane, and Arthur R. Miller, *Civil Procedure* (St. Paul, MN: West, 1985).

38. The American Bar Association provides information on the basic steps in a civil trial, at https://www.americanbar.org/groups/public_education/resources/law_related_education_network/how_courts_work/cases/ (accessed July 29, 2024).

39. William T. Schantz, *The American Legal Environment* (St. Paul, MN: West, 1976), 169.

40. Friedenthal et al., *Civil Procedure*, 380.

41. J. Skelly Wright, "The Pretrial Conference," in *American Court Systems: Readings in Judicial Process and Behavior*, ed. Sheldon Goldman and Austin Sarat (San Francisco, CA: Freeman, 1978), 120.

42. See *Edmondson v. Leesville Concrete Co.*, 500 U.S. 614 (1991), and *J. E. B v. Alabama Ex Rel. T. B.*, 511 U.S. 127 (1994), respectively. The Supreme Court declined to hear a case from

Minnesota that raised the question of whether the same principle should be extended to religion. See Linda Greenhouse, "Fierce Combat on Fewer Battlefields," *New York Times*, July 3, 1994, E4.

43. See "Point-Counterpoint, Jurors Asking Questions," *Judicature* 100, no. 1 (2016): 6873, https://judicature.duke.edu/wp-content/uploads/2021/11/Point-Counterpoint_Spring2016.pdf (accessed July 17, 2024).

44. Kim Bellware, Dan Rosenzweig-Ziff, and Will Sommer, "Alex Jones Ordered to Sell Personal Assets over Sandy Hook Judgment," *Washington Post*, June 14, 2024, https://www.washingtonpost.com/style/media/2024/06/14/alex-jones-infowars-sandy-hook-liquidate/ (accessed July 18, 2024).

45. Madeline Halpert, "Bankruptcy Trustee Plans to Shut Down Alex Jones' Infowars," *BBC*, June 14, 2024, https://www.bbc.com/news/articles/cn0003l7gl6o (accessed July 18, 2024).

CHAPTER 12

1. Richard J. Richardson and Kenneth N. Vines, *The Politics of Federal Courts* (Boston, MA: Little, Brown, 1970). Although Richardson and Vines developed their model primarily for federal courts, we believe that their hypotheses and conclusions are equally true for state judges.

2. Edward H. Levi, *An Introduction to Legal Reasoning* (Chicago, IL: University of Chicago Press, 1948), 1–2.

3. *Lane v. Wilson*, 307 U.S. 268 (1939); and *Gomillion v. Lightfoot*, 364 U.S. 339 (1960).

4. *Lane*, 307 U.S. at 275.

5. *Gomillion*, 364 U.S. at 342.

6. Donald J. Farole Jr., "Problem Solving and the American Bench: A National Survey of Trial Court Judges," *Justice System Journal* 30 (2009): 50–69.

7. Chad Westerland, Jeffrey A. Segal, Lee Epstein, Charles M. Cameron, and Scott Comparato, "Strategic Defiance and Compliance in the U.S. Courts of Appeals," *American Journal of Political Science* 54 (2010): 891.

8. Walter F. Murphy, *Elements of Judicial Strategy* (Chicago, IL: University of Chicago Press, 1964), 204.

9. Jeffrey A. Segal and Robert M. Howard, "How Supreme Court Justices Respond to Litigant Requests to Overturn Precedents," *Judicature* 85 (2001): 151.

10. Data reported by *SCOTUSblog*, a leading US Supreme Court information resource. Accessed July 31, 2024, https://www.scotusblog.com/statistics/

11. Michael A. Bailey and Forrest Maltzman, "Does Legal Doctrine Matter? Unpacking Law and Policy Preferences on the U.S. Supreme Court," *American Political Science Review* 102 (2008): 369.

12. Henry Sumner Maine, *Ancient Law* (Boston, MA: Beacon Press, 1963), 3–19.

13. Henry J. Abraham, *The Judicial Process*, 7th ed. (New York, NY: Oxford University Press, 1998), chap. 9.

14. Evers v. Jackson Municipal Separate School District, 232 F. Supp. 241 (1964).

15. Ibid., 249.

16. Ibid., 255.

17. Richardson and Vines, *The Politics of Federal Courts*, 8–9.

18. Steven Vago, *Law and Society*, 5th ed. (Englewood Cliffs, NJ: Prentice Hall, 1997), 354.

19. Steven Vago, *Law and Society*, 6th ed. (Upper Saddle River, NJ: Prentice Hall, 2000), chap. 9.

20. Oliver Wendell Holmes Jr., *The Common Law* (Boston, MA: Little, Brown, 1881), 1–2.

21. Jerome Frank, *Courts on Trial: Myth and Reality in American Justice* (Princeton, NJ: Princeton University Press, 1950), 151.

22. Richardson and Vines, *The Politics of Federal Courts*, 10.

23. Donald Dale Jackson, *Judges* (New York, NY: Atheneum, 1974), 18.

24. One study noted that between 1959 and 1998, some 140 books, articles, dissertations, and conference papers reported empirical data showing a link between judges' political party affiliation and their judicial behavior. Daniel R. Pinello, "Linking Party to Judicial Ideology in American Courts: A Meta-Analysis," *Justice System Journal* 20 (1999): 219–54.

25. Some studies suggest that age, socioeconomic status, and religion may influence some judges in some of their cases, but the associations are weak. See, for example, Sheldon Goldman, "Voting Behavior on the United States Courts of Appeals Revisited," *American Political Science Review* 69 (1975): 491–506; John R. Schmidhauser, "The Justices of the Supreme Court: A Collective Portrait," *Midwest Journal of Political Science* 3 (1959): 1–57; and Donald Leavitt, "Political Party and Class Influences on the Attitudes of Justices of the Supreme Court in the Twentieth Century," paper delivered at the annual meeting of the Midwest Political Science Association, Chicago, 1972. Other studies suggest that these background factors have virtually no explanatory power—for example, J. Woodford Howard, *Courts of Appeals in the Federal Judicial System* (Princeton, NJ: Princeton University Press, 1981), chap. 6. For a more detailed discussion of this subject and a literature review, see C. K. Rowland and Robert A. Carp, *Politics and Judgment in Federal District Courts* (Lawrence: University Press of Kansas, 1996), chap. 2.

26. David W. Adamany, "The Party Variable in Judges' Voting: Conceptual Notes and a Case Study," *American Political Science Review* 63 (1969): 59.

27. These figures are based on data collected by Robert A. Carp and Kenneth L. Manning.

28. For a more extensive discussion of the odds ratio and methodology used in this study, see Rowland and Carp, *Politics and Judgment in Federal District Courts*, 180–81.

29. Marcus E. Hendershot and H. Christian Tecklenburg, "Controlling for District Court Judges' Preferences," *Justice System Journal* 32 (2011): 88.

30. Marc Sennewald, Kenneth L. Manning, and Robert Carp, "The Polarization of the Judiciary," *Party Politics* 23 (2017): 657–65.

31. For a good review of the early literature on this subject, see Goldman, "Voting Behavior on the United States Courts of Appeals Revisited," 491, no. 2. See also Howard, *Courts of Appeals in the Federal Judicial System,* chap. 6. See also Donald R. Songer, Reginald S. Sheehan, and Susan B. Haire, *Continuity and Change on the United States Courts of Appeals* (Ann Arbor: University of Michigan Press, 2000), 110–19.

32. Sheldon Goldman, "Voting Behavior on the United States Courts of Appeals, 1961–1964," *American Political Science Review* 60 (1966): 384.

33. See, for example, Donald Songer, "Consensual and Nonconsensual Decisions in Unanimous Opinions of the United States Courts of Appeals," *American Journal of Political Science*

26 (1982): 225–39; Donald Songer and Sue Davis, "The Impact of Party and Region on Voting Decisions in the United States Courts of Appeals, 1955–1986," *Western Political Quarterly* 43 (1990): 317–34; and Ronald Stidham, Robert A. Carp, and Donald R. Songer, "The Voting Behavior of President Clinton's Judicial Appointees," *Judicature* 80 (1996): 16–21.

34. Cass R. Sunstein, David Schkade, Lisa M. Ellman, and Andres Sawicki, *Are Judges Political? An Empirical Investigation of the Federal Judiciary* (Washington, DC: Brookings Institution Press, 2006), 8.

35. Christopher E. Smith, "Polarization and Change in the Federal Courts: En Banc Decisions in the U.S. Courts of Appeals," *Judicature* 74 (1990): 137.

36. Though one research team has suggested that there may even be ideological elements in some unanimous decisions. See Lee Epstein, William M. Landes, and Richard A. Posner, "Are Even Unanimous Decisions in the United States Supreme Court Ideological?" *Northwestern University Law Review* 106 (2012): 699–714.

37. "Stat Pack for the Supreme Court's 202021 Term," *SCOTUSblog*, July 2, 2021, https://www.scotusblog.com/wp-content/uploads/2021/07/Final-Stat-Pack-07.02.2021.pdf.

38. Ibid.

39. Leavitt, "Political Party and Class Influences on the Attitudes of Justices of the Supreme Court in the Twentieth Century," 18–19.

40. Ibid.

41. Lee Epstein, Thomas G. Walker, and William J. Dixon, "The Supreme Court and Criminal Justice Disputes: A Neo-Institutional Perspective," *American Journal of Political Science* 33 (1989): 838.

42. S. Sidney Ulmer, "Are Background Models Time-Bound?" *American Political Science Review* 80 (1986): 957–67; and "Scalia's Sharp Words Seem Aimed at Obama," *Houston Chronicle*, May 20, 2012, A30.

43. Keith T. Poole and Howard L. Rosenthal, *Ideology and Congress* (Piscataway, NJ: Transaction Publishers, 2007).

44. Lawrence Baum and Neal Devins, "Split Definitive: For the First Time in a Century, the Supreme Court Is Divided Solely by Political Party," *Slate. com*, November 11, 2011, http://www.slate.com/articles/news_and_politics/jurisprudence/2011/11/supreme_court_s_partisan_divide_and_obama_s_health_care_law.html.

45. Adam Liptak, "The Upshot: The Polarized Court," *New York Times*, May 10, 2014, http://www.nytimes.com/2014/05/11/upshot/the-polarized-court.html.

46. 576 U.S. _____ (2015).

47. Ibid.

48. "Scalia's Sharp Words Seem Aimed at Obama," A30.

49. 536 U.S. 765 (2002).

50. James L. Gibson, "'New-Style' Judicial Campaigns and the Legitimacy of State High Courts," *Journal of Politics* 71 (2009): 1285.

51. John Kennedy, "DeSantis Appoints Third Florida Supreme Court Justice, Completing Conservative Makeover," *Florida Times-Union*, January 22, 2019, https://www.heraldtribune.com/news/20190122/desantis-appoints-third-florida-supreme-court-justice-completing-conservative-makeover.

52. Kyle Kondik and J. Miles Coleman, "Redistricting in America, Part Three: The Republicans' Southern Prizes," University of Virginia—Center for Politics' *Crystal Ball*, August 5, 2021, https://centerforpolitics.org/crystal-b

all/articles/redistricting-in-america-part-three-the-republicans-southern-prizes/.

53. Laurel White, "Wisconsin Supreme Court Upholds GOP-Backed Lame-Duck Laws Limiting Power of Governor, AG," *Wisconsin Public Radio*, July 9, 2020, https://www.wpr.org/wisconsin-supreme-court-upholds-gop-backed-lame-duck-laws-limiting-power-governor-ag.

54. Shawn Johnson, "Wisconsin Supreme Court Sides with Republicans in Dispute over Walker Appointees," *Wisconsin Public Radio*, April 30, 2019, https://www.wpr.org/wisconsin-supreme-court-sides-republicans-dispute-over-walker-appointees.

55. Todd Richmond, "Wisconsin Supreme Court Strikes Down Governor's Mask Mandate," *Associated Press*, March 31, 2021, https://apnews.com/article/legislature-madison-wisconsin-coronavirus-pandemic-strikes-9f05a7331f7957721799b23ea381fead; Todd Richmond, "Wisconsin High Court Tosses Out Governor's Stay-Home Order," *Associated Press*, May 13, 2020, https://apnews.com/article/virus-outbreak-us-news-ap-top-news-wisconsin-courts-69eeec35356f6c25cf63b855886237c3.

56. Reid J. Epstein, "Liberal Wins Wisconsin Court Race, in Victory for Abortion Rights Backers," *New York Times*, April 4, 2023, https://www.nytimes.com/2023/04/04/us/politics/wisconsin-supreme-court-protasiewicz.html

57. S. Sidney Ulmer, "The Political Party Variable in the Michigan Supreme Court," *Journal of Public Law* 11 (1962): 352–62; and Malcolm M. Feeley, "Another Look at the 'Party Variable' in Judicial Decision-Making: An Analysis of the Michigan Supreme Court," *Polity* 4 (1971): 91–104.

58. John S. Klemanski and Julie K. Walters, "Defeating an Incumbent Chief Justice: The 2008 Michigan Supreme Court Election," *Judicature* 94 (2011): 233–38.

59. Philip L. Dubois, "The Illusion of Judicial Consensus Revisited: Partisan Conflict on an Intermediate State Court of Appeals," *American Journal of Political Science* 32 (1988): 946–67.

60. Ibid., 953–54.

61. For a good bibliography of the literature on partisan voting patterns among state judges, see ibid., 965–67. See also the literature review in this article: Paul R. Brace and Melinda Gann Hall, "Studying Courts Comparatively: The View from the American States," *Political Research Quarterly* 48 (1995): 5–29.

62. Laura Langer and Teena Wilhelm, "The Ideology of State Supreme Court Chief Justices," *Judicature* 89 (2005): 86.

63. Richardson and Vines, *The Politics of Federal Courts*, 71.

64. For a more elaborate discussion of this phenomenon, see Robert A. Carp and K. Rowland, *Policymaking and Politics in the Federal District Courts* (Knoxville: University of Tennessee Press, 1983), chap. 4.

65. Richardson and Vines, *The Politics of Federal Courts*, 73.

66. Ibid., 72.

67. For example, see Robert A. Carp and Russell Wheeler, "Sink or Swim: The Socialization of a Federal District Judge," *Journal of Public Law* 21 (1972): 359–93. See also Robert A. Carp, "The Influence of Local Needs and Conditions on the Administration of Federal Justice," paper delivered at the annual meeting of the Southwestern Political Science Association, Dallas, 1971.

68. See, for example, Angus Campbell, Philip E. Converse, Warren E. Miller, and Donald E. Stokes, *The American Voter* (New York, NY: Wiley, 1960); Everett Carll Ladd Jr. and Charles D. Hadley, *Transformations of the American Party System*, 2nd ed. (New York, NY: W. W. Norton, 1978); V. O. Key Jr., *Public Opinion and American Democracy* (New York, NY: Knopf, 1967); and Robert S. Erikson and Kent L. Tedin, *American Public Opinion: Its Origins, Content, and Impact*, 8th ed. (Boston, MA: Pearson, 2010).

69. Barbara Hinckley, *Stability and Change in Congress* (New York, NY: Harper and Row, 1978); Randall B. Ripley, *Congress: Process and Policy*, 2nd ed. (New York, NY: W. W. Norton, 1978); V. O. Key Jr., *Politics, Parties, and Pressure Groups*, 5th ed. (New York, NY: Crowell, 1964), especially chaps. 9 and 24; and J. H. Fenton, "Liberal–Conservative Divisions by Sections of the United States," *Annals* 344 (1962): 122–27.

70. John R. Schmidhauser, "Judicial Behavior and the Sectional Crisis of 1837–1860," *Journal of Politics* 23 (1961): 615–40. To be more precise, Schmidhauser found that justices' party affiliations and their geographic orientations were highly interrelated. Because the four justices who were most supportive of southern regional interests were all southern Democrats, and because the two justices with the strongest pro-northern voting patterns were northern Whigs, Schmidhauser concluded that the effects of party and region were virtually inseparable.

71. Leavitt, "Political Party and Class Influences on the Attitudes of Justices of the Supreme Court in the Twentieth Century."

72. James F. Simon, *In His Own Image* (New York, NY: David McKay, 1973), 103–4.

73. For a good review of this literature and also for some key empirical findings, see Songer, Sheehan, and Haire, *Continuity and Change on the United States Courts of Appeals*, 119–25.

74. Howard, Courts of Appeals in the Federal Judicial System, 55, 79, 156.

75. Susan Brodie Haire, "Judges' Decisions in the United States Courts of Appeals: A Reassessment of Geographic Patterns in Judicial Behavior" (Ph.D. diss., University of South Carolina, 1993), 160.

76. Steve Alumbaugh and C. K. Rowland, "The Links between Platform-Based Appointment Criteria and Trial Judges' Abortion Judgments," *Judicature* 74 (1990): 161.

77. Vilhelm Aubert, "Conscientious Objectors before Norwegian Military Courts," in *Judicial Decision-Making*, ed. Glendon Schubert (New York, NY: Free Press of Glencoe, 1963), 206–7.

78. For a review of the literature in this realm and also for some excellent historical data, see Songer, Sheehan, and Haire, *Continuity and Change on the United States Courts of Appeals*, 125–28.

79. For example, see Goldman, "Voting Behavior on the United States Courts of Appeals, 1961–1964," 370–85.

80. Haire, "Judges' Decisions in the United States Courts of Appeals," 163, and chap. 5.

81. Sara C. Benesh and Malia Reddick, "Overruled: An Event History of Lower Court Reaction to Supreme Court Alteration of Precedent," *Journal of Politics* 64 (2002): 534–50.

82. Based on data collected by Robert A. Carp, Kenneth L. Manning, and Ronald Stidham.

83. Gary Fields and Jess Bravin, "Federal Judges Aren't as Lenient as

Lawmakers Say, Studies Show," *Wall Street Journal*, October 30, 2003.

84. Carp and Wheeler, "Sink or Swim," 376.

85. Adam Liptak, "Judges Seek to Ban Secret Settlements in South Carolina," *New York Times*, September 2, 2002.

86. Howard, Courts of Appeals in the Federal Judicial System, 234.

87. For example, see Carp and Rowland, *Policymaking and Politics in the Federal District Courts*, 106–16. This discussion is based on material taken from Martin A. Levin, *Urban Politics and the Criminal Courts* (Chicago, IL: University of Chicago Press, 1977).

88. This discussion is based on material taken from Levin, *Urban Politics and the Criminal Courts.*

89. Ibid., 136–42.

90. Ibid.

91. Ibid., 142–47.

92. Glick, *Courts, Politics, and Justice*, 90. As quoted in William Mishler and Reginald S. Sheehan, "The Supreme Court as a Countermajoritarian Institution? The Impact of Public Opinion on Supreme Court Decisions," *American Political Science Review* 87 (1993): 89.

93. As quoted in Mishler and Sheehan, "The Supreme Court as a Countermajoritarian Institution?" 87–101.

94. 539 U.S. 558 (2003).

95. 478 U.S. 186 (1986).

96. John H. Cushman Jr., "O'Connor Not Retiring," *Houston Chronicle*, July 7, 2003.

97. Liptak, "Judges Seek to Ban Secret Settlements in South Carolina."

98. Brown v. Board of Education, 349 U.S. 294 (1955).

99. *Baker v. Carr*, 369 U.S. 186 (1962).

100. *Miller v. California*, 413 U.S. 15 (1973).

101. *Trop v. Dulles*, 356 U.S. 86 (1958).

102. Lawrence Baum, *The Supreme Court*, 5th ed. (Washington, DC: CQ Press, 1995), 151. For a good discussion of this subject, see David G. Barnum, "Supreme Court and Public Opinion: Judicial Decision Making in the Post–New Deal Period," *Journal of Politics* 47 (1985): 652–66.

103. *Marbury v. Madison*, 1 Cranch 137 (1803); *Brown v. Board of Education*, 347 U.S. 483 (1954); *Roe v. Wade*, 410 U.S. 113 (1973); and *Lawrence v. Texas*, 539 U.S. 558 (2003).

104. For examples of these earlier studies, see Glen T. Broach et al., "State Political Culture and Sentence Severity in Federal District Courts," *Criminology* 16 (1978): 373–82; and Ronald Stidham and Robert A. Carp, "Trial Courts' Responses to Supreme Court Policy Changes: Three Case Studies," *Law and Policy Quarterly* 4 (1982): 215–335.

105. Lee Epstein and Andrew D. Martin, "Does Public Opinion Influence the Supreme Court? Possibly Yes (But We're Not Sure Why)," *University of Pennsylvania Journal of Constitutional Law* 13 (2010): 263–81.

106. Mishler and Sheehan, "The Supreme Court as a Countermajoritarian Institution?" 96.

107. Ibid., 87–101; and William Mishler and Reginald Sheehan, "Popular Influence on Supreme Court Decisions: A Response to Helmut Norpoth and Jeffrey A. Segal," *American Political Science Review* 88 (1994): 716–24.

108. Mishler and Sheehan, "The Supreme Court as a Countermajoritarian Institution?" 96.

109. Michael W. Giles, Bethany Blackstone, and Richard L. Vining Jr., "The Supreme Court in American Democracy: Unraveling the Linkages

between Public Opinion and Judicial Decision Making," *Journal of Politics* 70 (2008): 293.

110. See, for example, Ashlyn Kuersten, Kenneth L. Manning, and Robert A. Carp, "The Political Context of Lower Court Decision Making," paper delivered at the annual meeting of the Southern Political Science Association, Savannah, Georgia, 1999; and Kenneth L. Manning, Ashlyn K. Kuersten, and Robert A. Carp, "Public Opinion and the Political Context of Lower Court Decision Making," paper delivered at the annual meeting of the American Political Science Association, Washington, DC, 2000.

111. James H. Kuklinski and John E. Stanga, "Political Participation and Government Responsiveness: The Behavior of California Superior Courts," *American Political Science Review* 73 (1979): 1090–99.

112. Melinda Gann Hall, "Electoral Politics and Strategic Voting in State Supreme Courts," *Journal of Politics* 54 (1992): 427.

113. Paul Brace and Brent D. Boyea, "State Public Opinion, the Death Penalty, and the Practice of Electing Judges," *American Journal of Political Science* 52 (2008): 360.

114. "Dallas Judge Apologizes for 'Poor Choice of Words,'" *Montrose Voice*, December 23, 1988, 5.

115. Lisa Belkin, "Texas Judge Eases Sentence for Killer of 2 Homosexuals," *New York Times*, December 17, 1988, https://timesmachine.nytimes.com/timesmachine/1988/12/17/507088.html?pageNumber=8

116. "Texas Judge Censured Over Remarks on Homosexuals," *Los Angeles Times*, November 29, 1989, https://www.latimes.com/archives/la-xpm-1989-11-29-mn-168-story.html

117. Ibid.

118. "Overheard," *Newsweek*, January 2, 1989, 13. Hampton lost an election bid in 1992 for a position on the state courts of appeals, though he continued to serve as a state district court judge until his retirement in 1996. See "Gay Rights Groups Hail Defeat of Judge in Texas," *New York Times*, December 4, 1992, https://timesmachine.nytimes.com/timesmachine/1992/12/04/892692.html?pageNumber=52

119. Brent D. Boyea, "Does Seniority Matter? The Conditional Influence of State Methods of Judicial Retention," *Social Science Quarterly* 91 (2010): 209.

120. For example, in 2003, the Supreme Court ruled that in employment discrimination suits authorized by Congress, employees do not need direct evidence of bias to bring a lawsuit against an employer; indirect evidence is sufficient. *Desert Palace, Inc. v. Costa*, 539 U.S. 90 (2003).

121. Jim Abrams, "U.S. House Votes to Protect 'Under God' in the Pledge," *Houston Chronicle*, September 24, 2004.

122. However, many constitutional scholars argue that the right of the federal courts to hear such cases stems directly from Article III of the Constitution, and that therefore Congress could not legally curtail court jurisdiction over these subjects except by initiating an amendment to the Constitution.

123. Tom S. Clark, "The Separation of Powers, Court Curbing, and Judicial Legitimacy," *American Journal of Political Science* 53 (2009): 971–89.

124. See, for example, Stephen L. Wasby, *The Impact of the United States Supreme Court* (Homewood, IL: Dorsey Press, 1970), especially 255–56; and Harrell R. Rodgers Jr. and Charles S. Bullock III, *Coercion to Compliance* (Lexington, MA: Heath, 1976).

125. National Labor Relations Board v. Jones and Laughlin Steel Corp., 301 U.S. 1 (1937); and West Coast Hotel Co. v. Parrish, 300 U.S. 379 (1937).

126. Stidham and Carp, "Trial Courts' Responses to Supreme Court Policy Changes," 218–22.

127. Clay Robison, "Perry's Prediction on Suit Draws Fire," *Houston Chronicle*, June 9, 2004.

128. G. Alan Tarr and Mary Cornelia Aldis Porter, *State Supreme Courts in State and Nation* (New Haven, CT: Yale University Press, 1988), chap. 2.

129. Ibid., 45.

130. Roger D. Groot, "The Effects of an Intermediate Appellate Court on the Supreme Court Product: The North Carolina Experience," *Wake Forest Law Review* 7 (1971): 548–72.

131. Tarr and Porter, State Supreme Courts in State and Nation, 51.

132. 539 U.S. 558 (2003).

133. Keith B. Richburg, "Calif. Ruling Shows Hurdles Remain for Gay Marriage," *Washington Post*, May 27, 2009.

134. 576 U.S. (2015).

135. E. J. Dionne Jr., "Obama Hopes Sotomayor Is the Remedy for Roberts," *Houston Chronicle*, May 28, 2009, B9.

136. This example is based on Jim Carlton and Amy Dockser Marcus, "Undocumented Worker's Suit Is Upheld," *Wall Street Journal*, February 25, 1991. The case citation is *E.E.O.C. v. Tortilleria La Mejor*, 758 F. Supp. 585 (E.D. Cal. 1991).

137. Carp and Rowland, Policymaking and Politics in the Federal District Courts, 37.

138. Jess Bravin, "Split Supreme Court Narrows Use of Wetlands Act," *Wall Street Journal*, June 20, 2006. This was in the combined set of cases: *Rapanos v. United States* and *Carabell v. U.S. Army Corps of Engineers* (nos. 04-1034 and 04-1384). See http://www.law.cornell.edu/supct/html/04–1034.ZS.html.

139. For Chief Justice Roberts's concurring opinion, see http://www.law.cornell.edu/supct/html/04-1034.ZC.html.

140. However, on matters of local economic regulation, voting differences among judges are still sharp (see Table 12.1). Only at the national level have federal judges tended to refrain from substituting their own views for those of elected officials.

141. Carp and Rowland, Policymaking and Politics in the Federal District Courts, 39.

142. At the state level, whether high court ambiguity is thought to be greater on civil rights and liberties issues or in the labor and economic realm varies from one jurisdiction to another. Note the several areas discussed in Chapter 3 of this book, under the heading "Norm Enforcement in the State Courts," in which state courts have taken the lead in bringing about policymaking innovations.

143. William J. Kitchin, *Federal District Judges: An Analysis of Judicial Perceptions* (Baltimore, MD: Collage Press, 1978), 104.

144. Carp and Rowland, Policymaking and Politics in the Federal District Courts, 40.

145. Roth v. United States and Alberts v. California, 354 U.S. 476 (1957).

146. See https://www.merriam-webster.com/dictionary/prurient

147. *Jacobellis v. Ohio*, 378 U.S. 184 (1964).

148. *Miller v. California*, 413 U.S. 15 (1973).

149. *Jacobellis v. Ohio*, 378 U.S. 184 (1964) at 197.

150. Laura Parker, "Federal Judge in Florida Rules 2 Live Crew Album Is

Obscene," *Houston Chronicle*, June 7, 1990.

151. Chuck Philips, "Appeals Court Voids Obscenity Ruling on 2 Live Crew Album," *Los Angeles Times*, May 8, 1992, http://www.articles.latimes.com/1992-05-08/news/mn-1911_1_live-crew.

152. "U.S. Judge Blocks Arkansas Law That Would Allow Librarians to Be Charged for Loaning 'Obscene' Books to Minors," *CBS News*, July 29, 2023, https://www.cbsnews.com/news/arkansas-law-blocked-librarians-criminal-charges-loaning-obscene-books-minors/

153. Ann Davis, " Locker-Room Antics Can Spark Lawsuits Alleging Harassment," *Wall Street Journal*, June 5, 1997.

154. Pat Eaton-Robb, "Judge Rules Cheerleading Is Not a Sport," *Houston Chronicle*, July 25, 2010, A16.

155. John P. McAlpin, "Father Not Allowed to Donate Embryos," *Houston Chronicle*, August 15, 2001.

156. Kitchin, Federal District Judges, 107.

157. Ibid.

158. Ibid.

159. Glick, Courts, Politics, and Justice, 335.

160. Rick A. Swanson, "Judicial Roles in State High Courts," *Judicature* 94 (2011): 177.

161. Carp and Rowland, Policymaking and Politics in the Federal District Courts, 14.

CHAPTER 13

1. From an interview with an appeals court judge, as quoted in J. Woodford Howard Jr., *Courts of Appeals in the Federal Judicial System* (Princeton, NJ: Princeton University Press, 1981), 135.

2. However, for a discussion of the causes of dissent in state supreme courts and how such causes may differ from those at the federal level, see Paul Brace and Melinda Gann Hall, "Neo-Institutionalism and Dissent in State Supreme Courts," *Journal of Politics* 52 (1990): 54–70.

3. See *A Reporter's Guide to Applications Pending Before the Supreme Court of the United States*, document accessed July 28, 2021, and available at https://www.supremecourt.gov/publicinfo/reportersguide.pdf.

4. "Stat Pack for the Supreme Court's 202021 Term," *SCOTUSblog*, July 2, 2021, https://www.scotusblog.com/wp-content/uploads/2021/07/Final-Stat-Pack-07.02.2021.pdf.

5. The Supreme Court Case Selections Act of 1988, Public Law No. 100-352 (1988).

6. Alabama, for example, imposes a burdensome original jurisdiction on its supreme court, and Arizona requires its high court to hear appeals in a wide variety of cases. However, Florida has given its supreme court broad discretion in case selection. See G. Alan Tarr and Mary Cornelia Aldis Porter, *State Supreme Courts in State and Nation* (New Haven, CT: Yale University Press, 1988), 49.

7. Joseph Tanenhaus, Marvin Schick, Matthew Muraskin, and Daniel Rosen, "The Supreme Court's Certiorari Jurisdiction: Cue Theory," in *Judicial Decision-Making*, ed. Glendon Schubert (New York, NY: Free Press, 1963), 111–32.

8. See, for example, S. Sidney Ulmer, "The Decision to Grant Certiorari as an Indicator to Decision 'On the Merits,'" *Polity* 4 (1972): 429–47. Nevertheless, in a later study, Ulmer found

that despite the inordinate willingness of the high court to hear cases brought by the US government, such willingness did not translate into subsequent support for the government's position, at least in civil liberties cases. See S. Sidney Ulmer, "Governmental Litigants, Underdogs, and Civil Liberties in the Supreme Court: 1903–1968 Terms," *Journal of Politics* 47 (1985): 899–909.

9. See, for example, Donald R. Songer, "Concern for Policy Outputs as a Cue for Supreme Court Decisions on Certiorari," *Journal of Politics* 41 (1979): 1185–94; and S. Sidney Ulmer, "Selecting Cases for Supreme Court Review: An Underdog Model," *American Political Science Review* 72 (1978): 902–1010.

10. Virginia C. Armstrong and Charles A. Johnson, "Certiorari Decisions by the Warren and Burger Courts: Is Cue Theory Time Bound?" *Polity* 15 (1982): 141–50.

11. Jeffrey A. Segal and Harold J. Spaeth, "Rehnquist Court Disposition of Lower Court Decisions: Affirmation Not Reversal," *Judicature* 74 (1990): 84–88.

12. Henry R. Glick, *Courts, Politics, and Justice*, 3rd ed. (New York, NY: McGraw-Hill, 1993), 280.

13. A good discussion of the nature of conflict on the US Supreme Court can be found in Phillip J. Cooper, *Battles on the Bench: Conflict inside the Supreme Court* (Lawrence: University Press of Kansas, 1995).

14. J. Woodford Howard Jr., "On the Fluidity of Judicial Choice," *American Political Science Review* 62 (1968): 43–57.

15. *The Brennan Center for Justice: Diversity on the Bench*, accessed July 28, 2021, at https://www.brennancenter.org/issues/strengthen-our-courts/promote-fair-courts/diversity-bench.

16. See, for example, Jonathan P. Kastellac, "Racial Diversity and Judicial Influence on Appellate Courts," *American Journal of Political Science* 57 (2013): 167–83; Christina L. Boyd, Lee Epstein, and Andrew D. Martin, "Untangling the Causal Effects of Sex on Judging," *American Journal of Political Science* 54 (2010): 389–411.

17. See, for example, Jan Crawford Greenburg, Supreme Conflict: The Inside Story of the Struggle for Control of the United States Supreme Court (New York, NY: Penguin Group, 2008); Edward Lazarus, Closed Chambers: The Rise, Fall, and Future of the Modern Supreme Court (New York, NY: Penguin Group, 2005); Walter F. Murphy, Elements of Judicial Strategy (Chicago, IL: University of Chicago Press, 1964); and Bob Woodward and Scott Armstrong, The Brethren: Inside the Supreme Court (New York, NY: Simon & Schuster, 1979).

18. In the parlance of judicial scholars, this is referred to as the social leadership function. See David J. Danelski, "The Influence of the Chief Justice in the Decisional Process," in *Courts, Judges, and Politics*, 3rd ed., ed. Walter F. Murphy and C. Herman Pritchett (New York, NY: Random House, 1979), 695–703. For an empirical analysis of the phenomena discussed by Danelski, see Stacia L. Haynie, "Leadership and Consensus on the U.S. Supreme Court," *Journal of Politics* 54 (1992): 1158–69.

19. Henry Robert Glick, *Supreme Courts in State Politics* (New York, NY: Basic Books, 1971), 59.

20. This is termed the *task leadership function*. See Danelski, "The Influence of the Chief Justice in the Decisional Process."

21. Howard, Courts of Appeals in the Federal Judicial System, 230–31.

22. Adam Liptak, "Chief Justice Praises the Courts' Responses to the Pandemic," *New York Times*, December 31, 2020, https://www.nytimes.com/2020/12/31/us/supreme-court-coronavirus.html.

23. David Slayton, administrative director of the state's court administration office, as quoted by Jolie McCullough, "A Texas Man Was Sent to Trial with the Coronavirus. Jurors Weren't Told They Were Exposed until after Deliberations Ended," *Texas Tribune*, January 5, 2021, https://www.texas-tribune.org/2021/01/05/texas-jury-trials-coronavirus/.

24. As quoted by the National Center for State Courts, *Coronavirus and the Courts*, accessed July 28, 2021, https://www.ncsc.org/newsroom/public-health-emergency.

25. Murphy, Elements of Judicial Strategy, 44.

26. As quoted in ibid.

27. Glick, Supreme Courts in State Politics, 89.

28. James F. Spriggs II, Forrest Maltzman, and Paul J. Wahlbeck, "Bargaining on the U.S. Supreme Court: Justices' Responses to Majority Opinion Drafts," *Journal of Politics* 61 (1999): 503.

29. Jeffrey R. Lax and Charles M. Cameron, "Bargaining and Opinion Assignment on the U.S. Supreme Court," *The Journal of Law, Economics, & Organization* 23 (2007): 276.

30. *Roe v. Wade*, 410 U.S. 113 (1973); and *Doe v. Bolton*, 410 U.S. 179 (1973).

31. Woodward and Armstrong, *The Brethren*, chaps. titled "1971 Term" and "1972 Term."

32. Ibid., 233.

33. Glick, Supreme Courts in State Politics, 66.

34. Murphy, Elements of Judicial Strategy, 57.

35. Howard, Courts of Appeals in the Federal Judicial System, 209.

36. David Von Drehle, "Antonin Scalia's Lasting Influence," *Time*, February 13, 2016, https://time.com/4220770/antonin-scalia-influence/

37. Northwest Austin Municipal Utility District Number One v. Holder, Docket No. 08-322 (2009).

38. Nina Totenberg, "Supreme Court Closes Deeply Divided Term," *National Public Radio*, July 2, 2009, http://www.npr.org/templates/story/story.php?storyId5106185978.

39. 594 U.S. ____ (2021).

40. Nina Totenberg, "The Supreme Court Deals a New Blow to Voting Rights, Upholding Arizona Restrictions," *National Public Radio*, July 1, 2021, https://www.npr.org/2021/07/01/998758022/the-supreme-court-upheld-upholds-arizona-measures-that-restrict-voting.

41. As quoted in Charles Fairman, *Mr. Justice Miller and the Supreme Court, 1862–1890* (Cambridge, MA: Harvard University Press, 1939), 320.

42. Adam Liptak and Alicia Parlapiano, "Conservatives in Charge, the Supreme Court Moved Right," *New York Times*, June 28, 2018, https://www.nytimes.com/interactive/2018/06/28/us/politics/supreme-court-2017-term-moved-right.html.

43. John Paul Stevens, *Five Chiefs: A Supreme Court Memoir* (New York: Little, Brown and Company, 2011).

44. John O. McGinnis, "The Decider," *Wall Street Journal*, August 27, 2009, http://online.wsj.com/article/SB10001424052970203706604574371430415946724.html.

45. Lee Epstein and Tonja Jacobi, "Super Medians," *Stanford Law Review* 61 (2008): 37–100.
46. Adam Liptak, "A Supreme Court Term Marked by a Conservative Majority in Flux," *New York Times*, July 2, 2021, https://www.nytimes.com/2021/07/02/us/supreme-court-conservative-voting-rights.html.
47. Keep in mind that typically over 40 percent of cases each term are decided unanimously. In 2020–2021, 43 percent of cases were decided by a unanimous decision; the average over the previous decade was 47 percent. See "Stat Pack for the Supreme Court's 202021 Term," https://www.scotus-blog.com/wp-content/uploads/2021/07/Final-Stat-Pack-07.02.2021.pdf.
48. Jess Bravin, "John Roberts and Brett Kavanaugh Are Now the Supreme Court's Swing Votes," *Wall Street Journal*, July 7, 2023, https://www.wsj.com/articles/john-roberts-and-brett-kavanaugh-are-now-the-supreme-courts-swing-votes-8f90c4f6
49. Webster v. Reproductive Health Services, 492 U.S. 490 (1989).
50. David A. Kaplan, "A Legacy of Strife: Marshall's Papers Shed Light on the Court—and the Library of Congress," *Newsweek*, June 7, 1993, 69.
51. Benjamin Weiser and Bob Woodward, "*Roe* Decision Nearly Overturned 4 Years Ago, Justice's Files Show," *Houston Chronicle*, May 24, 1993.
52. Joan Biskupic, "Exclusive: How Samuel Alito Got Canceled from the Supreme Court Social Media Majority," *CNN.com*, July 31, 2024, https://www.cnn.com/2024/07/31/politics/samuel-alito-supreme-court-netchoice-social-media-biskupic/index.html
53. *Clinton v. Jones*, 520 U.S. 681 (1997).
54. Henry Robert Glick and Kenneth N. Vines, *State Court Systems* (Englewood Cliffs, NJ: Prentice-Hall, 1973), 79.
55. Murphy, Elements of Judicial Strategy, 63–64.
56. 576 U.S. (2015), Scalia dissenting.
57. *Lawrence v. Texas*, 539 U.S. 558 (2003), Scalia dissenting.
58. 576 U.S. (2015), Scalia dissenting.
59. Theodore Eisenberg and Geoffrey P. Miller, "Reversal, Dissent, and Variability in State Supreme Courts: The Centrality of Jurisdictional Source," *Boston University Law Review* 89 (2009): 1451–1504.
60. Ibid.
61. Edward Fitzpatrick, "Scalia's Virulence Undercuts His Influence, and That's No Jiggery-Pokery," *Providence Journal*, July 1, 2015, http://www.provi-dencejournal.com/article/20150701/NEWS/150709908.
62. As quoted in Howard, Courts of Appeals in the Federal Judicial System, 209.
63. Woodward and Armstrong, *The Brethren*, 187, 188.
64. 567 U.S. (2012).
65. Jan Crawford, "Roberts Switched Views to Uphold Health Care Law," *CBS News*, July 1, 2012, http://www.cbsnews.com/8301-3460_162-57464549/roberts-switched-views-to-uphold-health-care-law/.
66. Nina Totenberg, "Federal Judge Richard Posner: The GOP Has Made Me Less Conservative," *National Public Radio,* July 5, 2012, http://www.npr.org/blogs/itsallpolitics/2012/07/05/156319272/federal-judge-richard-posner-the-gop-has-made-me-less-conservative.
67. Murphy, Elements of Judicial Strategy, 61.

68. As quoted in Howard, Courts of Appeals in the Federal Judicial System, 209.

69. Totenberg, "Federal Judge Richard Posner: The GOP Has Made Me Less Conservative."

70. Danelski, "The Influence of the Chief Justice in the Decisional Process," 696.

71. David M. O'Brien, "The Supreme Court: From Warren to Burger to Rehnquist," *Political Science* 20 (1987): 12.

72. Stephen Wermiel, "Consensus Builder: Rehnquist Emerges as a Skillful Leader of the Court's Majority," *Wall Street Journal*, June 29, 1989.

73. For more on Rehnquist's leadership of the Court, see Mark Tushnet, *A Court Divided: The Rehnquist Court and the Future of Constitutional Law* (New York, NY: W. W. Norton, 2005).

74. Linda Greenhouse, "Roberts Is at Court's Helm, But He Isn't Yet in Control," *New York Times*, July 2, 2006.

75. Jeffrey Rosen, "The Trial of John Roberts," *New York Times*, September 12, 2009, http://www.nytimes.com/2009/09/13/opinion/13rosen.html.

76. Adam Liptak, "A Supreme Court Term Marked by a Conservative Majority in Flux," *New York Times,* July 2, 2021, https://www.nytimes.com/2021/07/02/us/supreme-court-conservative-voting-rights.html.

77. "Stat Pack for the Supreme Court's 202021 Term," *SCOTUSblog*, July 2, 2021, https://www.scotusblog.com/wp-content/uploads/2021/07/Final-Stat-Pack-07.02.2021.pdf.

78. Joan Biskupic, "Analysis: John Roberts Doesn't Want to Hear Any Dissent about His Supreme Court," *CNN*, July 2, 2023, https://www.cnn.com/2023/07/02/politics/john-roberts-scotus-dissent/index.html

79. Nina Totenberg, "Supreme Court Says Justices Were Interviewed about the Leaked Draft Opinion," *National Public Radio*, January 20, 2023, https://www.npr.org/2023/01/20/1150512960/supreme-court-justices-interviewed-leaked-opinion-report-roe-wade

80. Glenn Fine, "Why the Supreme Court's Leak Investigation Failed," *The Atlantic*, March 6, 2023, https://www.theatlantic.com/ideas/archive/2023/03/supreme-court-dobbs-leak-investigation-internal-oversight/673283/

81. Mark Sherman, "Most of Justice Thomas' $267,000 Loan for an RV Seems to Have Been Forgiven, Senate Democrats Say," *Associated Press*, October 25, 2023, https://apnews.com/article/supreme-court-clarence-thomas-motorcoach-loan-ethics-afed2073e0d7cf4a994256ce35d5063f

82. Rose Horowitch and Lawrence Hurley, "Supreme Court Draws Fire for Ethics Inaction," *NBC News*, April 26, 2023, https://www.nbcnews.com/politics/supreme-court/supreme-court-draws-fire-ethics-inaction-rcna81544

83. Ibid.

84. Cooper Burton, "The Supreme Court Starts Its New Term with Dismal Approval Ratings," *ABC News*, October 2, 2023, https://abcnews.go.com/538/supreme-court-starts-new-term-dismal-approval-ratings/story?id=103609006

85. Jeffrey M. Jones, "Supreme Court Approval Holds at Record Low," *Gallup*, August 2, 2023, https://news.gallup.com/poll/509234/supreme-court-approval-holds-record-low.aspx

86. Olivia Alafriz, "Supreme Court's Approval Rating Ticks Up, Poll Shows," *Politico.com*, April 3, 2024, https://www.politico.com/news/2024/04/03/supreme-court-approval-ratings-00150365

87. Justin Jouvenal, "Supreme Court Ethics Remain at Center Stage after Hard-Right Rulings," *Washington Post*, July 6, 2024, https://www.washingtonpost.com/politics/2024/07/06/supreme-court-ethics-public-trust/

88. Victoria Balara, "Fox News Poll: Supreme Court Approval Rating Drops to Record Low," *Fox News*, July 16, 2024, https://www.foxnews.com/official-polls/fox-news-poll-supreme-court-approval-rating-drops-record-low

89. Katie Rogers, "Warning of 'Extreme' Agenda, Biden Calls for Supreme Court Overhaul," *New York Times*, July 29, 2024, https://www.nytimes.com/2024/07/29/us/politics/biden-supreme-court-austin-texas.html

90. Victoria Balara, "Fox News Poll: Supreme Court Approval Rating Drops to Record Low," *Fox News*, July 16, 2024, https://www.foxnews.com/official-polls/fox-news-poll-supreme-court-approval-rating-drops-record-low

91. Katie Rogers, "Warning of 'Extreme' Agenda, Biden Calls for Supreme Court Overhaul," *New York Times*, July 29, 2024, https://www.nytimes.com/2024/07/29/us/politics/biden-supreme-court-austin-texas.html

92. Erwin Chemerinsky, "Time Is Running Out for John Roberts and the Supreme Court," *New York Times*, June 12, 2023, https://www.nytimes.com/2023/06/12/opinion/ethics-supreme-court-congress.html

93. William H. Rehnquist, *The Supreme Court* (New York: Knopf, 2001), 23435.

94. For a discussion of research findings about the discuss list and the US Supreme Court, see Gregory A. Caldeira and John R. Wright, "The Discuss List: Agenda Building in the Supreme Court," *Law and Society Review* 24 (1990): 809–36.

95. Arthur D. Hellman, "The Supreme Court's Shrunken 'Discuss List'" FedSoc Blog (The Federalist Society), November 22, 2023, https://fedsoc.org/commentary/fedsoc-blog/the-supreme-court-s-shrunken-discuss-list

96. For an excellent discussion of this subject, see David W. Rohde and Harold J. Spaeth, *Supreme Court Decision Making* (San Francisco, CA: Freeman, 1976), chap. 8.

97. Lee Epstein and Jeffrey A. Segal, "Measuring Issue Salience," *American Journal of Political Science* 44 (2000): 66–83.

98. Linda Greenhouse, "Chief Justice Roberts in His Own Voice: The Chief Justice's Self-Assignment of Majority Opinions," *Judicature* 97 (2013): 90–97.

99. 576 U.S. 473 (2015).

100. 567 U.S. 519 (2012).

101. However, some research has challenged the "conventional wisdom . . . that assignment of the majority opinion to the marginal member of the minimum winning original coalition might ensure its survival." In a study of the Warren Court, the researchers found that "although the marginal justice is substantially advantaged in opinion assignment, coalition maintenance is not thereby enhanced." Saul Brenner and Harold J. Spaeth, "Majority Opinion Assignments and the Maintenance of the Original Coalition on the Warren Court," *American Journal of Political Science* 32 (1988): 72–81. See also Saul Brenner, "Reassigning the Majority Opinion on the United States Supreme Court," *Justice System Journal* 11 (1986): 186–95.

102. For a good example, see Paul J. Wahlbeck, "Strategy and Constraints on Supreme Court Opinion Assignment," *University of Pennsylvania Law Review* 154 (2006): 1729–55.

103. Forrest Maltzman and Paul J. Wahlbeck, "May It Please the Chief? Opinion Assignments in the Rehnquist Court," *American Journal of Political Science* 40 (1996): 438.

104. Jeffrey Rosen, "The Supreme Court's Group Hug," *Time*, July 3, 2008, http://www.time.com/time/magazine/article/0,9171,1820165,00.html.

105. Donald Dale Jackson, *Judges* (New York, NY: Atheneum, 1974), 329.

106. As quoted in Danelski, "The Influence of the Chief Justice in the Decisional Process," 698. For a good discussion of the importance of Stone's leadership style as it affected future chief justiceships, see Thomas G. Walker, Lee Epstein, and William J. Dixon, "On the Mysterious Demise of Consensual Norms in the United States Supreme Court," *Journal of Politics* 50 (1988): 361–89.

107. For two excellent studies of the role and work of the chief judge of the US appeals courts, see Stephen L. Wasby, "The Work of a Circuit's Chief Judges," *Justice System Journal* 24 (2003): 63–90; and Virginia A. Hettinger, Stefanie A. Lindquist, and Wendy L. Martinek, "The Role and Impact of Chief Judges on the United States Courts of Appeals," *Justice System Journal* 24 (2003): 91–117.

108. As quoted in Howard, Courts of Appeals in the Federal Judicial System, 228.

109. Ibid., 229. In a few instances the chief judges have been accused of stacking the three-judge panels, which are supposed to operate on a more or less random, rotational basis. For example, see *Armstrong v. Board of Educ. of Birmingham*, 323 F.2d 333, 352–61 (5th Cir. 1963), 48 F.R.D. 141, 182 (1969). See also Burton M. Atkins and William Zavoina, "Judicial Leadership on the Court of Appeals: A Probability Analysis of Panel Assignment in Race Relations Cases on the Fifth Circuit," *American Journal of Political Science* 18 (1974): 701–11.

110. For an excellent study of the recruitment process for state supreme court chief justices, see Laura Langer, Jody McMullen, Nicholas P. Ray, and Daniel D. Stratton, "Recruitment of Chief Justices on State Supreme Courts: A Choice between Institutional and Personal Goals," *Journal of Politics* 65 (2003): 656–75.

111. Patrick Marley, "Voters Back Amendment on Chief Justice Selection," *Milwaukee Journal Sentinel*, April 7, 2015, http://www.jsonline.com/news/statepolitics/voters-back-amendment-on-chief-justice-selection-b99475888z1-298998481.html.

112. Victor E. Flango, Craig R. Ducat, and R. Neal McKnight, "Measuring Leadership through Opinion Assignments in Two State Supreme Courts," in *Judicial Conflict and Consensus: Behavioral Studies of American Appellate Courts*, ed. Sheldon Goldman and Charles Lamb (Lexington: University Press of Kentucky, 1986), 217.

113. Ibid., 218–19.

114. Tarr and Porter, State Supreme Courts in State and Nation, 186.

115. Ibid., 148.

116. Saul Brenner, "Fluidity on the United States Supreme Court: A Reexamination," *American Journal of Political Science* 24 (1980): 526–35.

117. For an article on this subject, and one that addresses some aspects not included in Brenner's earlier article, see Robert H. Dorff and Saul Brenner, "Conformity Voting on the United States Supreme Court," *Journal of Politics* 54 (1992): 762–75.

118. Forrest Maltzman and Paul J. Wahlbeck, "Strategic Policy Considerations and Voting Fluidity on the

Burger Court," *American Political Science Review* 90 (1996): 590–91.

119. For example, see Forrest Maltzman, James F. Spriggs, and Paul J. Wahlbeck, *Crafting Law on the Supreme Court: The Collegial Game* (New York, NY: Cambridge University Press, 2000); Goldman and Lamb, *Judicial Conflict and Consensus*, pts. 2 and 3; and Glick, *Supreme Courts in State Politics*.

120. Rick A. Swanson, "Judicial Perceptions of Voting Fluidity on State Supreme Courts," *Justice System Journal* 28 (2007): 199–218.

121. For an excellent statement of attitude theory, along with a summary of the relevant literature, see Jeffrey A. Segal and Harold J. Spaeth, *The Supreme Court and the Attitudinal Model* (New York, NY: Cambridge University Press, 1993); and Jeffrey A. Segal and Harold J. Spaeth, *The Supreme Court and the Attitudinal Model Revisited* (New York, NY: Cambridge University Press, 2002). For a sophisticated debate among judicial scholars about the utility of various forms of attitudinal models, see the first six articles in *American Journal of Political Science* 40 (1996): 971–1083.

122. Rohde and Spaeth, Supreme Court Decision Making, 75.

123. Segal and Spaeth, The Supreme Court and the Attitudinal Model.

124. C. K. Rowland and Robert A. Carp, *Politics & Judgment in Federal District Courts* (Lawrence: University Press of Kansas, 1996), especially chaps. 6 and 7.

125. Harold J. Spaeth, "The Attitudinal Model," in *Contemplating Courts*, ed. Lee Epstein (Washington, DC: CQ Press, 1995), 313.

126. Lee Epstein, William M. Landes, and Richard A. Posner, *The Behavior of Federal Judges* (Cambridge, MA: Harvard University Press, 2013).

127. Cass R. Sunstein, David Schkade, Lisa M. Ellman, and Andres Sawicki, *Are Judges Political? An Empirical Analysis of the Federal Judiciary* (Washington, DC: Brookings Institution Press, 2006).

128. Harold J. Spaeth, "Chief Justice Rehnquist: 'Poster Child' for the Attitudinal Model," *Judicature* 89 (2005): 108–15.

129. Glendon Schubert and David J. Danelski, eds., Comparative Judicial Behavior: Cross-Cultural Studies of Political Decision-Making in the East and West (New York, NY: Oxford University Press, 1969).

130. Lee Epstein and Thomas G. Walker, "The Role of the Supreme Court in American Society: Playing the Reconstruction Game," in *Contemplating Courts*, ed. Epstein, 322.

131. For example, see Lee Epstein and Jack Knight, *The Choices Justices Make* (Washington, DC: CQ Press, 1998).

132. Forrest Maltzman, James F. Spriggs II, and Paul J. Wahlbeck, *Crafting Law on the Supreme Court: The Collegial Game* (New York, NY: Cambridge University Press, 2000).

133. Thomas H. Hammond, Chris W. Bonneau, and Reginald S. Sheehan, *Strategic Behavior and Policy Choice on the U.S. Supreme Court* (Palo Alto, CA: Stanford University Press, 2005).

134. Robert Moog, "The Indian Supreme Court in the 1990s," *Judicature* 85 (2002): 268–76.

135. Lori Hausegger and Lawrence Baum, "Inviting Congressional Action: A Study of Supreme Court Motivations in Statutory Interpretation," *American Journal of Political Science* 43 (1999): 182.

136. 567 U.S. 519 (2012).

137. Ibid.

138. Greg Stohr, "Record Number of Amicus Briefs Filed in Health Care Cases," *Bloomberg News*, March 15, 2012, http://go.bloomberg.com/health-care-supreme-court/2012-03-15/record-number-of-amicus-briefs-filed-in-health-care-cases/.

139. The justices shared these thoughts during an unusual television interview broadcast by *ABC News* on July 7, 2003. See *Dallas Morning News*, "Two High Court Justices Grant Rare TV Interview," July 7, 2003, http://www.dallasnews.com/sharedcontent/dallas/politics/national/stories/070703dnnatjustices.53019.html.

140. Patrick D. Schmidt and David A. Yalof, "The 'Swing Voter' Revisited: Justice Anthony Kennedy and the First Amendment Right of Free Speech," *Political Research Quarterly* 57 (2004): 209–17.

141. Scott Lemieux, as quoted in *The Guardian* (UK), in "Which Way Will the U.S. Supreme Court Rule on Obamacare: Panel Predictions," June 27, 2012, http://www.guardian.co.uk/commentisfree/2012/jun/27/us-supreme-court-rule-Obamacare.

142. Adam Liptak, "Scalia Says He Had No 'Falling Out' with Chief Justice," *New York Times*, July 19, 2012, http://www.nytimes.com/2012/07/19/us/politics/justice-scalia-says-he-had-no-falling-out-with-chief-justice-roberts.html.

143. James B. Stewart, "In Obama's Victory, a Loss for Congress," *New York Times*, June 29, 2012, http://www.nytimes.com/2012/06/30/us/conservatives-see-silver-lining-in-health-ruling.html.

144. Ibid.

145. Joshua Green, "What Conservatives Have to Like in the Health-Care Ruling," *Business Week*, June 29, 2012, http://www.businessweek.com/articles/2012-06-29/what-conservatives-have-to-like-in-the-health-care-ruling.

146. *CBS News*, "Harvard Law Prof.: Roberts' Ruling Was Conservative," June 29, 2012, http://www.cbsnews.com/8301-505263_162-57463529/har-vard-law-prof.-roberts-ruling-was-conservative/.

147. Charles Lane, "Nominee's Rulings Lean Right," *Washington Post*, September 13, 2005, http://www.washingtonpost.com/wp-dyn/content/article/2005/09/12/AR2005091201511.html.

148. For more on this background, see James Taranto, "Heritage Rewrites History," *Wall Street Journal*, February 8, 2012, http://online.wsj.com/article/SB10001424052970204369404577211161144786448.html.

149. *Gallup.com*, "Americans' Views on the Healthcare Law," June 22, 2012, http://www.gallup.com/poll/155300/Gallup-Editors-Americans-Views-Health-care-Law.aspx.

150. Patricia Zengerle, "Most Americans Oppose Health Law but Like Provisions," *Reuters.com*, http://www.reuters.com/article/2012/06/25/us-usa-campaign-healthcare-idUSBRE85N01M20120625.

151. Miranda Nazzaro, "6 in 10 Hold Favorable View of Affordable Care Act in New Polling," *The Hill*, February 21, 2024, https://thehill.com/policy/healthcare/4480695-6-in-10-hold-favorable-view-of-affordable-care-act-in-new-polling/

152. For examples of these combined or integrated approaches, see Donald R. Songer and Susan Haire, "Integrating Alternative Approaches to the Study of Judicial Voting: Obscenity Cases in the U.S. Courts of Appeals," *American Journal of Political Science* 36 (1992): 963–82; Paul Brace and Melinda Gann Hall, "Integrated Models of Judicial Dissent," *Journal of Politics* 55 (1993): 914–35; and Carol Ann Traut and

Craig F. Emmert, "Expanding the Integrated Model of Judicial Decision Making: The California Justices and Capital Punishment," *Journal of Politics* 60 (1998): 1166–80.

CHAPTER 14

1. *Miranda v. Arizona*, 384 U.S. 436 (1966).
2. *Dobbs v. Jackson Women's Health Organization*, 597 U.S. 215 (2022).
3. For a good description of the bureaucratic theory, see Walter F. Murphy, "Chief Justice Taft and the Lower Court Bureaucracy: A Study in Judicial Administration," *Journal of Politics* 24 (1962): 453–76.
4. Richard J. Richardson and Kenneth N. Vines, *The Politics of Federal Courts* (Boston, MA: Little, Brown, 1970), 144.
5. Lawrence Baum, "Implementation of Judicial Decisions: An Organizational Analysis," *American Politics Quarterly* 4 (1976): 91.
6. The desegregation policy was announced in *Brown v. Board of Education of Topeka*, 347 U.S. 483 (1954). For a study of the lower federal courts involved in implementing *Brown*, see Jack W. Peltason, *Fifty-Eight Lonely Men* (New York. NY: Harcourt, Brace and World, 1961).
7. For an excellent account of the school desegregation struggle in Georgia, see Harrell R. Rodgers Jr. and Charles S. Bullock III, *Coercion to Compliance* (Lexington, MA: Lexington Books, 1976).
8. See Jennifer Barnes Bowie, Donald R. Songer, and John Szmer, *A View from the Bench and Chambers: Examining Judicial Process and Decision Making on the U.S. Courts of Appeals* (Charlottesville, VA: University of Virginia Press, 2014), 17980.
9. *Brown v. Board of Education of Topeka II*, 349 U.S. 294 (1955).
10. *Eknes-Tucker v. Governor of Alabama*, 80 F.4d 1205 (2023).
11. *Doe v. Ladapo* (2024), 31. Opinion available at https://storage.courtlistener.com/recap/gov.uscourts.flnd.460963/gov.uscourts.flnd.460963.223.0.pdf?utm_source=substack&utm_medium=email (accessed June 17, 2024).
12. Ibid., 38.
13. Ibid., 7172.
14. The statement was made by Justice Potter Stewart in *Jacobellis v. Ohio*, 378 U.S. 184 (1964).
15. *Furman v. Georgia*, 408 U.S. 238 (1972). A good account of the various views held by the justices, as well as the behind-the-scenes events leading to the final decision, may be found in Bob Woodward and Scott Armstrong, *The Brethren: Inside the Supreme Court* (New York, NY: Simon & Schuster, 1979), 205–20.
16. *Gregg v. Georgia*, 428 U.S. 153 (1976).
17. For a good discussion of this point, with pertinent examples, see Bradley C. Canon and Charles A. Johnson, *Judicial Policies: Implementation and Impact*, 2nd ed. (Washington, DC: CQ Press, 1999), 49–50.
18. Ibid., 29.
19. *Flowers v. Mississippi*, 588 U.S. 284 (2019), 304.
20. Ibid., 315.
21. Ibid., 306.
22. Ibid., 311.
23. Ibid., 316.
24. Texas Supreme Court, *Flowers v. Mississippi*, 287 So.3d 905 (2019).
25. For an excellent podcast regarding the Curtis Flowers case, see *In the Dark*, Season Two: https://features.a

pmreports.org/in-the-dark/season-two/.

26. *Searcy v. Strange*, Civil Action No. 14-0208-CG-N, U.S. District Court for the Southern District of Alabama, 2015.

27. See the discussion of Chief Justice Roy S. Moore's arguments and actions in Erik Eckholm, "Supreme Court Undercuts Alabama Chief Justice's Argument to Delay Same-Sex Marriages," *New York Times*, February 9, 2015, http://nyti.ms/1M7QCCw; Campbell Robertson, "U.S. Orders Alabama to License Gay Unions," *New York Times*, February 12, 2015, http:// nyti.ms/1zajnW5; and Campbell Robertson, "Alabama Court Orders a Halt to Same-Sex Marriage Licenses," *New York Times*, March 3, 2015, http:// nyti.ms/1GPuysx. Our discussion of the events preceding the U.S. Supreme Court's hearing of the same-sex marriage issue relies heavily on these three articles.

28. See John Gruhl, "The Supreme Court's Impact on the Law of Libel: Compliance by Lower Federal Courts," *Western Political Quarterly* 33 (1980): 517.

29. *Miranda v. Arizona*, 384 U.S. 436 (1966).

30. See Donald R. Songer and Reginald S. Sheehan, "Supreme Court Impact on Compliance and Outcomes: *Miranda* and *New York Times* in the United States Courts of Appeals," *Western Political Quarterly* 43 (1990): 307.

31. Michael A. Zilis and Xander Borne, "Defying the Supreme Court: The Impact of Overt Resistance to Landmark Legal Rulings," *Social Science Quarterly* 102 (2021): 920–38.

32. *Arizona v. Gant*, 556 U.S. 332 (2009).

33. Ibid. Also note the case facts described come from the case.

34. *United States v. Ferebee*, 957 F.3d 406 (2020).

35. Ibid. The case facts described come from the decision.

36. Ibid., 419.

37. See G. Alan Tarr, *Understanding State Constitutions* (Princeton, NJ: Princeton University Press, 1998), 166.

38. See Barry Latzer, "The Hidden Conservatism of the State Court Revolution," *Judicature* 74 (1991): 190–97; and Michael Esler, "State Supreme Court Commitment to State Law," *Judicature* 78 (1994): 25–32.

39. See Peltason, *Fifty-Eight Lonely Men*; and Richardson and Vines, *The Politics of Federal Courts*, 98–99.

40. *Griswold v. Connecticut*, 381 U.S. 479 (1965).

41. *Roe v. Wade*, 314 F. Supp. 1217 (1970).

42. Ronald Stidham and Robert A. Carp, "U.S. Trial Court Reactions to Changes in Civil Rights and Civil Liberties Policies," *Southeastern Political Review* 12 (1984): 7.

43. See, for example, Kathleen L. Barber, "Partisan Values in the Lower Courts: Reapportionment in Ohio and Michigan," *Case Western Reserve Law Review* 20 (1969): 406–7; Robert A. Carp and C. K. Rowland, *Policymaking and Politics in the Federal District Courts* (Knoxville, TN: University of Tennessee Press, 1983), chap. 2; C. K. Rowland and Robert A. Carp, "A Longitudinal Study of Party Effects on Federal District Court Policy Propensities," *American Journal of Political Science* 24 (1980): 301; and Ronald Stidham, Robert A. Carp, and C. K. Rowland, "Women's Rights before the Federal District Courts, 1971–1977," *American Politics Quarterly* 11 (1983): 214.

44. See, for example, Peltason, *Fifty-Eight Lonely Men*; Kenneth N. Vines, "Federal District Judges and Race Relations Cases in the South," *Journal of Politics* 26 (1964): 338–57;

Richardson and Vines, *The Politics of Federal Courts*, 93–100; and Michael W. Giles and Thomas G. Walker, "Judicial Policy-Making and Southern School Segregation," *Journal of Politics* 37 (1975): 917–36.

45. Michael W. Giles and Thomas G. Walker, "Judicial Policy-Making and Southern School Segregation," 931.

46. Ali S. Masood and Donald R. Songer, "Reevaluating the Implications of Decision-Making Models: The Role of Summary Decisions in U.S. Supreme Court Analysis," *Journal of Law and Courts* 1 (2013): 365.

47. Ali S. Masood, Benjamin J. Kassow, and Donald R. Songer, "The Aggregate Dynamics of Lower Court Responses to the US Supreme Court," *Journal of Law and Courts* 7 (2019): 182.

48. For a good discussion of this practice, with pertinent examples, see Leon Friedman, "Overruling the Court," *Hofstra Law Report* 11 (Spring 2002): 16–19.

49. Public Law 111–112, S. 181.

50. *Ledbetter v. Goodyear Tire & Rubber, Co.*, 550 U.S. 618 (2007).

51. See Kate Pickert, "Lilly Ledbetter," *Time*, January 29, 2009, https://time.com/archive/6914011/lilly-ledbetter/ (accessed July 6, 2024).

52. *Ledbetter v. Goodyear Tire & Rubber, Co.*, 550 U.S. 618 (2007), 661.

53. *Texas v. Johnson*, 491 U.S. 397 (1989).

54. "D.C. Flag Burning Tests New Law," *Congressional Quarterly Weekly Report*, November 4, 1989, 2952.

55. *United States v. Eichman*, 496 U.S. 310 (1990).

56. *Chisholm*, 2 Dallas 419 (1793); *Scott*, 19 Howard 393 (1857); *Pollock*, 158 U.S. 601 (1896); and *Oregon*, 400 U.S. 112 (1970).

57. See *Garland v. Cargill* (2024), 2. Opinion available at https://www.supremecourt.gov/opinions/23pdf/22-976_e29g.pdf.

58. Ibid., Justice Alito concurring opinion, 1.

59. See https://cohen.house.gov/media-center/press-releases/congressman-cohen-condemns-supreme-courts-bump-stock-ruling-urges.

60. See https://delauro.house.gov/media-center/press-releases/delauro-statement-supreme-court-ruling-bump-stocks.

61. See https://www.judiciary.senate.gov/press/releases/durbin-statement-on-supreme-court-bump-stocks-ruling.

62. See https://www.cnn.com/2024/06/14/politics/supreme-court-bump-stocks/index.html.

63. See https://www.tucsonsentinel.com/nationworld/report/062024_gop_bump_stocks/senate-republicans-scuttle-bump-stock-legislation/.

64. For a good discussion focusing on court-limiting legislation introduced in the House of Representatives between 1973 and 2000, see Lauren C. Bell and Kevin M. Scott, "Policy Statements or Symbolic Politics? Explaining Congressional Court-Limiting Attempts," *Judicature* 89 (2006): 196–201.

65. Jennifer Steinhauer, "Senate, for Just the 8th Time, Votes to Oust a Federal Judge," *New York Times*, December 8, 2010, https://www.nytimes.com/2010/12/09/us/politics/09judge.html (accessed July 6, 2024).

66. See the day-to-day coverage of the hearings in the *ABA Journal*, http://www.abajournal.com. Also see David Broder, "Peering Through the Judicial Camouflage," *Salt Lake Tribune*, July 30, 2009, http://www.sltrib.com.

67. Christina L. Boyd, Paul M. Collins, and Lori A. Ringhand, *Supreme Bias Gender and Race in U.S. Supreme Court Confirmation Hearings* (Stanford, CA: Stanford University Press, 2023).

68. See James E. Anderson, David W. Brady, and Charles S. Bullock III, *Public Policy and Politics in America* (North Scituate, MA: Duxbury Press, 1978), 291–92; and Charles S. Bullock III, "Equal Education Opportunity," in *Implementation of Civil Rights Policy*, ed. Charles S. Bullock III and Charles M. Lamb (Monterey, CA: Brooks/Cole, 1984), 57–58.

69. Bethany Blackstone, "An Analysis of Policy-Based Congressional Responses to the U.S. Supreme Court's Constitutional Decisions," *Law and Society Review* 47 (2013): 199228.

70. *Hamdan v. Rumsfeld*, 548 U.S. 557 (2006).

71. Canon and Johnson, *Judicial Policies*, 129.

72. Tyler Pager, "Biden Unveils Commission to Study Possible Expansion of Supreme Court," *Washington Post*, April 9, 2021, https://www.washington-post.com/politics/biden-to-unveil-commission-to-study-possible-expansion-of-supreme-court/2021/04/09/f644552c-9944-11eb-962b-78c1d8228819_story.html.

73. Charlie Savage, "Experts Debate Reducing the Supreme Court's Power to Strike Down Laws," *New York Times*, June 30, 2021, https://www.ny-times.com/2021/06/30/us/politics/supreme-court-commission.html.

74. See Robert A. Carp, Kenneth L. Manning, and Ronald Stidham, "Right On: The Decision-Making Behavior of George W. Bush's Judicial Appointees," *Judicature* 92 (2009): 312–19.

75. Katie Benner and Erica L. Green, "Justice Dept. Seeks to Pare Back Civil Rights Protections for Minorities," *New York Times*, January 5, 2021, https://www.nytimes.com/2021/01/05/us/politics/justice-department-dispa-rate-impact.html.

76. For an excellent study, focusing specifically on the solicitor general's filing of amicus curiae briefs, see Richard L. Pacelle Jr., "Amicus Curiae or Amicus Praesidentis? Reexamining the Role of the Solicitor General in Filing Amici," *Judicature* 89 (2006): 317–25.

77. This occurred in numerous instances during the Trump administration. See Jacqueline Thomsen, "Judges Face New Test: How to Get Trump Officials to Comply with Their Orders," *The National Law Journal*, December 2, 2020, https://www.law.com/nationallawjournal/2020/12/02/judges-face-new-test-how-to-get-trump-officials-to-comply-with-their-orders/. See also Debra Cassens Weiss, "Trump Administration Officials Appear to Defy Court Orders, Setting a Bad Precedent, Prof Says," *ABA Journal*, December 4, 2020, https://www.abajournal.com/news/article/trump-administration-officials-appear-to-defy-court-orders-setting-a-bad-precedent-prof-says (accessed July 6, 2024).

78. Danielle Douglas-Gabriel, "DeVos and Education Dept. Could Face New Sanctions for Violating a Court Order," *Washington Post*, January 8, 2020, https://www.washingtonpost.com/education/2020/01/08/devos-education-dept-could-face-new-sanctions-violating-court-order/ (accessed July 6, 2024).

79. Debra Cassens Weiss, "Federal Judge Orders Return of Deportation Flight Carrying 2 Plaintiffs in Asylum-Policy Challenge," *ABA Journal*, August 10, 2018, https://www.abajournal.com/news/article/federal_judge_orders_return_of_deportation_flight_carrying_two_plaintiffs_i (accessed July 6, 2024).

80. Arelis R. Hernández, "Judge Halts Mother-Daughter Deportation, Threatens to Hold Sessions in Contempt," *Washington Post*, August 9, 2018, https://www.washingtonpost.com/local/immigration/judge-halts-mother-daughter-deportation-threatens-to-hold-sessions-in-contempt/2018/08/09/a23a0580-9bd6-11e8-8d5e-c6c594024954_story.html (accessed July 6, 2024).

81. Ibid.

82. One study, for example, analyzed judicial implementation and impact from the standpoint of four populations: an interpreting population, an implementing population, a consumer population, and a secondary population. See Canon and Johnson, *Judicial Policies*.

83. See, for example, Frances K. Browne and Deborah L. Shapiro, "Punitive Damage Awards in New York since *State Farm*," http://www.brodybrowne.com/images/Punitive%20Damages_Browne.pdf.

84. *Gideon v. Wainwright*, 372 U.S. 335 (1963).

85. *Miranda v. Arizona*, 384 U.S. 436 (1966).

86. Our discussion of the use of such powers is drawn from Phillip J. Cooper, *Hard Judicial Choices* (New York, NY: Oxford University Press, 1988), 12–14, 342, 348–49.

87. Docket No. 11-182. Our discussion of the case is drawn heavily from material found at the Oyez Project at IIT Chicago–Kent College of Law, June 25, 2012, http://www.oyez.org/cases/2010-2019/2011_11_182.

88. *National Federation of Independent Business v. Sebelius*, 567 U.S. 519 (2012).

89. Docket No. 11-400. Our discussion of this case is drawn primarily from material found at the Affordable Care Act Cases, the Oyez Project at IIT Chicago–Kent College of Law, July 6, 2012, http://www.oyez.org/cases/2010-2019/2011/_11_400.

90. *King v. Burwell*, 576 U.S. 473 (2015).

91. *California v.* Texas, 593 U.S. 659 (2021).

92. *King v. Burwell*, 576 U.S. 473 (2015), 476.

93. Ibid., 498.

94. "Tracking Abortion Bans across the Country," *New York Times*, https://www.nytimes.com/interactive/2024/us/abortion-laws-roe-v-wade.html (accessed July 6, 2024).

95. Ibid.

96. *Idaho v. United States*, 603 U.S. ___ (2024). Available at https://www.supremecourt.gov/opinions/23pdf/23-726_6jgm.pdf (accessed July 6, 2024).

97. *United States v. Idaho*, 623 F.Supp.3d 1096 (2022).

98. *Idaho v. United States*, 603 U.S. ___ (2024), 3. Available at https://www.supremecourt.gov/opinions/23pdf/23-726_6jgm.pdf (accessed July 6, 2024).

99. Susan W. Johnson, "Stability and Change: Policy Evolution on the Supreme Court of Canada, 19452005," *Canadian Journal of Political Science* 52 (2019): 358.

100. Canon and Johnson, *Judicial Policies*, 206.

101. See Gerald N. Rosenberg, *The Hollow Hope: Can Courts Bring about Social Change?* (Chicago, IL: University of Chicago Press, 1991).

102. Ibid., 156.

103. See, for example, Canon and Johnson, *Judicial Policies*; Doug McAdam, *Political Process and the Development of Black Insurgency* (Chicago, IL: University of Chicago Press, 1982); and Aldon Morris, *The Origins of the Civil Rights Movement* (New York, NY: Free Press, 1984).

104. Linda Greenhouse, *Justice on the Brink* (New York, NY: Random House, 2021), 8.

105. Ibid., 21.

106. Ibid., 21.

107. *Shelby County v. Holder*, 570 U.S. 529 (2013), 577.

108. *Students for Fair Admissions, Inc. v. President and Fellows of Harvard College*, 600 U.S. 181 (2023).

109. Ibid., 230.

110. Julian Mark and Susan Syrluga, "Race Was Once Factored into College Admissions," *Washington Post*, June 24, 2024, https://www.washingtonpost.com/education/2024/06/29/affirmative-action-supreme-court-college-queens-harvard/ (accessed July 2, 2024).

111. Archibald Cox, *The Warren Court* (Cambridge, MA: Harvard University Press, 1968), 74.

112. *Mapp*, 367 U.S. 643 (1961); *Gideon*, 372 U.S. 335 (1963); *Miranda*, 384 U.S. 436 (1966).

113. See *United States v. Leon*, 468 U.S. 897 (1984); and *Massachusetts v. Sheppard*, 488 U.S. 981 (1984).

114. *Arizona v. Evans*, 514 U.S. 1 (1995) and *Herring v. United States*, 555 U.S. 135 (2008).

115. See the discussion of search and seizure in Otis H. Stephens Jr. and John M. Scheb II, *American Constitutional Law*, 2nd ed. (Belmont, CA: West/Wadsworth, 1999), 587–94.

116. *Hudson v. Michigan*, 547 U.S. 586 (2006).

117. *Gideon v. Wainwright*, 372 U.S. 335 (1963).

118. See Thomas K. Maher, "The Impact of *Gideon* on Justice in North Carolina—50 Years of Progress," *North Carolina State Bar Journal* (Spring 2012): 24–27, 40.

119. *Miranda v. Arizona*, 384 U.S. 436 (1966).

120. *Dickerson v. United States*, 530 U.S. 428 (2000).

121. Rosenberg, *Hollow Hope*, 343.

122. See Richard C. Cortner, "Strategies and Tactics of Litigants in Constitutional Cases," *Journal of Public Law* 17 (1968): 287–307; Jo Freeman, *The Politics of Women's Liberation* (New York, NY: David McKay, 1975); Leslie Friedman Goldstein, "Sex and the Burger Court: Recent Judicial Policy Making Toward Women," in *Race, Sex, and Policy Problems*, ed. Marian Lief Palley and Michael B. Preston (Lexington, MA: Lexington Books, 1979), 103–13; and Karen O'Connor, *Women's Organizations' Use of the Courts* (Lexington, MA: Heath, 1980).

123. *Obergefell v. Hodges*, 576 U.S. 644 (2015).

124. Erwin Chemerinsky, "Symposium: A Landmark Victory for Civil Rights," https://www.scotusblog.com/2015/06/symposium-a-landmark-victory-for-civil-rights/ (accessed July 2, 2024).

125. Ibid.

CHAPTER 15

1. "Rehnquist Says It's OK for a President to Pack High Court," Houston Chronicle, October 19, 1984.

INDEX

D

L

M

N

T

U

ABOUT THE AUTHORS

Robert A. Carp is professor emeritus of political science at the University of Houston. He is coauthor of *Policymaking and Politics in the Federal Courts; Politics and Judgment in Federal District Courts*; the *Federal Courts*, fourth edition, with Ronald Stidham; and numerous articles on judicial process.

Kenneth L. Manning is a professor and chair of the Department of Political Science at the University of Massachusetts Dartmouth. Manning's work on the politics of judicial decision-making and federal judicial selection has been published in the *American Journal of Political Science, Justice System Journal, Law and Policy, Social Science Quarterly*, and other respected journals.

Lisa M. Holmes is an associate professor of political science at the University of Vermont. She specializes in US politics with a focus on judicial politics, constitutional law, and gender and law. Her work has recently been published in *P.S.: Political Science and Politics, The Oxford Research Encyclopedia of Politics,* and *Judicature.* In 2023, she received the College of Arts and Science's Scholar-Teacher Award at the University of Vermont.

Jennifer Bowie is an associate professor of political science at the University of Richmond. Her research and teaching focuses on judicial decision-making and behavior on the US and comparative courts. She is a coauthor of *The View from the Bench and Chambers: Examining Judicial Process and Decision Making on the U.S. Courts of Appeals.* Her work has been published in a number of journals and edited volumes including *The Journal of Politics, Political Research Quarterly*, and the *Journal of Law and Courts.*